INTERNATIONAL ARBITRATION AND EU LAW

ELGAR ARBITRATION LAW AND PRACTICE

The Elgar Arbitration Law and Practice series is a library of works by leading practitioners and scholars covering key areas of commercial and investment arbitration. The titles in the series are analytical in approach, highlighting and unpicking the legal issues that are most critical and relevant to practice. Designed to be detailed, focussed reference works, the books in this series aim to offer an authoritative statement on the legal and procedural framework in both established and emerging areas of arbitral practice. The series will include texts covering the rules of specific arbitral bodies and national arbitration laws, regional approaches to commercial and investment arbitration, as well as sector-specific arbitration.

Titles in the series include:

International Commercial Arbitration and the Brussels I Regulation
Louise Hauberg Wilhelmsen

Investment Arbitration in Central and Eastern Europe
Law and Practice
Edited by Csongor Nagy

International Arbitration and EU Law
Edited by José Rafael Mata Dona and Nikos Lavranos

INTERNATIONAL ARBITRATION AND EU LAW

Edited by

JOSÉ RAFAEL MATA DONA

*Independent Practitioner, D.E.S. in European and International Law,
and member of the Brussels and Caracas Bars*

NIKOS LAVRANOS

*Guest Professor of International Investment Law, Free University of Brussels, Belgium,
Secretary-General of the European Federation for Investment Law and Arbitration (EFILA)
and founder of NL-Investmentconsulting, Of Counsel at Wöss & Partners*

ELGAR ARBITRATION LAW AND PRACTICE

Edward Elgar
PUBLISHING

Cheltenham, UK • Northampton, MA, USA

Published by
Edward Elgar Publishing Limited
The Lypiatts
15 Lansdown Road
Cheltenham
Glos GL50 2JA
UK

Edward Elgar Publishing, Inc.
William Pratt House
9 Dewey Court
Northampton
Massachusetts 01060
USA

A catalogue record for this book
is available from the British Library

Library of Congress Control Number: 2020952357

This book is available electronically in the **Elgar**online
Law subject collection
http://dx.doi.org/10.4337/9781788974004

ISBN 978 1 78897 399 1 (cased)
ISBN 978 1 78897 400 4 (eBook)

Typeset by Columns Design XML Ltd, Reading
Printed and bound by CPI Group (UK) Ltd, Croydon, CR0 4YY

CONTENTS

CONTENTS

EXTENDED TABLE OF CONTENTS

PART I THE PRE- AND THE POST-AWARD STAGE IN INTERNATIONAL COMMERCIAL ARBITRATION VIS-À-VIS EU LAW AND THE EUROPEAN ATTITUDE TOWARD ANTI-SUIT RELIEF

PART III   INTERSECTIONS BETWEEN INTERNATIONAL INVESTMENT ARBITRATION AND EU LAW

CONTRIBUTORS

Niuscha Bassiri is a partner at Hanotiau & van den Berg in Brussels. She has acted as counsel and arbitrator in commercial and investment arbitration matters spanning a variety of industry sectors for nearly two decades, with a combined amount in dispute exceeding USD 60 billion. Since 2014, she has continuously been ranked amongst the best of her generation worldwide by Who's Who Legal – Arbitration. Ms. Bassiri is a faculty member of the international arbitration LLM programme at the University of Miami and a lecturer at the ICHEC Business and Management School, Brussels.

George A. Bermann is the Columbia Law School Jean Monnet Professor of EU Law, Walter Gellhorn Professor of Law Director, Center for International Commercial and Investment Arbitration. He has a J.D. and a B.A. from Yale University and an LL.M. from Columbia Law School. He holds honorary degrees from the Universities of Fribourg in Switzerland, Versailles-St. Quentin in France and Universidad César Vallejo in Peru. He is an affiliated faculty member of the School of Law of Sciences Po in Paris and the MIDS Masters Program in International Dispute Settlement in Geneva. He is also a visiting professor at the Georgetown Law Center. At the Law School, he founded both the European Legal Studies Center and the *Columbia Journal of European Law*.

Alexander Blumrosen is an attorney admitted to the Bars of Paris and New York, and founder of the Polaris Law firm in Paris, France, where he specialises in arbitration (serving as arbitrator and counsel), litigation and privacy. He is a graduate of Georgetown University Law Center (JD), and the University of Paris I-Sorbonne (DEA). He was selected by the EU Commission and the U.S. Department of Commerce to be on the list of Privacy Shield arbitrators, and is on the 'Tech list' of the Silicon Valley Arbitration and Mediation Center (SVAMC). He is a former President of the International Technology Law Association (ITechLaw) and a life member of the Council on Foreign Relations.

Charles N. Brower is at present sitting as Judge ad hoc of the International Court of Justice in three ongoing contentious cases, the largest number of such appointments received by any of the four Americans ever so appointed. At the same time he continues as a Judge of the Iran-United States Tribunal, which position he has held since 1983. In 1987 he was granted temporary leave from that Tribunal in order to serve as Deputy Special Counsellor to the President of the United States with the rank of Deputy Assistant to the President (equivalent to Deputy Secretary of a Cabinet Department). Earlier (1969–1973) Judge Brower served in the Office of The Legal Adviser of the United States Department of State successively as Assistant Legal Adviser for European Affairs, as Deputy Legal Adviser and for a number of months as Acting Legal Adviser, hence the chief international lawyer for the United States Government. He also has served as Judge ad hoc of the Inter-American Court of Human Rights. Since 2001 he has been an Arbitrator Member of Twenty Essex (Chambers) in London, in which capacity he has served as international arbitrator in numerous investor/State and commercial cases as party-appointee, sole arbitrator, and President, Presiding Arbitrator and Chairman. From 1961 until 2005 he served at various times as associate, partner and special counsel of White & Case LLP, first in New York City, then in Washington, DC His many honors and awards include the Manley O. Hudson Medal of the American Society of International Law (for 'pre-eminent scholarship and achievement in international law … without regard to nationality'), the Pat Murphy Award of the Center for American and International Law's Institute for Transnational Arbitration, and Lifetime Achievement Awards of the Global Arbitration Review and the American Bar Association's Section of International Law. In the past he served on the Board of Governors of the American Bar Association, as a Member of the Association's House of Delegates for 15 years, as President of the American Society of International Law and Chairman of the Center for American and International Law's Institute for Transnational Arbitration. Uniquely, an 'elegant insect' newly discovered in Costa Rica was named *Barylypa broweri* in honor of his 'enthusiastic and outstanding legal defense of the hundreds of thousands of species … of the Santa Elena Peninsula serpentine barrens in northwestern Costa Rica', which defence included succeeding in having that area designated a United Nations World Heritage Site. Judge Brower's academic appointments have included Visiting Fellowship at Jesus College, University of Cambridge, a series of Visiting Fellowships at Cambridge's Lauterpacht Centre for International Law, appointment as Distinguished Visiting Research Professor of Law at George Washington University's Law School, and invitations to give various endowed lectures in Europe, the United States and Asia.

Luis Capiel is an Of Counsel at Herbert Smith Freehills, specialising in international arbitration. He has acted as counsel and arbitrator in a variety of cases, focusing on complex commercial and construction disputes. Luis is a German qualified lawyer, admitted to the Madrid and the Munich Bars. He holds a Law Degree from the Humbolt Universität zu Berlin and an LL.M. (First Class Honours) from The University of Auckland.

Stefano Castagna is a doctoral candidate in International Business Taxation, University of Economics and Business (Wirtschaftsuniversität Wien – WU), Vienna, Austria. Before entering the DIBT programme, he worked as a consultant, advising clients in transfer pricing, taxation, accounting and legal matters. He has also served as a delegate in sessions of different UN bodies, including UNCITRAL and the Intergovernmental Working Group of Experts on International Standards of Accounting and Reporting (ISAR). The author is licensed to practise law in the State of New York, USA. He holds a Law Degree (CLMG), and an MSc degree in Business Administration and Law (CLELI) from Bocconi University, Milano, Italy. He also holds an IBRLA LL.M from NYU School of Law, New York, USA.

Dodo Chochitaichvili is a Belgian qualified lawyer specialised in dispute resolution. She advises and represents clients before Belgian courts in a variety of legal matters (commercial and general contract law, torts, liabilities, consumer law, competition law) and sectors. Her practice also focuses on national and international arbitrations, and arbitration-related court proceedings and includes acting as arbitrator. She speaks French, Georgian and English.

Oliver Cojo is an Associate at Herbert Smith Freehills, specialising in international arbitration. He is an adjunct professor at IE University and co-chair of the young practitioners group of the Spanish Arbitration Club (CEA-40). Oliver is a Spanish qualified lawyer, admitted to the Madrid Bar. He holds an LL.M. from Maastricht University and a Degree in Law and Business Management from Universidad de Valladolid.

Quentin Declève is an Associate at Van Bael & Bellis and a Member of the Brussels Bar. His practice focuses on international litigation and arbitration, as well as on EU and national competition law and international trade law. He also represents clients before the EU Courts and before Belgian civil and commercial courts. He is the founder and editor of the International Litigation Blog (www.international-litigation-blog.com) and has worked as an assistant in EU law at Université Saint-Louis in Brussels. He holds degrees from Université Catholique de Louvain and Columbia Law School.

Monica Feria-Tinta is a barrister at Twenty Essex, a leading commercial barrister's chambers in London. Monica is recognised in legal directories as a leading barrister in public international law at the English Bar. She appears at all levels in English and international courts and tribunals. Her arbitration practice covers both commercial and investment arbitration. In addition to acting as Counsel, she also accepts appointments as arbitrator. Monica is a world expert on enforcement of awards, and the author of a forthcoming book on the subject with Oxford University Press. She is a Partner Fellow at the Lauterpacht Centre for International Law, University of Cambridge, where she is guest lecturer on the topic of investment law, and a member of the Chartered Institute of Arbitrators. She was 'Barrister of the Year' finalist in The Lawyer's Awards in 2020. She holds an LLM (LSE) and the Diploma of the Hague Academy in International Law.

Anne-Karin Grill is an experienced international arbitration lawyer and well-versed in other forms of alternative dispute resolution (ADR), especially mediation. She advises clients in commercial arbitration proceedings in accordance with the rules of key arbitral institutions and has an excellent track-record in investor-state arbitration. In addition to her advocacy work before international tribunals, Anne-Karin serves as arbitrator and acts as CEDR accredited mediator in multi-jurisdictional commercial disputes. Anne-Karin is a Fellow of the Chartered Institute of Arbitrators (FCIArb) and serves as member of the ICC International Court of Arbitration. Upon the nomination of the Republic of Austria, she was appointed to the ICSID Panel of Conciliators. Anne-Karin lectures at the University of Vienna, Austria, and in renowned international legal programmes.

Emily Hay is Counsel at Hanotiau & van den Berg, Brussels, Belgium, practising in international commercial and investment treaty arbitration. She acts as arbitrator, counsel and tribunal secretary under a wide variety of institutional rules and across industry sectors. Ms. Hay also advises on data protection and privacy law, in particular under the GDPR. She holds an LL.M in Advanced Studies in International Law (cum laude) from Leiden University, the Netherlands, and a BA LL.B (First Class Honours) from Macquarie University, Australia. Ms. Hay is registered to practise in both New South Wales and Brussels (B-list).

Bo Ra Hoebeke is a Managing Associate at Linklaters in Amsterdam and over the past 12 years has focused exclusively on commercial and investment arbitration and arbitration-related court proceedings. She has advised and represented both national and international clients, as well as states and governmental bodies. Bo Ra also advises companies on the corporate structuring of their foreign investments and the protections offered by investment treaties. Bo Ra has been involved in disputes under a wide variety of arbitration rules (including UNCITRAL, ICC, SIAC, LCIA, SCC, CEPANI and NAI rules). She is regularly involved in high-profile arbitration-related court proceedings, such as the setting aside and enforcement of arbitral awards and proceedings relating to interim measures in support of arbitration. Her experience in court proceedings related to arbitration also includes setting aside proceedings regarding major investment arbitration cases. Bo Ra is a member of the Arbitration Commission (Netherlands) of the International Chamber of Commerce (ICC). She is also ITA Reporter for the Netherlands and regularly publishes and lectures on international arbitration.

David Ingle is a Senior Associate in Allen & Overy's Madrid office specialising in commercial and investment treaty arbitration. David is qualified to practise in England and Wales and is admitted to the Texas bar. He has acted as counsel for a range of clients in numerous international commercial and investment treaty arbitrations and has regularly appeared as advocate in disputes arising under the Energy Charter Treaty. David also lectures on English law and common law at the Universidad Carlos III de Madrid. Before relocating to Madrid, David practised in the A&O London arbitration team and also spent six months on secondment to the Prague office.

Toni Kalliokoski works as Counsel at Dittmar & Indrenius law firm in Helsinki, Finland. He specialises in competition litigation (antitrust damages) and complex commercial disputes. He received his LL.M. degree from the University of Helsinki in 2007 and has numerous academic publications especially in the field of antitrust damages.

Sophie J. Lamb QC is a litigation partner in the London office of Latham & Watkins and Global Co-Chair of the firm's International Arbitration Practice. Ms. Lamb QC regularly appears as advocate in all arbitral fora, before international tribunals and in the English courts, including in anti-suit matters. She is also widely recognised for her experience in international investment and inter-state disputes. Ms. Lamb QC holds an LL.M. from the London School of Economics, an LL.B. from the Université de Bourgogne and an LL.B. from the University of Manchester, and has lectured on a variety of subjects in the field of international dispute resolution at the world's leading universities and business schools.

Emanuela Martin holds Bachelor Degrees in Swiss and Romanian law and received her Master's degree in International and European Law from the University of Geneva, Switzerland, with a particular focus on International Dispute Settlement, Intellectual Property and Transnational Commercial matters. She has worked as an academic intern for projects partnering the World Intellectual Property Organization and the Geneva Centre for International Dispute Settlement. Emanuela is Legal Project Manager at Lévy Kaufmann-Kohler.

Dorieke Overduin holds a LL.M degree from Georgetown University Law Centre and is a fellow at the Institute of International Economic Law. Previously, she worked as a senior legal advisor to the Netherlands' Ministry of Economic Affairs and Climate Policy, was involved in legal aspects of trade and investment policy and related issues in international and European law. All opinions expressed in this chapter are personal to the author and are not to be attributed to the position of the Dutch government.

Robert Price is an associate in the Litigation & Trial Department in the London office of Latham & Watkins. He is a solicitor advocate and a member of the firm's International Arbitration, Public International Law and White Collar Defence & Investigations Practices. Mr. Price's practice focuses on commercial arbitration, investment treaty arbitration and complex litigation in the courts of England and Wales and overseas. Mr. Price holds a Graduate Diploma in Law from the College of Law, and a B.A. in Ancient and Modern History from the University of Oxford.

Friedrich Rosenfeld is partner at Hanefeld, a dispute resolution boutique based in Hamburg and Paris. He regularly acts as an arbitrator in international arbitration proceedings. Friedrich is also Global Adjunct Professor at NYU Law in Paris, Visiting Professor at the International Hellenic University in Thessaloniki and Lecturer at Bucerius Law School. In spring 2020, he was invited to teach international commercial arbitration as Global Professor of Law from Practice at NYU School of Law in New York.

Adriana San Román Rivera is founding partner of Wöss & Partners. Being double qualified, both as lawyer and financial analyst, her first career was in corporate banking, specialising in financial engineering and risk analysis, followed by a second career as an attorney engaged in the structuring of infrastructure projects, anti-dumping and antitrust investigations. Nowadays, she is party counsel in complex damages arbitrations and a leading damages expert having acted, amongst others, in a US$340 million landmark ICDR arbitration as damages expert appointed by Pemex. She is currently handling large international arbitrations with respect to oil platforms, energy tariff disputes, construction and energy projects. Mrs. San Román is attorney at law with highest honors, holds an M.A. in Finance & Investment at the University of Exeter, where she was a Ford foundation scholar, and also passed the first level of the Chartered Financial Analyst exam of the CFA Institute in New York. She is co-author of the leading monograph on damages, *Damages in International Arbitration under Complex Long-term Contracts*, member of the ICCA-ASIL Task Force on Damages in International Arbitration and co-author and lecturer of the 'Advanced Seminar on Damages in International Arbitration'.

Juan Manuel Sánchez Pueyo is a Managing Associate at Linklaters Madrid who specialises in commercial and investment arbitration, and has participated in numerous highly complex and high value matters. He acts as counsel in arbitrations and arbitration-related court proceedings, such as setting aside and enforcement proceedings. Juan has participated as counsel in disputes under a wide variety of arbitration rules (including UNCITRAL, ICC, SIAC, CEPANI and NAI rules). Juan also has experience in court proceedings and regularly advises clients regarding crisis management and litigation strategy. He works for both the Linklaters Dutch and Spanish Dispute Resolution practices, whilst being based in the Madrid office. Juan holds a degree in Law and a degree in Political Science and Public Administration, in addition to a Master's Degree in Commercial and Company law. He has been accepted to the Spanish Bar (2014) and Dutch Bar (2015, EU Lawyer). Juan is also member of the board of the Dutch Chapter of the CEA (Spanish Arbitration Club).

S.I. Strong (PhD, Cambridge; DPhil, Oxford; JD, Duke) is currently an Associate Professor of Law at the University of Sydney and specialises in international commercial arbitration and large-scale (class and collective) suits. Dr. Strong has published over 100 award-winning books and articles in Europe, Asia and the Americas and acted as a dual-qualified practitioner (US attorney and English solicitor) with major international law firms in London, New York and Chicago prior to entering academia. Dr. Strong currently sits as an arbitrator in a variety of international commercial matters.

Jeffrey Sullivan is a partner in the London office of Gibson Dunn & Crutcher, where he is a member of the firm's International Arbitration Group. Jeff's practice has a particular focus on disputes arising in the energy, extractive industries and infrastructure sectors. Jeff has acted as counsel and lead advocate in approximately 30 bilateral investment treaty and Energy Charter Treaty arbitrations, acting for both States and investors. He has also appeared as lead counsel in several ICSID annulment proceedings. He is admitted to practise in both Washington DC and England and Wales.

Isabelle Van Damme is Partner at Van Bael & Bellis and a Member of the Brussels Bar. Her practice focuses on WTO law, EU law and public international law. Isabelle previously worked as a référendaire in the chambers of Advocate General Sharpston, at the CJEU, worked at a Geneva-based firm specialised in WTO law and taught at the University of Cambridge, Clare College. She holds degrees from the University of Ghent, Georgetown University Law Center and the University of Cambridge. Her main publications include a monograph on *Treaty Interpretation by the WTO Appellate Body* (OUP) and *The Oxford Handbook of International Trade Law* (OUP).

Maria-Clara Van den Bossche is Associate in the Litigation and Arbitration practice group of Loyens & Loeff Belgium. She specialises in complex and international civil and commercial dispute resolution. Maria-Clara has a particular focus on class actions, enforcement and public international law. She has broad experience in enforcement of foreign judgments and arbitral awards, including against sovereign entities. She advises and represents clients in court litigation in various fields, including market practices. Through her involvement in most of the class actions initiated in Belgium and several publications on this topic, Maria-Clara has gained extensive expertise in this field. Maria-Clara is the President of the Dutch-speaking Brussels bar association (VPG).

Olivier van der Haegen is Partner in the Litigation and Arbitration practice group of Loyens & Loeff Belgium. Olivier acts as counsel in international arbitration proceedings, either ad hoc or under institutional rules, and handles litigations before Belgian courts in the real estate, construction, energy, food and media industries. Olivier also regularly acts in court proceedings relating to setting aside, recognition and/or enforcement of international (investment-treaty) arbitral awards or foreign judgments. He is member of Cepani (the Belgian arbitration institute), Cepani 40 Steering Committee and the IAI (International Arbitration Institute). He is recognised as 'Future Leader' by Who's Who Legal Arbitration and ranked as 'Next generation lawyer' by the Legal 500 Dispute Resolution.

Piotr Wiliński is an Assistant Professor at the Erasmus University. He specialises in international commercial arbitration, with a special focus on arbitral tribunal's powers and duties. Next to his role in academia, he works in International Arbitration practice group of Houthoff.

Bryce Williams is an associate in the London office of Latham & Watkins and a member of the firm's International Arbitration and Public International Law Practices. Mr. Williams has acted as counsel and tribunal secretary in international commercial and investment arbitrations under all of the major arbitral rules. Mr. Williams holds an LL.M. in International Dispute Settlement (MIDS) from the Graduate Institute and University of Geneva and an LL.B. (Hons) and Bachelor of International Studies, both from the University of Sydney.

Herfried Wöss is founding partner of Wöss & Partners, president and co-arbitrator of arbitral tribunals with respect to multi-million infrastructure and energy disputes, as well as complex damages cases under the LCIA, ICC, ICDR and other arbitration rules. He is also party counsel in large energy tariff, power plant construction, complex damages arbitrations and investment arbitrations. Dr. Wöss has acted as adjudicator with respect to Peru's largest infrastructure project and advises third-party funders on the feasibility of investment arbitrations. Dr. Wöss is an Austrian jurist, licensed in Mexico and Special Legal Consultant in Washington DC. Dr. Wöss holds a *Magister iuris,* a Doctorate in International and European Economic Law *(summa cum laude)* at the Johannes Kepler Universität in Linz, Austria, and an LL.M. in International Business Legal Studies at the University of Exeter, UK. He was Visiting Scholar at the Georgetown University Law Center from 2012–13, where he authored the leading monograph on damages, *Damages in International Arbitration under Complex Long-term Contracts* (Oxford University Press, 2014). He is co-author and lecturer of the 'Advanced Seminar on Damages in International Arbitration'.

Patricia Živković is a Lecturer in Law at the University of Aberdeen (Scotland, UK). She specialises in dispute resolution, with an emphasis on international commercial arbitration. She actively fosters the usage of alternative dispute resolution mechanisms by co-chairing the Young Croatian Arbitration Practitioners, an association for younger members of the arbitration community in Croatia, which she also co-founded, and is also a published author on various topics in the field of international arbitration.

FOREWORD

Charles N. Brower

The invasive species of European Union law has slithered into the realm of international arbitration, commercial and investor/State disputes alike, so far and for so long that it has necessitated this book to guide even veteran *arbitrazhniks* through the resulting maze of potential traps. Its co-editors, José Rafael Mata Dona and Nikos Lavranos, are to be commended for having assembled the 30 illustrious experts who have authored and co-authored the 20 essays collected in this book that recount in detail the interfaces of the numerous facets of 'EU law' with the comparatively simpler institution of international arbitration.

The incredible number and variety of such interfaces are readily apparent from the potpourri of subjects treated by the volume's chapters:

Agency, annulment, anti-suit relief, anti-trust, CETA (Comprehensive Economic and Trade Agreement), challenges, consumer protection, collective redress, damages, data protection, European Convention on Human Rights, Energy Charter Treaty, enforcement of awards, investor/State dispute settlement, investment under intra-EU bilateral investment treaties, mediation, Multilateral Investment Court, government procurement, recognition of arbitral awards, and taxes.

The influence of EU Law thus has crept into various areas traditionally connected to commercial arbitration. In this respect the Court of Justice of the European Union (CJEU) has played a particularly important role, e.g., regarding pre- and post-award stages, anti-suit relief, collective redress, anti-trust and damages, to name just a few. The various chapters covering these subjects illustrate the depth and breadth of EU law's consequent impact on the development of commercial arbitral jurisprudence, reflecting the drive of EU institutions towards ever greater harmonization, and the resulting constraint on party autonomy and on the margin of appreciation available to commercial arbitral tribunals and to municipal courts of EU Member States.

It all began much more simply with the signature in 1957 by just six western European States of the Treaty of Rome, which established what then became known as the European Economic Community (EEC). It followed, and in a sense built upon, the European Coal and Steel Community, which had been established by the same six States – Belgium, France, Italy, Luxembourg, the Netherlands and 'West Germany' (the Federal Republic of Germany) – via the Treaty of Paris in 1951. In those early EEC days, the obligations of the Treaty of Rome were exclusively internal to the Community, with few substantive obligations that might affect outside investors in a Member State, in particular Articles 85 *et seq.* 'Rules on Competition', 91 'Dumping Practices' and 92 *et seq.* 'Aids Granted by States'.

The next major Treaty in the chain, the 1993 Maastricht Treaty, officially titled 'The Treaty On European Union', promoted the previous EEC to be the 'European Union' consisting of 12 States Parties – Denmark, Greece, Ireland, Portugal, Spain and the United Kingdom joined the original six – and added two significant provisions, namely a 'monetary union' and a 'single currency'. That treaty changed none of the substance of the Articles of the Treaty of Rome noted above as potentially affecting outside investors in Member States.

An enormous, and portentous, addition to the competence of the Union in respect of international arbitration came with the most recent of the Union's treaties, however, namely the entry into force of the 2009 Treaty of Lisbon, in which 27 States Parties amended both the Treaty of Rome and the Maastricht Treaty. In what is the resulting 'Consolidated Texts of the EU Treaties as Amended by the Treaty of Lisbon', at Article 207, the Treaty of Lisbon added just three words, i.e., 'foreign direct investment', to the Union's competences, under the new title of 'External Action By The Union':

> The common commercial policy shall be based on uniform principles, particularly with regard to … the commercial aspects of *foreign direct investment* … (Emphasis added.)

With these three words the Union opened the door to a radical revision of the Union system with respect to foreign (including intra-EU) investments and the resolution of disputes arising out of them. The *Achmea* judgment of the CJEU declared that the arbitration clauses of long-existing bilateral investment treaties between Member States of the European Union are contrary to European Union law, due to the Union's post-Lisbon competence over 'foreign direct investment', and following that the Union on 5 May 2020 prevailed on 23 of its Member States to sign an Agreement for the Termination of Bilateral Investment Treaties between the Member States of the European Union (the 'Brexiting' United Kingdom and four others – Austria, Finland, Ireland and Sweden – declined to sign). Apart from the Union announcing that it would pursue the non-signers legally to force them to comply, it long ago had proposed an EU Investment Court System, along the lines of treaties it already had concluded with Vietnam, Singapore and Canada (CETA), which would provide for 15 judges chosen by Member States and an appeals mechanism. Indeed, in 'Negotiation Directives for a Convention Establishing a Multilateral Court for the Settlement of Investment Disputes' dated 1 March 2018, the EU Council in paragraph 4 had commanded Member States that negotiations for establishment of that Court:

> … [S]hould be conducted under the auspices of the United Nations Commission on International Trade Law (UNCITRAL). In the event of a vote, the Member States which are Members of the United Nations Commission on International Trade Law shall exercise their voting rights in accordance with these directives and previously agreed EU positions.

Thus, for the very first time, EU expansionism co-opted an unrelated United Nations organization for its own purposes, to wit, so that it might impinge quite directly on the international arbitration of investment disputes. The present effort of the EU and its Member States in Working Group III of UNCITRAL is to achieve agreement, if possible, within that Working Group III, on a Convention that would bind EU Member States to the proposed Investment Court System and allow non-Member States to opt into it, to do which such States would have to strip themselves of bilateral investment promotion and protection treaties insofar as they currently provide for conventional investor/State arbitration. In this respect the EU seeks to project its preferences upon the entire world of foreign investment.

How far the six-Member EEC has come over more than half a century to be not only the 27 Member EU, but also an expansionist power, seeking to draw non-EU-Member States and non-EU bodies into the vortex of its operations! Thank heavens that José Rafael Mata Dona and Nikos Lavranos not only have observed this trend, but also have recruited such an array of distinguished experts to inform and educate those who must deal with all of the growing aspects of coping with the EU in all of its manifestations. They are to be warmly praised for causing this volume to be produced!

PREFACE

The inception and the production of this book has been a long and complicated journey.

The idea was to present the increasing influence of EU law in many different areas of commercial arbitration and investment treaty arbitration in one volume. Obviously, a selection of topics had to be made and many other topics had to be left out but which equally would have deserved a place in this book.

The editors wish to thank all authors for their contribution to this book and their patience.

We also wish to thank Shantanu Kanade for his assistance in the editing process.

We are also indebted to the publisher for supporting this project from the beginning until the end.

We hope that the readers find this book valuable and welcome any suggestions for future editions.

The Editors
José Rafael Mata Dona and Nikos Lavranos
Brussels, July 2020

TABLE OF CASES

INTERNATIONAL

Arbitral Awards (ICSID)

Arbitral Awards (Non-ICSID)

Caribbean Court of Justice

Inter-American Court of Human Rights

Iran-US Claims Tribunal

Other Tribunals

Permanent Court of Arbitration

Permanent Court of International Justice/International Court of Justice

EUROPEAN CASES

Court of Justice of the European Union

European Commission of Human Rights

European Court of Human Rights

NATIONAL COURTS

Argentina

Australia

Austria

Belgium

Canada

Cyprus

Czech Republic

Denmark

Finland

France

Russian Federation

Singapore

Spain

Sweden

Switzerland

United Kingdom

United States

Uruguay

TABLE OF LEGISLATION

EU Recommendations

EU Regulations

NATIONAL LEGISLATION

Austria

Belgium

Bulgaria

Croatia

MISCELLANEOUS

Part I

THE PRE- AND THE POST-AWARD STAGE IN INTERNATIONAL COMMERCIAL ARBITRATION VIS-À-VIS EU LAW AND THE EUROPEAN ATTITUDE TOWARD ANTI-SUIT RELIEF

1

INTERACTION BETWEEN INTERNATIONAL COMMERCIAL ARBITRATION AND EU LAW BEFORE THE AWARD IS RENDERED

Piotr Wiliński[*]

A. INTRODUCTION

1.01 For decades international arbitration and European Union law ('EU law') managed to develop independently.[1] It has been largely so, because of the success of the New York Convention and decisions made on the European level not to interfere with the international (commercial) arbitration regime. In recent years, however, the amount of interaction proliferated. This can be observed on different levels, discussed in detail by authors in this book. This contribution identifies and maps areas where EU law needs to be taken into account by the parties, arbitral tribunal or courts before the arbitral award is rendered. It concludes that EU law is equally relevant both (i) at the jurisdictional stage as well as (ii) at the merits phase of the arbitral process.

B. JURISDICTIONAL PHASE OF THE ARBITRAL PROCESS AND EU LAW

1.02 When it comes to the jurisdictional phase, EU law comes into play in cases when the validity of international agreement to arbitrate is being tested not only by the arbitral tribunal but also by the court of a Member State, which may create the risk of conflicting decisions (section B.2) – the risk which is intended to be excluded by the arbitration exception in Brussels regime

---

[*] Date of submission: 24/05/2020.

[1] George A Bermann, 'Navigating EU Law and the Law of International Arbitration' (2012) 28(3) *Arbitration International* 397.

(section B.3). Initially, however, one should not forget that EU law becomes of relevance when parties are drafting international agreement to arbitrate (section B.1).

1. Limits to party autonomy imposed by EU law

Party autonomy is a cornerstone of international commercial arbitration, which 'has gained **1.03** extensive acceptance in national systems of law'.[2] Parties are using their autonomy to tailor the arbitral process to their needs. In doing so, they effectively contract out from the national court system of resolving disputes and – instead – commission the adjudicative function to the arbitral tribunal.[3] Party autonomy is not absolute, however.

One of the limits to party autonomy at the stage of drafting of an international agreement to **1.04** arbitrate is subject-matter arbitrability, which is inevitably affected by a number of rules of EU law. The notion of subject-matter arbitrability can be found in Article II(1) of the New York Convention which encapsulates the essential elements of a valid international agreement to arbitrate.

According to Article II(1) of the New York Convention: **1.05**

> Each Contracting State shall recognize an agreement in writing under which the parties undertake to submit to arbitration all or any differences which have arisen or which may arise between them in respect of a defined legal relationship, whether contractual or not, concerning a subject matter capable of settlement by arbitration.

As can be observed above, one of the conditions that has to be fulfilled so that the international **1.06** agreement to arbitrate is recognized and enforced under the New York Convention is that subject-matter of a dispute brought before the arbitral tribunal is capable of settlement by arbitration. In principle, one should consider that if the subject-matter of the dispute is non-arbitrable, it would bar the tribunal from deciding the dispute, because it is effectively reserved for a court's jurisdiction.[4] Consequently, the arbitral tribunal deciding on non-arbitrable matter endangers enforceability of the award at the post-award stage.[5]

Subject-matter arbitrability analysed at the pre-award stage may trigger complex choice-of-law **1.07** questions as to what is applicable law to determine whether the dispute is capable of settlement by arbitration.[6] Although Article II of the New York Convention does not anchor the requirement of 'subject matter capable of settlement by arbitration' to any national law and as such may constitute the autonomous international standard of subject-matter arbitrability,[7] the

---

2   Nigel Blackaby and others, *Redfern and Hunter on International Commercial Arbitration* (OUP 2015) para 3.97.
3   See also Piotr Wiliński, *Excess of Powers in International Commercial Arbitration* (Eleven International Publishing 2021) (forthcoming) 457–8.
4   See also Gary Born, *International Commercial Arbitration* (Kluwer Law International 2014) 950–51.
5   See Convention on the Recognition and Enforcement of Foreign Arbitral Awards (adopted 10 June 1958), entered into force 7 June 1959 (Art XII)) 330 UNTS 3 ('New York Convention'), Art V(2)(a). For further reading see also Chapter 2.
6   For further reading, see e.g., Bernard Hanotiau, 'What Law Governs the Issue of Arbitrability?' (1996) 12(4) *Arbitration International* 391; Dorothee Schramm and others 'Article II', in Herbert Kronke and others (eds), *Recognition and Enforcement of Foreign Arbitral Awards: A Global Commentary on the New York Convention* (Kluwer Law International 2010) 72–3.
7   See Born (n 4) 611–12.

realistic view is that the local court reviewing the validity of international agreement to arbitrate under Article II(3) of the New York Convention would be able to apply its own rules on subject-matter arbitrability.[8] For the national courts in the European Union, this would also entail application of the mandatory rules of EU law.[9]

1.08 This is a sensible solution if one considers the use of arbitration as a vehicle to avoid application of (otherwise applicable) mandatory rules of law. For this reason, parties should be mindful which of the EU law rules might limit their autonomy to delegate the disputes to arbitration (which, in turn, might also potentially be investigated by the courts or arbitral tribunals *ex officio*).[10]

1.09 In a recent study, Hanefeld mapped three areas of EU law that might create an obstacle to parties' freedom:[11] (i) European competition law; (ii) European Agency Directive; and (iii) European sanctions.[12] Since the first part of this book is entirely dedicated to selected areas of intersection between EU law and International Commercial Arbitration,[13] it is sufficient to conclude that – following *Eco Swiss*,[14] *Ingmar*[15] and *Unamar*[16] – both primary and secondary EU legislation may be a source of overriding, mandatory rules that limit the parties' autonomy and affect the validity of arbitration agreement.[17] Additionally, and importantly, it will be the Member State courts themselves that effectuate application of these rules.[18]

1.10 Indeed, in the context of competition law, Requejo Isidro similarly observes that:

> The world of international commercial arbitration is determined by the will of the parties. In factual situations likely to be covered by EU competition law, the question arises whether and to what extent parties may contract out EU competition law for their arbitration. There is a risk if they do or they do so beyond what is deemed acceptable, that the arbitration clause is itself regarded as anticompetitive by the arbitrators or by a national court – provided an ex ante control is available.[19]

1.11 The section below will further discuss a potential court's scrutiny of the validity of the international agreement to arbitrate before the arbitration is commenced or at the early stage of arbitral proceedings.[20]

---

8   Schramm and others (n 6) 69–73. See also Jan Kleinheisterkamp, 'The Impact of Internationally Mandatory Laws on the Enforceability of Arbitration Agreements' (2009) 3 *World Arbitration & Mediation Review* 119.

9   See also section B.2 and section B.3 below.

10 See section B.2 and section C.

11 Inka Hanefeld, 'Limits to Party Autonomy Imposed by European Mandatory Law' in Franco Ferrari (ed), *Limits to Party Autonomy in International Commercial Arbitration* (Juris 2016) 401, 402.

12 Ibid., 401, 408–13.

13 For a short overview see section C below.

14 Case C-126/97 *Eco Swiss China Time Ltd v Benneton Int'l NV* [1999] ECR I-3055.

15 Case C-381/98 *Ingmar GB Ltd v Eaton Leonard Technologies Inc* [2000] ECR I-9305.

16 Case C-184/12 *United Antwerp Maritime Agencies (Unamar) NV v Navigation Maritime Bulgare* [2013] ECLI:EU: C:2013:663.

17 For further reading, see e.g., Francesca Ragno, 'Are EU Overriding Mandatory Provisions an Impediment to Arbitral Justice?' in Franco Ferrari (ed), *The Impact of EU Law on Commercial Arbitration* (Juris 2017) 139.

18 See also section B.2.

19 Marta Requejo Isidro, 'Claims for Damages and Arbitration: The 2014/104/EU Directive' in Franco Ferrari (ed), *The Impact of EU Law on Commercial Arbitration* (Juris 2017) 421, 444–5.

20 See section B.2.

2. Conflicting decisions on validity of the international agreement to arbitrate

Validity of agreement to arbitrate is one of the very first issues that need to be examined during **1.12** the jurisdictional phase of arbitral proceedings by the arbitral tribunal. The reason is clear – an arbitral tribunal may only resolve the dispute between parties if the source of its authority originates from the valid arbitration agreement.

The underlying principles of international commercial arbitration – the principle of **1.13** competence-competence and presumption of separability – strengthens the position of an arbitral tribunal to determine its own jurisdiction.[21] Consequently, any claim against the validity of the agreement to arbitrate should be initially addressed and resolved by the arbitral tribunal itself.

At the same time, an arbitral tribunal may not be the only forum required to address the **1.14** question of the validity of the international agreement to arbitrate. As already hinted above, the issue of the validity of agreement to arbitrate may also be raised before the national courts. It will occur when an agreement to arbitrate is invoked in court proceedings as a basis to challenge the court's jurisdiction.

This can happen in several instances. In the simple scenario, a party is bringing a claim before **1.15** a national court, because it is truly convinced that this court is a competent forum to resolve a dispute. In this case it would be for the other party to invoke that an earlier agreement to arbitrate bars the (otherwise valid) court's jurisdiction. The difficulty arises, however, in somewhat more complicated hypothetical at the outset of an already initiated arbitration proceedings. Here, the notice of arbitration has already been served (and even the arbitral tribunal may have already been constituted), but the respondent in arbitral proceedings brings its (counter)claims to an otherwise potentially competent national court. Again, the motivation for such an action may be a legitimate conviction that the agreement to arbitrate is invalid, hence the dispute needs to be resolved in court. At the same time, the respondent in ongoing arbitration may seize the national court for tactical reasons which effectively would frustrate the arbitral proceedings in its jurisdictional phase.

In order to assess whether an international arbitration agreement is valid, the national court **1.16** would need to test this agreement against the framework of Article II of the New York Convention, which would apply to the recognition and enforcement of an international agreement to arbitrate. Two provisos are relevant in this context, namely (i) Article II(1) of the New York Convention which – as explained above[22] – defines requirements that need to be fulfilled by the agreement to arbitrate in order for it to be recognized and enforced pursuant to the New York Convention and (ii) Article II(3) of the New York Convention, which provides that:

> The court of a Contracting State, when seized of an action in a matter in respect of which the parties have made an agreement within the meaning of this article, shall, at the request of one of the parties,

---

21 For further reading see e.g., Jan Paulsson, *The Idea of Arbitration* (OUP 2013) 53–72.
22 See section B.1.

refer the parties to arbitration, unless it finds that the said agreement is null and void, inoperative or incapable of being performed.

1.17 Article II(3) of the New York Convention mechanism therefore obliges a national court of a Contracting State (to the New York Convention) to refer parties to arbitration in cases where the existence of the agreement to arbitrate is invoked unless the court finds that the agreement to arbitrate is null and void, inoperative or incapable of being performed.

1.18 As explained above, the requirements of Article II(1) of the New York Convention will play a role, when the national court seized to hear the case needs to assess the validity of the international agreement to arbitrate pursuant to Article II(3) of the New York Convention. The close reading of Article II(1) of the New York Convention allows to identify constitutive elements of international agreement to arbitrate. Consequently, such an agreement can take the form of arbitration clause or submission agreement and should be, in principle, in writing. It is up to the parties to define the scope of (contractual or not) disputes that would be resolved in arbitration. At the same, at all times, the agreement to arbitrate needs to refer to the defined legal relationship. Finally, the disputes referred should be capable of being resolved in arbitration (subject-matter arbitrability). It means that whenever the existence of the valid agreement to arbitrate is invoked it would inevitably require the assessment of the arbitrability of the dispute. This is where EU law – and in particular mandatory rules of EU law (as perceived by the reviewing court) – may play a role.[23]

1.19 The subject-matter arbitrability issues are mostly of relevance at the post-award stage when supervisory courts review the compliance of the award with the rules of subject-matter arbitrability or (international) public policy (be it as it may courts at the seat or at the enforcement stage).[24] At the same time, however, a considerable risk exists that in the pre-award stage, the (otherwise competent) court – instead of deferring the matter to arbitration – would be tempted to accept its jurisdiction, in a perceived due observance of the public policy character of EU Law (and 'biased lack of reliance on international arbitration'[25]). It is particularly so, considering that 'the logic of EU law favours an expansive notion of public policy, while the logic of international arbitration law favours one that is markedly more restrictive'.[26]

1.20 Additionally, as observed by Kleinheisterkamp, the matters of subject-matter arbitrability might be raised by the courts *ex officio*:

> … the prevailing – and correct – view [is] that Article II(3) is to be interpreted as following the same logic as Article V(2)(a) and (b). Courts may rely on their *lex fori* for determining whether the dispute is capable of settlement by arbitration, at least when their own public policy is at stake. It is therefore fully in line with the structure of the New York Convention that courts can raise the issue ex officio

---

23 See also section C.
24 See Chapter 2.
25 Francesca Ragno, 'Inarbitrability: A Ghost Hovering over Europe' in Franco Ferrari (ed), *Limits to Party Autonomy in International Commercial Arbitration* (Juris 2016) 128, 161.
26 Bermann (n 1) 397, 420.

and expect assurance that the effectiveness of their internationally mandatory rules will not be cancelled by the arbitration agreement.[27]

Similarly, Ragno concludes that: **1.21**

> If the court seized is persuaded that denying the effectiveness of the arbitration clause is necessary to prevent the circumvention of the domestic *lois de police*, after Unamar the same court may feel authorized to adopt the same approach even in relation to agreements selecting an arbitral tribunal seated in an EU Member State and choosing the law of a (different) EU Member State.[28]

Indeed it seems plausible that following *Unamar*,[29] the national court may (mis)use its **1.22** discretion when reviewing the subject-matter arbitrability at the pre-award stage of the arbitral proceedings. It is, of course, justified to invalidate the agreement to arbitrate in cases where arbitration is used as a vehicle to evade mandatory rules of law, it is another matter, however, if the reviewing court invalidates parties' agreement to arbitrate since it does 'not perceive [arbitration] as a fully acceptable alternative dispute resolution mechanism where public policy *lato sensu* can be enforced ...'[30]

The consequences of the national court's determination of (non-)arbitrability of the dispute are **1.23** crucial when arbitral proceedings are already pending. In this case, the court which finds that the dispute may not be resolved in arbitration (i.e., agreement to arbitrate is null and void, inoperable or incapable of being performed),[31] will likely accept the jurisdiction to hear the case on the merits.

The court's decision, however, will not have an automatic effect on the arbitral tribunal which **1.24** – based on a competence-competence principle – may also accept the jurisdiction to hear effectively the same case.[32] This creates a risk of conflicting decisions on the same subject-matter (on the one hand the national court's judgment and, on the other hand, arbitral tribunal's award), the risk which is to be avoided.[33] Consequently, the better view is for the court to allow considerable deference to the parties' autonomy (to arbitrate the dispute) and only intervene in manifest instances where arbitration is used to evade law. Arguably, in the context of EU law, such a pre-award review is still unlikely to be needed, considering *ex post* scrutiny of the arbitral award performed in this context *ex officio* by one of the enforcement courts in the EU Member State under the New York Convention.[34]

---

27 Kleinheisterkamp (n 8) 91, 119.
28 Ragno, 'Inarbitrability' (n 25) 128, 156.
29 *Unamar*, para 52.
30 Ragno, 'Inarbitrability' (n 25) 128, 161.
31 Different authors have different ideas as to what would be the category under which subject-matter non-arbitrability should be subsumed pursuant to Art II(3) of the New York Convention. See e.g., Ragno, 'Inarbitrability' (n 25) 128, 157 (null and void); Born (n 4) 947–8 (incapable of being performed).
32 There are also different temporal configurations of this scenario, depending who decides first on the issue of its jurisdiction or what forum is first seized.
33 Situation which is usually remedied by the *lis pendens* rule.
34 See Arts V(2)(a) and V(2)(b) of the New York Convention. For further reading see Chapter 2.

3. Brussels I *bis*[35] and the arbitration exception

1.25 As mentioned above, it is truly undesirable for two different *fora* to decide on the same dispute matter. This may happen, however, in cases when the respondent in an ongoing arbitration brings an action before a national court other than at the seat of the arbitration, claiming the invalidity of an arbitration agreement.[36]

1.26 The solution on a domestic level (as well as on a European level)[37] – as far as the two parallel national courts' proceedings are concerned – can be found in adoption of the *lis pendens* principle, which in its simplest form allows the court first seized to decide the case, unless it finds it has no jurisdiction. Such a traditional *lis pendens*, however, assumes the parallel proceedings before *fora* of equal status, which is not a case when a national court and an arbitral tribunal are concurrently seized. In fact, such a solution was for long not considered to be necessary to institute at a European level,[38] because a design of the European regime allowing for free circulation of courts' judgments (the Brussels I regime) considered arbitration to be a self-contained system. Consequently, it was decided to specifically exclude arbitration and arbitration-related matters from the scope of its application.[39]

1.27 This, however, did not stop some unexpected clashes from occurring in the past, in particular in cases where the measures tailored in support of arbitration (such as anti-suit injunctions in *West Tankers*[40]) conflicted with the principle of mutual trust – a cornerstone of judicial cooperation in the European Union under the Brussels I regime. As detailed analysis of the interface between arbitration and Brussels I *bis* is given elsewhere in this book,[41] it suffices to say that the European Court of Justice was invited to decide on interpretation of the arbitration exception only on a limited number of occasions in the context of the Brussel I *bis* predecessors.[42] This case law, which is briefly outlined below, was effectively reflected upon and influenced the changes adopted in Brussels I *bis*.

---

35 Regulation No 1215/2012 of the European Parliament and of the Council of 12 December 2012 on jurisdiction and the recognition and enforcement of judgments in civil and commercial matters (recast), OJ L 351/1 ('Brussels I *bis* Regulation').

36 See above section B.2. See also Piotr Wiliński, 'Emergence of Lis Pendens Arbitralis in Europe' (2011) 15(3) *Kwartalnik ADR* 135.

37 The *lis pendens* principle is also transposed (albeit in quite elaborated form) on the European level of judicial cooperation through Section 9 of the Brussels I *bis*.

38 A separate *lis pendens* rule for arbitration-related matters was considered in the process of reform of Brussels I Regime but ultimately rejected in the Brussels I *bis*. For further reading see Wiliński, 'Lis Pendens Arbitralis' (n 36) 135; Filip De Ly, 'The Interface Between Arbitration and the Brussels Regulation' (2016) 5(3) *American University Business Law Review* 485.

39 See 1968 Brussels Convention on Jurisdiction and the Enforcement of Judgments in Civil and Commercial Matters (opened for signature 27 September 1968, entered into force 1 February 1973) OJ L 299 ('Brussels Convention') Art 1, second para, sub-s (4); Council Regulation (EC) No 44/2001 of 22 December 2000 on jurisdiction and the recognition and enforcement of judgments in civil and commercial matters, OJ L 12/1 ('old Brussels I Regulation') Art 1(2)(d); Brussels I *bis* Regulation (n 35) Art 1(2)(d).

40 C-185/07, *Allianz SpA v West Tankers Inc.* [2009] ECR I-00663.

41 See Chapter 3 at 3.71 onwards.

42 See, in particular, Case C-190/89, *Marc Rich & Co. AG v Societa Italiana Impianti PA* [1991] ECR 1-3855, C-391/95, *Van Uden Maritime BV, trading as Van Uden Africa Line v Kommanditgesellschaft in Firma Deco-Line* [1998] ECR I-7091, *West Tankers* (n 40).

In *Marc Rich*,[43] the European Court of Justice had to answer *inter alia* the preliminary question **1.28** of the English court as to the scope of the arbitration exception.[44] The case related to the sale of crude oil. The agreement to arbitrate had been incorporated in an exchange of telexes by the buyer. After the dispute related to contamination of cargo arose, an Italian seller brought an action in an Italian court seeking declaratory relief of non-liability. In turn, the buyer invoked an agreement to arbitrate as preventing the Italian court from accepting jurisdiction. Simultaneously the buyer commenced arbitration proceedings in London. After the Italian seller refused to appoint an arbitrator, the buyer sought the English court's assistance with the process of appointment. Before the English court, however, the Italian seller argued that the already commenced proceedings in Italy barred the English court's jurisdiction as the court second seized. Consequently, the European Court of Justice has been invited to decide on the scope of the arbitration exception under the Brussels Convention.[45] The European Court of Justice concluded that the arbitration exception is broad which means that:

> [b]y excluding arbitration from the scope of the Convention of 27 September 1968 on Jurisdiction and the Enforcement of Judgments in Civil and Commercial Matters, by virtue of Article 1(4) thereof, on the ground that it was already covered by international conventions, the Contracting Parties intended to exclude arbitration in its entirety, including proceedings brought before national courts.[46]

In the second case, *Van Uden*,[47] the European Court of Justice reiterated that arbitration **1.29** should be entirely excluded from the scope of the Brussels regime, when the arbitration is primarily related to the subject-matter. Yet, if it is of a secondary importance it may very well be covered by the Brussels regime. In this context, De Ly explains further that, 'the provisional measures normally do not relate to the conduct of arbitral proceedings but to the substantive interest of the parties and, therefore, are not covered by the arbitration exception'.[48]

The third and seminal case dealing with the arbitration exception was *West Tankers*[49] which **1.30** related to the anti-suit injunction issued in support of arbitration proceedings.[50] The argument was raised that, similarly to all other arbitration related issues, anti-suit injunctions in support of arbitration proceedings should be carved-out from the scope of the Brussels regime. The House of Lords in its application to the European Court of Justice argued that an anti-suit injunction is 'a valuable tool for the court of the seat of arbitration, exercising supervisory jurisdiction over the arbitration, as it promotes legal certainty and reduces the possibility of conflict between the arbitration award and the judgment of a national court'.[51] The European

---

43   *Marc Rich* (n 42).
44   For further reading, see also Dominique T Hascher, 'Recognition and Enforcement of Judgments on the Existence and Validity of an Arbitration Clause under the Brussels Convention' (1997) 13(1) *Arbitration International* 33.
45   The Brussels Convention (n 39) being a predecessor of the old Brussels I Regulation (n 39) and of the Brussels I *bis* Regulation (n 35).
46   *Marc Rich* (n 42).
47   *Van Uden* (n 42).
48   De Ly (n 38) 485, 493.
49   *West Tankers* (n 40). For a detailed analysis, see Chapter 3 at 3.63 onwards.
50   For the analysis of the *West Tankers* decision it is relevant to take into account two other, anti-suit injunction related decisions of the European Court of Justice, namely C-116/02, *Erich Gasser GmbH v MISAT Srl* [2003] ECR I-14693 and C-159/02 *Gregory Paul Turner v Felix Fareed Ismail Grovit, Harada Ltd and Changepoint SA* [2004] ECR I-3565. See also Chapter 3 at 3.56 onwards.
51   *West Tankers* (n 40) para 17.

Court of Justice remained unconvinced, however, and concluded that anti-suit injunctions are incompatible with the Brussels Regime. The *West Tankers* decision effectively disarmed the (primarily) English law from its effective mechanism limiting the risk of conflicting decisions on the same subject matter.

1.31 Consequently, it was possible that two or more judicial bodies would decide on the issue on the validity of the agreement to arbitrate. One could imagine, for example, parallel requests brought to (i) the court of an EU Member State at the seat (for a positive declaratory judgment on existence of agreement to arbitrate), (ii) a court of another EU Member State outside the seat of arbitration (seized to hear the dispute or asked for a negative declaratory judgment that the agreement to arbitrate is invalid), and finally (iii) an arbitral tribunal based on competence to decide on its own competence.

1.32 Importantly, the declaratory judgment of the country of the seat (which has a leading role in overseeing the arbitral process) would not benefit from a recognition under the Brussels regime (since carved out by the arbitration exception) and yet declaratory (or merits) judgment from the court of another Member State that invalidates the agreement to arbitrate would have to be recognized and enforced within the EU.[52] Such a result was undesirable, because it created a conflicting enforcement obligations, on the one hand, under the Brussels regime (assuming that a court of a Member State invalidated the agreement to arbitrate) and, on the other hand, under the New York Convention (assuming the tribunal accepts jurisdiction and renders an (jurisdictional) award).

1.33 All of the abovementioned case law has been taken into account in the drafting process of the Brussels I *bis* Regulation.[53] Of particular importance is the Recital 12 of the Brussels I *bis* which reads that:

> This Regulation should not apply to arbitration. Nothing in this Regulation should prevent the courts of a Member State, when seized of an action in a matter in respect of which the parties have entered into an arbitration agreement, from referring the parties to arbitration, from staying or dismissing the proceedings, or from examining whether the arbitration agreement is null and void, inoperative or incapable of being performed, in accordance with their national law.

> A ruling given by a court of a Member State as to whether or not an arbitration agreement is null and void, inoperative or incapable of being performed should not be subject to the rules of recognition and enforcement laid down in this Regulation, regardless of whether the court decided on this as a principal issue or as an incidental question.

> On the other hand, where a court of a Member State, exercising jurisdiction under this Regulation or under national law, has determined that an arbitration agreement is null and void, inoperative or

---

52   See *National Navigation Co v Endesa Generacion SA* [2009] EWCA Civ 1397. In principle, the aim of the Brussels I *bis* Regime is to allow a free movement of courts' judgments in the European Union. Consequently, based on a principle of mutual trust, which is a cornerstone of a judicial cooperation, '… judgments given in a Member State should be recognised in all Member States without the need for any special procedure.' (Brussels I *bis*, Recital 26). For further reading see also Xandra Kramer, 'Cross-Border Enforcement and the Brussels I-bis Regulation: Towards a New Balance between Mutual Trust and National Control over Fundamental Rights' (2013) 60(3) *Netherlands International Law Review* (NILR) 343-73.

53   For an overview of the evolution of the Brussels Regime, see Martin Illmer, 'The Arbitration Interface with Brussels I Recast: Past, Present and Future' in Franco Ferrari (ed), *The Impact of EU Law on Commercial Arbitration* (Juris 2017) 31.

incapable of being performed, this should not preclude that court's judgment on the substance of the matter from being recognised or, as the case may be, enforced in accordance with this Regulation. This should be without prejudice to the competence of the courts of the Member States to decide on the recognition and enforcement of arbitral awards in accordance with the Convention on the Recognition and Enforcement of Foreign Arbitral Awards, done at New York on 10 June 1958 ('the 1958 New York Convention'), which takes precedence over this Regulation.

The Recital 12 brings some important clarifications regarding arbitration and the Brussels regime.[54] What can be immediately observed is the broad scope of the arbitration exception mirroring the European Court of Justice decision in *Marc Rich*.[55] What is particularly telling, however, is paragraph four of the Recital 12 and related to it Article 73(2) of the Brussels I *bis* Regulation, which tackles the undesirable situation where the court of the EU Member State is faced with conflicting enforcement obligations. Pursuant to a solution envisaged under Brussels I *bis*, the court should give a precedence to the enforcement obligations arising from the New York Convention over similar enforcement obligations resulting from the Brussels I *bis* Regulation.[56]   **1.34**

At the same time, however, it is necessary to highlight that this solution might be insufficient at the seat of arbitration (provided that the enforcement of the arbitral award is not governed by the New York Convention). Additionally, it might create a situation where the court (outside the seat) and the arbitral tribunal are in a race who renders the decision on validity of the agreement to arbitrate first, because the Brussels I *bis* solution would only favour the arbitral decision if it is already 'enforcement-ready'.   **1.35**

All in all, the solution introduced by the Brussels I *bis* should be endorsed, as it recalibrates the balance between arbitration and the Brussels regime by aligning it with a broad arbitration exception. It is yet to be seen, however, how the solution will work in practice and would it be sufficient to truly deal with the risk of conflicting decisions on validity of the agreement to arbitrate.   **1.36**

C. MERITS PHASE OF ARBITRAL PROCESS

After potential hurdles at the outset of the arbitration proceedings, EU law may also play a role during the merits stage of the procedure. Two issues are of particular importance: the arbitrability of EU Law before the arbitral tribunal (see section C.1) and the way an arbitral tribunal is dealing with matters of EU law (section C.2).   **1.37**

---

54 For a detailed analysis of the Recital 12 of the Brussels I *bis* Regulation see De Ly (n 38) 485. See also Julio César Betancourt, 'International Commercial Arbitration and Private Agreement to Abide under Recital 12, Paragraph 2, of the Recast Brussels Regulation' (2018) 33 *Spain Arbitration Review* 69.

55 *Marc Rich* (n 42).

56 See also Chapter 3 at 3.71 onwards.

1. Subject-matter arbitrability of EU law

1.38   Subject-matter arbitrability has already been discussed above as an issue determining tribunal's jurisdiction.[57] The issue deserves separate attention, however, also when the merits phase of the proceedings is analysed. This is because the subject-matter arbitrability may also relate to the main contract and a dispute arising out of or related to it. That being said, as aptly observed by Hanotiau and Caprasse, '[a]rbitrability is part of public policy. The scope of arbitrable matters has been expanding continuously with the consequence that today, arbitrability is the rule, inarbitrability is the exception'.[58] In turn, it is now generally accepted that the arbitrators are allowed to deal with and apply EU law, including rules of the EU law related e.g., competition law.[59] At the same time, it is also clear that there are a number of norms prescribed on the EU law level that are of public policy character and this affects the post-award review of the arbitral award.[60]

1.39   Indeed, according to the European Court of Justice decision in *Eco Swiss*:

> A national court to which application is made for annulment of an arbitration award must grant that application if it considers that the award in question is in fact contrary to Article 85 of the EC Treaty (now Article 81 EC), where its domestic rules of procedure require it to grant an application for annulment founded on failure to observe national rules of public policy.[61]

1.40   The same rule would apply at the enforcement stage where, pursuant to Article V(2)(a) and (b) of the New York Convention, the subject-matter arbitrability and public policy may be reviewed by the enforcement court *ex officio*.[62]

1.41   All in all, the problem that arises is related to the scope of the review of the arbitral tribunal's findings on public policy rules of EU law.[63] Since this issue is subject to further study in other

---

57   See section B.1 and section B.2.

58   Bernard Hanotiau and Olivier Caprasse, 'Public Policy in International Commercial Arbitration', in Emmanuel Gaillard and Domenico Di Pietro (eds), *Enforcement of Arbitration Agreements and International Arbitral Awards: The New York Convention in Practice* (Cameron May 2008) 819. See, however, *Accentuate Ltd v Asigra Inc* [2009] EWHC (Comm) 2655, [89] where the court concluded that mandatory provisions of EU law are not arbitrable as reported and criticized in Born (n 4) 972.

59   See section C.2. See also Born (n 4) 992:

> In Europe, EU law provides that disputes directly concerning the validity or existence of registered intellectual property rights are non-arbitrable, instead being subject to the exclusive jurisdiction of specified national courts. Aside from this core area of nonarbitrability, disputes involving patent and other intellectual property claims are generally arbitrable in the EU.

> Blackaby (n 2) para 2.137. For further reading see also Gordon Blanke and Phillip Landolt (eds), *EU and US Antitrust Arbitration: A Handbook for Practitioners* (Kluwer Law International 2011).

60   As also explained in section B.1 the EU rules of public policy character may formalize both in primary and secondary EU legislation. See also Ragno, 'Are EU Overriding Mandatory Provisions an Impediment to Arbitral Justice?' (n 17) 139, 140.

61   *Eco Swiss* (n 14).

62   See Born (n 4) 3698.

63   Of particular relevance, see e.g., *Eco Swiss* (n 14) and C-567/14, *Genentech Inc. v Hoechst GmbH and Sanofi-Aventis Deutschland GmbH* [2016] ECLI:EU:C:2016:526. For a commentary, see e.g., Jacob Grierson, 'The Court of Justice of the European Union and International Arbitration' (2019) 2 *b-Arbitra (Belgian Review of Arbitration)* 309, 320–22 (explaining that CJEU in *Genetech* missed a chance to clarify applicable scope of the review of arbitral award post *Eco*

contributions in this book, at this point it is sufficient to note that the reason why it is problematic to deal with the public policy rules of EU law is because there is a considerable discrepancy between EU law and international arbitration law approaches to public policy.[64] As aptly observed by Bermann:

> It is small wonder, then, that the EU and international arbitration legal orders harbour public policy notions of strikingly different amplitude, and that each regards maintaining its favoured amplitude as critical to its own success. As the connectedness between the two regimes becomes more evident, however, important fault lines are coming into view, as when a broadly conceived EU public policy renders international arbitral awards far more susceptible to annulment, non-recognition and non-enforcement than first principles of international arbitration law normally allow. The dissonance is felt most palpably by Member State courts, as they stand directly in the cross-fire between the demands of EU public policy, on the one hand, and the duty to affirm and enforce international arbitral awards, on the other.[65]

Therefore although the arbitral tribunal should not shy away from applying EU law, it should do so with considerable care having in mind the fate of the award at the post award-stage.[66] **1.42**

2. Application of EU Law by the arbitral tribunals

As a general rule, arbitral tribunals have a rather broad discretion to apply rules of EU law, even those of a public policy character.[67] Also, it is a well-settled principle of international arbitration that an arbitral award is final and binding and the merits review is *not* allowed during the setting-aside or enforcement proceedings at the post-award stage.[68] There are few caveats with regard to the process of application of EU law by the arbitral tribunal, however. **1.43**

In this context, one should reflect further whether (i) a tribunal is allowed (or even obliged) to invoke mandatory EU law *ex officio*, (ii) in case of doubts as to the interpretation of EU law, the arbitral tribunal may refer the matter with a preliminary question to the Court of Justice of the **1.44**

Swiss); Paschalis Paschalidis, 'Genetech: EU Law Confronted with International Arbitration' (2016) 5(1) *European International Arbitration Review* 59. See, however, C-284/16 *Slovak Republic v Achmea* [2018] ECLI:EU:C:2018:158, para 54:

> It is true that, in relation to commercial arbitration, the Court has held that the requirements of efficient arbitration proceedings justify the review of arbitral awards by the courts of the Member States being limited in scope, provided that the fundamental provisions of EU law can be examined in the course of that review and, if necessary, be the subject of a reference to the Court for a preliminary ruling.

64 Bermann (n 1) 397, 420, 'Discrepancies in the scope of public policy between the EU and international arbitration regimes thus cannot be dismissed as of academic interest only.'

65 Ibid., 397, 444.

66 For further reading, see Chapter 2.

67 See e.g., Isidro (n 19) 421, 444–5, 'That arbitrators can – as a rule – adjudicate damage claims in the field of competition law is no longer contested in the EU.'; Helmut Brokelmann, 'The Rail Track Judgment of the LG Dortmunt: Are Cartel Damages Claims Arbitrable?' (2018) 31 *Spain Arbitration Review* 9, 'The arbitrability of disputes involving the application of competition law is today a settled matter in the European Union.'

68 For further reading, see Chapter 2.

European Union, and (iii) a tribunal (seated in the EU Member State) is obliged to follow rules of private international law as set out in Rome I Regulation[69] and Rome II Regulation.[70]

1.45 As to the first point, there are strong arguments in favour of *ex officio* application of EU law that are particularly related to the tribunal's duty to render an enforceable award.[71] It is so, because the court at the post-award stage will always take into account whether public policy rules have been observed by an arbitral tribunal.[72] These would inevitably include rules of EU law. If an arbitral tribunal follows parties' pleadings alone, where applicable mandatory norms of EU law (e.g., competition law) were not raised for some reason, its award might effectively be quashed at the post-award stage in cases where it accomplices to evasion of EU law.[73] In any event, when the issue of mandatory rules of EU law is raised *ex officio*, the tribunal should not surprise the parties and should always give the parties opportunity to address it.[74]

1.46 As to the second point, although arbitral tribunals should comply with the rules of EU law and apply it, they cannot request a determination on a point of EU law to the Court of Justice of the European Union based on Article 267 of the Treaty on the Functioning of the European Union.[75] This question has been raised on several occasions and rejected by the CJEU,[76] most

---

69   Regulation 593/2008 of the European Parliament and the Council of 17 June 2008 on the Law Applicable to Contractual Obligations, 2008 OJ L 177/6 (Rome I).

70   Regulation 864/2007 of the European Parliament and the Council of 11 July 2007 on the Law Applicable to Non-Contractual Obligations, 2008 OJ L 177/6 (Rome II).

71   Some institutional rules expressly state that the tribunal has such a duty, see e.g., Art 42 of the 2017 (as well as 2021) ICC Rules, '[T]he arbitral tribunal shall act in the spirit of the Rules and shall make every effort to make sure that the award is enforceable at law'; Art 32(2) of the 2014 LCIA Rules, '[T]he Arbitral Tribunal … shall make every reasonable effort to ensure that any award is legally recognised and enforceable at the arbitral seat'. See also Born (n 4) 1993, 'One of the arbitrator's most significant obligations is to render an award that is enforceable.'; Blackaby (n 2) para 11.11; Hanefeld (n 11) 401, 416.

72   *Eco Swiss* (n 14).

73   It is also not uncommon to argue that the arbitral tribunal has a duty to apply EU law. See e.g., Gordon Blanke, 'Defining the Limits of Scrutiny of Awards Based on Alleged Violations of European Competition Law' (2006) 23(3) *Journal of International Arbitration*, 249, 252:

>   In light of the foregoing, it can safely be stated that current arbitration practice within the EU Member States confirms the 'capacity' of the international arbitrator to invoke of his own motion relevant EC competition law issues in order to guarantee the making of an effective and enforceable arbitral award. Furthermore, in the aftermath of Eco Swiss, it also appears that the arbitrator has become subject to a duty to apply Community public policy, which includes [the EC competition law rules], ex officio.

>   Born (n 4) 1993, 'There is substantial commentary to the effect that an arbitral tribunal has the power – and the obligation – to apply mandatory national laws ex officio, even if not invoked by the parties.'. See, however, Hanefeld (n 11) 401, 416–17 (emphasizing lack of an important arbitral tribunal's power to request a preliminary ruling to the CJEU). Also, Denis Bensaude, 'Thalès Air Defence BV v GIE Euromissiles: Defining the Limits of Scrutiny of Awards Based on Alleged Violations of European Competition Law' (2005) 22(3) *Journal of International Arbitration* 239, 243:

>   Most importantly, the Thalès Air Defence decision makes clear that an award will not be subject to annulment based merely on an arbitral tribunal's failure to raise *sua sponte* potential violations of European competition law arising from the agreements at issue. This is an important clarification, as certain commentators suggested that Eco Swiss could be interpreted to impose such an obligation on arbitral tribunals.

74   See also Chapter 2. For further reading, see i.a. Piotr Wiliński, 'Excess of Powers' (n 3) 437–8; Hanefeld (n 11) 401, 417.

75   Consolidated version of the Treaty on the Functioning of the European Union, 2012 OJ C 326/47 (TFEU).

76   See i.a. C-108/81 *Nordsee Deutsche Hochseefischerei GmbH v Reederei Mond Nordstern AG & Co KG and Reederei Friedrich Busse Hochseefischerei Nordstern AG & Co KG* [1982] ECR 1982-01095, *Eco Swiss* (n 14) para 22; Case C-555/13 *Merck Canada Inc v Accord Healthcare Ltd and Others* [2014] ECLI:EU:C:2014:92, paras 17–19. For further reading see i.a. Jurgen Basedow, 'EU Law in International Arbitration: Referrals to the European Court of Justice' (2015)

recently in the context of investment arbitration in *Achmea* where the Court of Justice of the European Union concluded that:

> . . . a tribunal such as that referred to in Article 8 of the BIT cannot be regarded as a 'court or tribunal of a Member State' within the meaning of Article 267 TFEU, and is not therefore entitled to make a reference to the Court for a preliminary ruling.[77]

One might question whether such a limitation may not have a negative effect on the **1.47** uniformity of interpretation of EU law, in particular its overriding mandatory norms. At the same time, it appears to be well-settled in case law that arbitral tribunals constituted based on the parties' agreement to arbitrate cannot make a reference to the Court of Justice for a preliminary ruling.

The third point relevant under this section relates to a question whether an arbitral tribunal **1.48** seated in the EU has a duty to follow private international rules set out in Rome I Regulation and Rome II Regulation. Such a qualification should be rejected, however, as coming too close to the merits review. Additionally, this type of suggestion identifying the 'tribunal's duties' might be raised at the post-award stage (e.g., allegations of 'excess of mandate') and potentially broaden the scope of the court's scrutiny. In this context, it should be reiterated that the tribunal has a broad discretion in the process of application of law, including the process of choosing applicable law. Depending on applicable law and arbitration rules, the tribunal (in absence of the parties' choice) might be given a power to determine what private international law rules apply, or else, directly determine that governing law.[78] Of course, Rome I Regulation and Rome II Regulation should not be neglected in this process, as they will prove to be significant and useful tools in the process of application of law. Yet, from the practical standpoint, the process of application or non-application of the Rome I Regulation or Rome II Regulation would unlikely affect the fate of the award at the post-award stage (no review on the merits).[79]

All in all, there are many instances where an arbitral tribunal may be faced with EU law. In **1.49** general, the tribunal's discretion to determine and apply the law shields it from extended review at the post-award stage. At the same time, it is prudent for an arbitral tribunal to stay alert on influence of EU law throughout the whole arbitral process.

32(4) *Journal of International Arbitration* 367; Paschalis Paschalidis, 'Arbitral Tribunals and Preliminary References to the EU Court of Justice' (2017) 33(4) *Arbitration International* 663; Maciej Szpunar, 'Referrals of Preliminary Questions by Arbitral Tribunals to the CJEU' in Franco Ferrari (ed), *The Impact of EU Law on Commercial Arbitration* (Juris 2017) 85.

77 *Achmea* (n 63) para 49.

78 See e.g., Art 21(1) of the 2017 (as well as 2021) ICC Rules; Art 35(1) of the 2010 UNCITRAL Rules; Art 33(1) of the 1976 UNCITRAL Rules.

79 For further reading on the application of the Rome Regulation(s) in international commercial arbitration, see i.a. Burcu Yüksel, 'The Relevance of the Rome I Regulation to International Commercial Arbitration in the European Union' (2011) 7(1) *Journal of Private International Law* 149; Davor Babić, 'Rome I Regulation: Binding Authority for Arbitral Tribunals in the European Union?' (2017) 13(1) *Journal of Private International Law* 71; Pedro A De Miguel Asensio, 'The Rome I and Rome II Regulations in International Commercial Arbitration' in Franco Ferrari (ed), *The Impact of EU Law on Commercial Arbitration* (Juris 2017) 177; Friedrich Rosenfeld, 'The Rome Regulations in International Arbitration: The Road Not Taken' in Franco Ferrari (ed), *The Impact of EU Law on Commercial Arbitration* (Juris 2017) 245.

D. CONCLUSIONS

1.50 The purpose of this chapter was to flag the instances where EU law is of relevance in the context of international arbitration. As has been observed, there are many avenues where international arbitration and EU law intersect in the evermore intertwined international legal order. The arbitral tribunals should be mindful of the fact in what instances EU law is relevant, both at the jurisdictional as well as at the merits phase. Contributions in this book might offer an invaluable guidance in this process by providing directions and identifying pitfalls one can face when applying EU law in international commercial arbitration.

2

THE IMPACT OF EU LAW ON CHALLENGES, RECOGNITION AND ENFORCEMENT OF INTERNATIONAL COMMERCIAL AWARDS

Bo Ra Hoebeke and Juan Manuel Sánchez Pueyo[1]

A. INTRODUCTION

This chapter aims to provide insight into how EU law impacts the post-award stage of **2.01** international commercial arbitration from mainly two perspectives: the ((in)consistencies in) post-award regimes in the EU Member States and how these regimes are applied by national courts throughout the EU. Similarly to the previous chapter regarding the impact of EU law in the pre-award stage, this contribution addresses the reconciliation of two different starting points (or views): on the one hand, that 'arbitration' is a topic that is best left to the discretion of the EU Member States; on the other hand, that EU law should apply in a uniform and consistent manner throughout the entire EU.

In that light, this chapter focuses on (possible) (procedural) inconsistencies, as well as the **2.02** consistencies, in the post-award regimes throughout the EU, that may have an impact on

---

1 The authors are grateful for the assistance and input provided by their colleagues Mr. Georgios Fasfalis and Mr. Juan Pablo Valdivia Pizarro. Date of submission: 24/06/2020.

whether EU law is tested and applied in a uniform and consistent manner by the national courts in the EU. In view of the fact that other Chapters already cover how certain EU law issues (e.g., consumer protection) impact the post-award stage in depth, this Chapter focuses on the procedural side of annulment and enforcement proceedings throughout the EU.

2.03 We will first briefly describe the impact of EU law on national regimes dealing with the post-award stage in respect of international commercial arbitral awards (see Section B). Thereafter, we will address the procedural side of the national regimes for the annulment as well as the recognition and enforcement of international commercial arbitral awards, and whether such procedural aspects may have an impact on how and to what extent national courts (can) apply EU law in the post-award stage (see Section C). Section D addresses the grounds for challenging arbitral awards and for the refusal of recognition and enforcement of arbitral awards and how the way in which these are tested and applied by the national courts may impact how such courts (can) test EU law in the post-award stage. Finally, Section E will briefly address milestone decisions in respect of the impact of EU law on the post-award stage in respect of international commercial arbitral awards.

B. THE IMPACT OF EU LAW ON EU MEMBER STATES' NATIONAL REGIMES

2.04 Similar to how EU Member States generally have considerable discretion as to the structuring and regulation of court proceedings, EU law does not provide for the harmonisation of national procedures for the annulment and enforcement of commercial arbitral awards. However, the EU's traditional deference to the existing international arbitration regimes, such as the New York Convention has shaped and promoted a large degree of consistency as to the national post-award procedures throughout the EU.

1. The influence of the New York Convention and the ECICA

2.05 A large number of national arbitration laws in EU Member States are either based on the UNCITRAL Model Law or, to a certain extent, modelled on it.[2] In turn, the grounds for the setting aside of arbitral awards contained in the UNCITRAL Model Law are essentially the same as the refusal grounds contained in the United Nations Convention on the Recognition and Enforcement of Foreign Arbitral Awards, concluded in New York in 1958, usually referred to as the New York Convention ('NYC'). Moreover, all EU Member States are also signatories to the NYC. As a result, the NYC is of great importance to the understanding of the EU Member States' post-award regimes.

2.06 Another relevant instrument in the understanding of the development of national post-award procedures within the EU is the European Convention on International Commercial Arbitration concluded in Geneva in 1961 ('ECICA'). The ECICA was first proposed in the 1950s, but was only concluded in 1961, three years after the NYC, and entered into force on 7 January 1964. The ECICA covers a broader range of procedural aspects than the NYC, including on what grounds the setting aside of an arbitral award in one Contracting State could constitute a

---

2 See, e.g., Austria, Belgium, Bulgaria, Croatia, Cyprus, Denmark, Estonia, Germany, Greece, Hungary, Ireland, Lithuania, Malta, Slovakia, Slovenia and Spain. See also France that provides for a comparable regime.

ground for the refusal of recognition or enforcement in another Contracting State (or not). However, the ECICA has not received much attention from the arbitration community. Some attempts have been made in the past to try to revamp its importance, both from institutions[3] and commentators[4], but the attention given to the ECICA in the European arbitration community has not substantially increased, notwithstanding the fact that, in practice, the ECICA is sometimes applied.[5]

Prior to the conclusion of the NYC and the ECICA, in 1957, the Treaty of Rome, pursuant to **2.07** which the European Economic Community was created, established in Article 220 that the Member States were to enter into negotiation with a view to securing the 'simplification of formalities governing the reciprocal recognition and enforcement of judgments of courts or tribunals and of arbitration awards'. These negotiations crystallized in the 1968 Brussels Convention on Jurisdiction and the Enforcement of Judgments in Civil and Commercial Matters ('Brussels Convention'). Notably, Member States left out of the Brussels Convention any attempt to simplify the formalities governing the reciprocal recognition and enforcement of arbitral awards.

According to the report by P Jenard on the Brussels Convention, published in the Official **2.08** Journal of the European Communities, it seemed preferable to exclude arbitration at the time the Brussels Convention was being drafted, despite the fact that arbitration was expressly referred to in Article 220 of the Treaty of Rome. The reason, according to the Jenard report, was that there were already many international agreements on arbitration, such as the NYC and the ECICA, that had been prepared by the Council of Europe and were expected to 'facilitate the recognition and enforcement of arbitral awards to an even greater extent than the New York Convention'.[6]

For this reason, with respect to arbitration, the Brussels Convention concisely stated in Article **2.09** 1(4) that it 'shall not apply to (...) arbitration'. Thus, the Brussels Convention was not intended to apply to the recognition and enforcement of arbitral awards, was not intended to apply for the purpose of determining the jurisdiction of courts and tribunals in respect of litigation relating to arbitration and, finally, was not intended to apply to the recognition of judgments rendered in such proceedings.

---

3 See Committee for Trade, Industry and Enterprise Development of the Economic Commission for Europe; Revision of the 1961 European Convention on International Commercial Arbitration, Note by the Secretariat on the fifth session, dated 30 March 2001.

4 See Gerold Zeiler and Alfred Siwy, *The European Convention on International Commercial Arbitration: A Commentary* (Kluwer Law International 2018).

5 See e.g., Supreme Court of Austria, *Kajo-Erzeugnisse Essenzen GmbH v DO Zdravilisce Radenska*, 20 October 1993 and 23 February 1998 (Yearbook Commercial Arbitration 1999 – vol XXIVa); Supreme Court of Austria, *Buyer (Austria) v Seller (Serbia and Montenegro)*, 26 January 2005, 3 Ob 221/04b; Commercial Court for the Kemerovskaya Region, Russian Federation, *Ciments Français v Holding Company Sibirskiy Cement OJSC*, 20 July 2011 (Yearbook Commercial Arbitration 2011 – vol XXXVI).

6 Report by P Jenard on the Convention of 27 September 1968 on jurisdiction and the enforcement of judgments in civil and commercial matters [1979] Official Journal of the European Community, no C 59/13.

2. The Brussels (recast) regime and arbitration

2.10 The Brussels (recast) regime's impact on arbitration (related proceedings) is discussed in detail in Chapters 1 and 3. Therefore, we will only succinctly describe this issue to the extent relevant to the post-award regimes of the EU Member States, i.e., the recognition and enforcement of court decisions in respect of the annulment or enforcement of (commercial) arbitral awards. In that respect, it is clear that the Brussels (recast) regime does not apply: court decisions rendered in national proceedings related to the annulment of arbitral awards and court decisions in respect of the recognition and enforcement of arbitral awards cannot be recognised and enforced within the EU on the basis of the Brussels (recast) regime.[7]

2.11 Despite this explicit exclusion of arbitration from the scope of the Brussels regime, difficulties began to arise in matters where there was overlap between the jurisdiction of the Member State courts on one hand, and that of arbitral tribunals constituted in a Member State, on the other.[8] These clashes between EU law and arbitration became patent, first, as a result of the expansion of the European Community in 1973, with Denmark, the United Kingdom and Ireland's membership.[9] Further discussion on this issue arose in light of Greece's accession to the Brussels Convention in 1982.[10]

2.12 After these events, the European Court of Justice (ECJ) became the main EU institution dealing with the problems arising from the interaction between the Brussels regime and arbitration. On 25 July 1991, the ECJ rendered its preliminary ruling in the case *Marc Rich*.[11] This was the first case in which the ECJ addressed the exclusionary approach towards arbitration taken in the Brussels Convention, and it dealt with ancillary proceedings in relation

---

7   See Regulation (EU) No 1215/2012 of the European Parliament and of the Council of 12 December 2012 on jurisdiction and the recognition and enforcement of judgments in civil and commercial matters (recast) [2012] OJ L 351/1, Rec 12(4):

    This Regulation should not apply to any action or ancillary proceedings relating to, in particular, the establishment of an arbitral tribunal, the powers of arbitrators, the conduct of an arbitration procedure or any other aspects of such a procedure, nor to any action or judgment concerning the annulment, review, appeal, recognition or enforcement of an arbitral award.

    See Jenard Report (n 6) 13; Peter Schlosser, Report on the Convention of October 9, 1978, signed in Luxembourg, on the accession of the Kingdom of Denmark, Ireland and the United Kingdom to the Convention on Jurisdiction and the Enforcement of Judgments in Civil and Commercial Matters and to the Protocol on its interpretation by the Court of Justice [1979] OJ C 59/71, 93; Case C-391/95, *Van Uden Maritime BV, trading as Van Uden Africa Line v Kommanditgesellschaft Firma Deco-Line and Another* [1998] ECR I-07091, para 32; District Court of Rotterdam 22 June 2009, ECLI:NL:RBROT:2009:BI9014, *SNP Petrom SA v NIS Oil Industry of Serbia, NIS Jugopetrol S&S* 2010, 3, ground no 4.5.

8   Alexander R Markus and Sandrine Giroud, 'A Swiss Perspective on West Tankers and Its Aftermath: What about the Lugano Convention?' (2010) 28(2) *ASA Bulletin (Association Suisse de l'Arbitrage)* 233. Due to Ireland's and the UK's common law tradition, the interpretation of the arbitration exclusion provision found in the original Brussels Convention was seen by these countries as more extensive. Despite the divergence of view, the Schlosser Report reflected a consensus for a broad exclusion of arbitration from the Brussels Convention, highlighting that it does not apply to judgments concerning the validity of an arbitration agreement, where the arbitration agreement is invalid, or where parties are ordered to discontinue arbitration (see Schlosser Report (n 7) para 64).

9   See Markus and Giroud (n 8).

10   Report on the Accession of the Hellenic Republic to the Community Convention on Jurisdiction and the Enforcement of Judgments in Civil and Commercial Matters [1986] OJ C 298/1, para 35.

11   Case C-190/89, *Marc Rich & Co AG v Società Italiana Impianti PA* [1991] ECR I-03855.

to an arbitration. Thereafter, the ECJ issued a number of seminal decisions that clarified and shaped the boundaries between EU law and arbitration. In 1995, the ECJ rendered its judgment in the *Van Uden* case,[12] dealing with the applicability of the Brussels Convention to court proceedings regarding preliminary measures requested by a party in relation to arbitration proceedings. Thereafter, in 2002 and 2009 respectively, the ECJ issued decisions in the *Turner*[13] and *West Tankers* cases.[14] As discussed in more detail in Chapter 3 of this book, these two decisions addressed the issue of anti-suit injunctions. The outcome of the ECJ decisions in these two cases was that the proceedings against which an anti-suit injunction in favour of arbitration are directed fall within the scope of the Brussels I Regulation and that the anti-suit injunction in favour of arbitration was incompatible with the Regulation.[15]

The next key development in this area was the entry into force of the Regulation 1215/2012 on jurisdiction and the recognition and enforcement of judgments in civil and commercial matters (recast) ('Brussels I Regulation (recast)'), which was drafted considering the ECJ case law mentioned above. As also discussed in Chapter 1, the Brussels I Regulation (recast) offered important clarifications as to the interaction between EU law and arbitration.[16] **2.13**

Of particular relevance for the post-award phase is paragraph 3 of Recital 12, which deals with the potential conflict that may arise when a Member State court has the duty to enforce a judgment under the Regulation and, at the same time, the duty to enforce an arbitral award relating to the same dispute under the NYC. Recital 12, paragraph 3, explains that the court's obligation to enforce the first judgment will be without prejudice of the court's competence to decide on the recognition and enforcement of arbitral awards under the NYC. **2.14**

---

12   See *Van Uden* (n 7).
13   Case C-159/02, *Gregory Paul Turner v Felix Fareed Ismail Grovit, Harada Ltd. and Changepoint SA* [2004] ECR I-3565.
14   Case C-185/07, *Allianz SpA v West Tankers Inc.* [2009] ECR I-00663.
15   See Markus and Giroud (n 8).
16   The Brussels I Regulation (recast) included a new Art 73, that specified that it 'shall not affect the application of the 1958 New York Convention'. Moreover, it included a new recital in its preamble, which intended to elaborate further on the succinct exclusion of arbitration contained in both the 1968 Brussels Convention on jurisdiction and the enforcement of judgments in civil and commercial matters [1972] OJ L 299/32 and the Council Regulation (EC) No 44/2001 of 22 December 2000 on jurisdiction and the recognition and enforcement of judgments in civil and commercial matters [2001] OJ L 12 /1 (Brussels I regulation). Recital 12 of the Brussels I Regulation (recast) clarified the following issues with respect to arbitration:

The Brussels I Regulation (recast) should not:

prevent the courts of a Member State, when seized of an action in a matter in respect of which the parties have entered into an arbitration agreement, from referring the parties to arbitration, from staying or dismissing the proceedings, or from examining whether the arbitration agreement is null and void, inoperative or incapable of being performed, in accordance with their national law

- A ruling given by a court of a Member State as to whether or not an arbitration agreement is null and void, inoperative or incapable of being performed should not be subject to Brussels I Regulation (recast).
- Where a court of a Member State, with jurisdiction under the Brussels I Regulation (recast) or under national law, has determined that an arbitration agreement is null and void, inoperative or incapable of being performed, this should not preclude that court's judgment on the substance of the matter from being recognized or, as the case may be, enforced in accordance with the Brussels I Regulation (recast). This should be without prejudice to the competence of the courts of the Member States to decide on the recognition and enforcement of arbitral awards in accordance with the Convention on the Recognition and Enforcement of Foreign Arbitral Awards (opened for signature 10 June 1958, entered into force 7 June 1959) 330 UNTS 4 ('the New York Convention'), which takes precedence over this Regulation.

2.15 Finally, as also discussed in more detail in Chapter 3, after the implementation of the Brussels I Regulation (recast), the ECJ had to decide again on a preliminary question in relation to anti-suit injunction in the *Gazprom* case.[17] The practical implications of the ECJ decision in the *Gazprom* case are that, while arbitral tribunals have the power under EU law to issue anti-suit injunctions against parties that are in breach of the arbitration agreement conferring jurisdiction upon the arbitral tribunal, courts of the Member States cannot issue anti-suit injunctions when the breach of the arbitration agreement is the result of proceedings being initiated in the courts of another Member State.

2.16 In light of the above, it seems that the Brussels (recast) regime will only impact the post-award stage in very specific circumstances, such as those referred to in paragraph 3 of Recital 12 of the Brussels I Regulation (recast).

C. PROCEEDINGS IMPACTING THE REVIEW OF EU LAW

2.17 Whether and to what extent EU law may have an impact in the post-award stage heavily depends on whether and to what extent national courts are allowed to assess issues of EU law in annulment proceedings (if available) in the various EU Member States (see sub section C.1), and in enforcement proceedings in respect of international commercial arbitral awards (see sub section C.2).

1. Annulment proceedings: (in)consistencies throughout the EU

2.18 The main procedure in which an arbitral award can be challenged is the annulment (or setting aside) procedure. In annulment proceedings the national courts have, in any event, *some* room to assess and test an arbitral award and through that court review how EU law may impact the post-award phase.

2.19 The first question is whether all EU Member States provide for an annulment procedure in respect of international commercial arbitral awards.[18] Surprisingly, this is not entirely clear: in Latvia, the arbitration act does not provide for setting aside proceedings in respect of any arbitral awards, domestic or international. However, the Latvian Constitutional Court seems to have ensured that parties can challenge an arbitral tribunal's jurisdiction before the national courts. [19] In addition, in some EU Member States the parties can – to some extent – exclude setting aside proceedings. For example, in Belgium setting aside proceedings are available, but it is possible that parties agree to waive the right to institute setting aside proceedings if none

---

17   Case C-536/13, *'Gazprom' OAO v Lietuvos Respublika* [2014] ECLI:EU:C:2014:2414.

18   In this respect, this publication does not take Brexit into account, also considering that the relevant regimes regard either national law or the New York Convention.

19   Toms Krūmiňš, 'Arbitration in Latvia: A Cautionary Tale?' (2017) 34(2) *Journal of International Arbitration* 327; Ģirts Lejiņš and Eva Kalnina, 'National Report for Latvia (2018 through 2020)' in Lise Bosman (ed), *ICCA International Handbook on Commercial Arbitration* (ICCA & Kluwer Law International 2020, Suppl 110, April 2020) 41. In 2014, the Latvian Constitutional Court found Latvian arbitration law, to the extent it denies a person the right to contest a tribunal's jurisdiction before a court, to be inconsistent with section 92 of the Latvian constitution (which incorporates the right of access to courts). It also suggested to the Latvian legislature to introduce grounds for the setting aside of arbitral awards (Latvian Constitutional Court, Case No 2014-09-01, 28 November 2014).

of the parties are Belgian.[20] A similar waiver is available in Sweden and France.[21] Also, the English Arbitration Act allows, in respect of domestic and international arbitral awards, parties to *partially* waive the right to institute setting aside proceedings, in respect of the national courts' review of the substance of the award. However, the English Arbitration Act does not allow such waiver in respect of the court's review of jurisdictional objections and procedural complaints.[22]

If setting aside proceedings are not available or if the parties can agree to (partially) exclude setting aside proceedings, this may essentially mean that the parties can (partially) opt out of the national courts' review of the arbitral award, also in respect of EU law. Logically, this affects the potential impact of EU law in the post-award stage. Of course, if the enforcement of the arbitral award is requested within the EU, this review by the courts is likely to take place in that context. However, there may well be circumstances in which this is not the case, even though the merits of the award do regard issues of (fundamental) EU law. Put in extreme terms, this opens up the possibility to (partially) contract out of the national courts' review (on the merits) as to the compliance with (fundamental) EU law, either through the choice of the formal seat of the arbitration (e.g. Latvia) or through the parties' agreement to (partially) exclude setting aside proceedings (as allowed in Belgium, Sweden, France and England and Wales or Northern Ireland). **2.20**

Secondly, the potential impact of EU law in setting aside proceedings further depends on, for example, what practical room is provided to applicants in setting aside proceedings to prepare and present their case and whether the procedure as such facilitates and provides an incentive to national courts to interfere (with a view to ensuring the correct application of EU law). **2.21**

In respect of how setting aside proceedings are practically provided for, a large degree of uniformity exists within EU Member States. Generally, in several EU Member States parties have three months after the arbitral award was made to prepare the filing of the application for the setting aside. However, in many EU Member States this term is shorter. For example, Sweden changed the three-month term into a two-month term.[23] Also, in Poland,[24] Portugal,[25] Slovakia,[26] Spain[27] and Hungary[28] the parties only have two months to bring setting **2.22**

---

20 Belgian Judicial Code, Art 1718; see also 'Chapter 16: Annulment of International Arbitral Awards' in Gary B Born, *International Arbitration: Law and Practice* (2nd edn, Kluwer Law International 2015) 341.

21 Sweden, Swedish Arbitration Act (SFS 1999:116; updated as per SFS 2018:1954), S 51, 'If none of the parties is domiciled or has its place of business in Sweden, such parties may in a commercial relationship through an express written agreement exclude or limit the application of the grounds for setting aside an award as are set forth in Section 34.' See, in respect of France, Code of Civil Procedure (CCP) Art 1522.

22 See Born (n 20) 341. Of course, strictly speaking, the English Arbitration Act would not be relevant to this analysis of the EU Member States' regimes for annulment proceedings as the UK is not an EU Member State anymore.

23 Sweden, Swedish Arbitration Act (SFS 1999:116; updated as per SFS 2018:1954), S 34; see Aren Goldsmith, Harry Nettlau, 'The Revised Swedish Arbitration Act: Some Noteworthy Developments' (Kluwer Arbitration Blog, 19 May 2019) <http://arbitrationblog.kluwerarbitration.com/2019/05/19/the-revised-swedish-arbitration-act-some-noteworthy-developments/> accessed 24 June 2020.

24 Polish CCP, Art 1208(1).

25 Portuguese Voluntary Arbitration Law, Art 46(6).

26 Slovak Arbitration Law, S 41.

27 Spanish Arbitration Law, Art 41(4).

28 Act LX on arbitration, S 47(3).

aside proceedings. Estonia,[29] France,[30] Luxembourg,[31] Lithuania[32] and Romania[33] grant the parties only one month for preparing the setting aside application. However, in Luxembourg, this term is triggered by the notification of the order of execution to the parties (and not the rendering, sending or receipt of the arbitral award itself), and a Luxembourg court may only set aside an arbitral award after the exequatur has been granted.[34] Interestingly, Ireland's 56-day term seems quite strict but represents, in fact, in case of an application based on public policy grounds, an open ended term, as the term starts from the date on which circumstances giving rise to the application became known or ought reasonably to have become known to the party concerned.[35]

2.23 Whether a shorter term to institute setting aside proceedings, in practice, indeed leads to less room for parties to prepare (and institute) setting aside proceedings may also depend on other features of the procedure. For example, in the Netherlands, parties in fact have *more than* the three full months as from the date on which the arbitral award was sent to the parties,[36] based on the assumption that the arbitral award is 'sent' only four weeks after the date of the arbitral award.[37] However, this feature is more or less counterbalanced by Dutch case law that, in principle, requires a claimant in setting aside proceedings to state in the document initiating the proceedings *all* setting aside grounds in respect of *all* parts of the arbitral award against which the grounds are directed.[38] Thus, the (almost) four-month term in the Netherlands within which a claimant essentially needs to prepare its setting aside claim in full may seem generous, but may – in practice – provide less room for a claimant to prepare its setting aside claim when compared to a regime that requires that setting aside proceedings are instituted within a shorter period but allows a claimant to further adduce setting aside grounds in the course of the proceedings.[39]

2.24 Thirdly, the potential impact of EU law in setting aside proceedings may also vary on the basis of how many instances the setting aside proceedings cover, and whether there is a (central/higher) court that can give direction to case law regarding setting aside claims.

2.25 Generally, within most of the EU Member States such application for the setting aside of an arbitral award is decided on by at least one lower (factual) court, with the possibility to lodge

---

29   Estonian CCP, Art 752(1).
30   See French CCP, Art 1519. If foreign parties are involved, in which case the time limits extend by two months, by virtue of Art 643(2) French CCP.
31   Luxembourg CCP, Art 1246.
32   Law on Commercial Arbitration of Lithuania, Art 50(5).
33   Romanian CCP, Art 611.
34   Luxembourg CCP, Art 1246.
35   Irish Arbitration Act, Art 12.
36   Dutch Code of Civil Procedure ('DCCP'), Art 1064a(2).
37   DCCP, Art 1058(2). See GJ Meijer, AIM van Mierlo, *Parlementaire Geschiedenis Arbitragewet* (Wolters Kluwer 2015) 119-20; GJ Meijer, *Tekst & Commentaar Burgerlijke Rechtsvordering* (Wolters Kluwer 2018); DCCP, Art 1058 note 1c, cf Amsterdam District Court 19 November 2019, ECLI:NL:GHAMS:2019:4121, *Korbusiness BV* (2020) 19 *Tijdschrift voor Arbitrage*, ground no 4.4; Arnhem-Leeuwarden Court of Appeal 8 October 2019, ECLI:NL:GHARL:2019:8203, *Stichting Amphia* (2020) 13 *Tijdschrift voor Arbitrage*, ground no 4.2.
38   DCCP, Art 1064a(4).
39   See e.g., Czech Republic. According to a 2012 Czech Supreme Court decision, a party requesting that the award be set aside can raise additional grounds for setting aside at any point before the first oral hearing (Czech Supreme Court, File No 23 Cdo 3728/2011, 9 May 2012).

appeal to the highest court in that jurisdiction. Also, in this respect there are some exceptions. For example, in Austria, Bulgaria and Malta the highest (supreme) court is competent to hear setting aside applications (in the case of Austria, unless it regards labour or consumer disputes[40]),[41] whereas in Ireland and Spain such applications are decided in one instance by a lower court but *without* appeal to the national Supreme Court.[42] In the Netherlands, the 2015 Arbitration Act abandoned the three-layer review of setting aside applications and limited setting aside proceedings to only one factual instance (Court of Appeal), with the possibility to institute appeal in cassation before the Dutch Supreme Court (which appeal can be excluded unless one of the parties is a consumer).[43]

Finally, some procedural mechanisms within the national regimes for annulment proceedings **2.26** may provide the national courts with more room to address issues of EU law. For example, where a court can remit the dispute to the arbitral tribunal in order to address an issue of fundamental EU law,[44] the court may be more easily inclined to address that issue in setting aside proceedings than when the court only has the option of setting aside the arbitral award on that basis. The same applies in respect of the possibility to *partially* set aside an arbitral award:[45] in case a court can merely partially set aside an arbitral award it may also be more easily inclined to sustain a setting aside claim.

Notwithstanding the aforementioned, the possible impact of EU law in setting aside pro- **2.27** ceedings will – to a large(r) extent – depend on how a national court fulfils its supervising role

---

40   Christian W Konrad, Philipp A Peters, 'Challenging and Enforcing Arbitration Awards 2019' (*Global Arbitration Review*, 15th May 2019) <https://globalarbitrationreview.com/jurisdiction/1005933/austria> accessed 24 June 2020.

41   See regarding Bulgaria, Law on International Commercial Arbitration, Prom SG 60/1988, Amend SG 8/24 Jan 2017, Art 47 and regarding Malta, Arbitration Act 1996 (Cap 387), Art 57(b). In the case of Malta, the highest court is the Court of Appeal.

42   Ireland, Arbitration Act 2010, Number 1 of 2010, Ss 9(1)(a) and 11(b)(1); Michael M Collins, 'National Report for Ireland (2019 through 2020)' in Lise Bosman (ed), *ICCA International Handbook on Commercial Arbitration* (ICCA & Kluwer Law International 2020, Suppl 110, April 2020) 2. Spain, Arbitration Law 60/2003 (with 2009 and 2011 amendments) Arts 8(5) and 42(2).

43   DCCP, Art 1064a(5).

44   Netherlands, Code of Civil Procedure, Art 1065a(1):

  The Court of Appeal may, at the request of a party or on its own motion, suspend the setting aside proceedings for a period of time to be determined by the Court of Appeal to put the arbitral tribunal in a position to reverse the ground for setting aside by reopening the arbitral proceedings or by taking other measures as the arbitral tribunal considers appropriate …

  See also Belgium, Judicial Code, Art 1717(6); Croatia, Law on Arbitration, Art 36(4); Cyprus, The International Commercial Arbitration Law, 1987, No 101, Art 34(4); Denmark, Arbitration Act 2005, S 37(5); Finland, Arbitration Act (1992/967) amended in 2015, S 42; Hungary, Act LX of 2017 on Arbitration, Art 47(4); Ireland, Arbitration Act 2010, No 1 of 2010, S 6(a) and Sch 1; Lithuania, Law on Commercial Arbitration, 2012, Art 50(6); Malta, Arbitration Act 1996 (Cap 387), Art 55 Malta Arbitration Act; Poland, Code of Civil Procedure, Art 1209; Portugal, Voluntary Arbitration Law, Art 46(8); Slovenia, Law on Arbitration, Art 40(5); Sweden, Swedish Arbitration Act (SFS 1999:116; updated as per SFS 2018:1954), S 35.

45   Netherlands, Code of Civil Procedure, Art 1065(5):

  If a ground for setting aside only concerns a part of the arbitral award, then the award shall not be set aside in respect of the remaining part, insofar as this, taking into account the content and purport of the award, is not inseparably connected with the part to be set aside.

  See also Austria, Code of Civil Procedure, Art 611(3); Belgium, Judicial Code, Art 1717(3)(a)(iii); Croatia, Law on Arbitration, Art 36(2)(1)(d); Cyprus, The International Commercial Arbitration Law, 1987, No. 101, Art 34(2)(a)(3) and Art 34(4); Denmark, Arbitration Act 2005, S 37(3); Estonia, Code of Civil Procedure, Art 751(3).

in setting aside proceedings. This, in turn, depends to a large degree on the setting aside grounds that are available in that jurisdiction and how these setting aside grounds are – in practice – applied by the national courts. In that light, Section D addresses, per setting aside/refusal ground, where relevant, the question of whether the national courts of the EU Member States may *ex officio* apply that ground and whether they are to apply *restraint* in testing and applying these grounds.

2. Enforcement proceedings: (in)consistencies throughout the EU

2.28 When discussing the enforcement of awards, a distinction needs to be made between domestic awards and non-domestic or foreign awards, which distinction is not (always) the same as the distinction between 'international' and 'non international' awards.

2.29 Each jurisdiction, including all EU Member States,[46] has its own laws and case law as to what is considered a *domestic* award and the requirements to enforce them. Most jurisdictions consider 'domestic' awards to be awards rendered in arbitral proceedings of which the formal venue is located within the respective jurisdiction. There are exceptions, such as France, where an arbitration is considered international when international commercial interests are at play.[47] In that case, whether an arbitration is domestic or international is determined by the interest underlying the dispute.[48]

2.30 In some jurisdictions, such as Belgium, the Netherlands and Germany, a domestic award becomes enforceable only after the competent national court has granted leave for enforcement.[49] In others, the award is automatically enforceable after it is rendered. For instance, under Austrian law, an arbitral award has the same rank as a judgment of an Austrian national court, and the award is an enforceable title. The same applies, for example, under Spanish, Swedish and Portuguese law.

2.31 In those jurisdictions where leave for enforcement is necessary, a request for leave should be brought before a court of first instance. This is the case in, for example, Belgium, Finland, Greece and the Netherlands.[50] However, in the case of Poland, such a request should be brought before an appellate court.[51] In some jurisdictions, for example, the Netherlands, the procedure to seek leave for enforcement may be initiated and carried out *ex parte*.[52] In the Netherlands, such leave for enforcement is, thus, usually obtained (in the first instance) in only a few hours or days on the basis of a simple request filed with the competent Dutch court, which request – generally – will be granted by the court without hearing the parties (and

---

46 For an overview of the Member States national laws differentiation between international and domestic awards see T Cole and others, *Legal Instruments and Practice of Arbitration in the EU* (EU Directorate General for Internal Policies 2014) Annex B.

47 French Code of Civil Procedure, Art 1504.

48 See French Court of Cassation 1st Civil Chamber, 13 March 2007; and French Court of Cassation 1st Civil Chamber, 20 November 2013.

49 See e.g., Belgian Judicial Code, Art 1719; Zivilprozessordnung (ZPO), S 1062(1) no 4; DCCP, Art 1062(2).

50 See Art 1710 of the Belgian Judicial Code; S 43 FAA, Art 918(2)(d) GCCP; Art 1062(1) DCCP.

51 Polish CCP, Art 1213(1)(1).

52 See e.g., Luxembourg (see Guy Harles, 'National Report for Luxembourg (2018 through 2020)' in Lise Bosman (ed), *ICCA International Handbook on Commercial Arbitration* (Kluwer Law International 2020, Suppl 109, February 2020) 23).

without requesting any (further) briefing by the parties).[53] In other jurisdictions *ex parte* proceedings are allowed, but the party against whom enforcement is sought, is granted the opportunity to appear in the proceedings in case it becomes aware of them.[54]

The exequatur procedure in respect of domestic arbitral awards may also differ as to the **2.32** possibility to challenge the exequatur or the refusal thereof. In the Netherlands, in principle, no appeal is possible *against* the granting of leave to enforce a domestic award other than (further) pursuing the challenge of that award,[55] whereas the *refusal* to grant a leave to enforce can be appealed before the Court of Appeals and, subsequently, the Supreme Court.[56]

As to *foreign* or *non-domestic* awards, the starting point is that Article III NYC essentially **2.33** leaves it up to the national legislation *how* enforcement proceedings take place, provided that the enforcement of a foreign arbitral award is not subject to 'substantially more onerous conditions' than those applicable to the enforcement of domestic awards.[57]

In case of recognition and enforcement of a foreign award in Austria, Bulgaria, Finland or **2.34** Greece,[58] the competent court is a court of first instance, with an appeal mechanism available.[59] In other EU Member States (e.g., Italy, Lithuania, the Netherlands, Poland, Portugal and Sweden[60]), appellate courts are responsible for the recognition and enforcement of foreign awards. In Spain, the competent court for recognition of foreign awards is the Civil and Criminal Chamber of the Superior Court of Justice of the relevant administrative region, while enforcement matters are heard by the relevant court of first instance.[61] Recognition and

---

53   DCCP, Art 1062. See also (n 50).
54   See Art 1720(3) of the Belgian Judicial Code. See also, Marc Dal, 'National Report for Belgium (2019 through 2020)' in Lise Bosman (ed), *ICCA International Handbook on Commercial Arbitration* (ICCA & Kluwer Law International International 2020, Suppl 110, April 2020) 1–57.
55   DCCP, Art 1062(3). Art 1063(2) DCCP limits the refusal grounds to only public policy in case no setting aside proceedings were (timely) instituted.
56   DCCP, Art 1063(4) and (5).
57   Art III NYC reads as follows:

> Each Contracting State shall recognize arbitral awards as binding and enforce them in accordance with the rules of procedure of the territory where the award is relied upon, under the conditions laid down in the following articles. There shall not be imposed substantially more onerous conditions or higher fees or charges on the recognition or enforcement of arbitral awards to which this Convention applies than are imposed on the recognition or enforcement of domestic arbitral awards.

58   Austrian Enforcement Act, Art 409; see also ACCP, Art 614(1); Bulgarian LICA, Art 51 and Bulgarian PILC Arts 118–119; Finnish AA, S 54; Greek CCP, Art 905.
59   See e.g., Austrian Enforcement Act, Arts 78 and 411(1); Austrian CCP, Arts 514–528a, esp 521a; Bulgarian CCP, Art 258(1); Finnish Code of Judicial Procedure, Ch 25 Art 1, Ch 25a Art 5 and Ch 30 Arts 1 and 2.
60   Italian CCP, Art 839; Law on Courts of the Republic of Lithuania, Art 21(2); Lithuanian CCP, Art 809(1); Lithuanian LC, Art 51(2)A; DCCP, Arts 1075(2) and 1076(6); Polish CCP, Art 1213(1)(1); Portuguese LVA, Art 59; Swedish AA, Ss 56 and 59. In principle, appeal in cassation is available in these jurisdictions. However, there is no recourse available against a court's decision under the New York Convention, which recognizes and enforces a foreign arbitral award in the Netherlands (see Dutch Supreme Court, 25 June 2010, *Rosneft v Yukos* (2011) 40 *Tijdschrift voor Arbitrage*; Dutch Supreme Court 31 March 2017, *Nelux v Respondents* (2017) 25 *Tijdschrift voor Arbitrage*).
61   Spanish AL, Art 8(6).

enforcement of foreign awards may be *ex parte* (e.g., in Austria, France, Greece or Italy)[62] or *adversarial* (e.g., in Croatia, Cyprus, Finland, Germany, the Netherlands, Portugal or Sweden).[63]

2.35 The legal framework regarding enforcement of domestic awards equally applies to foreign awards in some jurisdictions, such as Belgium or Denmark.[64] In other jurisdictions, the applicable framework may well differ if foreign awards are concerned.

2.36 For example, in the Netherlands, the procedure in respect of foreign arbitral awards starts directly with the Court of Appeal and is *not* an *ex parte* procedure (like the first instance exequatur procedure in respect of domestic arbitral awards).[65] However, also in respect of *foreign* arbitral awards, based on Article III NYC, in principle, no appeal in cassation is possible against the granting of a leave to enforce.[66] In practice, this means that in the Netherlands – generally – in respect of *foreign* arbitral awards the party against whom the enforcement is sought, will appear in the proceedings and written and oral submissions will be made by the parties. Thus, from a procedural perspective, if EU law issues are at play, it is likely that these will be addressed by the parties before the Dutch court in enforcement proceedings regarding *foreign* arbitral awards, whereas this is *not* the case in the Dutch *ex parte* enforcement proceedings (in the first instance) regarding *domestic* arbitral awards.[67]

2.37 That being said, if obtaining an exequatur is required for the enforcement of international arbitral awards, the possible impact of EU law in the post-award stage through enforcement proceedings will – to a large(r) extent – depend on the refusal grounds available in the relevant jurisdiction and how these are – in practice – applied by the national courts.

D. GROUNDS FOR SETTING ASIDE AND ENFORCEMENT PROCEEDINGS

1. General notes on setting aside and refusal grounds

2.38 As already mentioned, within the EU the national provisions are largely similar in respect of the grounds that an applicant can invoke in order to annul an arbitral award as many EU Member States either adopted the Model Law or based their national arbitration act on the

---

62 Austrian Enforcement Act, Art 410; French CCP, Art 1516; Athens Court of Appeal No 29/2010; Italian CCP, Article 839.

63 Croatian AA, Art 49(2); Cypriot Foreign Courts Judgments Law, Art 5; Finnish AA, Art 55(1); ZPO, S 1063(1); DCCP, Arts 986-88; Portuguese LVA, Art 57(2); Swedish AA, S 57.

64 Belgian Judicial Code, Art 1719; Danish Arbitration Act, S 38.

65 DCCP, Arts 1075–1076.

66 Dutch Supreme Court 25 June 2020, Rosneft/Yukos Capital NJ 2012/55. This is not the case if, in the country of origin, no setting aside proceedings are or were available, without the unavailability thereof being the result of the parties' agreeing to exclude setting aside proceedings. As follows from the above, within the EU, this essentially could only regard Latvia.

67 However, based on the 'second' three-month term to institute setting aside proceedings that starts running upon service of the arbitral award *together with* a leave to enforce upon the award debtor, in respect of domestic arbitral awards, the discussion between the parties will (most likely) indeed take place in the setting aside proceedings that can still be instituted after the leave is granted.

Model Law.[68] Considering that the setting aside grounds contained in the Model Law are based on the refusal grounds contained in the NYC,[69] within the EU the setting aside grounds and refusal grounds are largely similar.

However, some setting aside grounds in certain jurisdictions seem quite similar to those in the **2.39** Model Law, but – upon closer examination – differ in some respect. For example, in the

---

68 United Nations Commission on International Trade Law (UNCITRAL) Model Law on International Commercial Arbitration 1985, with amendments as adopted in 2006, Art 34(2):

An arbitral award may be set aside by the court specified in article 6 only if:

a) the party making the application furnishes proof that:
   i. a party to the arbitration agreement referred to in article 7 was under some incapacity; or the said agreement is not valid under the law to which the parties have subjected it or, failing any indication thereon, under the law of this State; or
   ii. the party making the application was not given proper notice of the appointment of an arbitrator or of the arbitral proceedings or was otherwise unable to present his case; or
   iii. the award deals with a dispute not contemplated by or not falling within the terms of the submission to arbitration, or contains decisions on matters beyond the scope of the submission to arbitration, provided that, if the decisions on matters submitted to arbitration can be separated from those not so submitted, only that part of the award which contains decisions on matters not submitted to arbitration may be set aside; or
   iv. the composition of the arbitral tribunal or the arbitral procedure was not in accordance with the agreement of the parties, unless such agreement was in conflict with a provision of this Law from which the parties cannot derogate, or, failing such agreement, was not in accordance with this Law; or
b) the court finds that:
   i. the subject-matter of the dispute is not capable of settlement by arbitration under the law of this State; or
   ii. the award is in conflict with the public policy of this State.

69 See New York Convention (n 16) Art V:

1. Recognition and enforcement of the award may be refused, at the request of the party against whom it is invoked, only if that party furnishes to the competent authority where the recognition and enforcement is sought, proof that:
   a) The parties to the agreement referred to in article II were, under the law applicable to them, under some incapacity, or the said agreement is not valid under the law to which the parties have subjected it or, failing any indication thereon, under the law of the country where the award was made; or
   b) The party against whom the award is invoked was not given proper notice of the appointment of the arbitrator or of the arbitration proceedings or was otherwise unable to present his case; or
   c) The award deals with a difference not contemplated by or not falling within the terms of the submission to arbitration, or it contains decisions on matters beyond the scope of the submission to arbitration, provided that, if the decisions on matters submitted to arbitration can be separated from those not so submitted, that part of the award which contains decisions on matters submitted to arbitration may be recognized and enforced; or
   d) The composition of the arbitral authority or the arbitral procedure was not in accordance with the agreement of the parties, or, failing such agreement, was not in accordance with the law of the country where the arbitration took place; or
   e) The award has not yet become binding on the parties or has been set aside or suspended by a competent authority of the country in which, or under the law of which, that award was made.
2. Recognition and enforcement of an arbitral award may also be refused if the competent authority in the country where recognition and enforcement is sought finds that:
   (a) The subject matter of the difference is not capable of settlement by arbitration under the law of that country; or
   (b) The recognition or enforcement of the award would be contrary to the public policy of that country.

See also Born (n 20) 3186–7.

Netherlands, case law specified the setting aside ground regarding an arbitral tribunal's violation of its mandate such that, in serious instances only, the tribunal's omission to address an essential defence may provide a ground to set aside an arbitral award.[70] Obviously, such setting aside grounds may provide room and ways for the courts to scrutinise an arbitral award, also in respect of the application of EU law by the arbitral tribunal (or lack thereof).

2.40 Notwithstanding, irrespective of how the national arbitration laws formulate the setting aside grounds, in respect of the (possible) impact of EU law in setting aside proceedings, it is also relevant how these setting aside grounds are – in practice – applied by the national courts.

2.41 In this respect, it must also be noted that both the NYC and the Model Law intend for the grounds for refusal of recognition and enforcement 'to be construed narrowly'.[71] In respect of *enforcement* such a restrained approach in interpreting and applying the refusal grounds also results from the NYC itself. While the NYC exhaustively lists the grounds upon which enforcement and recognition of an award can be refused, and leaves up to the national courts (i.e., the competent authorities) to consider whether the requirements for those grounds have been met, the NYC:

> simply requires that unless they are found to be fundamentally defective, awards must be enforced. The appraisal of defects is ultimately left to the discernment of national courts, as are the consequences of annulment by the courts of the place of arbitration. In a phrase, it is impossible to violate the New York Convention by enforcing an award, only when not doing so.[72]

2.42 Moreover, as it follows from the text of Articles V(1) and (2) NYC, even if grounds for refusal are proven or found, a national court (i.e., the competent authority), is not obliged to refuse enforcement. Commentators have extensively discussed this point, which relates to the use by the drafters of the NYC of the word 'may'. Whereas the English, Spanish, Chinese and Russian texts, which are all to be deemed authentic, use permissive language similar to 'may be refused', some commentators argued that the French text used imperative language which imposed an obligation to refuse enforcement.[73] This view has become minoritarian, and the permissive interpretation of Articles V(1) and (2) NYC seems to be generally accepted.[74]

2.43 The following paragraphs of Section D address, in respect of the setting aside/refusal grounds that are generally common in the EU Member States, how the national courts of the EU Member States apply these grounds and how that may (or may not) provide room for the testing and/or application of EU law in the post-award stage. Section E, thereafter, will briefly address milestone decisions on the impact of EU law on the post-award stage in respect of international commercial arbitral awards.

---

70 GJ Meijer, *Tekst & Commentaar Burgerlijke Rechtsvordering* (n 37); DCCP, Art 1065, note 4h.

71 See AJ van den Berg, *The New York Arbitration Convention of 1958* (Kluwer Law International 1981) 267-68.

72 Jan Paulsson, 'Chapter 1 - Essential Features', in Marike Paulsson, *The 1958 New York Convention in Action* (Kluwer Law International 2016) 2.

73 See, for a detailed discussion as to the different text of the NYC in support of the permissive interpretation, Jan Paulsson, 'May or must under the New York Convention: An Exercise in Syntax and Linguistics' (1998) 14 *Arbitration International* 227.

74 See Nigel Blackaby, Constantine Partasides and others, *Redfern and Hunter on International Arbitration* (6th edn, OUP 2015) 623.

2. Non-arbitrability of the subject matter

Pursuant to the NYC, non-arbitrability constitutes a(n exceptional) ground for the refusal to **2.44** enforce arbitral awards. Under Article V(2)(a) NYC, 'recognition and enforcement of an arbitral award may (…) be refused if the competent authority in the country where recognition and enforcement is sought finds that the subject matter of the difference is not capable of settlement by arbitration under the law of that country'. Article 34(2)(b)(i) of the Model Law, modelled after Article V(2)(a) NYC, also provides that an award may be set aside if the court finds that 'the subject-matter of the dispute is not capable of settlement by arbitration' under the law of the seat of arbitration, i.e., where setting aside proceedings take place.[75]

Shortly put, arbitrability regards the question of whether the subject matter of the dispute can **2.45** be settled by means of arbitration or whether national courts have exclusive jurisdiction in that respect. In the context of challenging arbitral awards (in setting aside proceedings), in essentially all EU Member States the non-arbitrability of the subject matter of the arbitration agreement is considered to provide grounds to challenge the award.[76] In almost all EU Member States the courts are allowed to test this ground *ex officio*. In this respect, for example, the Czech Republic and Romania form an exception: in those jurisdictions courts do not seem to test non-arbitrability *ex officio*.[77]

However, in Bulgaria, Finland and Sweden non-arbitrability is not captured in a setting aside **2.46** ground, but is considered to lead to the nullity or invalidity of the arbitral award, which can be invoked outside the context of setting aside proceedings.[78] This also means that in the aforementioned jurisdictions a claim based on non-arbitrability is not subject to the rather strict time limit within which setting aside proceedings should be instituted. In addition, within the EU the national courts generally are allowed to assess *de novo* whether grounds exist to accept that the subject matter of the arbitration agreement is non-arbitrable.

In the context of enforcement proceedings on the basis of the New York Convention, **2.47** non-arbitrability constitutes a ground to refuse the recognition and enforcement of an arbitral award. Pursuant to Article V(2)(a) NYC a national court can refuse recognition and enforcement if the matter decided upon by the arbitral tribunal is non-arbitrable on the basis of the law of that court. In respect of the national court of an EU Member State, such law includes EU law, and, therefore, EU law is, in principle, relevant to the assessment of whether a matter is non-arbitrable. As also follows from the formulation of Article V(2)(a) NYC, the NYC

---

75   It should be noted that non-arbitrability (and public policy) under the NYC and the Model Law can be examined *ex officio*, unlike other grounds for refusal to enforce or set aside arbitral awards.

76   As mentioned, no setting aside proceedings are available in Latvia, but in 2014 the Latvian Constitutional Court ruled that a party can challenge arbitration agreements before the Latvian courts. In that context, it makes sense that such challenge of a tribunal's jurisdiction also would cover a plea regarding the non-arbitrability of the subject matter.

77   See, for instance, Stefan Dudas, 'Chapter 4 – Setting Aside of Arbitral Awards' in Crenguta Leaua and Flavius-Antoniu Baias (eds), *Arbitration in Romania: A Practitioner's Guide*, (Kluwer Law International 2016) 216, para 4.02. As will be set out in more detail below, within the EU there seems to be a (strong) consensus that the national courts are *not* to assess *ex officio* whether an arbitral award is based on a valid arbitration agreement.

78   See, for instance, Assen Alexiev, 'National Report for Bulgaria (2018 through 2019)' in Lise Bosman (ed), *ICCA International Handbook on Commercial Arbitration* (Kluwer 2020, Suppl 104, February 2019) 62. Gisela Knuts, 'Chapter 9 – Recourse to the Courts against an Arbitral Award', in Ulf Franke, Annette Magnusson and others (eds), *International Arbitration in Sweden: A Practitioner's Guide* (Kluwer Law International 2013) 241.

allows national courts to assess this refusal ground *ex officio*. In addition, it seems to be generally accepted that the court in enforcement proceedings may assess this ground *de novo*,[79] although the burden of proof in respect of the non-arbitrability remains with the party opposing the enforcement.[80]

2.48   Thus, the issue of non-arbitrability seems to provide a rather wide stage for possible court interference at the post-award stage and for the national courts to assess the arbitral award on the basis of EU law. However, in practice, the impact or relevance of EU law in respect of the scope of review – i.e., arbitrability – seems to be limited: EU law issues that tend to come up at the post-award stage seem to generally relate to public policy issues rather than the question whether the subject matter of a dispute can be subjected to arbitration.

3.   The validity and scope of the arbitration agreement

2.49   Article V(1)(a) NYC provides for another ground for the refusal to enforce an arbitral award. According to this provision, recognition and enforcement may be refused, if one of the parties furnishes proof that the parties to the arbitration agreement 'were, under the law applicable to them, under some incapacity, or the said agreement is not valid under the law to which the parties have subjected it or, failing any indication thereon, under the law of the country where the award was made.' This provision is mirrored in Article 34(2)(a)(i) of the Model Law, which provides that an award may be set aside if one of the parties was 'under some incapacity' or in case the arbitration agreement 'is not valid under the law to which the parties have subjected it or, failing any indication thereon, under the law' of the seat of arbitration, where setting aside proceedings are pending.

2.50   As to the testing of whether an arbitral award is based on a valid arbitration agreement in setting aside proceedings, there seems to be a uniform approach within the EU: in all EU Member States this forms a setting aside ground, but this ground is *not* tested or applied *ex officio*.

2.51   However, the Dutch Supreme Court, on 8 November 2019,[81] rendered a decision in which it confirmed that the Dutch courts should *ex officio* test whether a leave for enforcement[82] in respect of a Dutch arbitral award rendered against a consumer should be refused on the basis that the relevant arbitration clause is 'unfair' within the meaning of the Council Directive 93/13/EEC of 5 April 1993 on unfair terms in consumer contracts. The latter would lead to

---

79   See Born (n 20) 3702.

80   Ibid., 3422.

81   Dutch Supreme Court, 8 November 2019, ECLI:NL:HR:2019:1731, *Stichting Intermaris*, ground no 2.7. The case regarded a request made by the District Court Amsterdam in enforcement proceedings for a preliminary ruling by the Dutch Supreme Court.

82   Under Dutch law, the test applicable in respect of the court's decision to grant leave for enforcement in cases instituting setting aside proceedings is (still) possible and essentially requires the Dutch courts to test whether it is likely that the award will be set aside. As a result, the Supreme Court's findings in the aforementioned case are also relevant to setting aside proceedings.

the conclusion that the arbitral award is likely to be set aside on the basis of a lack of a valid arbitration agreement (Article 1065(1)(a) DCCP).[83]

In addition, the EU Member States are largely consistent in that the national courts assess *de* **2.52** *novo* whether a valid arbitration agreement underlies the arbitral award. However, in practice, in some jurisdictions (more than in others) the courts accord deference to the findings and decisions by the arbitral tribunal in respect of the factual and legal basis underlying the jurisdictional decisions.[84] This is especially the case where such review would boil down to an appeal on the merits of the tribunal's decision.[85] In addition, in some jurisdictions a *de novo* review by the courts may not be fully unrestricted. This is the case in the Netherlands, where, in principle, only limited room exists for the parties to add new arguments that did not form part of the (jurisdictional) debate that took place in the arbitration.[86] However, in the recent Dutch Supreme Court decision referred to above, the Dutch Supreme Court explicitly stated that the courts should not merely apply a marginal review, meaning that the court cannot rely on the assessment of the case that was made by the arbitral tribunal, but should assess – for itself – whether the clause is 'unfair', irrespective of whether *in the arbitration* the defence and arguments were raised by the consumer or not.[87]

EU law is likely to be relevant as part of the 'national laws' of the EU Member States from **2.53** which the arbitral award originates and where setting aside proceedings are instituted (Art 34(2)(a)(i) Model Law and Art V(1)(c) NYC). Considering that the courts generally apply – and possibly, in respect of consumer law, also *ex officio* and in an unrestrained manner[88] – a *de novo* assessment this may lead to a significant impact of EU law in the post-award stage, where EU law may be relevant for the assessment of whether a valid arbitration agreement underlies the arbitral award.

Thus, in summary, in setting aside annulment proceedings substantial room seems to exist for **2.54** the testing of EU law in the context of the assessment of whether an arbitral award is based on a valid arbitration agreement by the national courts. However, this may vary depending on the degree that the national courts are allowed to, in that respect, test (in full) also the merits of the debate in the arbitration, which may also depend on what part of EU law is invoked (e.g., whether it relates to consumer law or not).

---

83 Similarly, Dutch courts should *ex officio* test whether the contractual provision on the basis of which the claim was awarded against the consumer is 'unfair' within the meaning of the aforementioned Directive. If so, also in that case Dutch courts should refuse the leave for enforcement, as the arbitral award is then likely to be set aside on the basis of a violation of public policy (DCCP, Art 1065(1)(e)).

84 Born (n 20) 3207–8; see Madrid Audiencia Provincial, Judgment of 30 April 2007, SAP M 240/2007, grounds nos 2–3.

85 Madrid Audiencia Provincial, ibid.

86 Dutch Supreme Court, 27 March 2009, ECLI:NL:HR:2009:BG4003, *Hendrix Poultry Breeders BV v Burshan* NJ 2010/169 and Dutch Supreme Court 27 March 2009, ECLI:NL:HR:2009:BG6443, *Smit Bloembollen BV v Ruwa Bulbs BV*, NJ 2010/170.

87 See *Stichting Intermaris* (n 81) ground no 2.7. In that case, the consumer had not appeared in the arbitration.

88 Ibid.

4. Inability of a party to present its case

2.55 Testing whether a party was able to present its case aims to ensure that due process is observed in arbitral proceedings. Article V(1)(b) NYC provides that a national court may refuse recognition and enforcement of an award if the party against whom the award is 'invoked was not given proper notice of the appointment of the arbitrator or of the arbitration proceedings or was otherwise unable to present his case'. This ground is often raised by parties opposing the recognition and enforcement of awards, but some say that it is rarely successfully invoked. Similarly, Article 34(2)(a)(ii) of the Model Law, states that an arbitral award may be set aside if the party making the application proves that 'the party making the application was (…) unable to present his case'.

2.56 EU law does include precepts regulating due process rights. The European Convention of Human Rights ('ECHR') contains precepts protecting due process rights. This instrument needs to be considered together with the jurisprudence of the European Court of Human Rights and the former European Commission of Human Rights. As discussed in more detail in Chapter 4, Article 6(1) of the ECHR establishes a number of rights, including the right to an effective remedy, to a fair hearing and to representation before a tribunal. Further, it follows from the decisions of the European Commission on Human Rights that arbitration proceedings fall within the scope of application of the ECHR, to the extent that the organs of a State exercise certain control as to the fairness and correctness of arbitration proceedings, e.g., when national courts hear annulment proceedings or decide on the recognition of awards.

2.57 As also exhibited in Chapter 4, an arbitral tribunal can be a 'tribunal' within the meaning of Article 6(1) of the ECHR. Case law under Article 6(1) of the ECHR shows that an arbitral tribunal must afford an applicant the safeguards in Article 6(1) ECHR in case of compulsory arbitration. Also, in case of voluntary arbitration, the arbitral tribunal must afford the same safeguards, unless such rights are validly waived.

2.58 Therefore, it seems clear that a party seeking the annulment of an arbitral award before a national court of a Member State may invoke a violation of its rights ensuing from Article 6(1) of the ECHR. In fact, it follows from the decision of the European Commission on Human Rights that Member States' national courts, when deciding on the annulment of an arbitral award, should exercise 'a certain control and guarantee as to the fairness and correctness of the arbitration proceedings',[89] which includes ensuring that the party's rights have not been violated.

2.59 Another question, in the context of enforcement proceedings on the basis of the New York Convention, is whether EU law notions of due process could be invoked by a party resisting enforcement on the basis of Article V(1)(b) NYC. Article V(1)(b) NYC does not establish on the basis of which notions of due process a national court needs to assess whether a party has been unable to present its case. Obvious options are the notions of due process of the country where the award was made or the notions of due process of the national court deciding on the recognition and enforcement of the award. It could be argued that courts will look at the due process notion of the country where the award was made, assuming that violations of due

---

89 *Jakob Boss Sohn KG v the Federal Republic of Germany*, App No. 18479/91, ECmHR, 2 December 1991.

process under the law of the national court where enforcement is sought, would be considered a violation of public policy of that country under Article V(2)(b) NYC. In principle, then the national courts must consider EU law notions of due process when Article V(1)(b) is invoked to the extent that the award has been made in an EU Member State. Arguably, this would include rights arising from Article 6(1) of the ECHR.

Besides these instances, national courts' approaches as to what is considered a violation of due **2.60** process, irrespective of the due process notions they choose to apply, may vary according to their tradition and perceptions. As a result, national courts of Member States may be influenced by EU law when assessing whether a party has been able to present its case, even if EU law precepts may not be directly applicable to the assessment.

5. Public policy

Under Article V(2)(b) NYC, an award may be refused enforcement if 'recognition or **2.61** enforcement of the award would be contrary to the public policy' of the State where enforcement is being sought. Article 34(2)(b)(ii) Model Law also dictates that an award may be set aside, if the setting aside court finds that 'the award is in conflict with the public policy' of the setting aside State.[90] Most national courts have annulled awards on the basis of public policy only in limited, exceptional matters.

In the context of setting aside proceedings, the regimes of almost all EU Member States as to **2.62** the assessment of public policy issues are largely similar: a violation of public policy constitutes a ground for the setting aside of an arbitral award, which is tested *ex officio* by the national courts. The setting aside regimes of Bulgaria and the Czech Republic, however, do not seem to contain a setting aside ground based on a violation of public policy, whereas Malta seems to define, in a restrictive manner, what constitutes public policy in its Arbitration Act.[91] The other side of the spectrum is represented by Finland and Sweden where an arbitral award that violates public policy is null and void, which assessment is not dependent on one of the parties having instituted setting aside proceedings.[92]

Generally, the EU Member States all acknowledge that national courts should apply a **2.63** substantial degree of restraint when assessing whether an arbitral award violates public policy. However, in respect of specific areas, in some jurisdictions a full – unrestrained – assessment of a public policy violation may be allowed, for example, in respect of the right to be heard.[93] In addition, the aforementioned restraint is also expressed in court decisions confirming that the setting aside of an arbitral award based on a violation of public policy is only justified in case of,

---

90   Public policy (and non-arbitrability) may be examined *ex officio* under both the NYC and the Model Law; see also (n 75) regarding non-arbitrability.

91   See Assen Alexiev (n 78); Miloš Olík, 'National Report for the Czech Republic (2018 through 2020)' in Lise Bosman (ed), *ICCA International Handbook on Commercial Arbitration* (ICCA & Kluwer Law International 2020, Suppl 109, February 2020) 62. Art 58 of the Malta Arbitration Act states that for the purposes of the said Article an award is in conflict with the public policy of Malta where (a) the award was induced or affected by fraud or corruption; or (b) a breach of the rules of natural justice occurred in connection with the making of the award.

92   Finland, Finnish Arbitration Act, Art 40(1)(2); Sweden, Swedish Arbitration Act (SFS 1999:116; updated as per SFS 2018:1954), S 33.

93   Dutch Supreme Court, 25 May 2007, *Spaanderman v Anova Food* NJ 2007/294.

for example, a 'flagrant, effective and concrete' breach of public policy.[94] In essence, the public policy ground is only accepted by Member States' national courts in cases where there is a serious breach of standards of international commerce or of the fundamental values of the State.[95]

2.64   According to the ECJ, recourse to the public policy exception must relate to infringements that would have constituted 'a manifest breach of a rule of law regarded as essential in the legal order of the State in which enforcement is sought or of a right recognised as being fundamental within that legal order'.[96]

2.65   In the context of both setting aside proceedings and enforcement proceedings the question arises whether a violation of a fundamental rule of mandatory law also includes the incorrect application of such rules. Concisely put, this would apply in case of 'serious errors of mandatory law, leading to results that significantly undermine or frustrate statutory objectives in a socially unacceptable manner'.[97] In some jurisdictions, it is clear that the same would apply in respect of an incorrect application of EU law.[98] This aligns with the position that almost all EU Member States acknowledge that a legal error, as such, does not provide grounds to set aside an arbitral award, and that that can only be the case in extreme cases of errors in law. However, the aforementioned recent decision by the Dutch Supreme Court also made clear that in the Netherlands, the Dutch courts in enforcement proceedings (and in setting aside proceedings) are to fully test whether the clause on which a claim against a consumer is based is 'unfair' within the meaning of Directive 93/13/EEC, irrespective of the assessment and findings of the arbitral tribunal.[99] Thus, it seems that in the Netherlands ample room exists for the courts' intervention in the post-award stage on the basis of an incorrect application of EU consumer law.[100]

---

94   *SA Thalès Air Defence v GIE Euromissile and SA EADS France*, Paris Court of Appeal, 1er Ch sect C, 18 November 2004.

95   'Legal Instruments and Practice of Arbitration in the EU: Study for the Juri Committee' (European Parliament 2014) 33.

96   Case C-7/98, *Dieter Krombach v André Bamberski*, [2000] ECR I-01935.

97   Born (n 20) 3330; see also Supreme Court of Denmark, Case 142/2014, *Taewoon Inc. v AH Industries A/S*.

98   See e.g., Denis Bensaude, 'Thalès Air Defence BV v. GIE Euromissile: Defining the Limits of Scrutiny of Awards Based on Alleged Violations of European Competition Law' (2005) vol 22 issue 3 *Journal of International Arbitration* 243.

99   See *Stichting Intermaris* (n 81) in which the Dutch Supreme Court indicated that the leave for enforcement should also be refused in case it is likely that the arbitral award will be set aside on the basis of a violation of public policy (DCCP, Art 1065(1)(e)) due to the fact that the clause on the basis of which the claim was awarded against the consumer is 'unfair' within the meaning of the Council Directive 93/13/EEC of 5 April 1993 on unfair terms in consumer contracts [1993] OJ L 95/29.

100   The approach taken by the Dutch Supreme Court can be said to be – to some extent – in line with earlier case law from the Dutch Supreme Court. The Dutch Supreme Court has consistently reiterated the starting principle that the courts should apply restraint in respect of the setting aside grounds contained in Art 1065(1) DCCP. Previously, the Dutch Supreme Court had accepted only two exceptions in that regard, in the sense that in case of these two exceptions the courts should not apply restraint. One exception relates to the existence of a valid arbitration agreement (based on the fundamental right of access to national courts), in relation to which courts can exceptionally test in full certain aspects of an arbitral tribunal decision. The other exception relates to public policy, but only where the setting aside was claimed based on a violation of the right to be heard. However, in respect of the 'right to be heard' exception, notably, this should, in principle, not lead to a (full) re-assessment of the merits of the case as the courts' full review is (strictly) limited to an assessment of whether the arbitral tribunal violated the procedural principle of respecting the parties' right to be heard. In this respect, *Stichting Intermaris* can be said to have gone a step beyond this; allowing a full and unrestrained assessment of the merits of the case as to the question of whether a clause is 'unfair' within the meaning of Directive 93/13/EEC.

Notwithstanding that national courts, have, in general, interpreted this ground narrowly,[101] the **2.66** public policy ground generally provides 'some' room for a party (or court) to argue the relevance of EU law at the post-award stage. As also follows from the court decisions summarised in Section E below, the term 'public policy' is sufficiently vague for purposes of introducing various issues of EU law into the post-award stage under the header 'public policy'.

E. MILESTONE CASES

In this last section, we will briefly discuss some of the milestone decisions of the ECJ and **2.67** national courts in order to provide further insight into how EU law impacts the post-award stage of international commercial arbitration.

1. Eco Swiss China Time Ltd. v Benetton International

The *Eco Swiss*[102] case is regularly cited as supporting the argument that norms underlying EU **2.68** competition law enjoy public policy status. Eco Swiss and Bulova initiated arbitration proceedings against Benetton for breach of an agreement. The arbitral tribunal issued a partial final award and a final award, finding in favour of Eco Swiss and Bulova and determining that Benetton had breached the relevant agreement. Benetton then sought to have the awards annulled, arguing as its main stance that the underlying agreement was void under Article 101 of the TFEU and that, thus, the awards, which sought to enforce the agreement at hand, violated EU competition law.

However, Benetton had failed in: (i) initiating the annulment proceedings against the partial **2.69** final award within the three-month limit prescribed by Dutch law; and (ii) presenting the argument during the arbitral proceedings, that the agreement upon which the claim was based was itself invalid under EU competition law, in particular Article 101 of the TFEU. The Dutch court seized of hearing this challenge against the award referred several questions to the ECJ for a preliminary ruling.

In its decision, the ECJ highlighted the importance of EU competition law provisions, as **2.70** contained in Article 101 of the TFEU.[103] It then went on and stated that the provisions of Article 101 of the TFEU 'may be regarded as a matter of public policy within the meaning of the New York Convention'.[104]

The ECJ concluded that if a Member State treats a violation of domestic public policy as a **2.71** ground for annulling an award, it should also do so in respect to EU public policy.[105] Thus, the ECJ basically left it up to the national post-award stage regimes how Article 101 of the TFEU is taken into account in the court's review of arbitral awards, as long as the treatment is the

---

101   See Legal Instruments and Practice of Arbitration in the EU (n 95) 33.
102   Case C-126/97, *Eco Swiss China Time Ltd. v Benetton International NV* [1999] ECR I-3079.
103   Ibid., para 36.
104   Ibid., para 39.
105   Ibid., para 38.

same as the way in which other issues of public policy are reviewed in post-award proceedings. Notwithstanding, although this was not made explicit by the ECJ, commentaries generally accept that a court of a Member State must apply *ex officio* the mandatory provisions of EU law that are directly applicable under its domestic legal system.[106]

2. SA Thalès Air Defence v GIE Euromissile and SA EADS France

2.72   In *Thalès Air Defence*,[107] Thalès, after being ordered to pay EUR 100 million in damages to Euromissile in an award, initiated annulment proceedings before the Paris Court of Appeal. Thalès alleged that the underlying contract between the parties was against EU competition law, and that the enforcement of the award would be contrary to international public policy. The Paris Court of Appeal rejected Thalès' request, and explained that, under French law, for an award to be set aside on the ground that it violates international public policy, including a violation of EU competition law, the violation must be flagrant, effective and concrete. In its decision, the Paris Court of Appeal, in line with the *Eco Swiss* decision, stated that EU competition law forms an integral part of the French concept of international public policy. However, it considered that, in the circumstances of the case, the violation of public policy was not sufficient as to justify a deviation from the fundamental principle that the courts should not re-assess the merits of the case in setting aside proceedings (*revision au fond*) nor the setting aside of the final award.

3. SNF v Cytec Industrie

2.73   The arbitral tribunal hearing the dispute between SNF and Cytec Industries rendered a partial award and a final award in favour of Cytec. Cytec sought to enforce the award in France, while SNF challenged the award by initiating setting aside proceedings in Belgium, where the award was rendered, and opposing the recognition and enforcement of the award in France. The recognition and enforcement of the award was granted in France by the Paris Court of Appeal in March 2006.[108]

2.74   One year later, both the partial and the final awards were annulled in Belgium by the Court of First Instance in Brussels. The key difference between these decisions was to what extent the respective national courts were willing to review the merits of the dispute in order to see whether the awards infringed EU competition law. Following the decision in *Thalès*, the French court refused to dive into the merits of the dispute, and stated that it would only refuse recognition and enforcement of the award if the violation of public policy was flagrant, effective, and concrete. Meanwhile, the Brussels' Court of Appeal's decision of 22 June 2009 was actually aligned with the French position, stating that a judge should not inspect the arbitrator's reasoning and should not replace the arbitral tribunal assessment of the case with its own, taking a somewhat closer approach to that of the French courts.

---

106   See Diederik de Groot, 'Arbitrage en Europees mededingingsrecht – een voorlopige balans dertien jaar na Eco Swiss/Benetton' (2012) 64 *Tijdschrift voor Arbitrage*.

107   See *Thalès Air Defence* (n 94).

108   The Paris Court of Appeal decision was later on confirmed by the French Supreme Court on 4 June 2008.

Interestingly, in the meantime, in 2005 the Court of Appeal in The Hague (the Netherlands), **2.75**
had rendered a decision in the case between Marketing Displays International Inc. and VR
Van Raalte Reclame B.V. that expressed the opposite view, similar to the decision by the Court
of First Instance in Brussels.[109]

4. Elisa María Mostaza Claro v Centro Móvil Milenium

In *Mostaza Claro*,[110] a Spanish telecom company instituted arbitration against Mostaza Claro. **2.76**
Although the subscription agreement contained an arbitration clause, the arbitral institution
gave Ms Mostaza Claro the right to have a dispute heard in court rather than an arbitral forum.
Mostaza Claro did not invoke that right and participated in the arbitration.

Having lost in the arbitration, Mostaza Claro initiated annulment proceedings before a **2.77**
Spanish court, arguing that the arbitration agreement was invalid under EU consumer law as it
should be considered an 'unfair contract term' within the meaning of the Directive on Unfair
Terms in Consumer Contracts.

The ECJ ruled that the Member State court seized of an action for the annulment of an **2.78**
arbitration award must set aside the award if it finds that there was a failure to comply with EU
rules of a public policy nature. This included compliance with the 'unfair term' under the
Directive 93/13/EEC, even if this objection was never raised by the consumer in the
arbitration.[111] In addition, the Court relied on the principle of equivalence, finding as it had
done in *Eco Swiss*, that the national court should grant an application for annulment of an
arbitration award where such an application is founded on failure to comply with Community
rules of public policy, as much as it is required to do so in relation to a violation of its own
domestic public policy norms.[112]

Having said that, the ECJ went on to find that the 'nature and importance of the public **2.79**
interest underlying the protection which the Directive [93/13] confers on consumers' justifies
that the national courts should assess of their own motion whether a contractual term is unfair
(on the basis of Directive 93/13), or, in other words, *ex officio*.[113] The ECJ has not expressed in
clear terms whether national annulment courts should test *in full* whether EU consumer law is
violated, which may lead to different perspectives by national courts.[114]

---

109 The Hague Court of Appeal, 24 March 2005, ECLI:NL:GHSGR:2005:AT8982, *Marketing Displays International Inc.
     v VR Van Raalte Reclame BV*, Bb 2006/41.
110 Case C-168/05, *Mostaza Claro v Centro Móvil Milenium SL* [2006] ECR I-10421.
111 Ibid., paras 30–31.
112 Ibid., para 35.
113 Ibid., para 38.
114 As reflected above in relation to another area of EU law, i.e., EU competition law, the approaches taken by French,
     Belgian and Dutch courts with regard to the extent to which EU competition law is tested in post-award proceedings
     significantly vary (see *SNF v Cytec Industrie* (n 107) and *Marketing Displays International Inc. v VR Van Raalte Reclame
     BV* (n 109)).

5. Asturcom Telecomunicaciones SL v Cristina Rodríguez Nogueira

2.80 In *Asturcom*,[115] the Court qualified its *Mostaza Claro* position. The facts of both cases were similar, with the exception that in *Asturcom*, the consumer had not participated in the arbitral proceedings, the tribunal issued its award by default, and the consumer took no steps whatsoever to have the award annulled. Additionally, the consumer ignored the award altogether, which led to the claimant seeking enforcement before a Spanish court, which made a preliminary reference to the CJEU.

2.81 After some considerations with respect to the principles of effectiveness and equivalence, [116] the ECJ reiterated that the unfair consumer contract terms directive forms part of EU public policy, and that national courts must ensure that the directive's purposes are achieved both effectively and in a fashion equivalent to the comparable provisions of national law.[117] The ECJ reinstated its earlier decision in *Mostaza Claro*, stating that it has 'held that the national court is required to assess of its own motion whether a contractual term is unfair [for a consumer]'.[118] The ECJ, therefore, requires an *ex officio* test of the relevant consumer protection rules by the national annulment courts.

2.82 While the ECJ has not set a requirement of full review on the merits, it has been suggested that this decision, together with Mostaza Claro, could leave 'the door ajar for an unwished-for review on the merits'.[119] Indeed, as mentioned above, some Member States' national courts, like the Dutch Supreme Court, are opening the door for a review on the merits, requiring a full review on the merits regarding the adherence to EU consumer protection law.[120]

F. CONCLUSION

2.83 Our conclusion is that generally the national post-award stages within the EU is consistent and provides a good basis to ensure that EU law is applied in a uniform and consistent manner throughout the EU. However, this is not guaranteed as there are still some striking procedural differences between the national post-award regimes throughout the EU that may give rise to inconsistencies on whether and to what extent (compliance with) EU law is (consistently) tested by national courts in the post-award stage. This may also depend on the specific EU law area involved. In addition, no clarity exists in respect of the question of exactly which parts of EU law should – in the end – *always* be tested (in full) by the national courts in the post-award stage notwithstanding the parties' agreement to arbitrate. Thus, the current state of affairs is that there is a certain (limited) degree of *inconsistency* and *uncertainty* as to the (possible) impact of EU law in the post-award stage in respect of international commercial arbitral awards.

---

115 Case C-40/08, *Asturcom Telecomunicaciones SL v Rodriguez Nogueira* [2009] ECR I-9579.
116 Ibid., paras 30–38.
117 Ibid., paras 52–56.
118 Ibid, para 32.
119 Maud Piers, 'Consumer Arbitration in the EU: A Forced Marriage with Incompatible Expectations' (2011) 2(1) *Journal of International Dispute Settlement*, 209, 228. See also, Bernd U Graf and Arthur E Appleton, 'ECJ Case C 40/08 Asturcom – EU Unfair Terms Law Confirmed as a Matter of Public Policy' (2010) vol 28 issue 2 *ASA Bulletin* 417.
120 See Section D above, with reference to *Stichting Intermaris* (n 81).

On the one hand, one may question whether the rationale of leaving 'arbitration' out of the **2.84** scope of EU law justifies such inconsistency and uncertainty where it comes to the core provisions of EU law that are fundamental to the functioning of the unified and single market that the EU represents. On the other hand, attributing such 'fundamental' status to a large range of EU law provisions, and making these provisions subject to (a full) review by national courts (in the post-award stage) notwithstanding that parties agreed to arbitration, would effectively deprive commercial parties of the tool of ('one shot') arbitration. Considering that arbitration has proven – over the past decades – to be a very mature and useful tool for international dispute resolution, together with the difficulties that some national courts face in handling their case load, this, in the end, could even be detrimental to the functioning of the EU single market.

In any event, in the authors' view, clarity – at the EU level – as to exactly which 'fundamental' **2.85** EU law provisions the EU Member States should guarantee a certain degree of review by national courts through their own (national) post-award regimes, would be useful in order to avoid (lengthy) proceedings in that respect.

3

THE RELATIONSHIP BETWEEN ANTI-SUIT RELIEF, EU LAW AND THE NEW YORK CONVENTION

Sophie J. Lamb QC, Bryce Williams and Robert Price[*]

A. INTRODUCTION

3.01 Parallel proceedings are an increasingly common feature of international arbitration. One can speculate as to the drivers of this phenomenon – the increased use of arbitration, the inventiveness of counsel, the diversity of actors and interests engaged in international arbitration proceedings (including governmental interests), the significance of the disputed subject matter and so on. Irrespective of the drivers, the fact is that many financially significant disputes involve more than one dispute element. However, the coordination between courts and tribunals dealing with these elements is often limited, and the tools available to address jurisdictional conflicts are imperfect. Courts and tribunals legitimately diverge on which coordination tools are appropriate to deploy, and when.

3.02 A powerful though blunt tool used to counter abusive parallel proceedings is the anti-suit injunction. Anti-suit injunctions involve an order directing a party to discontinue, or refrain from commencing or pursuing proceedings in another jurisdiction. This kind of relief may be issued in order to enforce an arbitration agreement or a choice of court agreement, or to

---

[*] Date of submission: 8/1/2020.

minimise prejudice to the primary proceedings.[1] Failure to comply with an injunction issued by a court can entail contempt of the issuing court, punishable by sanctions including fines, and imprisonment in the case of individuals.[2] Anti-suit injunctions are used primarily by courts in common law jurisdictions (including in England and Wales since the fifteenth century). They are also increasingly issued by arbitral tribunals and emergency arbitrators to protect and support their own or contemplated arbitral proceedings.

Given the proliferation of parallel proceedings, the schism between common law and civil law **3.03** attitudes toward anti-suit relief,[3] and the uncertain application of the Brussels regime[4] to the litigation/arbitration interface, it is perhaps unsurprising that the anti-suit injunction was the trigger and vehicle through which the now vexed relationship between European Union (EU) law, international law and international arbitration came to be examined.

An important dimension to this relationship is the interaction between anti-suit relief, the **3.04** Brussels regime and the New York Convention[5] (to which all EU Member States are members).[6] Anti-suit relief and a stay of proceedings pursuant to Article II(3) of the New York Convention may achieve a similar outcome, but each allocates the power to determine that outcome to different decision-makers.[7] Complexities also arise in the absence of anti-suit relief, when parallel court and arbitral proceedings may produce inconsistent decisions, each of which may be *prima facie* entitled to recognition in third (EU member) state courts pursuant to the Brussels regime and the New York Convention respectively.[8]

This chapter will first discuss the modern English experience of anti-suit relief by exploring **3.05** examples of its varied deployment and versatility. It will then briefly examine why such relief has proven controversial, including its perceived impact on comity between judicial bodies. Against that background, this chapter will then examine the evolving European attitude toward anti-suit relief in the arbitral context and its impact on the practice of Member State

---

1 The power of the English courts to issue an anti-suit injunction against a party acting unconscionably (that is, oppressively or vexatiously) but not in breach of an arbitration agreement or choice of court agreement was recognised by the House of Lords in *South Carolina Insurance Co v Assurantie Maatschappij 'de Zeven Provincien' NV* [1987] AC 24.

2 In *Mobile Telecommunications Co KSC v HRH Prince Hussam Bin Abdulaziz Au Saud* [2018] EWHC 3749 (Comm), the Respondent was sentenced to 12 months' imprisonment for breaching an anti-suit injunction designed to protect arbitral proceedings.

3 See Case C-159/02 *Turner v Grovit* [2003] ECR I-3567, Opinion of AG Ruiz-Jarabo, para 26 ('*Turner (AG Opinion)*') – 'Such restraining orders date back to the 15th century, although their significance has evolved, always being linked to the concept of equity and inspired by the views of common-law judges'.

4 That is, collectively, 1968 Brussels Convention on Jurisdiction and the Enforcement of Judgments in Civil and Commercial Matters (opened for signature 27 September 1968, entered into force 1 February 1973) [1972] OJ L 299/32 ('Brussels Convention'); Council Regulation (EC) 44/2001 on jurisdiction and the recognition and enforcement of judgments in civil and commercial matters [2000] OJ L12/1 ('Brussels Regulation'); European Parliament and Council Regulation (EU) 1215/2012 on jurisdiction and the recognition and enforcement of judgments in civil and commercial matters (recast) [2012] OJ L351/1 ('Brussels Recast Regulation').

5 Convention on the Recognition and Enforcement of Foreign Arbitral Awards (opened for signature 10 June 1958, entered into force 7 June 1959) (New York Convention).

6 Explored further in Sections D.6 and D.7 below.

7 To the courts at the seat of arbitration, the arbitral tribunal, or otherwise interested third-state courts (in the case of anti-suit relief), or the courts hearing the substantive parallel proceedings (further to Art II(3) of the New York Convention)).

8 Explored further in Section D.7 below.

courts, principally the English courts. As part of that analysis, this chapter will explore the issues that emerged from the landmark decision of the Court of Justice of the European Union (CJEU)[9] in *West Tankers*,[10] and will also reflect on the CJEU's decision in *Gazprom*.[11] This chapter will conclude with some predictions for a post-Brexit and post-*Achmea* Europe.[12]

B. THE MODERN ENGLISH EXPERIENCE OF ANTI-SUIT RELIEF

3.06 English courts have become a focal point for the resolution of issues concerning parallel proceedings. The prevalence of English law as the law governing many international commercial contracts,[13] the long English tradition of trade and maritime arbitration, and favourable perception of the English courts' neutrality and quality have all contributed to their popularity in resolving these issues.

3.07 The power of the English courts to order anti-suit relief in support of domestic court proceedings was already well established by the turn of the twentieth century.[14] This kind of anti-suit relief was a discretionary, equitable remedy, issued against parties over whom the courts had personal jurisdiction.[15]

3.08 Nevertheless, historically, the English courts had declined to specifically enforce arbitration agreements given that to do so 'amounted to ousting the jurisdiction of the courts of law [and thus] was invalid, and therefore equity would not enforce [them]'.[16] As Lord Justice Fletcher Moulton observed in *Pena Copper*, 'that practically reduce[d] the arbitration clauses – the ordinary arbitration clauses – to nullities'.[17] English civil procedure legislation (passed in the

---

9   Over the course of the period studied, the court hearing references for preliminary rulings from Member States' courts has changed its nomenclature (from the Court of Justice of the European Communities to the Court of Justice, a court of the Court of Justice of the European Union). For ease of comprehension, the same nomenclature (CJEU) is used throughout.

10   Case C-185/07 *Allianz SpA, Generali Assicurazioni Generali SpA v West Tankers Inc* [2009] ECR I-00686 (*'West Tankers (CJEU)'*).

11   Case C-536/13 *'Gazprom' OAO v Lietuvos Respublika* [2015] ECLI:EU:C:2015:316 (*'Gazprom (CJEU)'*).

12   Case C-284/16 *Slowakische Republik v Achmea BV* [2018] ECLI:EU:C:2018:158 (*'Achmea (CJEU)'*).

13   A 2014 study of more than 4,000 international commercial contracts referred to in International Chamber of Commerce (ICC) arbitral awards found that English law was the most attractive law for international commercial parties (including third-party (that is, non-English) parties). Gilles Cuniberti, 'The International Market for Contracts: The Most Attractive Contract Laws' (2014) 34 *NWJILB* 455.

14   In *Pena Copper Mines Ltd v Rio Tinto Co Ltd* [1911-13] All ER Rep 209, [216] (*'Pena Copper'*), Lord Justice Farwell, referring to *Carron Iron Co v MacLaren* [1855] 5 HL Cas 416 and *Lord Portarlington v Soulby* (1834) 3 My & K 104, observed 'it is clear that there has always been jurisdiction to restrain foreign actions'.

15   In *Pena Copper* (n 14), Lord Justice Fletcher Moulton concluded that the Court:

    ought to exercise our powers in personam to prevent that line of conduct taking effect which is certainly contrary to their contractual duties. Of course if it was a question of discretion – and it certainly is – I agree with what the Master of the Rolls has said, to the effect that this is a case in which certainly we ought to exercise our discretion.

16   *Pena Copper* (n 14) 214.

17   Ibid.

mid-nineteenth century[18]) introduced an indirect means to enforce an arbitration agreement by staying domestic court proceedings.[19] But the issue of competing foreign proceedings remained.

In the landmark case of *Pena Copper* (1911),[20] the English Court of Appeal addressed this issue. The Court found that there was: **3.09**

> ... a plain bargain between the parties that their rights should be governed by English law, and that any dispute should be determined in one way only – namely, by reference to arbitration, the award of the arbitrator being a condition precedent to any liability of either party ... there is probably an express negative [obligation (that is, not to sue elsewhere)], but there is certainly an implied negative.[21]

In that context, it was appropriate for the Court to 'exercise [its] powers in personam to prevent that line of conduct [the foreign suit] taking effect which is certainly contrary to [the parties'] contractual duties', by way of an anti-suit injunction.[22] As the Court of Appeal later explained in *Tracomin*, the *agreement to arbitrate* was the source of the Court's jurisdiction – 'the fact that they have agreed to submit disputes to English arbitration amounts either to a sufficient submission to the English courts or, alternatively, the creation of a sufficiently close nexus between them and the jurisdiction of the English courts to entitle us to exercise that jurisdiction'.[23] **3.10**

The power to order anti-suit relief derives from a broader power of the courts to grant injunctions when it is 'just and convenient to do so', a power codified in section 37 of the Senior Courts Act 1981 (UK) and its antecedents. It exists alongside other tools of the Court to control multiple proceedings, including anti-suit relief in the context of choice of court agreements,[24] the principle of *forum non conveniens* (when a court stays its own proceedings if it considers there is a more convenient forum for the dispute)[25] and stays of domestic proceedings in favour of arbitration (now reflected in Article II(3) of the New York Convention).[26] **3.11**

Consistent with the development of jurisprudence in respect of these other tools, notions of comity, not expressly considered in *Pena Copper*, have played a role in the exercise of the Court's discretion. The question of comity is returned to in Section C, below. By the 1980s, the Court of Appeal in *Tracomin* observed that the jurisdiction to grant anti-suit relief in support of an arbitration agreement was to 'be used sparingly' and 'with great caution'.[27] In **3.12**

---

18   Long before the Geneva Protocol on Arbitration Clauses (opened for signature 24 September 1923) and the New York Convention (n 5).

19   *Pena Copper* (n 14) 214.

20   Ibid.

21   Ibid., 212.

22   Ibid., 214–15.

23   *Tracomin SA v Sudan Oil Seeds Co Ltd (No 2)* [1983] 3 All ER 140, 144 (*'Tracomin'*).

24   As in *Turner v Grovit* [2001] UKHL 65, [2002] 1 WLR 107 [26] (*'Turner (HOL)'*), discussed in Section D.3 below.

25   *Spiliada Maritime Corp v Cansulex Ltd* [1987] AC 460.

26   As in *Fili Shipping Co Ltd v Premium Nafta Products Ltd* [2007] UKHL 40, [2007] 4 All ER 951.

27   *Tracomin* (n 23) 144.

1994, in *The 'Angelic Grace'* case, explored in Sections C.2 and D.2 below, this trend was reversed.[28] In Lord Justice Millett's view, returning to the reasoning in *Pena Copper*:

> ... the time has come to lay aside the ritual incantation that this is a jurisdiction which should only be exercised sparingly and with great caution. There have been many statements of great authority warning of the danger of giving an appearance of undue interference with the proceedings of a foreign Court ... [b]ut in my judgment there is no good reason for diffidence in granting an injunction to restrain foreign proceedings on the clear and simple ground that the defendant has promised not to bring them.[29]

3.13 *The 'Angelic Grace'* was nevertheless decided before the Arbitration Act 1996 (UK), which had been introduced, in part, to respond to 'international criticism that the [English] courts intervene more than they should in the arbitral process'.[30] The Act did not adopt in full the Model Law developed by the UN Commission on International Trade Law (UNCITRAL), but 'very close regard was paid to the Model Law, and ... both the structure and the content [of the Act] ... owe much to [the UNCITRAL] model'.[31] For example, in relation to the scope of permissible court intervention in arbitral proceedings, section 1(c) of the Act provides that 'in matters governed by this Part, the court should not intervene except as provided by this Part'. This mirrors Article 5 of the UNCITRAL Model Law (with the exception that the Model Law prescribes 'no court *shall*' intervene, rather than '*should*').[32]

3.14 Likewise, section 44 of the Act (Court Powers Exercisable in Support of Arbitral Proceedings) was drafted to correspond (in part) to Article 9 of the Model Law (Arbitration agreement and interim measures by court). Section 44 prescribes that English courts have the same powers in respect of arbitral proceedings as they do in respect of court proceedings in relation to certain matters, including the granting of interim injunctions. That section provides, in part:

> 44(1) Unless otherwise agreed by the parties, the court has for the purposes of and in relation to arbitral proceedings the same power of making orders about the matters listed below as it has for the purposes of and in relation to legal proceedings.
>
> (2) Those matters are—
>
> (a) the taking of the evidence of witnesses;
> ...
> (e) the granting of an interim injunction or the appointment of a receiver.
>
> (3) If the case is one of urgency, the court may, on the application of a party or proposed party to the arbitral proceedings, make such orders as it thinks necessary for the purpose of preserving evidence or assets.

---

28 *Aggeliki Charis Compania Maritima SA v Pagnan SpA (The 'Angelic Grace')* [1995] 1 Lloyd's Rep 87 (CA) ('*Angelic Grace (COA)*').
29 Ibid., 96.
30 Departmental Advisory Committee on Arbitration Law, *Report on the Arbitration Bill* (HL 1996) ('DAC Report') [21].
31 DAC Report, Ibid., [4].
32 In *AES Ust-Kamenogorsk Hydropower Plant LLP v Ust-Kamenogorsk Hydropower Plant JSC* [2013] UKSC 35, [2013] 1 WLR 1889 ('*Ust-Kamenogorsk*') [33], the Supreme Court observed that this difference 'implies a need for caution, rather than an absolute prohibition, before any court intervention'.

The relationship between this specific provision of the Arbitration Act and the Court's general **3.15** and wider power under the Senior Courts Act to grant injunctions (including *final* anti-suit injunctions in support of arbitration) inevitably came to be explored. As the Court of Appeal observed in *Cetelem*:

> ... [t]he relationship between the powers of the court under section 37 of the [Senior Courts Act] and section 44 of the 1996 Act will at some stage require detailed consideration because there is a tension (to put it no higher) between the apparently wide powers conferred on the court by section 37 and the much narrower powers conferred on the court by section 44. The resolution of that tension must await another day.[33]

Given this lack of clarity, some creative reasoning flourished in the lower courts. For example, **3.16** in *Starlight Shipping*, the Court worked on the assumption that 'assets' able to be preserved under section 44 of the Arbitration Act extended to contractual rights, including the 'contractual right to have disputes referred to arbitration'.[34]

The issue finally came for consideration by the UK Supreme Court in the context of the **3.17** question of whether anti-suit relief is available to prevent litigation overseas, even if neither party intends to pursue the arbitration route. Looking squarely at the Arbitration Act, the answer appeared to be 'no', if requiring as a predicate to injunctive relief, existing or contemplated arbitration proceedings.[35] In *Ust-Kamenogorsk*, Lord Mance confirmed that a wider power indeed survived and exists beyond the Act:

> ... [w]here an injunction is sought to restrain foreign proceedings in breach of an arbitration agreement ... the source of the power to grant such an injunction is to be found not in section 44 of the 1996 Act, but in section 37 of the 1981 Act. Such an injunction is not 'for the purposes of and in relation to arbitral proceedings', but for the purposes of and in relation to the negative promise contained in the arbitration agreement not to bring foreign proceedings, which applies and is enforceable regardless of whether or not arbitral proceedings are on foot or proposed.[36]

The Supreme Court also cited with approval Lord Justice Millett's concerns expressed in *The* **3.18** *'Angelic Grace'* with respect to the 'ritual incantation' of comity, extracted above.[37] In doing so,

---

33   *Cetelem SA v Roust Holdings Ltd* [2005] EWCA Civ 618, [2005] 1 WLR 3555 [74] ('*Cetelem*').

34   *Starlight Shipping Co v Tai Ping Insurance Co Ltd* [2007] EWHC 1893 (Comm), [2008] 1 All ER (Comm) 593 [21] ('*Starlight Shipping*'). The approach was followed in *Sheffield United Football Club Ltd v West Ham United Football Club plc* [2008] EWHC 2855 (Comm), [2009] 1 Lloyd's Rep 167, but doubted in *Ust-Kamenogorsk* (n 32) [47]–[48].

35   *Ust-Kamenogorsk* (n 32).

36   Ibid., [48].

37   *Angelic Grace (COA)* (n 28) 96; *Ust-Kamenogorsk* (n 32) [25]. Note that *Ust-Kamenogorsk* involved proceedings in Kazakhstan, and is therefore unrelated to the EU and uninfluenced by the decisions of the CJEU such as *West Tankers* and *Gazprom*. The 'incantation' formulation has nevertheless also received criticism. For example, in *Comandate Marine Corp v Pan Australia Shipping Pty Ltd* [2006] FCAFC 192, [2008] 1 Lloyd's Rep 119, Justice Allsop of the Federal Court of Australia observed that:

> ... [t]he anti-suit injunction, in form, is not directed to the court. This much is obvious. If it were otherwise, there would be a direct interference with an arm of government of a sovereign State. Nevertheless, to order a party not to approach a court of competent jurisdiction is an indirect interference with that court. That is not to say anti-suit injunctions should not be issued. But it is to recognise that in a potentially complex exercise of discretion comity is not an 'incantation', as Millett LJ put it in *The 'Angelic Grace'* [1995] 1 Lloyd's Rep 87 [96], but a real consideration, in particular if legitimate national legislation (such as that protecting or regulating a body of commercial law eg

the Court reaffirmed its willingness to intervene to grant anti-suit relief to enforce an arbitration agreement (when outside of the restraints imposed by the Brussels regime, discussed further in Section D below).

C. THE VERSATILITY AND CONTROVERSY OF ANTI-SUIT RELIEF

1. Types of anti-suit relief in the arbitral context

3.19 As the *Ust-Kamenogorsk* case illustrates, courts and tribunals, in England and elsewhere, have been confronted with requests for anti-suit relief in a variety of contexts. In the most common and straightforward case, a party (Party A) initiates proceedings in a foreign court[38] in breach of an arbitration agreement with the other party (Party B). Party B applies to the courts at the seat of arbitration to issue an injunction restraining Party A from commencing or continuing proceedings in the foreign court.[39] Critically the relief sought is directed to the party in breach of the arbitration agreement and not the foreign court. *The 'Angelic Grace'*,[40] in which the claimant in a London-seated arbitration sought an injunction from the English courts against a defendant that had issued proceedings in Italy, is a classic example of this type of relief.

3.20 In similar fashion, Party B could apply to the arbitral tribunal rather than the courts at the seat of arbitration to issue the injunction (in the form of an award or order). An illustration of this example would be the *Gazprom* award, discussed further below in Section D.6, in which the arbitral tribunal ordered the respondent to withdraw certain claims made before the Lithuanian courts.[41]

3.21 If the foreign court proceedings in breach of the arbitration agreement have already run to judgment, a party may seek an 'anti-enforcement' injunction from the seat court or the arbitral tribunal to prevent the party in breach from enforcing the foreign court judgment (in the foreign jurisdiction or elsewhere). This was the situation in Ecobank, in which an employee had already obtained judgments in the Togolese and Ivorian courts against *Ecobank* (in breach of an arbitration agreement between the employee and the bank).[42] However, as *Ecobank* demonstrates, timing can play a decisive role in the balance of equities and the question of comity, a matter returned to in Section C.2 below.

3.22 Injunctions may also be directed against the arbitration, rather than the foreign court proceedings. These injunctions, sought from a favourable national court (generally not of the seat), work to disrupt the arbitral proceedings and are often sought in tandem with the

---

insurance law or bill of lading carriage) applies and if parties have conducted themselves and contracted against that background or in that framework.

38   That is, a court other than the courts at the seat of the arbitration.
39   An alternative would be to apply to the foreign court to refer the parties to arbitration pursuant to Art II(3) of the New York Convention (if the foreign state is a party to that Convention, or similar principles apply). This would be the approach if proceedings were initiated in the courts at the purported seat of the arbitration.
40   *Angelic Grace (COA)* (n 28).
41   *Gazprom OAO v Ministry of Energy of the Republic of Lithuania* (SCC Case No V (125/2011), Final Award, 31 July 2012, para. 292(ii) ('*Gazprom (Arbitral Award)*').
42   *Ecobank Transnational Inc v Tanoh* [2015] EWCA Civ 1309, [2016] 1 WLR 2231 ('*Ecobank*').

commencement of substantive proceedings in that court.[43] This anti-arbitration injunction can purport to bind the parties, the arbitral institution and even the members of the tribunal.

In many cases, a government-linked respondent is the applicant for anti-arbitration relief, as in *BCB v Belize*.[44] In that case, the Belizean government compulsorily acquired loan and debenture facilities owed to the British Caribbean Bank (BCB).[45] In addition to pursuing relief in the Belizean courts, BCB brought arbitration proceedings against the government of Belize under the UK-Belize bilateral investment treaty (BIT).[46] In response, the government of Belize sought and obtained an anti-arbitration injunction from the courts of Belize restraining BCB from pursuing the BIT proceedings.[47] The Belizean Court of Appeal upheld the injunction, finding that the right to arbitrate under the BIT was only enlivened upon the completion of the domestic proceedings.[48] This finding was reversed by the Caribbean Court of Justice (CCJ), which discharged the injunction. The CCJ concluded that, while there was 'no unqualified or indefeasible right to arbitrate',[49] there was no requirement in the BIT to exhaust local remedies.[50] Further, it was appropriate for the arbitral tribunal, pursuant to the *kompetenz-kompetenz* doctrine, to assess its own jurisdiction.[51]

3.23

The decision reflects a sustained shift in the relationship between domestic courts and arbitration, in which courts have tended to limit the availability of anti-arbitration injunctions to exceptional cases.[52]

3.24

---

43   In some instances, arbitrations have been seated in the relevant jurisdiction, and as such the relevant court has had a legitimate supervisory role over the arbitral proceedings. However, this role has been abused to protect a governmental or government-owned respondent. In the *Himpurna* case, Pertamina, an entity owned by the government of Indonesia (the respondent), sought and obtained an anti-arbitration injunction in respect of an arbitration seated in Jakarta. Nevertheless, the tribunal ignored the injunction and relocated its hearings to The Hague. (*Himpurna California Energy Ltd v Republic of Indonesia*, Interim Award and Final Award, 26 September 1999 and 16 October 1999 in Albert Jan van den Berg (ed), *Yearbook Commercial Arbitration 2000* (Kluwer Law International, 2000) vol 25).
     In the unusual case of *YPF v AESU*, the courts of Uruguay (the seat of the arbitration) and the courts of Argentina (the courts nominated in the arbitration agreement as having exclusive jurisdiction to hear annulment applications) issued conflicting orders to the parties and to the arbitral tribunal – to proceed with, and to stop, the next phase of the arbitration, respectively. 'Lat Am courts clash over gas exports award' *Global Arbitration Review* (11 March 2016).

44   *British Caribbean Bank Ltd v The Attorney General of Belize* [2013] CCJ 4 ('*BCB v Belize (CCJ)*'). See also, the decisions of the Argentine courts in *Entidad Binacional Yacyretá v Eriday UTE* (Federal District Court of Buenos Aires, 27 September 2004; Federal First Instance Court of Administrative Matters, 18 April 2005), imposing an anti-arbitration injunction, and threatening a fine of USD 7 million (increasing by USD 1 million daily) against Eriday UTE if it proceeded with an arbitration against an Argentine state-linked entity.

45   *BCB v Belize (CCJ)* (n 44) [2].

46   Ibid., [7].

47   Ibid., [10]–[11].

48   Ibid., [12].

49   Ibid., [23].

50   Ibid., [21]–[22].

51   Ibid., [23].

52   See, e.g., *Elektrim SA v Vivendi Universal SA* [2007] EWHC 571, [2007] 2 Lloyd's Rep 8 [74]–[75] ('*Elektrim*'); *Claxton Engineering Services Ltd v TXM Olaj-És Gázkutató KFT* [2011] EWHC 345 (Comm); [2011] 2 All ER (Comm) 128 [27]–[44] ('*Claxton (Injunction)*'); *Sabbagh v Khoury* [2018] EWHC 1330 (Comm) ('*Sabbagh (EWHC)*'). In *Sabbagh v Khoury* [2019] EWCA Civ 1219 ('*Sabbagh (COA)*') [90], the English Court of Appeal observed that 'it is clear from the principles of international arbitration embodied in the New York Convention and from the English authorities that the court must show great caution and restraint before granting such an [anti-arbitration] injunction'.

3.25 Anti-arbitration relief has also been sought from seat courts against parallel arbitrations. In *Elektrim v Vivendi*,[53] the parties to an ongoing arbitration under the London Court of International Arbitration (LCIA) Rules prepared a settlement agreement (with disputes in relation to that agreement to be settled by ICC arbitration seated in Geneva). The parties disputed the validity of the settlement agreement, and a separate ICC arbitration was commenced. The party disputing the validity of the settlement agreement sought a temporary injunction from the English courts in respect of the LCIA arbitration concerning the dispute under the original agreement. That party argued that an injunction was required as if the settlement agreement was held to be valid in the ICC arbitration, the LCIA arbitration was without object (as the dispute under the original agreement had been validly settled by the settlement agreement). Justice Aikens denied the relief, concluding that '[i]t is simply inevitable that there will be multi-party, multi-tribunal litigation or arbitration in the circumstances of the war for the PTC shares that is going on'.[54]

3.26 Proceedings have also sought to be restrained by way of anti-suit relief when they tend to obstruct or undermine the primary proceedings, even though they do not have the same object as the primary proceedings (that is, the same or closely-related substantive claims). As such, these secondary proceedings are not brought in breach of the underlying arbitration agreement.[55] Nevertheless, tribunals have sought to restrain these proceedings in order to protect the procedural integrity of the proceedings under their supervision.[56] The cases of *Hydro v Albania*[57] and *Nova v Romania*[58] illustrate this type of relief.

3.27 Both *Hydro* and *Nova* concerned investors[59] that had commenced arbitration proceedings before the International Centre for Settlement of Investment Disputes (ICSID) (under the Italy-Albania BIT and Netherlands-Romania BIT, respectively). While the arbitration proceedings were ongoing, Albania and Romania, the respondents to the ICSID proceedings, commenced domestic criminal proceedings against the investors. Albania and Romania also sought to extradite the investors from England to face the criminal proceedings. In response, the investors sought provisional measures against Albania and Romania in order to suspend the extradition process. Both sets of ICSID tribunals acceded to the requests on the basis that the investors were material witnesses and were the only people properly able to instruct counsel. As such, the investors' detention in the respondent state would undermine the integrity of the arbitration proceedings.[60]

---

53 *Elektrim* (n 52).
54 Ibid., [80].
55 See, e.g., *Hydro Srl v Republic of Albania*, ICSID Case No. ARB/15/28, Order on Provisional Measures, 3 March 2016, para 3.23 ('*Hydro*').
56 See, e.g., ibid., para 3.18.
57 Ibid.
58 *Nova Group Investments, BV v Romania*, ICSID Case No. ARB/16/19, Procedural Order No. 7, Decision on Claimant's Request for Provisional Measures, 29 March 2017 ('*Nova*'); *Nova Group Investments, BV v Romania*, ICSID Case No. ARB/16/19, Procedural Order No. 8, Decision on Respondent's Request for Reconsideration of Procedural Order No. 7, 18 April 2017.
59 'Investors' is used in this and following paragraphs to refer to either the corporate entities (the claimants in the ICSID proceedings) or the individuals behind the corporate entities (subject to the criminal and extradition proceedings), depending on the context.
60 *Hydro* (n 55) para 3.18; *Nova* (n 58) para 301, 307.

The investors in the *Hydro* case successfully enforced the tribunal's order in England, where **3.28**
the Westminster Magistrates' Court stayed the extradition proceedings, recognising that the
extradition would 'prejudice the [investors'] rights to be allowed to continue with their business
interests and engage with the arbitral proceedings'.[61] However, in *Nova*, the Westminster
Magistrates' Court refused to stay extradition proceedings, including on the basis that the
criminal proceedings underway in Romania, an EU Member State, were to be accorded greater
deference given the comity between Member State courts.[62] Permission for judicial review
against that decision was refused. Nevertheless, the High Court noted that the investor's abuse
of process arguments could be heard in a later appeal against the substantive extradition
decision. In obiter, Justice Males observed that:

> ... [Nova's investors'] abuse of process argument raises a serious issue worthy of consideration by this
> court if necessary. It may require consideration of what should be the approach of the English court to
> what is in effect an anti-suit injunction issued by an international arbitration tribunal to restrain the
> pursuit of extradition proceedings. Such an argument would need to take account of (what I have
> assumed to be) the binding obligation on Romania as a matter of international law to comply with the
> recommendation of the arbitral tribunal, and the policy of the English court to support arbitration.
> However, there are likely to be other factors which will also have to be considered. These include such
> matters as the seriousness of the charges against the claimant, the public policy in support of
> extradition, and (if there is an issue about this) the claimant's ability to obtain a fair trial in Romania
> bearing in mind his allegation that the proceedings there are politically motivated. There may well be
> other factors also.[63]

Nevertheless, permission to appeal on the abuse of process argument against the substantive **3.29**
decision was also refused, the English High Court having found that the ICSID tribunal's
provisional measures were:

> ... issued by an international arbitral tribunal which was seized of an arbitration in which [Adamescu,
> the individual investor behind Nova] was not even a party, could not oust [the extradition process,
> under 'well-established machinery with origins in EU law'], or properly cause the extradition

---

61 *Government of Albania v Francesco Becchetti* (Westminster Magistrates' Court, 20 May 2016) [54].

62 The decision (including the order or its reasoning) has not been officially reported. Emilie Gonin, 'How Effective are
ICSID Provisional Measures at Suspending Criminal Proceedings before Domestic Courts: The English Example?'
(Wolters Kluwer, 30 September 2017) <http://arbitrationblog.kluwerarbitration.com/2017/09/30/effective-icsid-
provisional-measures-suspending-criminal-proceedings-domestic-courts-english-example/> accessed 8 January 2020.
  The basis for the decision is summarised in *Adamescu v Bucharest Appeal Court Criminal Division, Romania* [2019]
EWHC 525 (Admin), [26] ('*Adamescu (EWHC)*'). The lower court had:

  ... concluded that the [ICSID tribunal's provisional measures order] was not binding on the magistrates' court,
  [Adamescu] was not a party to the arbitration directly but was merely a witness for one of the parties, previous
  authority relied on by the appellant could be distinguished, it was a matter for the requesting authority whether to
  proceed with extradition in light of the [ICSID order], that there were no reasonable grounds for suspecting that the
  requesting authority was abusing the procedures of the domestic court, that there would be no prejudice to
  [Adamescu] (as opposed to Nova) in continuing to determine the extradition request, and that by continuing to deal
  with the extradition request the domestic court was not facilitating any alleged breach of the [ICSID order].

63 *R (on the application of Adamescu) v Westminster Magistrates Court* [2018] EWHC 593 (Admin) [16]. Cf, the refusal of
an extradition order (and refusals of permission to appeal against that refusal) referred to in *Turkey v Talip Buyuk, Hamdi
Akin Celik and Ali Ipek* [2019] EWHC 1184 (Admin).

process to be halted. Enforcement of the [provisional measures] is a matter for the ICSID tribunal when it gives its final award (which it has not yet done) and not for the magistrates' court.[64]

3.30 These examples illustrate the diversity of fora from which anti-suit relief may be sought and the diversity of different situations in which it has been deployed to respond.

2. Controversy surrounding anti-suit relief in the arbitral context

3.31 Nevertheless, the resort to anti-suit relief in its diverse forms remains controversial in theory and in practice.

3.32 Formally, the relief is directed to a party before the court or arbitral tribunal. However, in substance, anti-suit relief requires the forum to assess and decide upon the proper scope of another arbitral or judicial body's jurisdiction, generally without any authority over the other body, or basis for priority over that body's assessment of its own jurisdiction. In doing so, it undermines the power of that body to decide upon its own jurisdiction (a power which extends to both arbitral and judicial bodies) pursuant to the *kompetenz-kompetenz* doctrine and, at least in the judicial context, the 'comity' that exists as between judicial organs in different legal systems. If targeted at a foreign seated arbitration, anti-arbitration relief may be perceived to be an indirect affront to the supervisory powers of the courts at the seat of the arbitration.[65]

3.33 Anti-suit relief has been described as 'unilateral' and 'confrontational'.[66] Its impact on the proper coordination of multiple proceedings can be weakened, and in some instances, eliminated, as the injuncted parties (and undermined forum) refuse to recognise the relief or respond with antagonistic counter-relief (that is, anti-anti-suit relief).[67] If all courts and

---

64 *Adamescu (EWHC)* (n 62) [31]. Adamescu's application to the European Court of Human Rights (ECtHR) in respect of the decision by the Romanian courts to issue an arrest order was dismissed in April 2019, as the ECtHR found the application did not disclose any violation of the European Convention on Human Rights (*B.A.A. v Romania*, App no 70621/16, 18 April 2019).

65 Indeed, in ordering an anti-arbitration injunction in respect of proceedings seated in Lebanon, Justice Knowles noted that the arbitrators' positive jurisdictional findings:

… would always be subject to any conclusion reached on subsequent judicial consideration. In the present case there has been that subsequent judicial consideration. It has not been by a supervisory court but it has been by a court properly fulfilling its role in litigation properly before it, and in addressing a question put to it and argued before it by the parties who contended that there was an agreement to arbitrate … This is an exceptional case in many respects, and on a close appreciation of its circumstances I hope it will be understood that it is not one that involves any undue assertion of the jurisdiction of the courts of England and Wales. *Sabbagh (EWHC)* (n 52) [49]–[50].

The Court of Appeal in that case (*Sabbagh (COA)* (n 52) [109]) further observed that '[a]n anti-arbitration injunction does not involve an interference with the jurisdiction of a foreign court, except in the very indirect way of relieving it of its role as the supervisory court for the arbitration.'

See also, the distinction between the recommended approaches to parallel proceedings in seat and non-seat courts in the International Law Association's Final Report on Lis Pendens and Arbitration. International Law Association, *Report of the Seventy-Second Conference (Toronto): Final Report on Lis Pendens and Arbitration* (ILA 2006) ('ILA Report') 181–2, 184.

66 Gabrielle Kaufmann-Kohler, 'Multiple Proceedings in International Arbitration: Blessing or Plague?' (Herbert Smith Freehills and Singapore Management University School of Law Asian Arbitration Lecture, 24 November 2015) ('Kaufmann-Kohler').

67 In *KBC v Pertamina*, KBC sought to enforce an award rendered by a Swiss-seated tribunal in Texas. Pertamina, an entity owned by the government of Indonesia, sought to annul the award in Indonesia. KBC obtained a temporary order

tribunals were willing to grant such relief 'chaos would ensue',[68] and as Advocate General (AG) Kokott in *West Tankers* ventured, 'ultimately the jurisdiction which could impose higher penalties for failure to comply with the injunction would prevail'.[69]

The English courts have acknowledged but consistently rejected these arguments. In rejecting **3.34** these concerns, the English courts have emphasised that an anti-suit injunction is not issued against another sovereign court. Rather it is issued against the party in breach restraining that party from commencing or continuing proceedings.[70]

Further, English courts tend to emphasise the contractual nature of the relief[71] – the point of **3.35** the anti-suit injunction (in support of arbitration) is to enforce the negative aspect of the promise to arbitrate the parties' dispute, as Lord Mance explained in *Ust-Kamenogorsk*:

> An agreement to arbitrate disputes has positive and negative aspects. A party seeking relief within the scope of the arbitration agreement undertakes to do so in arbitration in whatever forum is prescribed. The (often silent) concomitant is that neither party will seek such relief in any other forum. [...] the negative aspect is as fundamental as the positive. There is no reason why a party to either should be free to engage the other party in a different forum merely because neither party wishes to bring proceedings in the agreed forum.[72]

The English courts thus take the view that anti-suit injunctions, as a *personal* remedy meant to **3.36** *enforce the promise* of a party in breach of an arbitration agreement, do not offend the principle of comity.

---

in Texas restraining Pertamina from continuing the Indonesian proceedings. Pertamina then obtained an injunction in Indonesia against KBC enforcing the award in the US, and had the award annulled. KBC's temporary order was replaced by an injunction. Both the Indonesian decision annulling the award and injuncting the Texan proceedings, and the Texan decision to grant the injunction, were ultimately reversed on appeal (*Karaha Bodas Company, L.L.C. v Perusahaan Pertambangan Minyak Dan Gas Bumi Negara (Pertamina)*, United States District Court, Southern District of Texas, Houston Division, 26 April 2002, 22 July 2002 and 17 April 2003 and United States Court of Appeals, Fifth Circuit, 18 June 2003, in Albert Jan van den Berg (ed), *Yearbook Commercial Arbitration 2003* (Kluwer Law International, 2003) vol 28).

68 *Turner (AG Opinion)* (n 3) para 33.

69 Case C-185/07 *Allianz SpA, Generali Assicurazioni Generali SpA v West Tankers Inc.* ECR I-00666 Opinion of AG Kokott, para 72 ('*West Tankers (AG Opinion)*').

70 As Lord Hobhouse in *Turner (HOL)* (n 24) [26] explained:

> The making of a restraining order does not depend upon denying, or pre-empting, the jurisdiction of the foreign court. One of the errors made by the deputy judge in the present case was to treat the case as if it were about the jurisdiction of the Madrid court. Jurisdiction is a different concept. For the foreign court, its jurisdiction and whether to exercise that jurisdiction falls to be decided by the foreign court itself in accordance with its own laws (including Conventions to which the foreign country may be a party). The jurisdiction which the foreign court chooses to assume may thus include an extraterritorial (or exorbitant) jurisdiction which is not internationally recognised. International recognition of the jurisdiction assumed by the foreign court only becomes critical at the stage of the enforcement of the judgments and decisions of the foreign court by the courts of another country. Restraining orders come into the picture at an earlier stage and involve not a decision upon the jurisdiction of the foreign court but an assessment of the conduct of the relevant party in invoking that jurisdiction. English law makes these distinctions.

71 As noted in Section A above, relief may also be granted where the commencement or continuance of parallel proceedings is oppressive or vexatious notwithstanding it may not be in breach of contract.

72 *Ust-Kamenogorsk* (n 32) [21].

3.37 The notion of comity has nevertheless proven to be an amorphous touchstone – a few examples from the English courts illustrate the fluidity of the concept. In a classical exposition, Sir John Donaldson, Master of the Rolls, in *British Airways Board*, described judicial comity as 'shorthand for good neighbourliness, common courtesy and mutual respect between those who labour in adjoining judicial vineyards'.[73]

3.38 In *The 'Angelic Grace'*, discussed above in Section B and further below in Section D.2, Lord Justice Leggatt suggested that *failing* to issue an anti-suit injunction would be contrary to the principle of comity:

> For my part, I do not contemplate that an Italian Judge would regard it as an interference with comity if the English Courts, having ruled on the scope of the English arbitration clause, then seek to enforce it by restraining the charterers by injunction from trying their luck in duplicated proceedings in the Italian Court. I can think of nothing more patronising than for the English Court to adopt the attitude that if the Italian Court declines jurisdiction, that would meet with the approval of the English Court, whereas if the Italian Court assumed jurisdiction, the English Court would then consider whether at that stage to intervene by injunction. That would be not only invidious but the reverse of comity.[74]

3.39 The timing of the grant of anti-suit relief leaves courts and tribunals with a difficult decision – intervene before the other court or tribunal rules on its own jurisdiction and prevent an inconsistent decision, or wait until the decision is made, which may remove the necessity of intervention at all, or alternatively, exacerbate the jurisdictional conflict and raise questions about the recognition of an inconsistent foreign judgment or award (discussed further in Section D.7 below). Justice Rix, the first instance judge in *The 'Angelic Grace'*, considered that 'much greater damage is done to the interests which that caution and that comity are intended to serve, if this Court adjourns these proceedings to await the outcome of a challenge to the jurisdiction in Italy … and then proceeds to issue an injunction'.[75]

3.40 In that respect, in *Ecobank v Tanoh*, Lord Justice Christopher Clarke discussed the practical dimension of the principle of comity in the context of anti-suit relief. Practical considerations weigh in favour of the early issue of anti-suit injunctions as they minimise the wastage of resources of the relevant courts:

> Comity has a warm ring. It is important to analyse what it means. We are not here concerned with judicial *amour propre* but with the operation of systems of law. Courts around the free world endeavour to do justice between citizens in accordance with applicable laws as expeditiously as they can with the resources available to them. This is an exercise in the fulfilment of which judges ought to be comrades in arms. The burdens imposed on courts are well known: long lists, size of cases, shortages of judges, expanding waiting times, and competing demands on resources. The administration of justice and the interests of litigants and of courts is usually prejudiced by late attempts to change course or to terminate the voyage. If successful they often mean that time, effort, and expense, often considerable,

---

73 *British Airways Board v Laker Airways Ltd* [1984] QB 142 (QB), 185–186. Nevertheless, in that case, the anti-suit injunction awarded was reversed by the House of Lords.

74 *Angelic Grace (COA)* (n 28) 95.

75 *Aggeliki Charis Compania Maritima SA v Pagnan SpA (The 'Angelic Grace')* [1994] 1 Lloyd's Rep 168 (QB) 182 ('*Angelic Grace (QB)*').

will have been wasted both by the parties and the courts and others. Comity between courts, and indeed considerations of public policy, require, where possible, the avoidance of such waste.[76]

In that case, an application for an *anti-enforcement* injunction (as the foreign proceedings had resulted in a judgment) was refused. As Lord Clarke explained: **3.41**

Timing is of considerable significance. The grant of an interlocutory injunction to prevent the commencement or continuance of a duplicate set of proceedings may well be a sound step which (a) gives effect to contractual rights and (b) avoids the cost and waste of rival proceedings operating in tandem and the risk of inconsistent judgments – results which considerations of comity would favour. In the case of an anti-enforcement injunction the application will, by definition, be made after the rival proceedings have run to judgment. The grant of an injunction will mean that the cost of those proceedings and the resources of the rival court will (unless the injunction is discharged) have been wasted. It will not avoid the risk of inconsistent decisions although it will preclude the respondent from enforcing the existing potentially inconsistent decision.[77]

If it is not exactly clear what the principle of comity requires, it is clear that traditionally, the English courts have not viewed the issuance of anti-suit injunctions as being against (and perhaps even view it as being prescribed by) the requirements of comity, especially when it is sought with expedition. **3.42**

Civil law courts (and civil law-minded tribunals) have preferred the defensive tool of *lis alibi pendens* (which requires an identity of parties, subject matter and cause of action), or where this standard is not met, *connexity* between closely related actions, to stay proceedings when another proceeding has already been initiated.[78] This approach underpins the mechanism adopted between courts in the Brussels regime.[79] **3.43**

Consistent with that approach, civil law courts have declined to enforce anti-suit injunctions issued by foreign (common law) courts. For example, the Düsseldorf Oberlandesgericht refused to enforce an anti-suit injunction issued by the English High Court in support of an arbitration under the LCIA Rules. In its judgment, the Düsseldorf court observed that the injunctions: **3.44**

... constitute an infringement of the jurisdiction of Germany because the German courts alone decide, in accordance with the procedural laws governing them and in accordance with existing international agreements, whether they are competent to adjudicate on a matter or whether they must respect the jurisdiction of another domestic or a foreign court (including arbitration courts). Furthermore, foreign courts cannot issue instructions as to whether and, if so, to what extent (in relation to time-limits and issues) a German court can and may take action in a particular case.

---

76 *Ecobank* (n 42) [132].
77 Ibid. [135].
78 Kaufmann-Kohler (n 66).
79 See, e.g., Arts 29–34 of the Brussels Recast Regulation (n 4). See further, ILA Report (n 65) 158–62.

The fact that the contested antisuit injunctions are not directly addressed to the German State or German courts, but to Mr G. as the plaintiff in the actions already instituted by him and in potential further actions in Germany, cannot affect this decision …[80]

3.45 Nevertheless, some civil law jurisdictions have modified their conventional tools to enhance the protection offered to locally-seated arbitrations and to limit deference to foreign courts (features associated with anti-suit relief). For example, under the traditional *lis pendens* rules in Switzerland, an arbitral tribunal seated in Switzerland would be required to stay its proceedings if a foreign court had already been seized of the dispute and a decision of that foreign court would be entitled to recognition in Switzerland.[81] This rule has a jurisdictional rather than purely procedural effect – as the Swiss Federal Tribunal has observed, it 'paralyses the jurisdiction of the second [tribunal]'.[82] In 2007, amendments to Swiss arbitration legislation 'intentionally gave discretionary power to arbitral tribunals in the context of parallel proceedings', mandating a tribunal seated in Switzerland to proceed notwithstanding ongoing foreign proceedings, unless there are serious reasons to stay the arbitration.[83] The Swiss courts will nevertheless refrain from actively interfering with the foreign proceedings by issuing anti-suit or equivalent relief.[84]

3.46 The foreignness of anti-suit relief to the civil law tradition has fed into the evolving relationship between EU law and arbitration. In particular it has driven the CJEU's decisions on court and tribunal-ordered anti-suit relief and the fallout from those decisions in Member State courts.

D. RELATIONSHIP BETWEEN THE CJEU AND ARBITRATION

1. Establishing the Brussels regime

3.47 In 1957, the European Economic Community (EEC) was established by the Treaty of Rome (what is now known as the Treaty on the Functioning of the European Union).[85] Article 220(4) of the Treaty provided that, 'Member States shall, so far as necessary, enter into

---

80 *Re the Enforcement of an English Anti-Suit Injunction* [1997] ILPr 320 (Oberlandesgericht (Regional Court of Appeal), Düsseldorf) [14]–[15]. There are some notable exceptions – see, e.g., Cass Civ 1re, 14 Octobre 2009, pourvoi n° 08-16.369, 08-16.549, Bulletin 2009 I n° 207.
81 Nevertheless, this latter criterion was often used as a stop-valve, with tribunals asserting that the foreign court's failure to give effect to a valid arbitration agreement would render the judgment ineligible for recognition in Switzerland.
82 *Fomento de Construcciones y Contratas SA v Colon Container Terminal SA*, 127 ATF III 279 (2001) (Swiss Federal Tribunal) ('*Fomento*').
83 These amendments were principally introduced in response to the *Fomento* decision, ibid., and the implications of the *lis pendens* rule in the context of the Lugano Convention (the Convention which effectively extends the Brussels Regulation to Switzerland, Iceland, Norway and Denmark), where judgments would be 'entitled to recognition' whether or not they gave effect to a valid arbitration agreement, a concern sought to be addressed in the Brussels Recast Regulation (n 4) (see Sections D.6 and D.7 below). See Rapport de la Commission des affaires juridiques du Conseil national, *Initiative parlementaire Modification de l'art. 186 de la loi fédérale sur le droit international privé* (17 February 2006, 02.415).
84 Matthias Scherer and Werner Jahnel, 'Anti-suit and Anti-arbitration Injunctions in International Arbitration: A Swiss Perspective' (2009) 12(4) *Int ALR* 66.
85 Treaty establishing the European Economic Community (opened for signature 25 March 1957, entered into force 1 January 1958) ('Treaty of Rome').

negotiations with each other with a view to securing for the benefit of their nationals … the simplification of formalities governing the reciprocal recognition and enforcement of judgments of courts or tribunals and of arbitration awards.[86] It was contemplated when the Treaty of Rome was signed that there would be a unified, comprehensive regime for the recognition and enforcement of judicial decisions and arbitral awards in Europe.

However, just over a decade later in 1968, the Convention on Jurisdiction and the Enforcement of Judgments in Civil and Commercial Matters (Brussels Convention) was signed.[87] The Brussels Convention addressed issues of jurisdiction and enforcement of court decisions, but Article 1(4) of the Convention excluded arbitration as a whole from its ambit. It was acknowledged, at that time, that this was a departure from the uniform scheme envisioned by the Treaty of Rome.[88] The exclusion of arbitration from the Brussels regime had been motivated by the emergence of international treaties on arbitration, in particular the European Convention on International Commercial Arbitration (European Convention), opened for signature in 1961, and the New York Convention, opened for signature in 1958 (and signed by five of the six EEC Member States). It was clear to the drafters of the Brussels Convention that conflicts with such treaties were to be avoided.[89] This exclusion was maintained when the Brussels Convention became an EU Regulation in 2000 (Brussels Regulation).[90]   **3.48**

Nevertheless, even at the time of the framing of the Brussels Convention, issues with the scope of the exclusion had been anticipated. On the UK's accession to the Convention, it asserted that the exclusion covered 'all disputes which the parties had effectively agreed should be settled by arbitration, including any secondary disputes connected with the agreed arbitration'.[91] The original EEC members took a more narrow view of the exclusion (and hence a wider operation for the Convention). The Schlosser report, prepared on the accession of the UK, identified these as '[t]wo divergent basic positions which it was not possible to reconcile'.[92] This rift has persisted in Member States' submissions to the CJEU over the past three decades, as issues concerning the interface between the Brussels regime and arbitration have come before Europe's highest court.   **3.49**

2. Early decisions on the interface between the Brussels regime and arbitration

The CJEU addressed the interface between arbitration and the Brussels Convention (as it was then) in *Marc Rich* and in *Van Uden*.[93]   **3.50**

---

86   Emphasis added.

87   Brussels Convention (n 4).

88   P Jenard, 'Report on the Convention on jurisdiction and the enforcement of judgments in civil and commercial matters' [1979] OJ C 59/1 13 ('Jenard Report').

89   Ibid., 13.

90   Brussels Regulation (n 4).

91   Peter Schlosser, 'Report on the Convention on the Association of the Kingdom of Denmark, Ireland and the United Kingdom of Great Britain and Northern Ireland to the Convention on jurisdiction and the enforcement of judgments in civil and commercial matters and to the Protocol on its interpretation by the Court of Justice', [1979] OJ C59/71 para 61 ('Schlosser Report').

92   Ibid., para 61.

93   Case C-190/89 *Marc Rich and Co AG v Società Italiana Impianti PA* [1991] ECR I-03894 ('*Marc Rich (CJEU)*').

3.51 In *Marc Rich*, the parties disputed whether an arbitration agreement (with a London seat) had been incorporated into the contract. One party had commenced proceedings in the Italian courts and asserted that the arbitration agreement had not been incorporated. The second party commenced arbitration proceedings in London shortly thereafter, and sought the assistance of the English courts to appoint an arbitrator given the default of the first party. That second party had also commenced proceedings in the Italian courts for a declaration that the Italian courts lacked jurisdiction. In the arbitrator appointment proceedings, Lord Justice Lloyd and Sir Roger Ormrod of the English Court of Appeal considered that there was 'reasonable doubt' as to the scope of the arbitration exception under the Brussels Convention and referred the question to the CJEU.[94]

3.52 AG Darmon recognised the impact of the CJEU's decision on 'the juridical stability which international arbitration enjoys within the territory of the Community'.[95] AG Darmon considered that the principal subject matter of the proceedings before the English courts concerned the appointment of an arbitrator, a matter excluded from the scope of the Convention. The existence of the arbitration agreement was a preliminary question, which could not affect whether the Convention applied or not. In any event, in AG Darmon's opinion, the existence of the arbitration agreement was also a matter outside the scope of the Convention, as were other court proceedings related to arbitration. AG Darmon reached this position acknowledging the risks of an irreconcilability between an arbitral award rendered in England and an Italian judgment on the substance of the case.[96]

3.53 The CJEU came to the same conclusion, finding that the parties to the Brussels Convention, wishing to avoid overlap with the European Convention and the New York Convention, 'intended to exclude arbitration in its entirety, including proceedings brought before national courts'.[97] Likewise, the CJEU found that when the main subject matter of the proceedings was excluded from the Brussels Convention, the existence of a preliminary matter within the scope of the Convention could not justify its application.[98]

3.54 Following the decision in *Marc Rich*, the English courts maintained their view that the Brussels Convention did not impose any hard limitation on their power to grant anti-suit injunctions in support of arbitral proceedings. In *The 'Angelic Grace'*,[99] the English courts issued an anti-suit injunction to restrain a party from breaching its arbitration agreement (in that case

---

94   *Marc Rich & Co AG v Società Italiana Impianti PA (The Atlantic Emperor) (No.1)* [1989] 1 Lloyd's Rep. 548 (CA) [15] (*'Marc Rich (COA)'*).

95   *Case C-190/89 Marc Rich and Co AG v Società Italiana Impianti PA* [1991] ECR I-03865, Opinion of AG Darmon (*'Marc Rich (AG Opinion)'*) para 5.

96   *Marc Rich (AG Opinion)* (n 95) para 102.

97   *Marc Rich (CJEU)* (n 93) para 18.

98   *Marc Rich*, ibid., para 26. In the interim, the Italian Corte di Cassazione had ruled that the arbitration agreement was not valid. Following the CJEU's decision, the appeal in the English courts against the decision to proceed with the appointment of an arbitrator was dismissed. Marc Rich sought an injunction restraining the Italian proceedings pending the appointment of an arbitrator by the English courts. In a twist of fate, this application was rejected. The Court of Appeal found that Marc Rich was estopped by the Italian decision, which was enforceable as Marc Rich had submitted to the jurisdiction of the Italian courts by pleading a defence on the merits of the Italian proceedings – a ground for recognition of the judgment separate from the Brussels regime (see *Marc Rich & Co AG v Società Italiana Impianti PA (The Atlantic Emperor) (No.2)* [1992] 1 Lloyd's Rep. 624 (CA) (*'Marc Rich (COA-2)'*).

99   *Angelic Grace (QB)* (n 75).

by issuing proceedings in the Italian courts) while arbitration proceedings were ongoing in London. In the first instance proceedings, Justice Rix was conscious to note the uncertainty concerning the Court's obligation to recognise the prospective Italian judgment under the Brussels regime when those proceedings had been brought in violation of an arbitration agreement. Nevertheless, Justice Rix considered that in the circumstances, his 'hope and sincere belief [was] that the Italian Courts would feel not at all perturbed' by the injunction, especially as the Italian courts had not yet ruled on the arbitration clause.[100] The Court of Appeal was less restrained – its position reflected in the 'ritual incantation' dictum extracted in Section C.2 above.

In *Van Uden*,[101] the question of the relationship between the Brussels regime and arbitration **3.55** returned to the CJEU, this time by way of a request for a preliminary ruling from the Dutch Supreme Court (Hoge Raad). In that case, the claimant in an arbitration seated in the Netherlands had sought (and obtained) interim measures from the Dutch courts – a preliminary payment of part of the claimed amount – against a respondent domiciled in Germany. Amongst a range of other issues, the CJEU was called upon to decide the application of the Brussels Convention to proceedings for interim measures relating to an ongoing arbitration. AG Léger[102] and the CJEU drew a distinction between proceedings ancillary to arbitration (like the proceedings in *Marc Rich* for the appointment of an arbitrator), and the interim measures proceedings at issue – which were not targeted at the arbitration per se, but rather 'parallel to such proceedings … [t]hey concern not arbitration as such but the protection of a wide variety of rights'.[103] As such, the CJEU concluded that the interim measures proceedings fell within the Convention given that the Convention's scope was 'determined not by [the nature of the proceedings] but by the nature of the rights which they serve to protect' (in this case, the claimant's underlying contractual rights to payment).[104]

3. Turner-ing the tide – establishing limits on anti-suit relief in the European context

Together, *Marc Rich* and *Van Uden* signposted the CJEU's approach to the scope of the **3.56** arbitration exception under the Brussels Convention, which was to be radically redefined in the *West Tankers* decision (discussed further below in Section D.4). The groundwork for *West Tankers* was nevertheless being laid by the CJEU in its decision in *Turner v Grovit*, which concerned the power to issue anti-suit injunctions in support of court proceedings.

In *Turner*,[105] Turner resigned and brought unfair dismissal proceedings in England following a **3.57** transfer of his employment to Spain and to another company in the corporate group. The companies responded by instituting proceedings for breach of contract in Spain. Turner sought anti-suit relief from the English courts against the Spanish proceedings.

---

100 Ibid., 182.
101 Case C-391/95 *Van Uden Maritime v Kommanditgesellschaft in Firma Deco-Line* [1998] ECR I-7122 ('*Van Uden (CJEU)*').
102 Case C-391/95 *Van Uden Maritime v Kommanditgesellschaft in Firma Deco-Line* [1998] ECR I-7093, Opinion of AG Léger ('*Van Uden (AG Opinion)*').
103 *Van Uden (CJEU)* (n 101) para 33.
104 Ibid.
105 Case C-159/02 *Turner v Grovit* [2004] ECR I-3578 ('*Turner (CJEU)*').

3.58   At first instance, the relief was denied on the basis that under the Brussels Convention, the Spanish courts were entitled to assess their own jurisdiction.[106] The Court of Appeal reversed this decision, and found that the Convention did not limit the power of the English courts to protect their own processes from abuse.[107] The House of Lords agreed, noting that the focus of its inquiry was on the behaviour of the party instituting the foreign proceedings, rather than the jurisdiction of the foreign court.[108] Nevertheless, the House of Lords referred the question of the consistency of the anti-suit relief with the Convention to the CJEU for a preliminary ruling.

3.59   In the opinion of AG Ruiz-Jarabo,[109] the practice of issuing anti-suit injunctions cast doubt on the reciprocal trust between the various national legal systems under the Brussels Convention. AG Ruiz-Jarabo observed that:

> … [i]f all European courts arrogated such a power to themselves, chaos would ensue. If that power were exercised only by English courts, they would be taking it upon themselves to exercise a distributive function which the Brussels Convention entrusts to less flexible, but more objective, criteria, which it imposes on everyone in the same way.[110]

3.60   The CJEU agreed. The Court noted that while an injunction was directed at the party and not at the foreign court, the injunction undermined the foreign court's jurisdiction to determine the dispute, as it was imposed by a court and backed by a penalty.[111] As such, the injunction was an interference with the foreign court's jurisdiction and incompatible with the Convention.

3.61   As *Turner* concerned a choice of court agreement, rather than an arbitration agreement, it was understood not to apply to arbitration agreements by virtue of the arbitration exception (now Article 1(2)(d) of the Brussels Regulation). *Turner* therefore did not prevent the English courts from issuing anti-suit injunctions when EU court proceedings were brought in breach of an arbitration agreement.

3.62   Indeed, in *Through Transport*,[112] the English Court of Appeal observed that the CJEU's decision in Turner did not apply directly to the case when one set of proceedings was outside the Brussels Convention/Regulation – 'there is nothing in the Convention to prevent the courts of a contracting state from granting an injunction to restrain a claimant from beginning proceedings in a contracting state which would be in breach of an arbitration clause'.[113] As such, the Court's approach in *The 'Angelic Grace'* continued to apply.[114] However, that approach did not last long before being challenged in the *West Tankers* case.

---

106   *Turner v Grovit* [1999] 1 All ER (Comm) 445 (Ch) [23].
107   *Turner v Grovit* [2000] QB 345 (CA) 357–8.
108   *Turner (HOL)* (n 24) [26].
109   *Turner (AG Opinion)* (n 3).
110   Ibid., para 33.
111   *Turner (CJEU)* (n 105) para 27.
112   *Through Transport Mutual Insurance Association (Eurasia) Ltd v New India Assurance Co Ltd (The Hari Bhum) (No.1)* [2004] EWCA Civ 1598, [2005] 1 All ER (Comm) 715 ('*Through Transport*').
113   Ibid., [84].
114   Ibid., [87]–[92]. Nevertheless, in that case the Court of Appeal reversed the first instance decision to issue an anti-suit injunction. The reversal turned on the particular facts of the case (a claim against an insolvent insurer was made pursuant

4. Arbitration and the Brussels regime collide – the West Tankers decision

West Tankers involved a collision between a vessel and a jetty (the latter owned by the charterers **3.63** of the vessel). The charterers/jetty owners partially recovered their losses against their insurance and brought arbitration proceedings under the charter party against the vessel owners for the uninsured remainder. In the interim, the insurers sued the vessel owners in the Italian courts for the amounts paid under the insurance pursuant to their right of subrogation (conferred under Italian law). The charterers/jetty owners sought an anti-suit injunction from the English courts to stop the Italian proceedings and to refer the matter to arbitration.

The question thus arose as to whether the CJEU's approach in *Turner* also applied to the **3.64** arbitral context. The English Court of Appeal in *Through Transport* had held that it did not. The House of Lords, in referring the question to the CJEU, agreed with that approach, but noted that European academic opinion was divided on the question.[115] Lord Hoffmann observed that arbitration was not self-sustaining and needed the support of the courts, such support being an important factor in the seat of arbitration chosen by parties. He noted that:

> … [t]he courts are there to serve the business community rather than the other way round. No one is obliged to choose London. The existence of the jurisdiction to restrain proceedings in breach of an arbitration agreement clearly does not deter parties to commercial agreements. On the contrary, it may be regarded as one of the advantages which the chosen seat of arbitration has to offer.[116]

AG Kokott considered that the decisive question was not whether the anti-suit injunction **3.65** proceedings were captured by the Regulation, but whether the proceedings against which the anti-suit injunction was directed (the Italian proceedings) were captured.[117] In her view, the principle of mutual trust could be infringed even if one of the proceedings (the English anti-suit proceedings) was not within the scope of the Regulation.[118] The national authorities of Member States, including in their application of national procedural rules, were not permitted to impair the practical effectiveness of EU law.[119] AG Kokott rejected the House of Lords' concerns about the competitiveness of European seats of arbitration, finding that 'aims of a purely economic nature cannot justify infringements of Community law'.[120] Again, AG Kokott recognised the risk of conflicting decisions, but was of the view that:

> … [a] unilateral anti-suit injunction is not, however, a suitable measure to rectify that situation. In particular, if other Member States were to follow the English example and also introduce anti-suit

---

to a Finnish statute against the insurer's club in Finnish courts; the Club Rules (as between the insolvent insurer and the club) contained an arbitration clause. In the circumstances, it was not appropriate to issue an injunction given that while the claim was subject to the arbitration clause, the claimant's commencement of proceedings was not in breach of that clause. The Court of Appeal expressly referred to 'the reasoning underlying the approach of the ECJ in *Turner v Grovit*' as a circumstance relevant to its decision not to grant an anti-suit injunction (at [97]).

115   *West Tankers Inc v RAS Riunione Adriatica di Sicurta SpA and others* [2007] UKHL 4, [2007] 1 All ER (Comm) 794 [27] ('*West Tankers (HOL)*').

116   Ibid., [20].

117   *West Tankers (AG Opinion)* (n 69) para 33.

118   Ibid., para 34.

119   Ibid., para 35.

120   Ibid., para 66.

injunctions, reciprocal injunctions would ensue. Ultimately the jurisdiction which could impose higher penalties for failure to comply with the injunction would prevail.[121]

3.66 The CJEU's reasoning followed AG Kokott's logic. The Italian proceedings fell within the scope of the Regulation, given their primary subject matter was the protection of the insurer's underlying rights to damages.[122] The preliminary question before the Italian tribunal as to the validity of the arbitration agreement also fell within the Regulation.[123] The English anti-suit injunction, while outside the scope of the Regulation, amounted to 'stripping the [Italian court] of the power to rule on its own jurisdiction under [the Brussels Regulation]'.[124] In doing so, it undermined the effectiveness of the Regulation and 'the attainment of the objectives of unification of the rules of conflict of jurisdiction in civil and commercial matters and the free movement of decision in those matters'.[125] This concern about the effectiveness of the European judicial system has assumed increasing importance in the CJEU's jurisprudence and foreshadows the CJEU's approach in the *Achmea* decision, discussed briefly in Section D.7 below.

3.67 The CJEU's 2009 decision in *West Tankers* generated significant controversy in the international arbitration community,[126] concerned primarily with the practical realities of arbitral proceedings rather than maintaining the ideological purity of the Brussels regime. As foreshadowed by Lord Hoffmann, the decision raised significant questions about the attractiveness of European cities as arbitral seats. It also generated discussion about the ideal interface between the Brussels regime and arbitration – with proposals both to expand and contract the arbitration exception (and thus the operation of the regime).[127]

5. The Claxton carve-out – limiting the effect of West Tankers

3.68 Nevertheless, the English courts were bound by the CJEU's decision in *West Tankers*, and could not issue anti-suit injunctions to protect arbitration agreements when one party breached the agreement by commencing proceedings in the courts of another EU Member State.

3.69 The English courts nevertheless continued to issue anti-suit injunction against parties commencing proceedings in a court outside of the EU, as they did in *Ust-Kamenogorsk* (in respect of Kazakh proceedings),[128] and *Shipowners' v Containerships* (Turkish proceedings).[129]

---

121 Ibid., para 72.
122 *West Tankers (CJEU)* (n 10) para 26.
123 Ibid., para 26.
124 Ibid., para 28.
125 Ibid., para 24.
126 In particular, amongst those practising in the UK. In Edwin Peel's view, 'There is little merit in detailed assessment of the reasoning of the court, and not only because, as is usually the case, there is not much of it.' (Edwin Peel, 'Arbitration and Anti-Suit Injunctions in the European Union' (2009) 125 *LQR* 365).
127 The development of the proposals is summarised in Case C-536/13 *'Gazprom' OAO v Lietuvos Respublika* [2014] ECLI:EU:C:2014:2414, Opinion of AG Wathelet, paras 113–124 ('*Gazprom (AG Opinion)*').
128 *Ust-Kamenogorsk* (n 32).
129 *Shipowners' Mutual Protection and Indemnity Association v Containerships Denizcilik Nakliyat ve Ticaret AS* [2016] EWCA Civ 386, [2016] 2 All ER (Comm) 851 ('*Shipowners*').

The English courts did not refrain from issuing anti-arbitration injunctions against European-   **3.70**
seated arbitral proceedings either. In *Claxton*, the English High Court had found, in a battle of
the forms scenario, that the parties had agreed upon the exclusive jurisdiction of the English
courts, and not arbitration in Hungary.[130] The Hungarian party then commenced arbitration
proceedings seeking an urgent interim award, declaring that the parties were subject to the
arbitration agreement and seeking damages for breach of that agreement. In Justice Hamblen's
view, the CJEU's decision in *West Tankers* did not affect the Court's power to interfere with
proceedings outside the scope of the Regulation, given that the effectiveness of the Regulation
was not impaired.[131] In that case, while anti-arbitration injunctions were generally 'best left to
the relevant supervisory courts of the country of the seat of the arbitration', it was appropriate
in the circumstances (particularly because the English court had already ruled that there was no
arbitration agreement) to issue an anti-arbitration injunction.[132]

6. Recasting the relationship – the new Brussels Recast Regulation and the Gazprom case

In 2015, the Brussels Recast Regulation commenced application, replacing the earlier Brussels   **3.71**
Regulation.[133] The Recast Regulation retained the previous Article 1(2)(d) in the Brussels
Regulation (the successor of Article 1(4) of the 1968 Brussels Convention), which was the
basis of the arbitration exception, and added a new Recital 12 and Article 73(2), both of which
further clarified the scope of the arbitration exception. Recital 12 expressly clarifies that the
Brussels Recast Regulation 'should not apply to arbitration', including:

> any action or ancillary proceedings relating to, in particular, the establishment of an arbitral tribunal,
> the powers of arbitrators, the conduct of an arbitration procedure or any other aspects of such a
> procedure, nor to any action or judgment concerning the annulment, review, appeal, recognition or
> enforcement of an arbitral award.

Some in the arbitration community were of the view that the Brussels Recast Regulation's   **3.72**
amendments swept away the *West Tankers* decision,[134] and permitted courts to issue anti-suit
injunctions in support of arbitration proceedings. Indeed, AG Wathelet was of that opinion in
the *Gazprom* case.

Gazprom concerned the distribution of gas in Lithuania by Gazprom, an energy company   **3.73**
majority owned by the government of Russia, through a company partly owned by Gazprom
and partly owned by the government of Lithuania. Gazprom and Lithuania were parties to a
shareholders' agreement in respect of the company, which included an arbitration clause.

---

130 *Claxton Engineering Services Ltd v TXM Olaj-És Gázkutató KFT* [2010] EWHC 2567 (Comm), [2011] 2 All ER (Comm) 38.
131 *Claxton (Injunction)* (n 52) [20]–[26].
132 Ibid., [32], [42].
133 Brussels Recast Regulation (n 4).
134 cf Adrian Briggs, *Civil Jurisdiction and Judgments* (6th ed, Routledge 2015) para 2.44. Briggs suggests that 'the idea that [the new Recital in the Recast Regulation] might have opened the door to the possibility of an anti-suit injunction (and the reversal of the effect of [*West Tankers*]) ordered in aid of the arbitration is most implausible'. See also, Simon Camilleri, 'Recital 12 of the Recast Regulation: A New Hope' (2013) 62 ICLQ 899, 916 ('*Camilleri*') – '… there still seems to be no place for the anti-suit injunction with Europe as 'mutual trust' is as important under the Recast Regulation as it was (or, for now, is) under Brussels I'.

3.74 The Lithuanian Ministry of Energy brought an action in the Lithuanian courts for an investigation of the joint venture company, on the basis that the general manager and directors appointed by Gazprom had not acted in the best interests of the company when the gas pricing formula (agreed between the company and Gazprom) had been amended.

3.75 Gazprom reacted by commencing an arbitration under the shareholders' agreement. Gazprom sought an anti-suit injunction against Lithuania in respect of the investigation proceedings, which was granted by the arbitral tribunal in part.[135] Meanwhile, the Lithuanian courts had determined that the matters raised in the investigation were not arbitrable and that the Lithuanian courts had jurisdiction over those matters. Gazprom then sought to enforce the tribunal's award in Lithuania. Enforcement was refused at first instance. Gazprom appealed, and in determining Gazprom's appeal, the Lithuanian Supreme Court requested a preliminary ruling from the CJEU on whether it could refuse to enforce the award on the basis that the award was inconsistent with the Brussels Regulation and/or the Recast Regulation.

3.76 AG Wathelet analysed the development of the Brussels Recast Regulation and concluded that the amendments to the Regulation were aimed at extending the arbitration exclusion to any proceedings in which the validity of an arbitration agreement was contested, reinstating the broad-brush view expressed by the CJEU in *Marc Rich* in 1991.[136] As such, if *West Tankers* had been decided under the Brussels Recast Regulation, the anti-suit injunction (issued by a court in support of an arbitration, and against proceedings in a court of another EU Member State) would have been permissible.[137] Further, and in addition, AG Wathelet observed that arbitral tribunals were not bound by the principle of mutual trust in the Recast Regulation (as a limit on their power to issue anti-suit injunctions).[138] In AG Wathelet's view, the principles in the Recast Regulation were not sufficiently fundamental to the European legal order to be considered 'public policy'.[139] As such, the Lithuanian courts were not entitled to refuse recognition and enforcement of the tribunal's award on that basis.

3.77 The CJEU, however, left open the position under the Brussels Recast Regulation, given the relevant matters had arisen before 10 January 2015 (the date the Recast Regulation commenced application).[140] Distinguishing its position in *West Tankers*, the Court found that because the anti-suit injunction was issued by an arbitral tribunal, rather than by a national court, it was incapable of affecting the mutual trust between courts,[141] and therefore was not precluded by the (original) Brussels Regulation.[142] The recognition and enforcement of the tribunal's award (governed by the New York Convention, and not by the Brussels Regulation)

---

135 *Gazprom (Arbitral Award)* (n 41).
136 *Gazprom (AG Opinion)* (n 127) para 141.
137 Ibid., paras 133–134.
138 Ibid., para 154.
139 Ibid., paras 180–188.
140 *Gazprom (CJEU)* (n 11) para 3.
141 Ibid., para 39.
142 Ibid., para 44.

would likewise not infringe the principle of mutual trust.[143] As such, Gazprom was able to successfully enforce the tribunal's anti-suit injunction in Lithuania.[144]

Gazprom has thus given rise to the situation in which an arbitral tribunal, but not a court of an EU Member State, has the power to issue anti-suit injunctions against parties that breach their arbitration agreement by commencing proceedings in a court of another Member State.[145] **3.78**

As the CJEU did not address the availability of anti-suit relief under the Brussels Recast Regulation, nor did it question the conclusion reached by AG Wathelet, it might have been expected that Member State courts would follow AG Wathelet's lead. **3.79**

However, in one of the first cases to consider the Brussels Recast Regulation, Justice Males of the English High Court was of the view that AG Wathelet's opinion was 'fundamentally flawed'.[146] In *Nori Holding*,[147] one party had brought court proceedings in Russia and Cyprus (the latter an EU Member State) in breach of an arbitration clause providing for LCIA arbitration in London. The other parties sought an anti-suit injunction in the English courts against these proceedings. Justice Males rejected the application in respect of the Cypriot proceedings, observing that Recital 12 did nothing to 'undermine, or even to address, the fundamental principles concerning the effectiveness of the Regulation … If the EU legislature intended to reverse the West Tankers decision, it chose an odd way in which to do so'.[148] **3.80**

Given the refusal to grant leave to appeal in *Nori Holding*, and the UK's departure from the EU,[149] the position of the higher English courts under the Recast Regulation may not be resolved for some time (or at all). Further, given the limited practice of issuing anti-suit relief in other common law jurisdictions within the EU (Ireland[150] and Cyprus[151]), the question may not return to the CJEU either. **3.81**

---

143 Ibid., paras 42–43.
144 Gazprom was also successful in defending the substance of the claims brought by Lithuania in separate arbitration proceedings. On 4 July 2019, the Svea Court of Appeal rejected an application by Lithuania to set aside the arbitral award in those proceedings. Tom Jones, 'Lithuania fails to revive US$2 billion claim against Gazprom' (*Global Arbitration Review*, 5 July 2019) <https://globalarbitrationreview.com/article/1194864/lithuania-fails-to-revive-ususd2-billion-claim-against-gazprom> accessed on 8 January 2020.
145 Query whether this position, in relation to English-seated arbitral tribunals, is consistent with s 48(5)(a) of the Arbitration Act 1996 (UK), which provides that an arbitral tribunal has the *same powers* as the court to order a party to do or refrain from doing anything.
146 *Nori Holding Ltd v Public Joint-Stock Company 'Bank Otkritie Financial Corporation'* [2018] EWHC 1343 (Comm), [2018] All ER (D) 30 (Jun) [91] (*'Nori Holding'*).
147 Ibid.
148 Ibid., [90].
149 On 31 January 2020, the UK left the EU with a transitional period until 31 December 2020. See the Agreement on the withdrawal of the United Kingdom of Great Britain and Northern Ireland from the European Union and the European Atomic Energy Community, 19 October 2019 ('UK Withdrawal Agreement').
150 In *Walters v Flannery* [2017] IEHC 736 [24], the High Court of Ireland noted that 'there is no Irish authority setting out the test for anti-suit injunctions in this jurisdiction', but that 'there exists instructive English case law on this issue'.
151 See *Finvision Holdings Ltd* (Decision of the Supreme Court of Cyprus, 10 July 2018), where it appears that the approach of the English courts is generally followed.

7.   A new frontier for jurisdictional conflicts – *Achmea*, the Recast Regulation and the New York Convention

3.82   A further expression of the difficult future for the relationship between arbitration, EU law and international law is reflected in the CJEU's landmark decision in *Achmea*.[152] *Achmea* concerned an arbitral award obtained by Achmea against Slovakia in a Frankfurt-seated arbitration, commenced pursuant to a BIT between the Netherlands and the former Czechoslovakia.

3.83   Slovakia brought an action before the courts in Germany to set aside the arbitral award, including on the basis the arbitration agreement was void and incompatible with EU law, and that the award was contrary to public policy. The German Federal Court of Justice referred the question of whether the arbitration agreement in the BIT was compatible with EU law to the CJEU.[153]

3.84   In the view of AG Wathelet, the systemic risk that intra-EU BITs represented to the uniformity and effectiveness of EU law had been greatly exaggerated.[154] AG Wathelet considered that an arbitral tribunal under an intra-EU BIT would be permitted to request the CJEU to give a preliminary ruling,[155] which would preserve the autonomy of EU law.[156]

3.85   The CJEU found that tribunals in arbitrations arising under BITs may be called upon to interpret and apply EU law,[157] but could not refer questions as to the interpretation of EU law to the CJEU, as they sat outside the EU judicial system.[158] As such, the autonomy of EU law could not be guaranteed and the mechanism for investor-state arbitration in the BIT was incompatible with EU law.[159]

3.86   In the wake of the decision, somewhat ironically, one can foresee the potential rise of anti-arbitration type relief, like that in *BCB v Belize*,[160] being sought by respondent states against investors pursuing intra-EU BIT proceedings. These measures could be taken in conjunction with Member States seeking to set aside intra-EU BIT awards, withdrawing cases brought by state-controlled entities against other Member States, and the termination of all

---

152   *Achmea (CJEU)* (n 12).
153   Ibid., para 23.
154   Case C-284/16 *Slowakische Republik v Achmea BV* [2017] ECLI:EU:C:2017:699, Opinion of AG Wathelet, para 44 ('*Achmea (AG Opinion)*').
155   As such a tribunal fell within the scope of Art 267 TFEU (Ibid., para 131).
156   Ibid., paras 133–135. Further, disputes between EU members states and individuals would not be captured by Art 344 of the TFEU and did not concern the interpretation or application of EU law, given the underlying causes of action derived from the BIT, and not EU law. AG Wathelet also observed that the autonomy of EU law was not undermined given the ultimate oversight by Member State courts of the arbitral process, and the recognition and enforcement of the resulting awards.
157   *Achmea (CJEU)* (n 12) para 42.
158   Ibid., para 49.
159   Ibid., para 60.
160   *BCB v Belize (CCJ)* (n 44), discussed in Section C.1 above.

intra-EU BITs through a plurilateral treaty,[161] as foreshadowed in their declarations of 15 and 16 January 2019 (*Achmea* declarations).[162]

The *Achmea* decision also brings into sharp relief the CJEU's perspective on the relationship **3.87** between EU law (in the form of the constitutional EU treaties,[163] and secondary legislation) and international law (of which the constitutional treaties form a part[164]). In *Achmea*, the CJEU justified EU law's 'autonomy' from international law by reference to 'the essential characteristics of the EU and its law'.[165] The CJEU recalled its earlier opinion in the *ECHR* case, in which it found that the 'founding treaties of the EU, unlike ordinary international treaties, established a new legal order'.[166] In that order, as the Member States have declared, 'Union law takes precedence over bilateral investment treaties concluded between Member States'.[167]

Nevertheless, outside that order, the relationship between EU law and international law **3.88** remains contentious. As the tribunal in *Vattenfall* noted, different approaches have been taken to reconciling conflicts between EU and international law – either by endorsing a harmonious interpretation, prioritising international law over EU law or finding that there is no conflict that requires resolution.[168]

In the anti-suit relief context, the CJEU has suggested that no direct conflict appears between **3.89** a Member State's obligation under Article II(3) of the New York Convention to 'refer the parties to arbitration' and the prohibition on anti-suit relief within the EU that flows from the Brussels regime.[169]

---

161 European Commission, 'EU Member States agree on a plurilateral treaty to terminate bilateral investment treaties' (24 October 2019).

162 Declaration of the Representatives of the Governments of the Member States of 15 January 2019 on the Legal Consequences of the Judgment of the Court of Justice in *Achmea* and on Investment Protection in the European Union (hereafter First *Achmea* Declaration); Declaration of the Representatives of the Governments of the Member States of 16 January 2019 on the Enforcement of the Judgment of the Court of Justice in *Achmea* and on Investment Protection in the European Union (hereafter Second *Achmea* Declaration); Declaration of the Representative of the Government of Hungary of 16 January 2019 on the Legal Consequences of the Judgment of the Court of Justice in *Achmea* and on Investment Protection in the European Union (hereafter Third *Achmea* Declaration) (collectively, '*Achmea* declarations').

163 Treaty of Rome (n 85) (subsequently retitled the Treaty on the Functioning of the European Union); and the Treaty on European Union (n 149) (collectively, 'EU Treaties').

164 See *Vattenfall AB and others v Germany*, ICSID Case No. ARB/12/12, Decision on the *Achmea* Issue, paras 146, 149–150 ('*Vattenfall*'). In *Electrabel SA v Republic of Hungary*, ICSID Case No. ARB/07/19, Decision on Jurisdiction, Applicable Law and Liability, paras 4.122–4.123 and *RREEF Infrastructure (GP) Ltd v Spain*, Decision on Jurisdiction, para 73, the tribunals found that EU secondary legislation, as well as the EU Treaties, formed part of the international legal order.

165 *Achmea (CJEU)* (n 12) para 33.

166 Ibid; Case Opinion 2/13 *Accession of the European Union to the European Convention for the Protection of Human Rights and Fundamental Freedoms* [2014] ECLI:EU:C:2014:2454, para 157.

167 First *Achmea* Declaration and Third *Achmea* Declaration (n 162).

168 *Vattenfall* (n 164) para 147.

169 In *West Tankers (CJEU)* (n 10) para 33, the CJEU observed that its finding that anti-suit injunctions were incompatible with the Brussels Regulation was 'supported by Article II(3) of the New York Convention', presumably as the obligation under that Article appears to be primarily directed to the court seized of the allegedly impermissible substantive proceedings.

3.90 In contrast, it was the view of Lord Justice Leggatt in *The 'Angelic Grace'* that Article II(3):

> ... does not confer an exclusive jurisdiction on the Court of the Contracting State concerned [that is, the Court hearing the substantive matter (in breach of the arbitration agreement)][to refer the Parties to arbitration]; and *it is consonant with that provision that the Court of another Contracting State should make an order procuring the same result* ...,[170]

a position reluctantly followed in subsequent cases, including the first instance decision in *West Tankers*.[171] The UK Supreme Court, in *Ust-Kamenogorsk* (after the CJEU decision in *West Tankers*) softened that approach, clarifying that '[n]othing in the New York Convention *requires* Contracting States to have in their law any equivalent power to that which section 37 includes in respect of foreign proceedings in breach of an arbitration agreement [that is, the power to issue anti-suit relief]'.[172]

3.91 The conflict in practice arises from the *consequences* of the prohibition on anti-suit relief – if the foreign court refuses to decline jurisdiction, both arbitral proceedings and court proceedings may continue on the substantive merits of a given case, which may lead to inconsistent decisions.[173] In the EU context, the arbitral award would be entitled to recognition and enforcement pursuant to the New York Convention, whereas the judgment would be recognised and enforced under the Brussels regime. The Recast Regulation attempts to regulate this conflict by giving the New York Convention priority over the Recast Regulation in Recital 12 (contrary to the default position reflected in *Achmea* and subsequently):

> ... where a court of a Member State, exercising jurisdiction under this Regulation or under national law, has determined that an arbitration agreement is null and void, inoperative or incapable of being performed, this should not preclude that court's judgment on the substance of the matter from being recognised or, as the case may be, enforced in accordance with this Regulation. This should be *without prejudice* to the competence of the courts of the Member States to decide on the recognition and enforcement of arbitral awards in accordance with the Convention on the Recognition and Enforcement of Foreign Arbitral Awards, done at New York on 10 June 1958 ('the 1958 New York Convention'), *which takes precedence over this Regulation.*

In her Opinion in that case, AG Kokott observed that, 'If an arbitration clause is clearly formulated and not open to any doubt as to its validity, *the national courts have no reason not to refer the parties to the arbitral body appointed in accordance with the New York Convention.*' (*West Tankers (AG Opinion)* (n 69) para 73). Emphasis added.

170 Emphasis added. *Angelic Grace (COA)* (n 28) 94.

171 *West Tankers Inc v Ras Riunione Adriatica di Sicurta SpA (The Front Comor)* [2005] EWHC 454 (Comm), [2005] 2 All ER (Comm) 240 [53]-[58]. AG Kokott shared that view with respect to exclusivity but not the permissibility of an anti-suit injunction (*West Tankers (AG Opinion)* (n 69) para 56).

172 Emphasis added. *Ust-Kamenogorsk* (n 32) [54]. The English Court of Appeal has conversely noted that nothing in the New York Convention *prohibits* the issuance of anti-arbitration injunctions (*Sabbagh (COA)* (n 52) [64]). The power to issue an anti-arbitration injunction also derives from section 37 of the Senior Courts Act 1981 (UK).

173 This issue had long been identified as implicating a conflict between the Brussels regime and the New York Convention – for example, at first instance in *Marc Rich* (cited in *Angelic Grace (QB)* (n 75) 179–80); see also, *West Tankers (HOL)* (n 115) [19], *West Tankers (AG Opinion)* (n 69) paras 71–73.

The position is reinforced by Article 73(2) of the Recast Regulation, which provides that the   **3.92**
Recast Regulation 'shall not affect the application of the 1958 New York Convention'.

While this clarification of the relationship between EU law and the New York Convention   **3.93**
may appear helpful, it may produce arbitrary outcomes in practice.[174] The enforcement of an
award at the seat of the arbitration is governed by domestic law, not the New York Convention
– meaning that the courts at the seat of an arbitration may be obliged to enforce the judgment
of a foreign court under the Brussels regime, notwithstanding their view that there was a valid
arbitration agreement. Likewise, a court may not refuse enforcement of a judgment under the
Brussels regime on the basis of a pending (but not yet rendered) award – which may produce
competition between courts and tribunals to render their decisions first.

E. REFLECTIONS AND A PREDICTION

The limitless creativity of counsel means that courts and tribunals will continue to be   **3.94**
challenged with new situations. This creativity is illustrated by the *TSIKinvest*,[175] *Evrobalt*[176]
and *Kompozit*[177] BIT cases against Moldova, in which each investor successfully invoked
emergency arbitration under the Stockholm Chamber of Commerce (SCC) Rules, seeking
interim relief, notwithstanding that the cooling-off period in the treaty had not elapsed and
emergency arbitration was not a feature of the SCC Rules when the treaty had been agreed.

Courts and tribunals faced with both familiar and new problems arising from parallel   **3.95**
proceedings must resolve a tension between the practical realities of the situation (including the
concomitant abuses of process, wastage of time and costs) and solutions that are doctrinally
acceptable (in particular, if extended beyond the immediate case to the myriad possible
counterfactual situations presented by parallel proceedings). Some tools attempt to resolve this
tension by way of judicial discretion (as for anti-suit injunctions), while others defer to
unyielding objective criteria (as in the case of the Brussels regime in respect of parallel court
proceedings).

The rifts between courts and tribunals on the appropriate means of addressing parallel   **3.96**
proceedings appear to be widening, rather than narrowing. In the EU context, the uncertain
boundaries of the Brussels regime and its interaction with arbitral proceedings (even after the
recasting of the Brussels Regulation) has added an additional layer of complexity to the
solution.

---

174   See, e.g., the discussion in *Camilleri* (n 134).
175   *TSIKinvest LLC v Republic of Moldova*, SCC Emergency Arbitration EA 2014/053.
176   *Evrobalt LLC v Republic of Moldova*, SCC Emergency Arbitration EA 2016/082.
177   *Kompozit LLC v Republic of Moldova*, SCC Emergency Arbitration EA 2016/095.

3.97   In common law arbitral jurisdictions outside of the EU,[178] the availability of anti-suit injunctions[179] and the unavailability of anti-arbitration injunctions[180] ensure that arbitration agreements are protected, which is conducive to international arbitration in general.

3.98   Within the EU, however, the case law from *West Tankers* and *Gazprom* leaves some uncertainty as to the future of international arbitration – in particular, how courts and tribunals can coherently and effectively manage parallel proceedings when at least one or all proceedings have an EU element.

3.99   The UK's departure from the EU exacerbates this uncertainty. The UK and EU have indicated a willingness to extend the application of the Recast Regulation through an agreed transition period.[181] Nevertheless, the position at the end of any transition period is much less clear. The evolutionary development of the Brussels regime (including the extension of the Brussels Convention and (original) Regulation to European Free Trade Association (EFTA) members through the Lugano Conventions) has resulted in a patchwork of instruments to which the UK has itself joined and/or has been subjected to as a Member State. The UK's future participation in some or any of these instruments, and its willingness to accept the CJEU's interpretative authority in respect of them, remains an open question in the long term.

3.100   Leaving the regime entirely may have significant downsides for non-arbitral proceedings. However, it would provide an opportunity for the expansion and revival of the English courts' practice of issuing anti-suit injunctions in support of international arbitrations. This practice may further augment the attractiveness of London as one of the preeminent centres of international arbitration. Lord Hoffmann identified this advantage in the context of arbitral seats outside the EU in *West Tankers*:

> If the Member States of the European Community are unable to offer a seat of arbitration capable of making orders restraining parties from acting in breach of the arbitration agreement, there is no shortage of other states which will. For example, New York, Bermuda and Singapore are also leading centres of arbitration and each of them exercises the jurisdiction which is challenged in this appeal. There seems to me to be no doctrinal necessity or practical advantage which requires the European Community handicap itself by denying its courts the right to exercise the same jurisdiction.[182]

---

178   And in England & Wales in respect of parallel proceedings brought in non-EU courts.

179   See *Shipowners* (n 129); *Ust-Kamenogorsk* (n 32).
      In respect of Singapore, e.g., see *Hilton International Manage (Maldives) Pvt Ltd v Sun Travels & Tours Pvt Ltd* [2018] SGHC 56; *BC Andaman Co Ltd v Xie Ning Yun* [2017] SGHC 64; *Maldives Airports Co Ltd and another v GMR Malé International Airport Pte Ltd* [2013] SGCA 16. In the latter case, Chief Justice Menon expressly approved the English Court of Appeal's decision in *The 'Angelic Grace'* (n 28) (at [42]).

180   See *BCB v Belize (CCJ)* (n 44).

181   UK Withdrawal Agreement (n 149), Art 67.

182   *West Tankers (HOL)* (n 115) [21]. This quote, from the Court's decision in 2007, is particularly prescient given the distance that Singapore has come in positioning itself as a premier centre of arbitration – including as a result of supportive executive and judicial attitudes towards arbitration.

Irrespective of the UK and the EU's future relationship, anti-suit relief will continue to be a   **3.101**
controversial and powerful, though 'imperfect', weapon.[183] Its effectiveness in responding to
new challenges presented by parallel proceedings (and creative counsel) is not guaranteed.
Courts and tribunals thus need to continue to develop new tools and adapt existing tools for
coordination and dialogue to ensure 'practical justice' can be achieved between the parties.[184]

---

183   Adopting Lord Goff's description of the related *forum non conveniens* principle in *Airbus Industrie GIE v Patel* [1999] 1
      AC 119 132 ('*Airbus*').
184   Ibid., 133.

Part II

SELECTED AREAS OF INTERSECTION BETWEEN EU LAW AND INTERNATIONAL COMMERCIAL ARBITRATION

4

ARBITRATION AND THE EUROPEAN CONVENTION ON HUMAN RIGHTS

Monica Feria-Tinta[1]

A. INTRODUCTION

There was a time when the European Convention on Human Rights ('European Convention' or 'ECHR') was deemed 'irrelevant to the theory and practice of international commercial arbitration'.[2] As a result – as aptly noted by Benedettelli – arbitration lawyers showed no interest in the case law developed by the Strasbourg organs.[3] More recently, however, commercial lawyers have discovered the European Convention on Human Rights as an increasingly attractive tool for the protection of international commercial arbitration rights.[4]   **4.01**

---

1   The author is grateful to Fiona Petersen for her research assistance in the preparation of this chapter. Date of submission: 12/6/2020.
2   As noted by Massimo V Benedettelli, 'The European Convention on Human Rights and Arbitration: The EU Law Perspective' in Franco Ferrari (ed), *The Impact of EU Law on Commercial Law* (Jurisnet LLC 2017) 463.
3   Ibid.
4   See, e.g., Stephen Fietta and James Upcher, 'Public International Law, Investment Treaties and Commercial Arbitration: an emerging system of complementarity?' (2013) 29(2) *Arbitration International* 187, 202.

73

4.02 This chapter looks at two important strands in the expanding jurisprudence of the European Court of Human Rights ('ECtHR' or 'the Court'), to that effect. These are namely in the areas of (i) due process guarantees enshrined in Article 6(1) in relation to arbitral procedures; and (ii) enforcement of arbitral awards.

4.03 The jurisprudence relating to arbitration emanating from the Strasbourg organs has a long evolving history, going as far back as 1962.[5] It is not the purpose of this chapter to attempt a definitive review of the jurisprudence in those areas. It rather seeks to take the pulse of the current evolution of this jurisprudence, identifying the key developments and the direction this jurisprudence is taking.

4.04 It has been suggested that the case law of the Court shows a pragmatic rather than a dogmatic approach.[6] It has also been suggested that the applicability of the European Convention to arbitral proceedings is a complex issue.[7] Indeed, the principles identified herein emerge in a very nuanced manner. Moreover, as new case law emerges, new questions arise.

4.05 Setting the contours of the key notions so far developed, however, is a useful tool, for litigators. In order to do so, this chapter is divided as follows: First, some procedural considerations are made. Secondly, the treatment of the relevance of Article 6(1) in relation to arbitration proceedings is discussed. Finally, the application of Article 1 of Protocol 1 (Right to Property) to the Convention so as to secure the enforcement of awards, is considered.

B. SOME PROCEDURAL CONSIDERATIONS

4.06 There are two procedural considerations worth making at the outset when discussing the applicability of the European Convention to arbitral proceedings and enforcement of awards. The first consideration corresponds to the *locus standi* (and the correlative substantive rights in which this *locus standi* is grounded) that the Convention permits. The second consideration corresponds to the broader question of the manner in which the application of Article 6(1) to arbitral proceedings fits within a claim that can only be brought against the State. Indeed, 'the defendant to a claim in Strasbourg has to be a contracting State'.[8]

1. *Locus standi* of individual and legal entities before the European Court

4.07 Article 1 of the European Convention on Human Rights reads as follows:

---

5   See *X v Germany* App no 1197/61 (Commission Decision, 5 March 1962).

6   Sébastien Besson, 'Arbitration and Human Rights' (2006) vol 24 issue 3 *ASA Bulletin (Association Suisse de l'Arbitrage)* 395–416, §35.

7   Nathalie Voser and Benjamin Gottlieb, 'How the European Court of Human Rights Interferes in (Sports) Arbitration' (Kluwer Arbitration Blog, 19 December 2018) <http://arbitrationblog.kluwerarbitration.com/2018/12/19/how-the-european-court-for-human-rights-interferes-in-sports-arbitration/> accessed 12 June 2020.

8   Adam Samuel, 'Arbitration, Alternative Dispute Resolution Generally and the European Convention on Human Rights, An Anglo-Centric View' (2004) 21(5) *Journal of International Arbitration* 413–38, 216.

Obligations to respect Human Rights

The High Contracting Parties shall secure to everyone within their jurisdiction the rights and freedoms defined in Section 1 of this Convention.

The term *everyone* has been interpreted by the ECtHR to cover both individuals (natural **4.08** persons) and legal persons.[9] This in effect means, that the substantive provisions of the ECHR protect not only individuals but also companies.[10] In addition, as seen below, Article 1 of Protocol 1, explicitly refers to legal persons as enjoying the right to property.[11]

The case of *Yukos v Russia* is one of the most widely known cases of a legal person having used **4.09** the contentious procedure under the European Convention. In this case, *Yukos*, the former Russian energy giant which ceased trading following tax proceedings taken against it by the Russian authorities, filed a claim against Russia in relation to the retroactive application of law and fairness proceedings in the imposition of massive fines for violations of tax regulations. The ECtHR found that there had been a violation and, in a landmark decision on just satisfaction, the Court made its largest ever award for pecuniary loss, ordering Russia to pay in the region of 1.9 billion Euros in compensation to the shareholders of Yukos.[12]

Thus, both individuals and companies can avail themselves of the procedural mechanisms **4.10** under the Convention including bringing claims under the Convention. As put by Emberland, in essence, companies are 'welcomed in the ECHR's legal order'.[13] To the extent that other regional human rights mechanisms (such as the Inter-American Court of Human Rights) have interpreted the protection under their relevant regional human rights instruments to cover human beings only, this feature of the European System is unique and I would suggest, is at the basis of the development of jurisprudence relevant to commercial arbitration rights.

2. The principle that State courts exercise a certain control and guarantee as to the fairness and correctness of the arbitration proceedings

Although arbitration proceedings are private proceedings whereby parties have voluntarily **4.11** renounced their right to have their civil rights determined in court proceedings (an instrument of the State) nevertheless, these private proceedings fall within the scope of application of the Convention (which binds State organs) to the extent that the State exercises a certain control and guarantee as to the fairness and correctness of the arbitration proceedings (i.e., State of the seat of the arbitration).

---

9   The first time that a corporate claim was brought before the European Court goes back to 1978, when a private media corporation brought a dispute against the United Kingdom. See *Sunday Times v United Kingdom* App no 6538/74 (ECtHR, 26 April 1979).

10 For a reading on the topic see, Marius Emberland, *The Human Rights of Companies: Exploring the Structure of ECHR Protection* (OUP 2006).

11 Art 1, Protocol 1 on the right to property reads, 'Every natural or legal person is entitled to the peaceful enjoyment of his possessions.'

12 *OAO Neftyanaya Kompaniya Yukos v Russia* App no 14902/04 (ECtHR, 31 July 2014).

13 See Emberland (n 10) 25.

4.12 In the decision *R. v. Switzerland*[14] the today defunct European Commission on Human Rights ('Commission') concluded that 'the state cannot be held responsible for the arbitrators' actions unless, and only in so far as, the national courts were required to intervene'.[15]

4.13 The Commission further held, in *Jakob Boss Sohne KG v Germany*, as follows:

> (…) the applicant company had voluntarily entered into an arbitration agreement and thereby renounced its right to have its civil rights determined in court proceedings for the conduct of which the State is responsible under the Convention. (…)

> This does not mean, however, that the respondent State's responsibility is completly excluded (…) as the arbitration award had to be recognized by the German courts and be given executory effect by them. The courts thereby exercised a certain control and guarantee as to the fairness and correctness of the arbitration proceedings which they considered to have been carried out in conformity with fundamental rights and in particular with the right of the applicant company to be heard.[16]

C. THE MANNER IN WHICH ARTICLE 6(1) ECHR IS RELEVANT TO ARBITRATION

4.14 Article 6(1) does not necessarily require 'access to a court of law of the classic kind, integrated within the standard judicial machinery of the country'.[17] An arbitral tribunal can be a 'tribunal' within the meaning of Article 6(1).[18]

4.15 Article 6(1) ECHR provides, in material part:

> In the determination of his civil rights and obligations … everyone is entitled to a fair and public hearing within a reasonable time by an independent and impartial tribunal established by law. Judgment shall be pronounced publicly but the press and public may be excluded from all or part of the trial in the interests of morals, public order or national security in a democratic society, where the interests of juveniles or the protection of the private life of the parties so require, or to the extent strictly necessary in the opinion of the court in special circumstances where publicity would prejudice the interests of justice.

1. Agreement to arbitrate as a waiver of Article 6

4.16 However, two rights are waived by entering into an arbitration agreement voluntarily. First, the arbitrating parties are considered to have waived their right of access to a court.[19] Second, it is argued that there is at least one of the rights listed in Article 6(1) whereby there is consensus

---

14 *R v Switzerland* App no 10881/84 (Commission Decision, 4 March 1987).
15 Ibid., as reported in *Yearbook of the European Convention on Human Rights* 1987 (Martinus Nijoff Publishers) 43.
16 *Jakob Boss Sohne KG v Germany* App no 18479/91 (Commission Decision, 2 December 1991).
17 This principle was held already since the 1980s by the Court. See *Lithgow and others v UK* Apps 9006/80; 9262/81; 9263/81; 9265/81; 9266/81; 9313/81; 9405/81 (ECtHR, Judgment of 8 July 1986) ('*Lithgow*') §201.
18 *Suda v Czech Republic* App no 1643/06 (ECtHR, 28 October 2010) ('*Suda*') §48.
19 Fredrik Ringquist, 'Do Procedural Human Rights Requirements Apply to Arbitration – A Study of Article 6 (1) of the European Convention on Human Rights and its Bearing upon Arbitration' (Master Thesis, University of Lund 2005) 33.

that waiver is automatic, namely the right to a public hearing.[20] As noted, 'this is considered to be a direct consequence of the private nature of arbitral proceedings'.[21]

In *Nordström*, the Commission stated as follows: 'In some respect – in particular as regards **4.17** publicity – it is clear that arbitral proceedings are often not even intended to be in conformity with Article 6 (Art. 6), and that the arbitration agreement entails a renunciation of the full application of that Article.'[22]

It cannot be said today, that an arbitral agreement entails a renunciation of 'the full application **4.18** of Article 6'. See the more recent position of ECtHR in *Suovaniemi*[23] (discussed in section 3, below). Even with an arbitration agreement, due process, equality of arms, are core rights governing an arbitral process and often referred to by the parties during the proceedings. A distinct question is whether their lack thereof can be attributable to the State. As seen above, Article 6 is opposable to the State (and not operating at the horizontal level only) only to the extent that the State exercises a control (i.e., if a party resorts to judicial intervention at the seat of the arbitration).

For a waiver to be the starting point, an agreement has to be free from constraint. In its first **4.19** case on the subject of Article 6(1) and arbitration, *X v Germany*, the Commission stated that arbitration agreements were not valid as waivers if '*la clause compromissoire … ne l'avait signée sous la contrainte*'.[24] In *Deweer*, the Court, similarly concluded that absence of constraint is a requirement for the validity of the waiver.[25]

Further, in order to elaborate on the manner in which Article 6 has been applied to arbitration **4.20** proceedings, it is necessary first, to turn to the distinction between *voluntary* and *compulsory* arbitration.

2. The distinction between voluntary and compulsory arbitration for the application of Article 6(1) safeguards

The European Court draws a crucial distinction between voluntary arbitration and compulsory **4.21** arbitration. This distinction was made first in the leading case of *Bramelid*, a decision made by the European Commission.[26]

---

20 Ibid., 36.
21 Ibid.
22 *Nordström-Janzon and Nordström-Lehtinen v the Netherlands* (1996) DR 87-B, 112–17.
23 *Suovaniemi v Finland* App no 31737/96 (ECtHR, 23 February 1999) ('*Suovaniemi*').
24 *X v Germany* App no 1197/61 (Commission Decision, 5 March 1962) *Yearbook of the European Convention on Human Rights* 5, 96.
25 *Deweer v Belgium* (1980) Series A no 35, §49.
26 *Bramelid and Malström v Sweden* App nos 8588/79 and 8589/79 (Commission Decision, 12 October 1982).

4.22 If arbitration is compulsory, the arbitral tribunal must afford the safeguards secured by Article 6(1).[27] By contrast, where arbitration is voluntary, the arbitral tribunal must afford the safeguards secured by Article 6(1) *unless* those safeguards have been validly waived.[28]

4.23 The ECtHR's case law suggests that arbitration is only compulsory where the applicant has a binary choice between accepting arbitration or ceasing their activities completely.[29] The ECtHR is generally reluctant to find that a contractual clause requiring arbitration means that arbitration is compulsory. The ECtHR tends to reason that the party could have negotiated a contract without the arbitration clause.[30]

4.24 As observed by Besson, the boundaries of compulsory arbitration can be uncertain in some cases.[31] However, the recent cases *Ali Riza*; *Mutu and Pechstein*; *Tabbane*; *Eiffage*; and *Transado* illustrate the ECtHR's more recent approach to determining whether arbitration is compulsory or voluntary.

a.   Compulsory arbitration

4.25 The case of *Ali Riza* concerned two disputes.[32] The first was a dispute between a professional footballer and a Turkish football club in relation to alleged breaches of the employment contract (§§11–114). The second dispute was between a referee and the Central Referee Committee ('CRC') of the Turkish Football Federation ('TFF'). The CRC had downgraded the referee's status from 'top-level referee' to 'provincial referee' (§§38–39). It was common ground that arbitration was compulsory for both the footballer and the referee (§175).

4.26 At the relevant time, professional football in Turkey was regulated by Law no. 3813 of 17 June 1992 on the Establishment and Duties of the Turkish Football Federation ('the TFF Rules'). The TFF Rules applied to all professional footballers in Turkey; the footballer had no choice in this matter. The TFF rules provided that the TFF's Arbitration Committee had compulsory jurisdiction in respect of contractual disputes (§§169, 170 and 176).

4.27 At the relevant time, Article 59(3) of the Turkish Constitution provided: 'decisions of sport federations relating to administration and discipline of sports activities may be challenged only through compulsory arbitration. Decisions of arbitration committees are final and shall not be appealed to any judicial authority' (§105). The decision of the CRC was a 'decision of a sports federation relating to administration and discipline of sports activities' so arbitration was compulsory for the referee. The referee had no choice in this matter. In addition, the relevant

---

27   *Suda* (n 18) §49; *Mutu and Pechstein v Switzerland* App nos 40575/10 and 67474/10 (ECtHR 2 October 2018) ('*Mutu and Pechstein*') §95.

28   *Suda* (n 18) §48; *Mutu and Pechstein* (n 27) §96; *Tabbane v Switzerland* App no 41069/12 (ECtHR, 31 March 2016) ('*Tabbane*') §27.

29   *Mutu and Pechstein* (n 27) §113; *Ali Riza and Others v Turkey* App nos 30226/10 and 5506/16 (ECtHR, 28 January 2020) ('*Ali Riza*') §§175–77.

30   *Mutu and Pechstein* (n 27) §§119-120; *Tabbane* (n 28) §29; *Eiffage v Switzerland* App no 1742/05 (ECtHR, 15 September 2009) ('*Eiffage*') 13; *Transado – Transportes Fluviais Do Sado SA v Portugal* no 35943/02 (ECtHR, 16 December 2003) ('*Transado*') 5.

31   Besson (n 6) §17.

32   There were a further three applicants, but their applications were found to be inadmissible: §5.

TFF rules provided that decisions of CRC could only be appealed to the TFF's Arbitration Committee (§177).

In the case of *Mutu and Pechstein*, Pechstein was a professional speed skater, affiliated to the **4.28** Deutsche Eisschnelllauf-Gemeinschaft, which was a member of the International Skating Union ('ISU'). Following anti-doping tests, the ISU's Disciplinary Commission suspended Pechstein from competing for two years. This decision was appealed to the Court of Arbitration for Sports ('CAS').

Under the ISU rules, Pechstein had to accept the compulsory and exclusive jurisdiction of CAS **4.29** in respect of disputes stemming from disciplinary proceedings. Otherwise, she could not take part in competitions. Essentially, Pechstein had a binary choice between 'accepting the arbitration clause and thus earning her living by practising her sport professionally, or not accepting it and being obliged to refrain completely from earning a living from her sport at that level' (§113). Therefore, even though acceptance of CAS's jurisdiction was imposed by the ISU regulations, not by law, the ECtHR considered that arbitration was compulsory for Pechstein (§115).

b. Voluntary arbitration

In contrast to Pechstein, the ECtHR considered that arbitration was voluntary for Mutu. **4.30** Mutu was a professional footballer. In 2003, he signed a contract with Chelsea Football Club. In 2004, he tested positive for cocaine. As a result, Chelsea Football Club terminated his employment contract and he was suspended from playing.

The Football Association Premier League Appeals Committee ('FAPLAC') decided that **4.31** Mutu had breached his employment contract without just cause. FAPLAC is affiliated to the Fédération Internationale de Football Association ('FIFA'). Mutu unsuccessfully appealed FAPLAC's decision to CAS.

In order to play football professionally, Mutu had to comply with the FIFA Regulations for the **4.32** Status and Transfer of Players 2001 ('FIFA Regulations'). While Article 42 of the FIFA Regulations provides for recourse to arbitration, the regulations do not oblige players to accept arbitration. Article 42 is 'without prejudice to the right of any player or club to seek redress before a civil court in disputes between clubs and players'.

Mutu's employment contract with Chelsea Football Club required Mutu to accept arbitration **4.33** but the ECtHR held that this did not mean that arbitration was compulsory for Mutu. While the ECtHR acknowledged that major football clubs have greater negotiating strength than individual players, Mutu had not proved that it was impossible for him to negotiate a contract without an arbitration clause, either with Chelsea Football Club or with another club. Further, Mutu had not proven that it was impossible for him to gain access to domestic courts by relying on Article 42 of the FIFA Regulations (§119). Therefore, unlike Pechstein, Mutu was not faced with a binary choice between accepting arbitration and playing professionally, on the one hand, or not accepting it and ceasing to play professionally. Thus, ECtHR held that Mutu had voluntarily accepted arbitration (§§116–120).

4.34 The ECtHR's approach to arbitration clauses in contracts is further illustrated by *Tabbane*, *Eiffage*, and *Transado*.

    (1)   In *Tabbane*, a businessman entered into a contract with the company, Colgate.

    (2)   In *Eiffage*, a group of civil engineering companies entered into a contract with the European Council for Nuclear Research after responding to a call for tender.

    (3)   In *Transado*, a company entered into a concession agreement with a public authority.

4.35 In all three cases, the contract contained an arbitration clause. In each case, the ECtHR held that the applicant had freely decided to enter into the contract and accept the arbitration clause. The ECtHR emphasised that the applicants – a businessman and commercial companies – had been 'free to establish commercial relations with partners of their choosing without affecting their freedom and capacity to engage, with other partners, in projects within their respective fields of activity' (summary in *Mutu and Pechstein* §§104–107; *Tabbane* §29; *Eiffage* p. 13; *Transado* p. 5). ·

3. Voluntary arbitration and waiver of rights under Article 6(1)

4.36 Where arbitration is voluntary, the arbitral tribunal must afford the safeguards in Article 6(1), *unless* the person has validly waived their rights under Article 6(1).

4.37 Waiver is valid if: (a) it is free; (b) unequivocal; (c) permissible; and (d) there are minimum guarantees 'commensurate to the importance of the right waived' (*Suda* §48; *Tabbane* §27).

a. Free

4.38 There is little case law on the meaning of 'free'. In *Tabbane*, the ECtHR found that the applicant's waiver was valid, noting that he was not under duress when he agreed to the arbitration clause (§29).

b. Unequivocal

4.39 A number of cases have considered the meaning of 'unequivocal' (e.g., *Suovaniemi*, pp 5–6; *Mutu and Pechstein* §122; *Tabbane* §30).

4.40 In determining whether the waiver is unequivocal, an important factor is whether the applicant complained about the alleged infringement of their rights during the arbitration. For example, in *Suovaniemi*, the applicant's waiver of the right to an independent and impartial tribunal was held to be unequivocal. This is because the applicant had refrained from challenging the arbitrator during the arbitral proceedings, despite being aware of grounds on which the arbitrator could be challenged.[33] In contrast, the ECtHR held that Mutu's waiver of the right to an independent and impartial tribunal was equivocal. This is because Mutu had (unsuccessfully) challenged one of the arbitrators, alleging that he lacked independence and impartiality (§122).

---

33   *Suovaniemi* (n 23) 5–6.

The wording of the arbitration clause is another factor which the ECtHR looks at when **4.41** deciding whether the waiver was unequivocal. For example, in *Tabbane*, the applicant's waiver was unequivocal because he had agreed to a contract which included the following clause: 'neither party shall have any right to appeal such decision to any court of law' (§30).

c. Permissible

Article 6(1) encompasses a number of procedural rights, including the principle of 'equality of **4.42** arms', a right to a fair and public hearing, a right to have that hearing within a reasonable time, a right to an independent and impartial tribunal, and a right to a reasoned decision. In *Suovaniemi*, the ECtHR contemplated that it may be permissible to waive some of these rights but not others.[34] It stated that it is permissible to waive the right to a public hearing[35] and the right to an impartial judge.[36]

It has been noted by publicists that the parties can also 'validly waive the right to obtain a **4.43** reasoned award if they specifically address this point in their agreement; but the mere signing of an arbitration agreement is not sufficient'.[37]

It is well established on the other hand, that a complete waiver is not permissible.[38] **4.44**

d. Minimum guarantees commensurate to the importance of the right waived

The ECtHR has held that the rights under Article 6(1) have such great importance in a **4.45** democratic society that a person cannot entirely lose all the benefits of Article 6(1) by agreeing to an arbitration clause (*Suda* §48). Where a party waives their rights under Article 6(1), they must be protected by minimum guarantees commensurate to the importance of the right waived (*Tabbane* §27). Such minimum guarantees were discussed by the ECtHR in *Tabbane* and *Suovaniemi*.

In *Tabbane*, the arbitrators decided that the seat of arbitration would be Geneva and thus, **4.46** Swiss law governed the arbitration. Section 192 of the Swiss Federal Law on Private International Law provides that parties who are not domiciled, habitually resident or established in Switzerland may exclude any appeal to Swiss courts from arbitral awards. The arbitration award was unfavourable to the applicant and he appealed it to the Swiss court. The Swiss court refused to examine the arbitration award because it considered that the right to appeal against any arbitral award had been validly waived in accordance with section 192.

The ECtHR held that the applicant's waiver had been attended by minimum safeguards, **4.47** reflecting the importance of the right waived. The ECtHR noted the following safeguards: (i) the applicant was able to select an arbitrator; (ii) that arbitrator, together with the other two arbitrators, was able to choose the seat of arbitration and thereby chose Swiss law as the

---

34 Ibid., 5.
35 Ibid.
36 Ibid., 6.
37 Besson (n 6) §21.
38 Philippe Frumer, *La renunciation aux droits et libertés, La Convention européenne des droits de l'homme á l'épreuve de la volonté individuelle* (Bruylant 2001) 110–12; D Poncet and A Cambi, 'Un arbitre independent et impartial aux termes de l'article 6. 1 de la Convention européenne des droits de l'homme, un point de vue de la Suisse', in *Mélanges en l'honneur de Pierre Lambert* (Bruylant 2000) 655, 670, cited in Besson (n 6) §20.

governing law; and (iii) when the applicant appealed the award to the Swiss court, the Swiss court had heard the applicant's arguments, taken into account the relevant facts and law and had produced a judgment which was adequately reasoned and not arbitrary (§ 31).

4.48 In *Suovaniemi*, the applicants complained that their rights under Article 6(1) had been violated because the national courts had upheld an arbitral award, even though two of the arbitrators allegedly lacked impartiality. The ECtHR held that the applicants had validly waived their right to an impartial tribunal and that such a waiver was accompanied by the necessary minimum safeguards. In particular, the ECtHR noted that the applicants were represented by counsel throughout the arbitration. Further, like in *Tabbane*, the domestic court had heard the applicants' arguments concerning the circumstances in which the waiver took place during the arbitration proceedings.[39]

4. Rights under Article 6(1) where arbitration is compulsory or where arbitration is voluntary and those rights have not been validly waived

4.49 The literature on the applicability of the standards under Article 6(1) suggests that with the exception of publicity (which is considered automatically waived as a result of the agreement to arbitrate, as seen above), all rights in Article 6(1) *prima facie*, apply to arbitral proceedings.[40]

4.50 Article 6(1) generally encompasses a number of rights including:

(1) a right to a hearing by a tribunal 'established by law';
(2) a right to an 'independent and impartial' tribunal;
(3) a right to an oral hearing;
(4) a right to a 'public' hearing;
(5) a right to a decision within a reasonable time;
(6) a right to obtain a reasoned decision.

4.51 It is considered below how these rights apply in the context of compulsory arbitration and voluntary arbitration where those rights have not been validly waived.

a. Established by law

4.52 In *Mutu and Pechstein*, the ECtHR explained what is meant by 'established by law' and why it is important. It stated (§138):

> ['Established by law'] reflects the principle of the rule of law, which is inherent in the system of protection established by the [ECHR]. An organ which has not been established in accordance with the will of the legislature would necessarily lack the legitimacy required in a democratic society to hear the cases of individuals. The phrase 'established by law' covers not only the legal basis for the very existence of a 'tribunal' but also the composition of the bench in each case ...

---

39 *Suovaniemi* (n 23) 6.
40 Ringquist (n 19) 37.

The criterion of 'established by law' has been applied in at least three cases: one case in which **4.53** the criterion was clearly fulfilled; one case in which it was clearly not fulfilled; and one case in which some of the judges expressed doubt about whether the criterion was fulfilled.

In *Ali Riza*, the arbitral tribunal was clearly 'established by law'. The legal framework **4.54** governing the Arbitration Committee was established by primary legislation. This legislation prescribed issues such as the Arbitration Committee's competence, composition, appointment procedure and the tenure of members (§§201–204).

In *Suda*, the arbitral tribunal was clearly not 'established by law' (§53). The applicant was a **4.55** minority shareholder in a public limited company. The company and its main shareholder had entered into an agreement to submit disputes to arbitral tribunal. The arbitrators on that tribunal were selected from a list drawn up by the company and the arbitral procedure was governed by rules established by the company (§6).

In *Mutu and Pechstein*, the majority found that the arbitral tribunal was 'established by law' but **4.56** two judges expressed doubt about this. The majority acknowledged that CAS is part of the International Council of Arbitration for Sport ('ICAS') which is a 'private-law foundation'. Nonetheless, the majority decided that CAS is established by law because it is 'endowed with full jurisdiction ... on the basis of legal rules' and its awards can be appealed to the Swiss Federal Court in certain circumstances specified in legislation (§149).

In a separate opinion, Judges Keller and Serghides questioned whether CAS is established by **4.57** law. They noted that CAS has no legal personality; rather, it is part of a private-law foundation, ICAS (§22). In the context of tribunals set up by executive decree, the ECtHR has held that 'the legislature need not regulate every detail ... by a formal Act of Parliament' but 'the legislature [must establish] at least the organisational framework for the judicial organisation' (*Lindner v Germany* (dec) no. 32813/96). Judges Keller and Serghides suggested that the same principle should apply to tribunals set up by private-law bodies (§23). They stated that the majority 'should have given some indications about the conditions in which private entities may be regarded as "tribunals established by law"'. (§25).

b. *Independent and impartial tribunal*

In *Mutu and Pechstein*, the ECtHR gave guidance on the meaning of 'independent and **4.58** impartial'. It stated:

> 140. In order to establish whether a tribunal can be considered 'independent', regard must be had, inter alia, to the manner of appointment of its members and their term of office, the existence of guarantees against outside pressure and the question whether the body presents an appearance of independence ...

> 141. Impartiality normally denotes the absence of prejudice or bias ... [T]he existence of impartiality must be determined according to a subjective test, that is on the basis of the personal conviction and conduct of a particular judge, by ascertaining whether he showed any personal prejudice or partiality in a given case, and also according to an objective test, that is, whether the court offered, in particular through its composition, guarantees sufficient to exclude any legitimate doubt about his impartiality ...

143 ... '[J]ustice must not only be done, it must also be seen to be done'. What is at stake is the confidence which the courts in a democratic society must inspire in the public ....

4.59   The ECtHR added:

in matters of commercial and sports arbitration to which consent has been given freely, lawfully and unequivocally, the notions of independence and impartiality may be construed flexibly, in so far as the very essence of the arbitration system is based on the appointment of the decision-making bodies ... by the parties to the dispute (§146).

4.60   Pechstein complained about lack of impartiality and independence in relation to one of the arbitrators who decided her case and in relation to CAS as an institution. The ECtHR dismissed her complaints.

4.61   As regards the individual arbitrator, Pechstein alleged that he was biased because he had always refused to be appointed as an arbitrator by any athlete accused of doping. The ECtHR held that there was no factual evidence to support this allegation (§150).

4.62   As regards CAS as an institution, Pechstein alleged that it lacked independence and impartiality for three reasons, as explained below.

(1)   Pechstein alleged that CAS is biased in favour of sports bodies because it is financed by sports bodies. The ECtHR dismissed this argument. It reasoned that domestic courts are financed by the State, but this does not mean they lack independence and impartiality in disputes between litigants and the State. By analogy, CAS does not lack independence and impartiality solely on account of its financing arrangements (§151).

(2)   Pechstein alleged that the mechanism for appointing arbitrators led to an imbalance between sports federations and athletes. At the relevant time, the process for becoming a CAS arbitrator was as follows. Parties can only choose an arbitrator from a list that is selected by ICAS. The majority of members of ICAS are representatives of sports federations. ICAS selects three-fifths of the arbitrators from nominations it receives from sports federations. ICAS chooses one-fifth of the arbitrators 'with a view to safeguarding the interests of athletes' and one-fifth with a view to selecting arbitrators who are independent from the sports federations. Arbitrators are on the list for a renewable term of four years, but ICAS has the power to remove an arbitrator who has failed to perform his duties and ICAS needs only give 'brief reasons' for this. Despite the sports bodies' influence over the selection of arbitrators, the ECtHR held that there was no violation of Article 6(1). This was because there were about 300 arbitrators on the list from which Pechstein could choose and Pechstein had not demonstrated that the individual arbitrators who decided her case lacked impartiality and independence (§157).

(3)   The CAS Secretary General has the power to make formal rectifications to the award. The CAS Secretary General is appointed by ICAS and the majority of ICAS are representatives of sports federations. Pechstein argued that this shows that CAS lacks independence and impartiality. The ECtHR dismissed this argument, because Pechstein had not shown that her award had been amended by the Secretary General (§158).

4.63   In a separate opinion in *Mutu and Pechstein*, Judges Keeler and Serghides strongly criticised the majority's reasoning. They argued that it is not necessary to prove that the *individual* arbitrator lacks independence and impartiality. Rather, there is a breach of Article 6(1) if the organisation's general structure lacks the appearance of independence and impartiality. The sports federations have a considerable influence over the selection of arbitrators. Therefore Judges Keeler and Serghides argued that Pechstein's Article 6(1) rights had been violated since CAS did not have the appearance of independence and impartiality (Opinion of Judges Keeler and Serghides §§12–16).

Mutu complained that one of the arbitrators who gave the award in 2009 had previously found **4.64** against him in an award in 2005. The ECtHR stated that an arbitrator would only be considered biased where they had decided an earlier dispute with identical facts and substantially identical issues (§162). The ECtHR held that the facts in the 2005 award and the 2009 award were the same, but the issues were different. The 2005 award concerned breach of contract whereas the 2009 award concerned damages for that breach. Thus, the ECtHR held there was no violation of Article 6(1) (§§160–164).

Ali Riza concerned disputes between a player and a Turkish football club and between a referee **4.65** and the CRC of the TFF (see para 4.25 above). These disputes were heard by the TFF's Arbitration Committee. Arbitration by the TFF's Arbitration Committee was compulsory for the applicants.

The ECtHR found that the Arbitration Committee lacked independence and impartiality, in **4.66** violation of Article 6(1), for the following reasons. The members of the Arbitration Committee are appointed by the Board of Directors. The Board of Directors is elected by the TFF Congress. Both the Congress and the Board of Directors are dominated by representatives of football clubs. This 'tip[s] the balance in favour of clubs' (§219). The Board of Directors also has significant influence over the CRC and had approved the CRC's decision which was being disputed by the applicant. The ECtHR concluded that there were legitimate reasons for doubting the independence and impartiality of the Arbitration Committee because the Board of Directors had 'vast powers' over the Arbitration Committee and there were not 'adequate safeguards protecting [the Arbitration Committee] against outside pressures, particularly from the Board of Directors' (§222). The ECtHR required Turkey to take measures to reform the Arbitration Committee to ensure its independence and impartiality (§242).

In a separate opinion, Judge Bošnjak agreed that Article 6(1) had been violated on account of **4.67** the Arbitration Committee's lack of independence and impartiality. However, he disagreed with the majority's reasoning. In his view, the Arbitration Committee lacked independence and impartiality for the following two reasons:

(1)   The members of the Arbitration Committee do not have immunity from actions brought against them in connection with the exercise of their duties as arbitrators (§§2–3).

(2)   The term of office of the Arbitration Committee members is linked to the duration of the mandate of the Board of Directors. If a conflict arises between the Board of Directors and the Arbitration Committee, the Board can resign, seek reappointment in the same composition and then appoint a new Arbitration Committee. This means it is unlikely that the Arbitration Committee will decide in a manner that is unfavourable to the Board of Directors (§§2 and 4).

4.68   In contrast to the majority, Judge Bošnjak considered that the over-representation of clubs relative to players and referees in Congress and the Board of Directors was not a problem (§§6–10). This is because the interests of clubs, players and referees do not necessarily clash, e.g., a representative of a club may previously have been a player. Nor are the interests of all clubs aligned; one club's loss may be another club's gain. In addition, Judge Bošnjak reasoned by analogy to domestic courts. He stated (§9):

> … [I]n several High Contracting Parties to the [ECHR], judges are appointed by the Parliament, which in turn comprises very few members from the lowest social strata. If, in a given court case, an unemployed and uneducated defendant with ethnic, racial or religious minority roots is facing a victim from the middle or upper social class, would that mean that the judge in his or her case is neither independent nor impartial simply because the composition of Parliament is much closer to the victim's background? The majority's logic, as I read it, would suggest that that could be the case. I would find it hard to share that view.

c.   Oral hearing

4.69   Parties can waive their right to an oral hearing beforehand.[41] As noted by Ringquist this follows from the fact that 'the right to an oral hearing can be waived in advance even in court proceedings'.[42]

d.   Public hearing

4.70   In *Mutu and Pechstein*, the ECtHR set out a number of exceptions to the principle of public hearings (§177).

(1)   '[T]he press and public may be excluded from all or part of the trial in the interests of morals, public order or national security in a democratic society, where the interests of juveniles or the protection of the private life of the parties so require, or to the extent strictly necessary in the opinion of the court in special circumstances where publicity would prejudice the interests of justice' (Art 6(1)).

(2)   A public hearing is not needed for proceedings devoted exclusively to legal or highly technical questions.

(3)   The right to a public hearing must be balanced against the right to a trial within a reasonable time.

4.71   Pechstein complained that her hearing before CAS and her hearing before the Swiss court were not public. The ECtHR held that the CAS hearing should have been in public. This is because the 'facts were disputed and sanction imposed on the applicant carried a degree of stigma and was likely to adversely affect her professional honour and reputation' (§182). In contrast, the ECtHR held that the hearing before the Swiss court did not need to be public. This is because the hearing before the Swiss court only concerned procedural safeguards applicable to CAS. These were highly technical legal questions, which did not involve any examination of facts (§§185–188).

---

41   Ringquist (n 19) 38.
42   Ibid.

In *Bramelid*, likewise, the Commission found that the applicants were entitled to a hearing **4.72** before a tribunal 'within the meaning of Article 6(1)' which included the right to a public hearing.[43] In said case, 'two individuals had to have recourse to arbitration by virtue of a legal obligation'.[44] The Commission also noted that the arbitration procedure had a direct bearing on the applicants' civil rights and obligations, and *'in particular that the outcome of those proceedings was crucial in deciding the ownership of the NK shares by the applicants'*.[45] It concluded that in those circumstances, the applicants' case 'was not heard publicly'.[46] It additionally found that the tribunal hearing the case was not 'an independent and impartial tribunal.' All, contrary to Article 6(1).

e.   A right to a decision within a reasonable time

In *Rychetsky*,[47] the Commission was asked to determine whether arbitral proceedings held in **4.73** Switzerland that had lasted eight years were in conformity with Article 6(1).[48] The Commission did not pronounce itself on the unreasonableness of the entire eight-year period.[49] It rather found it relevant to look only into the period after which the Swiss courts had been asked to intervene, which had been a period of six months. Said delay was not considered to be unreasonable.

f.   A right to obtain a reasoned award

As observed by Besson, the right to be heard encompasses the right to obtain a reasoned **4.74** award.[50] It is accepted, however, that 'the parties can validly waive the right to obtain a reasoned award if they specifically address this point in their agreement, but the mere signing of an arbitration agreement is not sufficient'.[51]

5.   Restrictions on Article 6(1)

The rights under Article 6(1) are not absolute. They may be subject to certain limitations. The **4.75** right of access to a tribunal 'calls for regulation by the State' and that regulation may 'vary in time and in place according to the needs and resources of the community and of individuals' (*Lithgow* (no. 9006/80, (*'Lithgow'*) §194). In laying down such a regulation, the Contracting States 'enjoy a certain margin of appreciation' (*Ali Riza* §172).

Any limitations on the rights under Article 6(1) must comply with the following requirements **4.76** (*Ali Riza* §172):

(1)   It must 'pursue a legitimate aim'.

(2)   There must be a 'reasonable relationship of proportionality between the means employed and the aim sought to be achieved'.

---

43   *Bramelid* (n 26) §30.
44   Ibid., §31.
45   Ibid., §29.
46   Ibid., §42.
47   *Rychetsky v Switzerland* App no 10881/84 (Commission Decision, 4 March 1987).
48   Ringquist (n 19) 38.
49   Ibid.
50   Besson (n 6) §21.
51   Ibid.

(3) It must not restrict the access to a tribunal 'in such a way or to such an extent that the very essence of the right is impaired'.

4.77 As discussed above, section 192 of the Swiss Federal Law on Private International Law provides that parties who are not domiciled, habitually resident or established in Switzerland may exclude any appeal to Swiss courts from arbitral awards. Essentially, where such parties have agreed to an exclusive arbitration clause, the effect of section 192 is that the Swiss courts will enforce that arbitration clause and refuse to hear the dispute. The ECtHR has held that section 192 is justified for the following reasons (*Mutu and Pechstein* §§97–99; *Tabbane* §§33–36):

(1) Section 192 pursues the following five legitimate aims. First, by enforcing exclusive arbitration clauses, it respects the parties' contractual freedom. Secondly, it increases the efficiency of arbitration by allowing litigants to avoid the cost and time of appeals to domestic courts. Thirdly, it is beneficial for Switzerland because it increases the attractiveness of Switzerland as an arbitral seat. Fourthly, is also beneficial for the Swiss domestic courts because they are spared from using their resources on hearing appeals from arbitral appeals. Fifthly, in the context of professional sports, it is beneficial for disputes to be resolved by a specialised international body, rather than by the domestic courts.

(2) The means employed by section 192 are proportionate to those legitimate aims. Parties are not compelled to exclude access to the domestic courts. Rather section 192 gives parties the option of freely choosing to exclude recourse to domestic courts. Furthermore, section 192(2) provides that if an award is to be enforced in Switzerland, the New York Convention for the Recognition and Enforcement of Foreign Arbitral Awards applies by analogy. This gives the domestic courts a degree of control because the domestic courts can refuse to recognise awards on certain grounds.

(3) Because section 192 pursues a legitimate aim in a proportionate manner, it does not infringe the very essence of Article 6(1).

4.78 Restrictions on Article 6(1) were considered by the ECtHR in *Lithgow*. Sir William Lithgow was the largest single shareholder in Kincaid (a manufacturer of marine diesel engines). Kincaid was nationalised by the Aircraft and Shipbuilding Industries Act 1977 ('the 1977 Act'). Although Sir William Lithgow received some compensation, he complained that the compensation was grossly inadequate. An Arbitration Tribunal was set up to resolve disputes concerning compensation. However, only Stockholders' Representatives, but not shareholders, had access to the Arbitration Tribunal. Sir William Lithgow alleged that the lack of individual access to the Arbitration Tribunal infringed Article 6(1). The ECtHR dismissed his claim. It held that 'the limitation on a direct right of access for every individual shareholder to the Arbitration Tribunal pursued the legitimate aim of avoiding a multiplicity of claims and proceedings brought by individual shareholders' (*Lithgow* §197). There was a reasonable relationship of proportionality between the means employed and this aim because the Stockholders' Representative represented the interests of individual shareholders. The 1977 Act provided for meetings at which the individual shareholders could give instructions to the Stockholders' Representative. Furthermore, the 1977 Act provided remedies to shareholders whose representative had failed to comply with their duties. Therefore, the very essence of Sir William Lithgow's rights under Article 6(1) had not been impaired (*Lithgow* §196).

D. ARTICLE 1 PROTOCOL 1

Article 1 Protocol 1 of the ECHR provides: **4.79**

> Every natural or legal person is entitled to the peaceful enjoyment of his possessions. No one shall be deprived of his possessions except in the public interest and subject to the conditions provided for by law and by the general principles of international law.

> The preceding provisions shall not, however, in any way impair the right of a State to enforce such laws as it deems necessary to control the use of property in accordance with the general interest or to secure the payment of taxes or other contributions or penalties.

It has been held by the ECtHR, that an arbitral award, like a judgment, can constitute a **4.80** 'possession' within the meaning of Article 1 Protocol 1 if it is 'sufficiently established to be enforceable'.[52]

Article 1 Protocol 1 requires the State to make use of all available legal means at its disposal in **4.81** order to enforce a binding arbitration award (provided that it constitutes a 'possession').[53] The State must make sure, in that sense, that the execution of an arbitral award is carried out without undue delay and that the overall system is effective both in law and in practice (*Kin-Stib* §83).

Where the State has interfered with a person's right to peaceful enjoyment of their possessions, **4.82** the Court considers whether 'a fair balance has been struck between the demands of the general interest of the community and the requirements of the protection of the individual's fundamental rights' (*Stran Greek Refineries* §69).

The unjustified refusal to enforce an arbitral award could therefore amount to an expropri- **4.83** ation.[54] A consideration, that may be relevant is whether there are other legal means available whereby enforcement can be secured (*Kin-Stib*, §84).

Two instructive examples where States have been found in breach of Article 1 Protocol 1 in **4.84** relation to the enforcement of arbitral awards are provided in *Stran Greek Refineries* and *Kin-Stib*.

In *Stran Greek Refineries*, the ECtHR found that Greece had breached Article 1 Protocol 1. **4.85** From 1967 to 1974, Greece was ruled by a military junta. In 1972, the first applicant made a contract with the Greek State, pursuant to which the applicant undertook to construct a crude oil refinery and the State undertook to purchase a plot of land suitable for building such a refinery. However, the State failed to do so. In 1975, democracy was restored. A law was enacted which allowed the new government to terminate preferential contracts concluded under the military regime ('the 1975 Law'). Using this law, the government terminated the contract with the applicant.

---

52 *Kin-Stib and Majkić v Serbia* App no 12312/05 (ECtHR, 20 April 2010) ('*Kin-Stib*') §83.
53 *Stran Greek Refineries and Stratis Andreadis v Greece* App no 13427/87 (ECtHR, 09 December 1994) ('*Stran Greek Refineries*') §§61–62.
54 Besson (n 6) § 8, citing *Stran Greek Refineries*, ibid.

4.86 The applicant claimed that the government owed it compensation for breach of its obligations during the period of validity of the contract. In 1980, the government submitted the dispute to arbitration and in 1984, the arbitral tribunal issued a final and binding award in favour of the applicant (the 'Award'). In 1987, Greece enacted a law which provided:

> (1) The true and lawful meaning of [the 1975 Law] is that, upon the termination of these contracts, all their terms, conditions and clauses, including the arbitration clause, are ipso jure repealed and the arbitration tribunal no longer has jurisdiction.
> (2) Arbitration awards covered by paragraph 1 shall no longer be valid or enforceable.
> (3) Any principal or ancillary claims against the Greek state ... which arise out of the contracts entered into between 21 April 1967 and 24 July 1974, ratified by statute and terminated by virtue of [the 1975 Law] are now proclaimed time-barred.

4.87 As a result, the Award was declared void and unenforceable. The ECtHR held that this was an interference with the applicants' possessions (§§58–67). This interference was not justified because 'it would be unjust if every legal relationship entered into with a dictatorial regime was regarded as invalid when the regime came to an end'. The ECtHR added 'the contract in question related to the construction of an oil refinery, which was of benefit to the economic infrastructure of the country' regardless of which government was in power (*Stran Greek Refineries* §71). Thus, Greece was under a duty to pay the applicants the sums awarded against it in the Award (§73). As noted by Fietta and Upcher, 'in a rare judgment awarding substantial compensation for breach of human rights under the ECHR, the Court ordered Greece to pay to the applicants the full amount contained in the arbitration award plus interest'.[55]

4.88 In *Kin-Stib*, on the other hand, the ECtHR found that Serbia had breached Article 1 Protocol 1. Kin-Stib, a company, brought arbitral proceedings against another company, Genex. This resulted in an arbitral award in Kin-Stib's favour, which was sufficiently established to be a possession. Genex only partially complied with the arbitral award. In 2004, the Serbian Commercial Court fined Genex for failing to comply fully with the award. However, in 2006, the Serbian Commercial Court terminated enforcement by means of imposing fines because the maximum statutory amount had been reached. In 2008, the Serbian Commercial Court stayed enforcement proceedings while Genex was being restructured. The ECtHR found that Serbia had not taken the necessary measures to fully enforce the arbitration award and had not provided any convincing reasons for that failure (§85). It ordered Serbia to pay EUR 38,000 in total to the applicants (§§91–102).

4.89 Both cases demonstrate that the European Convention can be used effectively to secure the enforcement of awards in certain cases.

---

55 Fietta and Upcher (n 4) 210.

E. CONCLUSION

In *Law and Practice of Commercial Arbitration in England*, Mustill and Boyd state that 'all **4.90** persons concerned with the conduct of arbitrations have a duty to ensure that they are familiar with the principles of human rights law'.[56]

The evolving jurisprudence under the ECHR relating to arbitral proceedings, can be complex, **4.91** fact-specific, and in a state of flux. However, as more cases come before the Court, different elements of the rights at stake are tested. It can be noticed – in that regard – that there has been an evolution in the jurisprudence of the Strasbourg organs. If in *Nordström*, the Commission held that an arbitration agreement per se constituted a full waiver of Article 6, the European Court contemplated in *Souvaniemi* that it may be permissible to waive some of these rights but not others. There is consensus today that a complete waiver of Article 6(1) is not permissible.

The case law under Article 6(1) of the ECHR, shows that the ECtHR draws a distinction **4.92** between voluntary and compulsory arbitration. Where arbitration is voluntary, the rights under Article 6(1) can be waived, if the waiver is free, unequivocal and permissible and there are minimum guarantees commensurate to the importance of the right. Where arbitration is compulsory or where rights have not been validly waived, the arbitral tribunal must afford the applicant the safeguards in Article 6(1). These include the right to an independent and impartial tribunal established by law, and in some circumstances, it can even be the right to a public hearing. Rights under Article 6(1) may be restricted but any restrictions must comply with three requirements: (1) it must pursue a legitimate aim; (2) there must be a reasonable relationship of proportionality between the means employed and the aim sought to be achieved; and (3) it must not restrict the access to a tribunal in such a way or to such an extent that the very essence of the right is impaired.

An important development has also been that the concept of expropriation can be applied to **4.93** non-enforcement of arbitral awards by domestic courts. In relation to Article 1 Protocol 1, an arbitral award can constitute a 'possession'. If so, the State must make use of all available legal means at its disposal in order to enforce the award effectively and without undue delay. In several instances, the European Court's intervention has secured the enforcement of awards which otherwise would have been denied to the applicants.

---

56   Michael J Mustill, Stewart Crauford Boyd, *Law and Practice of Commercial Arbitration in England* (2001 companion volume) (2nd edn, Butterworths 1989) 77.

5

THE ALLOCATION OF GDPR COMPLIANCE IN ARBITRATION

Alexander Blumrosen[*]

A. INTRODUCTION

5.01 There is a new challenge for the law and practice of international arbitration that comes from the adoption of the General Data Protection Regulation ('GDPR') by the European Union. This chapter will examine certain aspects of the collision between the obligations set out by the GDPR and the international arbitration process, which is both a legal and cultural shock, and which has not gone unnoticed. Arbitration is typically considered a private process that replaces the more public courthouse and operates with a contractual mandate from the parties of jurisdictional authority to definitively resolve disputes that would otherwise lie with the State. That mandate is possible by virtue of arbitration laws, which vary State to State, and by international treaties, in particular the NY Convention, that provide for recognition and enforcement of awards.

5.02 While arbitral tribunals often address questions of which State law applies to the resolution of a legal question raised by the parties in the arbitration, it is less frequent that arbitrators must address an intrusion into the arbitration proceedings of State law requirements that impact the organization of the arbitration proceeding. With the adoption of the GDPR, the rules protecting the privacy of personal data in the EU have been codified into a regulation of broad

---

[*] Date of submission 22/12/2020.

application that must be considered by parties, tribunals, arbitration institutions, and other actors in the arbitration process.

How is an arbitrator to get even a single night of sound sleep, reflecting on how the highly developed and regulated field of data privacy applies to a particular arbitration? **5.03**

While the terms of GDPR are very broad, and compliance failure can be severely sanctioned, it is possible as discussed hereafter for each of the actors in the arbitration process to limit their liability by allocating responsibility for compliance with the actors best positioned to ensure such compliance. However, GDPR compliance can also pose an existential threat to the very mission of the arbitrator, which is to render an award that is enforceable; in closing, this chapter will examine whether a violation of GDPR by any of the arbitration actors in a particular matter could undermine the enforceability of an otherwise valid award. **5.04**

B. BACKGROUND, RESOURCES AND IMPLEMENTATION IN THE FIELD

Since May 25, 2018, the EU General Data Privacy Regulation[1] has provided the legal framework for regulating the personal data of EU nationals within and without the EU. The purpose of the Regulation is to 'effectively protect the fundamental rights and freedoms of natural persons with regard to the processing of their personal data'.[2] The GDPR did not spring up overnight, but is the regulatory evolution of over 50 years of data privacy regulation in Europe, first by EU Member States in their national law,[3] then through national laws adopted in application of the EU Data Protection Directive of 1995.[4] **5.05**

Many of the regulatory principles and practices under the GDPR are a direct reflection of practice under the prior EU Directive, and the wealth of interpretive guidance from the EU Commission, through the Article 29 Working Party (WP29), or from EU Member State data protection authorities (DPAs) remains relevant to GDPR implementation. However, the way in which the GDPR addresses the following two issues has attracted great attention to the scope and potential impact of EU data privacy laws. **5.06**

First, the various different national laws adopted under the Directive have been harmonized, so that the new national laws which have been adopted under the Regulation all adhere to the stated requirements of the EU law, and diverge only in those limited areas where the EU legislator left some discretion to Member States. This is a sea change from practice under the Directive, which allowed unbridled discretion to each Member State providing the minimum requirements of the Directive were incorporated into national law, leading to wide variations between national laws and practice. One of the main goals of the GDPR was to harmonize EU **5.07**

---

1 Regulation (EU) 2016/679 of the European Parliament and the Council of 27 April 2016 on the Protection of Natural Persons with Regard to the Processing of Personal Data and on the Free Movement of Such Data, and Repealing Directive 95/46/EC (General Data Protection Regulation), 2016 OJ L 119/1 (GDPR).

2 GDPR, recitals 1–3.

3 See e.g. France, Law n° 78-17 of 6 January 1978 on computers, databases and liberties <https://www.cnil.fr/sites/default/files/typo/document/Act78-17VA.pdf> accessed 8 June 2020.

4 Directive 95/46/EC of the European Parliament and of the Council of 24 October 1995 on the protection of individuals with regard to the processing of personal data and on the free movement of such data [1995] OJ L281/31.

privacy laws to promote efficiency, compliance and predictability, and the new regime has been largely successful in meeting this goal.

5.08 Second, the sanctions regime under the Directive was mostly left to Member States, and was largely ineffective, both regarding the caps on the amount of fines as well as the resources of the Member States to police compliance. As a result, there was a great diversity of enforcement within the EU leading to market distortions as the burdens of compliance (or not) and sanctions (or not) on companies doing business in the EU were uneven. The GDPR radically changed the sanctions regime; administrative fines for certain violations may now be up to 20,000,000 Euros or up to 4 per cent of annual corporate revenue.[5]

5.09 Just as under the Directive during the period 1995–2018, the national privacy regulators retain jurisdiction to investigate, prosecute and assess fines for violations of the GDPR. Indeed, while the Regulation is an EU Regulation, there is no EU regulatory data protection regulatory authority charged with enforcement. However, to ensure continued guidance, the GDPR provides for a permanent EU committee, the European Data Protection Board (EDPB)[6] that continues the guidance and policy work that the WP29 accomplished under the Directive. Importantly, the body of guidance on every facet of EU data privacy law from these policy bodies since 1995 is a continuing source of information about how EU data privacy laws work.

5.10 The EU-wide adoption of a harmonized law increasing potential sanctions focused attention on the new law during the 18 months leading up to its implementation on May 25, 2018, as the Regulation in its final form had been adopted by the EU Parliament on April 27, 2016, thereby giving national regulators and companies over two years to prepare for compliance with the new rules.

5.11 The GDPR has led to a lively discussion in the arbitration community about whether the GDPR applies to actors in an international commercial arbitration, and if so, which actors in the arbitration process are responsible for ensuring compliance and what steps should be taken to do so.

5.12 In practice, however, while there is regulatory guidance on general principles, there is little arbitration-specific instruction or precedent about the specific steps that should be taken by parties, by tribunals, and by institutions, to properly allocate responsibility – and limit potential liability – for GDPR compliance.

5.13 The discussion in the arbitration community on how EU privacy laws can be implemented in an arbitration has been short in time, professional, and ultimately inconclusive. The last three

---

5   GDPR, Art 83.

6   The EDPB is responsible for the application of the General Data Protection Regulation (GDPR) as of 25 May 2018, and is made up of the head of each Data Protection Authority (DPA) and of the European Data Protection Supervisor (EDPS) or their representatives <https://ec.europa.eu/info/law/law-topic/data-protection/reform/rules-business-and-organisations/enforcement-and-sanctions/enforcement/what-european-data-protection-board-edpb_en> accessed 8 June 2020.

years has given rise to a series of well-documented articles,[7] law firm contributions,[8] and arbitration institution reflection in the form of recommendations and checklists[9] that capture the legal and regulatory environment of the GDPR in the context of an arbitration proceeding. Any study of the subject by practitioners and academics must start with these readily available resources.

The articles referenced above ask the important question, 'who may be liable for privacy compliance in an arbitration', and find that the broadly-worded GDPR principles, and the lack of arbitration-specific guidance, require a complicated fact-specific assessment of GDPR in each arbitration. Arbitrators who are serious about implementing quick and efficient procedures are understandably concerned that the complication of GDPR compliance in each case will quickly paralyze or even overwhelm their primary mission; getting the parties from the initial pleading in an arbitration to an enforceable award. This chapter will focus attention on the specific requirements of the GDPR, and who in an arbitration proceeding must address GDPR compliance. **5.14**

This chapter will (i) summarize briefly the traits of the new EU privacy regime, before turning to the (ii) unresolved issues that face the actors in the arbitration community as GDPR privacy protections become institutionalized in the arbitral process, focusing in particular on who should be responsible for implementing GDPR compliance in arbitration and the risk that non-compliance may pose to very validity of an arbitration award. **5.15**

C. SUMMARY OF EU GDPR REQUIREMENTS AS THEY APPLY TO ARBITRATION

For the reasons set out hereafter, it is beyond argument that the GDPR applies to international commercial arbitrations that involve the processing of personal data by processors located in the EU, including the data of non-EU nationals.[10] **5.16**

---

7   Kathleen Paisley, 'It's All About the Data: The Impact of the EU General Data Protection Regulation on International Arbitration' (2018) 41 *Fordham International Law Journal* 841 <https://ir.lawnet.fordham.edu/ilj/vol41/iss4/4> accessed 8 June 2020.

8   Baker Botts, 'Foreign Data Protection Laws in U.S. Litigation and International Arbitration' (Insights, 6 February 2020) <https://www.bakerbotts.com/insights/publications/2020/february/foreign-data-protection-laws-in-us-litigation-and-international-arbitrationcapabilities/cybersecurity/protocol_cybersecurity_intl_arb_july2017.pdf> accessed 8 June 2020; Natalia M Szlarb, 'European Union: GDPR And International Arbitration At A Crossroad' (Sheppard Mullin Richter & Hampton, 5 December 2019) <https://www.mondaq.com/unitedstates/arbitration-dispute-resolution/871962/gdpr-and-international-arbitration-at-a-crossroad> accessed 8 June 2020; Martin Zahariev, 'GDPR issues in commercial arbitration and how to mitigate them' (Kluwer Arbitration Blog, 7 September 2019) <http://arbitrationblog.kluwerarbitration.com/2019/09/07/gdpr-issues-in-commercial-arbitration-and-how-to-mitigate-them/> accessed 8 June 2020.

9   International Council for Commercial Arbitration, International Bar Association, 'The ICCA-IBA Roadmap to Data Protection in International Arbitration' (Public Consultation Draft, 28 February 2020) <https://www.arbitration-icca.org/media/14/18191123957287/roadmap_28.02.20.pdf> accessed 8 June 2020.

10 The EDPB guidelines 3/2018 on the territorial scope of the GDPR, Art 3 (Version 2.1, 12 November 2019) <https://edpb.europa.eu/our-work-tools/our-documents/guidelines/guidelines-32018-territorial-scope-gdpr-article-3-version_fr> accessed 8 June 2020, confirms at p. 10 that,

   The text of Article 3(1) does not restrict the application of the GDPR to the processing of personal data of individuals who are in the Union. The EDPB therefore considers that any personal data processing in the context of the activities of an establishment of a controller or processor in the Union would fall under the scope of the GDPR, regardless of the location or the nationality of the data subject whose personal data are being processed. This

5.17   There is some debate whether the GDPR applies with equal force to non-commercial arbitrations, such as those organized under bilateral or multilateral investment treaties, even when an arbitrator or other arbitration actor in such proceeding is located in the EU. A recent decision by a Permanent Court of Arbitration tribunal held that the GDPR does not come within the material scope in investor-state arbitration under Chapter II of NAFTA, as such arbitrations are organized under the NAFTA treaty to which neither the EU nor its Member States is a party.[11] In particular, the Regulation expressly excludes from the material scope of the Regulation the collection of data 'in the course of an activity which falls outside the scope of Union law'.[12]

5.18   But that does not settle the issue of national data protection legislation in investment treaty arbitration. In another recent case also pending before the Permanent Court of Arbitration, involving the Korea-United States Free Trade Agreement, the tribunal required compliance with the data privacy protections of the Korean Personal Information Protection Act (PIPA), holding that personal information contained in documentation produced in the arbitration must be redacted, even though much of the personal data was already in the public domain.[13]

5.19   Further, the territorial reach of the GDPR is broad, requiring that any entity located in the EU that processes personal data ensure the protections afforded to natural persons by the GDPR.[14] Accordingly, any party, counsel, arbitrator, expert or arbitral institution established in the EU is subject to the GDPR if they process personal data during the arbitration.[15]

---

approach is supported by recital 14 of the GDPR which states that '[t]he protection afforded by this Regulation should apply to natural persons, whatever their nationality or place of residence, in relation to the processing of their personal data.

11   PCA Case No 2018-54, *Tennant Energy LLC v Canada* (Tribunal's Communication to the Parties) 24 June 2019 <https://pcacases.com/web/sendAttach/3741> accessed 8 June 2020. The reasoning of this opinion has been criticized as being contrary to the plain meaning of the GDPR and to the guidance by the EDPB on the territorial scope of the Regulation. See e.g., Bhavit Baxi, 'Tennant Energy v. Canada, diluting the impact of GDPR in International Treaty Arbitration' (KSLR EU Law Blog, 15 October 2019) <https://blogs.kcl.ac.uk/kslreuropeanlawblog/?p=1415#.Xt4y4O exXb0> accessed 8 June 2020; Emily Hay, 'The Invisible Arm of GDPR in International Treaty Arbitration: Can't We Make It Go Away?' (Kluwer Arbitration Blog, 29 August 2019) <http://arbitrationblog.kluwerarbitration.com/2019/08/ 29/the-invisible-arm-of-gdpr-in-international-treaty-arbitration-cant-we-make-it-go-away/> accessed 8 June 2020.

12   GDPR, Art 2(a).

13   PCA Case No. 2018-51, *Elliott Associates LP (USA) v Republic of Korea* (Procedural Order no 4) 30 June 2019 <https://www.google.com/url?sa=t&rct=j&q=&esrc=s&source=web&cd=&ved=2ahUKEwjHxoOZkPPpAhXiyYUKHa 7CAuwQFjACegQIBBAB&url=https%3A%2F%2Fwww.italaw.com%2Fsites%2Fdefault%2Ffiles%2Fcase-documents %2Fitalaw10756.pdf&usg=AOvVaw1_jtDh1uqm5BOrgEjETv-q> accessed 8 June 2020.

14   GDPR, Art 3:

1. This Regulation applies to the processing of personal data in the context of the activities of an establishment of a controller or a processor in the Union, regardless of whether the processing takes place in the Union or not.
2. This Regulation applies to the processing of personal data of data subjects who are in the Union by a controller or processor not established in the Union, where the processing activities are related to: (a)the offering of goods or services, irrespective of whether a payment of the data subject is required, to such data subjects in the Union; or ….

15   The GDPR requires compliance even by entities located outside the EU that process the personal data of EU data subjects if such data is used for commercial purposes. It would seem unlikely that the paragraph 2 of this article would apply to arbitrations composed entirely of non-EU actors, simply because the personal data of EU data subjects is processed. Certainly, arbitration is a service, offered to consenting parties in exchange for payment, but the service is not offered to the EU data subjects themselves as specified in the GDPR, as would be for example a non-EU internet sales site targeting sales to EU consumers, but is rather a service offered to the economic actors that are parties to the arbitration and that have compiled the personal data and act accordingly as controllers or processors.

So what is 'personal data' under the GDPR? In the context of an arbitration, all 'personal data'   **5.20**
is subject to the GDPR, meaning:

> any information relating to an identified or identifiable natural person … in particular by reference to
> an identifier, such as a name, an identification number, location data, online identifier, or to one or
> more factors specific to the physical, physiological, genetic, mental, economic, cultural or social
> identity of that natural person.[16]

Examples of personal data provided by the European Commission include:[17]   **5.21**

- a name and a surname
- a home address
- an email address
- an identification card number
- location data
- an IP protocol address
- a cookie ID
- the advertising identifier of a phone

In short, the exchange of any information by which a specific individual can be identified is   **5.22**
personal data within the meaning of the Regulation. Such information can be in arbitration
exhibits, but also in briefs, witness statements, expert reports and of course the award. All of
these documents may accordingly fall within the scope of GDPR compliance obligations if the
personal data is 'processed' by one or more arbitration actors.

Does handling personal data in documents submitted in connection with an arbitration   **5.23**
constitute 'processing' under the GDPR? For those unfamiliar with EU data privacy, it would
be tempting to consider that 'processing' is an informatics or data IT function, far removed
from legal deliberations. But the GDPR defines processing very broadly to cover any:

> operations performed on personal data, including by manual or automated means, including the
> 'collection, recording, organization, structuring, storage, adaptation or alteration, retrieval, consult-
> ation, use, disclosure by transmission, dissemination or otherwise making available, alignment or
> combination, restriction, erasure or destruction of personal data.[18]

During arbitral proceedings, the collection and examination of documents, the transfer of
documents to counsel or an expert, the exchange of documents between the parties, or the
disclosure of evidence ordered by the tribunal must all be considered 'processing' activities
within the meaning of the Regulation.

---

16 GDPR, Art 4(1).
17 'What is personal data?' (European Commission website) <https://ec.europa.eu/info/law/law-topic/data-protection/
    reform/what-personal-data_en> accessed 8 June 2020.
18 GDPR, Art 4(2).

1. Liability

5.24 The person who processes personal data, by engaging in any of the activities above, is defined by the GDPR as being either a 'Data Controller' (or Controller), a 'Data Processor', or a 'Third party':

- A Controller is the 'the natural or legal person, public authority, agency or other body that, alone or jointly with others, determines the purposes and means of the processing of personal data'[19] and who has the principal obligation for compliance.
- A Processor is 'the natural or legal person, public authority, agency or other body which processes personal data on behalf of the controller'.
- A Third party is a 'person (other than the data subject, controller, and processor) who, under the direct authority of the controller or processor, are authorized to process personal data'.[20]

5.25 By this classification, the GDPR allocates responsibility for compliance 'to determine who shall be responsible for compliance with data protection rules, and how data subjects can exercise the rights in practice'.[21] This requires a factual analysis of each situation to identify which arbitral actor has made decisions about which data would be processed, when, how and for what purpose.

5.26 The controller must adhere to a number of requirements in connection with the processing under the GDPR. According to Article 5 of the Regulation, the controller must ensure that personal data be:

- processed lawfully, fairly and in a transparent manner;
- collected for specified, explicit and legitimate purposes;
- adequate, relevant and limited to what is necessary;
- accurate and, where necessary, kept up to date;
- kept in a form which permits identification of data subjects for no longer than is necessary;
- processed in a manner that ensures appropriate security of the personal data.

5.27 The Regulation prohibits the processing of certain categories of data, such as data revealing racial origin or religious and political beliefs, or genetic and biometric data, unless a specific listed exception applies, among which is the exception that the data is 'necessary for the establishment, exercise or defence of legal claims'.[22]

---

19   Ibid., Art 4(7).

20   Ibid., Art 4(10).

21   The Working Party on the Protection of Individuals with regard to the processing of personal data set up by Directive 95/46/EC of the European Parliament and of the Council of 24 October 1995 (Article 29 Data Protection Working Party), 'Opinion 1/2010 on the concepts of "controller" and "processor" WP 169 adopted on 16 February 2010 <https://ec.europa.eu/justice/article-29/documentation/opinion-recommendation/files/2010/wp169_en.pdf> accessed 8 June 2020.

22   GDPR, Art 9(2)(f). Given this exception, even sensitive personal data may be legitimately processed in an arbitration provided all other GDPR conditions are met.

Note that there can be more than one controller in an eco-system of onward data transfers, and **5.28** in some cases any one actor may be a controller for certain purposes, and also a processor or third party for others, depending on the data flow. In an arbitration, the principal data controller is the party, which has collected the data in the normal course of its business from its clients and vendors and is squarely responsible for that data under the GDPR. But counsel and arbitrators may also be controllers, even though they did not initially collect the data, because to perform their respective functions they have broad discretion and professional independence to decide how certain personal data produced in the proceeding should be used. As a result, they may be considered 'Joint Controllers', each with the legal obligation to verify that the personal data transferred to them is securely maintained while the data is in their custody.[23]

The GDPR requires that any processing of personal data must meet at least one of the **5.29** following six conditions, failing which the transfer cannot be considered legal:[24]

- made with the consent of the person to the processing of his or her data for one or more specific purposes;
- required for the performance of a contract;
- required to comply with a legal obligation;[25]
- required to safeguard the vital interests of the person concerned or another natural person;
- required for the performance of a public interest task or in the exercise of official authority vested in the controller;
- required for the purposes of legitimate interests of the controller or by a third party.

The conditions most commonly invoked to justify the lawful processing of data under the **5.30** GDPR in arbitration proceedings are that such processing is (1) necessary for the performance of a contract, (2) required to fulfil a legal obligation, or (3) for the purpose of the legitimate interests of the controller.[26]

A recommendation by the EU Article 29 Data Protection Working Party, on international **5.31** data transfers in the context of international litigation specifically identifies document discovery in international judicial proceedings as being necessary for the purposes of a controller's legitimate interests, providing the legal basis for the processing of data for that purpose.[27]

---

23 Joint controllers are required to transparently allocate their respective responsibilities for compliance with the GDPR, and they can do this contractually, through the adoption of data management protocols. However, the allocation agreed upon between joint controllers is not binding on the data subjects who may exercise their rights under the GDPR against every controller (Art 26(3) GDPR). In other words, contractually allocating responsibilities does not release any one controller from its responsibilities towards data subjects. The implication of Art 26 is that a joint controller may be liable for damages to the data subject for matters that the controller may have contractually determined, with other joint controllers, to be beyond the scope of its individual responsibility.

24 GDPR, Art 6.

25 Only legal obligations under EU law or the laws of an EU Member State, to the exclusion of obligations under non-EU law such as an order to produce documents from a US court in discovery proceedings. GDPR, Art 6(3).

26 If the transfer is based on 'legitimate interests', then the controller must be able to show that its legitimate interests are not overridden by the interests or rights and freedoms of the data subject.

27 Article 29 Data Protection Working Party, 'Working Document 1/2009 on pre-trial discovery for cross border civil Litigation' WP 158 <https://ec.europa.eu/justice/article-29/documentation/opinion-recommendation/files/2009/wp158_en.pdf> accessed 8 June 2020.

5.32 GDPR Article 23 authorizes Member States to establish exemptions that would allow the processing of data in other countries. A Member State may restrict this scope, in particular to ensure 'the protection of judicial independence and judicial proceedings', which may make it possible to limit the rights of the persons concerned.[28] An arbitration procedure in a Member State where these rights of the data subject have been restricted would reduce compliance measures by allowing arbitral tribunals to impose certain rules such as confidentiality orders while avoiding the need for extensive data processing and transfer protocols. The adoption of such exemptions under GDPR Article 23 give the adopting EU Member State a competitive advantage on privacy issues in the selection of the arbitration seat, but most EU Member States have not adopted such exemptions.

2. Substantive personal data processing requirements

5.33 Once a lawful basis for the transfer is established, the GDPR requires compliance with substantive personal data processing rules. Drawing from the principles of data protection included in the GDPR, any processing of personal data will need to comply with the following requirements:[29]

a. Security of personal data

5.34 Controllers and processors are required to adopt technical and organizational measures to ensure a level of security appropriate to the risk, including among other things, the anonymization and encryption of personal data.[30]

5.35 There are several initiatives to develop protocols[31] and platforms[32] for the secure sharing and exchange of documents in arbitration. Although these model protocols have not been developed specifically to meet the requirements of the GDPR, they provide a useful basis for a data security regime in arbitration as they identify non-GDPR bases for the potential liability

---

28 GDPR, Art 23(1)(f). Ireland was one of the first countries to adopt an exemption to allow the rights of data subjects to be limited in arbitral proceedings and allows for exceptions to the provisions of the rights of data subjects where necessary to the exercise or defence of a right in a court of law. See, Irish Data Protection Act 2018, S 60(3)(a)(iv):

> The rights and obligations provided for in Articles 12 to 22 and Article 34, and Article 5 [of the GDPR] in so far as any of its provisions correspond to the rights and obligations in Articles 12 to 22 ... are restricted ... to the extent that the restrictions are necessary and proportionate ... in contemplation of or for the establishment, exercise or defence of, a legal claim, prospective legal claim, legal proceedings or prospective legal proceedings whether before a court, statutory tribunal, statutory body or an administrative or out-of-court procedure.

29 In addition to those listed above, which are most likely to be raised in an arbitration, data subjects under the GDPR also have the right to access the data (Art 15), the right to restrict processing (Art 19), and the right to data portability (Art 20).

30 GDPR, Art 32.

31 See Debevoise and Plimpton, 'Protocol to Promote Cybersecurity in International Arbitration, 2017' <https://www.debevoise.com/~/media/files/capabilities/cybersecurity/protocol_cybersecurity_intl_arb_july2017.pdf> accessed 8 June 2020; ICCA, International Institute for Conflict Prevention and Resolution (CPR) and the New York City Bar Association, 'Cybersecurity Protocol for International Arbitration – Consultation Draft' (2018) 32 <https://www.jarbitration-icca.org/media/10/43322709923070/draft_cybersecurity_protocol_final_10_april.pdf> accessed 8 June 2020.

32 See e.g., the Stockholm Chamber of Commerce Platform <https://sccinstitute.com/scc-platform/> accessed 8 June 2020: 'The SCC Platform provides participants with a secure and efficient way of communicating and filing all case materials in the arbitration ... and will constitute the forum through which the SCC communicates with the parties, counsel and arbitrators throughout the proceedings.'

of arbitrators and arbitral institutions for failing to implement appropriate data security measures. The parties and their counsel, with the support of arbitral institutions, typically undertake the development of a security system, and it is only in the absence of an agreement between the parties that the arbitral tribunal may be requested to decide on appropriate security measures.

b. Right to transparency or the principle of respect of human rights

At the time of data collection, the controller must communicate to the data subject: (i) the contact details of the controller(s) and processor(s); (ii) the purpose and the legal basis of the processing; (iii) the legitimate interests pursued by the controller by the processing; (iv) where applicable, the intention to transfer personal data to a country, third parties and the existence or absence of an adequacy finding; (v) the duration of data retention and/or the criteria used to determine the duration; (vi) the existence of the right to apply to the data controller to access personal data, the correction or deletion of such data, or a limitation of the processing operation relating to the data subject, or the right to object to the processing, and the right to data portability; (vii) the existence of the right to withdraw one's consent at any time; and (viii) the right to lodge a complaint to a supervisory authority.[33]   **5.36**

This requirement is perhaps the most confounding for arbitrators, as they are far removed from the original collection of the data, and have no connection with the data subjects who are typically – if we look beyond the arbitration participants – the employees, vendors or customers of the parties. Article 14 of the GDPR provides for less burdensome disclosure requirements for the processing of personal data that are not directly collected from the person concerned,[34] and even these reduced obligations may be shifted by contract to the parties.[35]   **5.37**

c. Right of rectification and right to erasure

According to Article 16 of the GDPR, 'the data subject shall have the right to obtain from the controller without undue delay the rectification of inaccurate personal data concerning him or her'. Importantly, there is no exception to this Article 16 data subject right that could apply to an arbitration proceeding, unless a Member State exempts such data under Article 23 of the Regulation, and so arbitration data protection protocols will need to identify a process in the arbitration to accommodate any requests based on this provision. Article 17 of the GDPR establishes the grounds to obtain the *right to erasure* ('*right to be forgotten*'),[36] which by its terms will not apply if the personal data is transferred 'for the establishment, exercise or defence of legal claims',[37] and accordingly will likely arise less frequently in arbitration proceedings.   **5.38**

To complicate matters further in an international arbitration, it is common for transfers of data to locations outside the EU to be made, but such transfers must meet additional requirements.   **5.39**

---

33   GDPR, Art 13.
34   This is the case when counsel receives information from their client, as the attorney is bound by professional secrecy, and this explains why Art 14 provides for an exception to the obligation to provide information to the data subject where such data is confidential under a regulated obligation of professional secrecy.
35   The parties may consider specifying in their data management protocol that only the parties will be responsible for communicating the information required by the GDPR to the data subjects, the arbitrators and the arbitration institution being contractually exempt from such obligation.
36   The right to erasure provides that the data subjects have the right to require that the controller delete their personal data.
37   GDPR, Art 17(3)(e).

Transfers outside the EU may only be made to a country with adequate personal data safeguards,[38] or if the controller making the transfer use appropriate safeguards for the data under GDPR Article 46 by adopting the EU Standard Contract clauses or by adopting Binding Corporate Rules.[39] Until 2020 transfers to the United States or Switzerland could be made using the procedures of the Privacy Shield,[40] but this mechanism was judged by the EU Court of Justice to be unlawful under EU law,[41] and so until a new mechanism is adopted, Binding Corporate Rules or Standard Contractual Clauses will provide the principal means to make transfers outside the EU under the GDPR.[42]

5.40   However, if none of the above requirements is met, there is still one exception that can permit limited numbers of documents with personal data to be transferred outside the EU for the purposes of the arbitration; the GDPR allows transfers of data to a third country when the transfer is necessary 'for the establishment, exercise or defence of legal claims'.[43]

3.   Management of personal data in an arbitration

5.41   All of the arbitration actors must turn to data privacy issues at the start of the arbitration, to assess in the first instance whether the GDPR or another data protection statute applies, and to take preliminary steps to ensure compliance, bringing to bear their respective resources and experience. The main actors in the implementation of compliance should be (1) the parties, (2) the institution, and (3) the tribunal, in that order.

---

38   Ibid., Art 45.

39   Ibid., Art 46.

40   The Privacy Shield had replaced the EU-US Safe Harbour that was declared unlawful by the European Court of Justice on October 6, 2015 (Case C-362/14, *Maximillian Schrems v Data Protection Commissioner* [2015] ECLI:EU:C:2015:650) and provides the basis for the adequacy decision for data transfers to the United States taken by the EU Commission on July 12, 2016. See Commission Implementing Decision (EU) 2016/1250 of 12 July 2016 pursuant to Directive 95/46/EC of the European Parliament and of the Council on the adequacy of the protection provided by the EU-U.S. Privacy Shield [2016] OJ L 207/1. The Privacy Shield framework was considered adequate by the EU until 2020 in part because it provides recourse for GDPR claims by aggrieved data subjects including a *sui generis* arbitration panel defined at Annex I to Annex II of the 12 July 2016 adequacy decision that is administered by the American Arbitration Association (see International Centre for Dispute Resolution (ICDR) – American Arbitration Association (AAA) EU-US Privacy Shield Program – Independent Recourse Mechanism (IRM) <https://go.adr.org/privacyshield.html> accessed 8 June 2020).

41   CJEU Judgment C-311/18 ECLI:EU:C:2020:559 (Schrems II), 16 July 2020.

42   The EDPB in a post-Schrems II draft guidance has noted that even strict compliance with these mechanisms may not be enough; the transferor is required to make an assessment of destination country legislation, including national security surveillance laws, and to take any additional steps that may be needed to account for the intrusiveness of the destination country's legislation, such as using end-to-end encryption (see EDPB, 'Recommendations 01/2020 on measures that supplement transfer tools to ensure compliance with the EU level of protection of personal data', 10 November 2020 <https://edpb.europa.eu/sites/edpb/files/consultation/edpb_recommendations_202001_supplementarymeasurestransfer stools_en.pdf> accessed 22 December 2020).

43   GDPR Art 49(1)(e), though EDPB guidance provides that the exeptions in article 49 may only be invoked if the appropriate safeguards identified in Articles 46 and 47 are not available. See EDPB Guidelines 2/2018 on derogations of article 49 under Regulation 2016/679, 25 May 2018, p. 11, <https://edpb.europa.eu/our-work-tools/our-documents/ directrices/guidelines-22018-derogations-article-49-under-regulation_en>.

a. The parties

The parties are best positioned to understand which personal data in their possession or control **5.42** is to be communicated in an arbitration. After all, this is the party that decided that certain categories of data would be important for its business and then went about collecting, processing, using and storing the data in a way that it considered useful. Also, the party is in closest proximity with the data subject at the time of data collection, and so is uniquely positioned to explain to the data subject why the data was being collected, how the data would be used, and what rights the data subject has under law with respect to the collected data.

The party has organized the collection of personal data about its employees, and is in the best **5.43** position to inform them of company data protection, retention and security policy, by including this information transparently in employment agreements and internal regulations, procedures and training. As consent is only one of several legal bases justifying the lawful transfer of data, the party is able in their normal business operations to adopt a data protection policy referring to other legal bases for data collection such as 'performance of contract' or 'legitimate interests', and providing in such policies that the data relating to employees may be used in arbitral proceedings, and confirming that such data may be transferred abroad to a third country as long as such transfer complies with the GDPR.[44]

With respect to the party's customers, vendors and other persons whose data may end up in an **5.44** arbitration, again it is the party that collects the personal data, and uses the data in its business, that is able to set the conditions of initial collection and inform the data subjects of all the potential uses to which their data may be put. To a great degree, later controllers and processors such as the arbitrators to whom the data is transferred accept the data transfer subject to all the limitations and imperfections arising in the initial collection process.[45]

The privileged position of the party as the initial data collector is recognized implicitly in the **5.45** GDPR, as Articles 13 and 14 set out different standards of information to be provided to the data subject depending on whether the data is collected directly by the party (Art 13), or is data passed on to other and later controllers or processors who have no direct contact with the data subject. In the latter case, there are several important exceptions to the duty to inform the data subject of any further processing decided by the controller, including that the data subject already has all the information required, as this information would have been provided previously by the party collecting the data. This structure of the GDPR reinforces how

---

44   In accordance with GDPR, recital 39:

> Any processing of personal data should be lawful and fair. It should be transparent to natural persons that personal data concerning them are collected, used, consulted or otherwise processed and to what extent the personal data are or will be processed. [...] Natural persons should be made aware of risks, rules, safeguards and rights in relation to the processing of personal data and how to exercise their rights in relation to such processing. In particular, the specific purposes for which personal data are processed should be explicit and legitimate and determined at the time of the collection of the personal data.

45   For good reason, data management protocols, such as the model protocol included as annex D to the article above at note 7 envision the possibility of indemnification of all later controllers or processors by the initial controllers (who by definition set the ground rules for the collection and processing of the personal data). Arbitration institutions are well positioned to acknowledge in their recommendations and institutional rules the primary liability of the parties in the initial collection and processing of data and to include, as a default or on an opt-out basis, an indemnification provision in favour of the other arbitration participants for potential data protection claims.

important the initial data collection is, since proper compliance and full transparency at the time of collection can avoid any requirement that later processors or controllers return to the data subject for consent, or with further disclosures.

5.46 Indeed, one could argue based on the structure of GDPR Articles 13 and 14 that arbitration actors other than the party that made the initial collection of personal data should all be considered processors, and not controllers. The arbitrators, for instance, did not decide to collect the personal data; they did not adopt the procedures for the collection, nor did they have any role in informing the data subject at the time of collection, or in establishing the 'purposes and means' of the personal data processing. Rather, the arbitrators received the personal data from the parties, or from party counsel, with a precise mission that is arguably far removed from the control and processing of data: to use the data (including any personal data provided) for the sole purpose of understanding the parties' factual and legal arguments, and to thereafter draft and issue an award.

5.47 Identifying arbitrators, or other arbitration actors, as something less than controllers would be entirely welcome, ensure predictability and efficiency, and above all avoid cumbersome procedures; an arbitrator receiving a file containing personal data of EU nationals may find it difficult if not entirely impossible to contact data subjects identified in the parties' materials to inform them that their personal details are henceforth part of an arbitration.

5.48 Rather, it should be the party, with verification as needed by the arbitration institution if there is one, to limit, redact, anonymize or pseudonymize the data so that only personal data required for the purposes of the arbitration is sent to the arbitrators. If this is done, a large part of arbitrator compliance with GDPR will be limited to ensuring that the parties and party counsel have taken steps to restrict communication of personal data in the proceedings. To do so, it is useful for the arbitrators to get confirmation from the parties that the documents exchanged in the arbitration will be purged of irrelevant personal data, and that any personal data that is communicated is subject to appropriate confidentiality, security, data minimization and other safeguards consistent with GDPR protections.

5.49 Any other solution that would impose disclosure obligations to the data subject on arbitrators is simply unworkable.

b. *Arbitral institutions*

5.50 The International Chamber of Commerce (ICC) has recently updated its guidance to arbitrators and parties on data protection issues in ICC arbitrations.[46] This guidance seeks to provide full disclosure to all participants that their own data will be used in the arbitration, with guidance to arbitrators to obtain consent of the parties early in the proceedings, and reminds all arbitration participants of their duty to ensure security of all data in their possession during the

---

46   See ICC 'Note to the Parties and Arbitral Tribunals on the Conduct of Arbitration', 1 January 2019, <https://iccwbo.org/content/uploads/sites/3/2017/03/icc-note-to-parties-and-arbitral-tribunals-on-the-conduct-of-arbitration.pdf> accessed 8 June 2020.

arbitration. But the guidance also refers to the more difficult issue of the personal data of third parties that may be communicated with briefs or exhibits of the parties.[47]

Arbitration centres have a central role in assisting the parties, and the arbitrators, organize the communication of information that may include personal data. The institutions are well positioned to assist the parties, many of whom will have data protection officers (DPOs) well-versed in the rules of data protection, but who may have never participated in an arbitration. The institution can inform the parties what data protection rules apply in the arbitration, the nature of the information that the parties should expect to provide and can liaise with the parties' DPO on specific questions. **5.51**

In practice, the institutions should provide an informational checklist to the parties for compliance with GDPR in arbitration, with resources that can be provided to parties that may have a variety of different compliance needs based on their industry, the type of data collected and to be provided in the arbitration, and their existing compliance processes. The resources provided should enable the parties to determine whether it is in compliance with its own data protection obligations to date, and whether a Data Protection Impact Assessment (DPIA)[48] should be prepared in connection with planned arbitral disclosures. **5.52**

The checklist and the resources provided by the institution should assist the parties so that they can later certify to the arbitrators, in the data management protocol, that they are GDPR compliant in the collection and processing of personal data to be used in the arbitration. **5.53**

The institution should also provide resources to arbitrators in the form of model data management protocols that should be raised at a preliminary stage of the arbitration, fully discussed with the parties, and included in the Terms of Reference or similar undertaking signed by the parties.[49] **5.54**

c. *Arbitrators*

Arbitrators should successfully avoid having their principal mission disrupted by extensive compliance obligations under the GDPR if the other parties, and specifically the parties to the arbitration, engage fully in their own compliance efforts as discussed above. **5.55**

The first obligation of the arbitrator should be to ensure that the parties are themselves GDPR compliant; that the initial data collection was done according to GDPR rules; that all processing of such data in preparation for the arbitration was also compliant; that the GDPR rights of the data subject have been respected as from the initial collection. **5.56**

---

47 Ibid., para 85, 13:

Any individual, whose data is collected and processed in the context of an arbitration may at any time request the Secretariat and, as the case may be, the arbitral tribunal to exercise notably his right of access and that inaccurate data be corrected or suppressed, according to the applicable data protection regulations.

48 GDPR, Art 35. The preparation of a DPIA under the GDPR is required where a processing 'is likely to result in a high risk to the rights and freedoms of natural persons ...'.

49 For a model protocol, see Paisley (n 7) 931.

5.57 The second obligation of the arbitrator should be to ensure that the parties continue to be GDPR compliant throughout the arbitration, including if international transfers outside the EU are contemplated, and that they agree to abide by all institutional data protection and security rules in the arbitration. This is more than a representation of the party's past conduct and compliance but is a promise of continuing compliance in the arbitration.

5.58 Data subject rights are better managed by the parties that collected the initial data; for example, a data subject request for the erasure of data collected by a party, but transferred to arbitrators, should in the first instance be considered by the party as the initial controller, which could then consult as needed with the other arbitration actors in the proceeding.

5.59 A few other considerations should lessen considerably the GDPR burden on arbitrators.

5.60 First, the GDPR does not exclude arbitrations, and arbitrators, from its scope of application, although State court judicial functions can be excluded from GDPR compliance by Member States[50] in order to safeguard the independence of the judiciary (i.e., not subject to oversight by an executive agency), and the importance of this separation of powers to the constitutional organization of Member States has been confirmed, at least in France, as an important value.[51] By analogy, as arbitrators have a State-recognized adjudicatory function through the widespread adoption of the New York Convention, there is a good argument that at least certain adjudicatory functions of an arbitral tribunal should be beyond the oversight of any Data Protection Authority.

5.61 Secondly, while the GDPR does not create any specific exceptions for arbitration, nothing in the GDPR excludes any existing EU Member State arbitrator immunities. In France and most EU Member States, courts have developed doctrines of arbitrator immunity that prevent discontented litigants from seeking the liability of the arbitrator for having wrongly, or poorly, decided the matter.[52] This precedent is also confirmed, in ICC arbitrations, by the parties' acceptance that the arbitration award is their sole recourse, to the exclusion of any other claims,[53] and similar declarations are often included in other institutional arbitration rules.

5.62 Finally, arbitrators could look to the example of certain US courts that have appointed a Privacy Monitor, out of deference to EU laws, in order to oversee compliance by the non-EU

---

50 See GDPR, recitals 20 and 23.

51 French Constitutional Court, Decision no 2018-765 DC, 12 June 2018 <https://www.conseil-constitutionnel.fr/decision/2018/2018765DC.htm> accessed 8 June 2020.

52 The UK Arbitration Act of 1996 provides that, '[a]n arbitrator is not liable for anything done or omitted in the discharge or purported discharge of his functions as arbitrator unless the act or omission is shown to have been in bad faith.'; United States Court of Appeals, *Tamari v Conrad*, 12 April 1977, 552 F.2d 778 (7th Cir. 1977) 'the district court correctly dismissed the action because arbitrators are immune from suit with respect to questions involving their authority to resolve a dispute'; Pierre Lalive, 'Sur l'irresponsabilité arbitrale, Etudes de Procédure et d'arbitrage en l'honneur de J.-F. Poudret' (Faculté de Droit de l'Université de Lausanne 1999) 419–35. See generally Thomas Clay, *L'Arbitre* (Dalloz 2001).

53 See ICC Rules of Arbitration, Art 35.6:

> Every award shall be binding on the parties. By submitting the dispute to arbitration under the Rules, the parties undertake to carry out any award without delay and shall be deemed to have waived their right to any form of recourse insofar as such waiver can validly be made.

parties with GDPR requirements.[54] Appointing a monitor brings additional GDPR expertise to the organization of the discovery process, is consistent with the doctrine of international comity, and relieves the arbitration participants of some of the burden, and potentially the liability, of ensuring GDPR compliance.

D. THREATS TO THE ENFORCEABILITY OF THE ARBITRAL AWARD

A larger existential concern resulting from the greater fines and penalties under the GDPR is that the quickly growing body of EU data protection law could potentially interfere with the primary mission of arbitration, which is the issuance by an arbitral panel of binding awards capable of enforcement around the world. The New York Convention provides at Article V for just a few, but critical, exceptions to the enforcement of arbitration awards. In particular, Convention signatories are able to refuse enforcement of arbitration awards that violate public policy.[55] The Convention has been ratified by over 150 states, and so those few exceptions have global significance, as the inability to enforce an award throughout Convention signatories would render the award ineffectual. **5.63**

So the question becomes whether non-compliance with the GDPR in the arbitration proceedings could rise to the level, at the time of an enforcement action, of a violation of public policy. At this stage there is no case law from any signatory country on this issue, but the risk of such a characterization is real, as will be seen from a few examples taken from French case law. **5.64**

For example, an arbitration award issued outside France must be confirmed by the French courts to be enforceable, in a process called 'exequatur'. A complete review of the merits of the award by the French court at the time of enforcement is not allowed. However, an arbitration award will not be enforced 'if the enforcement of the award would shock unacceptably our juridical order, the offence being a manifest violation of an essential rule, or a fundamental principle'.[56] While the specific words used by the French Supreme Court to describe this doctrine has changed over the years, the substance remains, and affords national courts an extensive power of review over international arbitration awards on public policy grounds.[57] **5.65**

---

54 *Lataillade v. LVMH*, Case No. 1:16-cv-06637 (SDNY 2017); *Fortis Advisors v. Sillajen, Inc.*, N18C-09-127 EMD CCLD (Sup. Ct., Del. 2019); *Tiffany v. LVMH*, Case No. 2020-0768 (Chancery Court, Del. 2020); *Allianz Global Investors GMBH, et al. v. Bank of America Corp., et al.*, Case No. 1:18-cv-10364-LGS-SDA (SDNY 2020); *Glass Egg Digital Media Ltd., v. Gameloft Inc.*, Case No. 17-cv-04165-MMC (RMI) (N.D. Cal. 2020); *Gary Northrup v. Covidien LP and Medtronic Inc.*, Case No. 5:2019cv00299 (CD. Cal. 2019).

55 Article V.2:

    Recognition and enforcement of an arbitral award may also be refused if the competent authority in the country where recognition and enforcement is sought finds that:

    [...]

    (b) The recognition or enforcement of the award would be contrary to the public policy of that country.

56 *Thalès Air Defense v GIE Euromissile*, CA Paris, Judgment of 18 November 2004, JCP G [2005] II 10038. See also *SNF v Cytec*, Cass. 1e civ., Judgment of 4 June 2008 (requiring that a violation of international public policy in an arbitration award be 'obvious, effective and concrete' to avoid enforcement).

57 See, Denis Mouralis, 'Conformité des sentences internationales à l'ordre public : la Cour de cassation maintient le principe d'un contrôle limité' (2014) 16–21 *La Semaine Juridique – Édition Générale* 782 ; Cass. Civ. 16-25.657 and 16-26.445, 13 September 2017, 'it is up to the enforcement judge to assess whether recognition and enforcement of the award violates the French conception of international public order'.

5.66   There can even be a heightened level of review when the foreign award or judgment has a particularly close connection to France and affects the rights and interests of French nationals or residents, which could be the case if it was precisely the personal data of French data subjects that had not been properly protected in compliance with the GDRP in the contested arbitration award.[58]

5.67   It is quite possible that a French court could consider that the GDPR reflects essential rules the violation of which could lead to the refusal of arbitration award enforcement. True, the GDPR provides only for administrative fines, but French law modified at the time the GDPR was adopted carries significant criminal penalties for violations of data privacy rules,[59] reflecting the importance of the GDPR regulatory scheme in France.

5.68   National courts may also invoke, to refuse enforcement of an award,[60] the transfer in the arbitration of personal data outside the EU if done at the request of a foreign court, tribunal or administrative authority without complying with applicable international treaties,[61] such as the Hague Evidence Convention.[62] The increasing availability of discovery in international arbitration, especially through court orders from national courts in the US,[63] will create direct conflicts between the US court orders requiring production of documents, and the express transfer prohibitions of GDPR Article 48 and EU Member State blocking statutes. Accordingly, there is a risk that EU Member State national courts could refuse enforcement of

---

58   Patrick Courbe, 'L'ordre public de proximité, Mélanges offertes à Paul Lagarde' (Dalloz 2005) 227; Tristan Azzi, 'Précisions sur l'Ordre Public de Proximité' (2006) *La Semaine Juridique – Édition Générale* 10165.

59   A full list of French criminal law protections of data privacy appears on the site of the French Data Protection Authority <https://www.cnil.fr/fr/les-sanctions-penales> accessed 8 June 2020. For example, processing personal data without implementing the protections contained in Arts 23, 24, 30 and 32 of the GDPR can result in criminal fines up to 300,000 EUR and/or up to five years' imprisonment.

60   See, e.g., *Pierre Chapgier v Taithout Prévoyance*, no 07-11004, Tribunal de Grande Instance, Paris, May 14, 2008 (stating in dicta that a US court judgment obtained using illicit discovery in violation of the Convention would not be enforceable in France).

61   GDPR, Art 48. This provision acts as a 'blocking statute', prohibiting the transfer of personal data outside the EU in response to a court order except through an international treaty, and such blocking statutes often with criminal penalties also exist in EU Member States, such as France (see, Law n°68-678 of 26 July 1968 <https://www.legifrance.gouv.fr/affichTexte.do?cidTexte=JORFTEXT000000501326> accessed 8 June 2020), with criminal sanctions of up to six months' imprisonment and 18,000 EUR in fines. This law was invoked to sanction an attorney seeking discovery outside any treaty procedure for use in US litigation ('Christopher X', Cass. Civ. 2008 n° 07-83228 <https://www.legifrance.gouv.fr/affichJuriJudi.do?idTexte=JURITEXT000017837490> accessed 8 June 2020, although certain US courts do not give much weight to the foreign sovereign interests expressed in such statutes when applying the balancing test set out by the Supreme Court in *Aerospatiale v United States District Court*, 482 U.S. 522 (1987) (District courts have discretion to use Hague Evidence Convention procedures which are optional) (see e.g., *In re Air Cargo Shipping Servs Antitrust Litig*, 278 FRD 51 (EDNY 2010).
      Several courts have already had the opportunity to address the weight to be given the blocking statute provisions of GDPR Art 48 under the Aerospatiale balancing test, with mixed results. Compare *Giorgi Global Holdings v. Wieslaw Smulski*, No. 17-4416, 2020 BL 190347 (E.D.P.A. May 21, 2020) and *Finjan, Inc. v Zscaler, Inc.*, 2019 WL 618554 (N.D. Cal. 2019) with *Morgan Art Foundation Ltd v. McKenzie*, 2019 WL 2725625 (S.D. N.Y. 2019) and *In re Mercedes Benz Emissions Litigation*, 2020 WL 487288 (D. N.J. 2020).

62   The Hague Convention of 18 March 1970, on the Taking of Evidence Abroad in Civil or Commercial Matters, 847 UNST 241 <https://www.hcch.net/en/instruments/conventions/full-text/?cid=82> accessed 8 June 2020.

63   Discovery orders in international arbitration are increasingly available under 28 USC §1782(a). See, *HRC-Hainan Holding Co v Hu* 2020 US Dist LEXIS 32125 (ND Cal 25 February 2020)); see also *Servotronics Inc v Boeing Co* 2020 US App LEXIS 9872 (4th Cir 30 March 2020) and *Abdul Latif Jameel Transp Co v FedEx Corp* 939 F3d 710 (6th Cir 19 September 2019).

international arbitration awards that are based on unlawfully transferred personal data in violation of such rules in application of the public policy exception to enforcement discussed above.

Such a result would be unsatisfactory to any arbitrator, who of course may consider the effect foreign law may have in issuing an enforceable award and this may be added motivation for arbitrators to seek compliance with GDPR in the organization of their proceedings. **5.69**

E. CONCLUSION

The GDPR is a brave new world of EU regulatory compliance with the capacity to confound and confuse even the most well-intentioned arbitrator. The challenge will be for the arbitration participants to work together to incorporate the data protection rules of the GDPR into the norms of traditional arbitration practice so that addressing privacy issues becomes both simple and second nature. **5.70**

If the arbitrators need to pay close attention in order to understand how these new rules will impact the arbitration process without jeopardizing their award, the arbitration institutions must also have a central role in bridging the knowledge gap between the parties, who rely on the collected personal data for their business but who typically know little about arbitration, and the arbitrators who have little experience in data protection but who are motivated by their mission to issue an enforceable arbitration award. **5.71**

6

'CONSUMER PROTECTION' IN INTERNATIONAL ARBITRATION AND EU LAW

Niuscha Bassiri and Emily Hay[1]

A. INTRODUCTION

6.01 Working on the principle that '[c]onfident consumers create thriving markets',[2] consumer protection is a priority for the European Union. The protection of consumers is embedded in the EU treaties,[3] and the EU has pursued Europe-wide policies related to the protection of consumers for decades.[4] Efforts to put consumers at the heart of all EU policies continue to

---

1   The authors would like to thank Beatrice Van Tornout, a former associate at Hanotiau & van den Berg, for her valuable assistance in research for this contribution. Date of submission: 1/6/2020.

2   Letter from the former President of the European Commission, José Manuel Barroso, to the former President of the European Parliament, Jerzy Buzek, 28 September 2011, Memo/11/645 <http://europa.eu/rapid/press-release_MEMO-11-645_en.htm> accessed 1 June 2020.

3   Treaty on the Functioning of the European Union [2012] OJ C 326/47, Art 169(1):

> In order to promote the interests of consumers and to ensure a high level of consumer protection, the Union shall contribute to protecting the health, safety and economic interests of consumers, as well as to promoting their right to information, education, and to organise themselves in order to safeguard their interests.

4   See EU Council Resolution of 14 April 1975 on a preliminary programme of the European Economic Community for a consumer protection and information policy [1975] OJ C 92/1; Preliminary programme of the European Economic Community for a consumer protection and information policy [1975] OJ C 92/2 <https://eur-lex.europa.eu/legal-content/EN/TXT/?uri=OJ:C:1975:092:TOC> accessed 1 June 2020.

this day, under the 'European Consumer Agenda'.[5] In 2018 the EU launched a 'New Deal for Consumers' aimed at strengthening the enforcement of EU consumer law.[6]

The EU's approach to consumer protection touches on international arbitration in several **6.02** ways. Both hard and soft EU law create a number of limits upon the use of arbitration as a method of resolution of business-to-consumer ('B2C') disputes.

In particular, EU law does not look favourably upon pre-dispute arbitration agreements with **6.03** consumers.[7] Arbitration may be considered acceptable where there is (i) a post-dispute agreement to arbitrate; and (ii) the arbitration does not prevent consumers or traders from accessing the judicial system. However, even within these narrow limits, arbitration is not put forward under EU law as the panacea for the resolution of B2C disputes, especially in the online environment.

When dealing with consumer protection and B2C arbitration, it is inevitable that the online **6.04** context is considered. The volume and frequency of B2C transactions that are concluded online, both within and across national borders, leads to the need for appropriate dispute resolution mechanisms to handle the issues that arise. While arbitration rightly prides itself on being a cost-effective, flexible and efficient method of dispute resolution, the formalities involved in rendering a binding and enforceable decision entail costs that are generally disproportionate to the amount at stake in a B2C dispute.

The focus of this chapter is on the intersection between EU law on consumer protection and **6.05** international arbitration. Each national jurisdiction within the EU also has its own specific approach to consumer protection in arbitration. It goes beyond the scope of this chapter to address the specificities of the national context.

In Section B below, we consider some of the substantive provisions of EU law that implicate **6.06** consumer protection, including EU legislation and case law of the European Court of Justice ('ECJ'). Section C addresses in more detail some of the legal and procedural issues in B2C arbitration under EU law. Section D contains the conclusion.

---

5   Communication from the European Commission to the European Parliament, the Council, the Economic and Social Committee and the Committee of the Regions, 'A European Consumer Agenda – Boosting confidence and growth', 22 May 2012, COM(2012) 225 final, <https://eur-lex.europa.eu/legal-content/EN/TXT/PDF/?uri=CELEX: 52012DC0225&from=EN> accessed 1 June 2020.

6   Communication from the Commission to the European Parliament, the Council and the European Economic and Social Committee, 'A New Deal for Consumers', 11 April 2018, COM(2018) 183 final, <https://eur-lex.europa.eu/legal-content/EN/TXT/PDF/?uri=CELEX:52018DC0183&from=EN> accessed 1 June 2020.

7   Council Directive 93/13/EEC of 5 April 1993 on unfair terms in consumer contracts [1993] OJ L95/29 ('Unfair Terms Directive'), Art 3 and Annex para 1(q). See Section B.1.a. below.

B. THE EU LAW APPROACH

6.07 In this section, we will discuss the EU legal framework of consumer protection, with a focus on those 'hard law' areas that touch on international arbitration. We will first examine EU legislation (1), before turning to consider relevant case law of the European Court of Justice (2).

1. EU Legislation

6.08 EU legislation in this field severely limits parties from resorting to consumer arbitration where it relates to a pre-dispute agreement to arbitrate or would limit access to the EU judicial system. Agreements to arbitrate after a dispute has arisen are viewed favourably insofar as they do not exclude a consumer's right to access courts. In this regard, the European Union hosts an online platform which facilitates the resolution of consumer disputes by alternative dispute resolution, including arbitration.[8]

6.09 A recent definition of the term 'consumer' is included in Directive 2019/771 of the European Parliament and the Council of 20 May 2019 on certain aspects concerning contracts for the sale of goods ('Directive 2019/771'):[9]

> The definition of a consumer should cover natural persons who are acting outside their trade, business, craft or profession. However, Member States should also remain free to determine in the case of dual purpose contracts, where the contract is concluded for purposes that are partly within and partly outside the person's trade, and where the trade purpose is so limited as not to be predominant in the overall context of the contract, whether, and under which conditions, that person should also be considered a consumer.

a. Unfair Terms Directive

6.10 Council Directive 93/13/EEC of 5 April 1993 on unfair terms in consumer contracts ('Unfair Terms Directive') regulates contractual terms which are not individually negotiated by the consumer, in particular where there is a pre-formulated standard contract.[10] Such a term will be regarded as unfair 'if, contrary to the requirement of good faith, it causes a significant imbalance in the parties' rights and obligations arising under the contract, to the detriment of the consumer'.[11]

---

8   European Commission, 'Online Dispute Resolution', <https://ec.europa.eu/consumers/odr/main/index.cfm?event= main.home2.show&lng=EN> accessed 1 June 2020. See Directive 2013/11/EU of the European Parliament and of the Council of 21 May 2013 on alternative dispute resolution for consumer disputes and amending Regulation (EC) No 2006/2004 and Directive 2009/22/EC [2013] OJ L165/63 ('Consumer ADR Directive'); Regulation 524/2013 of the European Parliament and of the Council of 21 May 2013 on online dispute resolution for consumer disputes and amending Regulation (EC) No 2006/2004 and Directive 2009/22/EC [2013] OJ L165/1 ('Consumer ODR Regulation').

9   Directive (EU) 2019/771 of the European Parliament and the Council of 20 May 2019 on certain aspects concerning contracts for the sale of goods, amending Regulation (EU) 2017/2394 and Directive 2009/22/EC, and repealing Directive 1999/44/EC [2019] OJ L136/28 ('Directive 2019/771').

10   Unfair Terms Directive (n 7) art 3(2).

11   Ibid., art 3(1).

The Annex to the Unfair Terms Directive contains a list of terms which 'may be regarded as **6.11** unfair'.[12] Paragraph 1(q) identifies, in this regard, terms which have the object or effect of 'excluding or hindering the consumer's right to take legal action or exercise any other legal remedy, particularly by requiring the consumer to take disputes exclusively to arbitration not covered by legal provisions …'.[13] Since the Annex is an 'indicative and non-exhaustive list', it does not purport to definitively invalidate such terms or classify them as prima facie unfair. The assessment of fairness is to be carried out on a case-by-case basis.[14]

The terminology of 'arbitration not covered by legal provisions' is notoriously unclear.[15] It has **6.12** been suggested that it could refer to a procedure without legal safeguards similar to those that apply in court.[16] Other interpretations include that it prohibits decisions on the basis of principles of equity, unfair settlement terms, or uncontrolled freedom of action.[17]

As an EU Directive, this legislation does not have direct effect, but is implemented by **6.13** legislation in each EU Member State. Member States are obliged to lay down in national law that unfair terms shall not be binding on the consumer.[18] In addition, Member States must take necessary measures to ensure that the consumer does not lose the protection of the Unfair Terms Directive by virtue of a choice of law of a non-Member State where the relevant contract has a close connection with the territory of the Member States.[19]

Different EU Member States have taken different approaches to that implementation. In **6.14** France, for example, arbitration agreements cannot be enforced against consumers.[20] In Germany, an arbitration agreement with a consumer must be contained in a separate agreement personally signed by the parties.[21] In Belgium, the law is less strict as it does not

---

12   Ibid., art 3(3).

13   Ibid., Annex, para 1(q).

14   Alexander J Bělohlávek, *B2C Arbitration: Consumer Protection in Arbitration* (Juris Net 2012) 74–5. See, e.g., the *Mostaza Claro* case of the ECJ discussed further below.

15   Gary B. Born, *International Commercial Arbitration* (2nd ed, Kluwer 2014) 1019.

16   Christopher Kuner, 'Legal Obstacles to ADR in European Business-to-Consumer Electronic Commerce', <http://www.kuner.com/data/pay/adr.html> accessed 1 June 2020. See also Bělohlávek (n 14) 76.

17   Bělohlávek (n 14) 77.

18   Unfair Terms Directive (n 7) art 6(1).

19   Ibid., art 6(2).

20   Art 2061 of the French Civil Code (*Code Civil*) provides:

'La clause compromissoire doit avoir été acceptée par la partie à laquelle on l'oppose, à moins que celle-ci n'ait succédé aux droits et obligations de la partie qui l'a initialement acceptée. Lorsque l'une des parties n'a pas contracté dans le cadre de son activité professionnelle, la clause ne peut lui être oppose.

Informal translation:

The arbitration clause must be accepted by the party against which it is invoked, unless the latter has succeeded to the rights and obligations of the party which initially accepted it. To the extent that one party has not contracted in the context of their professional activity, the clause may not be invoked against them.

21   Art 1031(5) of the German Code of Civil Procedure (*Zivilprozeßordnung*) provides:

Schiedsvereinbarungen, an denen ein Verbraucher beteiligt ist, müssen in einer von den Parteien eigenhändig unterzeichneten Urkunde enthalten sein. Die schriftliche Form nach Satz 1 kann durch die elektronische Form nach § 126a des Bürgerlichen Gesetzbuchs ersetzt werden. Andere Vereinbarungen als solche, die sich auf das schiedsrichterliche Verfahren beziehen, darf die Urkunde oder das elektronische Dokument nicht enthalten; dies gilt nicht bei notarieller Beurkundung.

prohibit arbitration clauses in B2C contracts. Rather, only those clauses in a B2C contract which contain a prohibition on consumers seeking redress against traders are considered to be abusive.[22] However, Belgian courts consider that consumers should have a choice between arbitration and litigation and, therefore, tend to invalidate pre-dispute clauses that contain an arbitration clause to the exclusion of the courts.[23]

6.15 The Unfair Terms Directive has been amended by Directive (EU) 2019/2161 of 27 November 2019 of the European Parliament and of the Council of 27 November 2019 amending Council Directive 93/13/EEC and Directives 98/6/EC, 2005/29/EC and 2011/83/EU of the European Parliament and of the Council as regards the better enforcement and modernisation of Union consumer protection rules ('Directive 2019/2161'). It is part and parcel of the 'New Deal for Consumers' initiative. Directive 2019/2161 focusses, in particular, on the changed consumer behaviour of (cross-border) online shopping, but also on the protection of users of social media networks against traders. It aims at strengthening the enforcement of consumer protection laws by simultaneously modernising them. This Directive has to be transposed by 28 November 2021 and applied from 28 May 2022.

b. Consumer ADR Directive

6.16 Directive 2013/11/EU of the European Parliament and of the Council of 21 May 2013 on alternative dispute resolution for consumer disputes and amending Regulation (EC) No 2006/2004 and Directive 2009/22/EC ('Consumer ADR Directive') has as its purpose to ensure: 'that consumers can, on a voluntary basis, submit complaints against traders to entities offering independent, impartial, transparent, effective, fast and fair alternative dispute resolution procedures'.[24]

6.17 The Consumer ADR Directive obliges Member States to facilitate access by consumers to ADR procedures, and to ensure that ADR entities comply with the standards set in the Directive. Those standards relate, inter alia, to (i) the accessibility of ADR procedures online

---

Informal translation:

> Arbitration agreements to which a consumer is a party must be contained in a document which has been personally signed by the parties. The written form pursuant to subsection 1 may be substituted by electronic form pursuant to section 126 a of the Civil Code ('Bürgerliches Gesetzbuch – BGB'). No agreements other than those referring to the arbitral proceedings may be contained in such a document or electronic document; this shall not apply in the case of a notarial certification.

(Translation by translex.org, <https://www.trans-lex.org/600550/_/german-code-of-civil-procedure/#head_9> accessed 1 June 2020.)

22   Art VI.83(22) of the Belgian Economic Code provides:

> Dans les contrats conclus entre une entreprise et un consommateur, sont en tout cas abusives, les clauses et conditions ou les combinaisons de clauses et conditions qui ont pour objet de faire renoncer le consommateur, en cas de conflit, à tout moyen de recours contre l'entreprise.

Informal translation:

> In contracts concluded between businesses and consumers, clauses and conditions or the combination of clauses and conditions that prohibit, in case of a dispute, any means of redress against the trader are abusive.

23   Niuscha Bassiri and Maud Piers, 'Article 1676' in Niuscha Bassiri and Maarten Draye (eds), *Arbitration in Belgium: A Practitioner's Guide* (Kluwer 2016) para 32.
24   Consumer ADR Directive (n 8) art 1.

and offline, either free of charge or for a nominal fee;[25] (ii) the expertise, impartiality and independence of those conducting ADR;[26] and (iii) the fairness of the procedure.[27]

6.18 Importantly for arbitration, an ADR solution may only be binding on the parties if they were informed of its binding nature in advance and specifically accepted this.[28] Moreover, a pre-dispute agreement to submit complaints to an ADR entity is not binding on the consumer if it has the effect of depriving the consumer of their right to bring the dispute before the courts.[29]

6.19 In addition, in terms of the substance of a dispute, binding ADR may not deprive the consumer of the protection of mandatory laws in the consumer's Member State of habitual residence.[30]

6.20 In the EU, the most popular ADR method for solving disputes involving consumers is the ombudsman method. This method of ADR provides for the consumer to make a complaint directly with the trader. If the consumer is not satisfied with the trader's response, the former may escalate the matter to the ombudsman authority. The ombudsman authority will allocate the matter to a case manager at the authority, who will investigate it, including looking into evidence not provided by the complaining consumer. Thereafter, the case manager will first try to facilitate a settlement between the consumer and the trader, failing which the case manager will give a recommendation. If the consumer and the trader cannot agree on the recommendation, the case manager will record this. Pending the ombudsman proceedings, the statutory time limitations are stayed.[31]

6.21 Thus, under the ombudsman method, the role of the facilitator is three-fold: independent investigator, independent settlement facilitator, and independent decision-maker. Given that the ombudsman method is run by a centralised service authority per industry, the know-how is preserved and consistent decisions are the norm.[32]

c. Consumer ODR Regulation

6.22 Linked to the Consumer ADR Directive is Regulation 524/2013 of the European Parliament and of the Council of 21 May 2013 on online dispute resolution for consumer disputes and amending Regulation (EC) No 2006/2004 and Directive 2009/22/EC ('Consumer ODR Regulation').

---

25 Ibid., art 8.
26 Ibid., art 6.
27 Ibid., art 9.
28 Ibid., art 10(2).
29 Ibid., art 10(1).
30 Ibid., art 11.
31 See e.g., the 'Charter des Ombudsdienstes' of the Belgian Federal Agency for Food Safety <http://www.favv-afsca.be/ombudsdienstanbieter/charta/_documents/2009-02-20_Charta-des-Ombudsdienstes_de.pdf> and 'Ombudsdienst für Telekommunikation' in Belgium, Schlichtungsordnung, Fassung vom 9 October 2015 <http://www.ombudsmantelecom.be/de/wie-kann-beschwerde-eingereicht-werden.html?IDC=80> accessed 1 June 2020.
32 Pablo Cortés and Tony Cole, 'Legislating for an Effective and Legitimate System of Online Consumer Arbitration' in Maud Piers and Christian Aschauer (eds), *Arbitration in the Digital Age – The Brave New World of Arbitration* (Cambridge 2018) 238.

6.23 The Consumer ODR Regulation is aimed specifically at the online and cross-border sale of goods and supply of services. It provides for the establishment and operation of a European ODR platform for the online resolution of consumer disputes ('ODR Platform').

6.24 The ODR Platform is an interactive website and free of charge in all official languages of the EU institutions.[33] Consumers and traders are able to choose to submit a complaint to a competent ADR entity that has qualified and is listed under the Consumer ADR Directive. Parties have access to an electronic case management tool, and retain their right to access court.

6.25 Pursuant to the Consumer ODR Regulation, traders established in the EU engaging in online sales or service contracts, and EU online marketplaces, must provide a link to the ODR Platform on their website.[34]

6.26 The EU ODR Platform reported an average of 2000 complaints per month in its first two years of operation.[35] The top three most complained about sectors are (i) airlines (13.73 per cent of complaints); (ii) clothing and footwear (10.78 per cent of complaints); and (iii) information and communication technology goods (6.71 per cent of complaints).[36]

d. Future consumer legislation

6.27 The EU continues to actively monitor online dispute resolution in the context of consumer protection and will undoubtedly pass further legislation in this field. In February 2020, the European Parliament passed a Motion for a Resolution, noting that:[37]

> automated decision-making systems are being used in alternative dispute resolution mechanisms on various digital platforms to resolve disputes between consumers and traders; [and] call[ing] on the Commission to ensure that any upcoming review of Directive 2013/11/EU on alternative dispute resolution for consumer disputes and Regulation (EU) No 524/2013 on online dispute resolution for consumer disputes takes into account the use of automated decision-making and ensures that humans remain in control …

6.28 In terms of access to remedies, on 24 November 2020 the European Parliament endorsed the Representative Action Directive, as part of the New Deal for Consumers. This Directive will require Member States to put in place at least one effective procedural mechanism that allows qualified entities (e.g., consumer organisations or public bodies) to bring class action lawsuits on behalf of consumers.[38] It remains to be seen whether and how other developments regarding the arbitration of mass claims will be impacted by this initiative.

---

33 Consumer ODR Regulation (n 8) art 5.

34 Ibid., art 14.

35 See European Commission, 'Online Dispute Resolution Platform', <https://ec.europa.eu/consumers/odr/resources/public2/documents/trader_info_stats/ODR_Trader_Info_stat_EN.pdf> accessed 1 June 2020.

36 European Commission, 'Reports and Statistics', <https://ec.europa.eu/consumers/odr/main/?event=main.statistics.show> accessed 1 June 2020.

37 European Parliament, Motion for a Resolution, 6 February 2020, B9-0094/2020, <https://www.europarl.europa.eu/doceo/document/B-9-2020-0094_EN.pdf> accessed 1 June 2020, 4.

38 Position of the Council at first reading with a view to the adoption of a Directive of the European Parliament and of the Council on representative actions for the protection of the collective interests of consumers and repealing Directive 2009/22/EC, adopted by the Council on 4 November 2020, Interinstitutional File: 2018/0089(COD).

On the substantive law side, in the framework of the European Commission's Digital Single Market Strategy, the EU has adopted Directive 2019/771, which will apply from 1 January 2022. It focusses on consumer protection by setting common rules for B2C sales contracts concerning the conformity of goods with the contract, remedies in the event of a lack of conformity, modalities to exercise remedies, and commercial guarantees. In its Recital (5), the need for better protection of consumers is based on the fact that: **6.29**

> Technological evolution has led to a growing market for goods that incorporate or are inter-connected with digital content or digital services. Due to the increasing number of such devices and their rapidly growing uptake by consumers, action at Union level is needed in order to ensure that there is a high level of consumer protection and to increase legal certainty as regards the rules applicable to contracts for the sale of such products. Increasing legal certainty would help to reinforce the trust of consumers and sellers.

It is to be seen how this Directive will have an impact on the parties' choice of applicable law in B2C arbitrations. **6.30**

e. Rome I Regulation and Brussels I Regulation

The Regulation (EC) No 593/2008 of the European Parliament and the Council of 17 June 2008 on the law applicable to contractual obligations ('Rome I Regulation') governs the choice of law in the EU.[39] It excludes arbitration agreements from its scope.[40] However, it may still be relevant in the arbitration context by providing consumers with protection in relation to the determination of the governing law of a B2C contract. The default position is that such contracts shall be governed by the law of the country of the consumer's habitual residence.[41] Another governing law may be chosen, as long as it does not deprive the consumer of the protection afforded by mandatory provisions of their country of residence.[42] **6.31**

Regulation (EU) No. 1215/2012 of the European Parliament and of the Council of 12 December 2012 on jurisdiction and the recognition and enforcement of judgments in civil and commercial matters ('Brussels I Regulation') sets out the rules used to determine which courts of EU Member States have jurisdiction in a particular case.[43] The Brussels I Regulation does not apply to 'arbitration'.[44] There are different views possible as to the scope of this exclusion.[45] **6.32**

---

39   Regulation (EC) No 593/2008 of the European Parliament and the Council of 17 June 2008 on the law applicable to contractual obligations (Rome I) [2008] OJ L177/6.

40   Ibid., art 1(2)(e): 'The following shall be excluded from the scope of this Regulation: … (e) arbitration agreements and agreements on the choice of court'.

41   Ibid., art 6(1). There are certain conditions on the applicability of this default position, failing which the applicable law will be determined by arts 3 and 4 of Rome Regulation I, in accordance with art 6(3) thereof.

42   Ibid., art 6(2).

43   Regulation (EU) No. 1215/2012 of the European Parliament and of the Council of 12 December 2012 on jurisdiction and the recognition and enforcement of judgments in civil and commercial matters (recast) [2012] OJ L351/1.

44   Ibid., art 1(2)(d): 'This Regulation shall not apply to: … (d) arbitration'. See also Recital (12) thereof.

45   Robin Morse, 'The Substantive Scope of Application of Brussels I and Rome I: Jurisdiction Clauses, Arbitration Clauses and ADR Agreements' in John Meeusen, Marta Pertegás and Gert Straetmans (eds), *Enforcement of International Contracts in the European Union* (Intersentia 2004) 202; Philip de Ly, 'The Interface Between Arbitration And The Brussels Regulation' (2015) 5 *American University Business Law* Review 485; Neil Dowers and Zheng Sophia Tang, 'Arbitration in EU Jurisdiction Regulation: Brussels I Recast and a New Proposal' (2015) 3 *Groningen Journal of International Law* 125.

6.33 In terms of consumer protection, Article 18(1) of the Brussels I Regulation provides that a consumer may bring proceedings against the other party to a contract either in the courts of the Member State where that other party is domiciled, or in the courts of the place where the consumer is domiciled.[46] Article 19 of the Brussels I Regulation further provides that this right may only be departed from where an agreement: (i) is entered into after a dispute has arisen; (ii) allows the consumer to bring proceedings in other courts; or (iii) is entered into by both parties who are domiciled in the same Member State at the time of conclusion of the contract, and confers jurisdiction on the courts of that Member State.[47]

2. ECJ case law

6.34 The seminal cases of *Mostaza Claro* (2006)[48] and *Asturcom* (2009)[49] decided by the ECJ reinforce the significance of consumer protection in the EU legal order.

6.35 The 1999 decision in *Eco Swiss* should also be mentioned, which laid the groundwork for *Mostaza Claro* by finding that EU law prohibiting anti-competitive agreements may be considered a matter of public policy under the New York Convention on the Enforcement of Foreign Arbitral Awards of 1958 ('New York Convention').[50] The ECJ held that a national court reviewing an arbitration award in the context of an annulment application must annul the award where the court considers that the arbitration award is contrary to the prohibition on anti-competitive agreements in (what is now) Article 101 of the Treaty on the Functioning of the European Union (formerly Art 85(1) of the Treaty Establishing the European Community), in the same way that would be the case for a failure to observe national rules of public policy.[51]

a. Mostaza Claro

6.36 In *Mostaza Claro*, the ECJ considered an arbitration agreement between a consumer and a mobile telephone company. The Spanish referring court stated that there was no doubt that the arbitration agreement included an unfair contractual term and was therefore null and void. However, Ms. Claro did not plead the invalidity of the arbitration agreement during the arbitration proceedings. The question for the ECJ was whether the court hearing the action for the annulment of the arbitration award was required to annul the award if it found that the arbitration agreement contained an unfair term, even when it was not raised by the consumer

---

46 Brussels I Regulation (n 43) art 18(1).

47 Ibid., art 19.

48 Case C-168/05, *Mostaza Claro v Centro Móvil Milenium SL*, Judgment of 26 October 2006, ECLI:EU:C:2006:675.

49 Case C-40/08, *Asturcom Telecomunicaciones SL v Rodríguez Nogueira*, Judgment of 6 October 2009, ECLI:EU:C:2009:615.

50 Case C-126/97, *Eco Swiss China Time Ltd. v Benetton International NV*, Judgment of 1 June 1999, ECLI:EU:C:1999:269, para 39.

51 See ibid., para 37:

> ... where its domestic rules of procedure require a national court to grant an application for annulment of an arbitration award where such an application is founded on failure to observe national rules of public policy, it must also grant such an application where it is founded on failure to comply with the prohibition laid down in Article 85(1) of the Treaty.

See also ibid., para 39.

in the arbitration proceedings.[52] The ECJ held that the national court must annul an award where there was a failure to comply with EU rules of a public policy nature. This includes the mandatory provision of the Unfair Terms Directive, which provides that unfair terms shall not be binding on the consumer.[53] According to the ECJ, the national court is required to make this assessment of its own motion, in order to compensate for the imbalance which exists between the consumer and the seller or supplier.[54]

b. Asturcom

Mostaza Claro was followed by the ECJ's decision in *Asturcom* three years later. It also **6.37** concerned a contract with a consumer for a mobile telephone. However, unlike *Mostaza Claro*, the consumer did not participate in the arbitration proceedings and did not bring an annulment application, so the award had become final and binding. The question for the ECJ arose out of enforcement proceedings brought by Asturcom against the consumer.

The referring court found that the arbitration clause in the contract was unfair, because (i) the **6.38** costs incurred by the consumer in travelling to the seat of the arbitration were greater than the amount at issue in the dispute; (ii) the seat was located at a considerable distance from the consumer's place of residence; (iii) the seat was not indicated in the contract; and (iv) the institution at the seat drew up the contracts, which were used by the telecommunications providers.[55] The referring court asked the ECJ whether it should determine whether the arbitration agreement was void due to an unfair term and annul the award of its own motion, where the award was made in the absence of the consumer.[56]

The ECJ reiterated that Article 6(1) of the Unfair Terms Directive is a mandatory provision, **6.39** and stated that it must be regarded as having equal rank as national rules of public policy.[57] Therefore, in circumstances where a national court is seized of an action for enforcement and would be required (under domestic rules of procedure) to assess of its own motion whether an arbitration clause is in conflict with domestic rules of public policy, it is also obliged to assess of its own motion whether the arbitration clause is unfair under Article 6 of the Unfair Terms Directive.[58]

C. LEGAL AND PROCEDURAL ISSUES IN B2C ARBITRATION UNDER EU LAW

B2C arbitrations do not fit the neat picture of two freely consenting parties to the resolution of **6.40** a dispute for several reasons. Consumers often have little bargaining power with sellers or suppliers, meaning that they are not able to negotiate the terms on which goods are sold or services are supplied. A typical consumer does not have access to the same information as the seller or supplier about the terms they have agreed, including the legal implications thereof. Consumers also often have less resources at their disposal to address a dispute that does arise.

---

52 *Mostaza Claro* (n 48) para 20.
53 Ibid., paras 34, 36.
54 Ibid., para 38.
55 *Asturcom* (n 49) para 25.
56 Ibid., para 27.
57 Ibid., paras 51–52.
58 Ibid., para 53.

Businesses, on the other hand, have drafted their standard terms and conditions taking into account their own interests, and are likely to be 'repeat players' with greater familiarity with dispute resolution mechanisms.[59]

6.41 EU law attempts to compensate for the 'weaker position' of consumers by providing protections that 're-establish the equality' between them.[60] In practice, these limitations constrain the use of arbitration as a method of resolving B2C disputes in Europe.

6.42 In our view, while the EU law approach can be burdensome, on balance it is the right one. If the result of consumer protection laws in the EU is that there are limited options to pursue arbitration of B2C disputes, then it may not be the appropriate method of dispute resolution for this circumstance. From the consumer perspective, it is important to have a procedure that is accessible, simple, fast, effective, and low cost.[61] Consumers have to fully comprehend what kind of a procedure they have entered into, which is not evident in the case of arbitration. A survey in the US revealed the lack of consumer understanding of arbitration agreements; of the respondent consumers who believed that they had never concluded an arbitration clause 87 per cent had in fact entered into an arbitration agreement.[62] In jurisdictions where consumer arbitration is of little legal concern, there is no pretending that consumer protection is not neglected.

6.43 In the EU, another angle of criticism has to be taken into account when considering the future of B2C arbitration: current negative public opinion regarding investment arbitration. While commercial arbitration might have so far received an unwritten carve-out from this public sentiment, it appears rather doubtful to anticipate sympathies in favour of B2C arbitration, in particular, since consumer protection is equally of concern to those actors opposing investment arbitration.

6.44 These various issues, as well as the legal and procedural matters relevant to B2C arbitration identified below, lead to the conclusion that while arbitration can be flexible and cost-efficient compared to court litigation, it is not a natural fit for the specific needs of B2C disputes under EU law. Other methods of solving consumer disputes are the popular ombudsman method explained above. Suggestions have also been made to consider industry-specific online adjudication with non-binding decisions for consumer disputes, which appear to be similar to the ombudsman method.

---

59 Born (n 15) 1024; Llewellyn Joseph Gibbons, 'Creating a Market for Justice; a Market Incentive Solution to Regulating the Playing Field: Judicial Deference, Judicial Review, Due Process, and Fair Play in Online Consumer Arbitration' (2002–2003) 23 *Northwestern Journal of International Law and Business* 1, 13.

60 See *Mostaza Claro* (n 48) para 26; *Asturcom* (n 49) para 30.

61 Mirèze Philippe, 'ODR Redress System for Consumer Disputes: Clarifications, UNCITRAL Works & EU Regulation on ODR' (2014) 1 *Journal of Online Dispute Resolution* 57, 61. See also Born (n 15) 1024.

62 Jeff Sovern, Elayne E Greenberg, Paul F Kirgis and Yuxiang Liu, '"Whimsy Little Contracts" with Unexpected Consequences: An Empirical Analysis of Consumer Understanding of Arbitration Agreements' (2015) 75 *Maryland Law Review* 1, 1.

1. Differences across jurisdictions

Early in the new millennium, it was easier to believe that the internet was, or would become, a **6.45** domain beyond national borders and regulation.[63] In reality, national sovereignty has remained important to governance of the internet, with different nations and regions (such as the EU) asserting regulatory power over their corner of cyberspace. In this regard, the limitations upon B2C arbitration under EU law can be contrasted with other jurisdictions such as the US, which takes a market-based approach to consumer protection. In the US, mandatory recourse to arbitration is not generally an issue.[64] Being a more convenient dispute resolution procedure for many companies, arbitration is a common feature of B2C online terms and conditions in the US.

Many commentators criticise the US approach for providing inadequate protection to con- **6.46** sumers.[65] Others find the EU approach to be too heavy-handed, and open to abuse by consumers. As one author put it, 'consumer protection in practice often borders on the unbearable'.[66]

These differences can also be seen in the efforts of UNCITRAL from 2010 to 2016 to create a **6.47** global system of online dispute resolution for cross-border e-commerce disputes in both the B2C and business-to-business ('B2B') settings. Working Group III, whose task was to provide recommendations on ODR regarding e-commerce disputes involving consumer and commercial cases, completed its work with the issuance of mere non-binding 'Technical Notes on Online Dispute Resolution'. The Technical Notes contain a series of provisions about a neutral facilitating settlement; arbitration is not provided for, and UNCITRAL did not achieve the original objective of a global system.[67] The discussions stumbled upon the issue of B2C arbitration, where approaches to pre-dispute B2C consumer arbitration agreements across different jurisdictions could not be reconciled.[68]

Differences in regulation across countries and regions pose compliance challenges for com- **6.48** panies in various areas, of which consumer protection is only one. The result is that companies often have to adapt their standard terms and conditions provided to consumers to take account of such laws.

---

63   See Karen Sewart and Joseph Matthews, 'Online Arbitration of Cross-border, Business To Consumer Disputes' (2002) 56 *University of Miami Law Review* 1111, 1120.
64   Karolina Mania, 'American and European Perspectives on Arbitration Agreement in Online Consumer Contracts' (2019) 36 *Journal of International Arbitration* 659; Gabrielle Kaufmann-Kohler and Thomas Schultz, *Online Dispute Resolution: Challenges for Contemporary Justice* (Kluwer 2004) 178; Imre S Szalai and Judge John D Wessel, 'The Prevalence of Consumer Arbitration Agreements by America's Top Companies' (2019) 522 *UC Davis Law Review Online* 233, 235.
65   See e.g., Cortés and Cole (n 32) 225; Mania, ibid., 670.
66   Bělohlávek (n 14) 124.
67   The Working Group's materials can be found at <https://uncitral.un.org/en/working_groups/3/online_dispute> accessed 1 June 2020. The Technical Notes are available at <https://www.uncitral.org/pdf/english/texts/odr/V1700382_English_Technical_Notes_on_ODR.pdf> accessed 1 June 2020.
68   UNCITRAL, 'Report of Working Group III (Online Dispute Resolution) on the work of its thirty-third session', 11 March 2016, A/CN.9/868, available at <https://undocs.org/en/a/cn.9/868> accessed 1 June 2020, para 34. See Nadine Lederer, 'The UNCITRAL Technical Notes on Online Dispute Resolution – Paper Tiger or Game Changer?' (Kluwer Arbitration Blog, 11 January 2018) <http://arbitrationblog.kluwerarbitration.com/2018/01/11/new-found-emphasis-institutional-arbitration-india/> accessed 1 June 2020.

2. Validity of the arbitration agreement

6.49   The special status of consumers under EU law means that consideration must be given to whether the arbitration agreement constitutes an unfair contractual term. Under EU law, such a term is not enforceable against the consumer. The primary question is whether the arbitration agreement has the object or effect of 'excluding or hindering the consumer's right to take legal action or exercise any other legal remedy, particularly by requiring the consumer to take disputes exclusively to arbitration not covered by legal provisions ...'.[69] It may also be relevant to consider whether the arbitration agreement irrevocably binds the consumer 'to terms with which he had no real opportunity of becoming acquainted before the conclusion of the contract'.[70]

6.50   The unenforceability of an unfair contractual term is a mandatory rule of law. In order to be satisfied of their own jurisdiction and in the interests of the enforceability of an award, arbitral tribunals should therefore closely examine the validity of a B2C arbitration agreement. As per the ECJ's decision in *Mostaza Claro*, the assessment of whether the arbitration agreement is an unfair term should be carried out by the tribunal of its own motion, even if it is not raised by the consumer.[71] Moreover, the determination of whether there is an unfair term must be considered in light of the particular circumstances of the case.[72]

6.51   While B2C arbitration agreements are not prohibited outright by the Unfair Terms Directive, it remains a challenge to establish the existence of a valid arbitration agreement with a consumer. Moreover, for the precise conditions under which a B2C arbitration agreement will be held to be an unfair contractual term, it is necessary to consult the provisions of national law. The Unfair Terms Directive has been implemented by Member States, with variations in approach across jurisdictions. It is also important to keep in mind that some Member States have different regimes that apply to domestic and international arbitrations, that may impact upon the validity of the arbitration agreement in question.[73] For these reasons, and since businesses have an interest in taking a harmonised approach as far as possible, B2C arbitration clauses are rare in the EU.

6.52   National variations in the EU that apply different levels of restriction or formal requirements on B2C arbitration agreements are another obstacle to their use in practice.

6.53   For example, Section 1031(5) of the German Code of Civil Procedure requires that pre-dispute and post-dispute B2C arbitration agreements are recorded in a separate arbitration agreement or sufficiently segregated and individually signed in order to be upheld.[74] This form

---

69   Unfair Terms Directive (n 7), Annex, para 1(q).

70   Ibid., para 1(i). Where the Directive 2000/31/EC/ of the European Parliament and of the Council of 8 June 2000 on certain legal aspects of information society services, in particular electronic commerce, in the Internal Market (Directive on electronic commerce) [2000] OJ L178/1 applies, it may also be relevant to consider its requirements on mandatory consumer information.

71   *Mostaza Claro* (n 48) para 38.

72   Ibid., para 22.

73   Born (n 15) 1020.

74   Art 1031(5) of the German Code of Civil Procedure provides:

requirement can, in case of non-compliance, be cured by appearance at the arbitral oral hearing, pursuant to Article 1031(6) of the German Civil Procedure.[75] However, the allowance for objections to the form requirement up to the time of the oral hearing appears to be in contradiction with Article 1040(2) of the German Civil Procedure, which requires that any objections to the jurisdiction of the tribunal have to be raised at the latest with the statement of defence.[76] Therefore, it is recommended that consumers should raise objections regarding the lack of jurisdiction of the tribunal no later than with their statement of defence, failing which they might be considered precluded from raising such objections. When solving the conflict between Articles 1031(6) and 1040(2) of the German Code of Civil Procedure, courts should give preference to the rights of the consumer and apply the more generous rule, i.e., to be able to raise objections also after the statement of defence.

Unfair contractual terms for consumers could be considered invalid under German law if the arbitration agreement is in a standard form, which is surprising or places the consumer at an unreasonable disadvantage in accordance with Sections 305 et seq. of the German Civil Code. Examples of surprise or disadvantageous terms are the option of the trader to choose between arbitration or court proceedings, or where the seat of arbitration is in a foreign country.[77] German law does not, however, consider B2C arbitration agreements in standard forms per se **6.54**

Schiedsvereinbarungen, an denen ein Verbraucher beteiligt ist, müssen in einer von den Parteien eigenhändig unterzeichneten Urkunde enthalten sein. Die schriftliche Form nach Satz 1 kann durch die elektronische Form nach § 126a des Bürgerlichen Gesetzbuchs ersetzt werden. Andere Vereinbarungen als solche, die sich auf das schiedsrichterliche Verfahren beziehen, darf die Urkunde oder das elektronische Dokument nicht enthalten; dies gilt nicht bei notarieller Beurkundung.

Informal translation:

Arbitration agreements to which a consumer is a party must be contained in a document which has been personally signed by the parties. The written form pursuant to subsection 1 may be substituted by electronic form pursuant to Section 126a of the Civil Code. No agreements other than those referring to the arbitral proceedings may be contained in such a document or electronic document; this shall not apply in the case of a notarial certification.

75 Art 1031(6) of the German Code of Civil Procedure provides: 'Der Mangel der Form wird durch die Einlassung auf die schiedsgerichtliche Verhandlung zur Haupsache geheilt.' Informal translation: 'Any non-compliance with the form requirements is cured by entering into argument on the substance of the dispute in the arbitral proceedings.' Non-compliance with formal requirements may, in general, be cured already by filing a submission prior to the oral hearing without raising jurisdictional objections (see OLG Schleswig (2000) *Recht der Internationalem Wirtschaft* (RIW), 707).

76 Art 1040(2) of the German Code of Civil Procedure provides:

Die Rüge der Unzuständigkeit des Schiedsgerichts ist spätestens mit der Klagebeantwortung vorzubringen. Von der Erhebung einer solchen Rüge ist eine Partei nicht dadurch ausgeschlossen, dass sie einen Schiedsrichter bestellt oder an der Bestellung eines Schiedsrichters mitgewirkt hat. Die Rüge, das Schiedsgericht überschreite seine Befugnisse, ist zu erheben, sobald die Angelegenheit, von der dies behauptet wird, im schiedsrichterlichen Verfahren zur Erörterung kommt. Das Schiedsgericht kann in beiden Fällen eine spätere Rüge zulassen, wenn die Partei die Verspätung genügend entschuldigt.

Informal translation:

A plea that the arbitral tribunal does not have jurisdiction shall be raised not later than the submission of the statement of defence. A party is not precluded from raising such a plea by the fact that he has appointed, or participated in the appointment of, an arbitrator. A plea that the arbitral tribunal is exceeding the scope of its authority shall be raised as soon as the matter alleged to be beyond the scope of its authority is raised during the arbitral proceedings. The arbitral tribunal may, in either case, admit a later plea if it considers that the party has justified the delay.

77 German Supreme Court (BGH), Order of 24 September 1998 – III ZR 133/97.

invalid, as Section 1031(5) of the German Code of Civil Procedure mentioned above does not condition validity on B2C arbitration agreements being individually negotiated.

6.55 Together with national law, some guidance on unfairness can be drawn from the ECJ case of *Océano Grupo*, which dealt with whether a choice of court term was contrary to the Unfair Terms Directive. While not directly concerning arbitration, it may be relevant insofar as the Court decided that an exclusive jurisdiction clause that has not been individually negotiated, and that confers jurisdiction on a court where the seller or supplier has its place of business, must be regarded as unfair 'in so far as it causes, contrary to the requirement of good faith, a significant imbalance in the parties' rights and obligations arising under the contract, to the detriment of the consumer'.[78]

6.56 In the assessment of the balance in the parties' rights and obligations, it is relevant to consider, among other things, (i) whether the arbitration agreement was entered into before or after the dispute arose; and, if so, (ii) whether the arbitration agreement has the effect of depriving the consumer of their right to bring an action before the courts to settle the dispute. Under the Consumer ADR Directive, a B2C agreement to submit a complaint to an ADR entity (i.e., including an arbitral institution) is not binding on the consumer if it was entered into before the dispute arose and would deprive them of the right to go to court.[79] This reflects the 'principle of liberty' set out in the EU Commission's 1998 Recommendation on the principles applicable to the bodies responsible for out-of-court settlement of consumer disputes ('Commission Recommendation').[80] The Consumer ODR Regulation likewise includes a recital stating that ODR should not 'prevent parties from exercising their right of access to the judicial system'.[81]

6.57 The difficulty is that a valid arbitration agreement typically precludes parties from seeking to resolve the same dispute before a court. In the case of a foreign award to which the New York Convention applies, where a recognised arbitration agreement exists, a national court is required to refer the parties to arbitration if any of them request, 'unless it finds that the said agreement is null and void, inoperative or incapable of being performed'.[82]

6.58 Some question the wisdom of an approach which would invalidate all pre-dispute B2C arbitration agreements, both due to incompatibility with the New York Convention regime,[83] and the loss of predictability in a system relying on post-dispute agreements.[84] The assumption that an arbitration agreement is less favourable to a consumer than retaining the right to access court can also be questioned, depending on the type of arbitration procedure.[85] However, EU

---

78 Joined Cases C-240/98-C-244/98, *Océano Grupo Editorial SA v Rocío Murciano Quintero and Salvat Editores SA v José M Sánchez Alcón Prades and Others*, Judgment of 27 June 2000, ECLI:EU:C:2000:346, para 24. See Kaufmann-Kohler and Schultz (n 64) 176.

79 Consumer ADR Directive (n 8) art 10(1).

80 Commission Recommendation 98/257/EC of 30 March 1998 on the principles applicable to the bodies responsible for out-of-court settlement of consumer disputes [1998] OJ L115/31.

81 Consumer ODR Regulation (n 8) rec 26.

82 Convention on the Recognition and Enforcement of Foreign Arbitral Awards (opened for signature 10 June 1958, entered into force 7 June 1959) 330 UNTS 4 ('New York Convention'), art II(3).

83 Born (n 15) 1023.

84 Sewart and Matthews (n 63) 1136.

85 Kaufmann-Kohler and Schultz (n 64) 177.

law prioritises the liberty of consumers, and on this basis constrains arbitration insofar as it prevents a consumer from taking their dispute to court.

The requirement under EU consumer law for a post-dispute arbitration clause might also be **6.59** considered outdated in light of the New York Convention, which had, in 1958, been considered revolutionary for treating submission agreements and arbitration clauses equally. A post-dispute agreement to arbitrate could be classed as a submission agreement. At the beginning of the last century, arbitration clauses were considered problematic, precisely for the same reasons that pre-dispute B2C arbitration clauses are considered invalid under EU law.

The evaluation of whether there is a significant imbalance in the parties' rights and obligations, **6.60** as per the *Océano* case, should also take into account the fairness and effectiveness of the proceedings, in light of the remaining principles set out in the Commission Recommendation (see Section C.5 below).

3. Enforcement and public policy

Insofar as a B2C arbitration award is later sought to be enforced or is challenged as a foreign **6.61** award under the New York Convention, the ECJ's public policy considerations play an important role under Article V(2)(b) of the New York Convention.[86] Another relevant ground for challenging a B2C award or its enforcement is the invalidity of the arbitration agreement.[87]

As set out above, in the case of *Asturcom*, the ECJ decided that Article 6 of the Unfair Terms **6.62** Directive must be regarded as a provision 'of equal standing to national rules which rank, within the domestic legal system, as rules of public policy'.[88] The somewhat cryptic language of the judgment appears carefully worded to ascribe the desired legal value without going so far as to definitively classify consumer protection as a matter of public policy. According to some, the ECJ did not decide that consumer protection is a component of EU public policy.[89] Bělohlávek is of the view that the ECJ uses the term 'public policy' in the context of consumer protection but really means 'a specific *public interest* expressed through ... *overriding mandatory rules*'.[90] It is true that the ECJ ascribed the equal standing to Article 6 of the Unfair Terms Directive on the basis of 'the nature and importance of the public interest underlying the protection which [the Unfair Terms Directive] confers on consumers'.[91]

---

86 New York Convention, art V(2)(b) provides: 'Recognition and enforcement of an arbitral award may also be refused if the competent authority in the country where recognition and enforcement is sought finds that ... (b) The recognition and enforcement of the award would be contrary to the public policy of that country.'

87 New York Convention, art V(1)(a) provides:

Recognition and enforcement of the award may be refused, at the request of the party against whom it is invoked, only if that party furnishes to the competent authority where the recognition and enforcement is sought, proof that: (a) The parties to the agreement referred to in article II were, under the law applicable to them, under some incapacity, or the said agreement is not valid under the law to which the parties have subjected it or, failing any indication thereon, under the law of the country where the award was made ... .

88 *Asturcom* (n 49) para 52.

89 Bělohlávek (n 14) 391.

90 Ibid., 33.

91 *Asturcom* (n 49) para 52.

6.63 In practice, the nuance of the ECJ's wording is lost, in that consumer protection is commonly understood as part of 'European public policy'.[92] Moreover, whether formally classified as public policy or not, the same result is achieved, since equal ranking enables the review of a B2C arbitration award whenever public policy may be considered. This equation of consumer protection with public policy offered a convenient solution to the ECJ, as it guaranteed enforcement of consumer protection policy. Unlike other potentially more suitable grounds for challenging non-compliance with consumer protection, matters of public policy may be raised at any time, and by the court's own motion, under many national laws.[93]

6.64 In light of the *Mostaza Claro* and *Asturcom* decisions, domestic arbitral awards rendered in an EU Member State may be reviewed for compliance with Article 6 of the Unfair Terms Directive where national rules allow review for public policy.

6.65 Insofar as a B2C arbitration award with a legal seat in the EU is later sought to be enforced or is challenged as a foreign award under the New York Convention, another EU national court may consider whether the recognition or enforcement of the award would be 'contrary to the public policy of that country', including mandatory consumer protection EU laws, as per Article V(2)(b) of the Convention.[94] It should be noted that this will depend on national law and, in particular, the interpretation of Article V(2)(b) of the New York Convention by the courts in that jurisdiction.

4. Arbitrability of subject matter

6.66 Arbitrability requires that the subject matter is capable of settlement by arbitration, in the sense that national law forbids or restricts the ability to arbitrate certain types of dispute.[95] B2C disputes are, in principle, arbitrable under EU law, which does not have a blanket prohibition on B2C arbitration agreements.[96] This is supported by the *Mostaza Claro* and *Asturcom* decisions above, which held that it is for the national court to define the concept of unfair term, which must be considered in the particular circumstances of the case.[97] The fact that a determination is required demonstrates that B2C disputes are not inarbitrable.[98]

6.67 National law may place restrictions on the arbitrability of B2C disputes, or certain classes of such disputes, but this limitation does not derive from EU law.[99] For example, a codified non-arbitrability of the subject-matter is explicitly set out in Article 1030(2) of the German

---

92 See e.g., Dirk Otto and Omaia Elwan, 'Article V(2)' in Herbert Kronke, Patricia Nacimiento, Dirk Otto and Nicola Christine Port (eds), *Recognition and Enforcement of Foreign Arbitral Awards: A Global Commentary on the New York Convention* (Kluwer 2010) 384.

93 Maud Piers, 'Consumer Arbitration in the EU' (2011) 2 *Journal of International Dispute Settlement* 209, 225–27.

94 New York Convention, art V(2)(b).

95 Born (n 15) 948.

96 Gabrielle Kaufmann-Kohler, 'Online Dispute Resolution and its Significance for International Commercial Arbitration' in Gerald Aksen, Karl-Heinz Böckstiegel, Michael J Mustill, Paolo Michele Patocchi and Anne Marie Whitesell (eds), *Global Reflections on International Law, Commerce and Dispute Resolution: Liber Amoricum in Honour of Robert Briner* (ICC 2005) 444.

97 *Mostaza Claro* (n 48) paras 22–23; *Asturcom* (n 49) para 53.

98 Kaufmann-Kohler and Schultz (n 64) 171.

99 Ibid., 172.

Code of Civil Procedure regarding disputes on the existence of a lease of residential accommodation.[100]

Arbitrability is therefore not a primary consideration in terms of consumer protection under EU law. **6.68**

5. Principles for the conduct of proceedings

Issued in 1998, the Commission Recommendation covers all kinds of procedures which resolve a dispute 'through the active intervention of a third party, who proposes or imposes a solution'. Such solutions may be binding or may be settlement proposals.[101] The Recommendation provides that bodies responsible for the out-of-court settlement of consumer disputes should respect the principles of: (i) independence; (ii) transparency; (iii) adversarial procedure; (iv) effectiveness; (v) legality; (vi) liberty; and (vii) the right to be represented or assisted by a third party. **6.69**

Several of these principles are important for potential B2C arbitrations in the EU. While the Commission Recommendation itself is not binding, the principles it defines have inspired the provisions of hard law on these issues, as per the Consumer ADR Directive and the Consumer ODR Regulation. Moreover, the principles serve to shape views of validity and acceptability of certain types of arbitration agreement in national practice.[102] **6.70**

Taking the Commission Recommendation together with the legislation and case law set out in Section B above, there are a number of relevant principles to take into account for the conduct of B2C arbitral proceedings. Most of these principles apply to all types of arbitration, but are of particular relevance in the B2C context, due to the imbalance between the parties. **6.71**

a. Independence and impartiality

The first principle in the Commission Recommendation is of 'independence of the decision-making body … to guarantee the impartiality of its actions'.[103] Individuals acting as decision-makers must have: (i) the necessary abilities, experience and competence required to carry out their function; (ii) a period of office of sufficient duration to ensure independence; and (iii) if appointed by a company or a professional association, they must not have worked for that company (or the professional association or another member of the association) during the previous three years.[104] **6.72**

---

100 Otto and Elwan (n 92) 360. Art 1030(2) of the German Code of Civil Procedure provides: 'Eine Schiedsvereinbarung über Rechtsstreitigkeiten, die den Bestand eines Mietverhältnisses über Wohnraum im Inland betreffen, ist unwirksam. Dies gilt nicht, soweit es sich um Wohnraum der in § 549 Abs. 2 Nr. 1 und 3 des Bürgerlichen Gesetzbuchs bestimmten Art handelt.' The English translation reads: 'An arbitration agreement relating to disputes on the existence of a lease of residential accommodation within Germany shall be null and void. This does not apply to residential accommodation as specified in § 549 subsection 2 numbers (1) to (3) Civil Code.'

101 Commission Recommendation (n 80), recs.

102 Piers (n 93) 215.

103 Commission Recommendation (n 80) principle I.

104 Ibid.

6.73   In the context of B2C arbitration, one of the most difficult questions is the funding of the arbitration procedure, due to the small amounts at stake and the need to keep costs to an absolute minimum. Companies may have an interest in financing the dispute resolution body, in order to provide customers with reassurance. This means that industry selects the pool of arbitrators, and remunerates them, and these decision-makers often deal with dozens of cases at once. These combined factors can raise questions about the independence of decision-makers.[105]

b.   Transparency of procedures

6.74   Transparency is an aspect of the fairness of proceedings. It is especially important that consumers, perceived as the weaker party, are properly informed about arbitral proceedings that they agree to. Transparency requires, among other things, providing information about disputes that may be submitted to a particular body, and the rules governing the procedure, disclosure of potential costs, and the legal force of the decision.[106]

c.   Effectiveness

6.75   The effectiveness of arbitration is premised upon the binding nature of the resulting award, and the enforceability of that award with the same value as a court judgment.[107] A necessary part of producing a binding and enforceable outcome involves respecting certain formalities and principles of due process. These procedures entail time and costs that may be lower than those associated with court proceedings, but insufficiently low to be appealing for consumers. For example, initiating an arbitration claim often involves filing fees, time to draft submissions (or legal fees if represented), and hearings may take place at the legal seat of the proceeding, which may involve travel and further costs for the consumer.[108] Depending on the amount at stake, a simple cost-benefit analysis will often deter a claim.

6.76   From the consumer perspective, effectiveness may mean that dispute resolution is accessible online and across borders, and is simple, fast, and preferably at no cost.[109] In this regard, the Commission Recommendation sets out that in terms of consumer ADR procedures, effectiveness is ensured by a number of factors, including that the procedure is 'free of charges or of moderate costs', and that 'only short periods elapse between the referral of a matter and the decision'.[110] In line with this principle, the Consumer ADR Directive provides that ADR procedures should preferably be free of charge for the consumer. If costs are applied, they should not exceed a nominal fee in order that the procedure is 'accessible, attractive and inexpensive for consumers'.[111]

6.77   The necessary formalities involved in creating a binding award bring arbitration into tension with some of the essential elements of effectiveness of B2C dispute resolution mechanisms. There is the need for speedy resolution of the dispute on the one hand, and the need to respect

---

105   Kaufmann-Kohler (n 96) 452; Philippe Gilliéron, 'From Face-to-Face to Screen-to-Screen: Real Hope or True Fallacy?' (2008) 23 *Ohio State Journal on Dispute Resolution* 301, 319.
106   Commission Recommendation (n 80) principle II.
107   Kaufmann-Kohler and Schultz (n 64) 33.
108   Born (n 15) 1024; Bĕlohlávek (n 14) 381–2.
109   Philippe (n 61) 61. See also Born (n 15) 1024.
110   Commission Recommendation (n 80) principle IV.
111   Consumer ADR Directive (n 8) rec 41.

due process on the other.[112] Likewise, the measures of effectiveness under a traditional view of arbitration may hold less value to a consumer. Enforceability across international borders is one such factor. If the consumer has to go to court to enforce an arbitration award (and possibly in another jurisdiction), the effectiveness of the dispute resolution process will have largely been defeated.[113]

6. Challenges in the online context

As mentioned above, a defining characteristic of consumer protection in the past 20 years, and looking ahead to the future, is the proliferation of online B2C transactions. Due to the scale of online purchases by consumers, often across national borders, there is a strong need for efficient and effective means of resolving disputes arising from such transactions.[114]   **6.78**

While this chapter is focussed on consumer protection under EU law, there are a number of other limitations on B2C arbitration in the online context that are relevant to the fate of B2C arbitration in the EU.   **6.79**

Further issues to consider in the online context include: **6.80**

- Issues associated with obtaining electronic consent, in particular in relation to the requirement under the New York Convention that an arbitration agreement be 'in writing'.[115] National laws on the recognition of electronic consent may vary.
- The requirement to have original hard copies of an arbitral award, under the New York Convention and potentially national law.[116] This requirement adds extra cost in an already stretched situation.

Amongst those advocating for online B2C arbitration are also voices calling for a reform of the regulatory framework. The current regulatory framework for arbitration, whether online or offline, is tailored for commercial arbitration. In online arbitration, the imbalance that exists between consumers and traders can quickly translate into abusive practices.   **6.81**

A notable suggestion for workable online consumer arbitration contains the following four elements combining protection with security and efficiency: (i) total ban on pre-dispute B2C arbitration agreements to avoid the lack of equal arms and resources; (ii) possibility for the consumer to withdraw from arbitration at any time until the issuance of the award due to the lack of comprehension of the process and consequences for the consumer; (iii) enforceability of awards only if the arbitration is administered by a certified arbitration provider for credibility and due process purposes; and (iv) publication of anonymised awards for consistency and settlement purposes.[117]   **6.82**

---

112   Kaufmann-Kohler and Schultz (n 64) 32.
113   Sewart and Matthews (n 63) 1139.
114   Sewart and Matthews (n 63) 1111.
115   New York Convention, art II.
116   Ibid., art IV.
117   Cortés and Cole (n 32) 242–5. See also Amy J Schmitz, 'Building on OArb Attributes in Pursuit of Justice' in Piers and Aschauer (eds) (n 32).

7. Suitability of other dispute resolution mechanisms in the online environment

6.83 As foreseen by Kaufmann-Kohler and Schultz in 2005, while awareness of the benefits of online dispute resolution has spread, arbitration does not play a significant role as a dispute resolution mechanism in the B2C context, as compared to ombudsmen, mediation, negotiation, and 'non-binding' arbitration.[118]

6.84 The creation of the EU's ODR Platform is a case in point. While the ODR Platform lists various dispute resolution providers including for conciliation, mediation, and arbitration, options for arbitration are dwarfed by other mechanisms. While EU law places strong restrictions on B2C arbitration, the Consumer ODR Regulation recognises the benefits that alternative dispute resolution can present for resolving B2C disputes, especially in the online environment.

6.85 Another factor in favour of non-arbitration mechanisms is that dispute resolution providers listed on the ODR Platform must comply with the requirements of the Consumer ODR Regulation and Consumer ADR Directive,[119] which include that: (i) physical presence of the parties or their representatives may not be required, unless the parties agree;[120] (ii) the outcome of the procedure should be available within 90 days, with extensions possible only for 'highly complex disputes';[121] and (iii) the procedure must be free of charge or available at a nominal fee for consumers.[122]

6.86 In the context of B2B disputes, arbitration can be more suitable than reliance on local courts for a number of reasons, including: (i) the potential for greater cost efficiency; (ii) greater flexibility in procedure; (iii) the potential for speedy proceedings; (iv) accessibility; and (v) cross-border enforceability. Arbitration has been seen by some as the most promising form of alternative dispute resolution in cyberspace, since it is more effective than other consensual, non-adjudicative mechanisms of dispute resolution, and because national courts are not suited to the global character of cyberspace.[123]

6.87 However, the factors that make arbitration appealing in the B2B context do not apply in the same way to B2C disputes. As highlighted above, the dilemma in B2C disputes is to have a cost-effective means of resolving a dispute fairly, with a low monetary value and a commercially unsophisticated party.[124]

---

118 Kaufmann-Kohler and Schultz (n 64) 169. See also Thomas Schultz, 'Online Arbitration: Binding or Non-Binding?' (ADR Online Monthly, November 2002) available at <https://papers.ssrn.com/sol3/papers.cfm?abstract_id=898622> accessed 1 June 2020.

119 Rec 16 of the Consumer ODR Directive (n 8) states that:

> This Regulation should be considered in conjunction with Directive 2013/11/EU which requires Member States to ensure that all disputes between consumers resident and traders established in the Union which arise from the sale of goods or provisions of services can be submitted to an ADR entity.

120 Consumer ODR Regulation (n 8) art 10(b).
121 Ibid., arts 8(e) and 10(a).
122 Ibid., art 8(c).
123 Kaufmann-Kohler and Schultz (n 64) 27.
124 Born (n 15) 1025–6.

While arbitration is flexible as a dispute resolution mechanism and can be tailored to comply **6.88** with the requirements of EU law, other forms of resolution such as mediation and conciliation may be more fit for purpose.

D. CONCLUSION

In our view, while the EU law approach to B2C arbitration can be burdensome, on balance it is **6.89** the right one. If the result of consumer protection laws in the EU is that there are limited options to pursue arbitration of B2C disputes, then it may not be the appropriate method of dispute resolution for this type of relationship and transaction.

The EU's legislative framework has had the right instinct to keep B2C disputes out of court to **6.90** the extent possible and provide for alternatives to lengthy and expensive court proceedings. While at first sight online arbitration might seem to be the perfect fit for consumer disputes, it hides key unfair features vis-à-vis consumers. Unless and until a regulatory framework for online B2C arbitration is set up, ADR, and in particular the ombudsman method is the preferred method of dispute resolution.

7

DAMAGES IN INTERNATIONAL COMMERCIAL ARBITRATION

Herfried Wöss and Adriana San Román Rivera[*]

A. INTRODUCTION

7.01 This chapter deals with the structuring of damages claims in international commercial arbitration, in particular, with respect to income-generating contracts such as Joint Venture Agreements, Build-Operate Transfer Contracts, Public-Private Partnerships (PPPs) and concessions, which are the subject of important commercial arbitrations.

---

[*] Date of submission: 15/1/2020.

In this chapter we briefly recall the fundamental requirements of damages analysis referring to different rules of law, followed by the analysis of the key issues to be considered when framing a damages claim. Special consideration will be given to income-generating contracts. The measure of damages, as a legal notion defining what the applicable law allows to be compensated, merits particular comments as regards the differences between civil and common law. Furthermore, we will clarify the different functions of the but-for premise when framing a damages claim. This will be followed by an analysis of different topics that pose challenges in damages analysis such as loss of a chance, unjust enrichment and the difference between these concepts and lost profits.   **7.02**

With respect to quantification it is important to understand the distinction between concrete and abstract valuations and their relationship to modern valuation methods. In order to exemplify the different valuation methods, in this chapter illustrative cases are presented.   **7.03**

Interest as damages is another important aspect analysed in this chapter. The use of ex-post or hindsight information in the light of the full compensation principle will also be analysed. Cost allocation is an important element to be considered in the light of the full compensation principle. In this respect recent findings will be presented.   **7.04**

Damages analysis is contract specific as the damages case is a mirror-image of the liability case and it aims to determine the economic effect of the violation of a particular contract clause as compared to the situation that would have been in the absence of the breach. The framing of a damages claim is a highly analytical process whereby the but-for premise plays an essential role in order to answer the various questions that appear throughout it. There are no general recipes that apply to the different damages scenarios, but tools that enable a proper damages analysis.   **7.05**

Damages analysis of so-called income-generating contracts or investments was until recently a black hole in comparative[1] and international law. This chapter will follow the doctrine for damages claims in international arbitration in income-generating contracts or investments established in the Oxford University Press monograph *Damages in International Arbitration under Complex Long-term Contracts* and adds new topics, aspects and perspectives, as well as comments to contemporary discussions which provides further insight into this fascinating topic.   **7.06**

B. FULL COMPENSATION AND THE BUT-FOR PREMISE

The notion of full compensation and total reparation were used as synonyms during history and are based on philosophic and theological notions of Aristotle's distributive and commutative justice and Thomas Aquinas' Summa Theologica, further developed by the post-scholastics and natural lawyers. The notion of full compensation is expressly recognized in many important jurisdictions. The term total reparation as used in international law has been   **7.07**

---

1   Gerhard H Wächter, *M&A Litigation M&A Recht im Streit* (3rd rev edn, RWS Verlag Kommunikationsformum 2017) para 10.4, who stated in his seminal analysis of damages claims with respect to 'investment goods', that 'modern damages law has not established a doctrine that would allow a convincing and predictable application to the reduction of enterprise-value, investment goods or financial assets'; see also: Herfried Wöss, 'Schadenersatz' in Michael Nueber (ed.), *Handbuch Schiedsgerichtsbarkeit und ADR* (LexisNexis ARD ORAC 2021).

characterized by the famous *Factory at Chorzów* case, where the measure of damages adds distinct features to full compensation, which will be analysed in the respective chapter. These notions refer to both contractual and extra-contractual liability.

7.08 The compensation function of damages law has its origins in Greek philosophy. Aristotle (384–322 BC) dealt with compensation under the notion of 'corrective or commutative justice'. Commutative justice treats the wrong and the transfer of resources that undoes it, as a link between the injured party and the wrongdoer. Corrective and commutative justice seeks to subtract the unjust gain of one party to make up for the loss of the other party. In his Nicomachean ethics, Aristotle states that 'the law has regards only to the difference made by the harm done; they are on the same footing, apart from the fact that one has perpetrated and the other suffered the harm'.[2] Roman law settled the focus on the interest of the claimant to give him the value what he was expected to receive which leads to the formula *'id quod interest'*.[3] A prominent member of the scholastics, Thomas Aquinas (1225–1274) said that a person might violate commutative justice either by interfering with another's property in a wrongful manner or simply by taking what belongs to another.[4]

7.09 The underlying notion of Aristotle, the scholastics and post-scholastics was full compensation, whereby at that time both terms were used synonymously. Hugo Grotius (1583–1645) established the leading natural law damages doctrine in Chapter 17 of his master work *'De iure belli ac pacis'* based on full compensation of damages and lost profits, which comprises the violation of legal positions including property, contract and the law.[5] Grotius' doctrine was further developed by another natural law scholar, Samuel Pufendorf (1632–1694) who was heavily influenced by Thomas Hobbes. Damages law was understood as a defence against the absolute prohibition of *'neminem laedere'* (not to hurt anybody).[6] At that time, damages law focused on the position of the injured party, though notions such as the requirement of culpability exclude the damaging party's liability according to the principle of 'everything or nothing'. This principle means that if the injured party does not prove culpability of the party in breach or other conditions it would not receive anything. The 18th century saw an important reception of Roman law in continental Europe which, however, did not change the basic premise of full compensation of the loss incurred.

7.10 The full compensation principle is recognized in most of the important jurisdictions for international arbitration. In 1848, the leading English case *Robinson v Harman* established that the aim of damages is to give the injured party the necessary amount of money to put him 'so far as money can do it, in the same position as he would have been in had the contract been performed'.[7] The US Second Restatement of Contracts establishes: '[t]he initial assumption is

---

2   Herfried Wöss, Adriana San Román, Pablo T Spiller, Santiago Dellepiane, *Damages in International Arbitration under Complex Long-term Contracts* (OUP 2014) 13–14, 18–19; Gerard J Hughes, *The Routledge Guidebook to Aristotle's Nicomachean Ethics* (Taylor & Francis Group 2013) V 4, 1132a2-6.

3   Borzu Sabahi, *Compensation and Restitution in Investor-State Arbitration* (OUP, International Economic Law Series) 21.

4   James Gordley, *Foundations of Private Law: Property, Tort, Contract, Unjust Enrichment* (OUP 2006) 423–34.

5   Hugo Grotius, *De iure*, lib II, cap XVII, §§IV f, cited in Feras Gisawi, *Der Grundsatz der Totalreparation*, Gundlagen der Rechtswissenschaft 25 (Mohr Siebeck 2015) 28–9.

6   Samuel Pufendorf, 'Ut nemo laedatur, et si quod damnum fuit datum, reparetur', title to *De iure belli ac pacis*, lib III, cap I, §2, cited in Gisawi (n 5) 44.

7   *Robinson v Harman* (1848) 13 PD 191 (CA) 200.

that the injured party is entitled to full compensation for his actual loss'.[8] In order to achieve this purpose, US Courts award the expectation interest which aims to put the injured party in the economic position he would be in but for the breach.[9]

French law recognizes the principle of full compensation or *reparation intégrale*. Full compen- **7.11** sation is the objective (*principle de réparation intégrale du préjudice*) and has to be in accordance with the loss suffered (*tout le préjudice mais rien que le préjudice*). The essence of the full compensation principle is to return the victim as closely 'as monetary possible to the position in which he would have been had the wrong not being done'.[10] German damages law is based on the principle of total reparation leading to the situation which would have existed if the damaging event had not occurred (§249 BGB). Article 7.4.2 (Full compensation) of the UNIDROIT Principles of International Commercial Contracts (PICC) reads: 'The aggrieved party is entitled to full compensation for harm sustained as the result of the non-performance. Such harm includes both any loss which it suffered and any gain of which it was deprived, taking into account any gain to the aggrieved party resulting from its avoidance of cost or harm.' Finally, Article 74 CISG reads: 'Damages for breach of contract by one party consist of a sum equal to the loss, including loss of profit, suffered by the other party as a consequence of the breach.'

According to those rules of law, the payment of an amount of money should place the injured **7.12** party in the economic position it would be in, if the damaging act had not occurred, which refers to the full compensation principle. Nowadays, the principle of full compensation is a general principle of law as proved in the treatise Global Sales and Contract Law of Schwenzer/Hachem/Kee which contains an extensive comparative law analysis.

The but-for premise developed by Friedrich Mommsen in his seminal monograph '*Doctrine of* **7.13** *Interest*' in 1855 refers to the economic difference between the actual economic situation caused by the breach of contract and the hypothetical situation but-for the breach. The application of the but-for premise is the means to achieve full compensation, as the injured party should only be compensated for the difference that was duly proved, subject to the limitations of the applicable rules of law. The full compensation principle through the but-for premise is the 'Leitmotif' when framing or analysing a damages claim. This will be explained in detail throughout this chapter.

C. THE BUT-FOR PREMISE AND ITS THREE-DIMENSIONAL FUNCTION

1. The but-for premise as a means to achieve full compensation

Mommsen developed the notion of 'interest' from the Roman law maxim *id quod interest*, **7.14** according to which the judge had to estimate claimant's losses and his material situation

---

8   Restatement (Second) of Contracts, ch 16, Topic 2, Introductory Note.

9   Ibid., § 344 (a) (Purpose of Remedies).

10 Solène Rowan, *Remedies for Breach of Contract: A Comparative Analysis of the Protection of Performance* (OUP 2012) 109; Konstanze Brieskorn, *Vertragshaftung und responsabilité contractuelle, Ein Vergleich zwischen deutschem und französischem Recht mit Blick auf das Vertragsrecht in Europa* (Mohr Siebeck 2010) 252.

which would have resulted if the fact for which the respondent was liable had not occurred. Under his doctrine, such interest is calculated through the but-for premise or 'differential hypothesis', which is the determination of the difference between the economic situation of the injured party caused by the breach of contract or violation and the hypothetical situation of the injured party without such breach or violation. Mommsen's but-for premise aims to place the injured party in the economic position it would be but for the breach or illegal act, which results in full compensation.[11]

7.15   This economic difference is nowadays known as the expectation interest. Mommsen's doctrine spread throughout Europe and was introduced into US law by Professor Lon Fuller and his assistant William Perdue at the beginning of the 20th century through the notions of expectation interest ('what would be the economic situation of the injured party in the absence of the breach?') and reliance interest ('what would be the economic position of the injured party if it had not entered into the contract?').[12]

7.16   Under the but-for premise the question is what would have happened in the absence of the breach. In order to answer this question, the but-for premise compares the hypothetical economic situation without the breach and the actual economic situation with the breach. However, limitations under the applicable law such as causality, culpability, foreseeability, the duty of mitigation and contributory negligence have to be considered.[13] Once liability has been proved and the differential hypothesis together with the limitations have been applied, the result is the 'actual loss' or expectation interest which has to be compensated in order to achieve full compensation.

7.17   The application of the but-for premise may lead to different results depending on the interest protected under the applicable law. It makes a difference if the applicable law protects the performance principle, that is the equivalent to specific performance under concrete valuation, or the economic interest leading to a difference in value using market values through the so-called abstract valuation.

2.   The but-for premise as a means to prove causality and loss

7.18   Under the but-for premise, the question to be asked is what would have happened in the absence of the breach which refers to but-for causality. If the claimant would be in the same economic situation without the breach, there would be no causation. Whether this situation is limited to an economic difference, known as difference in value, or to the exact position, also known as the cost of cure, depends on the contract and on the measure of damages applicable

---

11   Friedrich Mommsen, *Beiträge zum Obligationenrecht: Abth. Zur Lehre von dem Interesse* (EU Schwetschke und Sohn 1855) 27; 'Das Interesse ist allerdings ein Schadenersatz; und sofern man den Ausdruck Schadenersatz allein auf die vollständige Entschädigung bezieht, treffen beide Ausdrücke in ihrer Bedeutung zusammen' ('Interest means, however, damages; and if the expression damages is exclusively understood as full compensation, both terms coincide in their meaning').

12   Lon L Fuller and William R Perdue, 'The Reliance Interest in Contract Damages' (Pt 1) (1936) 52 Y*ale Law Journal*, 52–96, referring to Windscheid, the mentor of Friedrich Mommsen.

13   Adriana San Román, Herfried Wöss, 'Damages in International Arbitration with respect to Income Generating Assets or Investments in Commercial and Investment Arbitration' (2015) *Journal of Damages in International Arbitration* 37, and in Mark Kantor (ed), *Yukos Special* (2015) 5 *Transnational Dispute Management*.

or available under the applicable rules of law. The loss must be properly attributable to the breach. Liability is to the extent that losses would have been avoided in the absence of the breach. If the damage would have occurred even in the absence of the breach then there is no loss caused by the breach.[14]

Causation is not only a requirement for the recovery of damages, but also has implications on the amount or extent of damages to be recovered. If through the application of the but-for premise only partial causation is proved, this may lead to the substantial reduction of the damages claim. This situation is intimately related to contributory negligence of the injured party, where the difficulty lies in the construction by the respondent of hypothetical concurrent causation situations in order to reduce the scope of causation. For example, in the case of the violation of a non-competition obligation, the defendant may argue that the joint venture company would not have won the project even in the absence of the breach or that the company was badly managed by the managing partner.[15] **7.19**

Once the hypothetical situation has been reconstructed and compared to the actual situation, if there is an economic difference, there is a loss. That is why the but-for premise serves as a means to determine whether there is an actual loss. **7.20**

3. The but-for premise and quantification

The objective of the but-for method is to build a scenario that takes into account the World as it is except for the economic and financial implications that could arise from a hypothetical circumstance where the breach had not occurred. However, the application may not be that simple, in particular, because of lack of information and the inability to disentangle the effects of specific actions from other forces affecting the business.[16] **7.21**

In determining damages the technique may be determined by which method most appropriately allows the analyst to construct a but-for scenario or, in general, to account for specific assumptions that are necessary for an assessment of damages. There are different valuation methods which are often grouped into three approaches: (i) income approach such as the Discounted Cash Flow Method (DCF), the Adjusted Present Value (APV), the Capitalized Cash Flow (CCF); (ii) the market approach (publicly-traded multiples, transaction multiples and stock prices); and (iii) the asset or cost approach (liquidated value, book value and adjusted book value) of which the first two are *forward looking* and the third is *backward looking*. The choice of the *approach* depends on the nature of the asset being valued and the micro- and macroeconomic circumstances surrounding the valuation,[17] as well as the evidence available. **7.22**

In case of lost income stream, the expert may either reconstruct the income stream of the company or investment or the loss of value it would have had in the absence of the breach or refer to the income stream or value of similar companies. Any method that helps to reconstruct **7.23**

---

14 Wöss and others, *Damages in International Arbitration under Complex Long-term Contracts* (n 2) para 5.61 (footnotes omitted).

15 Ibid., para 5.63.

16 Ibid., paras 6.29–6.30.

17 Pablo T Spiller and Santiago Dellepiane in Wöss and others, *Damages in International Arbitration under Complex Long-term Contracts* (n 2) paras 6.145 ff.

the hypothetical situation is admissible, provided the assumptions are reasonable and correspond to the evidence available. Due care, however, has to be taken with respect to the asset that is being valued, and to avoid methods that are unrelated to the situation of the injured party.

D. DAMAGES CLAIMS IN INCOME-GENERATING CONTRACTS

7.24 There are basically two types of contract when structuring damages claims: the typical bilateral or synallagmatic contract whereby one party delivers a service or good and the other pays for it; the income-generating contract or synallagmatic triallagma, where there is no exchange of goods or services against the price but both parties contribute assets in order to obtain cash flows from a third party that is the market. The main difference is that in the first category, the cash flows derive from collateral transactions such as re-sales which are not the direct object of the original contract. The lost profits are consequential damages which, under most rules of law are considered direct damages under the foreseeability test or indirect if they fail such test. These sales are not regulated or governed by the original contract. In the synallagmatic triallagmas the cash flows arising from the sales to the third party, which is the market, are the object and are governed by the project agreement. The cash flows not obtained because of the breach of contract of one of the parties are always direct or positive damages.

7.25 It is important to mention that the cash flows frustrated by the breach of the contract may or may not be profits because they may not even recover the initial investment which means that there is no profit. This situation has particular relevance when dealing with the measure of damages under the different rules of law as will be explained below.

7.26 Complex long-term contracts are in essence complex contract packages, whereby the project agreement is in the centre. In case of a PPP the operator and the financiers invest in infrastructure, in order to offer services, for example, in the form of the operation of a hospital. The quality of those services is being measured through a complex points system and the payment is according to the quality of services delivered. In case the minimum services points are not being achieved, deductions and liquidated damages are being applied. If this situation continues, contract termination is the consequence. The cash flows for the financing of the project derive from the users of the hospital or their insurances, and sometimes from subsidies.

7.27 Complex long-term contracts are structured according to complex risk matrices, whereby the risk structure during the development phase is different from the design and engineering phases, or the construction or operation phases. The risks identified are allocated to the project participants and risk mitigation mechanisms are applied. The task is to structure a project that is flexible enough to resist the challenges of changes of market conditions but is sufficiently attractive to secure financing and to generate profits commensurate to the risks taken which means that contracts have to be feasible or 'bankable' and make sufficient 'cash flows' probable.

7.28 The essential issue with this kind of contract is the circumstance that the cash flows are being generated only during the operational phase of the project. The risk of a non-functioning plant is with the owner. It takes years from the start of operation until the recovery of the initial investments. Profits in their proper sense are often generated in a late phase of the project, provided the project develops as planned. This is important for the understanding of the term cash flows which are not necessarily lost profits but to a large extent the recovery of the original investment, though those cash flows may according to the structure of financing contain a profit margin. Moreover, it is important that the cash flows be reasonably certain as only cash flows that may reasonably be generated ('reasonable certainty of income') may be lost.

Income-generating contracts are in essence income-generating assets or investments and not **7.29** classical exchange contracts classified as contract types under many rules of law. They are atypical contracts in which the partners contribute assets in a partnership-like relationship and the underlying projects are being financed through cash-flows deriving from the market on a 'non-recourse' basis. This means that the project company only disposes of a reduced capital and the necessary means to execute the project. The project company is structured to handle one particular project often as a 'special purpose company'. The underlying cash flows may not be foreseen with precision but are often subject to fluctuations. Nevertheless, there are recognized methods of business planning and forecasting such as the DCF, that is universally used and also recurred to in damages analysis.

The complex long-term contract is, therefore, a contract tailor-made to a particular project, **7.30** subject to a clear risk allocation and the contractual structure aims to secure the cash flows in order to achieve the success of an investment project. The reduction or interruption of the cash flows through the breach of contract leads to a loss of the value of the special purpose company or the investment.[18]

In this respect, it has to be underlined that damages analysis of income-generating contracts **7.31** requires a different approach and the development of a doctrine, as pointedly stated by Gerhard H Wächter in his treatise on *M&A Litigation* where he states with respect to 'investment goods', that:

> modern damages law has not established a doctrine that would allow a convincing and predictable application to the reduction of enterprise-value, investment goods or financial assets. … Jurisprudence could not develop a doctrine applicable to [investment goods] on the basis of accidents of private vehicles and damages to private consumer goods.[19]

When framing damages claims with respect to income-generating contracts, special consider- **7.32** ation must be given to the measure of damages, the reasonable certainty of the income stream as condition for the existence of loss, risk assumption and the protective effect of the contractual provision violated fulfilling the foreseeability requirement. All these elements are particularly important and have to be considered when framing damages with respect to this type of contracts, as we shall see in the next section of this chapter.

E. FRAMING A DAMAGES CLAIM IN INCOME-GENERATING CONTRACTS

Damages are the principal remedy in international arbitration as common law does not **7.33** normally recognize specific performance, which is often impracticable or impossible to pursue

---

18 Ibid., ch 3 and paras 5.03–04, with further references.
19 Wächter (n 1) para 10.4.

in complex contracts even under civil law. In the following, we will give a short overview of the relevant issues under the applicable law that have to be taken into consideration when framing a damages claim arising from the breach of an income-generating contract, which is different from damages analysis with respect to typical sales and services contracts where vast legal literature exists in the principal jurisdictions that are relevant for international arbitration. This is different from damages analysis regarding investment goods.

1. Breach

7.34 In all the rules of law analysed, damages claims start with establishing the liability of the party in breach. The damages case is a mirror-image of the liability case. Damages is about establishing the economic 'situation' that would have existed had the breach not occurred. This situation varies according to the precise contractual provision violated which may lead to innumerable situations, in particular, with respect to highly complex contracts. The key issue of establishing liability is often exception clauses or grounds of justification under the applicable law where the party in breach will try to prove that its conduct was allowed and, therefore, not in breach of the contract.

2. Loss

7.35 Loss and expectation interest are two different sides of the same coin in the case of lost profits or lost cash flows. Expectation interest depends on the income stream that the injured party can prove with reasonable certainty it would have obtained in the absence of the breach. Discrepancies between the amount sought and proved undermine certainty and weaken the claim. The expectation interest is the amount that the injured party would have obtained but for the breach which is the difference between the actual scenario and the hypothetical scenario without the breach. This leads to two main requirements: (1) to prove that the income-stream would have existed with reasonable certainty in the absence of the breach of contract; and (2) the effect of the breach of contract on the income stream. The reasonable certainty of the income stream is obtained through the but-for method and the evidence available, which leads to the re-construction of the hypothetical course of events in the absence of the breach of contract.

3. Causality

7.36 The next requirement that appears in every rule of law is causality. The test of causality is whether the loss would have occurred without the breach. If the answer is yes, there would be no causality, but other factors would have caused the loss.

7.37 With respect to causality there are two special situations which arise under different rules of law, one is the hypothetical normal course of events which applies, amongst others, under German law, whereby extraordinary situations are being discarded; the other is the prevalence of alternative or interrupting causality whereby other causes such as economic crises may limit or interrupt causality which is prevalent under English and common law. For example, in a famous shipping case, the merchandise was rotten due to delay of the ship. However, the ship never arrived because it was destroyed by a war. Under the theory of the hypothetical normal course of events, the war would be discarded and liability established as the delayed ship owner had to carry with the risk of war and cannot claim *force majeure*. Applying the principle of alternative causality, there would be no liability of the shipowner as the war is a matter of alternative causality for which the shipowner is not responsible.

4. Fault

There is a tendency in comparative contract law to eliminate the principle of fault, whereby **7.38** strict liability is contrasted by a wide notion of *force majeure* as is the case with the Convention on Contracts for the International Sale of Goods (CISG) and the Principles of International Commercial Contracts (PICC). Under §1324 sentence 1 of the Austrian ABGB, the injured party may only claim 'full satisfaction' including lost profits in case of intentional or gross negligent conduct, though fault is being presumed under §1298 ABGB in case of contractual liability which leads to a shift of the burden of proof. Fault is also required under German and French law. There is no fault requirement in English and US law. Fault hardly plays a role in international arbitration in case of breach of contract.

5. Limitations

a. Foreseeability, adequacy and remoteness

The test of foreseeability is whether the party in breach should have known that the breach **7.39** would have caused a loss to the injured party at the moment of entering into the contract or at the moment of the breach. Foreseeability is relevant in subsequent or consequential contractual relationships, where, for example, a good was received with a defect and could not be resold which leads to lost profits which are normally foreseeable for the original non-performing seller. The situation is different with respect to income-generating contracts where the income stream lost through contractual non-performance is direct damages and always foreseeable as the generation of income stream is the purpose of such contract in order to finance an investment or infrastructure. In this respect it is important that risks assumed in a complex long-term contract are always risks foreseen. Therefore, contractual risk allocation and risk assumption plays an important role when claiming damages, which means that contractual clauses have to be carefully analysed and their scope of protection determined. The German and Austrian doctrine of the 'scope of protection of the norm' is a very useful tool to that respect as it helps to determine which damages are foreseeable or not under the contractual risk allocation and assumption.[20]

English law contains a sophisticated legal regime with respect to risk assumption[21] and the **7.40** application of the landmark *Hadley v Baxendale*[22] case, which is particularly relevant in construction and infrastructure project agreements.

---

20   Wöss and others, *Damages in International Arbitration under Complex Long-term Contracts* (n 2) para 4.261.
21   Adam Kramer, 'An Agreement-Centred Approach to Remoteness and Contract Damages', in Cohen and McKendrick (eds), *Comparative Remedies for Breach of Contract* (Hart Publishing 2005) 250; Ibid, 'Remoteness: New Problem with the Old Test' in Djakhongir Saidov and Ralph Cunnington (eds), *Contract Damages* (Hart Publishing 2008) 277–8.
22   *Hadley v Baxendale* (1854) 9 Exch 341, 354.

7.41 The test of foreseeability refers to whether the loss was foreseeable for the respondent at the moment of the breach or at the moment of entering into the contract, but it does not refer to the certainty of the amount of profits lost or the exact amount of damages.

7.42 Whereas the limitation of foreseeability is based on subjective criteria under many jurisdictions, the German and Austrian law theory of adequacy uses an objective approach, whereby 'An event in meaning of civil law is causal, if it is apt in general and not only under special and extraordinary, improbable circumstances beyond the ordinary course of things, to produce the effect in question.'[23]

7.43 These differences in the foreseeability approach have to be observed in particular with respect to consequential and indirect damages under typical synallagmatic contracts but are hardly relevant with respect to income-generating contracts or synallagmatic triallagmas where the purpose of the contract is precisely to generate sufficient cash flows in order to finance a project or an investment.

b. Contributory negligence and mitigation

7.44 Contributory negligence may result in additional losses not caused by the breach of contract but by actions or omissions of the injured party. Causation is not only a requirement *sine qua non* for liability, but also determines its scope and has a limitation function. Contributory negligence is in essence a causality issue contemporary to the breach of contract.

7.45 Another limitation is mitigation whereby the injured party has a duty to take action to mitigate damages that might occur after the breach of contract and have to be avoided by the injured party. What is important when looking at mitigation is the burden of proof as the mitigation scenario has to be proved by the party in breach which may lead to complex evidentiary issues as it requires the comparison of the hypothetical course of events without the breach with the hypothetical mitigation scenario. However, the reasonable cost of mitigation has always to be borne by the party in breach. Whereas contributory negligence is relevant at the moment of the breach of contract, mitigation arises after the breach of contract.

7.46 The result after the requirements have been fulfilled and limitations have been applied and quantification has taken place according to the evidence available, is the actual loss which has to be fully compensated. This is the same as the expectation interest, that is the difference between the actual economic situation and the situation but for the breach together with the aforementioned limitations.

F. MEASURE OF DAMAGES

1. Definition

7.47 When framing a damages claim special attention must be taken to the measure of damages under the applicable law. The applicable rules of law basically apply two different principles: (1) the performance principle under civil law; and (2) the difference in value under common

---

23   Wolfgang Fikentscher and Andreas Heinemann, *Schuldrecht* (10th edn, De Gruyter 2006) paras 625–629.

law. These are the benchmarks under these two systems. The performance principle seeks to determine the financial equivalent to performance or the cost of cure, whereas the difference in value refers to an economic equivalent based on market values. The performance principle refers to the *pacta sunt servanda* maxim where the will of the parties under the contract is protected and should be enforced either through specific performance or a financial equivalent. This leads to different results when applying the but-for premise due to the difference in the underlying benchmarks.[24]

There are two specific classifications with respect to the measure of damages: (1) expectation and reliance interest; and (2) loss and lost profits. It is important to mention that many civil and common law jurisdictions use the expectation and reliance interest measures of damages and even countries that do not expressly mention them, accept them, as is the case of France.[25] The notion of loss and lost profits is used primarily in civil law countries, PICC and CISG. However, Austria and Germany, which are civil law countries, PICC and CISG also admit the notions of expectation and reliance interest, apart from the use of the terms loss and lost profits.[26]   **7.48**

2. The problem of the use of *Damnum emergens* and *Lucrum Cessans*

The difference between *damnum emergens* (loss) and *lucrum cessans* (lost profits) was known in Roman law but not further developed. According to Prof. Reinhard Zimmermann: **7.49**

> [t]he classical [Roman] lawyers did little to develop and systematize [this] area of law. Assessment of quod interest was largely left to the individual iudex, about whose activity in turn, we hardly possess any sources. All we can do, therefore, is to list a variety of items that were capable of being included sub titulo quod interest.[27]

The headings of damages *damnum emergens* and *lucrum cessans* were introduced in the Middle Ages as a consequence of the prohibition of interest which was considered usury and a sin by the catholic church under canonical law. Upon pressure of the upcoming 'Italian' banks it was necessary to introduce substitute remedies in their favour in case of loans that were not duly paid back. Under the heading of *damnum emergens* the banker could claim the cost of capital and under the heading of *lucrum cessans* the lost profits or quasi-interest. With this the catholic   **7.50**

---

24 Ingeborg Schwenzer, Pascal Hachem and Christopher Kee, *Global Sales and Contract Law* (OUP 2012) paras 44.04, 44.06, 44.19, 44.27.

25 P Jourdain, 'Le dommage-intérêts alloués par le juge', Rapport français, in M Fontaine, G Viney (under the direction of), *Les sanctions de l'inexécution des obligations contractuelles, Estudes de droit comparé* (Bruylant 2001) 273–4.

26 Art (§)1293 Allgemeines Bürgerliches Gesetzbuch (ABGB); Brigitta Jud, *Schadenersatz bei mangelhafter Leistung* (Manzsche Verlags- und Universitätsbuchhandlung 2003) 85–6; Art 7.4.2 Principles of International Commercial Contracts (PICC); McKendrick, Art 7.4.2 in Stefan Vogenauer and Jan Kleinheisterkamp (eds), *Commentary on the UNIDROIT Principles of International Commercial Contracts (PICC)* (OUP 2009) para 22; Art 74 Convention on Contracts for the International Sale of Goods (CISG).

27 Reinhard Zimmermann, *The Law of Obligations – Roman Foundations of the Civilian Tradition* (OUP 1996) 826–7, 972–3.

church avoided to grant an exception from the prohibition of interest but met the needs of the upcoming banking industry by granting alternative remedies.[28]

7.51 The distinction between positive damages and lost profits does not cause a problem in case of typical exchange contracts such as sales and works contracts, where the cost of a replacement of a defective good be considered *damnum emergens* and the reduced lost profits for the delayed sale of the goods be claimed as *lucrum cessans*. However, the loss may be calculated with more precision as difference between two financial situations, whereby the purchase of the goods is considered as expenses which is contrasted with the income generated by the sale of the goods. What counts is the economic difference between an ordinarily executed business and the business subject to replacement order and belated sale because of non-delivery. The lost or reduced profit margin at the re-sale is not necessarily profit, but reduced cash flows. Moreover, it has to be observed that even in typical synallagmatic contracts the sales that could not be achieved because the goods received were not according to specification, under the loss and lost profits measure of damages, lost profits have to be adjusted because the sales proceeds serve to recover the cost of the goods originally bought or the initial investment.

7.52 In the case of the turn-key construction of a carton freezer that did not work according to specifications, the aimed level of sales was not achieved because the owner of the carton freezer could not deliver the frozen meat under the sale contracts to its clients. In this case, part of the sales proceeds was meant to pay for the investment in the carton freezer. The buyer, who would be the injured party, could not ask for the sales that could not be achieved due to the lack of performance of the contract and the investment in the carton freezer at the same time. The sales proceeds were aimed to recover the investment, so asking for the investment and the sales proceeds at the same time would result in double counting. In order to avoid double counting adjustments to the lost profits should be made. This shows that even under the synallagmatic contracts when using the measure of damages of loss and lost profits, adjustments should be made when claiming lost profits, otherwise, there would be overcompensation or double counting. Therefore, even in this kind of contract, using the loss and lost profits measure of damages can create problems.

7.53 Whereas in many jurisdictions this distinction may be neglected or is irrelevant, in other countries, in particular, in Latin America and North Africa a damages claim has mandatorily to be formulated as loss and lost profit claims. Moreover, it is very difficult to ask for lost profits without asking for loss and lost profits are perceived as something negative.

7.54 As already observed by Prof. Friedrich Mommsen in his 'Doctrine of Interest' in 1855, the notions of *damnum emergens* and *lucrum cessans* are an indication of possible damages. According to Mommsen what matters is the effect of the breach on the assets of the injured party, which leads to the expectation interest.[29] Franz Gschnitzer observes that 'the difference between loss suffered *(damnum emergens)* and lost profits *(lucrum cessans)* ... [is] venerable, but

---

28 Max Neumann, 'Geschichte des Wuchers in Deutschland bis zum Jahre 1654', *Zeitschrift für Kirchenrecht*, V Jahrgang (Laupp & Siebeck 1865) 49–50; AWB Simpson, *The History of the Common Law of Contract, The Rise of the Question of Assumpsit* (OUP 1975) 144.

29 Mommsen (n 11) 11–2.

cannot be justified anymore'.[30] According to Helmut Koziol, one of the most renowned comparative law damages scholars:

> The venerable distinction between positive damage and lost profits is addressed in §252 BGB [German Civil Code]. However, this does not have any further importance as it expressly establishes that the damage to be compensated includes the lost profits. ... Also the [Austrian] jurisprudence considers the strict differentiation not justified and has extended the notion of positive damages to such an extent, that the compensation of lost profits is only of residual importance. Positive damages include any chance of profit that according to the ordinary course of business occurs with reasonable certainty.[31]

Under French law and the jurisprudence of the *Cour de cassation* the distinction has been neglected and other terms such as *prejudice commercial* as collective term or *prejudice économique* are being used.[32]

The situation is even more complicated when dealing with income-generating contracts. In **7.55** income-generating contracts or synallagmatic triallagmas there is no exchange of goods or services. Both parties contribute assets and the income stream comes from a third party that is the market. Through the income stream, the parties recover their initial investment. Asking for the investment and the income stream at the same time would result in double counting. Therefore, only lost profits or lost cash flows can be claimed. As already mentioned, actual profits only arise once the investment and all debts arising from the project are being paid. The term lost profits used is therefore not necessarily precise and what is lost are normally the cash flows.

This brings us to the next classification of the measure of damages: **7.56**

3. Expectation interest and reliance interest

After what has been explained above, we can see that the classification between expectation **7.57** and reliance interest is more suitable for both types of contracts and corresponds to the modern doctrine of damages established by Friedrich Mommsen and the famous English case *Robinson v Harman*[33] which means 'putting the insured party in the position it would have been had the breach of contract not occurred' as expressly established in §249(1) of the German Civil Code (BGB). This refers to a comparison of two economic situations, the actual situation subject to the breach and the hypothetical situation but-for the breach.

With respect to the expectation interest, the question to be asked is 'what would be the **7.58** economic position of the injured party but for the breach?'. When comparing these two situations, the initial investment is already being taken into consideration so is there no need for adjustment. Moreover, with the but-for premise what is determined is the precise situation

30 Franz Gschnitzer, *Österreichisches Schuldrecht, Besonderer Teil und Schadenersatz* (2nd rev edn by Christoph Faistenberger, Heinz Barta, Bernhard Eccher, Springer Verlag 1988) 45.
31 Helmut Koziol, *Grundfragen des Schadenersatzrechts* (Jan Sramek Verlag, 2010) paras 5/37–38 (2011) 2(3) *Journal of European Tort Law* 336–8. The Austrian Supreme Court of Justice (Der Oberste Gerichtshof (OGH) 1 Ob 315/97.
32 Andrea Pinna, *La mesure du préjudice contractuel* (LGDJ, Université Panthéon-Assas Paris II 2007) para 8, 248.
33 *Robinson v Harman* (1848) 1 Exch 850 (Exch) 855.

that would have existed but for the contractual violation. This also means that the damages case is a mirror-image of the liability case as previously explained. This further means that the hypothetical situation has to be reconstructed which may be quite challenging in case of a complex long-term contract.

7.59 With respect to the reliance interest, the question to be answered is 'what would be the economic position of the injured party if it had not entered into the contract?'. This reliance interest was first defined by Prof. Rudolf von Ihering when referring to the damages claims with respect to null and avoidable contracts[34] and was further developed under English and US law as a general measure of damages.

7.60 The question arises what happens if the initial investment is not being recovered or what would happen if one applies the but-for premise and compares the actual economic situation and the economic situation but for the breach and the result is lower than the initial investment. That means that the initial investment would not have been recovered but for the breach. If reliance interest would be awarded in full, that would lead to overcompensation. This issue is solved under certain rules of law by the shift of the burden of proof where the party in breach would have to prove in all certainty that the injured party would not have recovered its initial investment but for the breach as is the case under English[35] and German law (presumption of profitability).[36]

7.61 Usually, the expectation interest would place the injured party in the position it would be but for the breach. Therefore, the only reason to award the complete reliance interest when the performance interest does not cover the reliance interest, would be in case of misrepresentation or tortious liability.

G. QUANTIFICATION: ABSTRACT AND CONCRETE VALUATION APPROACHES

7.62 Abstract valuation refers to market values and is the preferred method in commercial transactions where time is of the essence and it is often easier to refer to market values than to make an analysis of the individual situation of the injured party. Concrete valuation refers to the precise situation of the injured party and how to restore it to the position it would have been in had the breach of contract not occurred.

7.63 The difference between concrete and abstract valuation approaches can be illustrated in the English case *Ruxley Electronics & Construction v Forsyth*[37] where a swimming pool was constructed with insufficient depth in violation of the applicable specification. Claimant sought the destruction and reconstruction of the swimming pool at a cost that exceeded the original construction cost. This claim was rejected by the court due to lack of reasonableness and lack of relevance for the value of the house to which the swimming pool belonged. The

---

34 Rudolf von Ihering, 'Culpa in contrahendo oder Schadenersatz bei nichtigen oder nicht zur Perfektion gelangten Verträgen', *Jahrbücher für die Dogmatik des heutigen römischen und deutschen Privaterechts IV* (1861).

35 *Joint Venture Yashlar (Turkmenistan), Bridas SAPIC (Argentina) v The Government of Turkmenistan*, ICC Case 9151/ FMS/KGA, final award dated 18 May 2000 para 363 ('*Bridas v Turkmenistan*').

36 Fikentscher and Heinemann (n 23) para 439.

37 *Ruxley Electronics and Construction Ltd v Forsyth (Laddingford Enclosures Ltd v Forsyth)* [1996] 1 AC 344.

rationale behind the judgment was that the violation of the specification did not affect the value of the house with the swimming pool under the difference of value principle. If the case had been decided under French law, the claimant would theoretically and under the applicable performance principle have had a right to the destruction of the swimming pool and its reconstruction even if that would be unreasonable.[38] This derives from the *pacta sunt servanda* obligation under French law which leads to the compensation of the cost of cure.

Therefore, the protected interest under different applicable rules of law leads to different **7.64** amounts of damages even when the but-for premise is being applied. This is true for typical synallagmatic contracts as shown in the example above. Expectation interest may be calculated according to concrete or abstract valuation as established by the applicable rules of law. In this respect, German and Austrian law allows both concrete and abstract approaches to determine the expectation interest.

In case of income-generating contracts, the expectation interest is the economic difference **7.65** between the actual situation and the situation but for the breach. In this regard, the calculation of damages through the DCF method is concrete valuation because it takes into consideration the concrete economic situation of the injured party with and without the breach. If the income stream of a particular income-generating contract or asset cannot be determined through the income approach due to lack of reliable evidence, then the value of similar companies or assets may be considered, which refers to market values. The determination of the market value through the market approaches, transaction multiples and stock prices, refers to abstract valuation.

In case of income-generating contracts what matters is the loss of cash flows, both in the past **7.66** from the moment of the breach of contract to the award, and from the award to the end of the project. The breach affects the performance of the whole contract from the moment it occurred. The aim is to determine the economic difference between the actual course of events and the hypothetical course of events that would have existed in the absence of the breach of contract, which can be achieved through the differential hypothesis. With respect to future lost cash-flows, the DCF-method is the most common method used in valuation analysis. In the respective financial model, the financial parameters will be adjusted in the hypothetical sphere in order to reconstruct the probable cash flows that would have occurred if there had been no breach and according to the but-for premise compare these cash flows with the cash flows affected by the breach.

The DCF method is widely used by economists, investors, companies and it is also accepted **7.67** for the computation of damages. It is also recommended by international agencies such as the World Bank.[39] The DFC method is a forward-looking method and it considers the company's ability to generate future cash flows. It relies on four main drivers: (i) revenues; (ii) operating expenses; (iii) capital expenses; and (iv) discount rate. The DCF method needs the estimation of future cash flows (revenues) and outflows (costs and taxes).

---

38   Rowan (n 10) 119; Civ (3) 5 Dec 1979, JCP 1981.II.19605; Civ (3) 6 May 1981, Juris-Data no 1981-001783.
39   World Bank, 'Guidelines on the Treatment of Foreign Direct Investment' (1992) paras 5–6.

7.68 There are various ways of forecasting future cash flows. One is to base them on the historical performance of the company, which requires that the business being valued has a previous performance. If it does not have a historic performance, it is still feasible to estimate future cash flows based on business plans or analyst reports. However, it should be validated with market indicators or industry forecasts. For discounting future cash flows as of the date of valuation, the weighted average cost of capital (WACC) of an efficiently managed firm under a similar market as the discount rate is widely accepted.[40]

7.69 The distinction between concrete and abstract valuation cannot always be strictly applied when quantifying damages in income-generating contracts as in some cases valuation has elements of both concrete and abstract approaches. For example, with respect to the stock market approach one has to look at the stock market price of the company in question when it is listed on the stock exchange, which is concrete valuation. The analyst then examines the effect of the breach of contract on the share price of the company through a so-called 'event study' that is by reference to the share index, which is abstract valuation, and compares it with the actual stock price subject to the breach to obtain the expectation interest. We can see that the event study of the impact of the breach of contract on the share price of the injured company has both concrete and abstract valuation elements.

7.70 An example of an event study used for damages valuation is *Crystallex v Venezuela*.[41] In 2002 Crystallex and the CVG (Corporación Venezolana de Guayana) concluded the Mine Operation Contract (MOC), which laid down the framework of rights and responsibilities of the parties for the development of the Las Cristinas gold mining project. Under the MOC, Crystallex was required to bear all the responsibility for the development of the Las Cristinas project and all of its associated costs, and to construct the agreed social works and make an initial payment of US$15 million, while being entitled to the proceeds deriving from the sale of its gold production, subject to the payment of a sliding royalty to the CVG and all applicable taxes required under Venezuelan law. CVG assumed the obligations of, inter alia, securing the permits required for the development of the project and of issuing and processing all notices to the Ministry of Mines required in connection to the MOC. According to Clause 17.4 of the MOC '[t]he [CVG] shall be in charge of the formalities before the Ministry of Environment and Natural Resources.'

7.71 The MOC provided for an initial duration of 20 years, which was extendable for two ten-year periods, for a maximum lifetime of 40 years. The Venezuelan government did not grant the environmental permit to exploit the mine and the arbitral tribunal found that Venezuela violated the Fair and Equitable Treatment standard contained in the Canada–Venezuela BIT.

7.72 The experts valuated the value of Crystallex according to the relevant industry index until the date of the announcement that Crystallex would not get the environmental permit, which was accepted by the arbitral tribunal as 'build up'. The tribunal considered that the stock market approach reflects the market assessment of the present value of future profits, discounted for all

---

40 Pablo T Spiller and Santiago Dellepiane in Wöss and others, *Damages in International Arbitration under Complex Long-term Contracts* (n 2) paras 6.152, 6.155.

41 *Crystallex International Corporation v Bolivarian Republic of Venezuela*, ICSID Case No. ARB(AF)/11/2.

publicly known or unknown risks. The tribunal considered this method appropriate as Crystallex was a one asset company and the right to extract gold was its only asset.

Another method that uses elements of both concrete and abstract valuation is the transaction **7.73** multiples method. For example, when the damage is the total loss of the value of the company, it can be valued by certain multiple times the EBIDTA of that company. In this case, the multiple can be obtained through the multiple used in the market for valuating similar companies or the one that has been used in commercial transactions with similar companies, which is abstract valuation, and the EBIDTA would be the one of the company in question, which is an element of concrete valuation.

H. THE DATE OF THE BREACH VS. THE DATE OF THE AWARD

Most rules of law allow for the calculation of damages at the time of the judgment or the **7.74** award or the last hearing on the merits. The exception is English law which applies the 'date of breach rule'. However, even under English law there are exceptions to this rule. In the *Golden Victory*, the House of Lords stated that the assessment of damages should be at the date of the award as opposed to the date of the breach.[42] In the case of *Johnson v Agnew*, the House of Lords held that the breach-date-rule 'is not an absolute rule; if to follow would give rise to injustice, the court has power to fix such other date as may be appropriate in the circumstances'.[43]

Under US law, the trial date is normally the relevant date for determining damages. However, **7.75** courts may use dates beyond such date to consider future losses when this is necessary to place the claimant in the position it would have been but for the breach.[44] The French *Cour de cassation* establishes since 1942 that the damages have to be quantified as of the date of the judgment which is considered in accordance with the principle of *réparation intégrale*. This means that inflations and price increases or reduction between the date of the breach and the judgment have to be considered.[45]

German law establishes that the date of determination of damages is the date of the last **7.76** hearing of facts.[46] This provision benefits only the claimant and does not take into account any reduction of damages in favour of the respondent.[47] Under CISG, in case of concrete valuation, the date of the determination should be as late as possible, ideally, the date of the judgment.[48]

The expectation interest is not linked to any particular date of valuation. However, under the **7.77** full-compensation principle, the question to be answered is: What would be the economic

---

42 *Golden Strait Corp. v Nippon Yusen Kubishika Kaisha (The Golden Victory)* [2007] UKHL 12 (HL).

43 *Johnson v Agnew* [1979] 2 WLR 487 (HL) 499.

44 James O'Brian and Robert P Gray, 'Lost Profits Calculations: Methods and Procedures' in Nancy J Fannon (ed), *The Comprehensive Guide to Lost Profits Damages for Experts and Attorneys* (BVR 2011) 352–4.

45 Brieskorn, Vertragshaftung und responsabilité contractuelle (n 10) 285–6, with further references.

46 BGH NJW 96, 2652, 2654; BGH 12.07.1996 – V ZR 117/95.

47 Brieskorn, Vertragshaftung und responsabilité contractuelle (n 10) 284, with further references.

48 Schwenzer, Hachem, Kee (n 24).

situation of the injured party but for the breach at the moment of the award? Because the moment of the award is the date when the injured is supposed to be compensated. This means that lost cash flows are to be updated from the date of the breach to the date of the award and, when applicable, future cash flows from the date of the award till the end of the project must be discounted to the date of the award.

7.78   When the date of the breach is chosen, lost cash flows from the date of the breach till the end of the project should be discounted at the appropriate rate and then updated to the date of the award. The updating interest rate should not be lower than the discount rate in order to avoid under-compensation which would violate the full-compensation principle. If the discount rate is higher than the updating rate, this would lead to under-compensation of the injured party and would not place it in the economic position it would be in but for the breach. If the risk is already acknowledged in the discount rate, there is no reason why that same risk should not be taken into consideration in the interest rate used when updating the cash flows to the date of the award. There is no reason for eliminating the risk for the same period of time when updating the same cash flows. The same interest rate should be used for discounting and updating the cash flows in order to place the injured party in the position it would be but for the breach, in this way full compensation is achieved and under-compensation is avoided. With respect to the reliance interest, it is likely to be calculated at the date of the investment and then updated to the date of the award using the appropriate interest rate.

7.79   This is illustrated in the automotive Joint Venture arbitration,[49] where two automotive supplier companies signed a Joint Venture Agreement to produce automotive parts for a particular Original Equipment Manufacturer (OEM) and established a Joint Venture Company in 2004. The Joint Venture Company was to be managed by the joint venture partner A with technology to be provided by joint venture partner B. Both parties had a 50 per cent participation and made equal capital contributions to the Joint Venture Company. The Joint Venture Agreement contained a non-competition clause which prohibited the parties to enter into business relationships with competitors. Soon after the signing of the Joint Venture Agreement and the commencement of operations of the Joint Venture Company, the latter was invited by the OEM to participate in an international tender for the supply of automotive parts. For that purpose, the parties agreed in a business plan duly approved by the board of directors of the Joint Venture Company that established the necessary investments to be made, and the profits to be achieved at the end of the project in 2010.

7.80   Soon thereafter, the OEM informed the Joint Venture Company that it had won the tender and observed that there was a slight difference in the company name. It turned out that joint venture partner B had established another joint venture with competitor company C and incorporated another joint venture company in the same country with nearly the same company name which was awarded and executed the project until the end of the project in 2010. As a consequence, company A commenced arbitration claiming lost profits against company B for the violation of the non-competition clause established in the Joint Venture Agreement. The Tribunal found that company B violated the non-competition clause in the Joint Venture Agreement.

---

49   Wöss and others, *Damages in International Arbitration under Complex Long-term Contracts* (n 2) paras 3.214–25.

With respect to damages, company A claimed the profits forecasted in the business plan   **7.81**
showing that the actual sales of automobiles in which the parts to be produced by the Joint
Venture Company were going to be used exceeded the projections contained in the business
plan. However, the Tribunal instead of awarding 50 per cent of the profits calculated as of
2010 in the business plan, which corresponds to the 50 per cent participation of company A in
the joint venture, discounted the cash flows to the date of the breach in 2005 at a 13 per cent
discount rate and did not update the 2005 damages amount to 2010. The outcome was a 50 per
cent reduction of the damages amount and flagrant under-compensation taking into consideration that discounting means applying interest over interest in reverse compounding, that is the
claimant received US$2 million instead of the US$4 million the joint venture parties had
calculated when agreeing the business plan in 2005. This was in spite of the evidence provided
by the claimant that the project was a success and the number of automotive parts sold during
that period was higher than the one forecast in the business plan.

It goes without saying that one does not need to be a financial expert or economist in order to   **7.82**
understand that the result of discounting to the date of the award with a high interest rate and
not updating it with a similar interest rate is unfair and leads to significant under-
compensation. In the illustrative case the claimant was only awarded US$2 million in 2010
instead of the US$4 million it would have received had the respondent not breached the Joint
Venture Agreement. In fact there is no reason why the arbitrator discounted the cash flow to
the date of the breach when the project finished in 2010 and the award was in 2010 and it
could have awarded damages as of 2010 without the need for further calculations as the
numbers were in the business plan and supported by public evidence available. This proves that
there is a need for some arbitrators to be better prepared to analyse damages claims in order to
avoid unfairness.

Whereas the Tribunal did not further reason this issue, in international commercial and   **7.83**
investment arbitration under-compensation through differential interest rates is sometimes the
result of an article written in 1990, that is 29 years ago based on an example that hardly
resembles modern arbitration practice referring to Janis Joplin's songbook instead of a project
agreement.[50] The main point of the article is that as the claimant is hypothetically paid in the
past, it is relieved of the risks associated with an asset, hence pre-judgment interest should be
awarded at a risk-free rate. The point is that assuming that the claimant was paid in the past is
a financial exercise based on a hypothesis that never occurred, as the claimant did not receive
any payment in the past, but it will receive payment at or after the award. Moreover, it ignores
the but-for premise, and the full compensation principles which are recognized in the most
important jurisdiction, according to which the hypothetical development of the injured party's
business has to be reconstructed according to the evidence available and should prove with
reasonable certainty the profits that the injured party would have obtained but for the breach.[51]

Under-compensation in the form of using high discount rates and risk-free rates for updating   **7.84**
has first been analysed and explained by some of the leading international experts in large
investment and commercial arbitrations in a seminal article referring to the so-called 'invalid

---

50   Franklin M Fisher and R Craig Romaine, 'Janis Joplin's Yearbook and the Theory of Damages' (1990) 5(3) *Journal of*
     Accounting, Auditing and Finance 149.
51   Paul E Godek, 'Ex Ante vs. Ex Post: Janis Joplin's Yearbook Revisited', Law 360, 22 July 2015.

round trip'[52] and is further explained in Chapter 6 of the monograph *Damages in International Arbitration under Complex Long-term Contracts*.[53] What the proponents of the invalid round trip overlook is that damages determination is in essence a legal issue whereby the experts have to calculate the amount of money that would place the injured party in the financial position it would be had the wrongful act not been committed, at the date of the award or when it receives the payment.

I.   SHOULD THE DATE OF THE AWARD BE THE DATE OF VALUATION WHEN THE COMPANY STOPPED OPERATIONS CAUSED BY THE BREACH OF CONTRACT?

7.85   If the company stopped operations because of the breach of the contract, the same situation, already explained in the previous section, applies. What is important is the reconstruction of the hypothetical course of events, that is the experts would have to prepare projections of the corresponding future cash flows based on reasonable assumptions and the evidence available from the date of the breach till the date established by the experts. These cash flows can be discounted to the date of the breach at a reasonable interest rate determined by the experts and then update them to the date of the award at the same interest rate to avoid under-compensation. The more straightforward solution, however, would be to calculate damages at the date of the award, which means updating the cash flows from the date of the breach till the date of the award and discount future cash flows to the date of the award. The resulting cash flows are to be compared with the actual cash flows resulting from the breach which are zero because the company stopped operations. This is the expectation interest which should be awarded in order to place the injured party in the economic position but for the breach.

J.   LOSS OF A CHANCE, LOST PROFITS AND UNJUST ENRICHMENT

7.86   Loss of a chance means that the lost profits depend on an aleatory element or game of chance related to the performance of contract, which are exogenous circumstances not controlled by the parties. Damages are limited to the pro rata probability of obtaining profits. Loss of a chance is recognized under English law, French law, and PICC. Under German law, loss of a chance is not admissible according to the principle of all or nothing. US law limits loss of a chance to malpractice of professionals and prices not obtained.[54]

7.87   Loss of a chance is different from contractual lost profits or cash flows as the latter are not subject to aleatory elements or a game of chance, but to contingencies or risks. In case of an infrastructure project, the successful determination of the construction phase is a contingency and a risk that could affect the generation of lost profits during the operation phase. This risk is computed as part of the discount rate imposed on the future cash flows.

---

52   Manuel A Abdala, Pablo D López Zadicoff, and Pablo T Spiller, 'Invalid Round Trips in Setting Pre-Judgment Interest in International Arbitration' (2011) 5(1) *World Arbitration and Mediation Review*, 1–21.

53   Pablo T Spiller and Santiago Dellepiane in Wöss and others, *Damages in International Arbitration under Complex Long-term Contracts* (n 2) paras 6.107–117, 7.09–13.

54   Herfried Wöss, 'Damages and Loss of a Chance or Loss of Opportunity', 13 (2020) 1 *New York Dispute Resolution Lawyer*, 33-5; Harvey McGregor, *McGregor on Damages* (16th edn, Sweet & Maxwell 1997) 246–59; Pinna (n 32) para 287; Official comment number 2 to Art 7.4.3 (2); Fikentscher and Heinemann (n 23) para 631.

The arbitral tribunal in *Bridas v Turkmenistan* explains the difference between lost profits and   **7.88**
loss of a chance when stating that there is 'a considerable difference between the loss of a
specific contractual right and the loss of a general opportunity to trade in a speculative
market'.[55] For example, in the case of a carton freezer, lost profits referred to all the cash flows
that could have been obtained from the sales contracts that could not be executed due to the
non-performance of the carton freezer. Loss of a chance refers to the opportunity to make
more sales if the carton freezer had worked properly. Lost profits refer to sales under a
contractual right, and loss of a chance refers to a market opportunity that does not rely on a
contract.

Under CISG, there is also no compensation for loss of a chance. However, paragraph 3 of the   **7.89**
CISG Advisory Council Opinion No. 6 on the 'Calculation of Damages under CISG
Article 74' makes the following differentiation: The prohibition on damages for loss of chance
or opportunity does not apply when the aggrieved party purposely enters into a contract in
order to obtain a chance of earning a profit. In such case, the chance of profit is an asset, and
when a party chooses to enter into a contract to obtain such a chance, the party is entitled to
compensation when the promisor unjustifiably does not perform. Otherwise, a promisor could
breach that contract with impunity and avoid 'liability solely on the bases of the difficulty of
proving loss where it was clear at the time of formation that such loss would be impossible to
prove with reasonable certainty'. Moreover, allowing recovery in this circumstance would be
consistent with the full compensation principle of Article 74. It also finds support in Article
7.4.3 of the UNIDROIT Principles, which provides for recovery of damages for the loss of
chance of profit.

With respect to unjust enrichment, in cases where the party in breach did not fulfil its   **7.90**
obligation of payment to the injured party, in order for the injured party to ask for unjust
enrichment, he would have to know if the party in breach had invested the amount of money
not paid, where he had invested it and at what rate of return. This information is not normally
available. Damages law is about the loss to the injured party and not about the benefit that the
respondent obtains from the breach. With respect to lost profits in income-generating
contracts, the injured party must prove with reasonable certainty that there would have been
income stream but for the breach in order for damages to be recoverable as expectation interest.
Under the US doctrine of the efficient breach, the breach would be efficient if the party in
breach gains enough from the breach to receive a benefit after compensating the injured for the
resulting loss according to the subjective preferences of the injured party. That means that the
defendant must pay to the injured party the expectation interest and is entitled to keep any
additional benefit.[56]

K. THE USE OF EX-POST INFORMATION IN THE LIGHT OF THE FULL COMPENSATION PRINCIPLE

If the date of valuation is the date of the breach of contract but calculations are being made   **7.91**
some time after that date, and the use of hindsight information between the date of the breach

---

55   *Bridas v Turkmenistan* (n 35) para 60.
56   E Allan Farnsworth, *Contracts* (4th edn, Aspen Publishers 2004) 736.

of contract and the date of the calculation of damages results in a higher value than the one that would have been obtained without considering such information, not considering hindsight information would result in unfairness against the injured party as the respondent would obtain windfall profits. On the other hand, if the use of hindsight information would lower the value of the income-generating contract and this information is not being taken into consideration, it would result in unfairness against the respondent as the claimant would get the windfall profits. If there is hindsight information, it has to be used as it avoids uncertainty and places the injured party in the economic position it would be in but for the breach which would bring fairness to both sides at least during the period of time that hindsight information is available. The use of hindsight information could increase or decrease the damages, both scenarios could happen, but using hindsight information reduces speculation, because actual information is considered in both, the actual and the but-for scenarios.

7.92 If the decision is to use hindsight information, then it should be used in both, the actual and the but-for scenarios, in order to obtain consistency. If the decision is not to use hindsight information, then it should not be used in either the actual or in the but-for scenario, again for the sake of consistency. However, it must be considered that not using hindsight information in the actual scenario would bring unrealistic results, which would add speculation. It has to be noted, that the rejection of hindsight information in the US derives from criminal law and refers to ex-post qualification of a crime, that is criminal liability.[57] In this respect it has to be observed, that in the context of damages valuation, hindsight refers to the consideration of the economic circumstances between the date of the breach and the date of valuation, but it does not apply to the determination of liability, therefore the arguments against hindsight in criminal law are not applicable to the determination of damages.

L. INTEREST AS DAMAGES

7.93 Interest may be legal, contractual or compensatory.[58] Legal interest is the statutory rate of interest for the delay in payments and is found under the US, English, French and Mexican laws, PICC and CISG. This refers to the minimum interest rate which the injured party should receive from the moment of the determination of the damages to the actual payment. The award of interest for the deprivation of the use of money is internationally accepted except in countries under the Sharia legal system. However, legal interest does not refer to damages but to delay in payments. With respect to the contractual interest rates for delayed payments, these are not necessarily applicable to the payment of damages and require detailed examination of the contractual provisions as well as of the limitations under the applicable law.

7.94 Compensatory interest or interest as damages aims at making the injured party whole for the time passed between the moment of the determination of damages and their actual payment. The aim is to compensate the injured party for the loss of the use of money. Therefore, interest for breach of long-term contracts arise in damages claims as pre-award interest or as post-award interest. Interest as damages is also admissible in the rules of law above mentioned.

---

57 See, amongst many, Megan E Giroux and others, 'Hindsight Bias and Law' (2016) 224(3) *Zeitschrift für Psychologie* 190–203.

58 Wöss and others, *Damages in International Arbitration under Complex Long-term Contracts* (n 2) ch 7.

The English Arbitration Act gives arbitrators the authority to award simple or compound **7.95** interest at such dates and rates that it considers meet the justice of the case.[59] In England, according to a study by the Law Commission, courts typically award pre-judgment interest at 8 per cent.[60] In the US, statutory interest ranges from 6 to 15 per cent. Some federal courts award pre-judgment interest and post-judgment interest at the same rate. Other federal courts rely on the principle of reasonableness and fairness which gives a wide margin of discretion.[61] When federal courts approach compensatory interest issues without consulting state law, district courts exercise broader discretion in resolving claims in compensatory interest.[62] French law also grants the injured party the right to obtain interest as damages which follows the rule established by the *Cour de cassation* which is in accordance with the but-for premise according to which 'the nature of liability is to re-establish as exactly as possible the equilibrium that the damages destroyed and to put the aggrieved party into the same situation that it would have been if the damaging event had not occurred, 'Le propre de la responsabilité civile este de replacer la victime dans la situation oú ell se serait trouvée si l'acte dommageable ne s'était pas produit.'[63]

In Germany, compound interest is not admissible (§289 first sentence BGB), however, this **7.96** may be asked for as damages according to §§280(1) and (2) and 286 BGB. § 288 BGB states that an injured party 'may claim higher interest on a different legal basis'[64] which is interest as damages. Article 78 CISG provides: 'If either party fails to pay the price or any other sum that is in arrears, the other party is entitled to interest on it, without prejudice to any claim for damages recoverable under article 74.' The general principles most often applied to the issue of interest under CISG are: full compensation to the aggrieved party for the loss they have endured, reasonableness and restitution to the aggrieved party.[65]

Article 7.4.10 (Interest on Damages) PICC expressly states that interest on damages accrues **7.97** from the date of non-performance. Paragraph (3) of Article 7.4.9 (Interest for failure to pay money) PICC establishes that the aggrieved party is entitled to additional damages if the non-payment caused it a greater harm. According to official comment 3 to that article, the additional damages must be proved in accordance with certainty of loss and foreseeability.

Under several rules of law mentioned above, interest as damages or compensatory interest as **7.98** pre-judgment or pre-award interest is admissible. Therefore, it may be concluded that 'the relevant statutes typically envisage that the court may grant interest on damages for any period between the time when the cause of action arose and the judgment',[66] which should aim at full compensation.

---

59 Arbitration Act 1996, c.23 §49.
60 The Law Commission (Law Com no 287), Pre-judgment interest on debts and damages – Item 4 of the Eighth Programme of Law Reform: Compound Interest (2004) 21 <http://www.lawcom.gov.uk> accessed 15/1/2020.
61 John Y Gotanda, 'Damages in Private International Law' (2007) 326 *Recueil de cours* 209–12.
62 Ibid., 214, footnotes omitted.
63 Cour de cassation. Deuxième chambre civile, 9 July 1981, Bull civ II 156.
64 Volker Triebel, 'Awarding Interest in International Arbitration' (1989) 6 *Journal of International Arbitration* 18–19.
65 Gotanda, *Damages in Private International Law* (n 61) 241–2.
66 Schwenzer, Hachem, Kee (n 24) 693–4.

7.99   Interest in the context of damages are understood as interest as damages,[67] which means that they should serve to place the injured party in the economic position it would be but for the breach of contract. Interest are intended to represent the cost of operating a company or the cost of operating a project, which is the cost of capital, in particular, the Weighted Average Cost of Capital or WACC, which takes into consideration both the cost of credit as well as the cost of capital. If the company is operating only with credit, it would only recognize the cost of the debt. On the other hand, the same applies with respect to the capital cost. The weighted average cost of capital takes into consideration, amongst others, the risk of the company. This is an interest rate that considers many elements.

7.100   The cost of capital that should be taken when updating cash flows, is the WACC of an efficiently managed company in that same sector. Some professionals argue that when the investment is at an early stage, there is no WACC, however, as has been mentioned it is not the WACC of the early stage investment, but the WACC of an efficiently managed company in the same sector. On the other hand, it is the hypothetical situation of the injured party without the illegal measure which takes into consideration that the company is in operation. Therefore, the WACC of an efficiently managed company in that sector should be applied in discounting the cash flows and also in updating them. The WACC may change in time, which has to be considered by the experts accordingly.

M. COST ALLOCATION

7.101   There are basically three rules with respect to cost allocation: (1) each part bears its own cost ('pay your own way') and that the cost of the arbitral institution and the arbitral tribunal are shared in equal parts, or 50/50 per cent rule; (2) costs-follow-the-event rule; and (3) the rule of relative success whereby the success is being pondered for each of the claims made adjusted cost rule. With respect to the costs-follow-the-event rule, the rationale behind it is the full compensation principle, which means to place the injured in the economic position it would be in but for the breach. The question to ask is how to make the injured party whole. When the winner is the claimant or the injured party, it would be necessary that it recovers its cost and also its legal fees together with the damages. In this way, the injured party would be placed in the economic position in which he would have been but for the breach of contract. The UNCITRAL Rules established the costs-follow-the-event rule in 1976. In 2010, the UNCITRAL Rules went further by stating that the cost of the arbitration shall be borne by the unsuccessful party including the winning party's cost.

7.102   According to a survey published in GAR in 2017,[68] before 2013, 60 per cent of published investment arbitration cases were decided according to the 50/50 per cent rule, 23 per cent of the cases followed the costs-follow-the-event rule and 17 per cent followed the partially adjusted cost rule. After 2013, this same survey shows that the application of the 50/50 per cent rule dropped from 60 to 36 per cent of the cases. By contrast, there was an increase in the

---

67   Wöss and others, *Damages in International Arbitration under Complex Long-term Contracts* (n 2) ch 7.
68   Mathew Hodgson, Alastair Campbell, 'Damages and Cost in Investment Treaty Arbitration Revised' (GAR News, 14 December 2017) <https://globalarbitrationreview.com/article/1151755/damages-and-costs-in-investment-treaty-arbitration-revisited> accessed on 15 January 2020.

application of the costs-follow-the-event rule from 23 to 44 per cent of the cases. With regard to the partially-adjusted cost it increased from 17 to 20 per cent. This article also mentions that since 2013 in line with the costs-follow-the-event rule, successful claimants received an adjusted cost award in 65 per cent of the cases in comparison to 63 per cent when the successful parties were the respondents.

In civil law countries, in particular, Austria, Germany, Sweden and Switzerland, civil **7.103** procedure rules require a proportional allocation reflecting each party's relative success on the claims and defences. In the US, parties pay their own costs irrespective of the outcome and share the costs of the tribunal and the administering institution, which is based on the philosophy that access to justice is paramount and barriers to seeking justice should be eliminated. Under English law, the winner recovers his reasonable costs from the loser who also pays for the tribunal and the arbitral institution, which is based on the philosophy of indemnity. In England costs are usually awarded to the net winner. If a claimant recovered some monetary award, he is normally regarded as the successful party since he had to bring the arbitration in order to recover its damages. However, this principle is not always strictly applied.[69]

What is important to consider is what happens when the claimant is the unsuccessful party and **7.104** is condemned to pay the costs of arbitration and legal fees of the respondent? In this respect, it can be argued that this can have a positive impact, because it prevents unmeritorious claims. However, it also has a negative effect, because claimants might feel threatened specially when considering that costs in arbitration are high and the legal fees are also quite substantial. Therefore, it would be worth considering that when the claimant is the losing party, but the claim was meritorious, the application of the 50/50 per cent approach should apply as it would avoid reluctance from the claimants to present a damages claim in arbitration. On the other hand, when the claimant is the losing party and the respondent proves that the case is frivolous, the costs-follow-the-event rule should apply. It is important to bear in mind the full compensation principle which is a general principle of law and aims at placing the injured party in the economic position it would be but for the breach, but it does not refer to the economic position of the party in breach.

N. CONCLUSIONS

Full compensation is recognized as the guiding principle when framing, analysing or awarding **7.105** damages. This principle is recognized in all important jurisdictions for international arbitration. Full compensation means to place the injured party in the economic position it would be but for the breach of contract. The full compensation principle is achieved through the but-for premise or hypothesis. The but-for premise has three different functions: (i) it is the method to quantify damages by comparing the actual economic situation of the injured party with the hypothetical or but-for situation. The result would be the loss that has to be compensated, which is the expectation interest; (ii) this method aids to establish causality through the

---

69   Michael O'Reilly, '13th Annual Review of the Arbitration Act 1996, Time to Review the Arbitration Act 1996? Provision on Costs and Appeals: An Assessment from an International Perspective' (British Institute of International and Comparative Law, 2010) 2 <https://www.biicl.org/files/4936_biicl_13th_annual_mor.pdf> accessed on 5 March 2019.

question whether the loss would have occurred in the absence of the breach of contract; and (iii) the application of the but-for premise leads to full compensation. Quantifying the expectation interest means placing the injured party in the position it would be but for the breach, which is full compensation.

7.106 When framing a damages claim, there are different requirements and limitations under different applicable laws. Under all rules of law, liability is the starting point for the claim. Causality is another requirement. With respect to the loss in income-generating contracts, what is important is to prove the reasonable certainty of the income stream. If the income stream is not proved with reasonable certainty, there is no loss to be compensated. Limitations such as fault, adequacy, foreseeability and remoteness may limit in particular consequential damages, which, however, hardly play a role with respect to income-generating contracts where the purpose of the contract and the risk sphere allocation and the protective effect of the particular contractual provision are of utmost importance as risks allocated to the respondent are risks foreseen and have to be borne by the respondent. The purpose of the income-generating contract is precisely the generation of cash flows and the effect of the breach of contract is the loss of such cash flows or the loss of value of the undertaking generating such cash flows under the contract. With respect to limitations, as explained in this chapter contributory negligence and mitigation are causality issues whereby contributory negligence is relevant at the moment of the breach of contract, whereas mitigation refers to the time thereafter.

7.107 Another important aspect when framing a damages claim is the type of contract. There are basically bilateral works and services contracts and synallagmatic triallagmas or partnership-like relationships without an exchange of goods, services and money but whereby the parties contribute assets and the income stream derives from a third party which is the market. In this respect, the measure of damages plays an important role and establishes complexity as some rules of law only recognize the loss and lost profits or *damnum emergens* and *lucrum cessans* measure of damages, which as we have shown are an artificial distinction that arose from religious-political circumstances in the Middle Ages but do not provide a practical solution for damages analysis as already recognised by Prof. Friedrich Mommsen in 1855. Specially in income-generating contracts, claiming loss and lost profits at the same time would result in double counting as explained in detail in this chapter. For income-generating contracts of synallagmatic triallagmas, the measure of damages that works best is the expectation interest which answers the question, what would be the economic position of the injured party but for the breach? or the reliance interest which answers the question what would be the economic position of the injured party had it not entered into the contract?

7.108 The expectation interest is achieved through the application of the but-for premise, which means that the economic difference between the actual situation and the but-for situation is the loss that has to be compensated. This measure avoids double counting when calculating damages with respect to income-generating contracts.

7.109 With respect to the reliance interest, which is the so-called sunk investment or the investment that could be recovered due to the breach, the reliance interest should only be awarded if the injured party proves with reasonable certainty that without the breach it would have recovered the initial investment. However, in case the injured party cannot prove this because of a bad business, the injured party may not recover all of the sunk investment. However, the injured party may recover the reliance interest even without proving that it would have recovered the initial investment but for the breach if it proves tort or misrepresentation. English and German law shift the burden of proof to the respondent who would have to show in all probability that the injured party would not have recovered the initial investment in the absence of the breach of contract.

There is difference between lost profits, loss of a chance and unjust enrichment. Lost profits **7.110** arise under a particular situation even when they are subject to contingencies. Loss of a chance requires an exogenous aleatory requirement and may not be claimed under some rules of law such as German law. Unjust enrichment as damages is only recognized by few rules of law and is awarded under very particular circumstances, in particular, where no economic difference may be determined.

The traditional distinction between abstract and concrete valuation found under many rules of **7.111** law is only partially applicable to modern damages valuation methods for income-generating contracts and investments as explained in this chapter.

The key issues in damages valuation with respect to income-generating contracts are the date **7.112** of valuation, the use of hindsight information, and the discount and updating rates for the cash flows. All these elements should be considered in the light of the full compensation principle which is to place the injured party in the economic position it would have been in but for the breach.

Damages are the result of fulfilling all the requirements and the application of the limitations **7.113** under the applicable law, subject to the relevant burden and standard of proof which the injured party has to overcome in order to be awarded damages. If the claimant meets all these requirements, he should receive compensation for his actual loss, which corresponds to the full compensation principle.

8

ARBITRATION IN ANTITRUST DAMAGES CASES IN THE EUROPEAN UNION

Patricia Živković and Toni Kalliokoski[*]

A. INTRODUCTION

8.01 Over the past 20 years in Europe, private enforcement of competition law has slowly progressed from non-existent to an established and growing phenomenon.[1] Despite this, antitrust damages remain a rapidly developing area of the law. Its development has been characterized by the interaction between the competition law of the European Union ('EU') and the law on damages actions in the different EU Member States. The Court of Justice of the European Union ('ECJ') has given a number of rulings with sometimes surprising outcomes for national legal systems when EU competition law and national laws collide.

8.02 To facilitate and regulate antitrust damages claims, the EU adopted a Directive on antitrust damages[2] ('Directive' or 'Damages Directive'), which entered into force in December 2014 and has been implemented by the EU Member States. The Damages Directive aims to guarantee a minimum level of procedural, evidential and substantive standards throughout the Member

---

* Date of submission: 26/01/2020.

1 See e.g., Jean-François Laborde, 'Cartel Damages actions in Europe: How Courts have assessed cartel overcharges' (2019) 4 *Concurrences* 3, para 15ff; Damien Geradin, 'Collective Redress for Antitrust Damages in the European Union: Is This a Reality Now?' (2015) 22:5 *George Mason Law Review*, 1079.

2 Directive 2014/104/EU of the European Parliament and of the Council of 26 November 2014 on certain rules governing actions for damages under national law for infringements of the competition law provisions of the Member States and of the European Union [2014] OJ L 349/1.

States. The Directive is expected to further increase the number of antitrust damages cases in the coming years.

As antitrust damages claims become more common, more and more of these claims will be **8.03** resolved in arbitration. However, arbitration as a method of dispute resolution presents some unique issues with regard to antitrust damages. Some of these issues relate to the suitability of arbitration to non-contractual claims against multiple jointly and severally liable defendants, such as in cartel cases. This has already resulted in the courts of some Member States not enforcing arbitration clauses. Another set of issues is related to whether arbitral proceedings provide sufficient procedural and substantive protections, especially now that the Damages Directive has set certain minimum standards required by EU law. This chapter addresses these two issues in turn.

B. SCOPE OF ARBITRATION CLAUSES IN ANTITRUST DAMAGES CASES

In this section, we first briefly comment on the ECJ's decision in case C-352/13 *CDC* **8.04** *Hydrogen Peroxide* because national courts have had contradictory interpretations on its relevance to the scope of arbitration clauses in antitrust damages cases. We then review recent rulings on the scope of arbitration clauses in antitrust damages cases in the courts of EU Member States. This review shows that national courts in Germany, the Netherlands, England and Finland have so far reached different interpretations on whether antitrust damages cases fall within the scope of arbitration clauses, sometimes claiming jurisdiction but sometimes referring the parties to arbitration. The reasoning used by the courts also varies. This creates considerable additional uncertainty in what already tend to be complex damages cases.

The problems only seem to arise under particular circumstances. Baker has proposed a useful **8.05** categorization of the most common types of antitrust damages cases into (1) partnership disputes, (2) bilateral buyer/seller disputes, (3) disputes over conspiracies with strangers, and (4) competitors' disputes.[3] He notes that categories (1) and (2) are closest to 'typical' business disputes based on breach of contract. Category (3), cartels, is the most problematic because it includes third parties that are not party to the arbitration agreement but still jointly and severally liable. We will thus focus on this category. Category (4) is not likely to result in arbitration proceedings at all because there will be no contractual relationship between the parties.[4]

1. Court of Justice of the European Union

In case C-352/13 *CDC Hydrogen Peroxide*,[5] the ECJ was asked to provide a preliminary ruling **8.06** on the interpretation of jurisdiction and arbitration clauses in the context of the Brussels I

---

3   Don Baker, 'Parallel Proceedings before the Arbitral Tribunal and the Courts' in Gordon Blanke and Phillip Landolt (eds), *EU and US Antitrust Arbitration: A Handbook for Practitioners* (Kluwer Law International 2011) 1472–3.

4   In the antitrust damages context, indirect purchasers are another example of a group that would categorically fall outside arbitration because there is no contract between the indirect purchaser and the infringer.

5   C-352/13, *CDC Hydrogen Peroxide* [2015] ECLI:EU:C:2015:335, para 14.

Regulation[6] in a cartel damages case. The claim was brought by a special purpose vehicle of the Cartel Damage Claims company ('CDC') that had acquired the damages claims of various customers of the cartel companies. The purchase agreements that the customers had entered into with the cartel members contained different jurisdiction clauses and arbitration clauses. The ECJ did not give a ruling on arbitration clauses, citing insufficient information about the contents of the arbitration clauses.[7] However, the ECJ did provide a ruling on the interaction of jurisdiction clauses and the Brussels I Regulation in a cartel damages case.[8] The ECJ thus left open how arbitration clauses should be interpreted in such a situation, and national courts have already developed different interpretations.

8.07 As regards jurisdiction clauses within the scope of the Brussels I Regulation, the ECJ ruled that it was necessary to determine whether the jurisdiction clauses actually applied to the dispute at hand. The ECJ stated that a jurisdiction clause should only be interpreted to cover disputes arising from the legal relationship covered by the agreement that contains the clause. This is to prevent a party from being bound by a jurisdiction clause in a dispute not related to the agreement and therefore taking a party by surprise.[9] The ECJ gave two particular reasons why a jurisdiction clause may not apply to a cartel damages claim. First, a cartel damages claim is a tort claim, and therefore not based on the contract that contains the jurisdiction clause.[10] Second, if the claimant was not aware of the defendant's cartel infringement at the time the parties agreed on the jurisdiction clause, then the claimant could not reasonably foresee the possibility of cartel damages disputes. Therefore, the cartel damages claims are not based on the contractual relationship, and the jurisdiction clause does not apply.[11] However, if the jurisdiction clause specifically refers to antitrust damages, then it does apply.[12] The fundamental reason for the ECJ's decision seems to have been the lack of reasonable foreseeability.

8.08 So far, some national courts have interpreted the scope of *arbitration clauses* using the same arguments that the ECJ stated for *jurisdiction clauses covered by the Brussels I Regulation*. Other courts have rejected this approach. Unless the ECJ confronts this issue, Member State courts will continue to take different positions and adopt different tests. This will lead to an incoherent situation where arbitration clauses will be applicable in some Member States or in some antitrust damages cases but not in others. This is completely undesirable.

8.09 National courts should exercise caution when interpreting the ECJ's judgment in the context of the scope of arbitration clauses because the ECJ expressly avoided ruling on this question. Also, the two main reasons given by the ECJ for its decision concerning jurisdiction clauses, namely, the tort law nature of the damages claims and the lack of foreseeability regarding the

---

6   Council Regulation (EC) No 44/2001 of 22 December 2000 on jurisdiction and the recognition and enforcement of judgments in civil and commercial matters [2001] OJ L 12/1.
7   See *Hydrogen Peroxide* (n 5), para 58.
8   Ibid., paras 57–72.
9   Ibid., para 68.
10   Ibid., para 69.
11   Ibid., para 70.
12   Ibid., para 71. For a critique of this approach, see David Ashton, *Competition Damages Actions in the EU: Law and Practice* (2nd edn, Edward Elgar Publishing Limited 2018), 357–61.

damages claims, are generally not considered to prevent a dispute from falling within the scope of an arbitration clause.[13] Most likely, the ECJ did not intend to rule on arbitration clauses at all.

2. EU Member States

So far, at least six courts have ruled directly on the scope of arbitration clauses in antitrust damages claims. We will briefly introduce these cases and the reasoning behind the courts' decisions as background for our analysis. **8.10**

a. Cases where arbitration clauses were not enforced

On 4 July 2013, the District Court of Helsinki in Finland ruled that it had jurisdiction in an antitrust damages case despite arbitration clauses.[14] A special purpose vehicle of the Cartel Damage Claims company was pursuing claims acquired from two Finnish pulp and paper companies against a Finnish chemicals company. The chemicals supply agreements contained different arbitration clauses with different numbers of arbitrators, potentially leading to two separate arbitration proceedings. The District Court found that CDC's claim was based on the alleged price effects of the illegal cartel agreement, and not on a breach of the hydrogen peroxide supply agreements. Furthermore, because CDC's predecessors were not aware of the cartel when they agreed to the arbitration clauses, they could not have intended for the arbitration clauses to apply to disputes caused by the cartel. The court further noted that materially the same dispute must not be split into separate proceedings without a specific reason. Also, the court considered that when interpreting an arbitration clause, importance should be given to the possibility to resolve the entire dispute in single proceedings, as well as the possibility to resolve closely related disputes in the same or at least similar proceedings. The court ruled that the cartel damages claim was not within the scope of the arbitration clauses.[15] **8.11**

On 4 June 2014, the District Court of Amsterdam ruled that the dispute between the claimant's predecessors and the defendants did not fall within the scope of the arbitration clauses, and the District Court had jurisdiction.[16] A special purpose vehicle of CDC was pursuing claims acquired from purchasers of sodium chlorate against chemicals companies. The defendants argued that the District Court lacked jurisdiction because CDC's claims were related to contractual deliveries of sodium chlorate and covered by arbitration clauses. CDC argued that the agreements were not important because its claim was based on the defendants' price-fixing behaviour. The District Court found that despite their broad wording, the scope of the arbitration clauses did not cover infringements of competition law. Based on the wording of the arbitration clauses and the parties' business experience, it was not reasonable to expect that the customers were bound to submit a dispute concerning a cartel into arbitration. The **8.12**

---

13   See e.g., Gary Born, *International Commercial Arbitration* (2nd edn, Kluwer Law International 2014), 1318–19, 1357–66.

14   District Court of Helsinki, in *CDC Hydrogen Peroxide Cartel Damage Claims SA v Kemira Oyj*, interlocutory judgment 36492, 4 July 2013, case number L 11/16750.

15   This was somewhat surprising because the applicability of arbitration clauses has traditionally been very broad in Finland. For example, the Finnish Supreme Court found in its judgment KKO 2008:102 that damages claims based on a breach of contract that also amounted to fraud had to be resolved in arbitration and not in criminal proceedings due to an arbitration clause in a shareholders' agreement.

16   District Court of Amsterdam, in *CDC Project 13 SA v Akzo Nobel NV and others*, 4 June 2014, ECLI:NL: RBAMS:2014:3190.

court found that the antitrust violation was not connected to the supply agreements and, hence, to the arbitration clauses. The court further mentioned that the customers were not reasonably required to expect that disputes about secret cartel conduct by their suppliers would have to be settled in arbitration. Finally, the court noted that its findings could have been different if the parties had shown that the supply contracts were fundamentally relevant to the damages claim.

8.13 The Amsterdam District Court's decision was appealed to the Amsterdam Court of Appeal which affirmed the District Court's decision on 21 July 2015.[17] The defendants had relied on both jurisdiction clauses and arbitration clauses to challenge the jurisdiction of the Dutch courts. The Court of Appeal first applied on the jurisdiction clauses the reasoning of the ECJ's *CDC Hydrogen Peroxide* ruling.[18] The Court of Appeal found that, according to their wording, the jurisdiction clauses did not refer to disputes concerning liability for infringements of competition law, but referred generally to disputes arising in contractual relations. The injured companies could therefore not be deemed to have agreed to apply the jurisdiction clauses also to settle antitrust damages claims resulting from the defendants' participation in a cartel. Finally, the Court of Appeal noted laconically that there were no grounds to rule otherwise concerning the arbitration clauses: the customers had not agreed to apply the arbitration clauses to antitrust damages matters.

8.14 On 25 May 2016, the District Court of Rotterdam reached a similar conclusion as the above-mentioned Amsterdam courts.[19] The case concerned a lift cartel, and the claimant was a litigation vehicle where the claims of numerous customers of the cartel had been consolidated. Despite the similar outcome, the reasoning of the Rotterdam Court was somewhat different. First, the court found that the case was indeed connected to the lift purchase agreements. The court took into account what the parties could reasonably expect from each other in their contractual relationship. The court applied the ECJ's reasoning in the *CDC Hydrogen Peroxide* ruling on jurisdiction clauses to arbitration clauses. Consequently, arbitration clauses could only cover disputes that were foreseeable to the parties at the time they entered into the agreement. Furthermore, if the arbitration clauses were enforced, the claimant's claims against contract parties would be resolved in arbitration. However, the same claims against non-contract parties, on the basis of joint and several liability, would still be resolved by the District Court as there was no basis to resolve them in arbitration. The court considered that splitting the claim in this way would be a significant practical obstacle to enforcing the claimant's right to compensation. Such an obstacle would be contrary to the EU law principle of effectiveness. In any case, it would be unreasonable and unfair.

8.15 The main points raised by the Finnish and Dutch courts seem to be as follows:

(i)   Cartel damages claims were not contractual claims because they are based on an illegal infringement of competition law and not on the sales contracts between the cartelists and their customers. Therefore, the cartel damages claims were not within the scope of the arbitration clauses included in the sales contracts.

---

17   Amsterdam Court of Appeal, in *Kemira Chemicals Oy v CDC Project 13 SA*, 21 July 2015, ECLI:NL: GHAMS:2015:3006.
18   See *Hydrogen Peroxide* (n 5), paras 68–71.
19   District Court of Rotterdam, in *Stichting De Glazen Lift v Kone BV and others*, 5 May 2016, ECLI:NL: RBROT:2016:4164.

(ii)   The arbitration clauses only referred broadly to all disputes in general but not to competition infringements in particular. Therefore, it cannot be deduced that the arbitration clauses cover claims based on competition infringements.

(iii)   The claimants did not know their contract parties were involved in a cartel. The cartels were unforeseeable behaviour and fall outside what the parties could expect to happen in the usual course of their contractual relationship. Therefore, the claimants could not have intended the arbitration clauses to cover damages based on cartel behaviour, and thus could not be bound by the arbitration clauses in such cases.

(iv)   Enforcing the arbitration clauses would split the proceedings into different forums, which would make it (too) difficult for the claimants to enforce their rights.

(v)   Enforcing the arbitration clauses would be unreasonable and unfair to the claimants. This point mainly seems to be derived from all the other points together but invokes concerns with the effectiveness of the arbitration clauses rather than their scope.

There is some change in the reasoning over time. Before the ECJ's decision in *CDC Hydrogen Peroxide*, the reasoning includes an argument that cartel damages claims are based on illegal price manipulation by the cartel members, not on the purchase agreements between the cartel members and their customers. After *CDC Hydrogen Peroxide*, the courts have focused more on the fact that the claimants were not aware of the infringement when they entered into the agreements containing the arbitration clauses.   **8.16**

b.   Cases where arbitration clauses were enforced

Contrary to the Finnish and Dutch decisions, the High Court of England and Wales on 28 February 2017 found a cartel damages claim to fall within the scope of an arbitration clause.[20] The claimant was pursuing antitrust damages for losses caused by a cartel of producers of lithium-ion batteries used in mobile phones. The claimant and two of the defendants were parties to a supply contract which contained an arbitration clause.   **8.17**

The High Court took as the starting point that rational businessmen who had agreed on an arbitration clause would wish their disputes to be decided by the same tribunal, and not to be divided between different forums.[21] However, tort claims not related to the contract containing the arbitration clause do not fall within the scope of the arbitration clause and the above-mentioned 'one-stop adjudication'.[22] Therefore, it was necessary to determine if the contract and the tort claims were sufficiently closely connected. If they were, then the tort claim should be decided along with the contract claim in arbitration.[23] The supply contract that contained the arbitration clause also contained a clause requiring the parties to negotiate prices in good faith, making the alleged cartel a breach of the parties' contractual obligations.[24] Therefore, the claimant had not only a claim in tort but also a parallel contract claim.   **8.18**

The court found the tort and contract claims to be closely related. First, the matter required the interpretation of the supply agreement. Second, it was not relevant whether the claimant had   **8.19**

---

20   *Microsoft Mobile Oy (Ltd) v Sony Europe Ltd and Ors* [2017] EWHC 374 (Ch) (28 February 2017).

21   Ibid., [43–45].

22   Ibid., [47–53].

23   I.e., whether 'the tortious claims were so closely knitted together with the contractual claims that a rational or sensible businessman would expect them to be subject to determination by a single tribunal'. Ibid., [49].

24   Ibid., [70–71].

pleaded the matter only as a tort claim. It was not possible to circumvent an arbitration clause by selective pleading if the facts of the matter indicated a contract claim was also possible.[25] It was not in dispute that the application of the arbitration clause would cause the claim to become fragmented.[26] The court found that such fragmentation was not in breach of EU law, so there was no reason not to apply the arbitration clause.[27]

8.20 On 13 September 2017, the District Court of Dortmund ruled that damages claims based on a railway construction cartel were within the scope of arbitration clauses in sales agreements that contained an alleged cartel overcharge.[28] The Dortmund Court's reasoning was that there were arbitration clauses in the construction contracts between the parties. The claimant had brought a claim for antitrust damages. Under German law, antitrust damages are a type of claim that is capable of being settled in arbitration, and antitrust damages were covered by the arbitration clauses.

8.21 None of the arbitration clauses specifically mentioned antitrust damages. The court considered that arbitration clauses can cover damages claims based on tort, even if they are not based on a contract. However, although antitrust damages claims can be considered tort claims, they also coincide with the sales agreements that contain the alleged overcharge because there can be no overcharge without the sales agreement. Similarly to the English High Court, the Dortmund Court also considered that a claimant cannot evade arbitration by basing its claim only on tort instead of the underlying contract. Furthermore, splitting the proceedings for the same claim between arbitration and court proceedings was not justified. Therefore, the court found no reason to exempt the antitrust damages claims from the scope of the arbitration clauses.

8.22 The claimant had relied on the ECJ's decision in Case C-352/13 *CDC Hydrogen Peroxide* and asserted that the cartel damages claims were not foreseeable and therefore not within the scope of the arbitration clauses. The Dortmund Court pointed out that the consequences of many other types of unforeseeable conduct are covered by arbitration clauses. Furthermore, the Dortmund Court noted that the ECJ's judgment did not deal with arbitration clauses and that the ECJ's competence to rule on arbitration is in any case questionable.

c. Comparison of the national judgments

8.23 In just the six judgments described here, the various courts have presented different reasonings for their decisions to a large extent and reached different conclusions. This seems to reflect the novelty of this issue in the antitrust damages context.[29] Before detailing the differences, it should be noted that there are also a number of fundamental similarities between the judgments.

8.24 First, all the courts have dealt with the issue mainly as a question of how to interpret the scope of the arbitration clauses. Second, with the exception of the German court, the courts actually seem to agree that a cartel damages case does not normally fall into the scope of even broadly

---

25   Ibid., [72].

26   Ibid., [76–77].

27   Ibid., [81].

28   District Court of Dortmund, case 8 O 30/16 [Kart], on 13 September 2017, ECLI:DE:LGDO:2017:0913.16KART.00.

29   The question of whether tort or statutory claims are within the scope of an arbitration clause is itself not a new issue. It is a common question concerning the scope of arbitration clauses. See Born (n 13) 1357–66.

drafted arbitration clauses. Third, the courts mostly point out that it is important to be able to consolidate claims that are closely related to each other. Fourth, the courts seem to apply arguments concerning the scope of arbitration clauses and jurisdiction clauses interchangeably.

Despite these similarities, there are many differences. Some of the central ones we have **8.25** attempted to summarize in Table 8.1.

Table 8.1   Comparison of the national judgments

Court	Claim based on contracts?	Claim foreseeable?	Fragmentation of claims is ...
Helsinki District Court	No	No	Undesirable, affects the interpretation of an arbitration clause
Amsterdam District Court	No	No	N/A
Amsterdam Court of Appeal	N/A	No	N/A
Rotterdam District Court	Yes	No	Against EU law
High Court of England and Wales	Yes	N/A	Not against EU law
Dortmund District Court	Yes	No	N/A

With the exception of the foreseeability of the claim, the interpretations seem to vary almost **8.26** randomly, which increases our concern that, without some sort of EU level guidance, the national courts will continue to come to very different conclusions.

As regards the characterization of the claim, the English High Court engages in very detailed **8.27** analysis of the wording of the purchase agreements in light of English case law, and finds a breach of contract. The Rotterdam District Court also found that the dispute has a connection to the contracts between the cartel members and their customers but gave no explanation as to how it reached this conclusion. The Dortmund District Court found that there is a necessary connection to the contracts because otherwise no overcharge could be levied. The Amsterdam Court of Appeal did not take a position as it decided the matter on other grounds. The Helsinki District Court and the Amsterdam District Court both found that the claim was, ultimately, not in contract but in tort, and ruled that the dispute was therefore outside the scope of the arbitration clauses.

The main point of consistency between the decisions is the foreseeability of the dispute. With **8.28** the sole exception of the English High Court, all the courts found the cartel damages disputes not to have been reasonably foreseeable at the time the arbitration clause was agreed. The Finnish and Dutch courts found that the disputes were thus outside the scope of the arbitration clauses. The German court ruled that it did not matter because unforeseeable disputes can be settled in arbitration. The English court did not deal with this issue, and it seems the point was not raised. The lack of reasonable foreseeability is the most common reason that courts have used to interpret the scope of the arbitration clauses. Its importance seems to have increased after the ECJ's decision in Case C-352/13 *CDC Hydrogen Peroxide*. The reason that lack of foreseeability has been so commonly found is no doubt related to the fact that all these cases concern cartels, which are secret infringements.[30]

8.29   Some courts have specifically addressed the issue that enforcing the arbitration clauses would fragment the case into a number of separate proceedings. The District Court of Helsinki considered claim fragmentation negative as a matter of principle, not because it may or may not have been a breach of EU law. The court took this into account in its interpretation of whether the cartel damages dispute was within the scope of the arbitration clause, not as a separate EU law issue.[31] The Rotterdam District Court found that if the parties were referred to arbitration, the court would still have to deal with the same claims based on joint and several liability against non-contract parties and based on umbrella damages. This, coupled with the number of the parties, would result in a procedural situation that would cause considerable practical difficulties for the claimants to enforce their rights. The court found this would be contrary to the EU law principle of effectiveness.[32] The English High Court found that referring the anchor defendant to arbitration would cause the claim to fragment.[33] The court asked whether fragmentation was such an infringement of EU law as to render the arbitration clause inoperable.[34] The court could not find support for such a conclusion in the ECJ's judgment in *CDC Hydrogen Peroxide*, only in the Advocate General's Opinion, which the ECJ did not follow.[35]

8.30   Out of the six cases, the Dortmund District Court's judgment seems to best match the largely prevalent view that the scope of arbitration clauses should be interpreted broadly and in favour of arbitration.[36] Even the English High Court still seemed to take as the main rule that cartel damages claims are tort claims and not within the scope of even a broadly drafted arbitration clause. It was the specific good faith obligation that caused the High Court to consider the matter to fall within the scope of the arbitration clause.

8.31   The Finnish and Dutch courts, on the other hand, have rejected on various grounds the commonly held expansive, pro-arbitration interpretation of the scope of arbitration clauses. The diversity in the reasoning of the Finnish and Dutch courts could be a result of what was pleaded. However, we think the reason is also the lack of clear statutory law or settled case law on the subject. As a result, the courts have had to fall back on general principles, leading to variations in how the courts have argued their decisions. In all the cases, however, the outcome

---

30   It remains to be seen how courts would deal with claims based on anticompetitive distribution agreements or abuse of dominance where the anticompetitive effects are typically implemented by including anticompetitive terms into contracts between the infringer and the injured party. That way both parties are aware of the anticompetitive terms from the beginning.

31   It seems that the fragmentation issue was superfluous for the outcome since the court found the dispute was in any case not related to the purchase agreements and not reasonably foreseeable, and thus not within the scope of the arbitration clause.

32   See *Stichting De Glazen Lift* (n 19), para 2.20.1.

33   See *Microsoft Mobile Oy* (n 20), [76–77].

34   Ibid., [78].

35   Ibid., [79–81].

36   See e.g., Born (n 13) 1317–66.

has been identical, indicating that the courts have been unanimous on what they consider the correct outcome, even if they have applied different reasoning to reach that outcome.

It is unclear whether the Finnish and Dutch courts mean their decisions to apply narrowly to **8.32** antitrust damages cases or to all cases where similar circumstances are present. In the latter case, it could significantly affect the applicability of arbitration clauses in general. Here, we once again see the tension of whether antitrust damages should be treated as any other damages cases or whether they are a special type of damages action that requires new rules and interpretations.

C. ISSUES IN THE INTERACTION BETWEEN THE DAMAGES DIRECTIVE AND ANTITRUST DAMAGES CASES IN ARBITRATION

The Damages Directive provided minimum requirements for a level playing field in antitrust **8.33** damages claims within the EU. However, the Damages Directive does not cover jurisdiction, and its application to arbitration proceedings is yet to be determined. Unless a Member State has explicitly legislated that the national statutes which implement the Directive apply to arbitration, such statutes apply in arbitration only to the extent that they are considered public policy and failing to heed them would put the enforceability of the arbitral award at risk.

We raise here certain particular procedural and substantive issues where arbitration by its **8.34** nature may not be able to provide claimants with equally effective remedies as court proceedings. These weaker procedural and substantive standards could lead to 'remedy-stripping' in arbitration, which may affect the enforceability of the award.

First, the fragmentation of claims which stems from the contract-based nature of arbitration **8.35** might be in conflict with the claimant's right to bring a claim based on joint and several liability against the co-infringers. Secondly, arbitration has its limitations not only when in joining respondents, but also when joining claimants. Although the Directive does not deal with collective redress *per se*, there is a significant effort at the EU level to promote collective redress. We will touch upon the possibility to provide for solutions of collective redress in arbitration. Finally, the Directive provided minimum requirements regarding the disclosure of evidence and the binding force of national competition authorities' decisions, both of which push the procedural and evidential limits of arbitration as it is today.

1. Claim fragmentation in antitrust arbitration and joint and several liability under the Damages Directive

The Damages Directive provides for joint and several liability of co-infringers, allowing **8.36** claimants to sue any co-infringer for the entire amount of the harm. This functions well in court where the court has the power to join co-infringers (and co-claimants) in the same proceedings. However, problems arise if the claimant has arbitration clauses with some of the defendants, and the arbitration clauses are enforced. Unless all the parties agree to be joined into single arbitration proceedings, the case is likely to split into court proceedings with non-contract party defendants and one or more arbitration proceedings with contract party defendants.

8.37 A joint and several claim is connected to arbitration clauses in relation to the injured party's contract parties. At the same time, in relation to the cartel members with which the injured party did not have a contract, a joint and several claim will not be covered by an arbitration agreement as there is no contract in the first place, and hence no consensus on arbitration. If the arbitration clauses are enforced, it is almost certain that such a case will become fragmented into a number of separate and parallel arbitration proceedings against each of the claimant's contract parties for the simple reason that it is not possible to consolidate the proceedings.[37] The matter may well become further fragmented by court proceedings against non-contract parties concerning the same competition law infringement.[38] The injured party could even have multiple, mutually incompatible arbitration clauses with any one of the infringers, forcing the claimant to initiate multiple sets of arbitral proceedings against the same defendant.[39]

8.38 Normally, an expansive, pro-arbitration interpretation of the scope of an arbitration clause is rational because it allows for the efficiency of one-stop dispute resolution and avoids the risk of contradictory decisions.[40] Yet, under the circumstances described above, the same interpretation will lead to the opposite outcome, which we doubt is something that rational businesspersons would intend. The main reason for this complex procedural situation is simply that arbitration was never designed to deal with situations where tort-based joint and several liability extends to multiple parties, some of whom have no contractual relationship with the claimant.[41] It is worth noting that this fragmentation will happen to *every claimant*, further multiplying the number of cases that it is necessary to bring.

8.39 The question for courts that are called upon to decide whether to refer parties to arbitration is whether the fragmentation of claims should have an effect on the outcome of the decision. The Damages Directive promotes effective remedies, which can be severely weakened by referring the injured party to a number of different arbitration panels. The question for arbitration lawyers, on the other hand, is whether they can overcome this by providing a framework which would foster multi-party arbitration.

8.40 The willingness of courts to refer parties into arbitration also for non-contractual claims rests on the intention of the parties and the preference for one-stop adjudication. As discussed here, these criteria do not seem to be present in cases that lead to fragmented proceedings. We submit that claim fragmentation should be one of the issues considered by courts as they interpret the scope of an arbitration clause. In our opinion, claim fragmentation is not an EU law issue as such. It is possible that claim fragmentation may be considered contrary to the EU law principle of effectiveness. However, claim fragmentation should first and foremost be taken into account as part of the normal interpretation of the scope of an arbitration clause.

8.41 Normally, the possibility to settle non-contractual claims along with contractual claims in the same arbitral proceedings rests on the premise that the parties intended to solve their disputes in arbitration and that they would rather settle all parts of the same dispute in a

---

37 Nigel Blackaby and others, *Redfern and Hunter on International Arbitration* (6th edn, OUP 2015) 91; Born (n 13) 1374.
38 Also, if there are multiple defendants that are contract parties to the claimant, each of them is jointly and severally liable for the overcharge contained in the agreements between the claimant and its other contract parties.
39 For example, this was the case in the Finnish branch of the hydrogen peroxide cartel damages litigation. The arbitration clauses included in different hydrogen peroxide supply agreements had different numbers of arbitrators.
40 See Born (n 13) 1319, 1326, 1343–4.
41 See Blackaby (n 37) 141, 143–5.

single set of arbitral proceedings rather than solve the contractual claims in arbitration and the non-contractual claims in court. However, if enforcing the arbitration clauses would not lead to consolidated proceedings but to the fragmentation of the dispute, one-stop adjudication in arbitration becomes impossible. Instead, courts become the forum that is able to offer one-stop adjudication. It is arguable that the parties did not intend to arbitrate such cases. If one-stop adjudication and the intent to arbitrate are not present in cases of claim fragmentation, we find it questionable whether there are compelling reasons to arbitrate such disputes.[42] We submit that this approach is more fundamental, and founded on established arguments in the interpretation of arbitration clauses, than the approaches so far offered by various courts, i.e., that antitrust damages should not be covered by arbitration because they are non-contractual and/or not foreseeable.

This argument is also based on a public policy presumption that all co-infringers deserve a day **8.42** in court, as this is their due process right, notwithstanding the fact that a material legal rule on joint and several liability allows them to be held liable in arbitration. The issue of parallel arbitration and court proceedings against the contractual and non-contractual (non-signatories of the arbitration agreement) defendants is indeed an outstanding issue discussed in the doctrine and in practice.[43] Imperfect consolidation,[44] which allows intervention of a non-signatory in arbitration, may solve the issue to some extent, but at the same time the prevailing underlying principle of confidentiality and privity of arbitration might prevent co-infringers from doing that.

One way to view claim fragmentation is as a particular type of remedy-stripping. Typically, **8.43** remedy-stripping means drafting dispute resolution clauses in such a manner as to take away some of the remedies and procedural tools that would ordinarily be available.[45] Claim fragmentation, on the other hand, follows simply from the nature of arbitration, which prevents the consolidation of related cartel damage claims and makes it more difficult for injured parties to benefit from joint and several liability. To the extent that remedy-stripping is considered to affect the interpretation and validity of arbitration clauses, those same arguments could apply to claim fragmentation.

---

42 Unless both parties still agree to arbitrate after the fact, which would establish the intent to arbitrate even in the absence of one-stop adjudication.

43 Don Baker, 'Chapter 40: Parallel Proceedings before the Arbitral Tribunal and the Courts', in Gordon Blanke and Phillip Landolt (eds), *EU and US Antitrust Arbitration: A Handbook for Practitioners*, (vol 2, Kluwer Law International 2011), 1476–8.

44 See more in Don Baker, 'Chapter 44: Possible Rules to Enhance the Effectiveness of Arbitration of US Antitrust Claims', in Blanke and Landolt, ibid., 1555–6.

45 See e.g., David Schwarz, 'Understanding Remedy-Stripping Arbitration Clauses: Validity, Arbitrability and Preclusion Principles' (2003) 38 *University of San Francisco Law Review*. Remedy-stripping does not seem to be a widespread phenomenon in European antitrust damages cases. This could be because it is only recently that companies have had to worry about facing antitrust damages claims in Europe. Second, because treble damages, class actions, discovery and similar devices are not available in most of Europe, there has been little to strip away in the first place. This may change with the implementation of the Damages Directive into national law.

2. Collective redress in antitrust arbitration: Designing complex arbitration through a procedural framework and alternative vehicles

8.44 As stated above, proceedings on cartel damages cases involve multiple parties. There are at least two co-infringers and likely a large number of injured parties because the infringement tends to affect the entire market. The harm is then likely to be passed on to different levels of the production and distribution chain. Thus, the availability of a collective redress mechanism is particularly important in antitrust damages cases.

8.45 The availability of opt-out class actions for antitrust claims is one of the main features of the US legal system which fosters private enforcement of antitrust law.[46] The Damages Directive, however, did not oblige Member States to introduce procedural mechanisms for collective redress. Nevertheless, the European Commission is still pursuing the introduction of a collective redress mechanism though only for consumers.[47]

8.46 Introducing collective redress into arbitration would be difficult because arbitration is, by design, normally limited to a particular contractual relationship. In a collective redress situation, there would be a group of claimants and a group of respondents, but not all of them would necessarily be in contractual relations and their contracts would not necessarily contain the same or mutually compatible arbitration clauses. Also, collective redress in antitrust damages cases would be the most valuable for indirect purchasers because the harm is spread to more and more parties as it is passed down the distribution chain. This would be particularly difficult to construct in arbitration because an indirect purchaser would not have a contractual relation with one of the co-infringers but either with one of the direct purchasers or with another indirect purchaser if there are several levels in the distribution chain.

8.47 Simply put, to make arbitration a competitive dispute resolution mechanism for antitrust disputes, effective and efficient rules on multi-party, multi-contract proceedings should be introduced. Otherwise, claimants may have little or no incentive to pursue such claims individually due to the costs and legal risks involved.[48] The arbitration legal framework already provides for several procedural tools in this regard: arbitration rules usually contain a provision on complex arbitrations, i.e., multi-party and multi-contract claims. However, the involvement of multiple parties in arbitration heavily depends (and challenges) the consensual nature of arbitration. Arbitration rules usually regulate several aspects of complex arbitration: multiple parties, multiple contracts (and arbitration agreements), joinder and consolidation.[49]

---

46   Alison Jones, 'Private Enforcement of EU Competition Law: A Comparison with, and Lessons from, the US' in Maria Bergström, Marios Iacovides, Magnus Strand (eds), *Harmonising EU Competition Litigation: The New Directive and Beyond* (Hart Publishing 2016) 5.

47   Commission Recommendation of 11 June 2013 on common principles for injunctive and compensatory collective redress mechanisms in the Member States concerning violations of rights granted under Union Law (2013/396/EU) [2013] OJ L 201/60. In April 2018, the Commission published proposals that would support collective redress for consumers under a 'New Deal for Consumers'.

48   Donncadh Woods, Ailsa Sinclair and David Ashton, 'Private enforcement of Community competition law: modernisation and the road ahead' (2004) 2 *Competition Policy Newsletter* 34.

49   For example, Arts 7–10 of the 2017 ICC Rules; Arts 14, 15 and 18 of the 2018 VIAC Rules; Arts 13, 14, 15 of the 2017 SCC Rules; rr 6, 7 and 8 of the 2016 SIAC Rules.

These scenarios require a deep understanding of complex arbitrations and a proper application **8.48** of the relevant arbitration rules in a particular case. Of course, these obstacles can be overridden by an *explicit* consent and abandonment of all previous agreements on dispute resolution by *all* parties in the dispute. In order to effectively circumvent the discussion as to the consent to arbitration in antitrust arbitration and to avoid other legal issues discussed below, we foster the following alternatives: (1) the facilitation of *submission (post facto)* agreements to arbitrate for antitrust damages claims; (2) the creation of new vehicles which can facilitate antitrust arbitration within the existing framework; or (3) drafting anew tailor-made rules for collective redress in antitrust arbitration, instead of trying to subsume these claims under the current provisions on multiple parties and claims, joinder, or consolidation. None of these options is easy.

In the meanwhile, one interim solution for some situations is to use special purpose vehicles **8.49** that will acquire, consolidate and bring claims. This 'claim bundling' model has been pioneered in Europe by the CDC company. This model mimics collective redress by aggregating individual claims from numerous injured parties to achieve economies of scale. The main problem for this model in arbitration is that the bundled claims are likely to be linked to numerous contracts by numerous injured parties, likely with different dispute resolution clauses. Thus, the claim fragmentation issue discussed earlier is key for the viability of this model. If arbitration clauses are enforced, the bundling model does not work because the claims cannot be aggregated and the economies of scale are lost. This is probably why CDC has sought to pursue its claims in court and defendants have sought to enforce the arbitration clauses as seen in the Finnish and Dutch cases discussed earlier.

3. Information asymmetry and disclosure: Expanding the evidential standard in arbitration

Antitrust damages claims are considered to suffer from information asymmetry where the **8.50** infringer has much information concerning the infringement and its effects while the injured parties have little information. Many civil law countries in the EU have disclosure rules that require parties to specify individual documents and items for disclosure. This is considered to make it too difficult for claimants to obtain evidence. Therefore, disclosure rules were broadened in the Damages Directive to cover also categories of evidence:[50]

> Member States shall ensure that national courts are able to order the disclosure of specified items of evidence or relevant categories of evidence circumscribed as precisely and as narrowly as possible on the basis of reasonably available facts in the reasoned justification.[51]

The importance of disclosure in antitrust damages cases should be recognized in arbitration as **8.51** well, where it should outweigh the usual expectation of the parties to have expedited

---

50 In addition to expanded disclosure, the Damages Directive (n 2) Art 17(2) provides for a reversed burden of proof concerning the fact of damage in cartel cases. See also para 47 of the preamble of the Directive.

51 Ibid., Art 5(2).

proceedings. The arbitrators' discretion to order discovery has been subject to an unaccommodating climate in international arbitration practice.[52] Namely, the current stance on the discovery/disclosure of evidence in arbitration is that, unless parties agree otherwise, the arbitrators should have discretion to order only limited discovery/disclosure, more limited than what is available in litigation.[53]

8.52 This is compounded by the fact that courts will usually have much wider powers to order disclosure by third parties. Hence, it is necessary to determine whether the assistance of national courts to arbitral tribunals can be developed in this area.

8.53 The opposite situation to too limited disclosure, as described above, could happen if an arbitral tribunal were to order the disclosure of evidence that should not be disclosable according to the Directive, such as leniency statements and settlement submissions.

8.54 At this point, it is not clear if the issues outlined above would amount to violating public policy, and thereby risk setting aside an arbitral award.[54]

D. CONCLUSION

8.55 In this chapter, we have identified a number of issues concerning the scope of application of arbitration clauses in antitrust damages cases. Due to the small number of cases found for analysis, any conclusions must remain tentative. However, we believe that even at this stage, a number of important topics emerge.

8.56 The main observation is that Member State courts have already made different decisions on whether cartel damages claims fall within the scope of application of an arbitration clause. Without co-ordination, this is likely to be repeated in different Member States and in different courts as the number of antitrust damages cases inevitably increases around Europe. If left unchecked, this will create a highly undesirable situation where the same arbitration clause could be applicable in some Member States but not applicable in others. Unfortunately, unless the EU or the ECJ provides rules or guidelines or a test to ensure some level of uniformity in national decisions, we see no easy way to coordinate this matter between the Member States.

8.57 Another key finding is that the reasoning given in the decisions seems to be at odds with the established case law concerning the scope of arbitration clauses. Normally, one would have

---

52 Giacomo Rojas Elgueta, 'Understanding Discovery in International Commercial Arbitration Through Behavioral Law and Economics: A Journey Inside the Minds of Parties and Arbitrators' (2011) 16 *Harvard Negotiation Law Review* 172–4.

53 Ibid., 172–3.

54 See the decision in the Case C-360/09 *Pfleiderer AG v Bundeskartellam* [2011] ECLI:EU:C:2011:389:

> The provisions of European Union law on cartels, and in particular Council Regulation (EC) No 1/2003 of 16 December 2002 on the implementation of the rules on competition laid down in Articles 101 TFEU and 102 TFEU, *must be interpreted as not precluding a person who has been adversely affected by an infringement of European Union competition law and is seeking to obtain damages from being granted access to documents relating to a leniency procedure involving the perpetrator of that infringement.* It is, however, for the courts and tribunals of the Member States, on the basis of their national law, to determine the conditions under which such access must be permitted or refused by weighing the interests protected by European Union law (emphasis added).

expected the courts to refer the parties into arbitration. The courts clearly must have had significant concerns about referring the parties into arbitration because the courts were willing to go against the established interpretation of the scope of arbitration clauses.

The established expansive interpretation of arbitration clauses rests, among others, on the **8.58** parties' intent to arbitrate and the efficiencies gained by consolidating the entire dispute into arbitration. We submit that in cartel cases these requirements are rarely at hand. The infringing contract party has secretly conspired with third parties to cause the injured party harm. The structure of arbitration makes it very unlikely that the matter can be consolidated into single proceedings, and will instead fragment into multiple arbitrations and possible court proceedings. The benefits of one-stop adjudication are lost, and the disadvantages likely outweigh the traditional benefits of arbitration. Under such circumstances, there is reason to question the injured party's intent to arbitrate such disputes.

We have also highlighted certain procedural issues where it seems that arbitral proceedings **8.59** may be less effective than court proceedings. Whether such lesser effectiveness is enough to place arbitral awards at risk of being set aside is uncertain but it is clear that failing to heed EU competition law in arbitration brings risks. It remains to be seen if arbitration is flexible enough to be fashioned into something that parties in antitrust damages cases would voluntarily choose as opposed to the current situation where some parties, and courts, clearly feel that arbitration by its nature will impede the effective administration of justice.

9

COLLECTIVE REDRESS ARBITRATION IN THE EUROPEAN UNION

S.I. Strong[*]

A. INTRODUCTION

9.01 Over the last decade, collective redress has become increasingly important in the European Union (EU). Not only have the European Commission and the European Parliament both addressed collective redress on numerous occasions,[1] but non-governmental organizations such

---

* Date of submission: 2/4/2020.

1 Commission Recommendation of 11 June 2013 on common principles for injunctive and compensatory collective redress mechanisms in the Member States concerning violations of rights granted under Union Law ('Commission Recommendation') [2013] OJ L201/60; Communication from the Commission to the European Parliament, the Council, the European Economic and Social Committee and the Committee of the Regions, 'Towards a European Horizontal Framework for Collective Redress' ('Commission Communication') COM(2013) 401 final; European Parliament resolution of 2 February 2012 on 'Towards a Coherent European Approach to Collective Redress' ('Parliament resolution') (2011/2089(INI)) [2013] OJ C239 E/05; European Commission, Public Consultation 'Towards a Coherent European Approach to Collective Redress' SEC(2011) 173. In late 2018, European bodies began to debate the creation of a new procedure on collective consumer actions. European Parliament, Draft Report on the proposal for a directive of the European Parliament and of the Council on representative actions for the protection of the collective interests of consumers, and repealing Directive 2009/22/EC (COM(2018)0184 – C8-0149/2018 – 2018/0089(COD)), 2018/0089(COD) (reflecting new proposed rules allowing groups of consumers harmed by illegal practices to launch collective actions and seek compensation) A8-0447/2018; see also Rafael Amaro and others, *Collective Redress in the Member States of the European Union* (Study commissioned by the European Parliament) <http://www.europarl.europa.eu/RegData/etudes/STUD/2018/608829/IPOL_STU(2018)608829_EN.pdf> accessed 12 February 2019.

as the British Institute of International and Comparative Law (BIICL) have analysed collective redress procedures in the EU in great depth.[2]

As useful as these initiatives have been, most discussions about large-scale relief in the EU **9.02** focus primarily if not exclusively on actions arising in the judicial context, even though courts are not always the best or only place to resolve large-scale legal disputes.[3] However, the European emphasis on judicial mechanisms appears to be based on two fundamental misconceptions.

First, European scholars and policymakers fail to appreciate the factors that drive development **9.03** of large-scale arbitral mechanisms and the extent to which those features exist in certain European Member States. Second, European lawyers and lawmakers mistakenly believe that US-style class arbitration – a mechanism that is far too similar to US-style class litigation to attract European interest – is the only type of large-scale arbitration possible.[4] In fact, a number of large-scale arbitral procedures that do not mirror the US-style opt-out representative class mechanism have already been developed and are either already available in Europe or are amenable for adoption in Europe.[5]

This chapter seeks to clarify these two misperceptions so as to provide scholars and policy- **9.04** makers with the type of information that is vital to the proper development of European law and policy. The discussion begins in Section B with an analysis of the legal and social pressures that influence the development of large arbitration, so as to determine whether and to what extent new arbitral mechanisms might develop or flourish in EU Member States. Section C provides an overview of existing and anticipated forms of collective redress arbitration in Europe, and Section D ties together the various strands of argument and provides additional guidance regarding the development of large-scale arbitration in Europe.

Before beginning, it should be noted that the primary focus of this chapter is on arbitral **9.05** mechanisms rather than on consensual dispute resolution, often referred to as 'alternative dispute resolution' (ADR) and interpreted in European circles exclusively as consensual dispute

---

2 Eva Lein and others, *State of Collective Redress in the EU in the Context of the Implementation of the Commission Recommendation* (British Institute of International and Comparative Law 2018) ('BIICL Report'), <https://www.biicl.org/documents/1881_StudyontheStateofCollectiveRedress.pdf?showdocument=1> accessed 12 February 2019; Eva Lein and others (eds), *Collective Redress in Europe: Why and How?* (British Institute of International and Comparative Law 2015).

3 For example, the EU documents refer to arbitration only in passing. Commission Recommendation (n 1) recital 16 paras 25–28; Commission Communication (n 1) paras 1.1, 3.8; Parliament Resolution (n 1) recitals 10, 25. Similarly, BIICL's 1,000+ page report contains only a handful of references to arbitration. BIICL Report (n 2) 164, 299, 542, 552 (regarding an illegal insurance arbitration scheme in Estonia); ibid., 253, 354, 921 (regarding collective consumer arbitration in Spain); ibid., 512 (regarding a large-scale investment arbitration against Cyprus); ibid., 528 (regarding arbitration and Denmark's opt-out judicial procedure); ibid., 568, 948, 955, 957 (regarding Sweden's Skandia case); ibid., 613, 623, 632 (regarding Greece's opt-out regime and arbitration); ibid., 653, 672–5, 1006 (regarding the reservation of rights regarding arbitration in Hungary); ibid., 795 (regarding a voluntary reorganization arbitration in Malta); ibid., 856 (regarding Portugal's approval of voluntary collective arbitration).

4 Commission Communication (n 1) para 1.1; see Philippe Billiet and others (eds), *Class Actions and Arbitration in the European Union* (Maklu Publishers 2012).

5 SI Strong, *Class, Mass, and Collective Arbitration in National and International Law* (Oxford University Press 2013) 6–19 ('Strong, *Class, Mass, and Collective Arbitration*') (distinguishing class, mass and collective arbitration in various jurisdictions and identifying existing large-scale arbitral devices in Europe).

resolution (i.e., negotiation or mediation/conciliation) rather than as including both consensual dispute resolution and arbitration, as is the case in other jurisdictions.[6] However, some issues relating to settlement of large-scale disputes will be addressed as they become relevant.

B. FACTORS AFFECTING THE DEVELOPMENT OF COLLECTIVE REDRESS ARBITRATION IN THE EU

1. Historical lessons

9.06 When considering the future of collective redress arbitration in the EU, it is helpful to consider how large-scale arbitration arose in other contexts in order to determine whether similar conditions exist in Europe. At this point, two historical models exist: US-style class arbitration[7] and mass arbitration in the investment realm.[8] While European nations are unlikely to adopt either of these mechanisms as a matter of domestic or European law,[9] these exemplars provide useful insights into whether some indigenous form of large-scale arbitration might develop in Europe.

9.07 The first issue to note is that class arbitration – the first type of large-scale arbitral proceeding to arise historically and at this point the most mature of the various mechanisms – was not consciously created as an optimal procedure to resolve certain types of legal disputes. Instead, class arbitration arose by accident rather than design.

9.08 The genesis of class arbitration can be traced back to the US corporate community's longstanding opposition to judicial class actions under Rule 23 of the US Federal Rules of Civil Procedure and various state-court analogues. Businesses have traditionally believed that most

---

6 As it turns out, there are relatively few developments regarding collective settlements in the EU. Indeed, one report recently noted that:

> [o]nly six Member States have a proper alternative dispute mechanism focused on mass harm situations, or at least containing specific rules on ADR in the context of mass harm situations: Belgium, France, Italy, the Netherlands, Spain and the United Kingdom. The mechanisms in place include the possibility to settle a collective claim or to have the dispute resolved by consumer ombudsmen. Among those countries, the alternative dispute resolution mechanism is thought to be efficient in four of them – Belgium, France, the Netherlands and Spain.

Amaro and others (n 1) 38.

7 Although class arbitration is most closely associated with the US, it has been used in Colombia and has been legislatively and judicially contemplated in Canada. Strong, *Class, Mass, and Collective Arbitration* (n 5) 284–304.

8 Mass arbitration combines elements of representative and aggregative relief and has thus far been only seen in a single investment proceeding, *Abaclat v Argentine Republic*, ICSID Case No ARB/07/5, although the procedure has been cited with approval by a number of other tribunals. Ibid., 74–83 (discussing *Abaclat v Argentine Republic, Ambiente Ufficio v Argentine Republic*, ICSID Case No ARB/08/9, and *Alemani v Argentine Republic*, ICSID Case No. ARB/07/8); see also SI Strong, 'Heir of *Abaclat*? Mass and Multiparty Proceedings: Ambiente Ufficio SpA v Argentine Republic' (2014) 29 *ICSID Review-Foreign Investment Law Journal* 149. Mass arbitration could be seen in large-scale investment proceedings that are currently pending. *Theodoros Adamakopoulous v Republic of Cyprus*, ICSID Case No ARB/15/49 (involving 954 claimants) ('*Adamakopoulous*').

9 US-style class arbitration involves opt-out, representative proceedings similar to those used in US-style class actions, which have been traditionally disfavoured by European Member States. Strong, *Class, Mass, and Collective Arbitration* (n 5) 7. Mass arbitration, which is only found in international investment disputes, adopts opt-in procedures (thereby avoiding one of the primary objections to US-style class suits) but is characterized as a 'hybrid' proceeding due to other similarities to representative actions. Ibid., 76.

large-scale actions are frivolous in nature, even though empirical research suggests that most class claims are well-founded.[10] Nevertheless, beginning in the 1970s and 1980s, companies in the US sought to limit the availability of class actions through legislative reform.[11]

While the lobbying efforts were intensive, they were ultimately unsuccessful due to the central role that class suits play in US law and policy. As has been discussed at length elsewhere, class actions in the US not only fulfil a compensatory function but also act as an important means of regulation, helping control corporate misbehaviour with the assistance of 'private attorneys general', meaning private individuals who sue to enforce various substantive laws that provide private remedies as a means of upholding important public policies.[12]   **9.09**

After being rebuffed by state and federal legislatures, corporate actors decided to turn to arbitration as a means of limiting class suits. Initially, businesses thought that adopting arbitration provisions in settings that were likely to generate class suits would eliminate large-scale suits by forcing claimants into individual bilateral proceedings.[13] However, judges began to see this tactic for what it was – a means of circumventing longstanding US policies favouring the use of class suits to provide compensation for large numbers of individuals with small-value claims and to deter corporate wrongdoers – and used standard common law techniques to remedy the situation by developing judicially created forms of class arbitration.[14] In so doing, US judges were able to give effect not only to important public policies relating to class relief but also to policies supporting procedural autonomy and freedom of contract.[15]   **9.10**

The first reported class arbitrations in the US appeared in the early 1980s and were seen in ever-increasing numbers over the following decades.[16] The procedure reached its zenith between 2000 and 2010, when over 300 proceedings were filed with one arbitration provider   **9.11**

---

10   Deborah R Hensler and others, *Class Action Dilemmas: Public Goals for Private Gain* (Rand Corporation 2004) 22–37; Elizabeth Chamblee Burch, 'Securities Class Actions as Pragmatic *Ex Post* Regulation' (2008) 43 *Georgia Law Review* 63, 85.

11   Strong, *Class, Mass, and Collective Arbitration* (n 5) 8.

12   Patrick Luff, 'Risk Regulation and Regulatory Litigation' (2011) 64 *Rutgers Law Review* 73, 74–6, 113–14.

13   Strong, *Class, Mass, and Collective Arbitration* (n 5) 8; Jean R Sternlight and Elizabeth J Jensen, 'Using Arbitration to Eliminate Consumer Class Actions: Efficient Business Practice or Unconscionable Abuse?' (2004) 67 *Law and Contemporary Problems* 75 n1.

14   Strong, *Class, Mass, and Collective Arbitration* (n 5) 8.

15   Ibid., 8–9. Canada has also addressed this issue. *Kanitz v Rogers Cable Inc*, [2002] 58 OR (3d) 299; *Dell Computer Corp v Union des consommateurs*, 2007 SCC 34; *Bisaillon v Concordia University*, 2006 SCC 19; *Seidel v Telus Communications Inc*, 2011 SCC 15.

16   *Keating v Superior Court*, 645 P2d 1192 (California 1982), rev'd on other grounds sub nom *Southland Corp v Keating*, 465 US 1 (1984); *Lewis v Prudential-Bache Securities, Inc*, 225 Cal Rptr 69 (California Court of Appeal 1986); *Izzi v Mesquite Country Club*, 231 Cal Rptr 315 (California Court of Appeal 1986); *Dickler v Shearson Lehman Hutton, Inc*, 596 A2d 860, 866–7 (Pennsylvania Superior Court 1991); *Blue Cross of California v Superior Court*, 78 Cal Rptr 2d 779 (California Court of Appeal 1998); *Bazzle v Green Tree Financial Corp*, 569 SE2d 349, 360–61 (South Carolina 2002), vacated, 539 US 444 (2003).

alone.[17] However, the 2010s saw a decline in class arbitration due to the action of the US Supreme Court, which was becoming increasingly protective of business interests in a variety of contexts.[18]

9.12 The US Supreme Court limited class arbitration through two different means. First, beginning in 2011, the Court handed down a series of opinions allowing corporate entities to force individual claimants to waive their right to class relief in matters involving consumer law, labour law and antitrust law.[19] This move was quite controversial, since most commentators believed such waivers never would have been permitted had they been sought in litigation rather than arbitration.[20] Empirical studies suggest that not every potential corporate respondent has adopted arbitral waiver provisions in the wake of these opinions, a significant number have, particularly in the telecommunications and financial industries.[21]

9.13 Interestingly, a major US corporation – Johnson & Johnson – recently saw a shareholder proposal seeking to have shareholder disputes heard in arbitration, rather than litigation.[22] Somewhat unusually, the proposal included a waiver of class proceedings.[23] The US Securities and Exchange Commission issued a no-action letter, agreeing with management at Johnson & Johnson that the proposal was unacceptable, since it would likely have detrimental effects on the rights of shareholders.[24]

9.14 Second, the US Supreme Court handed down a series of cases involving the type of consent that was necessary to allow class arbitration to proceed.[25] While two cases noted that parties do not need to specifically state that arbitration may proceed on a class-wide basis (instead, consent to that particular procedure can be gleaned implicitly from the arbitration agreement, any arbitral rules that the parties have adopted and/or the underlying law), the final decision in

---

17   Strong, *Class, Mass, and Collective Arbitration* (n 5) 12 (noting that more than 300 class arbitration were filed with the American Arbitration Association between 2003 and 2010).

18   SI Strong, 'The Rise and Fall of Class Arbitration in the United States', in Ana Montesinos García (ed.), *La Tutela de los Derechos e Intereses Colectivos en la Justicia del Siglo XXI* (Tirant Lo Blanch 2019) 207 ('Strong, Rise and Fall').

19   *AT&T Mobility LLC v Concepcion*, 563 US 333 (2011) (involving consumer actions); *American Express Co v Italian Colors Restaurant*, 570 US 228 (2013) (involving antitrust actions); *Epic Systems Corp v Lewis*, 138 S Ct 1612 (2018) (involving labour actions).

20   Strong, *Class, Mass, and Collective Arbitration* (n 5) 249.

21   Alyssa S King, 'Too Much Power and Not Enough: Arbitrators Face the Class Dilemma' (2018) 21 *Lewis and Clark Law Review* 1031, 1042; Peter B Rutledge and Christopher R Drahozal, '"Sticky" Arbitration Clauses? The Use of Arbitration Clauses After *Concepcion* and *Amex*' (2014) 67 *Vanderbilt Law Review* 955, 1012–13.

22   Dave Michaels and Gabriel T Rubin, 'SEC Rejects Proposal for Mandatory Shareholder Action', *Wall Street Journal* (11 February 2019) <https://www.wsj.com/articles/sec-rejects-proposal-for-mandatory-shareholder-arbitration-11549 927631> accessed 12 February 2019.

23   Letter from Skadden, Arps, Slate, Meagher & Flom LLP on behalf of Johnson & Johnson to the US Securities and Exchange Commission dated 11 December 2018 (including the shareholder proposal containing the waiver of class suits) <https://www.sec.gov/divisions/corpfin/cf-noaction/14a-8/2018/dorisbehr121118-14a8-incoming.pdf> accessed 12 February 2019.

24   Public Statement on Shareholder Proposals Seeking to Require Mandatory Arbitration Bylaw Provisions, Jay Clayton, Chair of the US Securities and Exchange Commission <https://www.sec.gov/news/public-statement/clayton-statement-mandatory-arbitration-bylaw-provisions> accessed 12 February 2019; see also Michaels and Rubin (n 22).

25   *Stolt-Nielsen SA v AnimalFeeds International Corp*, 559 US 662 (2010) (dealing with implicit consent in arbitration agreements); *Oxford Health Plans LLC v Sutter*, 569 US 564 (2013) (dealing with implicit consent in arbitration agreements); *Lamps Plus, Inc v Varela*, 139 S Ct 1407 (2019) (dealing with implicit consent in arbitration agreements).

the series – *Lamps Plus, Inc v Varela* – cast doubt on that principle.[26] In a hotly contested five to four decision with several dissenting opinions, a majority of the Court held that ambiguous arbitration agreements could not lead to class arbitration, which meant that the claimants had to proceed on an individual, bilateral basis.[27] Even more critically, the majority opinion precludes reliance on standard rules of contract interpretation, most notably the *contra proferentem* doctrine, on the grounds that arbitration is based on consent, which cannot be identified through rules of contract construction.[28] Although this decision does not formally state that explicit consent is required for class arbitration to arise, the practical effect of the opinion is nearly the same, since it will seldom be the case that an arbitration agreement provides unambiguous yet implicit consent to such class proceedings.

Taken together, this short history suggests that class arbitration initially developed in the US because of the combination of three key factors: (1) respect for large-scale relief as an appropriate procedural mechanism; (2) trust of arbitration as a procedurally legitimate means of resolving both public and private legal disputes; and (3) the need to give effect to certain substantive laws and policies.[29] This conclusion is confirmed by the fact that the number of class arbitrations in the US only began to decline when a majority of the US Supreme Court began to express scepticism about both the propriety of and need for large-scale relief (including large-scale judicial relief) in the US legal system[30] as a matter of both public and private law.[31]   **9.15**

These three factors can be tested against the development of mass arbitration in the investment realm. Interestingly, mass arbitration also arose as a pseudo-common law device, in that the mechanism was first adopted by an arbitral tribunal without explicit authorization from the relevant lawmaking body (in this case, the International Centre for Settlement of Investment Disputes (ICSID)). As a result, mass arbitration has suffered from some of the same issues as US-style class arbitration, most notably the question of whether large-scale procedures can be based on implicit consent to claimants' ability to act as a group.[32]   **9.16**

At this point, the international legal community has witnessed several large-scale investment arbitrations, though only one – *Abaclat v Argentine Republic* – has technically been deemed 'mass' arbitration.[33] *Abaclat* saw 60,000 Italian bondholders bringing a single action against   **9.17**

---

26 Strong, Rise and Fall (n 18) 207.

27 *Lamps Plus, Inc*, 139 S Ct at 1419.

28 Ibid.

29 SI Strong, 'Class Arbitration Outside the United States: Reading the Tea Leaves', in Bernard Hanotiau and Eric A Schwartz (eds), *Dossier VII: Arbitration and Multiparty Contracts* (ICC Institute of World Business Law 2010) 183, 201–3 ('Strong, Tea Leaves').

30 Although it is beyond the scope of the current discussion, the US Supreme Court has taken several steps in recent years to limit the availability of judicial class actions, based on what many believe is a pro-business bias. *Lamps Plus, Inc v Varela*, 139 S Ct 1407, 1435 (2019) (Kagan, J., dissenting); *Comcast Corp v Behrend*, 569 US 27 (2013); *Wal-Mart Stores, Inc v Dukes*, 564 US 338 (2011); Judith Resnik, 'Fairness in Numbers: A Comment on *AT&T v Concepcion, Walmart v Dukes*, and *Turner v Rogers*' (2011) 125 *Harvard Law Review* 78, 80.

31 For example, the US Supreme Court repudiated the longstanding doctrine of 'effective vindication of statutory rights' in *American Express Co v Italian Colors Restaurant*, 570 US 228, 234–7 (2013) (involving antitrust law).

32 Strong, *Class, Mass, and Collective Arbitration* (n 5) 78 n341.

33 *Abaclat v Argentine Republic*, ICSID Case No ARB/07/5, Decision on Jurisdiction and Admissibility (4 August 2011) (Pierre Tercier, President; Georges Abi-Saab; Albert Jan van den Berg) ('*Abaclat Award*'); see also Strong, *Class, Mass,*

Argentina for injuries suffered as a result of Argentina's default on approximately $100 billion worth of sovereign debt in 2001 and thus resembled many US-style class suits, which also feature high numbers of similarly situated claimants with relatively small individual amounts in dispute. Although no other investment tribunal has adopted the term 'mass arbitration' to characterize its proceedings, *Abaclat* was cited with approval in several other large-scale investment arbitrations.[34] As a result, the decision in *Abaclat* cannot be dismissed as simply an anomaly. Indeed, the decision could be relied upon in at least one large-scale investment dispute that is currently pending.[35]

9.18 Turning to the three factors found relevant to the development and maintenance of class arbitration in the US, it appears as if the first element – longstanding respect for the legitimacy of large-scale proceedings – was not as strong in the investment realm as it was in the US context. None of the arbitrators in *Abaclat* were from the US and thus cannot be said to have been influenced by the historical US mindset regarding the propriety of and need for large-scale suits. Indeed, the two members of the majority – Pierre Tercier, President, and Albert Jan van den Berg, appointed by the claimants – were European.[36] This suggests that the first of the three factors – a longstanding history of respect for class or collective relief – need not be as strong as it is in the US for large-scale arbitration to arise in other settings.

9.19 The second element derived from the US analysis focuses on the need for strong support for the legitimacy of arbitration. Although arbitration obviously cannot be actively disfavoured for large-scale arbitration to develop, the decision in *Abaclat* again suggests that other jurisdictions do not need to be as pro-arbitration as the US for collective redress arbitration to arise.[37] For example, recent years have seen investment arbitration face a number of challenges to its legitimacy.[38] While this is not the forum to discuss such matters, it appears that the future development of collective redress arbitration in Europe does not depend on an overwhelmingly high amount of support for arbitration in the jurisdiction in question.

9.20 The third factor in the development of class arbitration in the US involved the need to give effect to certain substantive laws and policies. Unlike the previous two elements, the concept of substantive need seems to be critical to the development of mass arbitration in the investment

---

and Collective Arbitration (n 5) 75. On 28 October 2011, Professor Abi-Saab issued a dissenting opinion to the decision on jurisdiction and admissibility. The case was subsequently settled after proceedings had concluded but before a decision on the merits was issued. *Abaclat v Argentine Republic*, ICSID Case No ARB/07/5, Consent Award (29 December 2016) (Pierre Tercier, President; Albert Jan van den Berg; Santiago Torres Bernárdez).

34   These proceedings were characterized as 'multi-party' rather than 'mass' arbitrations. *Ambiente Ufficio SpA v Argentine Republic*, ICSID Case No ARB/08/9, Decision on Jurisdiction and Admissibility (8 February 2013) (Brunno Simma, President; Karl-Heinz Böckstiegel; Santiago Torres Bernárdez) (involving 90 claimants); *Alemanni v Argentine Republic*, ICSID Case No ARB/07/8, Decision on Jurisdiction and Admissibility (17 November 2014) (Franklin Berman, President; Karl-Heinz Böckstiegel; J Christopher Thomas) (involving 74 claimants).

35   *Adamakopoulous* (n 8) (involving 954 claimants).

36   The dissenting arbitrator – Georges Abi-Saab – is Egyptian.

37   The US has been said to exhibit one of the strongest policies in favour of arbitration in the world. Bernard Hanotiau, 'Groups of Companies in International Arbitration', in Loukas A Mistelis and Julian DM Lew (eds), *Pervasive Problems in International Arbitration* (Wolters Kluwer 2006) 287; Gary B Born, *International Commercial Arbitration* (Kluwer Law International 2014) 310–11, 969.

38   A number of these challenges fly in the face of empirical research. SI Strong, 'Truth in a Post-Truth Society: How Sticky Defaults, Status Quo Bias and the Sovereign Prerogative Influence the Perceived Legitimacy of International Arbitration' 2018 *University of Illinois Law Review* 533, 537.

realm and, by extension, to the development of large-scale arbitration in other jurisdictions.[39] For example, the majority in *Abaclat* indicated that mass arbitration was only appropriate in cases where:

> [c]ollective proceedings … constitute[] the only way to ensure an effective remedy in protection of a substantive right provided by contract or law; in other words, collective proceedings [a]re seen as necessary, where the absence of such mechanism would *de facto* … result [] in depriving the claimants of their substantive rights due to the lack of appropriate mechanism.[40]

Considering the dispute at hand, a majority of the panel in *Abaclat* noted that:

> not only would it be cost prohibitive for many Claimants to file individual claims but it would also be practically impossible for ICSID to deal separately with 60,000 individual arbitrations. Thus, the rejection of the admissibility of the present claims may equal a denial of justice. This would be shocking given that the investment at stake is protected under the BIT, which expressly provides for ICSID jurisdiction and arbitration.[41]

2. Applying the historical test to collective redress arbitration in Europe

Having identified the factors that are necessary to establish and maintain a system of large-scale arbitration, it is necessary to determine whether and to what extent those elements exist in Europe. Each of the three criteria identified in the previous sub-section are discussed separately below.

9.21

a. Collective redress as an appropriate procedural mechanism

The first issue to consider is the strength and extent of support for collective redress in the EU and various Member States. Over the last decade, views on this issue have changed significantly, as demonstrated by the recent spate of European and Member State legislation on collective redress.[42]

9.22

Historically, Europeans resisted large-scale litigation based on the belief that such measures had to resemble class actions in the US, which were seen as violating important procedural rights and encouraging litigiousness.[43] Resistance to large-scale litigation was also the result of Europe's longstanding emphasis on *ex ante* regulation, which made *ex post* regulatory mechanisms such as class actions and class arbitrations largely if not wholly unnecessary.[44] However, the situation appears to have changed, likely as a result of a changed perception about the need for large-scale redress, as discussed further below.[45]

9.23

---

39 Strong, Tea Leaves (n 29) 201–3.
40 *Abaclat Award* (n 33) para 484 (citing SI Strong, 'From Class to Collective: The De-Americanization of Class Arbitration' (2010) 26 *Arbitration International* 493); see also ibid., para 541 (noting the need for 'homogeneous rights of compensation for a homogeneous damage caused to them by potential homogeneous breaches by Argentina of homogeneous obligations provided for in the BIT').
41 Ibid., para 537.
42 Commission Recommendation (n 1); Commission Communication (n 1); Parliament Resolution (n 1).
43 SI Strong, 'Regulatory Litigation in the European Union: Does the U.S. Class Action Have a New Analogue?' (2012) 88 *Notre Dame Law Review* 899, 900 ('Strong, Regulatory Litigation').
44 Ibid.
45 See s B.2.c.

9.24 When considering the possible evolution of large-scale relief in a particular jurisdiction, it is tempting to think that group arbitration can only arise if collective redress is first available in that country's national courts.[46] Certainly it is true that states that have embraced collective redress litigation are more likely to conclude that large-scale relief is legitimate as a policy matter.

9.25 To some extent, it makes sense to develop collective redress arbitration only in jurisdictions where large-scale judicial relief is already allowed, since that will ensure that the arbitral procedures accord with that state's views about the protection of various procedural rights and about whether large-scale arbitration should be regulatory or merely compensatory. It is important not to move forward with reform efforts too quickly, since expanding collective relief in arbitration beyond what is considered necessary and appropriate in the relevant legal and social culture can lead to a backlash, as seen in the US.

9.26 However, states should avoid adopting an unduly narrow approach to the development of collective redress arbitration, since those jurisdictions that do not have a domestic form of collective judicial relief may be most in need of a mechanism allowing for group arbitration. Indeed, at least one European Member State – Ireland – is known to have developed a form of large-scale arbitration even in the absence of court rules or legislation authorizing similar relief in court.[47]

b. *Arbitration as a legitimate form of dispute resolution*

9.27 The second element of the historical test involves national or regional views on the legitimacy of arbitration. At this point, the attitude toward arbitration in the EU appears to be relatively positive, even if it is not entirely uniform.[48]

9.28 The one difference between the US and Europe appears to involve consumer disputes, which can be made subject to a pre-dispute arbitration agreement in the US but not in Europe.[49] While this could be potentially problematic for the development of collective redress arbitration in Europe, in that a large number of large-scale arbitrations in the US deal with consumer issues, large-scale arbitration result does not have to arise from a pre-dispute arbitration provision. Indeed, Spain has developed a type of collective consumer arbitration that is based on post-dispute arbitration agreements.[50]

---

46 Strong, Tea Leaves (n 29) 203–4.

47 SI Strong, 'Large-Scale Dispute Resolution in Jurisdictions Without Judicial Class Actions: Learning From the Irish Experience' (2016) 22 *ILSA Journal of International & Comparative Law* 341 ('Strong, Ireland').

48 For example, each Member State takes a slightly different view with respect to the question of arbitrability. Tony Cole and others, *Legal Instruments and Practice of Arbitration in the EU* (2014) 41–2 (commissioned by the European Parliament Directorate-General for Internal Policies, Policy Department C – Citizens' Rights and Constitutional Affairs) <http://www.europarl.europa.eu/RegData/etudes/STUD/2015/509988/IPOL_STU%282015%29509988_EN.pdf> accessed 12 February 2019.

49 Ibid., 206–8.

50 Real Decreto-ley 231/2008 de 15 de febrero, por el que se regula el Sistema Arbitral de Consumo, Boletín Oficial Del Estado, lunes 25 de febrero de 2008, Número 48, Página 11072, arts 56–62 ('Ley 231/2008'), *translation available in* Strong, *Class, Mass, and Collective Arbitration* (n 5) Appendix; see s III.A.

c. Need for collective redress arbitration

According to the historical analysis in the preceding sub-section, the most important element **9.29** predicting the development of large-scale arbitration involves the need to give effect to certain substantive laws and policies. In the past, European Member States did not experience this type of need, either in litigation or in arbitration, because European and domestic legislation provided a sufficiently comprehensive compensatory and regulatory regime on an *ex ante* basis.

The situation has changed in the last few years, however. Improvements in technology, **9.30** communication and transportation have resulted in a rising number of disputes that involve numerous similarly situated individuals with the same or substantively similar types of small-scale claims. These types of matters are particularly well-suited to large-scale dispute resolution, which may explain the shift towards collective redress in Europe.

However, the movement may also be due to the rise of what has been called 'unanticipated **9.31** procedural risk', where:

> the unanticipated risk refers not to the type of injury … , but instead to either the scope of injury (such as an unanticipated volume of harm) or the nature of the injury (such as an unexpectedly low value of each individual claim). In these situations, the state anticipated a particular type of harm (described in the relevant substantive norm) but did not anticipate the possibility that the method of addressing the harm (i.e., standard bilateral litigation or arbitration) would be incapable of sufficiently deterring the behavior in question.[51]

When considering whether there is a need for large-scale arbitration, it is necessary to consider **9.32** whether the courts in the country in question are sufficient to meet the demands of both claimants and the state. In some cases, that may be true. However, large-scale arbitration differs from large-scale litigation in several regards and may be more beneficial in some circumstances.[52] It is therefore useful to consider, at least briefly, how large-scale arbitration may be more advantageous to the parties or the state than large-scale litigation.[53]

As a general rule, large-scale arbitration is said to be superior to similar forms of litigation with **9.33** respect to jurisdictional concerns (since arbitration can unify diverse parties in a single forum); choice of procedure (since arbitration can overcome differences in national procedural rules and can minimize or eliminate the impact of certain problematic procedures, such as US-style discovery); choice of law (since arbitrators may be more inclined than judges to apply foreign law); ease of international enforcement (since arbitral awards, unlike judicial decisions, may be subject to international treaties facilitating enforcement of the decision on the merits);

---

51 Strong, Regulatory Litigation (n 43) 935–8; SI Strong, 'Mass Procedures as a Form of "Regulatory Arbitration" – *Abaclat v Argentine Republic* and the International Investment Regime' (2013) 38 *Journal of Corporation Law* 259, 314.

52 Strong, *Class, Mass, and Collective Arbitration* (n 5) 284–304.

53 Notably, this chapter does not claim that one type of procedure (judicial or arbitral) is superior to the other in all circumstances. Instead, this chapter suggests that arbitration and litigation are equally competent in vindicating the rights of parties, a position that has been advanced by others. Cole and others (n 48) 186 (noting that 'not only does arbitration not conflict with EU law, but it may offer another opportunity for giving effect to EU law in the sphere of private law').

neutrality and expertise of the relevant decisionmaker(s); and of course considerations relating to the finality of the decision and associated savings of time and money.[54]

9.34 As useful as these analyses are, they do not take the particular nuances of European law into account. Thus, for example, the Brussels Recast makes recognition and enforcement of judicial decisions relatively easy within the EU, thereby offsetting one of the primary benefits of arbitration in cross-border contexts.[55] Choice of law considerations are minimized or eliminated in inter-European disputes, at least in matters governed by European rather than national law, since European law would govern in both litigation and arbitration.[56] Procedural considerations still exist, particularly since each Member State has its own procedural rules relating to collective redress, but parties to inter-European disputes will not be tempted to use arbitration to avoid US-style discovery, as many parties in US courts should, since European courts do not permit this type of information-sharing mechanism.[57]

9.35 However, there are a number of reasons why European states and parties should prefer collective redress arbitration over similar types of litigation in both domestic and cross-border settings. For example, arbitration might allow consumer, employment and insurance claims from different Member States to be heard in a single forum through post-dispute arbitration agreements, thereby eliminating the possibility of piecemeal litigation under the Brussels Recast.[58] Arbitration could also eliminate some of the procedural discrepancies that might arise in cross-border cases as a result of increasingly diverse national procedures involving collective redress.[59] Finally, arbitration also allows large-scale disputes to be heard by neutrals who have experience in those types of procedures[60] and promotes judicial efficiency by relieving courts of the burden of having to administer these types of time-intensive cases.[61]

C. EUROPEAN FORMS OF LARGE-SCALE ARBITRATION

9.36 As judicial forms of collective redress have evolved in Europe, so too have analogous arbitral forms of large-scale relief. In accordance with the analysis in the previous section, large-scale

---

54 Strong, *Class, Mass, and Collective Arbitration* (n 5) 284–304.
55 Regulation (EU) No. 1215/2012 of the European Parliament and of the Council of 12 December 2012 on jurisdiction and the recognition and enforcement of judgments in civil and commercial matters (recast), [2012] O.J. L351/1 ('Brussels Recast'). The Brussels Recast updated what was known as the Brussels Regulation. ibid para 1; see also Council Regulation (EC) No. 44/2001 of 22 December 2001 on jurisdiction and the recognition and enforcement of judgments in civil and commercial matters, [2001] O.J. L12/1. Some reports suggest that relatively few collective redress procedures in Europe have a cross-border element. BIICL Report (n 2) 74 (citing an empirical study of 67 respondents who stated that 61 per cent of the matters in which they had been involved had no cross-border elements). Others claim that this is an increasingly important area of interest. Amaro and others (n 1) 39–42.
56 The EU is particularly active in the area of consumer law, employment law and competition law, which are three fields that are likely to generate a large-scale action. BIICL Report (n 2) 24.
57 Federal Rules of Civil Procedure, R 26 (US); Strong, *Class, Mass, and Collective Arbitration* (n 5) 296–7.
58 Brussels Recast (n 55) arts 10–23; see also Amaro and others (n 1) 11 (noting claimant-friendly rules of the Brussels Recast does not assist collective cases).
59 Amaro and others (n 1) 17; BIICL Report (n 2) 10–11 (providing a comprehensive analysis of collective redress procedures currently in place in the EU).
60 Although a growing number of Member States allow collective redress in their national courts, such actions still arise relatively infrequently, which means that judges are not very experienced in such matters.
61 BIICL Report (n 2) 44, 116 (noting collective redress procedures take longer than non-collective procedures).

arbitration in Europe has developed in response to core areas of substantive need, primarily involving consumer and corporate (shareholder) disputes.[62] However, there can also be said to be a need for procedural devices facilitating settlement of large-scale disputes, particularly given the EU's emphasis on consensual dispute resolution, often referred to as 'alternative dispute resolution' or ADR.[63] As it turns out, European parties have access to two different mechanisms supporting settlement of large-scale disputes, one developed in Europe and one developed by the United Nations Commission on International Trade Law (UNCITRAL). While it is impossible to analyse the procedures found in each of these three categories in detail in the space provided, the following subsections provide a brief overview of the various mechanisms currently available in Europe.[64]

1. Collective consumer arbitration – Spanish and Irish models

Consumer disputes are often considered particularly amenable to large-scale dispute resolution, since they often involve large numbers of similarly situated claimants with relatively small individual claims. It is therefore unsurprising that two different types of collective consumer arbitration have developed in Europe. **9.37**

The first such mechanism to arise involves a Spanish statute known as Ley (Law) 231/2008.[65] Ley 231/2008 applies only to consumer disputes arising out of a common factual scenario and provides a means by which groups of individual disputes can be heard collectively pursuant to post-dispute arbitration agreements.[66] **9.38**

Spanish consumers initiate arbitral proceedings by filing their dispute with the Consumer Arbitration Board in their geographic region. Typically, those matters proceed on a bilateral basis, but collective proceedings can arise if a sufficient number of actions are filed and the president of the relevant board decides such treatment is appropriate, either on his or her own initiative or in response to a request from a local consumer association.[67] Notice of a potential collective proceeding is subsequently sent to the respondent, who may decide to accept or decline the opportunity to proceed collectively. If the respondent decides not to proceed on a **9.39**

62　A number of other ad hoc procedures have appeared from time to time. Ibid., 164, 299, 542, 552 (regarding an illegal insurance arbitration scheme in Estonia); ibid., 253, 354, 921 (regarding collective consumer arbitration in Spain); ibid., 512 (regarding a large-scale investment arbitration against Cyprus); ibid., 528 (regarding arbitration and Denmark's opt-out judicial procedure); ibid., 568, 948, 955, 957 (regarding Sweden's Skandia case); ibid., 613, 623, 632 (regarding Greece's opt-out regime and arbitration); ibid., 653, 672–5, 1006 (regarding the reservation of rights regarding arbitration in Hungary); ibid., 795 (regarding a voluntary reorganization arbitration in Malta); ibid., 856 (regarding Portugal's approval of voluntary collective arbitration).

63　Directive 2013/11/EU of the European Parliament and of the Council of 21 May 2013 on alternative dispute resolution for consumer disputes and amending Regulation (EC) No 2006/2004 and Directive 2009/22/EC (Directive on consumer ADR) ('Directive 2013/11') [2013] OJ L165/63; Amaro and others (n 1) 12 (noting, '[a]lternative dispute resolution mechanisms deserve to be developed and better adapted' for use in European collective redress procedures).

64　Further reading on each of the devices is available elsewhere, as noted below.

65　Ley 231/2008 (n 50) arts 56–62. A detailed discussion of Ley 231/2008 in English, including a full translation of the text of the statute itself, can be found in SI Strong, 'Collective Consumer Arbitration in Spain: A Civil Law Response to U.S.-Style Class Arbitration', (2013) 30 *Journal of International Arbitration* 495 ('Strong, Spanish Statute'); see also Bernardo M Cremades and Rodrigo Cortés, 'Class Actions and Arbitration Procedures – Spain' in Philippe Billiet and others (eds), *Class Actions and Arbitration in the European Union* (Maklu Publishers 2012) 153.

66　Ley 231/2008 (n 50) art 56.

67　Ibid., art 58. The statute also offers the means of creating a nationwide collective action.

collective basis, individual proceedings continue on a bilateral basis. If, however, the respondent agrees to proceed on a collective basis, all pending arbitrations are transferred to the Consumer Arbitration Board with jurisdiction over the dispute.[68] The Consumer Arbitration Board also provides notice to other potential claimants through publication in the Official Journal of Spain[69] arbitral tribunal and the matter is heard on a collective basis.[70]

9.40 The Spanish approach to collective arbitration successfully overcomes a number of potential problems with large-scale arbitration in Europe. First, because proceedings falling within the terms of Ley 231/2008 arise on a post-dispute basis, they avoid any conflicts with the EU directive on unfair terms in consumer contracts, which has been interpreted in many Member States as prohibiting pre-dispute arbitration agreements in consumer matters.[71] Second, Ley 231/2008 eliminates concerns about the type of consent needed to establish large-scale proceedings, since respondents must give explicit consent to collective proceedings.[72]

9.41 This is not to say that Ley 231/2008 is perfect. For example, respondents may hesitate to proceed collectively because there is no way to know in advance how large the final group, and therefore the scope of financial exposure, will be.[73] This type of tactical concern has proven problematic in other contexts.[74]

9.42 The second type of large-scale consumer arbitration to arise in Europe arose on an ad hoc rather than statutory basis. The procedure was developed in Ireland, which does not have any formal means of providing large-scale relief in litigation or arbitration, despite an ongoing need for such mechanisms.[75] The procedure in question developed in 2015, when over 1,000 claimants filed individual actions in the Irish courts seeking relief relating to defective hip implants manufactured by DePuy Synthesis Companies.[76] The dispute was so extensive that the Irish High Court estimated that the claims would not be fully resolved until 2022 if the matter remained in the judicial system.[77] As a result, the court, working with the parties, approved use of a private dispute resolution device that would resolve the claims in a more efficient, just and orderly manner by providing parties with a reasonable understanding of what the likely quantum of damages were, thereby encouraging parties to settle the matter without a full hearing.

---

68 Ibid., art 60. The one exception is in cases where an arbitral tribunal has already been appointed in an individual dispute. Those matters continue on a bilateral basis.

69 Ibid., art 59(1). Other forms of notice may be used if necessary or useful.

70 Ibid., art 59(3).

71 Council Directive 93/13/EEC of 5 April 1993 on unfair terms in consumer contracts [1993] OJ L95/29; Jonathan Hill, *Cross-Border Consumer Contracts* (Oxford University Press 2008) 215.

72 Strong, *Class, Mass, and Collective Arbitration* (n 5) 340–44.

73 Strong, Spanish Statute (n 65) 503-06 (noting other problems with Ley 231/2008); see also Amaro and others (n 1) 244 (discussing collective consumer arbitration in Spain).

74 Respondents often resist large-scale arbitration as a strategic matter, based on the belief that forcing parties to proceed individually will reduce or eliminate the number of claims that are brought. Strong, *Class, Mass, and Collective Arbitration* (n 5) 290, 329.

75 Strong, Ireland (n 47) 344–57 (discussing various large-scale disputes dating back to the early 1990s).

76 DePuy is facing over $4 billion in claims and litigation costs worldwide. Colm Keena, 'Court Due to Hear Six Cases Against Artificial Hip Maker' *Irish Times* (4 January 2019) <https://www.irishtimes.com/news/crime-and-law/court-due-to-hear-six-cases-against-artificial-hip-maker-1.3746887> accessed 12 February 2019.

77 Strong, Ireland (n 47) 342.

The procedures agreed by the parties involved a retired High Court judge who oversees a team **9.43** of ten independent evaluators who examined medical reports submitted by the plaintiffs and identified appropriate settlement offers.[78] The independent evaluators are all senior barristers, who are traditionally known for their neutrality and technical expertise.

The process has been facilitated by the relative predictability of personal injury damages in **9.44** Ireland. Typically, personal injury and wrongful death claims in Ireland are handled on a preliminary basis by an administrative mechanism known as the Injuries Board.[79] The Board provides general estimates on damages using the 'Book of Quantum' and various costs estimators and eventually issues an award known as an assessment, which the parties may accept or reject.[80] If the parties reject the assessment, they may take the claim to court.

The programme was expected to deliver decisions on individual claims within six weeks of **9.45** receipt of the relevant documentation,[81] and early reports suggested that the vast majority of affected individuals chose to use the alternative dispute mechanism rather than proceed independently in court.[82] However, recent reports about the efficacy of the system have been somewhat mixed, suggesting that Ireland should undertake efforts to design a permanent collective redress system, either in litigation or arbitration, rather than relying on ad hoc measures.[83]

2. Corporate shareholder arbitration – German, Portuguese and Swedish models

A second field where large-scale disputes are common involves shareholder suits. Three **9.46** European Member States – Germany, Portugal and Sweden – either have adopted or are considering adopting measures allowing collective corporate (shareholder) claims to be heard in arbitration. Interestingly, this movement is counter to the trend in the US, where shareholder arbitration is disfavoured, likely because of attempts to limit such actions to individual bilateral proceedings rather than allowing large-scale proceedings.[84]

The most advanced mechanism exists in Germany.[85] Interestingly, the procedure is not **9.47** reflected in legislation but instead arose as a result of a 2009 decision from the German Federal

---

78   Ibid., 359.

79   The Injuries Board is a state-run entity that handles all personal injuries claims unless the parties settle the matter directly between themselves. Personal Injuries Assessment Board <https://www.piab.ie/eng/> accessed 10 May 2020.

80   Personal Injuries Board FAQs <https://www.piab.ie/eng/help-support/faqs/> accessed 12 February 2019.

81   Strong, Ireland (n 47) 362.

82   Aodhan O'Faolain, 'Woman (81) with DePuy Hip Replacement Awarded €321k by High Court', Independent (1 December 2017) (noting only two cases to date had gone to full trial) <https://www.independent.ie/irish-news/courts/woman-81-with-depuy-hip-replacement-awarded-321k-by-high-court-36370366.html> accessed 12 February 2019.

83   Keena (n 76) (noting that some solicitors' firms believed the alternative dispute mechanism was ineffective, whereas solicitors for the manufacturer indicated that 60 per cent of the claims that had been filed had been resolved). It is difficult to determine the effectiveness of the procedure because settled cases are subject to confidentiality provisions. Ibid.

84   Michaels and Rubin (n 22).

85   A full analysis of the German procedure can be found at Christian Borris, 'Arbitrability of Corporate Law Disputes in Germany' in CJM Klaassen and others (eds), *Onderneming en ADR* (Kluwer 2011) 55; Strong, *Class, Mass, and Collective Arbitration* (n 5) 86–101.

Court of Justice ('Bundesgerichtshof' or 'BGH') declaring corporate law disputes arbitrable.[86] Later that year, the German Institution of Arbitration ('Deutsche Institution für Schiedsgerichtsbarkeit' or 'DIS') created a new set of specialized arbitral rules known as the DIS Supplementary Rules for Corporate Law Disputes ('DIS Supplementary Rules') that reflected the mandatory procedural protections set forth by the BGH in its decision.[87]

9.48 The DIS Supplementary Rules are limited to corporate law disputes involving partnerships ('Personegesellschaften') and limited liability companies under German law ('GmbH').[88] At this point, all of the disputes heard under the DIS Supplementary Rules have been relatively modest in size, since large, publicly traded companies are excluded from the scope of the Rules. Nevertheless, the DIS Supplementary Rules provide useful insights into how to organize large-scale proceedings involving shareholder disputes.

9.49 Under the DIS Supplementary Rules, a corporation can bind current, future and former shareholders through an arbitration provision found in a corporation's articles of incorporation.[89] Shareholders do not need to be named as parties at the time the arbitration is filed but do need to receive notice as a 'Concerned Other' at an appropriate point during the proceedings if they are to enjoy both the benefit and the burden of any award that ensues (i.e., if the award is to have *res judicata* effect as to those individuals).[90]

9.50 Shareholders do not need to participate actively in the proceedings to be bound by the decision rendered by the arbitral tribunal, although all shareholders must be given the opportunity to participate and the corporation itself must be named as a party.[91] Shareholders who wish to participate in the proceedings may do so as full parties or compulsory intervenors.[92]

9.51 Some people may regard the concept of passive and initially unnamed parties to be uncomfortably similar to the opt-out, representative procedures used in US-style class actions and class arbitrations.[93] However, the two procedures are quite different, since all shareholders in DIS

---

86   *S v M*, Case No II ZR 255/08 (German Federal Court of Justice, 6 April 2009), Kriendler Digest for ITA Board of Reporters <www.kluwerarbitration.com> accessed 12 February 2019; Borris (n 85) 61.

87   DIS Supplementary Rules for Corporate Law Disputes ('DIS Supplementary Rules') effective 15 September 2009 <http://www.dis-arb.de/download/DIS_SRCoLD_%202009_Download.pdf> accessed 12 February 2019; Strong, *Class, Mass, and Collective Arbitration* (n 5) 86–101.

88   DIS Supplementary Rules (n 87).

89   The International Chamber of Commerce (ICC) adopts a similar approach to the arbitration of internal trust disputes, which can also involve large numbers of parties. 'ICC Arbitration Clause for Trust Disputes' (2018) 29 *ICC International Court of Arbitration Bulletin* 92, 94 <https://iccwbo.org/publication/icc-arbitration-clause-trust-disputes-explanatory-note/> accessed 12 February 2019; see also SI Strong, 'Arbitration of Internal Trust Disputes: The Next Frontier for International Commercial Arbitration?' in Lise Bosman (ed), *ICCA Congress Series No 20, Evolution and Adaptation: The Future of International Arbitration* (Wolters Kluwer, 2019) 971; SI Strong, 'Mandatory Arbitration of Internal Trust Disputes: Improving Arbitrability and Enforceability Through Proper Procedural Choices' (2012) 28 *Arbitration International* 591, 601–4.

90   DIS Supplementary Rules (n 87) ss 4, 11. The term 'Concerned Others' is defined in a comment to Section II of the DIS Supplementary Rules and includes all shareholders.

91   Ibid., ss 2, 4.

92   Ibid., s 4 (noting the rights and responsibilities of the two categories of parties).

93   Federal Rules of Civil Procedure, R 23 (US) (describing class actions); American Arbitration Association, Supplementary Rules for Class Arbitration, effective 8 October 2003 <https://www.adr.org/ClassArbitration> accessed 12 February 2019.

proceedings are explicitly given the opportunity to be involved before the action proceeds and are allowed to participate in the conduct of the proceedings in a much more involved manner than unnamed plaintiffs in US-style class actions and class arbitrations do. Indeed, arbitrations under the DIS Supplementary Rules are best characterized not as representative proceedings but as a type of *in rem* action.[94]

Germany's success with shareholder arbitration has triggered interest from other European **9.52** countries.[95] Indeed, Portugal is currently contemplating the adoption of a law relating to shareholder arbitration that is expected to be very similar to the German approach.[96] The new law, which is expected to go into effect in early 2019, will feature new statutory language as well as rules to be adapted by arbitral institutions.

Sweden has also had some experience with large-scale arbitration, albeit on an ad hoc basis. **9.53** Although Sweden offers large-scale relief in its national courts, in 2004 a major matter – *Grupptalan mot Skandia v Forsakringsaktiebolaget Skandia* – was resolved privately through arbitration rather than litigation.[97] The dispute saw 15,000 retirement plan-savers pursuing 'a private class action claim against Skandia, whose internal corporate practices in restructuring the business had [allegedly] favored the mother company and cost the Swedish branch a loss of 1 billion SEK'.[98] One of the primary reasons for proceeding in arbitration was to resolve the dispute more quickly than would have been possible in court.[99]

One of the more remarkable aspects of the Skandia matter involves funding. Most jurisdictions **9.54** do not allow contingent fee structures like those that make US-style class actions and class arbitrations possible.[100] In the Skandia case, the claimants created a non-profit organization (Group Action Against Skandia), that was responsible for raising funds to proceed with the action.[101] This approach is similar to that taken in *Abaclat* and demonstrates one way to

---

94 Strong, *Class, Mass, and Collective Arbitration* (n 5) 25, 86, 89, 93; see also DIS Supplementary Rules (n 87) comment to s 2.

95 Since 2009, the DIS has seen an increasing number of disputes heard under the Supplementary Rules. For example, between September 2009 and December 2013, seven proceedings were initiated under the DIS Supplementary Rules, whereas in 2014, six proceedings were initiated; in 2015, five proceedings were initiated; in 2016, 14 proceedings were initiated; and in 2017, eight proceedings were initiated. DIS, Statistics <http://www.dis-arb.de/en/39/content/statistics-id54> accessed 12 February 2019.

96 Pedro Metello de Nápoles and José Miguel Júdice, 'Portugal' in *The European Arbitration Review 2017* (Global Arbitration Review) 101–2.

97 BIICL Report (n 2) 947-48; Roman Khodykin, 'Why is Class Arbitration Unpopular Across the Pond?' in Arthur W Rovine (ed), *Contemporary Issues in International Arbitration and Mediation: The Fordham Papers 2013* (Brill 2014) 123, 134; see also Case No T 97-04, District Court of Stockholm, 5 January 2004 (Skandia).

98 BIICL Report (n 2) 568 n.275, 948 n.744 (noting the claimants prevailed).

99 Per Henrik Lindblom, 'National Report: Group Litigation in Sweden' (Global Class Actions Conference, Oxford, December 2007) 22 <http://globalclassactions.stanford.edu/sites/default/files/documents/Sweden_National_Report.pdf> accessed 12 February 2019. Although unanticipated complexities slowed the arbitral process, there is no indication that the process would not have been as slow or slower in court.

100 Amaro and others (n 1) 16; BIICL Report (n 2) 18–20 (noting problems regarding funding of collective redress actions in Europe); ibid 29-30 (discussing contingent fees in European collective redress); Strong, *Class, Mass, and Collective Arbitration* (n 5) 322–3.

101 Khodykin (n 97) 134. One board member assigned his claim for compensation to the non-profit, allowing the non-profit to become a party to the dispute. Lindblom (n 99) 22.

overcome one of the key concerns about large-scale dispute resolution, namely how to raise the finances necessary to proceed with the case.[102]

3. Settlement of large-scale disputes – Dutch and UNCITRAL models

9.55 The final category of cases to consider involves settlement agreements. Most class claims in the US are resolved through settlements,[103] although the number of settlements arising out of collective redress proceedings in Europe appears to be somewhat lower.[104]

9.56 There are some reports that an increasing number of settlement agreements are being repudiated, at least in some jurisdictions.[105] As a result, European parties may have a rising need for mechanisms that facilitate enforcement of negotiated or mediated settlement agreements, both in domestic and cross-border cases.[106]

9.57 At this point, parties to large-scale settlement agreements have two different options that they can pursue. The first involves the Dutch Act on Collective Settlements (WCAM), which provides judicial confirmation to large-scale settlement agreements.[107] The WCAM is available on an opt-out basis for parties from anywhere in the world who are involved in a domestic or cross-border dispute. The procedure is relatively straightforward and involves a petition to the Amsterdam Court of Appeal to declare the settlement binding; notice to those affected by the proposed settlement; an evidentiary hearing regarding any objections to the proposal; and issuance of the order, which may include court-suggested modifications to the terms of the settlement originally proposed by the parties.[108]

9.58 The WCAM is available in cases involving both negotiated and mediated (conciliated) agreements,[109] which makes it compatible with EU initiatives meant to encourage the development of consensual dispute resolution (such as mediation and conciliation) in the area of consumer law and in commercial and civil matters.[110] However, European parties to

---

102 Strong, *Class, Mass, and Collective Arbitration* (n 5) 323–4.

103 Ibid., 68, 233 n36.

104 BIICL Report (n 2) 15 (citing empirical study suggesting that 62 per cent of collective redress cases in Europe were resolved through settlement 0–29 per cent of the time).

105 SI Strong, 'Beyond International Commercial Arbitration? The Promise of International Commercial Mediation' (2014) 45 *Washington University Journal of Law and Policy* 11, 35.

106 Enforcement of international settlement agreements is considerably more difficult than enforcement of domestic settlement agreements. SI Strong, 'Realizing Rationality: An Empirical Assessment of International Commercial Mediation' (2016) 73 *Washington and Lee Law Review* 1973, 2053–6 (Strong, Empirical). The same is true in cases involving cross-border compensatory and injunctive relief in the context of collective relief in Europe. BIICL Report (n 2) 21–2.

107 BIICL Report (n 2) 807–15. Although the WCAM has been in place since 2005, parties have only sought to confirm a settlement agreement under the Act nine times. Ibid., 815. France appears to have a law regarding facilitation of collective settlements, although it is not as broad as WCAM. Amaro and others (n 1) 161.

108 BIICL Report (n 2) 813–14.

109 Mediation, sometimes known as conciliation, involves negotiations that are assisted by an independent, third-party neutral (the mediator or conciliator). Strong, Empirical (n 106) 1980–81. At this point, the terms mediation and conciliation are essentially synonymous. Ibid.

110 Directive 2013/11 (n 63); Directive 2008/52/EC, of the European Parliament and of the Council of 21 May 2008 on certain aspects of mediation in civil and commercial matters [2008] OJ L136/ 3.

large-scale mediated settlement agreements may also be able to take advantage of a new international instrument that was promulgated by UNCITRAL and opened for signature in 2019.

The United Nations Convention on International Settlement Agreements Resulting from Mediation (Singapore Convention on Mediation) seeks to minimize some of the differences between international arbitration and international mediation by providing a fast and easy way to enforce settlement agreements arising out of international commercial mediation.[111] Although the Singapore Convention on Mediation does not apply specifically to large-scale disputes (as does the WCAM), there would appear to be no obstacle to using the Convention in cases involving collective settlements, so long as the agreement compiles with the terms of the instrument.[112] The only major concern involves the type of dispute. The Singapore Convention on Mediation focuses on commercial matters, and some types of disputes, such as those involving consumers or employees, that are likely to generate demands for collective redress are specifically excluded from the scope of the instrument.[113] The Singapore Convention on Mediation is also inapplicable to settlement agreements that have been approved by a court and are enforceable as a judgment in the country where the court sits, which means that the Convention cannot be used to enforce settlements that are confirmed under WCAM.[114] **9.59**

At the time of writing, it is unclear when the Singapore Convention on Mediation will go into effect and whether the EU and/or various Member States will be among the early states parties.[115] However, claims under the Singapore Convention on Mediation are not dependent on the nationality of the parties but on the place of enforcement, so European parties may be able to rely on the Convention even before the EU and/or individual Member States to adhere to the instrument, so long as enforcement efforts take place in a country that has joined the Convention.[116] **9.60**

D. CONCLUSION

As the preceding paragraphs have shown, collective redress arbitration is already on the European continent, with more developments expected in the coming months and years. In some cases, the impetus for change will come from the legislature, as is seen with the examples from Spain[117] and Portugal.[118] Future initiatives could be generated by individual Member States or by the EU, which is becoming increasingly active in procedural matters involving **9.61**

---

111 UNCITRAL, Report of the United Nations Commission on International Trade Law Fifty-first session, UN Doc A/73/17 (2018) para 49 (finalization of the Convention) and Annex I ('Singapore Convention'); see also Timothy Schnabel, 'The Singapore Convention on Mediation: A Framework for the Cross-Border Recognition and Enforcement of Mediated Settlements' (2019) 19 *Pepperdine Dispute Resolution Law Journal* 1, 1.

112 Singapore Convention (n 111) arts 1, 4, 8(1).

113 Ibid., art 1(2).

114 Ibid., art 1(3)(a).

115 Ibid., art 14 (noting the Singapore Convention 'shall enter into force six months after deposit of the third instrument of ratification, acceptance, approval or accession'); Schnabel (n 111) 5–6, 59.

116 Singapore Convention (n 111) arts 4–5.

117 See s C.1.

118 See s C.2.

alternative dispute resolution.[119] Scholars may assist in promoting reform efforts at the European or Member State level.[120]

9.62 In other cases, reform will come from arbitral institutions, as is seen with the DIS Supplementary Rules.[121] Indeed, other arbitral institutions in Europe, such as the International Chamber of Commerce (ICC)[122] and the London Court of International Arbitration (LCIA)[123] may already be capable of supporting demands for collective redress arbitration, based on the language contained in their standard arbitral rules. The Paris Mediation and Arbitration Centre (CMAP) has developed a set of rules intended to facilitate the mediation of collective claims and has successfully assisted in at least one multiparty matter.[124] While neither the LCIA nor the ICC are known to have administered any large-scale proceedings in recent years, the ICC did administer a case involving over 140 parties in the late 1990s.[125] As a result, it is impossible to deny the possibility of a large-scale arbitration proceeding in Europe under the general arbitral rules of either organization.

9.63 Reform may also arise organically. For example, some European Member States may allow collective redress arbitration to develop on an ad hoc basis, as occurred in Ireland[126] and Sweden.[127]

9.64 Finally, parties to large-scale disputes in Europe may seek to resolve those matters through mediation or negotiation. Such efforts will be facilitated by collective confirmation procedures in the Netherlands under WCAM[128] and through enforcement actions under the Singapore Convention on Mediation.[129]

9.65 At the time of writing, several new proposals had been made with collective redress arbitration in the EU and individual Member States.[130] While it is impossible to say how those initiatives will develop, it appears that this is an area of law, policy and practice that will only become increasingly important over time.

---

119 E.g., Commission Recommendation (n 1); Commission Communication (n 1); Parliament Resolution (n 1).
120 E.g., Marcello Gaboardi, 'New Ways of Protection of Collective Interests: The Italian Class Litigation and Arbitration Through a Comparative Analysis' (2020) SSRN <https://papers.ssrn.com/sol3/results.cfm> accessed 6 August 2020.
121 See DIS Supplementary Rules (n 87).
122 ICC Arbitration Rules, rr 19, 22(2), effective 1 March 2017 <https://iccwbo.org/publication/arbitration-rules-and-mediation-rules/> accessed 12 February 2019.
123 LCIA Arbitration Rules, r 14.4, effective 1 October 2014 <http://www.lcia.org/Dispute_Resolution_Services/lcia-arbitration-rules-2014.aspx> accessed 12 February 2019.
124 Amaro and others (n 1) 161 (discussing also collective settlements under French national law).
125 'The Decision, Judgment of the Swiss Federal Court' (1999) 10 *American Review of International Arbitration* 559, 564–8; Yves Derains and Eric A Schwartz, *Guide to the ICC Rules of Arbitration* (Kluwer Law International 2005) 101–02; Barry R Ostrager and others, '*Andersen v Andersen:* The Claimants' Perspective' (1999) 10 *American Review of International Arbitration* 443, 443.
126 See s C.1.
127 See s C.2.
128 See above n 107.
129 Singapore Convention (n 111).
130 European Proposal (n 1); Amaro and others (n 1) 92 (discussing technology, particularly online dispute resolution, and collective arbitration).

10

THE LAW GOVERNING COMMERCIAL AGENCY AGREEMENTS

Dodo Chochitaichvili[*]

A. INTRODUCTION

Commercial agents play an important role as intermediaries in international trade in goods (or **10.01** services) between principals and clients. With their knowledge of the local market, commercial agents help principals to enter foreign markets in consideration of remuneration, usually in the form of commissions. A commercial agent is a self-employed intermediary, acting as natural or legal entity, who has continuing authority to negotiate the sale or the purchase of goods (or of services) on behalf of a principal, or to negotiate and conclude such transactions on behalf of and in the name of that principal. In this commercial representative model of intermediary, there is little investment made by the principal on the envisaged market, except the payment of the remuneration when a sales (or services) contract is made.

Commercial agents however appear as the vulnerable parties in the contractual relationship, **10.02** namely due to the fact that once the markets developed by the agents have been tested by

---

[*] Date of submission: 16/4/2020.

principals, the latter try to build direct contracts with clients and therefore oust commercial agents. This is the moment where the activity of commercial agents and legal relationships are frequently terminated, principals taking advantage of the sales and the brand image developed by the agents when the clients continue to generate volumes and orders for the principals.

10.03   The European Directive 86/653 on commercial agents[1] (the Agency Directive) sets up minimum requirements for the protection that Member States are to offer to commercial self-employed agents. The Agency Directive provides the minimum level of protection from which parties may not deviate, except after the dispute has arisen, but leaves some leeway for national laws thus allowing some degree of diversity among the Member States' legislations. In Belgium for instance, the legislature took a protective approach of such institution and allows commercial agents having their principal place of business in Belgium to bring their claim before a Belgian court and ask this court to apply Belgian law instead of the chosen law by the parties in their agreement.

10.04   In international context, commercial agency agreements constitute a fertile ground for conflict-of-laws issues. In that regard the Agency Directive has not been immune from difficulties of interpretation which the European Court of Justice (the ECJ) had the opportunity to clarify. In the *Unamar* case, the issue before the ECJ touched upon the conflict-of-laws between two national laws which both had correctly transposed the Agency Directive. The question raised by the national court was whether there is a possibility for a national court to apply its local rules in the capacity of mandatory rules to an international agency contract, against a law of another Member State which has correctly transposed the Agency Directive but in different terms than the *lex fori*.

10.05   There are many decisions of the ECJ in the matter of commercial agency and the present contribution does not intend to feature all the European decisions but rather to present the decisions which can no longer be ignored by practitioners in conflict-of-laws issues, such as the *Ingmar*, *Agro* and *Unamar* cases.[2] It should be mentioned in passing that it is no surprise that among these three main judgments on conflict-of-laws based on preliminary references for ruling addressed to the ECJ, two of them originated from Belgian courts.

10.06   This chapter first recalls the objectives of the Agency Directive and the special status of Articles 17–19 of said Directive which creates a mandatory regime for indemnification or compensation for commercial agents after termination of the agreement (B). It then examines the sources of conflict-of-laws (C) and the territorial scope of the Agency Directive by examining the *Ingmar* and *Agro* cases (D). Finally, it analyses the concept of overriding mandatory provisions through the *Unamar* case as well as the arbitrability of commercial agency agreements from a Belgian perspective (E) before concluding (F).

---

1   Council Directive of 18 December 1986 on the coordination of the laws of the Member States relating to self-employed commercial agents (86/653/EEC), OJ L 382/17.

2   The present contribution does not address the Convention of 14 March 1978 on the Law Applicable to Agency to which only Argentina, France, the Netherlands and Portugal have adhered (entry into force on 1st May 1992).

B. THE COUNCIL DIRECTIVE ON SELF-EMPLOYED COMMERCIAL AGENTS (THE AGENCY DIRECTIVE)

1. The objectives of the Agency Directive

10.07 The Agency Directive was introduced at the European level to respond to the need of approximation and harmonisation of the legal systems of the Member States and accordingly to tackle the differences in national laws concerning commercial representation, with the goal of legally protecting commercial agents vis-à-vis their principals. The objectives identified in the preamble of the Agency Directive are threefold: (i) to remedy the differences in national laws which affect the conditions of competition; (ii) to harmonise the rules across the Member States; and (iii) to ensure the protection of commercial agents.

10.08 In the *Ingmar* case, Advocate General Léger summarises well the objectives pursued by the European legislature through the mean of the Agency Directive:

> In harmonising the national laws which govern the relationship between commercial agents and their principals, the legislature intended to create equivalent conditions for the carrying-on of the profession of independent commercial agent for all those who pursue it within the Community. In the same way, the approximation of the different national legal frameworks seeks to ensure a minimum level of protection for commercial agents, which, as I have said, also amounts to promoting the exercise of competition, freedom of movement of persons and free movement of services, since economic operators are then subject to the same social constraints.[3]

10.09 The Agency Directive aims therefore at coordinating the laws of the Member States as regards the legal relationship between the parties to a commercial agency agreement and to offer protection to commercial agents.[4] The case law of the ECJ is indeed led by the idea that commercial agents must be protected against the applicable law of the agreement which waives or offers less protection than the European legislation and its transposition laws.

10.10 The Agency Directive provides for the scope and the definition of the commercial agent (Art. 1), the rights and obligations of the commercial agent (Art. 3) and of the principal (Art. 4), remuneration of the commercial agent (Arts 6–12), the conclusion and termination of the agency contract, which includes the provisions on indemnity and compensation of the commercial agent (Arts 13–20) and some general and final provisions (Arts 21–23). The Directive sets up a minimum level of protection for commercial agents with regard in particular to the payment of commissions and indemnity and compensation upon termination of the commercial agency agreement. The protection of the commercial agent is hence ensured by not allowing the parties to derogate to some provisions, considered as mandatory rules, to the detriment of the commercial agent before the agency agreement expires. This is the case for instance for the indemnity and the compensation rules provided by Articles 17 and 18 as explained below.

---

3   Case C-381/98 *Ingmar GB Ltd v Eaton Technologies Inc* [2000] Opinion of AG Léger, ECLI:EU:C:2000:230, para 65.
4   Case C-465/04 *Honyvem Informazioni Commerciali Srl v Marielle De Zotti* [2006] ECLI:EU:C:2006:199, para 18; Case C-215/97 *Barbara Bellone v Yokohama SpA* [1998] ECLI:EU:C:1998:189, para 10; Case C-456/98 *Centrosteel Srl v Adipol GmbH* [2000] ECLI:EU:C:2000:402, para 13.

2. Special status of compensation and indemnity regime (Arts 17–19 of the Agency Directive)

10.11 The ECJ already had the opportunity to emphasise the importance of the level of protection for commercial agents by the Agency Directive in the course of the creation of the single market.[5] Such protection derives especially from the compensation and indemnity regime set up in Articles 17 and 18 of the Agency Directive in favour of the commercial agent following the termination of the commercial agency agreement.[6] Articles 17 and 18 of the Agency Directive indeed address the right to receive equitable payment for new clients and increased business in view of the loss of commissions, as well as rules regarding the compensation for the damage suffered through the termination:

> 21. The purpose of Articles 17 to 19 of the Directive, in particular, is to protect the commercial agent after termination of the contract. The regime established by the Directive for that purpose is mandatory in nature. Article 17 requires Member States to put in place a mechanism for providing reparation to the commercial agent after termination of the contract. Admittedly, that article allows the Member States to choose between indemnification and compensation for damage. However, Articles 17 and 18 prescribe a precise framework within which the Member States may exercise their discretion as to the choice of methods for calculating the indemnity or compensation to be granted.

> 22. The mandatory nature of those articles is confirmed by the fact that, under Article 19 of the Directive, the parties may not derogate from them to the detriment of the commercial agent before the contract expires. (...)

> 23. Second, it should be borne in mind that, as is apparent from the second recital in the preamble to the Directive, the harmonising measures laid down by the Directive are intended, inter alia, to eliminate restrictions on the carrying-on of the activities of commercial agents, to make the conditions of competition within the Community uniform and to increase the security of commercial transactions (...).

> 24. The purpose of the regime established in Articles 17 to 19 of the Directive is thus to protect, for all commercial agents, freedom of establishment and the operation of undistorted competition in the internal market. The provisions must therefore be observed throughout the Community if those Treaty objectives are to be attained.[7]

10.12 The level of protection for commercial agents is confirmed by Article 19 of the Agency Directive which provides that the parties may not derogate from Articles 17 and 18 to the detriment of the commercial agent before the agency agreement expires but only once the agreement has come to an end. This means that it is not allowed by the parties to evade the application of the provisions related to the indemnity at the end of the agreement or compensation for the damage suffered in a way that would adversely affect the commercial agent's financial situation. In the *Ingmar* case, Advocate General Léger pointed out that a

---

5   Case C-184/12 *United Antwerp Maritime Agencies (Unamar) NV v Navigation Maritime Bulgare* [2013] ECLI:EU: C:2013:663, paras 39–40.

6   Note that in its judgment of 19 April 2018 on a request for a preliminary ruling the ECJ held that Art. 17 of the Agency Directive must be interpreted as meaning that indemnity and compensation regimes laid down in that Article in the event of termination of the commercial agency contract are applicable where termination occurs during the trial period provided for by the agreement (Case C-645/16 *Conseils et mise en relations (CMR) SARL v Demeures terre et tradition SARL* [2018] ECLI:EU:C:2018:262).

7   C-381/98 *Ingmar GB Ltd v Eaton Technologies Inc* [2000] ECLI:EU:C:2000:605, paras 21–24.

contractual clause by which the parties' intention was to remove their relationship from the scope of legislation designed to establish a uniform legal framework brings about a rupture in the harmonisation;[8]

> 68. The choice, by the parties, of a law which omitted the obligation to indemnify or which neglected it by establishing a less favourable regime, would reduce the protection available to the agent. In that case, the law would place him at a disadvantage as compared with his competitors while at the same time placing his principal at an advantage as compared with other principals. The rupture of the conditions for harmonising the legislation applicable would thereby bring about a disequilibrium in the competition between economic operators pursuing their activity within the Community, which would run counter to the objectives of the Directive; and

> 75. (…) It follows that Articles 17 and 18 cannot be disapplied in favour of rules which are less favourable to the commercial agent. On the other hand, any other provision which finds no counterpart in the Directive could prevail over the Directive if it were shown that it worked to the advantage of the commercial agent.[9]

This also means that once the agreement has expired or is terminated, the parties would be capable to agreeing on a less favourable regime for the commercial agent or to relieve the principal of any indemnification. **10.13**

The mandatory nature and thus the special status of Articles 17 and 18 of the Agency Directive and of the corresponding implementing national provisions have been confirmed in the *Unamar* case.[10] The right to compensation and indemnity derives from statutory law, not from contractual obligations. Applied in the conflict-of-laws context, Article 19 of the Agency Directive requires the application of mandatory provisions notwithstanding any choice to the contrary, even where that choice is the law of a non-Member State. **10.14**

C. THE SOURCES OF CONFLICT-OF-LAWS

1. The principle of freedom of choice of law

In order to improve the predictability of the outcome of litigation and certainty as to the law applicable, conflict-of-law rules were adopted by the EU to determine the law applicable to **10.15**

---

8 See *Ingmar* (AG Opinion) (n 3) para 68.
9 Ibid., para 75.
10 See *Unamar* (n 5) paras 39–40:

> 39. In that regard, Articles 17 and 18 of the directive are of crucial importance, as they define the level of protection which the European Union legislature considered reasonable to grant commercial agents in the course of the creation of the single market.

> 40. As the Court has already held, the regime established by Directive 86/653 for that purpose is mandatory in nature. Article 17 of that directive requires Member States to put in place a mechanism for providing compensation to the commercial agent after the termination of a contract. Admittedly, that article allows the Member States to choose between indemnification and compensation for damage. However, Articles 17 and 18 of the directive prescribe a precise framework within which the Member States may exercise their discretion as to the choice of methods for calculating the indemnity or compensation to be granted. Moreover, under Article 19 of the directive, the parties may not derogate from them to the detriment of the commercial agent before the contract expires (*Ingmar GB*, para 21).

contractual obligations. These rules were consolidated in the 1980 Rome Convention,[11] replaced in 2008 by the Rome I Regulation which are the sources of conflict law, in addition to each Member State's code of law on private international law.[12] For both private international law instruments, the parties' freedom to choose the applicable law is considered as the cornerstone of the system of conflict-of-law rules in matters of contractual obligations.[13] This principle referred to as the *principle of party autonomy* is laid down in Article 3 of the Rome Convention and of the Rome I Regulation[14] and allows the parties to organise in an independent manner their legal relationship by choosing the law applicable to their agreement. The principle of party autonomy is however not unlimited insofar as the Rome Convention and the Rome I Regulation provide for different exceptions, among which the mandatory rules.

10.16 In the absence of choice of law by the parties, Rome I Regulation determines the law applicable to the different categories of agreements, of which the agency agreement categorised as services agreement, referred to in Article 4.1(b). This article provides that the contract for the provision of services shall be governed by the law of the country where the service provider has his habitual residence.

2. The exceptions to the freedom of choice of law

10.17 To the principle of freedom of choice of law there are different exceptions which may intervene and demand respect, such as the mandatory provisions aiming to protect a weaker party:

- Article 3(3) of the Rome I Regulation addresses national situations and specifies that: 'Where all other elements relevant to the situation at the time of the choice are located in a country other than the country whose law has been chosen, the choice of the parties shall not prejudice the application of provisions of the law of that other country which cannot be derogated from by agreement.' In this instance, it is not allowed for parties in an agency agreement located in one Member State and producing effects in that Member State to depart from the mandatory rules of that Member State, when the parties have chosen the law of another country.[15]

---

11 1980 Rome Convention on the law applicable to contractual obligations [1998] OJ C 027/34-46.

12 Regulation (EC) No 593/2008 of the European Parliament and of the Council of 17 June 2008 on the law applicable to contractual obligations (Rome I) [2008] OJ L 177, 6-16. Pursuant to Art 28 of the Rome I Regulation, this Regulation applies to contracts concluded after 17 December 2009.

13 See especially recital 11 of the Rome I Regulation.

14 Rome Convention (n 11), Art 3 provides that:

> A contract shall be governed by the law chosen by the parties. The choice must be expressed or demonstrated with reasonable certainty by the terms of the contract or the circumstances of the case. By their choice the parties can select the law applicable to the whole or a part only of the contract.

Rome I Regulation (n 12), Art 3 contains almost identical terms:

> A contract shall be governed by the law chosen by the parties. The choice shall be made expressly or clearly demonstrated by the terms of the contract or the circumstances of the case. By their choice the parties can select the law applicable to the whole or to part only of the contract.

15 Note that in Belgium some provisions of the Belgian Agency Law are considered as mandatory rules since they are capable of immediate implementation by the Belgian judge, whatever the law chosen by the parties. Parties can nevertheless depart from some provisions of the Belgian Agency Law; therefore, the foreign law could be effective for

- Article 3(4) of the Rome I Regulation which is an innovation in comparison with the Rome Convention addresses intra-European situations: 'Where all other elements relevant to the situation at the time of the choice are located in one or more Member States, the parties' choice of applicable law other than that of a Member State shall not prejudice the application of provisions of Community law, where appropriate as implemented in the Member State of the forum, which cannot be derogated from by agreement.' This provision applies to situations which have been harmonised at the European level, such as to the Agency Directive and its transposition laws.
- Article 9 of the Rome I Regulation (equivalent to Art. 7 of the Rome Convention[16]) on Overriding mandatory provisions (*lois de police*) provides for:
    - The definition of Overriding mandatory provisions: '1. (…) are provisions the respect for which is regarded as crucial by a country for safeguarding its public interests, such as its political, social or economic organisation, to such an extent that they are applicable to any situation falling within their scope, irrespective of the law otherwise applicable to the contract under this Regulation.'
    - Mandatory provisions of the law of the forum: '2. Nothing in this Regulation shall restrict the application of the overriding mandatory provisions of the law of the forum.'
    - Mandatory provisions of the foreign law: '3. Effect may be given to the overriding mandatory provisions of the law of the country where the obligations arising out of the contract have to be or have been performed, in so far as those overriding mandatory provisions render the performance of the contract unlawful. In considering whether to give effect to those provisions, regard shall be had to their nature and purpose and to the consequences of their application or non-application.'

Recital 7 of the Rome I Regulation explains that considerations of public interest justify to give **10.18** to Member State courts the possibility, *in exceptional circumstances*, to apply exceptions based on public policy and overriding mandatory provisions.[17] Furthermore, Article 16 of the Rome Convention and Article 21 of the Rome I Regulation specify that the application of a provision of the law of any country specified by the Convention and the Regulation may be refused only if such application is manifestly incompatible with the public policy (*ordre public*) of the forum.

---

the provisions for which the Belgian Agency Law allows the parties to derogate. On the immediate implementation nature of the Belgian Agency Law, see Claude Verbraeken, Aimery de Schoutheete, Jules Stuyck, *Manuel des contrats de distribution commerciale* (Kluwer éditions juridiques 1997) 147, no 123; A Mottet Haugaard and T Faelli, 'Chronique de jurisprudence relative à la loi du 13 avril 1995 sur le contrat d'agence (1995–2004)' (2005) 3 *Le droit des affaires – Het ondernemingsrecht* (DAOR) 241.

16   Rome Convention (n 11), Art 7 on 'Mandatory rules':

1. When applying under this Convention the law of a country, effect may be given to the mandatory rules of the law of another country with which the situation has a close connection, if and in so far as, under the law of the latter country, those rules must be applied whatever the law applicable to the contract. In considering whether to give effect to these mandatory rules, regard shall be had to their nature and purpose and to the consequences of their application or non-application. 2. Nothing in this Convention shall restrict the application of the rules of the law of the forum in a situation where they are mandatory irrespective of the law otherwise applicable to the contract.

17   Ibid., recital 7 also makes a distinction between 'overriding mandatory provisions' (Art. 9) and 'provisions which cannot be derogated from by agreement' (Art. 3(4)). See S Poillot-Peruzzetto, 'L'impérativité européenne, du malaise du mouvement à la solidité du fondement' (2019) *Recueil Dalloz* 448–52.

10.19 Whether such mandatory provisions can override the choice of law, be it non-EU law or the law of another Member State which has correctly implemented the Directive, has been the subject of preliminary references for ruling submitted to the ECJ which are discussed below through the landmark *Ingmar, Argo* and *Unamar* decisions.

D. THE TERRITORIAL SCOPE OF THE AGENCY DIRECTIVE AND THE CONNECTING FACTOR

10.20 The Agency Directive is silent on its territorial scope, nor does it contain a rule on conflict-of-laws. It does not state where the commercial agent has to carry out his activities, nor where the principal needs to be established for the Agency Directive to apply. The question which arises then is whether the Agency Directive is intended to have only *intra-Union effects*, i.e., only within the internal market or, to the contrary, whether its effects extend beyond the borders of the internal market.[18] That question is also relevant when the parties agree on a governing law which is the law of a non-Member State and which offers a less protective legislation on commercial agency.

10.21 The question of the law applicable to contracting parties neither of which are established within the EU is a question related to territoriality.[19] The location of economic operators or of their conduct within the territory have been applied for the interpretation and application of several articles of the EU Treaty.[20] In the *Ingmar* case, Advocate General Léger was of the view that the existence of an element of connection with the European territory in a legal relationship, although contractual, justifies the application of the norm of European law:[21]

> So long as one of the parties to the contract is based in the Community, he may thus benefit from the Directive's harmonising effects where he intends to rely on its provisions in order to develop his activity in that territory. It is not necessary to make the territorial application of the Directive conditional on the presence of all the parties to the contract in the Community.[22]

10.22 In the *Agro* case, Advocate General Szpunar stated that the effects of the Directive can be searched in the wording of the Agency Directive itself. The recitals of the Agency Directive refer to terms such as the 'carrying-on of that activity within the Community or principal and commercial agents are established in different Member States' (second recital); 'trade in goods between Member States, single market, the proper functioning of the common market' (third recital), leading to the interpretation that the Agency Directive is restrained to situations within the internal market and does not to apply to situations all over the world.[23]

---

18 Case C-507/15 *Agro Foreign Trade & Agency Ltd v Petersime NV* [2017] Opinion of AG Szpunar, ECLI:EU:C:2016:809, para 33.
19 See *Ingmar* (AG Opinion) (n 3) para 20 ff.
20 See Joined Cases 89/85, 104/85, 114/85, 116/85, 117/85 and 125/85 to 129/85 *Ahlström and Others v Commission* [1988] ECR 5193.
21 See *Ingmar* (AG Opinion) (n 3) para 39.
22 Ibid., para 48.
23 See *Agro Foreign Trade* (AG Szpunar) (n 18) paras 37, 45–47 and the interesting developments made in his Opinion on the legislative history of the Agency Directive in point 4 which initially did not limit the commercial agents' activity within the internal market.

The Agency Directive must be interpreted as meaning that it is, in principle, territorially **10.23** applicable to a commercial agency agreement where the commercial agent is based in a Member State and pursues his activity in one or more Member States. As will be examined below, the connecting factor for the Agency Directive to apply is the activity of the agent and not the establishment of the principal.

1. The *Ingmar* case: the commercial agent has activities within the European Union

The ECJ rendered an important decision regarding the international application of the Agency **10.24** Directive in the *Ingmar* case. The facts of the case can be summed up as follows: the Court of Appeal of England and Wales of the United Kingdom (UK) made a reference to the ECJ for a preliminary ruling in the proceedings regarding *Ingmar GB Ltd* and *Eaton Leonard Technologies Inc* on the interpretation of the Agency Directive. Ingmar was the commercial agent for an American company, Eaton Leonard Technology, in the UK and the Republic of Ireland from 1989 to 1996. When the commercial agency agreement came to an end in 1996, Ingmar launched proceedings against Eaton to obtain payment of commissions and compensation for the damage suffered as a result of the termination of the contractual relationship based on the English legislation implementing the Agency Directive. Eaton responded to the claim by arguing that the applicable law could not be English law since the commercial agency agreement contained a clause stipulating that the agreement was governed by the law of the State of California (USA).

The High Court held that the English legislation did not apply since the agreement was **10.25** governed by the law of the State of California. Ingmar appealed the judgment before the Court of Appeal of England and Wales, which decided to refer the following question to the ECJ for preliminary ruling:

> Under English law, effect will be given to the applicable law as chosen by the parties, unless there is a public policy reason, such as an overriding provision, for not doing so. In such circumstances, are the provisions of Council Directive 86/653/EEC, as implemented in the laws of the Member States, and in particular those provisions relating to the payment of compensation to agents on termination of their agreements with principals, applicable when:
>
> (a) a principal appoints an exclusive agent in the United Kingdom and the Republic of Ireland for the sale of its products therein; and
> (b) in so far as sales of the products in the United Kingdom are concerned, the agent carries out its activities in the United Kingdom; and
> (c) the principal is a company incorporated in a non-EU State, and in particular in the State of California, USA, and situated there; and
> (d) the express applicable law of the contract between the parties is that of the State of California, USA?[24]

The English court sought to ascertain whether Articles 17 and 18 of the Agency Directive, **10.26** which guarantee certain rights to commercial agents after termination of agency agreements, must be applied where the commercial agent carried on his activity in a Member State

---

24 See *Ingmar* (n 7) para 13.

although the principal was established in a third country (non-Member State) and a clause in the agreement provided that the agreement was governed by the law of the country of the principal.

10.27   Recalling the principles laid down in judgment *Bellone*, i.e., the necessity to protect commercial agents and to harmonise the legislations between the Member States in order to eliminate restrictions on the carrying-on of the activities of commercial agents, to make the conditions of competition within the EU uniform and to increase the security of commercial transactions, the ECJ held that a principal established in a non-Member country, whose commercial agent carries on his activities within the EU, cannot evade the provisions of Articles 17 to 18 of the Agency Directive by the simple expedient of a choice-of-law clause. The Court outlined that the purpose of those provisions were to be applied where the situation is closely connected with the EU, in particular where the commercial agent carries on his activities in the territory of a Member State, irrespective of the law by which the parties intended the agreement to be governed.[25]

10.28   The answer to the preliminary question given by the ECJ is therefore that Articles 17 and 18 of the Agency Directive must be applied where the commercial agent carries on his activity in a Member State although (a) the principal is established in a non-Member State and (b) a clause of the commercial agency agreement stipulates that the agreement is governed by the law of that country.[26] By this decision, the ECJ emphasised that a commercial agent which has activities within the EU and a principal established outside the EU cannot exclude the mandatory rules of the Agency Directive by way of a contractual clause designating the law of a non-Member State.[27] As a result, the freedom of choice of the parties had to be limited, so that the commercial agency agreement would meet the minimum standards of protection established by the European harmonised rules for the relationship between agent and principal.[28]

---

25   See *Ingmar* (n 7) para 25.
26   Ibid., para 26.
27   See commentary on this case by L Idot, 'Des droits de l'agent commercial qui exerce son activité dans un Etat membre alors que son commettant est établi dans un pays tiers' (2001) *Rev crit DIP* 107. In Germany, the Bundergerichtshof upheld the decision of the Oberlandesgericht Stuttgart which refused to enforce the choice of court agreement of a third country (in this case, the courts in Virginia, US) when the law chosen by the parties (the law of Virginia) does not entitle the commercial agent to compensation for termination of the commercial agency agreement and when it appears that the court of the third country will not apply EU and national mandatory provisions and will reject the claim for compensation (Bundesgerichtshof (Germany), 5 September 2012, *Rev, Crit. Dr. Intern. Privé*, 2013, liv. 4, 890; Oberlandesgericht Stuttgart, 29 December 2011, 5 U 126/11, IHR 2012, 163–6).
28   See Johan Erauw, 'The law applicable to distribution agreements' in *Arbitration and Commercial Distribution: Reports of the Colloquium of CEPANI, November 17th 2005* (Bruylant 2005) 84 commenting that:

> [T]he principle providing that once a rule is harmonized on the European level, it becomes applicable to all international cases on a mandatory basis, is an over-assertion of the European rules. It is not because a regulation or directive relates to one of the European freedoms and is regarded as essential for the relations 'ad intra' that its application shall necessarily follow, regardless of the weight and the importance of the contacts 'ad extra'. In private international law there is flexibility, even vis-à-vis national public policy.

2. The *Agro* case: the commercial agent has activities outside the European Union

Whether the Agency Directive and its implementing laws apply to a commercial agent that **10.29** carries out activities outside the EU is a question that was the subject of a reference for a preliminary ruling before the ECJ. The reference has been made in the proceedings before the Commercial Court of Ghent (Belgium) between Agro Foreign Trade & Agency Ltd, a company incorporated in Turkey, and Petersime NV, a company incorporated in Belgium, regarding payment of various forms of compensation owed as a consequence of the termination by Petersime of the commercial agency agreement between the two companies. The reference concerned the interpretation of the Agency Directive but also the 1963 Association Agreement between the EEC and Turkey.[29]

The facts of the case can be summarised as follows: Agro operated in the importation and **10.30** distribution of agricultural products in Turkey, while Petersime was involved in the development, production and supply of hatcheries and accessories for the poultry market. In 1992, the parties concluded a commercial agency agreement by which Petersime appointed Agro as commercial agent for the exclusive sales of its products in Turkey. The agreement was governed by Belgian law and only the courts of Ghent (Belgium) had jurisdiction in case of disputes. In 2013, Petersime terminated the commercial agency contract and Agro brought legal proceedings before the Ghent Commercial Court seeking payment of compensation for termination of the agreement and a goodwill indemnity, the repossession of the remaining stock as well as the payment of outstanding claims.

The *Agro* case is diametrically opposed to the *Ingmar* case insofar as, in the latter case, the **10.31** commercial agent was located and carrying out his activities within the European Union and the principal was located outside the EU. In the *Agro* case, the principal was located in the EU, while the commercial agent was located and carrying out his activities outside the EU.[30]

The parties had divergent legal positions: while Agro relied on the protection provided by the **10.32** Law of 13 April 1995 on commercial agency agreement[31] (the Belgian Agency Law) given that the law applicable to the agreement was Belgian law, Petersime argued that Belgian law only applied to the extent that the commercial agent operated in Belgium, which was not the case here. It relied on Article 27 of the Belgian Agency Law which provides that without prejudice to the application of international conventions to which Belgium is a party, any activity of a commercial agent whose principal place of business is in Belgium shall be governed by Belgian law and shall be subject to the jurisdiction of the Belgian courts.

The Belgian court noted that the parties made an explicit choice of the applicable law, in this **10.33** case Belgian law, but that it did not imply that the Belgian Agency Law was applicable, since the territorial scope of that law seemed to be limited to commercial agents principally established in Belgium. Hence, the Belgian Agency Law was self-limiting and therefore its

---

29 The Association Agreement between the European Economic Community and Turkey, signed in Ankara on 12 September 1963 by the Republic of Turkey, on the one hand, and by the Member States of the EEC and the Community, on the other, and concluded, approved and confirmed on behalf of the Community by Council Decision 64/732/EEC of 23 December 1963, OJ 1973 C 113/1.

30 See *Agro Foreign Trade* (AG Szpunar) (n 18) para 42.

31 This Law is now inserted in the 2013 Belgian Code of Economic Law under Title 1 of Book X.

mandatory character did not apply where the commercial agent did not have its principal establishment in Belgium, regardless of the fact that the parties may have designated Belgian law in general as the applicable law.[32]

10.34   As a result, the Ghent Commercial Court decided to stay the proceedings and to refer the following question to the ECJ for a preliminary ruling:

> Is the Law of 1995, which transposes Directive 86/653 into Belgian national law, in accordance with that directive and/or the provisions of the Association Agreement which has as its express aim the accession of Turkey to the European Union and/or the obligations between Turkey and the European Union to eliminate restrictions with regard to the free movement of services between them, when that law provides that it only applies to commercial agents whose principal place of business is in Belgium, and does not apply when a principal established in Belgium and an agent established in Turkey have explicitly chosen Belgian law?

10.35   The question referred to the ECJ sought to clarify whether the Agency Directive and/or the Association Agreement must be interpreted as precluding the application of national legislation transposing that Directive, which excludes from its scope of application a commercial agency agreement in the context of which the commercial agent is established in Turkey, where it carries out activities under that agreement, and the principal is established in a Member State, so that, the commercial agent cannot rely on rights which that Agency Directive guarantees after the termination of a commercial agency agreement.

10.36   According to the ECJ, such a particular situation is not expressly referred to in Articles 17 and 18 of the Agency Directive and therefore, it is necessary to consider the wording and the objectives pursued by that Directive.[33] In other words, the question here is whether the protection provided in Articles 17 and 18 of the Agency Directive are mandatory if the principal is established in a Member State and the commercial agent is established and carries out its activities in a third country.

10.37   The ECJ held that the situation in the *Agro* case did not present a sufficiently close link with the EU for the purposes of the application of the provisions of the Agency Directive.[34] According to the ECJ, it is not necessary to provide to commercial agents who are established and who are carrying out their activities outside the EU the same protection as those who are established and/or carry out their activities within the EU, for the purposes of making uniform the conditions of competition between commercial agents within the EU. The ECJ held that, in those circumstances:

> a commercial agent carrying out activities under a commercial agency contract in Turkey, such as the applicant in the main proceedings, does [not] come within the scope of application of Directive 86/653, regardless of the fact that the principal is established in a Member State, and therefore should not necessarily benefit from the protection provided by that directive to commercial agents.

> Consequently, the Member States are not obliged to adopt harmonisation measures, solely under Directive 86/653, concerning commercial agents in situations like those at issue in the main

---

32   Case C-507/15 *Agro Foreign Trade & Agency Ltd v Petersime NV* [2017] ECLI:EU:C:2017:129, para 18.
33   Case C-40/14 *Utopia* [2014] ECLI:EU:C:2014:2389, para 27.
34   See *Agro Foreign Trade* (n 32) para 33.

proceedings. That directive therefore does not preclude national legislation such as that at issue in the main proceedings.[35]

With respect to the Association Agreement, the ECJ held that this agreement pursued a solely **10.38** economic purpose and that the interpretation of the provisions of the EU law concerning the internal market could not be automatically applied by analogy to the interpretation of an agreement concluded by the European Union with a non-Member State, Turkey in the present situation, unless there were express provisions to that effect laid down by the agreement itself.[36] Hence, the differences between the objectives between the Agency Directive and the Association Agreement precluded the application of the protection laid down by the Agency Directive to commercial agents established in Turkey, even if Turkey has transposed the Agency Directive into its national law.[37]

The conclusions of the ECJ are clear: in the context of which the commercial agent is **10.39** established and carries out activities outside the EU, this commercial agent cannot rely on rights which the Agency Directive guarantees to commercial agents after the termination of such a commercial agency agreement.[38]

The national court (the Belgian court in this instance) thereafter needed to decide whether the **10.40** law chosen by the parties, i.e., the Belgian law, includes the Belgian Agency Law or whether it is only Belgian common contract law that applies to the legal relationship of the parties, with the exception of the Belgian Agency Law. It is for the national court, which finds that Belgian law is applicable to the agreement between the parties, to decide precisely which provisions of the Belgian law govern the contractual relationship between the parties.[39] In the *Agro* case, the parties made a choice as to Belgian law being applicable and in that respect, no conflict-of-laws had to be considered. If the ECJ does not command the application of protective provisions of the Agency Directive, it does not prohibit the Member States to extend this protective regime

---

35   Ibid., paras 35–36. Note that the word 'not' is missing in the English translation of the text, while this word is included in the French version of the judgment. The negation of the sentence makes sense given the decision of the ECJ. See *Agro Foreign Trade* (AG Szpunar) (n 18) paras 34–35:

>   The directive aims to harmonise private law of the Member States. It contains some of the essential provisions of an agency contract. The law applicable to the agency contract is to be determined by the conflict-of-law rules applicable in the State of the competent court. The applicable law can be designated either – as in the case at issue – by the parties' choice of law clause or by the choice of law rules applicable in the absence of a choice made by the parties.

>   As a consequence, in principle, if the law applicable to the agency contract is the law of a Member State, national provisions implementing the directive apply. This does not mean, however, that a national legislature is totally precluded from restricting the territorial scope of the application of provisions implementing that directive. Yet, in doing so, the national legislature has to bear in mind in what kind of situations the application of the directive is mandatory.

36   See *Agro Foreign Trade* (n 32) paras 39–42.
37   Ibid., paras 44–45.
38   Ibid., para 52. According to AG Szpunar, a commercial agent exercising his activities in a non-EU country and also in an EU country is likely to be an internal-market situation for which the Agency Directive will apply (See *Agro Foreign Trade* (AG Szpunar) (n 18) fn 41).
39   See *Agro Foreign Trade* (AG Szpunar) (n 18) paras 25–30.

to situations having a link with their territories, such as the establishment of the principal.[40] Following the judgment on the preliminary ruling, the Ghent Commercial Court decided to apply Belgian law but gave effect to the mandatory provisions of the Turkish Commercial Code considering that Turkey had implemented the *Acquis Communautaire* by transposing the Agency Directive following the Association Agreement with the EU, that the case was closely connected to Turkey and that a minimum protection similar to the protection offered to EU agents should be offered to Turkish agents.[41] As a consequence, the relevant section of the Turkish Commercial Code on commercial agents was, according to the Court, a mandatory provision within the definition of Article 7.1 of the 1980 Rome Convention.[42]

10.41 In comparison, the 1961 Belgian Law on unilateral termination of exclusive distribution agreements made for indefinite duration provides that the distributor, upon termination of the distribution agreement producing effects *in all or part* of the Belgian territory, may bring a claim before the Belgian court of its registered seat.[43] In the event that the claim is brought before the Belgian court, the latter will exclusively apply Belgian law. The Belgian Supreme Court has already decided regarding the Belgian Distributorship Law that when the distribution produces exclusively effects *outside* the Belgian territory, the mandatory provisions of the Belgian Distributorship Law are applicable in the event of termination of the distribution agreement *only* where the agreement between the distributor and the supplier renders this law expressly applicable to the agreement between the parties.[44]

10.42 *Mutatis mutandis*, given that the material scope of the Belgian Distributorship Law is quite similar to the Belgian Agency Law, i.e., that the distributor or the commercial agent must be established on the Belgian territory, the Belgian Laws on exclusive distribution and on commercial agency are considered as self-limiting. In other words, a mere reference to Belgian law in the agreement is not sufficient to render applicable the law on commercial agency or the law on exclusive distribution applicable to the commercial agent or the distributor that are established outside Belgium and therefore, an express reference to the relevant law in the agreement is required. This has been confirmed in a decision of the International Court of Arbitration of the ICC of 15 February 2010 in which a commercial agency having its principal place of establishment in Switzerland had been carrying out his activities, on an exclusive basis, in that country for a principal domiciled in Belgium.[45] The agreement provided for Belgian

---

40   For a commentary of the *Agro* case, see Cyril Nourissat, 'La directive sur les agents commerciaux ne saurait bénéficier à un agent exerçant hors de l'Union européenne même si la loi applicable au contrat est d'un Etat member' (2017) 4 *AJ Contrat* 186 ff.

41   Ghent Commercial Tribunal, Decision of 14 March 2019 (2019) *Revue@dipr.be*, 66.

42   See (n 16) for Art. 7.1 of the 1980 Rome Convention.

43   The Law of 27 July 1961 on unilateral termination of exclusive distribution agreements made for indefinite duration (the Belgian Distributorship Law) is now inserted in Chapter 3 of Book X of the 2013 Belgian Code of Economic Law. Art. X.39 of this Code provides that:

   The distributor may, upon termination of a distribution agreement effective within the entire Belgian territory or a part thereof, in any event summon the supplier in Belgium either before the court of his own domicile, or before the court of the domicile or registered office of the supplier. In case the dispute is brought before a Belgian court, this court shall exclusively apply Belgian law.

44   Belgian Supreme Court, Decision of 6 April 2006 (2006) I *Pasicrisie* 210.

45   International Court of Arbitration of the ICC, Decision of 15 February 2020 (2012) 3 *Revue de Droit Commercial Belge – Tijdschrift voor Belgisch Handelsrecht* (*RDC-TBH*) 238–41, with note of Aimery de Schoutheete and Paul Vandepitte, 'Le caractère autolimité de la loi du 13 avril 1995 relative au contrat d'agence commerciale', 241: the authors consider

law. Following the termination of the agreement, the commercial agent claimed the special protection under the Belgian Agency Law, which the arbitral tribunal refused, considering that this Law only benefits activities of the commercial agents who are established on the Belgian territory, which was not the case here. The arbitral tribunal concluded that Belgian common law was applicable, so that the claimant could not benefit from the mandatory provisions of the Belgian Agency Law, nor of the Agency Directive which had not been implemented or at least had not been made equivalent in Swiss law.

E. OVERRIDING MANDATORY RULES: THE *UNAMAR* CASE

1. Introduction

The *Unamar* case deals with an intra-European situation in which the question of applying the correct law of one of two Member States, both of which had implemented the Agency Directive, arose before Belgian courts. This case is different from the cases examined above given that the issue addressed to the ECJ was to determine which law of the two Member States should be applied, considering that both Member States had correctly transposed the Agency Directive but which offer a different degree of protection to the commercial agent. **10.43**

With the *Unamar* case, the ECJ clarified the notion of *overriding mandatory provisions* but also adopted a strict approach which invites the national court to rule whether the law of the forum is of mandatory nature. It is not sufficient for the national court to observe that the national legislature wanted the application of the mandatory rules whatever the choice of law by the parties, yet the national court must observe, on the basis of a detailed assessment, that the rules were adopted to protect a crucial public interest of the State.[46] **10.44**

The facts of the case can be summarised as follows: in 2005, an agency agreement was entered into between Unamar, a Belgian commercial agent, and NMB, a Bulgarian principal, for the **10.45**

---

that, based on the *Ingmar* case, if the commercial agent established in Switzerland had been carrying out his activities in the EU, the mandatory regime of the domestic law implementing Arts 17 and 18 of the Agency Directive applies. Considering that in this case the chosen law was Belgian law, the authors conclude that the mandatory provisions of the Belgian Agency Law should be applied. The same applies if the commercial agency had been carrying out partially his activities in the EU but only for that part carried out in the EU. The authors note however that such approach has been criticised for the fact that the rules chosen by the parties which would be more favourable for the agent than Arts 17 and 18 of the Agency Directive would therefore not be applicable. In a decision of 4 June 2015, the Liege Court of Appeal decided to apply Arts 20 and 21 of the Belgian Agency Law, implementing the mandatory provisions of the Agency Directive, when the law applicable to the contract was Belgian law (without expressly referring to the Belgian Agency Law), while the commercial agent did not have its principal establishment in Belgium but activities were carried out in the French overseas departments, which are part of the EU although they are located outside the European continent (See Liege Court of Appeal, Decision of 4 June 2015 (2017) 12 *Revue de Jurisprudence de Liège, Mons et Bruxelles (JLMB)* 564).

46 Pascal Hollander, 'L'arrêt Unamar de la Cour de justice: une bombe atomique sur le droit belge de la distribution commerciale ?' (2014) *JT*, 299. In the *Unamar* case, the European Commission adopted a strict approach by stating that unilateral reliance on mandatory rules by a State is contrary to the principles underlying the Rome Convention, in particular the fundamental principle of the precedence given to the law chosen contractually by the parties, insofar as the law is one of the Member State which has implemented in its national legal order the binding provisions of the Agency Directive (See *Unamar* (n 5) para 35).

operation of NMB's container liner shipping service.[47] The agreement provided that Bulgarian law was the governing law and that any dispute arising out of the agreement would be resolved by the arbitration chamber of the Chamber of commerce and industry in Sofia (Bulgaria).[48] The agreement was supposed to be renewed every year for the period of one more year.

10.46 In 2008, NMB informed its agents that, due to financial reasons, it was forced to terminate their contractual relationship. Unamar considered that the agency agreement was unlawfully terminated and brought an action in Belgium before the Antwerp Commercial Court for payment of various forms of compensation provided under the Belgian Agency Law. Unamar claimed compensation in lieu of notice, eviction indemnity and damages for compensation for dismissal of staff. NMB in turn brought an action before the same court against Unamar for payment of outstanding freight. The two cases were conjoined.

10.47 NMB raised a plea for lack of jurisdiction before the Antwerp Commercial Court arguing that the Belgian court did not have jurisdiction to hear the dispute given the arbitration clause contained in the commercial agency agreement.

10.48 In its judgment, the Antwerp Commercial Court decided that the plea invoked by NMB was unfounded. The Commercial Court ruled in favour of the agent and referred to Article 27 of the Belgian Agency Law which provides that Belgian law applies and Belgian courts have jurisdiction when the commercial agent has his principal place of business in Belgium. As regards the applicable law in the two disputes brought before it, the Antwerp Commercial Court ruled, inter alia, that Article 27 of the Belgian Agency Law was a unilateral conflict-of-law rule which was directly applicable as a mandatory rule and which thus rendered ineffective the choice of foreign law.[49] It also considered that commercial agency disputes were not subject to arbitration, unless the commercial agency agreement provided for Belgian law or an equivalent law, which was not the case of Bulgarian law since the latter, although correctly transposed in Bulgaria, did not apparently offer the same protection to commercial agents than the one offered by the Belgian Agency Law which goes beyond the minimal protection provided by the Agency Directive.[50]

10.49 NMB lodged an appeal against this judgment before the Antwerp Court of Appeal which ruled that the plea on the lack of jurisdiction was founded as the commercial agency agreement contained a valid arbitration clause and that it could not therefore rule on the claim for payment of compensation made by Unamar. In addition, the Antwerp Court of Appeal held

---

47   It should be noted that the Belgian Agency Law has extended the commercial agency regime to shipping service, which is not as such referred to in the Agency Directive. For instance, the definition of commercial agency under Belgian Agency Law does not refer to the sale or the purchase of goods (Art. 1 of the Directive). This is explained by the fact that the Directive gives a margin of appreciation to the Member States for the transposition of the Directive. Some countries have also extended the scope to include the services agreement (e.g., France, Italy, Portugal, Spain), while other countries limit to sales agency (e.g., UK, Denmark, Greece, Sweden, Finland).

48   On commercial agency agreements under Belgian law, see Claude Verbraeken and Aimery De Schoutheete, 'La loi du 13 avril 1995 relative au contrat d'agence commerciale' (1995) *Journal des tribunaux (JT)*, 461–9; M Willemart and S Willemart, *Le contrat d'agence commerciale (loi du 13 avril 1995 modifiée par celles des 4 mai 1999, 1er juin 1999 et 21 février 2005)* (Larcier 2005).

49   See Y Van Couter, E Van Parys and G Driesen, 'Artikel 27 Handelsagentuurwet' in *Handels-en Economisch Recht. Commentaar met overzicht van rechtspraak en rechtsleer*, Kluwer, 13–24.

50   Pascal Hollander (n 46), 297 ff.

that the Belgian Agency Law was not part of public policy, nor of Belgian international public policy within the meaning of Article 7(2) of the Rome Convention, and that Bulgarian law provided the minimum protection of the Agency Directive, so that the mandatory rules of the Belgian Agency Law should not apply. As a result, the principle of freedom of contract had to prevail and Bulgarian law was applicable.[51]

Unamar challenged the decision of the Antwerp Court of Appeal before the Belgian Supreme Court which took into consideration the following elements:[52] **10.50**

- with respect to jurisdiction, the New York Convention on the Recognition and Enforcement of Foreign Arbitral Awards of 10 June 1958 (the New York Convention) does not prevent the national judge to reject the application of an arbitration clause valid pursuant to a foreign law, on the basis of the *lex fori* that considers that the object of the dispute cannot be subject to arbitration;
- with respect to the Belgian Agency Law, according to the legislative history (*travaux préparatoires*) of this Law, Articles 18, 20 and 21 of the said Law should be regarded as mandatory rules of law pursuant to the mandatory nature of the Agency Directive which it implements into national law. Therefore, it follows from Article 27 of the Belgian Agency Law which provides that 'subject to the application of international conventions to which Belgium is part of, any activity of the commercial agent having its principal place of business in Belgium is subject to Belgian law and within the jurisdiction of Belgian courts', that its objective is to provide a wide protection, i.e., the protection of the mandatory rules of Belgian law, whatever the applicable law to the commercial agency agreement.[53]

2. Reference for a preliminary ruling

In those circumstances, the Belgian Supreme Court stayed the proceedings on the question of the arbitrability of the dispute, considering that the answer required to have another question **10.51**

51 Dirk De Meulemeester, 'Unamar: Arbitration clause drowned by gold plated provision in Belgian law on commercial agency?' (Kluwer Arbitration Blog, 3 December 2013) <http://arbitrationblog.kluwerarbitration.com/2013/12/03/unamar-arbitration-clause-drowned-by-gold-plated-provision-in-belgian-law-on-commercial-agency/> accessed 16 April 2020.
52 Belgian Supreme Court, Decision of 5 April 2012, (2012) I *Pasicrisie* 760.
53 It should be noted that Art. 27 of the Belgian Agency Law is equivalent to Art. X.25 of the 2013 Belgian Economic Code, which replaced Art. 27. Preparatory work mentions that Art. 27 does not intend to exclude arbitration of commercial agency disputes, but that in general the Belgian courts are competent to deal with such disputes (see Niuscha Bassiri and Maud Piers, 'Commentary of Article 1676 of the Belgian Judicial Code' in Niuscha Bassiri, Maarten Draye (eds), *Arbitration in Belgium, A Practitioner's Guide* (Wolters Kluwer 2016) 23). In this case, the provisions on commercial agent's indemnity pursuant to Belgian Agency Law exceed the level of protection granted by the Agency Directive and Bulgarian law. For instance, under the Belgian Agency Law, the commercial agent has the possibility to claim additional compensation for damages suffered in relation with the dismissal of the staff. Such compensation does not seem to exist under Bulgarian law which limits the indemnity to the average of value of one year's remuneration calculated over the last five years of the agreement's duration.

preliminary decided upon the interpretation of Article 7(2) of the Rome Convention.[54] It referred the following question to the ECJ:[55]

> Having regard, not least, to the classification under Belgian law of the provisions at issue in this case (Articles 18, 20 and 21 of the [Law on] commercial agency contracts) as special mandatory rules of law within the terms of Article 7(2) of the Rome Convention, must Articles 3 and 7(2) of the Rome Convention, read, as appropriate, in conjunction with [Directive 86/653], be interpreted as meaning that special mandatory rules of law of the forum that offer wider protection than the minimum laid down by [Directive 86/653] may be applied to the contract, even if it appears that the law applicable to the contract is the law of another Member State of the European Union in which the minimum protection provided by [Directive 86/653] has also been implemented?

10.52   The ECJ summarised the question as follows: must Articles 3 and 7(2) of the Rome Convention be interpreted as meaning that the law of a Member State which meets the requirement for minimum protection laid down by the Agency Directive and which has been chosen by the parties to a commercial agency agreement (*lex contractus*) may be disregarded by the court before which the dispute has been brought, established in another Member State, in favour of the law of the forum (*lex fori*) on the ground of the mandatory nature, in the legal order of that Member State, of the rules governing the position of self-employed commercial agents?

10.53   Hence the question submitted to the ECJ is whether the Belgian Agency Law could be considered as mandatory law under Article 7(2) of the Rome Convention. The ECJ was in particular asked to give guidance on whether the law of a Member State, which had correctly implemented the Agency Directive and went beyond the minimum protection laid down by said Directive, may impose the wider protection if the *lex contractus* was the law of another Member State which had also correctly implemented said Directive.

3.   Analysis of the judgment of the ECJ: strict interpretation of mandatory rules (Art. 7(2) of the Rome Convention)

10.54   It will be examined below how the ECJ shed light on the definition of the notion of *overriding mandatory provisions*, gave guidance to the national judge on the test for determining whether a national law is of an overriding mandatory nature and determined the limits that prevent the national judge to classify national law as overriding mandatory rule.[56]

a.   Preliminary remark

10.55   The reference for a preliminary ruling from the Belgian Supreme Court did not contain aspects of jurisdiction and the ECJ was only requested to determine the law applicable under the Rome Convention. The Belgian Supreme Court took the view that it had jurisdiction to decide

---

54   Art. 3 of the Rome Convention provides for the freedom of choice of law by the parties, but at the same time, Art. 7(2) states that the chosen law by the parties cannot restrict the application of the rules of the law of the forum in a situation where they are mandatory.

55   See *Unamar* (n 5) para 26.

56   Gisela Rühl, 'Commercial Agents, Minimum Harmonization and Overriding Mandatory Provisions in the European Union: The Unamar Case (Case C 184/12, Unamar, ECLI:EU:2013:663)' (2016) 53 *Common Market Law Review* 209–24.

the dispute on the basis of Article II(3) of the New York Convention. The ECJ recalled that, in that regard and according to settled case law of the Court, it was solely for the national judge before which the dispute was brought and which must assume responsibility of the subsequential judicial decision, to decide the need for a preliminary ruling and the relevance of the questions. The ECJ therefore held that it intended to answer the question without prejudice to the question of jurisdiction and therefore the impact on the arbitration clause.[57] The close link between the arbitration clause contained in the commercial agency agreement and the law applicable to the agreement is addressed below.

b. Definition of overriding mandatory provisions

Confirming the mandatory nature of Articles 17 and 18 of the Agency Directive, the ECJ held that whether a national court may reject the law chosen by the parties in favour of its national law transposing Articles 17 and 18 of the Agency Directive, reference must be made to Article 7 of the Rome Convention. In that regard, the Court made the following observations:[58]   **10.56**

- Article 7(1) of the Rome Convention refers to mandatory rules of foreign law and allows the State of the forum to apply the mandatory rules of another country with which the situation has a close connection instead of the law applicable to the agreement. In considering whether to give effect to these mandatory rules, regard has to be had to their nature and purpose and to the consequences of their application or non-application. Consequently, the application by the national court of mandatory rules of foreign law may arise only under expressly defined conditions;[59]
- Article 7(2) of the Rome Convention refers to mandatory rules of the law of the forum and allows the law of the forum to be applied whatever the law applicable to the agreement. There is no particular condition for the application of the mandatory rules of the law of the forum.[60]

However, the ECJ pointed out that even though national rules can be qualified as public order or mandatory rules, they still must comply with European Union rules and exceptions must constitute overriding reasons relating to the public interest:[61]   **10.57**

(...) the possibility of pleading the existence of mandatory rules under Article 7(2) of the Rome Convention does not affect the obligation of the Member States to ensure the conformity of those rules with European Union law. According to the case-law of the Court, the fact that national rules

---

57   See *Unamar* (n 5) para 28; Case C184/12, Unamar (Opinion of AG Wahl) ECLI:EU:C:2013:301, paras 22–23.

58   The ECJ recalled that it has jurisdiction to rule on reference for a preliminary ruling concerning the Rome Convention under the first protocol which entered into force on 1 August 2004 (See *Unamar* (n 5) para 27).

59   See *Unamar* (n 5) paras 42, 43 and 45. See also the developments of AG Szpunar in the Case C-135/15 *Republik Griechenland v Grigorios Nikiforidis* [2016] ECLI:EU:C:2016:281, on Art. 7(1) of the Rome Convention and Rome I Regulation.

60   See *Unamar* (n 5) paras 42, 44 and 45.

61   See comments on the *Unamar* case: Erinda Mehmeti and Jinske Verhellen, 'Wilsautonomie en dwingend recht in het Europees contractenrecht: hoe dwingend is dwingend recht wanneer partijen kiezen?' (2014) 1 *b-Arbitra* 199–209; Louis D'Avout, 'Les directives européennes, les lois de police de transposition et leur application aux contrats internationaux' (2014) 1 *Recueil Dalloz* 60–64 and Cyril Nourissat, 'De l'art délicat de manier les lois de police en présence d'un contrat d'agence commerciale intra-européen ...' (2013) *La Semaine Juridique Edition Générale* (*JCPG*) 2222-6; J Carruthers, 'Commercial agency and the conflict of laws – What place for party autonomy?', in Danny Busch, Laura Macgregor and Peter Watts (eds), *Agency Law in Commercial Practice* (OUP 2016).

are categorised as public order legislation does not mean that they are exempt from compliance with the provisions of the Treaty; if it did, the primacy and uniform application of European Union law would be undermined. The considerations underlying such national legislation can be taken into account by European Union law only in terms of the exceptions to European Union freedoms expressly provided for by the Treaty and, where appropriate, on the ground that they constitute overriding reasons relating to the public interest (Joined Cases C-369/96 and C-376/96 Arblade and Others[1999] ECR I-8453, paragraph 31).[62]

10.58 Recalling the importance of the fundamental principle of the freedom of choice of law provided by Article 3 of the Rome Convention and Article 3 of the Rome I Regulation, the ECJ confirmed overriding mandatory provisions within the meaning of Article 7 of the Rome Convention and held that the exceptions of mandatory rules should receive a strict interpretation:

> 47. In that connection, it must be recalled that the classification of national provisions by a Member State as public order legislation applies to *national provisions compliance with which has been deemed to be so crucial for the protection of the political, social or economic order in the Member State concerned as to require compliance therewith by all persons present on the national territory of that Member State and all legal relationships within that State (Arblade and Others*, para 30, and Case C-319/06 *Commission v Luxembourg* [1999] ECR I-4323, para 29).

> 48. That interpretation is also consistent with the wording of Article 9(1) of the Rome I Regulation, which is, however, not applicable *ratione temporis* to the dispute in the main proceedings. According to that article, *overriding mandatory provisions are provisions the respect for which is regarded as crucial by a country for safeguarding its public interests, such as its political, social or economic organisation, to such an extent that they are applicable to any situation falling within their scope, irrespective of the law otherwise applicable to the contract under this regulation.*

> 49. Thus, to give full effect to the principle of the freedom of contract of the parties to a contract, which is the cornerstone of the Rome Convention, (…) *the plea relating to the existence of a mandatory rule (…) must be interpreted strictly.* (emphasis added)

10.59 Note that a little later, referring to the *Unamar* case, the ECJ reasserted that the freedom of contract of the parties as to the choice of the applicable law constitutes the general principle laid down by the Rome I Regulation and that as a derogating measure, Article 9 of the Rome I Regulation must be interpreted strictly.[63]

10.60 The question that remains to be answered is:[64] can rules of private law which aim at protecting private interest (in contrast to public interest), and therefore weaker parties, be classified as overriding mandatory rules? The ECJ outlined that a national law was mandatory in nature insofar as it appeared that the legislature had adopted it in order to protect an interest judged to be essential by the concerned Member State:[65]

---

62 See *Unamar* (n 5) para 46 and the cited case law.
63 Case C-135/15 *Republik Griechenland v Grigorios Nikiforidis* [2016] ECLI:EU:C:2016:774, paras 43–44. The exception of overriding mandatory rules is now enshrined in Art. 9 of the Rome I Regulation and was already developed in the *Arblade* case (See Joined Cases C-369/96 and C-376/96 *Arblade* [1999] I-08453).
64 See Rühl (n 56) para 5.1.2.
65 See *Unamar* (n 5) para 50.

(...) such a case might be one where the transposition in the Member State of the forum, by extending the scope of a directive or by choosing to make wider use of the discretion afforded by that directive, offers greater protection to commercial agents by virtue of the particular interest which the Member State pays to that category of nationals.

The ECJ decides that provisions of national law which aim at protecting commercial agents **10.61** can be of mandatory nature if the national judge finds it to be crucial, in the legal order concerned, to grant the commercial agent protection going beyond the one provided for by the Agency Directive.[66] The specificity of the *Unamar* case relates to the fact that the Belgian Agency Law extended the protection of the Agency Directive to commercial agents not covered by the said Directive (i.e., the extension was to the shipping services). As a result, it could be argued that if the national rules do not serve to implement the purpose of the Agency Directive which is to protect the freedom of establishment and the operation of undistorted competition in the internal market, it would be quite unlikely that private rules which only protect a category of persons, such as here the category of commercial agents, be classified as overriding mandatory rules.[67]

In the *Nikiforidis* case, Advocate General Szpunar explained that the concept of overriding **10.62** mandatory provisions are provisions which serve to attain the special interest of the State concerned, which themselves determine their scope and *which cannot be restricted even where conflict-of-laws rules designate other law as applicable to the assessment of the legal relationship concerned*.[68] They differ from the public interest since their existence arose from growing State interference with private law relationships, although there is a strong link between overriding mandatory provisions and public policy (referred to in Article 21 of the Rome I Regulation). Public policy:

> is based on the idea of excluding the application of foreign law where it would result in a manifest breach of the public policy of the State of the forum. It therefore serves to eliminate certain effects – which are undesirable from the point of view of protecting public policy – of applying foreign law. However, overriding mandatory provisions protect public policy in a different way. They directly affect the legal relationship concerned. They shape its content, irrespective of the rules of foreign law which govern that relationship.[69]

Applying these principles, it follows that foreign law chosen by the parties to a commercial **10.63** agency agreement can be excluded by the national judge in favour of its national law because of the mandatory nature only if the national judge finds that, in the context of the transposition of the Agency Directive, the legislature of the forum had found crucial, within the concerned legal order, to grant the commercial agent a protection going beyond the one provided by that Directive, taking into account the nature and the purpose of such provisions.[70]

---

66 Ibid., para 52.
67 See Rühl (n 56) para 5.1.2; D'Avout (n 61) note 2, 62.
68 See *Nikiforidis* (n 59) para 65.
69 Ibid., paras 69–70.
70 Patrick Kileste and Cécile Staudt, 'Jurisprudence récente relative aux règles de droit international privé applicable aux contrats de distribution: arrêts *Corman-Collins* et *Unamar*' (2015) 9 *Revue de Jurisprudence de Liège, Mons et Bruxelles (JLMB)* 403.

c. Test for classification by the national court

10.64 The ECJ gave guidance to the national court as to how to conduct the test for classifying national rules as overriding mandatory rules. First of all, it recalled that the national court must take into account a restrictive interpretation of the national mandatory rule as referred to in Article 7 of the Rome Convention and in Article 9 of Rome I Regulation:

> 49. Thus, to give full effect *to the principle of the freedom of contract of the parties to a contract, which is the cornerstone of the Rome Convention, reiterated in the Rome I Regulation*, it must be ensured that the choice freely made by the parties as regards the law applicable to their contractual relationship is respected in accordance with Article 3(1) of the Rome Convention, so that *the plea relating to the existence of a 'mandatory rule'* within the meaning of the legislation of the Member State concerned, as referred to in Article 7(2) of that convention, *must be interpreted strictly.* (emphasis added)

10.65 Secondly, the national court must take into account the exact terms of the national law but also the general structure and all the circumstances in which that law was adopted in order to determine whether it is mandatory in nature insofar as it appears that the legislature adopted it in order to protect an interest judged to be essential by the concerned Member State.[71]

10.66 Based on these considerations, the ECJ described the methodology to be used by the national courts when they apply the law of the forum by reference to Article 7(2) of the Rome Convention and Article 9(2) of the Rome I Regulation: Articles 3 and 7(2) of the Rome Convention must be interpreted as meaning that the law of a Member State, which meets the minimum protection requirements laid down by the Agency Directive and which has been chosen by the parties to a commercial agency agreement, may be rejected by the court of another Member State before which the case has been brought in favour of the law of the forum owing to the mandatory nature, in the legal order of that Member State, of the rules governing the situation of self-employed commercial agents. This may happen only if the court before which the case has been brought finds, *on the basis of a detailed assessment*, that, in the course of that implementation, the legislature of the State of the forum held it to be *crucial*, in the legal order concerned, to grant the commercial agent a protection going beyond that provided for by that Directive, taking account of the nature and the objective of such mandatory provisions.[72] Hence, a thorough analysis, taking into account the legislative history of the concerned national provision as well as the wording must be conducted before applying Article 7 of the Rome Convention and Article 9 of the Rome I Regulation.

d. Limits: compliance with the harmonised Agency Directive

10.67 The ECJ circumscribed the test for classification of national provisions as mandatory provisions by adding that the national court must not compromise the harmonising effect of

---

71   See *Unamar* (n 5) para 50.

72   See *Unamar* (n 5) para 52. The *Unamar* case law has been confirmed in C-149/18 *Agostinho da Silva Martins v Dekra Claims Services Portugal SA* [2019] ECLI:EU:C:2019:84, para 31, in which the request for a preliminary ruling concerned the determination of the law applicable to an obligation to pay compensation arising as the result of a car accident that occurred in Spain:

> [W]ith regard to the possible identification of an 'overriding mandatory provision' … the referring court must find, on the basis of a detailed analysis of the wording, general scheme, objectives and the context in which that provision was adopted, that it is of such importance in the national legal order that it justifies a departure from the applicable law …

the Agency Directive or the uniform application of the Rome Convention at the European Union level. Hence, in the course of the assessment, the national court must take into account that – unlike the *Ingmar* case where the law which was rejected was the law of a third country – here the law which is to be rejected in favour of the law of the forum is that of another Member State which has correctly transposed the Agency Directive.[73] In this way the ECJ drew the attention of the national court to respect even more the law chosen by the parties when it is the law of another Member State having correctly transposed the Agency Directive.[74]

In addition, the possibility of pleading the existence of mandatory rules under Article 7(2) of **10.68** the Rome Convention does not affect the Member States' obligation to ensure conformity of those rules with European Union law; if those rules were exempt from compliance with European Union law, *the primacy and uniform application of European Union law would be undermined.*[75]

The question of free movement in Europe should also be taken into consideration: is there an **10.69** obstacle to the freedom when a national judge declares invalid the chosen mechanism by the parties to resolve their dispute on the sole ground that the national law is of mandatory nature, especially when the national law received a generous qualification of mandatory law or when the conflict of laws involve a minimum harmonisation Directive?[76]

As Advocate General Wahl pointed out, the question then arises whether the harmonisation of **10.70** national legislation brought about by an EU Directive may have an impact on the effectiveness of the mandatory provisions of the forum in relation to the laws of other Member States where national laws adopted to implement that directive are at issue.[77] The reply depends, according to Advocate General Wahl, on whether the directive created a full or minimum harmonisation.

In the minimum harmonised directive, Member States can extend the scope and the level of **10.71** protection provided by the directive to protect interests which they consider to be fundamental. This may therefore result in significant differences between national transposition laws.[78] Advocate General Wahl therefore held that the national provisions which extend the scope and the level of protection may be granted the mandatory nature and therefore supplant pursuant to Article 7(2) of the Rome Convention, the provisions of the chosen law by the parties, even if that law correctly implements the directive.[79] By contrast, in a full harmonised directive, the national transposition laws are equivalent and therefore the rule must be assessed only pursuant to the criteria established by the EU legislature. In fully harmonised situations,

---

73 See *Unamar* (n 5) para 51.
74 Pascal Hollander, 'Développements récents concernant les conflits de juridictions et de lois et l'arbitrage en matière de contrats de distribution commerciale', in Catherine Delforge (coord), *Actualités en matière de rédaction des contrats de distribution* (Bruylant 2014) 108.
75 See *Unamar* (n 5) para 46.
76 D'Avout (n 61) 63.
77 See *Unamar* (Opinion of AG Wahl) (n 57) para 39.
78 In the Agency Directive, the Member States are free to choose between the indemnity and compensation regime and opt for different methods of calculation.
79 See *Unamar* (Opinion of AG Wahl) (n 57) para 41.

mandatory provisions of a Member State cannot exclude, by application of Article 7(2) of the Rome Convention, the provisions of the law of another Member State.[80]

10.72 Even if the ECJ did not expressly address the distinction of minimum and full harmonisation in its judgment,[81] it can be deducted that the Agency Directive provides for minimum harmonisation as it grants commercial agents only minimum protection in the event of termination of the agency agreement and excludes from its scope self-employed commercial agents operating in the field of provision of services. Consequently, according to Advocate General Wahl, the national provisions which go beyond the scope and the minimum protection laid down in the directive must be applied instead of the law of another Member State chosen by the parties to their agreement.[82] The Antwerp Court of Appeal decided that the fact that Bulgarian law did not quite offer the same protection as the one granted by the Belgian Agency Law was not relevant given that Bulgarian law has correctly transposed the Agency Directive and offers the minimum protection to maritime agents.

10.73 It is quite remarkable to face conflict-of-laws between national European legislations while they originate from the common stem. In accordance with the principles of mutual recognition, it would be expected that the national court would comply with the law of another Member State chosen by the parties. Any court decision that would qualify its national law as mandatory law overriding the law of another Member State and therefore depart from the analysis, should provide a detailed analysis and serious grounds in that regard.[83]

10.74 It appears from the literature and comments on the *Unamar* case that the limits where the classification of mandatory rules will not be held are: (i) areas of full harmonisation of national legislation, i.e., areas where Member States are requested to adopt national laws laying down a scope and level of protection which, if not identical, are equivalent; (ii) in areas of minimum harmonisation where the differences between the chosen law and the law of the forum are gradual, if the chosen law intensifies only the level of protection requested by an EU Directive without extending the scope of protection to cases not covered by the Directive, or if the otherwise applicable law has not correctly implemented the standard Directive.[84]

---

80 Ibid., para 42.

81 For a critical comment on this point, see D'Avout (n 61) 64, who states that the ECJ has not solved the problem of conflict-of-laws of the transposition laws as it did not sufficiently examine the nature and the context of the directive.

82 See *Unamar* (Opinion of AG Wahl) (n 57) para 44. Some scholars read the ECJ's judgment as stating that there is a strong presumption *against* mandatory law in the light of the correct implementation by Bulgarian law and the national courts have to conduct a detailed and proper analysis of the legislative works of the Belgian Agency Law. What is exactly the nature of the 'gold-plated provisions' of the Belgian Agency Law is not entirely clear among scholars. See more details in Geert van Calster, *European Private International Law* (2nd edn, Bloomsbury 2016) 223.

83 D'Avout (n 61) 61; Marie-Laure Niboyer and Géraud de Geouffre de la Pradelle, *Droit international privé* (4th edn, LGDJ 2013) no 262.

84 See Rühl (n 56) para 5.3 referring to Jan Lüttringhaus, 'Eingriffsnormen im internationalen Unionsprivat- und Prozessrecht: Von Ingmar zu Unamar' (2014) 34 *IPRax* 150; Johannes Schilling, 'Eingriffsnormen im europäischen Richtlinienrecht - Anmerkung zu EuGH, 17.10.2013 – C-184/12, EU:C:2013:663 – Unamar' (2014) *Zeitschrift für Europäisches Privatrecht* 850; Laura M von Bochove, 'Overriding Mandatory Rules as a Vehicle for Weaker Party Protection in European Private International Law' (2014) 7(3) *Erasmus Law Review* 155.

e. Subsequent procedure in Belgium

Those who were expecting that the ECJ would assess the Belgian Agency Law and give its **10.75** qualification may be disappointed.[85] The ECJ only gave guidance to the national judge in the perspective of judicial subsidiarity.

Following the ECJ's judgment, the Belgian Supreme Court quashed the decision of the **10.76** Antwerp Court of Appeal, which declared without jurisdiction to hear the dispute and expressed that the dispute was subject to Bulgarian law. According to the Supreme Court, the Appeal Court did not duly justify its decision for the lack of jurisdiction.[86] However, in the annulment decision, the Supreme Court did not provide any explanation as to why the Belgian Agency Law would be mandatory law and simply referred to the operative part of the judgment of the ECJ.[87] It is not easy to interpret the annulment decision of the Supreme Court's decision as meaning that the Belgian Agency Law is of mandatory nature which requires to protect the commercial agent beyond the protection offered by the Agency Directive or if it quashed the decision of the Antwerp Court of Appeal for the reason that this Court did not carry out a detailed assessment of the transposition law pursuant to the test for classification.[88] The case has been sent by the Supreme Court to the Brussels Court of Appeal.[89]

Whether the indemnity regime of the Belgian Agency Law is a mandatory rule within the **10.77** meaning given by the ECJ is debatable among the Belgian legal community.[90] The Brussels Court of Appeal must now appreciate the mandatory nature taking into account that the assessment should not compromise either the harmonising effect of the Agency Directive, nor the uniform application of the Rome Convention and the fact that, unlike the *Ingmar* case in which the law of a third country was rejected, in this proceeding, consideration must be given to the law of another Member State which has correctly transposed the Directive.[91] Hence, the

---

85   For instance, the ECJ has taken the assessment in the *Arblade* case (See Joined Cases C-369/96 and C-376/96 *Arblade* [1999] I-08453).

86   Belgian Supreme Court, Decision of 12 September 2014, C.11.0430.N. Ultimately, the case was sent to another court of appeal according to the Belgian judicial procedure; in this case, before the Brussels Court of Appeal. See Geert van Calster, 'Belgian supreme court holds on gold-plated provisions in Unamar. Appeal judgment annulled, case to be revisited' <https://gavclaw.com/2014/09/26/belgian-supreme-court-holds-on-gold-plated-provisions-in-unamar-appeal-judgment-annulled-case-to-be-revisited/> accessed 16 April 2020.

87   See note under this case by Stefan Cnudde, 'Het arrest *Unamar*: op weg naar een spaarzamer gebruik door de forumrechter van de eigen voorrangsregels om het door partijen gekozen recht van een andere EU-lidstaat opzij te schuiven?' (2015) 9 *Rechtspraak Antwerpen Brussel Gent (RABG)* 663.

88   D'Avout (n 61) 64.

89   At the time of writing this contribution, to our knowledge no decision has been rendered yet by the Brussels Court of Appeal in this case.

90   *Contra* see for instance the Paris Court of Appeal, Decision of 6 May 2014, no 12/21230, *Uma Holding*, (2012) *Recueil de jurisprudence Dalloz* 2541, in which the agency agreement was governed by Malaysian law, identical to English law. This Court held that the shipping services do not fall within the scope of the Directive and if French law has extended the scope to those kind of services, this was only for internal public order. Consequently, the provisions of French law could not be considered as mandatory law for the purposes of setting aside an international arbitral award, no matter that the agent exercises its activities within the EU. The Court concluded that there was no violation of public order from the fact that Malaysian law did not provide an indemnity in favour of the commercial agent ((2015) Chroniques, *Revue trimestrielle de droit commercial (RTDCom)* 622).

91   Kim Swert, 'Het internationaal dwingendrechtelijk karakter van de Belgisch agentuurwet' (note under the Unamar case) (2014) 12 *RABG* 818; Judith Mary, 'Suite, et non fin, de la jurisprudence sur le contrat d'agence commerciale en Europe face aux lois de police' (2015) 1 (*RDC-TBH*) 74.

ECJ stressed on the necessity to observe the chosen law by the parties, which is the law of another Member State.[92]

10.78   Some authors[93] in Belgium have held that the Belgian Agency Law is not likely to pass the *Unamar* test for the following reasons: (a) the Belgian Agency Law and in particular its mandatory provisions which go beyond the protection granted by the Agency Directive does not endanger the protection of public interest of Belgium such as its political, social or economic order; (b) only some provisions of the Agency Law are mandatory, so that derogations are permitted to other provisions which are not categorised as mandatory by the Belgian legislature; (c) the mandatory nature of the Agency Law is intended to protect only the private interests and the commercial agent is allowed to waive his protection, e.g., following the termination of the commercial agency agreement and (d) it was never submitted that the Agency Law was of public order.[94]

10.79   Some authors also insist on the compliance with the principle of freedom of choice: when the parties have chosen the law of a Member State which has correctly transposed the Agency Directive, the European protection is guaranteed and there is no reason to apply a different law on commercial agency.[95]

10.80   Other authors consider that the simple fact that a State enacts a national provision as an internationally protective mandatory provision, i.e., a provision which applies whatever the applicable law to the agreement, means that the State has considered that the application of that provision was crucial for the safeguarding of public interest.[96]

10.81   To the contrary, the French Supreme Court held that the French Agency Law was mandatory law within the internal legal order and not mandatory law within the international legal order.[97]

---

92   Pascal Hollander (n 46); see Pascal Hollander on the application of Article 3.4 of Rome I Regulation to commercial agency legislation: Pascal Hollander, 'Questions de droit international privé et d'arbitrage touchant à la distribution commerciale', in Pascal Hollander (ed), *Le droit de la distribution* (Anthemis 2009) 271 ff.

93   See Hollander (n 74) 108.

94   The Belgian Supreme Court has constantly defined public order as: '(...) is of public law only what touches upon the essential interests of the State or of the community or sets, in private law, the legal basis on which rests the society's economic or moral order' (informal translation) (e.g., Decision of 15 March 1968 (1968) I *Pasicrisie* 894); see Caroline Verbruggen, 'Commentary of Article 1717 of the Belgian Judicial Code', in Niuscha Bassiri, Maarten Draye (eds), *Arbitration in Belgium, A Practitioner's Guide* (Wolters Kluwer 2016) 479; the definition given by the ECJ to overriding mandatory provisions is close to the definition of public order under Belgian law (see Hollander (n 74) 107, no 29).

95   Koen de Bock and Henri de Waele, 'Internationale handelsagentuur', in Diane Struyven (ed), *Bestendig Handboek Distributierecht* (Kluwer 2002) 38–9, no 3040; Mehmeti and Verhellen (n 61), 207–9.

96   Arnaud Nuyts, 'Les lois de police et dispositions impératives dans le règlement Rome I' (2009) *RDC-TBH* 560, who qualifies the Belgian Agency Law as mandatory law as it expressly provides for the internationally mandatory nature of some protective provisions.

97   French Supreme Court, Decision of 5 January 2016, no 14-10.628 (*ArcelorMittal*) and note of Cyril Nourissat, 'Loi applicable au contrat d'agent commercial: rappels et précisions' (2016) *Actualité juridique Contrats d'affaires* (*AJCA*) 162–3: a protective law of internal legal order cannot safeguard the State's public interest but rather categories of interests, such as the categories of commercial agents here. Constant case law from the French Supreme Court (Decision of 28 November 2000, no 98-11.335, case *Allium*): the rule requiring compensation payment due to unilateral

One recent Belgian case submitted to the Ghent Court of Appeal illustrates the application of **10.82** the principles laid down in the *Unamar* case.[98] An agency agreement was entered into between an Italian commercial agent and a Belgian principal, and provided for Belgian law with Belgian jurisdiction. Following the termination of the agreement by the principal, the agent brought legal proceedings before the Ghent Commercial Court to claim the payment of outstanding commissions and compensation. The legal action was brought two years after the termination of the agreement; according to the agent, the Italian limitation period was applicable in this case as it was longer than the Belgian limitation period and offered better protection to the agent, and hence it should be classified as overriding mandatory rule. The court recalled that effect may be given to the overriding mandatory provision of the law of the country where the obligations arising out of the contract have to be or have been performed, insofar as this overriding mandatory provision renders the performance of the contract unlawful (Article 9.3 of Rome I Regulation). Furthermore, the Court held that the agent did not prove that the provisions of Italian law were of overriding mandatory nature within the definition of Article 9.1 of Rome I Regulation. The decision not to apply Italian law is aligned with the decision of the ECJ of 31 January 2019 which considered that a national provision, such as the limitation period for actions seeking compensation, cannot be considered to be an overriding mandatory provision, unless the court finds, on the basis of a detailed analysis of the wording, general scheme, objectives and the context in which that provision was adopted, that it is of such importance in the national legal order that it justifies a departure from the law applicable.[99] It could however be questionable whether the court was right in putting the burden of proof of the existence of overriding mandatory provision on the agent while it is, according to the case law of the ECJ, upon the national judge to determine whether or not the provision is of mandatory law according to the interpretation given by law of the country where the contract is performed (foreign law), even though parties can indeed play a role in assisting the judge in this task.[100]

f. Impact on arbitration agreements

The interaction between the application of public policy rules, mandatory law and the principle **10.83** of party autonomy is a delicate one which the arbitral tribunals or national courts must take into account. It is generally speaking considered that matters which are capable of settlement can be submitted to arbitration: this reflects the notion of arbitrability.[101] The dispute that can be or not be submitted to arbitration, by virtue of their object (*objective arbitrability*) or the quality of the parties (*subjective arbitrability*) are determined by each state. The limits drawn by the legislature are often inspired by considerations of public order and mandatory law. Hence, matters which relate to criminal law or to some extent to insolvency law or family law are

---

termination of the agency agreement was to be qualified as protecting the national public policy of France but not as a rule of strict compliance for international cases, thus giving precedence to the chosen law by the parties.

98   Ghent Court of Appeal, Decision of 19 June 2019 (2019) 17 *RABG* 1486 with note of Wim Wijsmans and Hans Van Gompel, 'Het bijzonder dwingend recht van artikel 9.3 Rome I-Verordening toegepast op een de beëindiging van een handelsagentuur', 1511–6.

99   See *Agostinho da Silva Martins* (n 72) para 35.

100   Wijsmans and Van Gompel (n 98) paras 12–13.

101   Convention on the Recognition and Enforcement of Foreign Arbitral Awards (opened for signature 10 June 1958, entered into force 7 June 1959) (New York Convention), Art II and V.1(a).

considered inarbitrable. A matter that is classified as inarbitrable means that arbitration is not the suitable dispute resolution mechanism for the disputes arising out of this matter.[102]

10.84 The expression *favor arbitrandum* has been used to describe the progressive widening of the area of arbitrability.[103] This concept has evolved over time and has been linked with (overriding) mandatory provisions and public policy.[104] The evolution has emerged to consider that arbitration in a matter concerning public order or mandatory provisions is not in itself prohibited and is not equivalent to the waiver of the protected rights; instead the arbitrators have now the obligation to apply rules of public order under penalty of having their award set-aside.[105] Matters which relate to (overriding) mandatory provisions or to public policy are not necessarily inarbitrable per se.[106] A distinction has therefore been created between disputes which implies the application of public order rules (which do not prohibit their arbitrability) and a jurisdiction public order which are reserved only to state courts.[107]

10.85 In Belgium the 2013 arbitration reform confirmed the *favor arbitrandum* by widening the concept of arbitrability. The new Belgian Law on Arbitration introduced a provision according to which (i) any disputes involving *an economic interest*[108] may be submitted to arbitration and (ii) claims regarding disputes that do not involve an economic interest with regard to which a settlement agreement may also be submitted to arbitration.[109]

10.86 The *travaux préparatoires* of the 2013 reform in Belgium specify that this double criteria of arbitrability of a dispute is influenced by Swiss law and German law, and should be interpreted broadly. According to the Belgian legislature, this double criteria also puts eventually an end to the controversy about the arbitrability of disputes in presence of rules of public order.

10.87 Article II(1) of the New York Convention refers to party autonomy which allows the parties to choose the law governing to their legal relationship, whether contractual or not, concerning a *subject-matter capable of settlement by arbitration*. It follows therefrom that it is in the light of the law chosen by the parties that should be assessed whether the dispute is arbitrable or not to determine the validity of the arbitration clause.[110] By contrast, recognition and enforcement of an arbitral award under the New York Convention is addressed by the application of the law applicable to the agreement to which the parties have subjected it or under the law of the country where the award was made, as well as where a state court finds that the subject matter is not capable of settlement by arbitration under the law of the country where recognition and

---

102 Jan Engelmann, *International Commercial Arbitration and the Commercial Agency Directive: A Perspective from Law and Economics* (Springer 2017) 26.
103 Caroline Verbruggen, 'Réflexions sur la *'Favor Arbitrandum'* en droit belge', in Dirk De Meulemeester, Maxime Berlingin, Benoît Kohl (eds), *Liber amicorum, 50 years of solutions, CEPANI 1969-2019* (Wolters Kluwer 2019) 315–30.
104 See Engelmann (n 102) 25.
105 See Verbruggen (n 103) 315–30.
106 See Engelmann (n 102) 26.
107 See Verbruggen (n 103) 315–30.
108 The literal translation is 'pecuniary claim' in Art. 1676 of the Belgian Judicial Code.
109 Art. 1676 §1 of the Belgian Judicial Code. Art. 1676 §2 specifies that whosoever has the capacity or is empowered to make a settlement may conclude an arbitration agreement.
110 See Engelmann (n 102) para 136.

enforcement is sought (*lex fori*) or even where recognition or enforcement of the award would be contrary to the public policy of that country.[111]

The national judge may need upstream to control the arbitrability of the dispute in different **10.88** instances (plea for lack of jurisdiction, enforcement procedure or setting-aside procedure). It is the *lex fori* that prevails in comparative law in these instances.[112] By contrast, arbitral tribunals have no *lex fori*[113] and the concept of *favor arbitrandum* implies that the arbitral tribunal must refer to the law applicable to the arbitration clause; it is usually considered that the parties have submitted the arbitration clause to the law governing their agreement.

In the *Unamar* case, the commercial agency agreement contained an arbitration clause **10.89** instituted in favour of the arbitration chamber of the Chamber of commerce and industry in Sofia (Bulgaria). The Belgian Supreme Court did not raise a preliminary question in connection with the arbitration clause as its approach has been to invalidate an arbitration agreement contained in commercial agency agreements when some conditions are met.[114] Hence, the ECJ left the issue of jurisdiction open by stating that it intended to answer the question referred without prejudice to the question of jurisdiction.[115]

Advocate General Wahl recalled that it was clear from the Supreme Court's reasoning that **10.90** there is a close link between the determination of the law applicable to the agreement and the possibility the national court has of rejecting the arbitration clause – for instance, because according to the *lex fori* of the national court the subject-matter of the dispute is not arbitrable – and, accordingly, declaring that it has jurisdiction.[116]

---

111   See New York Convention (n 101), Art V.2(a) and (b).

112   Laure Bernheim-Van de Casteele argues that the *lex contractus* to assess the arbitrability would be inappropriate as the response to it would depend on the law chosen by the parties while the goal is to precisely examine the restrictions of the parties' freedom to have recourse to arbitration; see Laure Bernheim-Van de Casteele, *Les principes fondamentaux de l'arbitrage*, Francarbi (Bruylant 2012) paras 183–186.

113   Ibid., para 187.

114   Pascal Hollander, 'L'arbitrabilité des litiges relatifs aux contrats de distribution commerciale en droit belge', in *L'arbitrage et la distribution commerciale* (Bruylant 2005) 25–58, spec. 29–53; M Traest, 'Encore … un arrêt de la Cour de cassation sur l'arbitrabilité des litiges relatifs a` la résiliation, sous l'empire de la loi du 27 juillet 1961, des concessions de vente exclusive' (note sous Cass., 14 janvier 2010) (2013) *Revue critique de jurisprudence belge* (*RCJB*) 255–76.

115   See *Unamar* (n 5) para 28. It is worth recalling the principles laid down in C-9/12 *Corman-Collins* [2013] ECLI:EU:C:2013:860, which concerned the exclusive distribution agreements under Belgian law and which principles can be transposed to the Belgian Agency Law. The Belgian legislator has enacted a rule on exclusive jurisdiction in favour of Belgian judicial courts both for distribution and agency agreements which are performed in Belgium. The question of coexistence of these exclusive jurisdiction provisions with Brussels I Regulation was addressed in the *Corman-Collins* case. The ECJ held that Art. 2 of the Brussels I Regulation must be interpreted as meaning that, where the defendant is domiciled in a Member State other than that in which the court seized is situated, it precludes the application of a national rule of jurisdiction such as that provided by the Belgian Distributorship Law. This means that when the defendant is domiciled in a Member State, the Belgian internal rules of conflict-of-laws cannot apply. The question of whether such solution can be transposed to a law which is qualified as mandatory law remains however open. By contrast, in France, in the *Monster Cable* case, the claimant (an exclusive distributor) took an action before the French courts while the exclusive distribution agreement contained a jurisdiction clause in favour of the courts of San Francisco. The French Supreme Court held that a jurisdiction clause was intended for all disputes arising from the agreement and should consequently be applied, even though mandatory rules were applicable to the dispute (22 October 2008, no 07-15.823, *Bull* 2008, I, no 233).

116   See *Unamar* (Opinion of AG Wahl) (n 57) 23.

10.91 The Belgian Supreme Court held in its judgment deciding to make a reference for a preliminary ruling that Article II(1) and (3) of the 1958 New York Convention[117] do not exclude that the court, when seized of an action regarding an agreement governed by a foreign law chosen by the parties, rejects the application of an arbitration clause valid under that foreign law. Such rejection can however be pronounced only on the basis of a rule of law of the forum (*lex fori*) which considers that the subject-matter of the dispute is not capable of settlement by arbitration.[118] This highlights the practice of the Belgian courts which consists in examining the arbitrability nature at the stage of the plea of jurisdiction and which, almost systematically, results in declaring not arbitrable the disputes of commercial distribution agreements governed by foreign law.[119] The Belgian Supreme Court has decided already in a few cases that the Belgian Agency Law can prevail over the law chosen by the parties in their agreement. Such practice may however evolve as it will be explained below.

10.92 Until recently, with respect to exclusive distribution agreements, it has been considered in Belgium that the recourse to arbitration is allowed as long as the dispute is not about the unilateral termination of this agreement which is addressed specifically by the Belgian Distributorship Law. Hence, a dispute about the conditions under which the right of the principal to renew the agreement can be exercised could have been brought to arbitration. The possibility of recourse to arbitration for unilateral termination of exclusive distribution agreements is controversial. Such possibility exists if the agreement is subject to Belgian law; in that case the arbitration clause will need to be confirmed at the end of the termination of the agreement.[120] In a decision of 14 January 2010, the Belgian Supreme Court held that when an arbitration agreement is subject to foreign law in an exclusive distribution agreement, the judge seized by a plea for lack of jurisdiction must exclude arbitration when the dispute cannot be withdrawn from the national judge's power in accordance with the relevant legal rules of the *lex fori*.[121] Hence according to the Belgian Supreme Court the question of arbitrability of the dispute cannot be assessed only on the basis of the law governing the agreement for a national court to decline its jurisdiction. This means that Belgian courts determine, irrespective of the chosen law by the parties to the agreement, how the mandatory rules of the Belgian Distributorship Law may apply in particular cases.[122]

---

117 See New York Convention (n 101).

118 Belgian Supreme Court, Decision of 5 April 2012 (2012) I *Pasicrisie* 760.

119 See Hollander (n 74) 113; see also Pascal Hollander, 'Les pièges de la procédure arbitrale pour les habitués des tribunaux' in *Les pièges de la procédure civile et arbitrale dans la pratique* (Larcier 2019) 143, in which he recalls that an arbitration agreement concluded before the occurrence of the dispute and submitted to a foreign law which does not contain a protection equivalent to the protection granted under Belgian law to the weak party is not null and void, but renders the dispute not arbitrable; the non-arbitrable nature of the dispute is a ground for annulment under Art. 1717 § 3 (b) of the Belgian Judicial Code.

120 Guy Keutgen and Georges-Albert Dal, *L'arbitrage en droit belge et international, Tome I – Le droit belge* (3rd edn, Bruylant 2015) 143 para 135.

121 Dave Mertens, 'Over de arbitreerbaarheid van concessiegeschillen. Eindelijk een uitgemaakte zaak?' (noot onder Cass. 14 januari 2010) (2010–11) *Rechtskundig weekblad (RW)* 1087–91.

122 Herman Verbist and Johan Erauw, 'Arbitrability of exclusive distributorship agreements with application of foreign law confirmed by Belgian courts after the reform of the Belgian arbitration law of 2013' (2019) 1 *b-Arbitra* 278.

This practice was also confirmed by the Belgian Supreme Court for disputes involving commercial agency agreements in the *Air Transat* case.[123] In that case, the law chosen by the parties was the law of the province of Quebec, which according to the Court of Appeal of Brussels, did not offer the same guarantees as the Belgian Agency Law. Pursuant to the Opinion of the Belgian Advocate General Van Ingelgem in this case,[124] the Belgian Supreme Court seems to accept the jurisdiction of arbitrators for matters regarding the termination of exclusive distribution agreements – which law is also considered as mandatory under Belgian law[125] – provided that the protective regime of the mandatory law on exclusive distribution agreements is guaranteed by the arbitrators and that the arbitrators are bound to apply Belgian law or any other law which offers a similar protection to the exclusive distributor. Applying the same reasoning to commercial agency agreements, it was considered in this case that the law of the province of Quebec (*lex contractus*) did not offer a similar protection as the one provided by the Belgian Agency Law, so that the latter (*lex fori*) should apply and override the arbitration clause.[126]   **10.93**

The Belgian Agency Law may therefore constitute a ground to 'invalidate' the arbitration clause. The decision of the Belgian Supreme Court to refer the preliminary question to the ECJ in the *Unamar* case considered that the judge can reject the application of an arbitration clause valid under the *lex contractus* by applying the *lex fori* which does not allow the dispute to be subject to arbitration. By suggesting to apply its case law on the application of mandatory rules to disregard the arbitration clause, it could be argued that the Supreme Court could have considered that Bulgarian law did not offer the same protection as the Belgian Agency Law. Therefore, it is not surprising that the Belgian Supreme Court only asked the question of the application of Belgian Agency Law as mandatory law to ensure the validity of this *precondition* for the application of the jurisdiction of the Belgian judicial courts. Such position in Belgian law contrasts with the French position[127] and has been criticised since a Member State should avoid to artificially establish the jurisdiction of a national court by systematically qualifying its mandatory rules as international mandatory rule, in disregard of the contractual dispute resolution mechanisms chosen by the parties.[128]   **10.94**

---

123   Dave Mertens, 'Handelsagentuur en arbitrage' (note under Cass. 3 November 2011) (2011-12) *RW* 1647-1650; see also Arnaud Nuyts, *La concession de vente exclusive, l'agence commerciale et l'arbitrage* (Bruylant 1996).

124   Opinion of AG Van Ingelgem in the *Air Transat* case <www.juridat.be> accessed 16 April 2020.

125   Law of 27 July 1961 on the unilateral termination of exclusive distribution agreements of indefinite duration, now enshrined in Chapter 3 of Book X of the 2013 Belgian Code of Economic Law (the Belgian Distributorship Law). The Belgian Distributorship Law provides as a mandatory provision that in case the distributorship agreement is terminated by the principal to the detriment of the distributor, the latter may – when the part of the activities were performed in Belgium – claim for that part a compensation before Belgian courts against the principal. Once the Belgian court is seized, the latter must apply exclusively Belgian law; see Belgian Supreme Court, Decision of 28 June 1979 (1979) I *Pasicrisie* 1260; Belgian Supreme Court, Decision of 22 December 1988 (1989) *Journal des tribunaux* (*JT*) 458; Belgian Supreme Court, Decision of 16 November 2006 (2006) I *Pasicrisie* 2351.

126   In a decision of 6 November 2012, the Brussels Commercial Tribunal held that Arts 11, 18 and 20 of the 1995 Belgian Agency Law provide for a special protection for commercial agents having their principal place of business in Belgium. This protection is mandatory so that the parties may not depart from it to the detriment of the commercial agent before the commercial agency agreement is terminated. As a consequence, the clause submitting the dispute relating to the termination of a commercial agency agreement to arbitration governed by Swiss law cannot be given effect since this law does not offer a similar protection to that of Belgian law (Brussels Commercial Tribunal, Decision of 6 November 2012 (2014) 8 *Nieuw Juridisch Weekblad* no 301, 364–6).

127   French Supreme Court, Decision of 8 July 2010, no 09-67013, obs T Clay; (2010) *Rev arb* 513 (note R Dupeyré).

128   D'Avout (n 61) 62.

10.95   Two recent published Belgian courts decisions have applied the new criterion of arbitrability in exclusive distribution agreements. The first decision contained an arbitration clause in favour of the Rules of the Stockholm Chamber of Commerce and Swedish law as the law governing to the agreement,[129] while the second decision concerned also an exclusive distribution agreement with reference to the Rules of the Arbitration Board of Central Chamber of Commerce in Helsinki and Finish law as the governing law.[130] In both cases the Belgian courts accepted the plea for lack of jurisdiction in favour of arbitration. The courts noted that the disputes were of pecuniary matters and that the 2013 arbitration reform excluded the restriction with respect to public policy provisions when the dispute is of a pecuniary matter; hence the idea of the new Belgian Arbitration Act was to allow arbitrations in pecuniary matters, even if they are of a public policy nature.

10.96   By comparison, a case where the commercial agency agreement contained an arbitration clause with a seat in New York, the law of New York as governing law, and in which a commercial agent conducted the procurement of sea freight business in Austria and other countries of the EU for the principal based in New York arose before the Austrian courts. The commercial agent filed a claim against the principal before an Austrian court for compensation under the Austrian commercial agent's law. The Austrian Supreme Court decided that in accordance with the choice of law by the parties, a court must refer the parties to arbitration if there is an arbitration clause, unless the arbitration clause is null and void. An arbitration clause can be declared ineffective if the parties intended to bypass the application of mandatory rules. Having recalled the European case law on the mandatory nature of the Agency Directive (*Ingmar* and *Unamar*), the Austrian Supreme Court ruled that the commercial agent had a mandatory claim for compensation and that such right would not be recognised, and therefore enforced, under the law of New York. It concluded that the arbitration clause was not effective as the refusal of recognition of the arbitration clause remained the only possibility to secure the international mandatory scope of application of Articles 17 and 18 of the Agency Directive in favour of the agent. Therefore, according to the Supreme Court, the agent's claim under the Austrian commercial agent's law could be submitted before the Austrian courts.[131]

F. CONCLUSION

10.97   The recent developments of European case law show that the Agency Directive raises questions on conflict-of-laws and its territorial scope. With the *Unamar* case, it could be expected that the possibility to oust foreign law chosen by the parties for their contractual relationship would be limited in internal market cases. The principle of freedom of choice

---

129   Commercial Court of Hainaut (division of Tournai), Decision of 21 December 2016 (2019) 1 *b-Arbitra* 247.

130   Commercial Court of Antwerp (division of Hasselt), Decision of 13 July 2017 (2019) 1 *b-Arbitra* 253.

131   Austrian Supreme Court, 1st March 2017, OGH 5 Ob 72/16y; see comments from Tobias Gosch, 'Another Win for European Commercial Agents: Overriding Mandatory Austrian Law Provisions to Supersede Arbitration Agreement' (Kluwer Arbitration Blog 2017) <http://arbitrationblog.kluwerarbitration.com/2017/08/10/another-win-european-commercial-agents-overriding-mandatory-austrian-law-provisions-supersede-arbitration-agreement/> accessed 16 April 2020, who notes that the Austrian Supreme Court does not provide a detailed assessment and an explanation as to why the transposed Agency Directive provisions with an extended scope of applicability to the procurement of sea freight business in Austria are national overriding mandatory principles, and therefore why it is crucial that this category of agents should also be entitled to a compensatory claim on the basis of national overriding mandatory provision; see also van Calster (n 82) ch 3, s 3.2.8.3.

cannot indeed be ignored by a national court in favour of a wide application of the mandatory rules of the law of the forum. Unilateral and overriding application of the mandatory law transposed by a Member State should receive a strict interpretation and will depend *in fine* on the proof of existence of a legislative objective particularly mandatory at the national level and that this objective is necessary at least for the preservation of state structures.[132]

The analysis of the ECJ's case law was also the opportunity to recall that mandatory laws do **10.98** not escape the general rule pursuant to which national rules must be compatible with the requirements of the European legal order because of the principle of primacy of European law and international law as well as the objectives of harmonisation and uniformity.[133] When called to take the test of classification, the national judge must balance between the national law and the chosen law in dual interest of the Rome Convention (and Rome I Regulation) and the principles of common market which prohibit discriminatory restrictions in order to avoid protectionism.[134] A detailed assessment and a comparative approach of the legislations concerned is now expected from the national courts.[135]

From *Ingmar* to *Unamar* cases, one can imply that Articles 17 and 18 of the Agency Directive **10.99** are to be considered mandatory rules in the sense that whenever a commercial agent carries out his activities within the internal market, the protection of Articles 17 and 18 of the Agency Directive is granted, irrespective of the law applicable to the agreement between the parties. *A contrario*, these Articles are not mandatory if a commercial agent carries out his activities outside the internal market. A Member State may therefore restrict the territorial scope of protection of these Articles to commercial agents carrying out their activities within the internal market.[136]

As can be seen from the Belgian case law, the lively debate on the arbitrability of commercial **10.100** agency agreements and distribution agreements have been linked to the applicable law of these agreements. The main point of discussion has been how the Belgian courts should decide the issue of arbitrability of these agreements: is it the law that governs the agreement (in which case, the party autonomy applies) or under the *lex fori* (or even the Belgian procedural law)?[137] It has been argued in the doctrine that the fact that the parties cannot derogate on the jurisdiction of the Belgian courts by choosing a (foreign) applicable law and arbitration created a confusion between two different issues that are *jurisdiction* and the *applicable law*.[138] Hence,

---

132 D'Avout (n 61) 63. This author explains that the only way to justify that a directive can have an impact on the conflict-of-laws is to have a directive being derogatory to the conflict of laws regulation and exempt the transposition laws from the duty to comply with Rome I Regulation, as indicated in Art. 23 of this Regulation on the relationship with other provisions of Community law, 'With the exception of Article 7, this Regulation shall not prejudice the application of provisions of Community law which, in relation to particular matters, lay down conflict-of-law rules relating to contractual obligations.'

133 Confirmed in Belgium by the Belgian Supreme Court in the case *Le Ski*, Decision of 27 May 1971 (1971) I *Pasicrisie* 914.

134 Cyril Nourissat, 'Le contrat d'agence commercial en droit international privé. Retour sur quelques apports récents' (2014) *AJCA* 369; Michaël Karpenshif et Cyril Nourissat, *Les grands arrêts de la jurisprudence de l'Union européenne* (2nd edn, Presses Universitaires de France 2014) no 103.

135 Cyril Nourissat (n 134) 369.

136 See *Agro Foreign Trade* (AG Szpunar) (n 18) para 44.

137 Verbist and Erauw (n 122) 278.

138 Ibid.

some authors call for abandoning the condition of selection of Belgian law to address the question of arbitrability given that arbitrators will need to take into account in any case the mandatory provisions of the Belgian Agency Law, even if it would be against the law chosen by the parties.[139] In the context of the European case law, it is questionable whether Member States will now use the *Unamar* case to invalidate arbitration clauses on the basis of the concept of overriding mandatory rules in order to safeguard the application of their own overriding mandatory provisions through national courts. In addressing that question it remains to be seen if there is a fundamental interest that a commercial agent located in a country where specific protection is granted by the legislature needs to be protected under the law of that country, so that the law of another Member State chosen by the parties should not apply. Only time will tell how the test for classification of national rules set up by the ECJ will be conducted.

---

139   Verbist and Erauw (n 122) 283, referring to Olivier Caprasse, 'Les grands arrêts de la cour de cassation belge en droit de l'arbitrage' (2013) 1 *b-Arbitra*142.

11

THE POTENTIAL IMPACT OF DIRECTIVE 2014/24/EU ON CONSTRUCTION ARBITRATION IN EUROPE

Luis Capiel and Oliver Cojo[*]

A. INTRODUCTION

We live in a time where scepticism surrounding the European Union (EU) is on the rise, as shown by Brexit and the proliferation of euro-sceptic political parties in many countries. This trend is unfortunate because mistrust of the EU is often unfounded or, at the very least, its underlying reasons are not always properly understood.   **11.01**

The work of the EU has been a decisive factor in keeping the peace and bringing prosperity to EU countries and beyond. That work and the decisions taken to implement it are obviously not above reproach but, although that may sometimes be the case, the entire EU project need not be completely upended or disbanded as a result. Criticism of the EU's decisions that merit disapproval must be raised properly and have solid grounds to persuade decision-makers that the cons generated outweigh the pros. Only then can an attempt be made to steer change.   **11.02**

This book aims to show how EU law and international arbitration interact. It will therefore show how the EU has done its bit in assuring the success of the international arbitration industry, but it will also identify those areas of EU policy that require change, illustrate why and explain how. It is therefore a privilege for us to be part of this book.   **11.03**

We have been asked to write about construction arbitration in Europe and Directive 2014/24/EU on public procurement (the 'Directive'). Even though the impact that the   **11.04**

---

[*] Date of submission: 2/4/2020.

Directive may have on construction arbitration in the EU is not initially evident, we have accepted the challenge to be part of this commendable project.

11.05 Since the Directive may be unfamiliar to some readers, an overview of the Directive and of its scope of application are provided first (Section B). We then go on to analyse the potential impact of the Directive on construction arbitration in Europe (Section C). One consequence may be an increase in the number of complex arbitrations involving multiple parties or multiple contracts; thus some of the challenges posed by arbitrations of that kind and certain recommendations are also set out (Section D). Finally, we present our conclusions (Section E).

B. THE DIRECTIVE: OVERVIEW AND SCOPE OF APPLICATION

11.06 The Directive is part of a package of new directives on public procurement. The other directives that make up this package are Directive 2014/23/EU on the award of concession contracts and Directive 2014/25/EU on procurement by entities operating in the water, energy, transport and postal service sectors.

11.07 These directives are framed within 'Europe 2020', a strategy set out by the European Commission in its communication of 3 March 2010 aimed at fostering smart, sustainable and inclusive growth in the EU. According to the communication, public procurement is a means for achieving that goal since, for instance, it may help to improve framework conditions for businesses to innovate and foster smart growth.

11.08 The communication also states that public procurement policy must ensure the most efficient use of public funds and that procurement markets must be kept open EU-wide. On that basis, the Directive aims to improve the efficiency of public procurement procedures; in its recitals it states that the rules adopted by the previous directives 'should be revised and modernized to increase the efficiency of public spending, facilitating in particular the participation of small- and medium-sized enterprises (SMEs) in public procurement, and to enable procurers to make better use of the public procurement in support of common societal goals'.[1] Further, the Directive acknowledges the need to 'draw up coordinating national procurement procedures' that ensure competition and give practical effect to principles such as equal treatment, non-discrimination, mutual recognition, proportionality and transparency.[2]

11.09 That said, the concept of public procurement that underlies the Directive should first be clarified. The concept is defined as 'the acquisition by means of a public contract of works, supplies or services by one or more contracting authorities from economic operators chosen by those contracting authorities, whether or not the works, supplies or services are intended for a public purpose'.[3] To fully understand this definition, it is also important to clarify the notions of public contracts, contracting authorities and economic operators.

---

1   Directive 2014/24/EU on public procurement [2014] OJ L 94 ('Directive 2014/24/EU'), recital 2.
2   Ibid., recital 1.
3   Ibid., art 1.2.

Public contracts are defined as written instruments, concluded between contracting authorities **11.10** and economic operators, which contain a pecuniary interest and have as their object the execution of works, the supply of products or the provision of services.[4] The Directive also specifically defines public works contracts, public supply contracts and public service contracts. In particular, public works contracts are those that have as their object the execution, or the design and execution, of works related to the activities listed in Annex II of the Directive (which refers to a series of construction-related activities) or simply of a work, which is defined as 'the outcome of building or civil engineering works taken as a whole which is sufficient in itself to fulfil an economic or technical function'.[5]

Contracting authorities are defined as 'State, regional or local authorities, bodies governed by **11.11** public law or associations formed by one or more such authorities or one or more such bodies governed by public law.'[6] In this regard, the Directive indicates that the term 'bodies governed by public law' is to be understood in accordance with the case law of the Court of Justice of the European Union and clarifies that a body operating under normal market conditions, aiming to generate profit and bearing losses as a result of its activity, should not be considered as such.[7]

Economic operators are defined as 'any natural or legal person or public entity or group of such **11.12** persons and/or entities, including any temporary association of undertakings, which offers the execution of works and/or a work, the supply of products or the provision of services on the market'.[8] In this regard, the Directive specifies that the concept should be interpreted broadly and that groups of economic operators may participate in procurement procedures without having to adopt any legal form.[9]

The Directive does not apply to all kinds of public procurement procedures, only to those **11.13** relating to contracts exceeding certain thresholds.[10] In particular, the value of a public works contract must be equal to or greater than €5,186,000 for the Directive to be applicable.[11] This threshold is lower than in the previous directive, in which it was set at €6,242,000, which means that a greater number of public procurement processes are now being subject to the Directive.[12]

Further, contracts such as those awarded by contracting authorities operating in the water, **11.14** energy or transport sectors are excluded from the scope of application of the Directive.[13] Public contracts for arbitration services and for legal services in arbitration or judicial proceedings are also excluded on the basis that they 'are usually provided by bodies or individuals which are agreed on, or selected, in a manner which cannot be governed by procurement rules'.[14]

---

4   Ibid., art 2.1.5.
5   Ibid., art 2.1.7.
6   Ibid., art 2.1.1.
7   Ibid., rec 10.
8   Ibid., art 2.1.10.
9   Ibid., recs 14–15.
10 Ibid., art 1.1.
11 Ibid., art 4. The figures are net of VAT.
12 Directive 2004/18/EC on the coordination of procedures for the award of public works contracts, public supply contracts and public service contracts [2004] OJ L 134/114, art 7.
13 Directive 2014/24/EU, rec 21.
14 Ibid., recs 24–25 and art 10.c–10.d.

C. POTENTIAL IMPACT OF THE DIRECTIVE ON CONSTRUCTION ARBITRATION IN EUROPE

11.15 Construction is key to economic growth and may comprise a wide variety of projects, with different levels of complexity, specialisation, phases and need for cooperation. It is not uncommon for disputes to arise during the performance of such projects, which are often submitted to alternative dispute resolution methods and may ultimately end in arbitration. In fact, arbitration is widely popular in the construction sector. According to the 2013 International Arbitration Survey, '[i]n the Construction sector, arbitration is overwhelmingly cited as the preferred option, ahead of litigation'.[15] According to the 2018 International Arbitration Survey, 82 per cent of respondents expected an increase in cross-border construction arbitration.[16]

11.16 This is not surprising considering the manifold advantages of arbitration compared to traditional litigation. For instance, arbitration gives parties an opportunity to appoint arbitrators with specialised knowledge and experience in construction. Additionally, parties can tailor the rules of procedure to the particularities of construction disputes, where for example a document production phase may be essential, whereas in litigation they must follow rigid procedural rules. Other aspects that make arbitration more desirable are the finality of awards and confidentiality, circumstances that may be given significant weight in the context of construction disputes.

11.17 As explained above, public procurement procedures relating to a number of construction contracts are subject to the Directive. Insofar as disputes arising from those contracts may be submitted to arbitration, the Directive may also end up having an impact on arbitration. This potential impact is examined in this section in light of certain provisions of the Directive.

1. The Directive may contribute to the growth of construction arbitration at EU level

11.18 The first potential impact stems from the fact that the Directive intends to foster competition and openness in procurement markets at EU level. One of the objectives of the Directive is indeed to open public procurement procedures up to operators of other EU countries.[17]

11.19 This objective is enshrined in the principles of equal treatment and non-discrimination, to which the Directive intends to give practical effect as explained above. This is attempted by establishing, for instance, that contracting authorities shall treat economic operators equally

---

15 QMUL, SIA and PwC, *2013 International Arbitration Survey: Corporate choices in International Arbitration. Industry perspectives* (2013) 7 <http://www.arbitration.qmul.ac.uk/media/arbitration/docs/pwc-international-arbitration-study 2013.pdf> accessed 26 June 2019.

16 QMUL, SIA and White & Case, *2018 International Arbitration Survey: The Evolution of International Arbitration* (2018) 29 ('QMUL, SIA and White & Case, The Evolution of International Arbitration') <http://www.arbitration.qmul.ac.uk/ media/arbitration/docs/2018-International-Arbitration-Survey—The-Evolution-of-International-Arbitration-(2).PDF> accessed 26 June 2019.

17 Rui Medeiros, 'The New Directive 2014/24/EU on Public Procurement: A First Overview', in Luís Valadares Tavares, Rui Medeiros, David Coelho (eds), *The new directive 2014/24/EU on Public Procurement* (2014) 33 <https:// www.servulo.com/xms/files/00_SITE_NOVO/Arquivo/THE_NEW_DIRECTIVE_2014_Rui_Medeiros.pdf> accessed 26 June 2019.

and without discrimination, or by stating that procurement procedures shall not be designed with the aim of narrowing the competition by favouring or disfavouring certain economic operators.[18]

More specifically, although along the same lines, the Directive states that: **11.20**

> [e]conomic operators that, under the law of the Member State in which they are established, are entitled to provide the relevant service shall not be rejected solely on the ground that, under the law of the Member State in which the contract is awarded, they would be required to be either natural or legal persons.[19]

The increasing participation of foreign operators in procurement procedures makes it more **11.21** likely that disputes arising from the contracts entered into as a result of those procedures will be submitted to arbitration. This is because, as stated by a scholar, 'arbitration is the ordinary and normal method of settling disputes of international trade'.[20] In fact, when a contract is entered into by parties from different countries, arbitration no longer represents an alternative to ordinary jurisdiction: it is the only reasonable option.[21] That is confirmed by statistical data. According to the 2018 International Arbitration Survey, 97 per cent of respondents perceived arbitration as their preferred method of resolving cross-border disputes.[22]

Arbitration has two fundamental advantages over court litigation for the resolution of disputes **11.22** involving parties from different countries. On the one hand, arbitration is regarded as a more neutral option because resorting to ordinary jurisdiction would generally require one of them to litigate in the courts of its counterparty.[23] This is something that parties are generally unwilling to accept not (only) due to a potential bias of the court against the foreign party, but because the party 'playing at home' has a clear advantage as, for instance, it is likely to be more familiar with how the court system operates, its procedures or at least is likely to know reliable local attorneys to represent it in proceedings before that court.

On the other hand, arbitration is more effective than court litigation because, generally, awards **11.23** are more easily enforceable than judgments issued by national courts due to the New York Convention of 1958. Nonetheless, this advantage is not overly salient in the context of the EU where enforcement of judgments is facilitated by Regulation (EU) No. 1215/2012 on jurisdiction and the recognition and enforcement of judgments in civil and commercial matters.

In sum, the increasing cross-border interaction of public procurement procedures fostered by **11.24** the Directive is expected to result in more construction contracts between economic operators from one EU country and the contracting authorities from another. The parties to those

---

18 Directive 2014/24/EU (n 1) art 19.1.
19 Ibid.
20 Gary Born, *International Commercial Arbitration* (Kluwer Law International 2014) 93, citing Pierre Lalive, 'Transnational (or Truly International) Public Policy and International Arbitration', in Pieter Sanders (ed), *Comparative Arbitration Practice and Public Policy in Arbitration* (Kluwer Law International 1987) 293.
21 David Arias, 'El Arbitraje Internacional' [2013] 29 *Revista Jurídica de Castilla y León* 3.
22 QMUL, SIA and White & Case, The Evolution of International Arbitration (n 16) 5.
23 Litigating in the courts of a third country is another option, although it does not seem to make much economic sense.

contracts are likely to agree on an arbitration clause to resolve their disputes primarily because both will view arbitration as a more neutral option to resolve a dispute than court litigation. Therefore, the Directive may contribute to the growth of construction arbitration at EU level.

2. The Directive may lead to more multi-party or multi-contract arbitrations

11.25 Another potential impact that the Directive may have on arbitration is connected to another goal that it seemingly tries to achieve: dividing projects into different lots. This goal is not expressly stated in the Directive, but it can be inferred from its content.

11.26 For instance, it is stated that contracting authorities shall provide an explanation in the procurement documents of the main reasons for not subdividing a contract into different lots.[24] Division may even be mandatory in some cases if Member States so provide. The Directive establishes that Member States may render it obligatory to award contracts in the form of separate lots under conditions to be specified in accordance with their national law and having regard for EU law.[25] Further, facilitating the participation of SMEs in public procurement procedures is stated as one of the objectives of the Directive.[26] It is expected that achieving this objective will be fostered by dividing contracts into lots.

11.27 Subdividing a project into lots is likely to result in the project having several economic operators responsible for carrying out works that are interconnected with each other. Therefore, a delay or any issue emerging in connection with the works of one lot may trigger a 'domino effect' and have an impact on the works of other lots. That is likely to provide fertile ground for the emergence of multiple disputes between the contracting authority and the various economic operators or even among the economic operators themselves.

11.28 For the reasons explained in the previous section, it would not be surprising for the construction contracts relating to each lot to have arbitration clauses. In that context, the parties may want to have the various disputes decided in single arbitration proceedings. This would probably make sense most of the time from a purely economic viewpoint.[27] However, some of the parties may be reluctant to that possibility once the dispute has started for strategic reasons. Let us imagine that A enters into two contracts with B and C to perform different parts of a construction project. The works performed by B are delayed and, as a result, the works of C are also delayed. A could bring claims against B and C to seek compensation for the delays incurred. However, A would probably be unsuccessful in holding B and C liable in the same arbitration because the claim against C would be possibly weakened by the claim brought against B (which is to be based on the existence of delays caused by B). Therefore, it is likely that A would rather have its disputes with B and C decided in different arbitrations. Conversely, C would probably be most interested in having both disputes decided in single arbitration proceedings.

---

24   Directive 2014/24/EU (n 1) art 46.1.
25   Ibid., art 46.4.
26   Directive 2014/24/EU (n 1) rec 2.
27   Philippe Leboulanger, 'Multi-Contract Arbitration' [1996] 16(4) *Journal of International Arbitration* 62–3.

In any case, as the Directive intends to encourage several construction contracts being entered **11.29** into with different economic operators in the context of a single project and as the disputes generated by those contracts will sometimes end up in the same arbitration, the number of complex arbitrations involving multiple parties or multiple contracts may increase as a result of the Directive.

D. TARGETING THE CHALLENGES OF MULTI-PARTY OR MULTI-CONTRACT ARBITRATIONS

Complex arbitrations have their own particularities and give rise to specific challenges. In **11.30** particular, these challenges arise in relation to (i) how to bring to a single arbitration disputes arising from multiple contracts or involving different parties; and (ii) how to appoint the members of an arbitral tribunal when multiple parties are involved.

1. Bringing together disputes involving multiple contracts or multiple parties

In essence, disputes arising from multiple contracts or involving multiple parties may be **11.31** brought to a single arbitration in two ways: (i) by consolidating various arbitrations that have been initiated separately; and (ii) by initiating an arbitration in which the parties to the different contracts take part either from the beginning or after being joined.

Consolidation is permitted under many rules in certain scenarios. These scenarios are not **11.32** exactly the same under all rules, although, as it stands, one common denominator is that the arbitrations must be pending under the same rules in order for them to be consolidated. In 2017, the Singapore International Arbitration Centre (SIAC) set out an initiative for a protocol promoting cross-consolidation of arbitrations under different rules, although, as far as we are aware, not much has come out of that proposal yet.[28]

As mentioned before, the provisions on this point vary across rules, but consolidation of **11.33** various arbitrations pending before the same institution is generally possible when the parties involved agree to it. If that is not the case, consolidation may still be an option under some rules when all the arbitrations have been commenced under the same or at least compatible arbitration agreements. In any case, additional requirements (such as same parties, same arbitrators, same legal relationship or same seat) may need to be fulfilled for consolidation to be viable under the rules that allow for this option.[29]

The second option described in paragraph 11.31 above is also contemplated by various **11.34** arbitration rules. As with consolidation, the requirements for joinder are not the same under all of those rules, although an agreement amongst the parties to have the different disputes decided together and arbitration agreements that are at least compatible are again elements that may be decisive for this option to be available.[30]

---

28 SIAC, 'Proposal on Cross-Institution Consolidation Protocol' (19 December 2017) <http://siac.org.sg/69-siac-news/551-proposal-on-cross-institution-consolidation-protocol> accessed 26 June 2019.
29 ICC Rules (2021), art 10; LCIA Rules (2020), art 22 A; VIAC Rules (2018), art 15.
30 ICC Rules (2021), arts 7 and 9; LCIA Rules (2020), arts 1.2 and 22.1.x.

11.35   In light of the above, the reader may wonder if any measure could be taken to try to increase the likelihood of disputes arising from construction contracts subscribed with different economic operators in the context of a single project being brought together in the same arbitration. As explained above, having those disputes decided together probably makes sense most of the time from a purely economic viewpoint. This may therefore contribute to the Directive's goal of having a public procurement policy that ensures the most efficient use of public resources.

11.36   In our opinion, the likelihood of the above disputes being brought together in the same arbitration would increase by including thoughtful and carefully drafted arbitration clauses in construction contracts. The wording of arbitration clauses is sometimes overlooked, despite this being a most important element when drafting contracts. Arbitration clauses must be tailored to the nature of the contractual relationship, the particularities and needs of the parties, and the potential disputes. Therefore, the task of drafting an arbitration clause becomes essential when facing potential complex arbitrations involving multiple contracts or multiple parties.

11.37   In this regard, it has been suggested that '[i]n a multilateral relationship, whether involving a single contract or several related contracts, it may be appropriate or necessary to have a multi-party arbitration clause'.[31] The previous paragraphs may provide some hints as to what the arbitration clauses included in the various construction contracts should look like to increase the likelihood of disputes arising from those contracts being decided together.

11.38   The first step is to make sure that all the arbitration clauses provide for the application of the same arbitration rules and that such arbitration rules allow for consolidation and joinder, as described in paragraph 11.31. Then, the arbitration clauses should be adapted to the requirements established in those rules for those options to be available. Although this may vary depending on the rules chosen, the safest avenue would be to state in the arbitration clauses that the parties consent to having the disputes arising from the different construction contracts decided in the same arbitration and for the arbitration clauses themselves to be identical, or at least compatible.

2.   Appointment of arbitrators

11.39   When various disputes arising from different contracts and involving multiple parties are brought to the same arbitration, one sensitive issue is the method for the appointment of arbitrators.

11.40   The fact that the parties may appoint the persons who are to resolve their dispute is one of the fundamental advantages of arbitration over court litigation. As explained by one author, allowing the parties to choose the arbitrators is the surest way to have 'decision-makers who are competent, experienced and available, and who will adopt a genuinely international and neutral

---

31   Jean-Louis Devolvé and others, 'Final Report on Multi-Party Arbitrations' [1995] 6(1) ICC *International Court of Arbitration Bulletin*, para 113.

set of arbitral procedures' because the parties 'have the greatest incentive to make an appropriate selection and the most information on which to base such a choice'.[32]

In international commercial arbitrations, arbitral tribunals are normally composed of three **11.41** arbitrators, two of them nominated by each of the parties and the third selected jointly by the parties themselves, by the other two arbitrators or by the arbitration institution.[33] It has been contended that one of the advantages of offering each of the parties an opportunity to nominate an arbitrator is to increase the perceived confidence in the arbitral tribunal since, arguably, the party-nominated arbitrator is there to ensure that the other members of the arbitral tribunal fully understand that party's case.[34] This is, however, highly controversial. In fact, the recently published Code of Good Practices of the Spanish Arbitration Club establishes that:

> [t]he arbitrators appointed unilaterally by one party do not have the duty or the special function to guarantee that the case of the party that appointed them is correctly understood by the other members of the arbitral tribunal, nor any other duty or special function in relation to the case of the party that appointed them, unless otherwise agreed by the parties.[35]

In any case, the above method of forming arbitral tribunals works well in arbitration **11.42** proceedings involving two parties, but it generates a number of complications in the case of multi-party arbitrations. It seems unfeasible to give every single party the chance to nominate one arbitrator and it could be seen as unfair to give a group of claimants and a group of respondents an opportunity to appoint the same number of arbitrators without regard to the number of parties on the claimant and respondent side.[36] This was precisely the issue raised in the *Dutco* case.

In that case, Dutco initiated arbitration proceedings administered by the ICC and seated in **11.43** Paris, against BKMI and Siemens, in relation to alleged breaches of a consortium agreement between the three companies. The object of the consortium agreement was the construction of a cement plant in Oman, pursuant to a turnkey contract subscribed by BKMI with the owner. According to the consortium agreement, Dutco and Siemens were to perform the construction works. The parties also included the following dispute settlement clause:

> 'All disputes arising out of this Agreement, which cannot be settled amicably among the members, shall be finally settled in accordance with the rules of conciliation and arbitration of the International Chamber of Commerce by three arbitrators appointed in accordance with those rules. The seat of the Arbitration Court shall be Paris.[37]

---

32   Born (n 20) 1640.
33   Nigel Blackaby, Constantine Partasides QC, Alan Redfern, and Martin Hunter, *Redfern and Hunter on International Arbitration* (6th edn, OUP 2015) 239.
34   Ibid.
35   Club Español del Arbitraje [Spanish Arbitration Club] (CEA), *Code of Good Practices* (2019) para 73:

> *Los árbitros designados unilateralmente por una parte no tienen el deber o función especial de asegurarse de que el caso de la parte que los designó sea adecuadamente entendido por el resto de miembros del tribunal arbitral, ni ningún otro deber o función especial en relación con el caso de la parte que los designó, salvo acuerdo en contrario de las partes.*

36   Julian DM Lew, Loukas A Mistelis, and Stefan Michael Kröll, *Comparative International Commercial Arbitration* (Wolters Kluwer Law & Business 2003) 380.
37   Eric Schwartz, 'Multi-Party Arbitration and the ICC' [1993] 10(3) *Journal of International Arbitration* 5, 11.

11.44 According to Article 2(4) of the ICC Rules in force at the time, each party (claimant and respondent) was to nominate an arbitrator and, in case one of them failed to do so, the appointment was to be made by the court.[38] Moreover, the ICC Rules determined that the third arbitrator was to be appointed by the court, unless the parties had provided for the party-appointed arbitrators to agree on the third arbitrator within a given time limit. If the two arbitrators failed to appoint the chairman within that time limit, the third arbitrator would be appointed by the court. However, the ICC Rules made no reference to proceedings with multiple claimants or respondents.

11.45 In accordance with the described provision and common practice, Dutco nominated one arbitrator in its request for arbitration. However, the respondents (BKMI and Siemens) alleged in their response to the request for arbitration that Dutco should submit separate requests for arbitration to them so that each one could appoint an arbitrator. The ICC rejected that request and determined that the respondents should jointly nominate their arbitrator and that, if they failed to do so, the arbitrator would be appointed by the ICC. The respondents finally made a joint nomination, while reserving all their rights regarding the tribunal's constitution. After the chairman's nomination by the ICC, the respondents requested that the arbitral tribunal issue an award acknowledging a violation of the arbitration agreement due to the manner in which it had been constituted. Pursuant to this request, the arbitral tribunal issued an interim award ruling that it had been properly constituted.

11.46 Soon after, the respondents submitted a request to set aside the tribunal's interim award before the Paris Court of Appeals, which rejected it on the basis that the ICC Rules provided that the co-arbitrator had to be nominated respectively by the claimant or group of claimants and the respondent or group of respondents.[39] Nevertheless, the *Cour de Cassation* annulled the Court of Appeals' judgment as it considered that the parties were entitled to equal treatment in the constitution of the arbitral tribunal, and that such right was a matter of public policy and could only be waived after the dispute had arisen.[40] In the *Cour de Cassation's* view, it was unfair to compel two respondents to jointly nominate one co-arbitrator, when the claimant had nominated its own co-arbitrator, and thus the ICC should have appointed all the members of the tribunal in that case.

---

38   ICC Rules (1988), art 2.4:

> Where the dispute is to be referred to three arbitrators, each party shall nominate in the Request for Arbitration and the Answer thereto respectively one arbitrator for confirmation by the Court. Such person shall be independent of the party nominating him. If a party fails to nominate an arbitrator, the appointment shall be made by the Court. The third arbitrator, who will act as chairman of the arbitral tribunal, shall be appointed by the Court, unless the parties have provided that the arbitrators nominated by them shall agree on the third arbitrator within a fixed time-limit. In such a case the Court shall confirm the appointment of such third arbitrator. Should the two arbitrators fail, within the time-limit fixed by the parties or the Court, to reach agreement on the third arbitrator, he shall be appointed by the Court.

39   *MI Industrieanlagen GmbH, Siemens AG v. DUTCO Construction Co (Private) Ltd*, Cour d' Appel [Court of Appeal] of Paris, Not Indicated, 5 May 1989' [1990] XV *Yearbook Commercial Arbitration* 124–27.

40   *BKMI Industrienlagen GmbH & Siemens AG v. Dutco Construction*, Cour de Cassation (1er Chambre Civile), Pourvoi N° 89-18708 89-18726, 7 January 1992' [1993] XVIII, *Yearbook Commercial Arbitration* 140–14.

As a result of the foregoing, the subsequent version of the ICC Rules introduced a provision **11.47** for the constitution of arbitral tribunals in multi-party arbitrations in accordance with the tenets of the *Cour de Cassation*.[41] The principle set out by the *Cour de Cassation* has also been adopted in the arbitration laws of a number of countries, such as Spain.[42]

There are therefore some arbitration rules and arbitration laws that establish provisions to **11.48** tackle the challenges that may arise in relation to the constitution of arbitral tribunals in multi-party arbitrations. This should be taken into account when the arbitration clauses of the various construction contracts are drafted since it may be advisable to provide for the application of those arbitration rules or laws. In the alternative, similar provisions may be established in the arbitration clauses so as to avoid a situation where the participation of multiple parties in the same arbitration ends up obstructing the appointment process or leading to undesired outcomes as in the *Dutco* case.

The arbitration clauses could also establish appointment mechanisms that guarantee equality **11.49** in the constitution of the arbitral tribunal to all the intervening parties. For example, establishing lists of candidates that all parties may rank so that the candidates with the highest ranking are appointed. However, it should be borne in mind that this mechanism may hinder a subsequent consolidation or joining of parties.

What should be discouraged in any event is arbitration clauses providing that arbitral tribunals **11.50** may have more than three members so that each intervening party can appoint one arbitrator. That is likely to result in increased costs and delays (due to the challenges of squaring the schedules of more than three arbitrators). In addition, the parties may end up not enjoying the benefit they had initially sought – being able to appoint their respective arbitrator – if the arbitration court decides to itself appoint all members of the tribunal in application of the principle set out in the *Dutco* case.

E. CONCLUSION

It is possible that the European legislator did not consider the impact that the Directive could **11.51** have on construction arbitration. In fact, the interconnection between the Directive and construction arbitration is not readily evident. However, for the reasons explained above, the Directive could contribute to a rise in the number of (complex) construction arbitrations in the EU.

Complex arbitrations involving multiple parties or multiple contracts generate specific chal- **11.52** lenges that can be tackled by adopting certain measures. This contribution has identified some of those measures at the stage of drafting the arbitration clause.

---

41 ICC Rules (1998), art 10; ICC Rules (2017), art 12. The new version of the ICC Rules (2021) seems to go one step further by adding the following paragraph to art 12: 'Notwithstanding any agreement by the parties on the method of constitution of the arbitral tribunal, in exceptional circumstances the Court may appoint each member of the arbitral tribunal to avoid a significant risk of unequal treatment and unfairness that may affect the validity of the award'.

42 Spanish Arbitration Act, art 15(2)(b).

11.53 These measures could be implemented at the outset of the public procurement procedures governed by the Directive, in anticipation of the problems that may arise if the disputes end up in complex arbitrations. For instance, the bid specifications could provide that the arbitration clauses to be included in the contracts with the successful bidders should contain some of the elements outlined above.

Part III

INTERSECTIONS BETWEEN INTERNATIONAL INVESTMENT ARBITRATION AND EU LAW

12

GENERAL ASPECTS OF INVESTOR-STATE DISPUTE SETTLEMENT

George A. Bermann[*]

A. COMPETENCE OVER FOREIGN DIRECT INVESTMENT IN THE EUROPEAN UNION

12.01 No discussion of the European Union (EU) as actor in the international investment arena can fail to take into account issues of competence and, in particular, the allocation of competence between the EU and its Member States. The distribution of competences in foreign direct investment (FDI) between the EU and its Member States has been evolving, and evolving quickly. That distribution has historically been governed by the general EU law principle of conferral, meaning that 'the Union shall act only within the limits of the competences conferred upon it by the Member States in the Treaties to attain the objectives set out therein'.[1] By virtue of this provision, any action by the EU must be founded on a specific legal basis in the Treaty of European Union ('TEU'), establishing the EU, or the Treaty on the Functioning of the European Union (TFEU), governing the EU's activities, whether it be internal action or action in the international field.[2] The principle of conferral is complemented by the EU principle of subsidiarity, according to which the EU should not undertake action,

---

[*] Date of submission: 1/5/2020.

[1] Consolidated Version of the Treaty on European Union [2008] OJ C115/13 (TEU), Art 5(2) (formerly Art 5 of the Treaty on European Community).

[2] Opinion 2/94 pursuant to Art 228(6) of the EC Treaty (Accession by the Communities to the Convention for the Protection of Human Rights and Fundamental Freedoms) [1996] ECR I-1759.

even within its sphere of authority, if the objectives of that action can be adequately achieved at the Member State level.[3] That said, there has been a progressive expansion of EU external competence including, notably, in the foreign investment field. This expansion has been initiated by the Court of Justice of the European Union (CJEU) through case law on several fronts. The situation has radically changed with the entry into force of the 2009 Treaty of Lisbon, establishing a general EU competence over FDI, as described below.[4]

1. The EU's Exclusive Competence

The Treaty of Lisbon,[5] enacted on December 1, 2009, brought numerous changes to the EU legal system, among them Article 216(1) TFEU according to which: **12.02**

> [t]he Union may conclude an agreement with one or more third countries or international organizations where the Treaties so provide or where the conclusion of an agreement is necessary in order to achieve, within the framework of the Union's policies, one of the objectives referred to in the Treaties, or is provided for in a legally binding Union act or is likely to affect common rules or alter their scope.

Similarly, Article 3 TFEU, which identifies the areas in which the EU enjoys exclusive competence, states that: **12.03**

> '[t]he Union shall also have exclusive competence for the conclusion of an international agreement when its conclusion is provided for in a legislative act of the Union or is necessary to enable the Union to exercise its internal competence, or in so far as its conclusion may affect common rules or alter their scope.

These provisions represent a powerful affirmation of the doctrine of implied powers.

However, the change of most immediate interest was the express inclusion of FDI within the common commercial policy (CCP) over which the EU enjoys exclusive competence.[6] Article 207 TFEU expressly provides: **12.04**

---

3 TEU (n 1), Art 5:

   Under the principle of subsidiarity, in areas which do not fall within its exclusive competence, the Union shall act only if and in so far as the objectives of the proposed action cannot be sufficiently achieved by the Member States, either at central level or at regional and local level, but can rather, by reason of the scale or effects of the proposed action, be better achieved at Union level.

4 Treaty of Lisbon amending the Treaty on European Union and the Treaty establishing the European Community, signed at Lisbon on 13 December 2007 [2007] OJ C306/1.

5 Ibid.

6 The reasons and underlying policies that led to this shift in competence are still debated and range from economic (increasing strategic importance of international investment), political (the need to enhance EU bargaining power on the world stage) and legal (the need to develop uniform protection standards for investors) reasons, while a key role was played by the Commission which persistently pushed the issue onto the evolving trade agenda (in this sense see Sophie Meunier, 'Integration by Stealth: How the European Union Gained Competence over Foreign Direct Investment,' (2017) 55 *Journal of Common Market Studies* 593). For an evolution of the EU's legal competences in international investment policy and a history of the deliberations that led to the adoption of Arts III-314 and IIII-315 of the Treaty Establishing a Constitution for Europe (2004) OJ C310, later transposed as Arts 206–207 TFEU, see Johann Basedow, 'A Legal History of the EU's International Investment Policy' (2016) 17 *Journal of World Investment and Trade* 743.

The common commercial policy shall be based on uniform principles, particularly with regard to changes in tariff rates, the conclusion of tariff and trade agreements relating to trade in goods and services, and the commercial aspects of intellectual property, *foreign direct investment*, the achievement of uniformity in measures of liberalization, export policy and measures to protect trade such as those to be taken in the event of dumping or subsidies. The common commercial policy shall be conducted in the context of the principles and objectives of the Union's external action. (emphasis added)

a. The scope of EU competence

12.05 However, inclusion of FDI within the CCP did not enable the EU to take action on all matters relating to the regulation of foreign investment regulation. Article 207(6) bars the exercise of exclusive competence to the detriment of the allocation of competences between the Union and the Member States as set out in Articles 4(1) and 5(1)(2) TEU. It further precludes harmonization of the laws of the Member States on any given matter, even if harmonization is designed to implement an agreement with a third country, whenever the Treaty, as in the fields of education and health, expressly prohibits harmonization. The purpose of these provisions was to prevent the CCP from subverting the division of internal competences between the EU and the Member States.[7]

12.06 In understanding these limitations, it is helpful to distinguish among three scenarios. First, the EU enjoys sole competence to conclude international agreements, including free trade agreements ('FTAs') and investment agreements, to the extent the content of the agreement falls squarely and unreservedly within the scope of Article 207(1) TFEU.

12.07 Second, where an agreement also addresses matters falling within the exclusive competence of the Member States, it must take the form of a 'mixed agreement,' requiring Member State assent. Conclusion of mixed agreements entails two parallel ratification processes, one by the EU and the other by the Parliaments of the Member States.[8]

12.08 Less clear is the third scenario: international agreements containing rules that fall under shared competences without touching upon the Member States' exclusive competences. As to these, the question is whether the EU is empowered to act on behalf of the Member States during the stages of negotiation and conclusion of the agreement. The question has arisen squarely in the recent debate surrounding the EU's Comprehensive Economic and Trade Agreement (CETA) with Canada,[9] which was first negotiated as an EU-only agreement, but later concluded as a mixed-agreement, put at risk of deadlock upon Belgium's initial refusal to ratify it,[10] and ultimately subject to partial provisional application pending ratification by all the

---

7 See Markus Krajewski, 'The Reform of the Common Commercial Policy' in Andrea Biondi, Piet Eeckhout Stefanie Ripley (eds) *EU Law After Lisbon* (OUP 2012).

8 Ramses A Wessel, 'The EU as a Party to International Agreements: Shared Competences, Mixed Responsibilities' in Aland Dashwood and Marc Maresceau (eds) *Law and Practice of EU External Relations: Salient Features of a Changing Landscape* (CUP 2008) 175, 152–87.

9 The Comprehensive Economic and Trade Agreement between the EU and Canada (CETA), [2017] OJ L11/23. [hereinafter CETA].

10 Déclaration du Royaume de Belgique relative aux conditions de pleins pouvoirs par l'Etat fédéral et les Entités fédérées pour la signature du CETA <http://liege.mpoc.be/doc/europe/-AECG-CETA/Belgique_Declarationpour-la-signature-du-CETA_27-oct-2016.pdf> accessed 29 November 2018. See also Dylan Geraets, 'Changes in EU Trade Policy After Opinion 2/15' (2018) 13 *Global Trade and Customs Journal* 13.

Member States.[11] In May 2019, further to a request by Belgium, the CJEU issued Opinion 1/17, affirming CETA's compatibility with EU law,[12] in line with Advocate-General Bot's earlier conclusions.[13] In the aftermath of the watershed case of *Slovak Republic v Achmea BV*[14] that held intra-EU BITs to be incompatible with EU law, as will be discussed below, this caught many by surprise. For the purposes of this section, this case will be discussed in connection with the scope of EU competency. The broader implications of this opinion are discussed in a later section of this chapter examining what the *Achmea* judgment means for the future of intra-EU BITs under Section B.2, *infra*.

The same question as to EU competence had previously lain at the heart of the Commission's **12.09** request to the CJEU for an opinion on whether the EU has competence to conclude the EU-Singapore Free Trade Agreement (EUSFTA) on its own, notwithstanding the fact that the agreement covered shared competences. Implicated was an entire new generation of potential investment agreements, including those with the US, South Korea, Japan, and Vietnam, that the EU was negotiating in the wake of the Global Europe Trade Strategy of 2006.[15] The resulting CJEU Opinion 2/15 provided some clarification and became a point of reference for all future EU investment and FTA agreements.[16] However, Opinion 2/15 expressly limited its holding to the question whether 'the content of the agreement's provisions is compatible with the nature of the competence of the European Union to sign and conclude the envisaged agreement', thereby leaving open the question of whether 'the content of the agreement's provisions is compatible with EU law',[17] as was subsequently decided in Opinion 1/17.

b. The CJEU's Opinion 1/17

What is most striking about Opinion 1/17 is that, in finding that the international investment **12.10** court system established by CETA was compatible with the autonomy of the EU legal order, the Court employed reasoning equally applicable to such courts as might be established under other treaties, such as, for instance, the EUSFTA. Pertinently, the CJEU accepted the hierarchical superiority of such an investment court, on the understanding that that court

---

11 EU, 'Council Decision on the Provisional Application of the Comprehensive Economic and Trade Agreement (CETA) Between Canada, of the One Part, and the European Union and Its Member States, of the Other Part' (10974/16, 5 October 2016) <http://data.consilium.europa.eu/doc/document/ST-10974-2016-INIT/en/pdf> accessed 29 November 2018.

12 Opinion 1/17 (Compatibility of the ISDS mechanism under CETA with EU Law) [2019] ECLI:EU:C:2019:341. See also Christian Riffel, 'The CETA Opinion of the European Court of Justice and its Implications – Not That Selfish After All' (2019) 22(3) *J. of Intl. Economic Law* 503.

13 Opinion 1/17 (n 12).

14 Case C-284/16 *Slowakische Republik v Achmea BV* [2018] OJ C 161/7 (also cited in ECLI:EU:C:2018:158) (*Achmea* Judgment).

15 Commission, 'Global Europe: Competing in the World-A Contribution to EU's Growth and Jobs Strategy' (Communication) COM (2006) 567 final.

16 Opinion 2/15 (Competence of the EU to sign the EU-Singapore FTA) [2018] ECLI:EU:C:2017:376; Nikos Lavranos, 'CJEU Opinion 1/17: Keeping International Law and EU Law Strictly Apart' (2019) 4 *European Investment Law and Arbitration Review* 240; Giovanni Gruni, 'Towards a Sustainable World Trade Law? The Commercial Policy of the European Union After Opinion 2/15 ECJ' [2018] 13 *Global Trade and Customs Journal* 4.

17 Opinion 2/15 (n 16), paras 30, 290.

cannot interpret EU law. They are bound to 'follow the prevailing interpretation' given by domestic or EU courts, which they must treat as if a matter of fact. In this regard, the Court observed that:

> [a]n international agreement providing for the creation of a court responsible for the interpretation of its provisions and whose decisions are binding on the European Union, is, in principle, compatible with EU law. Indeed, the competence of the European Union in the field of international relations and its capacity to conclude international agreements necessarily entail the power to submit to the decisions of a court that is created or designated by such agreements as regards the interpretation and application of their provisions …[18]

12.11 In this respect, this decision stands in stark contrast to the CJEU's blockage of the accession of the EU to the European Economic Area Court, the Unified Patent Court, and the European Court of Human Rights on the basis of their alleged incompatibility with the autonomy of EU law, on the ground that Articles 344 and 267 TFEU were meant to secure the CJEU's monopoly in the definitive interpretation of EU law.[19] Article 344 TFEU bars Member States from submitting a dispute concerning the interpretation or application of the Treaties to any method of settlement other than those provided for in the Treaties, in order to ensure the consistent and uniform application of EU law, thereby preserving the autonomy of the EU legal system which it is the responsibility of the Court to ensure.[20] In the *Achmea* judgment, it was this autonomy that the CJEU considered to be threatened by the inability of international arbitral tribunals to seek interpretations of EU law from the CEU due to those tribunals not constituting courts or tribunals of a Member State within the meaning of Article 267, which sets out the preliminary ruling procedure.[21] Opinion 1/17, however, differentiates CETA from the applicable treaty in *Achmea*, on the basis that the interpretative power of the investment court is limited to construing the terms of CETA, with EU law treated strictly as a matter of fact.[22]

12.12 To link this discussion back to the competence of the EU to act on behalf of the Member States during the stages of negotiation and conclusion of an agreement, the CJEU's analysis of this particular point was far more limited in comparison to Opinion 2/15. What is clear from Opinion 1/17, however, is that the EU may not enter into any agreements that set up an investment court or tribunal that purports to decide matters of EU law or 'to call into question the level of protection of public interest determined by the [EU] following a democratic process'.[23] On this latter point, the CJEU stated, in no uncertain terms, that:

> If the Union were to enter into an international agreement capable of having the consequence that the Union – or a Member State in the course of implementing EU law – has to amend or withdraw legislation because of an assessment made by a tribunal standing outside the EU judicial system of the level of protection of a public interest established, in accordance with the EU constitutional

---

18 Opinion 1/17 (n 12), para 106, citing Opinion 2/13 (Accession of the Union to the ECHR) (2014) EU:C:2014:2454, para 182; see also Opinion 1/91 (EEA Agreement—I) [1991] EU:C:1991:490, paras 40 and 70, and Opinion 1/09 (Agreement on the creation of a unified patent litigation system), [2011] EU:C:2011:123, para 74.
19 See Opinion 2/13 (Accession of the Union to the ECHR), Opinion 1/91 and Opinion 1/09 (n 18).
20 *Achmea* (n 14), para 32.
21 Ibid., para 46.
22 Opinion 1/17 (n 12), para 118.
23 Ibid., paras 148, 156.

framework, by the EU institutions, it would have to be concluded that such an agreement undermines the capacity of the Union to operate autonomously within its unique constitutional framework.[24]

The EU's insistence that any agreement to which it accedes contain safeguards to prevent non-EU bodies from issuing authoritative interpretations of EU law and to retain both its and Member States' authority to independently prescribe the level of protection of a public welfare goal reflects how, paradoxically, the EU's autonomy, which lies at the heart of its legal regime, restricts its competence to enter into any agreements that would impinge upon this very autonomy. **12.13**

c. The CJEU's Opinion 2/15

In the earlier Opinion 2/15, the CJEU adhered to the 'centre of gravity' doctrine developed in its previous case law for determining whether an international agreement falls within the scope of the CCP, and therefore is subject to the EU's exclusive authority.[25] Under that approach, whenever an agreement comprises more than one measure, reference is to be had to the principal one, so that it may be considered as founded 'on a single legal basis […] required by the […] predominant […] component [unless they are] inseparably linked without one being secondary and indirect in relation to the other'.[26] In this event, there is no need to find an additional legal basis sufficient to support what may then be regarded as the measure's 'incidental' provisions. The net effect of this jurisprudence is to reduce the need for mixed agreements, thereby expanding the EU's exclusive competence. This is precisely what happened with Opinion 2/15. **12.14**

An initial matter in Opinion 2/15 was the definition of the term 'foreign direct investment' and what might constitute 'indirect' investments. The CJEU adopted the prevailing view that indirect investments are essentially short-term investments, otherwise known as 'portfolio investments,' by which foreign investors do not exercise influence over management of the enterprise or retain lasting and direct economic links enabling them effectively to do so.[27] Although the Commission asserted implied competence over portfolio investments,[28] the Court understood Article 207(1) TFEU more narrowly, holding that portfolio investments essentially constitute movement of capital, which lies outside the scope of the CCP and within **12.15**

---

24 Ibid., para 150.
25 Case C-155/07 *European Parliament v Council of the European Union* [2008] ECLI:EU:C:2008:605, paras 34–37; Case C-300/89 *Commission of the European Communities v Council of the European Communities* [1991] ECR I-2867, paras 17–21.
26 Case C-377/12 *European Commission v Council of the European Union* [2014] ECLI:EU:C:2014:1903, para 34; *Parliament v Council* (n 25), paras 34–37; Case C-414/11 *Daiichi Sankyo and Sanofi-Aventis Deutschland* [2013] ECLI:EU:C:2013:520, paras 50–52; Case C-137/12 *European Commission v Council of the European Union* [2013] ECLI:EU:C:2013:675, paras 56–58. See also Opinion 2/15 (n 16), paras 36–38.
27 See Opinion 2/15 (n 16); Commission, 'Communication from the Commission to the European Parliament, the Council, the European Economic and Social Committee and the Committee of the Regions – Towards a Comprehensive European International Investment Policy', COM (2010) 343 final, 2–3.
28 Opinion 2/15 (n 16), para 16; see also David Kleimann and Gesa Kübek, 'The Future of EU External Trade Policy – Opinion 2/15: Report from the Hearing' (*EU Law Analysis*, 4 October 2016) <www.eulawanalysis.blogspot.co.uk> accessed 29 November 2018, and Dominik Moskvan, 'The European Union's Competence on Foreign Investment: 'New and Improved?' (2017)18 *San Diego International Law Journal* 241, 253–4.

the shared competences of the EU and Member States, notably free movement of capital.[29] Any international agreement covering that matter consequently had to be concluded as a mixed agreement.

12.16 Having excluded governance of indirect investment from the CCP, the Court turned to the scope of the EU's authority over foreign direct investment. Importantly, it concluded that the CCP could cover all measures that have an impact on foreign investment, including investment protection, or that contribute to the 'legal certainty of investors'.[30] In other words, the Court underscored the important point that EU competence under Article 207(1) TFEU encompasses not only market access through foreign investment, but protection of foreign investments themselves,[31] even where an investment affects property rights whose governance is reserved to Member States under Article 345 TFEU.[32] '[W]hilst the Member States remain free to exercise their competences regarding property law [...] they are nonetheless not absolved from compliance with fundamental rights',[33] such as the principle of non-discrimination (vis-à-vis other Member State investors) and general principles of EU law comprising also the right to property, including the right to compensation for the taking of property.[34]

12.17 Opinion 2/15 broadened the scope of Article 207(1) TFEU in regard to foreign direct investment in other respects as well. The CJEU held that all aspects of trade in goods (including national treatment, trade facilitation and customs, technical barriers to trade, sanitary and phytosanitary barriers, competition and government procurement),[35] trade in services (including financial services and mutual recognition of professionals),[36] as well as certain non-economic objectives (such as minimum labour standards and environmental protection),[37] all fall within the scope of CCP. Although the CJEU further acknowledged that transport services are generally excluded from the scope of CCP in accordance with Articles 4 and 207(5) TFEU, it concluded that commitments regarding international

---

29 Opinion 2/15 (n 16), paras 225–256 and 305; see also Nikos Lavranos, 'Mixed Exclusivity: The CJEU's Opinion on the EU-Singapore FTA' (2017) 2 *European Investment Law and Arbitration Review* 3.

30 Ibid., para 94.

31 As argued in Joachim Karl, 'The Competence for Foreign Direct Investment – New Powers for the European Union?' (2006) 5 *Journal of World Investment and Trade* 413, 421–2.

32 Art 345 TFEU had been previously interpreted as excluding investment protection from EU exclusive competence, as referenced by Angelos Dimopoulos, 'Creating an EU Investment Policy: Challenges for the Post-Lisbon Era of External Relations' in Paul James Cardwell (ed), *EU External Relations Law and Policy in the Post-Lisbon Era* (TMC Asser Press 2012), 401; see also Moskvan (n 28), 254–5.

33 Opinion 2/15 (n 16), para 107.

34 See Federico Ortino and Piet Eeckhout, 'Towards an EU Policy on Foreign Direct Investment' in Biondi, Eeckhout and Ripley (eds) (n 7) 312, 319–20. As to the regulation of expropriation of foreign investment, Dimopoulos (n 32), 113–16, suggests that Arts 114, 115, and 352 TFEU provide for the shared competence for the inclusion of provisions protecting non-direct investments in international agreements from both EU and national measures.

35 Opinion 2/15 (n 16), paras 40–48.

36 Ibid., para 55.

37 Indeed, 'the objective of sustainable development henceforth forms an integral part of the common commercial policy': Opinion 2/15 (n 16), paras 147, 162–167.

maritime transport,[38] rail transport[39] and road transport[40] may nonetheless affect or alter common rules in those areas and were therefore included within the EU's exclusive competence. The CJEU further held that Article 207(1) TFEU covers the 'commercial aspects of intellectual property,' due to the fact that intellectual property rights may have direct and immediate effects on foreign trade and 'seek […] to facilitate the production and commercialization of innovative and creative products […] to increase the benefit from trade and investment'.[41]

Notwithstanding these expansive interpretations of Article 207(1) TFEU, the CJEU took a **12.18** quite different view of the EU's competence to negotiate and enter into the EUSFTA's provisions on investor-state dispute settlement (ISDS) without the Member States' consent. According to the Court, an ISDS regime could not be considered as merely incidental to the EUSFTA's substantive obligations since it removes disputes over foreign investment from the jurisdiction of Member State courts and 'cannot, therefore, be established without the Member States' consent'.[42] Although the CJEU did not identify a precise legal basis under the Lisbon Treaty for its conclusion,[43] the Opinion is unequivocal and represents an obvious warning that any international agreement establishing a similar investor protection regime would fall within the shared competences of the EU and Member States. While this was not expressly discussed by the CJEU in Opinion 1/17, Advocate-General Bot cited this aspect of Opinion 2/15 approvingly, noting that 'the Court [had] not, however, examine[d] the issue of the compatibility of the ISDS mechanism provided for in an agreement on international investment with EU law, from the perspective of the preservation of its own jurisdiction':[44]

> The Court has made clear that the exclusive competence enjoyed by the European Union under Article 207 TFEU in relation to foreign direct investment extends to all the substantive provisions usually found in a bilateral investment treaty. However, the European Union shares its competence with the Member States in relation to the provisions on the settlement of disputes between investors and States. In that regard, in Opinion 2/15, the Court observed that the system in question 'removes disputes from the jurisdiction of the courts of the Member States' and that that system must, therefore, be established with the Member States' consent.[45]

In what appears to anticipate its eventual findings in Opinion 1/17, the Court in Opinion 2/15 **12.19** observed that while

> the competence of the European Union to conclude international agreements necessarily entails the power to submit to the decisions of a body which, whilst not formally a court, essentially performs

---

38   Ibid., paras 175–194. The Court excluded from its analysis only inland waterways transport services due to their limited scope in the context of the EUSFTA: Opinion 2/15 (n 16), paras 216–217.

39   Ibid., paras 195–203.

40   Ibid., paras 204–212.

41   Ibid., paras 125, 111–130.

42   Ibid., para 292.

43   See for instance David Kleimann and Gesa Kübek, 'The Signing, Provisional Application, and Conclusion of Trade and Investment Agreements in the EU: The Case of CETA and Opinion 2/15' (2018) 45 *Legal Issues of Economic Integration* 13, 41.

44   Opinion 1/17 (n 12), Opinion of Advocate-General Bot [2019] ECLI:EU:C:2019:72, para 48.

45   Ibid., para 47.

judicial functions, such as the Dispute Settlement Body created within the framework of the WTO Agreement ...[46]

it was not necessary, for its purposes, to decide 'whether the provisions of the envisaged agreement are compatible with EU law'.[47]

12.20 Opinion 2/15 further confirmed that under the Lisbon Treaty, Member States may not contract internationally in the area of FDI, insofar as the exercise falls squarely and unreservedly within the sphere of common commercial policy as defined in Article 207(1) TFEU. Subject to the possibility of delegation of authority to the Member States, as in the case of the 2012 EU Regulation establishing transitional arrangements for BITs between Member States and third countries,[48] Member States are prohibited from adopting acts, including international agreements, producing legal effects in the area of foreign direct investment and they are positively obligated to terminate any existing BIT that has been superseded by a new EU investment agreement.[49]

12.21 Its limitations notwithstanding, Opinion 2/15 (which must be read together with the narrower findings arrived at in Opinion 1/17) substantially enhances the scope of the EU's exclusive authority to conclude future international trade agreements.

B. INTRA-EU INVESTMENT LAW AND POLICY

12.22 While the EU is a recent player in FDI, the Member States have been active in this domain for decades, entering into a great many BITs with third countries, or 'extra-EU BITs'. As a matter of practice, they did not enter into BITs with one another, both because they deemed them unnecessary and because such agreements would, in any event, appear to run afoul of internal market and non-discrimination principles of EU law.[50] However, some of the countries with which the Member States concluded BITs subsequently acceded to the EU, becoming EU Member States themselves.[51] At that point, the BITs with those countries came to be known popularly as 'intra-EU BITs'. There were at one point over 190 of them.

---

46 Opinion 2/15 (n 16), para 299.
47 Ibid., paras 30, 290 and 300.
48 Regulation (EU) 1219/2012 of the European Parliament and of the Council of 12 December 2012 establishing transitional arrangements for bilateral investment agreements between Member States and third countries [2012] OJ L351/40 which, in the words of the Court, 'empowers the Member States, subject to strict conditions, to maintain in force, or even to conclude, bilateral agreements with a third State concerning direct investment as long as an agreement between the European Union and that third State concerning direct investment does not exist' (Opinion 2/15 (n 16), para 250).
49 Opinion 2/15 (n 16), paras 252–256. See Hannes Lenk, 'More Trade and Less Investment for Future EU Trade and Investment Policy' (2018) 19 *Journal of World Investment & Trade* 305, 315. In the instant case, no further action was needed since Art 9(10) EUSFTA set out Singapore's intention to consider the existing BITs as terminated.
50 Hanno Wehland, 'Intra-EU Investment Agreements and Arbitration: Is European Community Law an Obstacle?', (2009) 58 *International and Comparative Law Quarterly* 297.
51 Philip FJS Strik, *Shaping the Single European Market in the Field of Foreign Direct Investment* (Hart Publishing 2016), 188.

1. European Commission policy on intra-EU BITs

Prior to the accession to the EU of the new Central and Eastern European States, the **12.23** Commission raised no objections to their BITs with existing Member States. But following accession, the Commission began challenging the intra-EU BITs in earnest. The Commission first voiced its opposition in a letter of January 2006 addressed to the Czech Minister of Finance and introduced by the Czech Republic in support of its arguments as Respondent State in the case of *Eastern Sugar v Czech Republic*.[52] The letter stated:

> [W]here the EC Treaty or secondary legislation are in conflict with some of these BITs' provisions – or should the EU adopt such rules in the future – Community law will automatically prevail over the nonconforming BIT provisions. [...] [I]ntra-EU BITs should be terminated insofar as the matters fall under Community competence. However, the effective prevalence of the EU *acquis* does not entail, at the same time, the automatic termination of the concerned BITs or, necessarily, the non-application of all their provisions.

The main message of the letter was that, even though intra-EU BITs were not automatically terminated by the accession of the new Member States to the EU, EU law rules prevailed over these treaties to the extent they overlapped with EU law. Therefore, the Commission took the view that the intra-EU BITs should be terminated by Member States following the procedures provided for in the BITs.[53]

Then, in November 2006, the Commission sent a note to the Economic and Financial **12.24** Committee of the Council with the following observations:

> There are still around 150 BITs between Member States in force [...] There appears to be no need for agreements of this kind in the single market and their legal character after accession is not entirely clear. It would appear that most of their content is superseded by Community law upon accession of the respective Member State. [...] Investors could practice 'forum shopping' by submitting claims to BIT arbitration instead of – or additionally to – national courts. This could lead to arbitration taking place without relevant questions of European Community's law being submitted to the ECJ, with unequal treatment of investors among Member States as a possible outcome.

> In order to avoid such legal uncertainties and unnecessary risks for Member States, it is strongly recommended that the Member States exchange notes to the effect that such BITs are no longer applicable, and also formally rescind such agreements. The Committee is invited to endorse this approach and Member States are asked to communicate to the Commission by 30 June 2007 which actions have been taken in that regard and which of their intra-EU investment agreements still remain to be terminated.[54]

With the rise of investor-State arbitrations under the intra-EU BITs, the Commission **12.25** adopted the practice of intervening as *amicus curiae* in those proceedings, contesting the validity of the agreements pursuant to which those proceedings were taking place, and thereby challenging the tribunals' jurisdiction. The Commission similarly made submissions to ad hoc

---

52 *Eastern Sugar BV v The Czech Republic*, SCC Case No 088/2004, Partial Award, 27 March 2007.
53 Ibid., para 119.
54 Ibid., para 126.

committees established under the aegis of the International Centre for Settlement of Investment Disputes ('ICSID'), as well as to national courts in enforcement proceedings.[55] The arbitral tribunals in whose proceedings the Commission intervened consistently rejected the Commission's assertions and upheld their jurisdiction under the treaties.[56] Typical was the Commission's *amicus curiae* submission in 2010 in the *Achmea v Slovakia* arbitration[57] which, for reasons outlined below,[58] was to become a landmark case. There, the Commission, as on numerous prior occasions, unsuccessfully claimed that the CJEU had exclusive competence to decide investment disputes by nationals of one Member State in the territory of another, and that the tribunals established pursuant to intra-EU BITs accordingly lacked jurisdiction to entertain investment claims under the BITs. The Commission termed the intra-EU BITs an 'anomaly within the EU internal market'.[59]

12.26 The Commission eventually decided to take legal steps.

12.27 The first occurred in 2010, after the ICSID tribunal in *Micula v Romania* condemned Romania for revoking a State aid that it had previously granted to Swedish investors.[60] Romania, having acceded to the EU and under pressure from the Commission, had revoked the aid in compliance with the EU prohibition on the grant of State aids within the EU without prior approval by the Commission. After partial payment of the resulting award by Romania, the Commission in May 2014 issued a 'suspension injunction' requiring Romania to suspend any further payment and admonishing Romania that any payments under the award would themselves amount to illegal State aids.[61] In March 2015, the Commission issued a final order concluding that payment of the *Micula* award would be an EU law infringement and indeed amount in itself to an unlawful State aid. It further ordered Romania not only to cease making any payments under the award, but also to recover all amounts already paid.[62] However, it bears mention that in June 2019 the General Court of the European Union ('GCEU') annulled the Commission's ruling, emphasizing that EU law should not be applied retrospectively to the pre-accession period and, accordingly, declining to recognize payment of

---

55 See e.g., Brief for *Amicus Curiae* the Commission of the European Union in Support of Defendant-Appellant, *Micula v Govt of Romania* 104 F Supp 3d 42 (DDC 2015) (EU Amicus Brief) <https://www.italaw.com/sites/default/files/case-documents/italaw9198.pdf> accessed 29 November 2018.

56 See eg *Electrabel SA v Republic of Hungary*, ICSID Case No ARB/07/19, Decision on Jurisdiction, Applicable Law and Liability, 30 November 2012; *European American Investment Bank AG (EURAM) v The Slovak Republic*, UNCITRAL, PCA Case No 2010-17, Award on Jurisdiction, 13 October 2011; *Charanne BV and Construction Investments SARL v The Kingdom of Spain*, SCC No V 062/2012, Award, 21 January 2016; *Blusun SA, Jean-Pierre Lecorcier and Michael Stein v Italian Republic*, ICSID Case No ARB/14/3, Award, 27 December 2016.

57 *Achmea BV v The Slovak Republic* (formerly *Eureko BV v The Slovak Republic*), UNCITRAL, PCA Case No 2008-13, Award on Jurisdiction, Arbitrability and Suspension, 26 October 2010.

58 Ibid.

59 EU Amicus Brief (n 55), para 177.

60 *Ioan Micula, Viorel Micula, SC European Food SA, SC Starmill SRL and SC Multipack SRL v Romania*, ICSID Case No ARB/05/20, Final Award, 11 December 2013.

61 Commission, 'State aid SA 38517(2014/C) (ex 2014/NN) – Implementation of Arbitral award Micula v Romania of 11 December 2013 – Invitation to submit comments pursuant to Article 108(2) of the Treaty on the Functioning of the European Union Text with EEA relevance' (2014) OJ C393/27 <https://eur-lex.europa.eu/legal-content/EN/TXT/?uri=uriserv:OJ.C_.2014.393.01.0027.01.ENG&toc=OJ:C:2014:393:TOC> accessed 29 November 2018.

62 Commission, 'State aid: Commission orders Romania to recover incompatible state aid granted in compensation for abolished investment aid scheme', Press Release IP/15/4725 (2015) <http://europa.eu/rapid/press-release_IP-15-4725_en.htm> accessed 29 November 2018.

the arbitral award as State aid under EU law.[63] As will be discussed further in Section B.3, *infra*, the matter is currently pending appeal before the CJEU.[64] The GCEU therefore may not have had the EU judiciary's final say upon the matter.

When Romania opposed a subsequent application by the foreign investors for enforcement of **12.28** the *Micula* award before the US District Court for the District of Columbia, the Commission once again appeared as *amicus curiae*. The District Court confirmed the award, largely on the basis of the GCEU ruling, and its judgment was subsequently affirmed by the Federal Court of Appeals for the District of Columbia Circuit.[65]

Secondly, in similar fashion, in November 2017, the Commission issued a decision finding **12.29** that the renewable energy reforms implemented by Spain in 2013 and 2014 were incompatible with EU law. It accordingly prohibited Spain from paying the awards that had been rendered against it by various investor-State tribunals in cases brought by investors from other Member States challenging those reforms. The Commission once again concluded that any payments made pursuant to awards rendered against Spain by an arbitral tribunal would constitute illegal State aid in violation of EU law.[66]

Between 2015 to 2017, beyond making *amicus curiae* submissions in various legal actions, the **12.30** Commission also initiated direct action itself by commencing infringement proceedings against Austria, the Netherlands, Romania, Slovakia and Sweden in June 2015, on account of their failure to terminate their intra-EU BITs.[67] As a result of the infringement proceedings brought against it by the Commission, Romania formally terminated all of its intra-EU BITs in March 2017.[68] Throughout this period, the European Commission consistently advanced a series of arguments in support of its position that intra-EU BITs were incompatible with EU law:

(1) First, the Commission invoked Articles 30 and 59 of the Vienna Convention on the Law of Treaties[69] for the proposition that the treaties of accession by which the Central and

---

63 Case Nos T-624/15, T-694/15, and T-704/15 *European Food SA and Others v European Commission* [2019] ECLI: EU:T:2019:423.

64 C-638/19 P, *Commission v European Food and Others* [Case in progress], <http://curia.europa.eu/juris/liste.jsf?num= C-638/19&language=en> accessed 16 February 2020.

65 See *Micula v Gov't of Romania*, 404 F. Supp. 3d 265 (D.D.C. 2019) and *Micula and others v Government of Romania*, No. 19-7127, slip op. at 1 (D.C. Cir. May 19, 2020).

66 Commission, 'State aid SA.40348 (2015/NN)—Spain Support for electricity generation from renewable energy sources, cogeneration and waste' C(2017) 7384 final <http://ec.europa.eu/competition/state_aid/cases/258770/258770_ 1945237_333_2.pdf>, paras 165–66:

> However, the Arbitration Tribunals are not competent to authorise the granting of State aid. That is an exclusive competence of the Commission. If they award compensation, such as in *Eiser v Spain*, or were to do so in the future, this compensation would be notifiable State aid pursuant to Article 108(3) TFEU and be subject to the standstill obligation. Finally, the Commission recalls that this Decision is part of Union law, and as such also binding on Arbitration Tribunals, where they apply Union law. The exclusive forum for challenging its validity are the European Courts.

67 Lucian Ilie, 'What is the Future of Intra-EU BITs?' (Kluwer Arbitration Blog, 21 January 2018) <http:// arbitrationblog.kluwerarbitration.com/2018/01/21/future-intra-eu-bits/> accessed 29 November 2018.

68 Ibid.

69 Vienna Convention on the Law of Treaties (adopted 23 May 1969, entered into force 27 January 1980) 1155 UNTS 331 (VCLT).

Eastern Europe States joined the TEU superseded the intra-EU BITs, all of which were entered into before they had acceded. As the BITs were at that point no longer valid, the tribunals constituted thereunder were, in the Commission's view, without jurisdiction to entertain the claims before them.

(2)   Second, arbitral tribunals in many cases stood, as in *Micula*,[70] to impose liability on Member States for withdrawing illegal State aids, despite the fact that EU law in fact required their withdrawal. According to the Commission, under the principle of supremacy of EU law, according to which EU law prevails over treaties concluded between Member States, Romania's obligations under EU State aid law took priority over its obligation under the Sweden-Romania BIT.[71]

(3)   Third, the Commission further asserted that the CJEU enjoys exclusive jurisdiction to rule on the interpretation and validity of EU law. While Member State courts may – and under some circumstances must – refer such issues to the CJEU via the EU's preliminary reference procedure, with the judgments rendered by the CJEU having binding effect in the ensuing national court proceedings, international arbitral tribunals may not do so. As a result, intra-EU BITs placed the uniformity and consistency of EU law in jeopardy.

(4)   Fourth, in support of its position, the Commission also invoked Article 344 TFEU, according to which 'Member States undertake not to submit a dispute concerning the interpretation of application of the Treaties to any other method of settlement than those provided for therein.' The Commission argued that this prohibition was not limited to disputes between Member States themselves.

(5)   Fifth, in addition, the Commission argued that the practical effect of an intra-EU BIT is to accord nationals of one Member State investing in another Member State more favorable treatment than investors from third Member States would enjoy, in violation of the EU law principle of non-discrimination laid down in Article 18 TFEU.

(6)   Sixth, importantly, the Commission buttressed its position on the ground that investment agreements were not needed within the EU single market, because EU law itself offered investors from one Member State protections in another Member State equivalent to those provided for by the BITs.[72] The means by which EU law might serve to protect intra-EU investments are inventoried in Section B.3, *infra*.

12.31   Although no international arbitral tribunal had endorsed the Commission's position, the views of the CJEU were, at the time, yet unknown. Eventually, however, the Court was called upon to speak, and it did so in the landmark decision of *Slovak Republic v Achmea BV*,[73] examined in the following section.

2. The *Achmea* judgment: The fate of arbitration clauses in intra-EU BITs

12.32   An ad hoc arbitral tribunal seated in Frankfurt and constituted under the UNCITRAL Arbitration Rules rendered an award in favour of Achmea, a Dutch investor, ordering Slovakia

---

70   *Micula v Romania* (n 60).

71   Commission, 'State aid SA 38517(2014/C) (ex 2014/NN) – Implementation of Arbitral award Micula v Romania of 11 December 2013.

72   Commission, 'Commission asks Member States to terminate their Intra-EU bilateral investment treaties', (Press Release IP/15/5198, 18 June 2015) <http://europa.eu/rapid/press-release_IP-15-5198_en.htm> accessed 29 November 2018.

73   *Achmea* (n 14).

to pay approximately 22.1 million euros in damages. Slovakia then filed a motion for annulment before the Higher Regional Court of Frankfurt.[74] The case went up to the German Federal Court of Justice, which eventually made a preliminary reference to the CJEU on the compatibility with EU law of the Netherlands-Slovakia BIT, and more particularly its provision for arbitration of intra-EU investment disputes.

While the Advocate-General concluded that the BIT was compatible in all respects with EU law, the CJEU decided otherwise, relying principally on Articles 344 and 267 TFEU.[75] **12.33**

As referenced in para 12.11 *infra*, the CJEU considered that the autonomy of EU law prescribed by Article 344 TFEU was impermissibly threatened by the inability of international arbitral tribunals to give interpretations of EU law, inasmuch as those tribunals are not courts or tribunals of a Member State within the meaning of Article 267,[76] and thus not able to refer questions of EU law to the CJEU.[77] The Court described the very limited review of arbitral awards by national courts – in this case the German courts – as insufficient to guarantee respect for EU law and its uniform interpretation by arbitral tribunals.[78] On these grounds, the CJEU concluded that the arbitration provision in Netherlands-Slovakia BIT, pursuant to which the *Achmea* award was rendered, was incompatible with EU law.[79] Upon receiving the CJEU's preliminary ruling, the German Federal Court of Justice proceeded to annul the *Achmea* award.[80] The Court specifically observed, however, that the investor might still resort to a Member State court on its claim against Slovakia.[81] **12.34**

Notwithstanding its condemnation of arbitration provisions in intra-EU BITs, the Court sought in *Achmea* to allay certain concerns surrounding it. First, the Court expressly distanced international investment arbitration from international commercial arbitration, remarking that the latter arises out of the freely expressed consent of the parties, whereas the former arises out of a treaty by which Member States removed access to national courts for the judicial remedies **12.35**

---

74 OLG Frankfurt am Main, AZ: 26 SchH 11/10.
75 *Achmea* (n 14):

> Arts. 267 and 344 TFEU must be interpreted as precluding a provision in an international agreement concluded between Member States, such as Art. 8 of the BIT, under which an investor from one of those Member States may, in the event of a dispute concerning investments in the other Member State, bring proceedings against the latter Member State before an arbitral tribunal whose jurisdiction that Member State has undertaken to accept.

76 Ibid., paras 32, 46.
77 Ibid., para 49.
78 Ibid., paras 53, 58, 59.
79 Ibid., paras 60, 63.
80 In doing so, the Court applied the German Civil Code, s 1059 (2) no 1 let a).
81 Bundesgerichtshof (German Federal Court of Justice), Decision of 31 October 2018 – I ZB 2/15, ECLI: DE:BGH:2018:311018BIZB2.15.0<http://juris.bundesgerichtshof.de/cgibin/rechtsprechung/document.py?Gericht=bgh&Art=en&sid=632d1a3c0f8c9b9a72c343835c1a371b&nr=89393&pos=0&anz=2> accessed 22 November 2018, para 72:

> Finally, the decision of the European Court of Justice of 6 March 2018 does not deny the defendant effective legal protection. The judgment of the European Court of Justice is based on the opinion that, with regard to the principle of mutual trust between the Member States concerning the recognition of the common values of the EU (Art 2 TEU) and the observance of EU law (...), the respondent can obtain effective legal protection before the courts of Slovakia as an investor.' [translated by the author]

prescribed by EU law.[82] It is not clear, however, why the inability of investor-State arbitral tribunals to make preliminary references to the CJEU is so problematic in terms of EU law autonomy, but the inability of international commercial arbitral tribunals to do so is not.

12.36 Second, the Court distinguished between intra-EU BITs, on the one hand, and international agreements entered into by the EU itself, on the other. According to the Court, in the latter circumstance, the EU is merely exercising its power to enter into international arrangements whereby it submits to the decisions of a court or tribunal established under such agreements. However, the courts or tribunals established under the EU's international investment agreements are also not courts or tribunals of a Member State, and they too will have occasion to opine on the interpretation or validity of EU law. The threat to EU law autonomy would therefore presumably still be present. Significantly, the Court added to its statement of approval of arbitration provisions in the EU's international investment agreements an important proviso, set out in paragraph 57, namely, that the EU's submission to the jurisdiction of such a court or tribunal could not be allowed to prejudice the autonomy of the EU legal order:

> It is true that, according to settled case-law of the Court, an international agreement providing for the establishment of a court responsible for the interpretation of its provisions and whose decisions are binding on the institutions, including the Court of Justice, is not in principle incompatible with EU law. The competence of the EU in the field of international relations and its capacity to conclude international agreements necessarily entail the power to submit to the decisions of a court which is created or designated by such agreements as regards the interpretation and application of their provisions, *provided that the autonomy of the EU and its legal order is respected.*[83]

12.37 The impact of the paragraph 57 proviso was clarified in the subsequent proceedings before the CJEU on CETA's compatibility with EU law discussed above, Opinion 1/17. In this Opinion, the CJEU concluded that CETA did not impair the autonomy of EU law,[84] in line with Advocate-General Bot's earlier opinion in the case, which had argued that such autonomy should not only be interpreted 'in such a way as to maintain specific characteristics of EU law,' but also 'to ensure the European Union's involvement in the development of international law and of a rules-based international legal order'.[85] At heart, the CJEU grounded its findings on the governing law provision in Article 8.31 CETA, which reads as follows:

1.   When rendering its decision, the Tribunal established under this Section shall apply this Agreement as interpreted in accordance with the Vienna Convention on the Law of Treaties [of 23 May 1969 (United Nations Treaty Series, Vol. 1155, p. 331; 'the Vienna Convention'], and other rules and principles of international law applicable between the Parties.

2.   The Tribunal shall not have jurisdiction to determine the legality of a measure, alleged to constitute a breach of this Agreement, under the domestic law of a Party. For greater certainty, in determining the consistency of a measure with this Agreement, the Tribunal may consider, as appropriate, the domestic law of a Party as a matter of fact. In doing so, the Tribunal shall follow the prevailing interpretation given to the domestic law by the

---

82   *Achmea* (n 14), para 55.
83   Ibid., para 57 (emphasis added).
84   Opinion 1/17 (n 12).
85   Opinion 1/17, Opinion of Advocate-General Bot (n 44), para 174.

courts or authorities of that Party and any meaning given to domestic law by the Tribunal shall not be binding upon the courts or the authorities of that Party.

3.   Where serious concerns arise as regards matters of interpretation that may affect investment, the Committee on Services and Investment may … recommend to the CETA Joint Committee the adoption of interpretations of this Agreement. An interpretation adopted by the CETA Joint Committee shall be binding on the Tribunal established under this Section. The CETA Joint Committee may decide that an interpretation shall have binding effect from a specific date.

Beyond assessing the envisaged ISDS mechanism's compatibility with the autonomy of the EU legal order, the Court also considered its compatibility with the general principle of equal treatment and the requirement of effectiveness of EU law as well as the right of access to an independent tribunal (to address all of Belgium's concerns). In its reasoning in Opinion 1/17, the Court did not draw on Article 344 TFEU, as this only applies to Member States ('Member States undertake not to …'), with no obligations for individuals, which foreign investors are. For several reasons, the Court found this mechanism to be compatible with all these respects of EU law. **12.38**

First, in assessing its compatibility with the autonomy of EU law, the CJEU clarified that the CETA Tribunals can stand outside the EU judicial system without breaching such autonomy. As set out in paragraph 12.10 *infra*, it reiterated that it was settled case law that 'an international agreement providing for the creation of a court responsible for the interpretation of its provisions and whose decisions are binding on the European Union, is, in principle, compatible with EU law',[86] which necessarily indicates that there ought to be certain safeguards to protect this. The CJEU declared that its own jurisdiction is not exclusive as far as international agreements are concerned and 'does not take precedence over either the jurisdiction of the courts and tribunals of the non-Member States with which those agreements were concluded or that of the international courts or tribunals that are established by such agreement.'[87] By so doing, the CJEU elected to treat international agreements as a part of the EU legal order separate from other rules of EU law; the jurisdiction granted to EU-affiliated courts and tribunals is only exclusive to EU law *senso strictu*, rather than international law. **12.39**

The CJEU have warned that such investment courts and tribunals could not have 'jurisdiction to issue awards finding that the treatment of a Canadian investor is incompatible with the CETA because of the level of protection of a public interest established by the EU institutions', as 'this could create a situation where, in order to avoid being repeatedly compelled by the CETA Tribunal to pay damages to the claimant investor, the achievement of that level of protection needs to be abandoned by the Union'.[88] The drafters of CETA, fortuitously, pre-empted this, by including a series of guarantees to ensure that the CJEU would remain the ultimate interpreter of EU law, even though CETA tribunals could not refer preliminary questions to it. Article 8.31(2) CETA bars CETA Tribunals from reviewing the legality of government measures under domestic law, instead CETA Tribunals apply only the **12.40**

---

86   Opinion 1/17 (n 12), para 106, citing Opinion 2/13, para 182, Opinion 1/91, paras 40 and 70, and Opinion 1/09, para 74.

87   Ibid., para 116.

88   Ibid., para 149.

CETA itself and international law, unlike the BIT in *Achmea* which invited tribunals to both interpret and apply EU law. Other safeguards include, inter alia, that the CETA Tribunals' jurisdiction is limited to matters of 'non-discriminatory treatment' and 'investment protection' (under Sections C and D of the Investment Chapter, respectively), as narrowly defined therein, to, amongst other things, exclude regulatory measures in the public interest), that they can at most award 'monetary compensation and any applicable interest' or the 'restitution of property' rather than invalidate EU or Member State acts, and that, as set out in Article 8.31(3), they will 'follow the prevailing interpretation given to domestic law by the courts or authorities of that Party,' treating EU and Member State law as fact not law.[89]

12.41 Moreover, CETA, by its own terms, lacks direct effect and its remedies ('monetary compensation and any applicable interest' or the 'restitution of property', as referenced above) do not supplant those available within the EU legal order, which would allow for preliminary references to the CJEU. In contrast, the CETA Tribunals are not able to make such references to the CJEU.

12.42 Second, turning then to the mechanism's compatibility with the general principle of equal treatment and requirement of effectiveness, the CJEU held that as the situation of Canadian investors investing within the EU is only comparable to EU investors investing in Canada, these are not 'situations that are comparable' to EU investors investing within the European Union.[90] The reason that Canadian investors have the possibility of relying on the provisions of CETA before a CETA Tribunal is that they are acting in their capacity as foreign investors.[91] On the requirement of effectiveness, the Court considered that the effectiveness of EU competition law would not be jeopardized by the CETA Tribunal's decisions (e.g., by awarding damages equivalent to the amount of fines imposed by the European Commission or a national competition authority), as 'EU law itself permits annulment of a fine when that fine is vitiated by a defect corresponding to that which could be identified by the CETA Tribunal'.[92]

12.43 Third, in assessing whether there was a right of access to an independent tribunal, the CJEU first observed that 'in the absence of rules designed to ensure that the CETA Tribunal and Appellate Tribunal are financially accessible to natural persons and small and medium-sized enterprises, the ISDS mechanism may, in practice, be accessible only to investors who have available to them significant financial resources', which would be inconsistent with the scope *ratione personae* of Section F, Chapter Eight CETA as well as the objective of free and fair trade, per Article 3(5) TEU.[93] However, Statement No 36 by the Commission and the Council on investment protection and the Investment Court System states that 'there will be better and easier access to this new court for the most vulnerable users, namely [small and medium-sized enterprises] and private individuals' and provides, to that end, that the 'adoption by the Joint Committee of additional rules … will be expedited so that these additional rules can be adopted as soon as possible' and that 'irrespective of the outcome of the discussions

---

89 Ibid., paras 21, 130 and 131.
90 Ibid., paras 179, 180.
91 Ibid., para 181.
92 Ibid., para 187.
93 Ibid., para 213.

within the Joint Committee, the Commission will propose appropriate measures of (co)-financing of actions of small and medium-sized enterprises before that Court'.[94] The CJEU was satisfied that these commitments would adequately address these concerns. Furthermore, the CJEU was of the view that there were sufficient safeguards in place to ensure the independence of the CETA Tribunals (regarding, inter alia, members' remuneration, appointment, removal, and the applicable rules of ethics), bearing in mind, that, as set out in Article 8.30.1 CETA, they 'shall not be affiliated with any government.'[95]

As the general reasoning of the CJEU applies far beyond CETA to any ISDS settlement **12.44** mechanism with third countries drafted in the same or similar style, these too withstand any charges of impinging upon the autonomy of the EU legal order. Under the provisions of CETA, CETA Tribunals are to interpret and apply only CETA itself and international law, unlike the BIT in *Achmea*, which invited tribunals to both interpret and apply EU law. Moreover, beyond this, the Court drew a dichotomy between CETA and the intra-EU BITs contemplated in *Achmea* on the basis of the principles of 'mutual trust' and 'sincere cooperation' between domestic courts within EU Member States, which, as a matter of EU law, are 'not applicable in relations between the Union and a non-Member State'.[96] In other words, while these principles governed intra-EU BITs, they did not apply to CETA, which involved Canada, a non-member State.

In a communication of July 19, 2018,[97] the Commission urged that the Member States draw **12.45** all necessary consequences from the *Achmea* judgment: National courts were under the obligation to annul inter-EU arbitral awards and to refuse their enforcement.[98] Furthermore, the Commission declared that the *Achmea* decision equally applies to the investor-State arbitration mechanism in Article 26 of the Energy Charter Treaty (ECT), regardless of the fact that the EU is also a signatory to the ECT.[99]

Accordingly, on January 15 and 16 2019,[100] the Member States jointly declared that investor- **12.46** State arbitration clauses between Member States are to be 'disapplied' and that all pending

---

94 Ibid., paras 8, 217; Council, 'Statement to be entered in Council Minutes-Statement by the Commission and the Council on investment protection and the Investment Court System (ICS)' [2017] OJ L11/20 <https://data.consilium.europa.eu/doc/document/ST-13463-2016-REV-1/en/pdf> accessed 20 February 2020.
95 Ibid., paras 238–243.
96 Ibid., para 129.
97 Commission, 'Communication from the Commission to the European Parliament and the Council – Protection of intra-EU investment' COM/2018/547 final <https://eur-lex.europa.eu/legal-content/EN/TXT/PDF/?uri=CELEX:52018DC0547&rid=8> accessed 10 February 2018.
98 Ibid., 3.
99 Ibid., 3,4.
100 Representatives of the Governments of the Member States of Belgium, Czech Republic, Germany, Ireland, Spain, Croatia, Cyprus, Bulgaria, Denmark, Estonia, Greece, France, Italy, Latvia, Lithuania, Austria, Portugal, Slovenia, Netherlands, Poland, Romania and United Kingdom, 'Declaration of Declaration of the Representatives of The Governments of The Member States, of 15 January 2019, on the legal consequences of the judgment of the Court of Justice In *Achmea* and on Investment Protection In The European Union' (January 2019) (Declaration) <https://ec.europa.eu/info/sites/info/files/business_economy_euro/banking_and_finance/documents/190117-bilateral-investment-treaties_en.pdf> accessed 10 February 2019; Representatives of the Governments of Finland, Luxembourg, Malta, Slovenia and Sweden, 'Declaration of the Representatives of the Governments of the Member States, of 16 January 2019, on the enforcement of the Judgment of the Court of Justice in Achmea and on Investment Protection in the

inter-EU investor-State arbitral proceedings shall be suspended, with no new proceedings initiated (the 2019 Declarations), though several Member States excluded these commitments as regards arbitration under the Energy Charter Treaty. Member States will also request their courts to set such arbitral awards aside or refuse their enforcement. However, awards already enforced or voluntarily complied with should not be challenged. The Member States also declared their intention to terminate all intra-EU BITs by December 6, 2020.[101] The Commission took this opportunity to reiterate that it would consider 'resuming or initiating infringement procedures' against Member States that do not terminate their intra-EU BITs.[102] On 28 October 2019, the Commission announced that Member States had reached agreement on a plurilateral treaty to terminate intra-EU BITs, which would pave the way towards a 'smooth and swift' ratification process.[103]

12.47 However, the Member States' declarations differ with regard to certain implications of the *Achmea* judgment, particularly in regard to the ECT. The Commission has regularly argued in ECT cases that there is a carve-out of intra-EU disputes from the coverage of the ECT, though it has been unsuccessful in doing so before all ECT tribunals that have addressed the matter.[104] In their declaration, the majority of the Member States declared that the *Achmea* ruling has the same implications for arbitration agreements founded on the ECT as for arbitration agreements founded on intra-EU BITs, and that any such agreements could not be given effect.[105] However, Finland, Hungary, Luxembourg, Malta, Slovenia, and Sweden maintained that the *Achmea* judgment is 'silent in the investor-state arbitration clause' in the ECT and that it would be inappropriate, absent a specific judgment, to infer its incompatibility with EU law.[106] Supporting that view is the fact that the ECT is an arrangement of which the EU itself is a member and that, the EU has thereby given its 'unconditional consent to the submission of a dispute to international arbitration,'[107] presumably including intra-EU disputes. Notably, in 2018, Spain asked the Svea Court of Appeal in Stockholm to seek a

---

European Union' (January 2019) (Second Declaration) <https://www.regeringen.se/48ee19/contentassets/d759689c0c804a9ea7af6b2de7320128/achmea-declaration.pdf> accessed 10 February 2019; Representative of the Government of Hungary, 'Declaration of the Representative of the Government of Hungary, of 16 January 2019, on the legal consequences of the Judgment of the Court of Justice in Achmea and on Investment Protection in the European Union' (January 2019) (Hungary Declaration) <http://www.kormany.hu/download/5/1b/81000/Hungarys%20Declaration%20on%20Achmea.pdf> accessed 10 February 2019.

101 Declaration (n 100), 5; Second Declaration (n 100), 5; Hungary Declaration (n 100), 3.
102 Ibid.
103 Commission, EU Member States agree on a plurilateral treaty to terminate bilateral investment treaties (Statement) (2019) <https://ec.europa.eu/info/sites/info/files/business_economy_euro/banking_and_finance/documents/191024-bilateral-investment-treaties_en.pdf> accessed 22 February 2020.
104 *Charanne BV and Construction Investments Sárl v Kingdom of Spain*, SCC Case No V 062/2012, Award, 21 January 2016, paras 444ff; *RREEF Infrastructure v Kingdom of Spain*, ICSID Case No ARB/13/30, Decision on Jurisdiction, 6 June 2016, paras 79 et. seq; *Eiser Infrastructure Ltd and Energia Solar Luxembourg Sarl v Kingdom of Spain*, ICSID Case No ARB/13/36; *Isolux Netherlands, BV v Kingdom of Spain*, SCC Case No V 2013/153, Final Award, paras 179ff; *Blusun SA, Jean-Pierre Lecorcier and Michael Stein v Italian Republic* (ICSID Case No ARB/14/3), Award, para 309.
105 Declaration (n 100), 3.
106 Second Declaration (n 100), 3; Hungary Declaration (n 100), 3.
107 Energy Charter Treaty (adopted 17 December 1994, entered into force 16 April 1998) 2080 UNTS 95 (ECT), art 26(3)(a).

preliminary ruling from the CJEU on the compatibility of the ECT with EU law.[108] However, in April 2019, the Swedish Court rejected this bid and refused a right to appeal against their decision.[109]

On 5 May 2020, the European Commission published the termination agreement for the **12.48** termination of intra-EU BITs, which was signed by 23 Member States,[110] though Austria, Finland, Ireland and Sweden are not listed as signatories to this treaty. Moreover, due to the exit of the United Kingdom from the EU on 31 January 2020, the UK also did not sign this treaty. Thus, the intra-EU BITs of those countries have not been terminated and continue to remain in force.

Moreover, it should be noted that the termination agreement explicitly states that it does not **12.49** apply to intra-EU ECT disputes. Instead, the EU and the Member States stated that this matter will be dealt with later.

3. Subsequent case law, in the wake of *Achmea*: The death of intra-EU BITs?

Shortly after the Member State declarations of January 2019, a Swedish court proceeded to **12.50** deny enforcement of the *Micula* award, despite its status as an ICSID award.[111] In doing so, it relied, not on *Achmea* as such, but on its obligation to demonstrate compliance with the Commission's ruling that payment of the *Micula* award would be incompatible with EU law and indeed constitute an illegal State aid in and of itself. As elaborated below,[112] the court justified its decision by reference to Article 54 of the Convention on the Settlement of Investment Disputes between States and Nationals of Other States (the ICSID Convention),[113] which requires Contracting States to enforce ICSID awards in the same manner in which they enforce judgments of their own State. The court found that, since a Swedish judgment in violation of EU law would likewise be denied enforcement, its refusal to enforce the *Micula* award comported with Article 54.

In a Swedish case the following month,[114] the court declined to annul an intra-EU award **12.51** issued in favour of a Luxembourg investor against Poland, but it did so on procedural grounds, namely that Poland had not raised the intra-EU objection before the tribunal on a timely basis.

---

108 Application of Spain to the Svea Court of Appeal to set aside the award rendered by the tribunal in *Novenergia II – Energy & Environment (SCA) (Grand Duchy of Luxembourg), SICAR v the Kingdom of Spain*, SCC Case No 2015/063. For a copy of the Final Arbitral Award made in Stockholm, Sweden on 15 February 2018, see, <https://www.italaw.com/sites/default/files/case-documents/italaw9715.pdf> accessed 20 February, 2020.

109 *Novenergia v Spain* (n 108).

110 Agreement for the Termination of Bilateral Investment Treaties between the Member States of the European Union (signed on 5 May 2020) <https://ec.europa.eu/info/sites/info/files/business_economy_euro/banking_and_finance/documents/200505-bilateral-investment-treaties-agreement_en.pdf> accessed 7 May 2020; Nikos Lavranos, 'Comment: When 23 EU member states terminate their intra EU BITs' (Borderlex, 6 May 2020) <https://borderlex.eu/2020/05/06/comment-when-23-eu-member-states-terminate-their-intra-eu-bits/> accessed 7 May 2020.

111 *Micula and others v Romania* (2019) Case Ä 2550-17 2019-01-23 (Nacka District Court).

112 *Poland v PL Holdings SARL*, Case Nos T 8538-17 & T 12033-17, Ruling of the Svea Court of Appeal, 22 February 2019.

113 Convention on the Settlement of Investment Disputes between States and Nationals of Other States (adopted 18 March 1965, entered into force 14 October 1966), 575 UNTS 159 (ICSID Convention).

114 *Poland v PL Holdings SARL* (n 112).

It did not decide whether *Achmea* would otherwise have compelled annulment. Interestingly though, the court rejected Poland's argument that its untimeliness should be excused due to *Achmea* allegedly having a public policy character. The Swedish appellate court made a preliminary reference to the CJEU on this very question and, as of this writing, that action is pending.

12.52 These decisions were prior to the GCEU's watershed decision in *Micula v Commission*, published a mere few months later in June 2019. As referenced in Section B.1, *supra*, in this latest development of the protracted saga, the GCEU annulled the European Commission's 2015 holding that Romania's payment of the *Micula* award would constitute illegal State aid within the meaning of Article 107 TFEU. The GCEU held that EU law should not be applied retrospectively to the pre-accession period, as the award recognized a right to compensation that the foreign investors had held before Romania acceded to the EU,[115] therefore rendering EU State aid rules inapplicable.[116] With regard to the intra-EU aspect of the applicable Sweden-Romania BIT, the General Court very briefly distinguished the facts before it from the *Achmea* judgment, ruling that 'the [*Micula*] arbitral tribunal was not bound to apply EU law to events occurring prior to the accession before it'.[117] This was in contrast to the *Achmea* tribunal, which was bound to apply EU law. As mentioned, the decision is currently pending appeal to the CJEU, which has yet to issue its opinion on the matter.

12.53 As briefly noted earlier in Section B.1, *infra*, Romania also appealed from the US District Court for the District of Columbia's decision of September 2019 to enforce the arbitral award in favour of the foreign investors against it.[118] The US District Court rejected Romania's and the Commission's reliance on the CJEU's *Achmea* judgment to argue that the Sweden-Romania BIT was an intra-EU BIT and, accordingly, invalid and unenforceable, leaving the US courts without the necessary subject matter jurisdiction under the US Foreign Sovereign Immunities Act of 1976. The Court, instead, held that Romania could not claim immunity before US Courts, as it had consented to the arbitration underlying the *Micula* award, by concluding the Sweden-Romania BIT, and relied on the GCEU's decision in the *Micula* saga (as summarized above) to distinguish *Achmea*. The US District Court also rejected Romania and the Commission's arguments on the applicability of the 'act of state' and 'foreign sovereign compulsions' under US law. In response to Romania's arguments that the foreign investors had never challenged the Commission's investigation into the legality of their alleged State aid, the US District Court was sufficiently persuaded by a declaration that the investors submitted (signed by a former GCEU judge), to the effect that neither the State aid investigation nor the subsequent injunction issued remained valid in view of the GCEU's most recent *Micula* decision; as Romania was not subject to EU law at the material time, the Commission had, in fact, lacked authority to take these preparatory steps in the first place. The US Court also dismissed Romania's claims that it had already fully paid the *Micula* award through a series of tax set-offs and executions that the foreign investors had initiated against various State-held

---

115   *European Food v Commission* (n 63), para 92.

116   Ibid., para 109

117   Ibid., para 87.

118   See *Ioan Micula, Viorel Micula, SC European Food SA, SC Starmill SRL and SC Multipack SRL v Romania*, ICSID Case No ARB/05/20, Memorandum Opinion of the United States District Court for the District of Colombia, 11 September 2019 <https://www.italaw.com/sites/default/files/case-documents/italaw10816.pdf> accessed 16 February 2020; Micula US Court Appeal (n 65).

accounts, observing that a substantial quantum of it remained outstanding. In May 2020, the Court of Appeals for the District of Columbia affirmed the district court ruling. While it addressed and rejected Romania's objections to certain procedural aspects of the lower court proceeding and judgment, it upheld without any discussion that court's ruling on subject matter jurisdiction, the effect of *Achmea*, the act of State and foreign sovereign compulsion. It simply said that the lower court's ruling was correct, and that its own judgment did not call for publication.[119]

While there have been reports that the Romanian government has elected to pay 912.5 million **12.54** lei (equivalent to approximately 200 million euros) to the investors to satisfy the *Micula* award,[120] the status of payment remains unclear – in any event, it appears that the appeals are still proceeding.

In that same year, ICSID tribunals also distinguished the *Achmea* judgment in two separate **12.55** arbitral awards, *United Utilities (Tallinn) B.V. v Republic of Estonia*[121] and *Magyar Farming Company Ltd v Hungary*,[122] which were decided in June and November 2019, respectively. Both tribunals held, in line with the '*kompetenz-kompetenz*' doctrine, that they had jurisdiction to decide the matters before them, irrespective of *Achmea*. They took the position that the *Achmea* judgment could not be used to restrict their authority under the applicable BITs, which should be analysed under public international law – rather than an exclusively EU lens, as the CJEU had done in *Achmea*.

In the first of these, *United Utilities v Estonia*, while the tribunal rejected all substantive claims **12.56** against Estonia (finding that there was no breach of the applicable fair and equitable treatment (FET) or non-impairment standards, or the umbrella clause under the Netherlands-Estonia BIT), it held that its jurisdiction 'arises from and is founded on the BIT and the ICSID Convention, as well as on the Parties' consent as required by these instruments,' and should therefore 'properly' be 'approached by analysing those agreements and the relevant facts from a public international law perspective,'[123] with reference to the VCLT. This was in contrast to the *Achmea* judgment, which viewed the issue solely through 'the lens of EU law'.[124] The tribunal distinguished *Achmea* on the basis that, first, the treaty applicable in *United Utilities* did not refer to domestic law, that, second, the *Achmea* judgment did not comment on the impact of instituting arbitral proceedings under the ICSID Convention, and that, third, Article 19 TEU arguably applies only to the extent that the interpretation and application of the EU treaties are required, and therefore the CJEU did not have exclusive authority over the matter at hand.[125] Moreover, absent the triggering of the suspension or termination processes

---

119 See *Micula and others v Government of Romania*, No. 19-7127, slip op. at 1 (D.C. Cir. May 19, 2020).

120 See Jack Ballantyne, 'Romania to pay out on Micula award?' (Global Arbitration Review, 16 December 2019) <https://globalarbitrationreview.com/article/1212205/romania-to-pay-out-on-micula-award> accessed 21 February 2020; Nicoleta Banila, 'Romanian gov to pay 912.5 mln lei (191 mln euro) as compensation in Micula state aid case', (SeeNews.com, 13 December 2019) <https://seenews.com/news/romanian-govt-to-pay-9125-mln-lei-191-mln-euro-as-compensation-in-micula-state-aid-case-680232> accessed 21 February 2020.

121 *United Utilities (Tallinn) BV and Aktsiaselts Tallinna Vesi v Republic of Estonia*, ICSID Case No ARB/14/24 Award, 21 June 2019.

122 *Magyar Farming Company Ltd, Kintyre Kft and Inicia Zrt v Hungary*, ICSID Case No ARB/17/27.

123 *United Utilities v Estonia* (n 121), para 532.

124 Ibid., para 539.

125 Ibid., para 540.

laid out in Article 65 VCLT, it could not be contended that the BIT terminated upon Estonia's accession to the EU.[126] The tribunal concluded that the BIT and TFEU did not share the 'same subject matter' or 'address the same rights and obligations,' primarily because 'the TFEU does not provide any mechanism for adjudicating disputes between EU Member States and foreign investors' – therefore, the BIT could continue to operate concurrently with the TFEU, notwithstanding the accession of Estonia to the EU.[127]

12.57   In the second, *Magyar Farming v Hungary*, prior to finding that Hungary had breached its BIT obligations by expropriating the claimant investors' investment without compensation, the ICSID tribunal also agreed that the validity of the applicable BIT must be assessed under international law.[128] It said that it was 'not convinced that it is bound by the [*Achmea* judgment] over the conflict between the BIT and the EU Treaties', as the ICSID Convention, Article 41, grants arbitral tribunals constituted thereunder '*kompetenz-kompetenz*'; on this view, an ICSID tribunal 'cannot abandon this mandate and blindly follow the determination of another adjudicatory body'.[129] It emphasized that, while the EU judiciary's authority extends to the interpretation and application of EU Treaties, it 'has no such (arguably) exclusive or ultimate mandate in respect of the interpretation of the BIT or the VCLT rules on treaty conflict'; indeed, in *Achmea*, the CJEU had not even purported to address whether the BIT and the EU Treaties governed the same subject matter as provided in Article 30 VCLT and, if so, whether there was a normative conflict between these treaties as understood under the VCLT.[130] The tribunal also held that, while the 2019 Declarations might arguably be viewed as a 'subsequent agreement between the parties regarding the interpretation of the treaty', as envisaged by Article 31(3)(a) VCLT, the investors had accepted Hungary's offer prior to *Achmea*.[131] Hence, according to ICSID Convention, Article 25, it was no longer open to Hungary to renege on this consent.[132] Beyond this, the 2019 Declarations were not the proper procedure to terminate or amend the BIT.[133] Finding, as the *United Utilities* tribunal did, that the BIT and the EU Treaties did not 'share the same subject matter',[134] the tribunal concluded that even if, *ex hypothesi*, they did, the presumption of non-conflict derives from the principle of harmonious interpretation of international law.[135] On this view, Articles 344 and 267 TFEU could be seen to carve out from the subject matter scope of Article 8 of the BIT potential investment disputes that also involve the 'interpretation or application of the [EU] Treaties' or 'interpretation of the [EU] Treaties, or the validity and interpretation of acts of the EU institutions', respectively.[136]

---

126   Ibid., para 538.
127   Ibid., paras 542–546.
128   *Magyar Farming v Hungary* (n 122), para 203.
129   Ibid., para 208.
130   Ibid., paras 209 and 210.
131   Ibid., para 217.
132   Ibid., para 217.
133   Ibid., paras 221ff.
134   Ibid., paras 228–238.
135   Ibid., para 240.
136   Ibid., paras 242–247.

4. Protection of intra-EU investment under EU law: Where do things stand?

If only because of the Commission's insistence that EU law provides adequate protection of **12.58** investments by a national of one Member State on the territory of another, it is pertinent to examine the actual scope of such protection and the means by which it can be secured. The reality of course is that there exists in EU law no single regime specifically designed for the protection of intra-EU investments, but rather a collection of disparate principles of general application. Even by the Commission's own admission, EU investors seeking protection of their investments in other Member States must avail themselves of the various general cross-border protections that EU law affords.

a. Investor protection under internal market principles

Investor protection within the EU is essentially predicated on a series of core general principles **12.59** of EU law, the most important of which are the free movement principles on which the internal market is built. Amongst those principles, free movement of capital and freedom of establishment figure most prominently.

i. Protection through free movement of capital

Cross-border investments within the EU cannot practically be effectuated in the absence of **12.60** free movement of capital.[137] The notion of 'capital movement' is not as such defined in the EU treaties. Directive 88/361/EEC does, however, provide a non-exclusive list of activities constituting capital movement.[138] Among the listed activities is direct investment, defined as the 'establishment and extension of branches or new undertakings belonging solely to the person providing the capital, and the acquisition in full of existing undertakings,' participation within 'new or existing undertaking with a view to establishing or maintaining lasting economic links,' reinvestment of profits, long term loans, investment in real estate 'dealing with or holding of shares, bonds or other financial instruments, insurances or even guarantees or securities provided'.[139] For its part, the CJEU considers that capital movement may take the form of a 'transfer of assets,' provided it entails a transfer of funds. However, that transfer cannot consist of mere 'payment'.[140] The CJEU has further held that investment is itself a distinctive purpose of capital movement.[141] It is commonly understood that direct investment entails the commitment of capital, the existence of a long-lasting link, and ordinarily a significant measure of managerial control of the undertaking by the provider of capital.[142]

---

137 Consolidated version of the Treaty on the Functioning of the European Union [2012] OJ C326/47 (TFEU), arts 63–66. Art 63(1) TFEU provides as follows: 'Within the framework of the provisions set out in this Chapter, all restrictions on the movement of capital between Member States and between Members States and third countries shall be prohibited'. See Steffen Hindelang and Niklas Maydell, 'The EU's Common Investment Policy – Connecting the Dots' in Marc Bungenberg, Joern Griebel and Steffen Hindelang (eds) *European Yearbook of International Economic Law – International Investment Law and EU Law* (Springer 2011) 1, 5–6.

138 Angelos Dimopoulos, *EU Foreign Investment Law* (OUP 2011) 37.

139 Nico Basener, *Investment Protection in the European Union* (Nomos Verlagsgesellschaft 2017) 119.

140 Joined Cases C-286/82 and C-26/83, *Graziana Luisi and Giuseppe Carbone v Ministero del Tesoro* [1984] ECR 377, para 21, 'payments are transfers of foreign exchange which constitute the consideration within the context of an underlying transaction, whilst movements of capital are financial operations essentially concerned with the investment of funds'.

141 Dimopoulos (n 138) 39.

142 Ibid., 38.

12.61   Free movement of capital does not only entail protection against measures based on national-ity,[143] but also protection against 'national measures [that] are liable to prevent or limit the acquisition of shares in the undertaking concerned or to deter investors of other Member States from investing their capital'.[144] However, restrictive Member State measures may be maintained if they are justified under Articles 64,[145] 65,[146] 66,[147] or 75[148] TFEU, though only on condition that they satisfy the principle of proportionality as outlined by the CJEU.[149] The CJEU employs a high level of scrutiny in assessing a Member State's reliance on any of these justifications.[150]

12.62   In January 2020, Advocate-General Campos Sánchez-Bordona delivered his Opinion in Case C-78/18 on the restrictions incorporated into a 2017 Hungarian law aimed at ensuring the transparency of financing that non-governmental organizations (NGOs) received from abroad.[151] Under this law, NGOs were required to register with the national authorities as 'organisations in receipt of support from abroad' if the amount of the donations they received from 'foreign provenance' in a given year reached a certain threshold. They were also expected to name donors whose support reached or exceeded HUF500,000 (approximately €1,500), stipulating the exact amount of the support. This information was to be published on a free, publicly accessible e-platform. The Commission had referred Hungary to the CJEU for failure to fulfil several obligations under EU law, including the principle of free movement of capital. The Advocate-General found this law to restrict the free movement of capital on the basis that it was capable of negatively affecting, first, the funding of associations and foundations established in Hungary which receive money from abroad (to which extent it also negatively affects the exercise of the freedom of association safeguarded by Art 12 EU Charter of Fundamental Rights), and, secondly, the rights to respect for private life and the protection of personal data (Arts 7 and 8 of the Charter) of those who make contributions from abroad to

---

143   Case C-367/98 *Commission of the European Communities v Portuguese Republic – Golden Shares* [2002] ECR I-4731, para 42. A Portuguese measure prohibiting the acquisition by investors from other Member States of more than a given number of shares in certain undertakings constitutes a discrimination based on nationality.

144   Ibid., paras 44, 47.

145   Art 64 (2) provides that 'the EU Parliament and the Council, acting in accordance with the ordinary legislative procedure, shall adopt the measures on the movement of capital to or from third countries involving direct investment ...'.

146   Art 65 enables Member States to 'apply the relevant provisions of their tax law', 'to take all requisite measures to prevent infringements of national law and regulations ... or to take measures which are justified on grounds of public policy or public security' provided that they do not 'constitute a means of arbitrary discrimination or a disguised restriction on the free movement of capital and payments'.

147   Art 66 enables the Council to take 'strictly necessary' measures 'with regard to third countries' in 'exceptional circumstances' when 'movements of capital to or from third countries cause, or threaten to cause serious difficulties for the operation of economic and monetary union'. Art 75 provides a special exception for restricting measures taken with regard to 'preventing and combating terrorism'.

148   Art 75 authorizes the Parliament and Council, in the interest of combating terrorism, to establish a framework for 'the freezing of funds, financial assets or economic gains belonging to, or owned or held by, natural or legal persons, groups or non-State entities'.

149   See e.g., Case C-423/98 *Alfredo Albore (Reference for a preliminary ruling: Corte d'appello di Napoli – Italy)* [2000] ECR I-5965, paras 21–22.

150   Case C-120/78 *Rewe–Zentral AG v Bundesmonopolverwaltung für Branntwein* [1979] ECR 649, para 8; Case C-54/99 *Association Eglise de la Scientologie de Paris* 2000 ECR I-01335, para 17.

151   Case C-78/18 *European Commission v Hungary (Transparency of Associations)* [2020] ECLI:EU:C:2020:1, Opinion of Advocate-General Campos Sánchez-Bordona.

the civil society organizations concerned.[152] While the CJEU has yet to express its views on the matter, it would appear that, at least for now, any measures aimed at promoting transparency (vis-à-vis foreign investments or otherwise) must have limits – insofar as these conflict with the free movement of capital and other associated rights, they may be invalidated. Decisions such as this confirm the potential for the principle of free movement of capital to afford protection to intra-EU investments.

Closely associated with free movement of capital is free movement of payment. Article 63(2) **12.63** TFEU guarantees the freedom of investors from one Member State to make payments or transfer currencies to another Member State. The CJEU has broadly defined a payment as 'consideration for a transaction'.[153] This freedom obviously enables investors to make cross-border payments to pay for expenses arising out of their investment. As with other freedoms, any measure restricting this freedom must be justified by the State in accordance with the proportionality principle.

ii. Protection through freedom of establishment

Freedom of establishment, under Article 49 TFEU, guarantees the right of individuals or legal **12.64** entities from one Member State to 'establish' their activity on the territory of another Member State. For the CJEU, an 'establishment' may be any activity entailing 'actual pursuit of an economic activity through a fixed establishment in another Member State for an indefinite period',[154] a formulation sufficiently broad to encompass the vast majority of investments.[155] Requirements of stability and duration serve to distinguish freedom of establishment from free movement of services.[156] The freedom extends both to individuals who are nationals of a Member State, regardless of domicile, and to 'companies or firms formed in accordance with the laws of a Member State and having their registered office, central administration or principal place of business in the Union'.[157]

Rules governing the right to establish and manage undertakings are not harmonized at the EU **12.65** level, leaving Member States largely free to determine the requirements for incorporation of local companies.[158] At the same time, the free establishment principle imposes an obligation on Member States to allow enterprises established in another Member State to set up agencies, branches or subsidiaries on its territory and accord them full rights.[159]

---

152 Ibid., para 115.
153 Joined Cases C-286/82 and C-26/83 *Luisi and Carbone* (n 140), para 21.
154 Case C-221/89, *The Queen v Secretary of State for Transport, ex parte Factortame Ltd and others (Reference for a preliminary ruling: High Court of Justice, Queen's Bench Division – United Kingdom)* [1991] ECR I-03905, para 20.
155 Basener (n 139) 112.
156 Friedl Weiss and Clemens Kaupa, *European Union Internal Market Law* (CUP 2014) 201; Catherine Barnard, *The Substantive Law of the EU: The Four Freedoms* (OUP 2016) 382.
157 TFEU (n 137), Art 54.
158 Weiss and Kaupa (n 156), 220; Case 81/87 *The Queen v HM Treasury and Commissioners of Inland Revenue, ex parte Daily Mail and General Trust plc (Reference for a preliminary ruling: High Court of Justice, Queen's Bench Division – United Kingdom)* [1988] ECR 05483, para 19.
159 Weiss and Kaupa (n 156) 220, 223; Case C-212/97 *Centros Ltd v Erhvervs- og Selskabsstyrelsen (Reference for a preliminary ruling: Højesteret – Denmark)* [1999] ECR I-01459, para 17.

12.66 Freedom of establishment within the EU also prohibits direct or indirect discrimination based on nationality[160] as well as non-discriminatory measures liable to 'hinder or render less attractive the exercise of fundamental freedoms guaranteed by the Treaty'.[161] Such measures would potentially include virtually any domestic regulatory measure.[162] However, States may justify such measures on grounds of public policy, public security or public health,[163] provided they are proportionate to the objective sought to be achieved.[164]

12.67 Clearly, overlaps may arise between the free movement of capital and freedom of establishment in connection with direct investments, such as when a State measure affects the acquisition of shares. Because non-EU nationals are entitled to invoke free movement of capital, but not freedom of establishment, the characterization of the measure may be decisive for them.[165] Under CJEU case law, the principles governing freedom of establishment prevail when the acquisition of shares gives a shareholder definite influence over a company's management decisions.[166] On the other hand, investments that do not give that level of control fall under the free movement of capital principle.

iii. Ancillary protection under EU law

12.68 Although free movement of capital and freedom of establishment are the main pillars of intra-EU investment protection within the EU legal order, a number of other EU law principles may also come into play to supplement that protection.

Free movement of goods

12.69 Investors within the EU may invoke, in connection with their investments in another Member State, Articles 34 and 35 TFEU, which prohibit quantitative restrictions, as well as measures having an equivalent effect, on cross-border imports and exports between Member States. For example, a foreign investor may argue that a measure taken by the host State to which it is exporting goods in connection with its investment is *de facto* hindering its export activity.[167] Protection may be had against both distinctly applicable measures (i.e., measures that on their face distinguish between nationals of the enacting State and nationals of other Member

---

160 *Centros*, ibid., para 28.

161 Case C-55/94 *Reinhard Gebhard v Consiglio dell'Ordine degli Avvocati e Procuratori di Milano (Reference for a preliminary ruling: Consiglio Nazionale Forense – Italy)* [1995] ECR I-4165, para 37.

162 Anna de Luca, 'The Legal Framework for Foreign Investments in the EU' in Leon Trackman and Nicola Ranieri (eds), *Regionalism in International Investment Law* (OUP 2013) 120, 125.

163 TFEU (n 137), Art 52.

164 See e.g., in Case C-442/02, *CaixaBank France v Ministère de l'Économie, des Finances et de l'Industrie (Reference for a preliminary ruling: Conseil d'État – France)* [2004] ECR I-8961, para 21 for a proportionate measure protecting consumers. See generally, Basener (n 139), 116.

165 de Luca (n 162), 139.

166 Case C-196/04 *Cadbury Schweppes plc and Cadbury Schweppes Overseas Ltd v Commissioners of Inland Revenue (Reference for a preliminary ruling: Special Commissioners of Income Tax, London – United Kingdom)* [2006] ECR I-7995, para 31.

167 Case C-393/92 *Municipality of Almelo and others v NV Energiebedrijf Ijsselmij (Reference for a preliminary ruling: Gerechtshof Arnhem – Netherlands)* 1994 ECR I-1477, para 28 (goods are products that 'can be valued in money' and that 'are capable, as such, of forming the subject of commercial transactions'); Case C-8/74 *Procureur du Roi v Benoît and Gustave Dassonville. Reference for a preliminary ruling: Tribunal de première instance de Bruxelles – Belgium* [1974] ECR 837, measures that ban certain imports or that are 'capable of hindering, directly or indirectly, actually or potentially, intra-community trade' fall under the scope of Arts 34 and 35.

States)[168] and indistinctly applicable measures (i.e., measures that do not).[169] Measures that would otherwise run afoul of Articles 34 or 35 may, however, be justified under Article 36 TFEU if they are adopted to serve a legitimate public policy purpose, are not used as a means of protectionism, and meet the requirements of proportionality. In the leading case, announcing what has become known as the '*Cassis de Dijon*' doctrine, the CJEU ruled that even indistinctly applicable measures may only be justified if they serve mandatory requirements that 'relat[e] in particular to the effectiveness of fiscal supervision, the protection of public health, the fairness of commercial transactions and the defence of the consumer' and comport with the principle of proportionality.[170]

Depending on the nature of an investment, free movement of goods may be critical to the investment's operations and thereby its success. **12.70**

Free movement of services

Investors established in one Member State may also invoke the free movement of services in support of their right to provide services in, or avail themselves of services from, another Member State in connection with an investment. Unlike freedom of establishment, free movement of services may be asserted by investors who are not established in the host State and entitled to invoke freedom of establishment.[171] The scope of the protection afforded by free movement of services, as well as the exceptions to that principle, are broadly comparable to those applicable to the free movement of goods. Clearly, an investment may be highly dependent on the availability of cross-border services, much as they may be dependent on cross-border movement of goods. **12.71**

Non-discrimination

National treatment, which is a cardinal feature of foreign investment protection, is also a central principle of internal market EU law. Article 18 TFEU provides simply that '[w]ithin the scope of application of the Treaties, and without prejudice to any special provisions contained therein, any discrimination on grounds of nationality shall be prohibited'. CJEU case law requires an objective justification for treating 'comparable situations' differently,[172] and considers undertakings to be in 'comparable situations' if their products or services are substitutes, compete with one another, or otherwise find themselves in 'fairly comparable circumstances'.[173] In these circumstances, disparate treatment must be justified by a legitimate interest and satisfy the requirements of proportionality.[174] **12.72**

---

168 See, e.g., *Commission of the European Communities v Ireland* (Failure to fulfil an obligation – Measures heaving an effect equivalent to quantitative restrictions) [1981] ECR 01625, an Irish measure that prohibited the sale of imported souvenir products unless they had an indication of their country of origin or the word 'foreign' clearly differentiated between domestic and foreign products.

169 *Rewe–Zentral AG* (n 150).

170 Ibid., paras 12–13, the Court rejected the justification based on the protection of the public health.

171 Weiss and Kaupa (n 156) 250–51.

172 Case C-303/05 *Advocaten voor de Wereld VZW v Leden van de Ministerraad (Reference for a preliminary ruling: Arbitragehof – Belgium)* [2007] ECR I-3633, para 56.

173 Case C-127/07 *Société Arcelor Atlantique et Lorraine and Others v Premier ministre, Ministre de l'Écologie et du Développement durable and Ministre de l'Économie, des Finances et de l'Industrie (Reference for a preliminary ruling: Conseil d'État – France)* [2008] ECR I-9895, para 36.

174 Basener (n 139), 445.

General principles of law

12.73 There exist, above and beyond specific articles of the TFEU, certain so-called general principles of law, i.e., unwritten norms of a general character articulated in CJEU case law. General principles of law are applicable to all measures taken by Member States within the sphere of EU law.

12.74 Several general principles of law strongly resonate with principles that are either stated in or deduced from the protections generally set forth in BITs and other international agreements on foreign investment. These norms, all of which relate in some way to the rule of law, include notably the principles of legal certainty, proportionality, legitimate expectations, access to justice and adequacy of legal remedies.[175] Even the vocabulary in which these norms are cast are echoed across the board in investor-State awards.

12.75 To give the protection of legitimate expectations as an example, in the *Hauer* case, the CJEU held that 'any economic operator ... to whom an institution has given justified assurances may rely on the principle of the protection of legitimate expectations' if those assurances are not respected, and in the case of *CNTA v Commission*,[176] it held that the Commission had violated the legitimate expectations of 'traders' by abolishing a compensatory program without providing any transitional period.[177] However, the CJEU, like investor-State tribunals,[178] has reiterated that economic actors cannot legitimately expect that the regulatory framework under which they operate will not be altered over time, especially 'in an area such as that of the common organization of the markets, the objective of which involves constant adjustments to reflect changes in economic circumstances'.[179] The CJEU has also clearly announced that investors cannot rely on commitments by public officials if they are unlawful, unless the investor acted in good faith and could not have reasonably foreseen that the measure on which it based its expectations was unlawful.[180]

---

175   See e.g., TEU (n 1), Art 19 and Charter of Fundamental Rights of the European Union [2000] OJ C364/01 (ChFR), Art 47. See generally Teis Tonsgaard and Steffen Hindelang, 'The Day After: Alternatives to Intra-EU BITs' (2016) 17(6) *Journal of World Investment and Trade* 984, 994–5 (each time that the EU or Member States apply EU law, they have to respect those principles).

176   Case C-74/74 *Comptoir national technique agricole (CNTA) SA v Commission of the European Communities* [1975] ECR 533, paras 42–44.

177   See generally Basener (n 139), 459 (2017).

178   See e.g., tribunals in *Parkerings-Compagniet AS v Republic of Lithuania*, ICSID Case No ARB/05/8, Award, 11 September 2007, para 332: 'As a matter of fact, any businessman or investor knows that laws will evolve over time. ... Lithuania gave no specific assurance or guarantee to Parkerings that no modification of law, with possible incidence on the investment, would occur'; *Sergei Paushok, CJSC Golden East Company and CJSC Vostokneftegaz Company v The Government of Mongolia*, UNCITRAL, Award on Jurisdiction and Liability, 28 April 2011, paras 226ff; *EDF (Services) Ltd v Romania*, ICSID Case No ARB/05/13, Award, 8 October 2009, para 177; *Link-Trading Joint Stock Company v Department for Customs Control of the Republic of Moldova*, UNCITRAL, Award on Jurisdiction, 16 February 2001; *Gami Investments, Inc v The Government of the United Mexican States*, UNCITRAL, Final Award, 15 November 2004, para 114; *Glamis Gold, Ltd v The United States of America*, UNCITRAL; *Continental Casualty Company v The Argentine Republic*, ICSID Case No ARB/03/9, Award, 8 June 2009, paras 623ff; *Total SA v The Argentine Republic*, ICSID Case No ARB/04/01, Decision on Liability, 27 December 2010, para 309; *El Paso Energy International Company v The Argentine Republic*, ICSID Case No. ARB/03/15, Award, 31 October 2011, paras 358ff.

179   Joined Cases C-37/02 and C-38/02 *Di Lenardo Adriano Srl and Dilexport Srl v Ministero del Commercio con l'Estero (Reference for a preliminary ruling: Tribunale amministrativo regionale per il Veneto – Italy)* [2004] ECR I-6911, para 70.

180   Basener (n 139), 460.

Legal remedies under EU law

Unlike intra-EU BITs, which provide, among other avenues, investor-State arbitration as a   **12.76**
dispute resolution mechanism, EU law presumes that if a Member State investor seeks relief
from violations of law committed by a Member State in which it invested, it will (absent a valid
choice of forum or arbitration clause in a contract with the State) do so in domestic courts,[181]
most likely, however, in the very courts of the host State. When enforcing EU law, national
courts must comply with the minimum procedural standards established by CJEU case law. In
the interest of preserving the consistency and uniformity of EU law, national courts may, and
at the highest levels of the national judiciary must, make a preliminary reference to the CJEU
for an interpretation of EU law as needed.[182]

Where the challenged measure was taken by an EU rather than a Member State institution,   **12.77**
the investor may proceed directly to the CJEU, naming the relevant EU institution as
defendant, to establish one of the grounds on which the Court may annul an EU measure,
namely 'lack of competence, infringement of an essential procedural requirement, infringement
of the Treaties or of any rule of law relating to their application, or misuse of powers'.[183]
Importantly, however, the rules of standing applicable to direct actions by private parties in the
Court are very strict. Thus, EU investors may proceed directly in the CJEU only if the
challenged measure was 'addressed to that person, … is of direct and individual concern to
them, [or is] a regulatory act which is of direct concern to them and does not entail
implementing measure.[184] Any such action is subject to a two-month limitations period.[185]
Investors may also seek damages from the EU[186] or a Member State,[187] as the case may be.
Lastly, the Commission itself can bring an infringement action against a State,[188] which may
result in an order addressed to the State to rectify the situation and, in exceptional cases,
imposition of a fine. An investor may conceivably derive benefit from any such order.

b. Investment protection under the EU Charter of Fundamental Rights

The EU Charter of Fundamental Rights (ChFR) confers on Member State nationals certain   **12.78**
rights that may serve to promote and protect their investment in another Member State,
though to some extent its protections mirror principles contained in the principles set out
above. For example, Article 20 ChFR echoes the prohibition in Article 18 TFEU of
discrimination on the basis of nationality. Article 20 ChFR, however, extends its protection
against nationality to all persons, not only EU nationals.

---

181   TEU (n 1), art 19(1).
182   Ibid., Art 267 (3).
183   Ibid., Art 263(2).
184   Ibid., Art 263(4).
185   Ibid., Art 236(6).
186   Ibid., Art 340(2).
187   Joined Cases C-6/90 and C-9/90 *Andrea Francovich and Danila Bonifaci and others v Italian Republic. References for a preliminary ruling: Pretura di Vicenza and Pretura di Bassano del Grappa – Italy* [1991] ECR I-5357.
188   TFEU (n 137), Art 258. See e.g., Case C-416/17 *European Commission v French Republic* [2018] ECLI:EU:C:2018:811 (condemnation of France for a breach of Art 267(3) for the failure of the French Conseil d'Etat to make a necessary preliminary reference).

12.79 Subject to the obligations set out in the Charter are not only the institutions of the EU, but also the institutions of the Member States whenever they 'implement EU law'.[189] Most salient in this regard are Articles 15, 16, and 17 ChFR, protecting, respectively, the freedom to choose an occupation and engage in work, the freedom to conduct a business in accordance with EU and national laws, and the right to own, use, or dispose of lawfully acquired property (including intellectual property), as well as the right not to be deprived of one's property except in the public interest and in accordance with the conditions, such as fair compensation, provided for by law. The CJEU has given these principles a broad interpretation.[190]

12.80 Of these rights, the ones most potentially relevant to protection of an EU national's investment in another Member State are those established by Articles 16 and 17. Article 16 entitles individuals and enterprises, including of course investors, to initiate and conduct a business activity, without undue interference.[191] The CJEU held that it even protects a business against measures imposing undue and unfair costs.[192] Again, restrictions are capable of being justified, this time under Art. 52(1) ChFR, provided the measure is based on EU or Member State law, was enacted to achieve a legitimate public interest, and respects the principle of proportionality.[193]

12.81 Of no less potential relevance to cross-border investment activity is Article 17 ChFR which establishes the right to protection of private property, a right that is obviously an essential aspect of investment protection. (Art 17 ChFR interestingly contains no nationality requirement and can therefore also be invoked by a non-EU investor in the EU.) According to the CJEU, the notion of 'property' encompasses 'rights with an asset value creating an established legal position under the legal system, enabling the holder to exercise those rights autonomously and for his benefit'.[194] Shares in a company obviously constitute 'property',[195] though market position, market opportunity and economic activity as such do not.[196] The latter may, however, derive protection from Article 16 ChFR. Article 17 ChFR must, however, be read in conjunction with Article 375 TFEU which entitles Member States to establish their own property ownership system.[197]

12.82 Property protection under Article 17 ChFR, as interpreted by the CJEU, includes protection against both direct and indirect expropriation, and more generally against illegitimate or disproportionate interferences with the use of property.[198] A State lawfully expropriates, whether directly or indirectly, if it acts in the public interest and on a precise legal basis, if the

---

189 ChFR (n 175), Art 51.

190 Basener (n 139), 125–6.

191 See e.g., Case C-280/93, *Federal Republic of Germany v Council of the European Union* [1994] ECR I-4973, para 80, referring to the market position of banana importers in Germany.

192 Case C-283/11, *Sky Österreich GmbH v Österreichischer Rundfunk (Request for a preliminary ruling from the Bundeskommunikationssenat)* [2013] ECLI:EU:C:2013:28, paras 45 ff.

193 Ibid., para 50.

194 Ibid., para 34.

195 Basener (n 139), 424.

196 Ibid., para 426.

197 Case C-309/96, *Daniele Annibaldi v Sindaco del Comune di Guidonia and Presidente Regione Lazio (Reference for a preliminary ruling: Pretura circondariale di Roma – Italy)* [1997] ECR I-7493, para 93.

198 Case C-483/99, *Commission of the European Communities v French Republic* 2002 ECR I-4781, para 44.

measure is proportionate, and if the property owner is afforded adequate and timely compensation. For the CJEU, a direct expropriation must entail a transfer of title.[199] To constitute an indirect expropriation, a measure must produce effects that, due to the severity of its interference with property rights and the impact on the use, possession or disposal of property, may be regarded as the equivalent of a direct expropriation.[200] The threshold for finding an indirect expropriation under EU law is high.[201] The CJEU has, for instance, held that a state measure prohibiting the use of a certain terminology for the description of kinds of Italian wines did not qualify as an 'indirect expropriation.'[202] The general contours of protection from expropriation under the ChFR are not dissimilar from the protections that foreign investors enjoy under international investment agreements.

5. Does EU law offer sufficient protection to investors?

Whether EU law, as just outlined, offers sufficient protection to investors from one EU **12.83** Member State in another EU Member State is a much-debated question. There is undoubtedly a resemblance between the standards of protection under ISDS and under EU law. However, there remains scepticism that the EU law standards are as protective of investors as the ISDS standards.[203] One cited difference is that the EU law standards are subject to a broad public interest exception, which may more readily allow measures to be justified.[204] There may well also be differences in practice, with investor-State arbitrators seen as interpreting and applying protective standards somewhat more expansively. This may be especially the case with indirect expropriation, for which the CJEU would appear to adopt a higher threshold than most arbitral tribunals do.[205] On other doctrinal fronts, such as protection of legitimate expectations, differences between arbitral and CJEU jurisprudence are less visible.[206]

On the other hand, EU law may present certain advantages. With the CJEU on the top of the **12.84** judicial hierarchy, and armed with preliminary ruling jurisdiction, the likelihood of consistency in analysis and outcome is considerable. Indeed, lack of consistency is one of the major criticisms currently levelled at ISDS, with creation of a genuine appellate mechanism being

---

199   Joined Cases C-20/00 and C-64/00 *Booker Aquacultur Ltd and Hydro Seafood GSP Ltd v The Scottish Ministers (Reference for a preliminary ruling: Court of Session (Scotland) – United Kingdom)* 2003 ECR I-7411, paras 80, 81.

200   Basener (n 139); See e.g., Case C-44/79 *Liselotte Hauer v Land Rheinland-Pfalz (Reference for a preliminary ruling: Verwaltungsgericht Neustadt an der Weinstraße – Germany)* 1979 ECR I-3727, para 19, which requires that the property rights are rendered 'totally valueless' and considering that arbitral tribunals are less strict and ask only for a 'substantial interference' with the property rights.

201   *Booker Aquacultur* (n 199), para 85: 'full or partial compensation can be appropriate in certain circumstances but there is no general principle requirement compensation to be paid in all circumstances'; Case C-347/03 *Regione autonoma Friuli-Venezia Giulia and Agenzia regionale per lo sviluppo rurale (ERSA) v Ministero delle Politiche Agricole e Forestali (Reference for a preliminary ruling: Tribunale amministrativo regionale del Lazio – Italy)* [2003] ECR I-7411, para 123: 'the lack of any compensation for the dispossessed wine producers ... does not in itself constitute a circumstance demonstrating incompatibility between the prohibition at issue ... and the right to property'.

202   *ERSA*, ibid., para 123.

203   Strik (n 51), 194.

204   Mavluda Sattorova, 'Investor Rights under EU Law and International Investment Law' (2016) *Journal of World Investment and Trade* 899.

205   Tonsgaard and Hindelang (n 175).

206   *Parkerings v Lithuania* (n 178); *CMS Gas Transmission Company v Republic of Argentina*, ICSID Case No ARB/01/08, Award, 12 May 2005.

taken very seriously as a remedy. Lastly, on certain less-central issues – such as free movement of the factors of production – protection under EU law may even surpass that afforded by the intra-EU BITs.

12.85   Still, EU law lacks a distinct investor protection regime. Protection of EU investors within the EU is at present implemented within a very general EU law framework of protection against government action consisting of pieces of EU primary and secondary law, along with the domestic law of the Member States.[207] In recognition of this, there is already afoot a move at the EU level to improve the clarity, uniformity and accessibility of the standards of investor protection under EU law. With a view to strengthening its position that EU law provides foreign investors from other Member States comparable protections, the Commission in July 2018, issued guidance to enable EU investors to invoke their rights before national adminis-trations and courts and to assist the Member States in affording investment protection in compliance with EU law.[208]

12.86   A significant difference between the two systems is of course the central role of international arbitration in ISDS as compared to reliance on national court systems within the EU, and in host States in particular. As will become clear below, there is much debate over the strengths and weaknesses – and the overall appropriateness – of international arbitration as a dispute resolution mechanism in the foreign investment arena. All in all, it is quite difficult to determine whether there is a deficit of protection under EU law. There is not even consensus over whether, in order to meet the comparability test, EU law standards must be as fully protective of investors as ISDS standards or need be only sufficiently protective.

6.   Possible future scenarios: Where might we be going?

12.87   The EU's growing hostility to ISDS inevitably raises the question of alternatives. Reform is very much on the mind both of the EU and its Member States. In April 2016, Austria, Finland, France, Germany and the Netherlands issued a so-called 'Non-Paper',[209] proposing a single agreement among the Member States to phase out all existing intra-EU BITs, while putting in place a unified investment protection regime within the EU.[210] As concerns substantive protection, the Non-Paper contemplates precise EU-level regulations, reaffirming a Member State's right to regulate and guaranteeing protection subject to FET, full protection and security, and compensation in case of expropriation.[211] Regarding procedural protection, the Non-Paper acknowledges that investment disputes should be primarily subject to Member

---

207   Tonsgaard and Hindelang (n 175).

208   Commission, 'Commission provides guidance on protection of cross-border EU investments' (Press Release IP/18/4528, 19 July 2018) <http://europa.eu/rapid/press-release_IP-18-4528_en.htm> accessed 29 November 2018.

209   Non-paper from Austria, Finland, France, Germany and the Netherlands (7 April 2016), available at: <https://www.tni.org/files/article-downloads/intra-eu-bits2-18-05_0.pdf> accessed 24 May 2020 ('Non-Paper').

210   Ibid., paras 3, 4.

211   Ibid., para 8; cf. Nikos Lavranos, 'After Achmea: The Need for an EU Investment Protection Regulation' (Kluwer Arbitration Blog, 17 March 2018) <http://arbitrationblog.kluwerarbitration.com/2018/03/17/achmea-need-eu-investment-protection-regulation/> accessed 29 November 2018. For a contrary view, see Marcin Orecki, 'Foreign Investments in Poland in Light of the Achmea Case and "Reform" of Polish Judicial System – Catch 22 Situation?' (Kluwer Arbitration Blog, 22 April 2018) <http://arbitrationblog.kluwerarbitration.com/2018/04/22/foreign-investments-poland-light-achmea-case-reform-polish-judicial-system-catch-22-situation/> accessed 28 November 2018.

States' domestic courts, subject to the EU's existing preliminary reference system.[212] In addition, the Non-Paper advocates a greater use of investor-State mediation.[213]

At the same time, the Non-Paper acknowledges the shortcomings that exist among Member State judicial systems. It reports that they 'can give rise to concern in terms of length of proceedings, quality of the judiciary and the perception of judicial independence'.[214] Among the remedies considered are: (a) use of the provision in Article 273 TFEU for submission to the CJEU of disputes between Member States; (b) creation of a settlement mechanism similar to the Unified Patent Court; and (c) referral of disputes for decision to the Permanent Court of Arbitration.[215] The latter two options would, however, have implications for the autonomy of the EU legal order to which the CJEU in its *Achmea* judgment attached such importance. Ultimately, however, the proposals in the Non-Paper have not as yet been pursued by the EU institutions. **12.88**

An alternative would be to maintain the intra-EU BITs but reserve their enforcement exclusively to the national courts within the EU. This is precisely what the German Federal Court in effect suggested in its judgment following the CJEU's ruling in *Achmea*. The court there emphasized that the *Achmea* judgment did not condemn the Slovakia-Netherlands BIT as such, but only its arbitration provision: **12.89**

> Finally, the decision of the European Court of Justice of 6 March 2018 does not deny the defendant effective legal protection. … [Achmea] can obtain effective legal protection before the courts of Slovakia as an investor.[216]

The Member State court alternative has certain drawbacks. There is obviously residual concern that host State domestic courts may be biased in favour of their own State. Proceedings would also necessarily be conducted in accordance with the civil procedure norms of the forum State, which may or may not be adaptive. Moreover, there is a real likelihood that national courts would interpret and apply common intra-EU BIT provisions differently, leading to disparate levels of investor protection of EU investors from Member State to Member State. The EU institutions did not rally to this approach either, the Commission energetically pursuing termination of all intra-EU BITs. As noted, termination of all intra-EU BITs is, for the EU, the way forward. **12.90**

---

212 Non-Paper (n 209), para 9.
213 Ibid., para 10.
214 Ibid., para 11.
215 Ibid., para 12.
216 Bundesgerichtshof (German Federal Court of Justice), Decision I ZB 2/15 (n 81), para 72:

> Schließlich wird der Antragsgegnerin durch die Entscheidung des Gerichtshofs der Europäischen Union vom 6. März 2018 nicht effektiver Rechtsschutz verwehrt. Das Urteil des Gerichtshofs ist von der Auffassung getragen, im Hinblick auf den Grundsatz des gegenseitigen Vertrauens zwischen den Mitgliedstaaten hinsichtlich der Anerkennung der gemeinsamen Werte der Union (Art. 2 EUV) und der Beachtung des Unionsrechts (…) könne die Antragsgegnerin als Investorin effektiven Rechtsschutz vor den Gerichten der Slowakei erhalten. Eine Aberkennung materieller Ansprüche der Antragsgegnerin ist mit der Entscheidung des Gerichtshofs und der sich darauf ergebenden Aufhebung des Schiedsspruchs im Streitfall nicht verbunden. Der Antragsgegnerin wird infolge der Aufhebung des Schiedsspruchs auch keine Vermögensposition entzogen.

12.91 Some attention has also been given to methods of amicable dispute settlement. The level of receptiveness to amicable dispute resolution among Member States is uneven. Most Member States that provide mediation services of one kind or another place them on a fully voluntary basis and limit them to commercial and civil matters. Only a few, among them Spain, Luxembourg and Poland, provide mediation in administrative proceedings.[217] The Netherlands and Estonia provide general mediation services for disputes arising in the field of public law.[218] Other Member States, such as Hungary, explicitly exclude mediation in administrative law matters.[219]

12.92 At the EU level, a 'Mediation Directive,' providing for enforcement of settlement agreements in cross-border disputes, is confined to civil and commercial matters and considered as inapplicable to investor-State disputes.[220] Two 'Remedies Directives' are limited in application to disputes over the award of concession contracts and public procurement.[221]

12.93 The Commission is not, however, oblivious to the potential of mediation as a dispute settlement mechanism in the foreign investment arena.[222] In 2017, it launched what it called an Inception Impact Assessment for the prevention and amicable resolution of investment disputes within the single market, setting out its preliminary thinking on the matter and inviting feedback.[223] In that document, the Commission contemplated four possible scenarios: (1) creation of so-called 'Investment Contact Points' between national administrations to assist investors to avoid the escalation of disputes with the relevant host State authority; (2) establishment of an EU legal framework for mediation between investors and the relevant national authorities having a minimum level of quality and transparency; (3) setting up permanent mediation agencies in each Member State that administer mediations or conduct mediations themselves; and (4) development of an EU-wide mediation service that would likewise either administer mediations or conduct mediations themselves.[224] A distinct advantage of any such solution is that, the results of mediation not being binding, it would in principle pose no threat to the autonomy of the EU legal order, as the Commission and the CJEU conceive of it. As will be discussed *infra*, the Commission on 11 October 2019

---

217 For the Member States framework regarding mediation see European Commission, e-Justice portal, available at: <https://e-justice.europa.eu/content_mediation_in_member_states-64-en.do> accessed 22 November 2018.

218 Ibid.

219 Ibid.

220 Directive 2008/52/EC of the European Parliament and of the Council of 21 May 2008 on certain aspects of mediation in civil and commercial matters [2008] OJ L136/3, Art 2 (1).

221 Council Directive 92/13/EEC of 25 February 1992 coordinating the laws, regulations and administrative provisions relating to the application of Community rules on the procurement procedures of entities operating in the water, energy, transport and telecommunications sectors [1992] OJ L76/14; Council Directive 89/665/EEC of 21 December 1989 on the coordination of the laws, regulations and administrative provisions relating to the application of review procedures to the award of public supply and public works contracts [1989] OJ L395/33, as amended by Directive 2014/23/EU of the European Parliament and of the Council of 26 February 2014 on the award of concession contracts Text with EEA relevance [2014] OJ L94/1 and Directive 2007/66/EC of the European Parliament and of the Council of 11 December 2007 amending Council Directives 89/665/EEC and 92/13/EEC with regard to improving the effectiveness of review procedures concerning the award of public contracts (Text with EEA relevance) OJ L335/31.

222 Commission, 'Inception Impact Assessment-Prevention and amicable resolution of investment disputes within the single market' (2017) Ref. Ares (2017) 3735364, 3.

223 Ibid.

224 Ibid.

submitted a proposal on rules for the mediation of investment disputes,[225] 'an area which traditional investment agreements have largely overlooked',[226] for the EU Council and Member States to approve, before it is put before Canada to consider in the relevant CETA Committees. Mediation has its obvious strengths, most notably in respect of costs and formality, though it does not of course guarantee a settlement outcome. It would not in any case supplant adjudicatory-style mechanisms altogether. It can be counted on at best to supplement them.

C. EXTRA-EU INVESTMENT LAW AND POLICY

With the Lisbon Treaty's extension of the common commercial policy to foreign investment, **12.94** the EU is shaping itself into a foreign investment law and policy bloc, much as the way it operates in the international trade arena. Prior to the Lisbon Treaty's entry into force, the conclusion of international investment agreements with third countries remained within the competence of the Member States. Due to the great number of BITs concluded between individual Member States and third countries, and the differences among them, there developed not only 'an uneven playing field for EU companies investing abroad',[227] but also an uneven playing field for foreign nationals investing in Europe. The movement to a largely unified regime would naturally entail the ultimate termination not only of the Member States' intra-EU BITs, but of their extra-EU BITs as well.[228]

1. EU policy and practice in international investment agreements

Under the EU's exclusive competence in the field of FDI, subject to delegation of authority to **12.95** the Member States, it is the EU that, going forward, will negotiate and enter into investment treaties with third countries. Through its unparalleled consolidation of bargaining power in the field, the EU will necessarily be a formidable player. Based on 2019 reports, the FDI stock of the EU represented the equivalent of 53.9 per cent of the EU GDP for inbound investment and 61.4 per cent for outbound investment, representing in turn roughly one-third of the worldwide FDI stock.[229] Interestingly, it is not European business that pressed for a unified

---

225 Commission, 'Proposal for a Council Decision on the position to be taken on behalf of the European Union in the Committee on Services and Investment established under the Comprehensive Economic and Trade Agreement (CETA) between Canada, of the one part, and the European Union and its Member States, of the other part as regards the adoption of rules for mediation for use by disputing parties in investment disputes' COM/2019/460 final (Commission Proposal on CETA Mediation Rules).

226 Commission, 'Commission presents procedural proposals for the Investment Court System in CETA' (11 October 2019) (News Archive) <https://trade.ec.europa.eu/doclib/press/index.cfm?id=2070> accessed 22 February 2020 (Commission Proposals for the CETA ICS).

227 Commission, 'Communication from The Commission to The Council, The European Parliament, The European Economic and Social Committee and The Committee of the Regions Towards a Comprehensive European International Investment Policy' COM (2010) 343 final, 5.

228 Alison Ross, 'Achmea: Where Do We Stand Now?', 13 *Global Arbitration Review* 12, 17.

229 See United Nations Conference on Trade and Development (UNCTAD), 'World Investment Report 2019, Country fact sheet: Developed economies' <https://unctad.org/Sections/dite_dir/docs/WIR2019/wir19_fs_dvd_en.pdf> accessed 21 February 2020.

foreign investment policy at the EU level,[230] but rather the Commission, acting as 'policy entrepreneur … to extend Union competences even in the face of Member State opposition'.[231]

a. The EU framework of foreign investment protection

12.96 Activity of the EU in foreign investment protection policy is at a relatively early stage, but coming into focus.

12.97 Under EU law, the EU's entry into international investment agreements is subject to the ordinary legislative procedure, as set out in Article 218(6)(a)(v) TFEU. Conclusion of any such agreement accordingly requires not only Council, but also Parliamentary assent.[232] Well aware of its role, the European Parliament is taking a keen interest in investment agreement negotiations,[233] and even before the Lisbon Treaty entered into force began claiming access to negotiation documents.[234] The procedural path to the conclusion of EU-IIAs is therefore characterized by the interplay among Commission, Council and Parliament, with EU policy shaped by this dialogue. With a view to enhancing transparency and inclusiveness in treaty negotiations, the Commission in late 2017 also published a proposal for the establishment of an Advisory Group on EU Trade Agreements.[235]

12.98 In late 2018, the Parliament, Commission and Council reached an agreement to establish a body analogous to the Committee on Foreign Investment in the United States (CFIUS) charged with reviewing certain foreign investment transactions to determine their effect on national security.[236] In March 2019, Regulation 2019/452, which establishes a framework for the screening of foreign direct investments into the EU (the FDI Regulation), was published.[237] This instrument applies to transactions from 11 October 2020.[238] This marks the first time that foreign direct investment will be regulated at the EU level. Unlike reviews by the CFIUS, the FDI Regulation does not establish a central screening mechanism or require Member States that do not have such a mechanism to implement one, and subjects such mechanisms to considerations of 'security or public order'.[239] Where, however, Member States

---

230 Johann Basedow, 'The European Union's New International Investment Policy: Product of Commission Entrepreneurship or Business Lobbying?' (2016) 21 *European Foreign Affairs Review* 469, 491.

231 Ibid.

232 See also Catharine Titi, 'International Investment Law and the European Union: Towards a New Generation of International Investment Agreements' (2015) 26 *EJIL* 639, 646.

233 Catherine Titi, 'A stronger role for the European Parliament in the design of the EU's investment policy as a legitimacy safeguard' (2017) 209 *Columbia FDI Perspectives* – Perspectives on topical foreign direct investment issues 1, 1–2.

234 European Parliament resolution of 24 April 2008 on the free trade agreement between the EC and the Gulf Cooperation Council (2009/C 259 E/15) [2008] OJ C259 E/83, para 27.

235 See Commission, 'State of the Union 2017 – Trade Package: Commission unveils initiatives for a balanced and progressive trade policy' (Press Release IP/17/3182, 14 September 2017) <https://trade.ec.europa.eu/doclib/press/index.cfm?id=1715&title=State-of-the-Union-2017-Trade-Package-Commission-unveils-initiatives-for-a-balanced-and-progressive-trade-policy> accessed 24 May 2020.

236 European Parliament, 'Agreement reached on screening of foreign direct investment for EU security' <http://www.europarl.europa.eu/news/en/press-room/20181120IPR19506/agreement-reached-on-screening-of-foreign-direct-investment-for-eu-security> accessed 26 November 2018.

237 Regulation (EU) 2019/452 of the European Parliament and of the Council of 19 March 2019 establishing a framework for the screening of foreign direct investments into the Union (PE/72/2018/REV/1) [2019] OJ L79I/1.

238 Ibid., Art 17.

239 A 'screening mechanism' is defined as 'an instrument of general application, such as a law or regulation, and accompanying administrative requirements, implementing rules or guidelines, setting out the terms, conditions and

have existing screening mechanisms in place, these must include the necessary measures to identify and prevent circumvention.[240] Moreover, new or existing Member State's screening mechanisms must also be transparent and non-discriminatory.[241] The final decision on such screening rests with the Member States, which remain sovereign in this area. Prior to this, while nearly half of the EU Member States already had such a mechanism in place, they differed greatly in scope and procedure.[242] This most recent initiative must be understood against the backdrop of the substantial growth of Chinese FDI inflows over recent years.[243] In light of this, even especially investment-friendly countries such as Germany have revised their policies.[244] It is with respect to China that the trade-off between openness to investment and national security (as well as human rights and environmental protection concerns) is most acute.[245] China has its own national security review system that pre-dates many of the European ones.[246] To date, the EU-China framework is governed by numerous BITs and an outdated bilateral agreement,[247] and replacing them will be a major exercise.

i. Treaty-making: Negotiation and ratification

Unlike other major actors in the foreign investment law arena, the EU does not as yet have a **12.99** Model BIT. Its agreements, whether in the form of a bilateral investment treaty or an investor chapter within a free trade agreement, are individually negotiated. Under general EU practice,[248] for any prospective international treaty, the Commission requests of the Council a negotiating mandate, under which the Commission conducts its negotiations with third countries. It is pursuant to a Council negotiation mandate that the Commission conducted its negotiations with Singapore, Canada, and other countries. It is also pursuant to a Council negotiation mandate that negotiations have begun in contemplation of a convention establishing a multilateral court for the settlement of investment disputes.[249]

---

procedures to assess, investigate, authorise, condition, prohibit or unwind foreign direct investments on grounds of security or public order', see ibid., Art. 2(4); see also ibid., Art 1(1).

240 Ibid., Art 3(6).

241 Ibid., Art 3(2).

242 Commission, Proposal for a Regulation of the European Parliament and of the Council establishing a framework for screening of foreign direct investments into the European Union COM (2017) 487 final, 2–3.

243 Thilo Hanemann and Mikko Huotari, 'Record Flows and Global Imbalances – Chinese Investment in Europe in 2016' (Merics Paper on China Update No 3 January 2017, Mercator Institute for China Studies) 4 <http://rhg.com/wp-content/uploads/2017/01/RHG_Merics_COFDI_EU_2016.pdf> accessed 26 November 2018.

244 European Council on Foreign Relations, Germany's turnabout on Chinese takeovers <https://www.ecfr.eu/Art./commentary_germanys_turnabout_on_chinese_takeovers_7251> accessed 26 November 2018.

245 See Commission, 'European Commission services' Position Paper on the Sustainability Impact Assessment in support of negotiations of an Investment Agreement between the European Union and the People's Republic of China' (May 2018), 6–7 <http://trade.ec.europa.eu/doclib/docs/2018/may/tradoc_156863.pdf> accessed 26 November 2018.

246 Cathleen Hartge, 'China's National Security Review: Motivations and the Implications for Investors' (2013) 49 *Stanford Journal of International Law* 239, 242.

247 Wenhua Shan and Sheng Zhan, 'The Potential EU-China BIT: Issues and Implications' in Bungenberg, August Reinisch, Christian Tietje (eds), *EU and investment agreements: Open Questions and Remaining Challenges* (Nomos 2013) 87, 99.

248 TFEU (n 137), Art 218.2 provides: 'The Council shall authorise the opening of negotiations, adopt negotiating directives, authorise the signing of agreements and conclude them.'

249 Council, 'Negotiating directives for a Convention establishing a multilateral court for the settlement of investment disputes' (12981/17 ADD 1 DCL 1, 2018), footnote 1 <http://data.consilium.europa.eu/doc/document/ST-12981-2017-ADD-1-DCL-1/en/pdf> accessed 29 November 2018.

12.100   The EU wasted little time in exercising its exclusive competence in connection with extra-EU investment agreements. Initially, two very ambitious agreements – one with Canada in the CETA and the other with the US in the Transatlantic Trade and Investment Partnership (TTIP) – attracted especially great interest and public scrutiny. Negotiations over a series of other bilateral arrangements were also launched.[250]

ii.   The residual role of the Member States

12.101   Even after the Lisbon Treaty, EU Member States retain a significant role in the realm of international investment agreements, defined with some specificity in an EU regulation establishing transitional arrangements for Member State BITs with third countries.[251] The Regulation imposes certain reporting requirements on the Member States.[252] With respect to existing BITs, Member States must report to the Commission all such agreements with third countries signed before December 1, 2009, or the date of their accession, that they wish to maintain in force or enter into force. Any such BITs with a third country may be maintained in force or enter into force until such time as the EU enters into an investment agreement with that country. However, the Commission has the right to assess whether any of those BITs or their provisions 'constitute a serious obstacle to the negotiation or conclusion by the Union of bilateral investment agreements with third countries'.[253] If the Commission finds that one or more of the provisions of such a BIT constitutes such an obstacle, consultations between the Commission and the Member State must take place,[254] following which the Commission may instruct the State as to the steps to be taken.[255] A Member State's failure to report or failure to take the required actions could trigger the Commission's infringement action procedure.[256]

12.102   The ground rules are broadly similar for extra-EU BITs entered into by a Member State between December 1, 2009 and the date of entry into force of the Regulation. In order for those BITs to be maintained, the Commission must find that their maintenance would not conflict with EU law or the EU's external relations objectives, that the Commission does not itself intend to open negotiations with the third country concerned, and that maintenance of the Member State BIT would not prejudice the EU's negotiation or conclusion of bilateral

---

250   Currently, agreements with the following countries are in place: Albania, Algeria, Andorra, Armenia, Bosnia and Herzegovina, Botswana, Chile, Egypt, Eswatini, Faroe Islands, Georgia, Iceland, Israel, Japan, Jordan, Kosovo, Lebanon, Liechtenstein, Lesotho, Macedonia, Mexico, Moldova, Montenegro, Morocco, Mozambique, Namibia, Norway, Palestinian Authorities, San Marino, Serbia, South Africa, South Korea, Switzerland, Syria, Tunisia, Turkey. Agreements with the following countries are partly in place: Antigua and Barbuda, Armenia, Bahamas, Barbados, Belize, Botswana, Cameroon, Canada, Colombia, Côte d'Ivoire, Comoros, Costa Rica, Cuba, Dominica, Dominican Republic, Ecuador, El Salvador, Ethiopia, Fiji, Ghana, Grenada, Guatemala, Guyana, Honduras, Iraq, Jamaica, Kazakhstan, Madagascar, Mauritius, Namibia, Nicaragua, Panama, Papua New Guinea, Peru, Samoa, Seychelles, South Africa, St. Kitts and Nevis, St. Lucia, St. Vincent and the Grenadines, Sudan, Suriname, Trinidad and Tobago, Ukraine, Zambia and Zimbabwe.
            Many more agreements are either pending, being updated or negotiated. For a complete list of Agreements including their current status and full text, please see Commission, 'Negotiations and Agreements' <http://ec.europa.eu/trade/policy/countries-and-regions/negotiations-and-agreements/> accessed 14 February 2019.
251   Regulation (EU) No 1219/2012 of the European Parliament (n 48).
252   Dimopoulos (n 138).
253   Regulation (EU) No 1219/2012 of the European Parliament (n 48), Art 5.
254   Ibid., Art 6(2).
255   Ibid., Art 6(3).
256   Frank Hoffmeister and Günes Ünüvar, 'From BITs and Pieces Towards European Investment Agreements' in Bungenberg, August Reinisch, Christian Tietje (n 247) 57, 70–71.

investment agreements with third countries.[257] If these conditions are met, maintenance of the agreements is authorized,[258] but absent authorization, the Member State 'shall not take any further steps towards the conclusion of such an agreement, and shall withdraw or reverse those steps which have been taken'.[259]

More remarkable is the possibility under the Regulation for Member States, despite the **12.103** exclusivity of the EU's competence under the Lisbon Treaty, to enter into new BITs with third countries going forward. A State that wishes to enter into negotiations with a third country, either to amend an existing agreement or to conclude a new one, must notify the Commission of its intentions in writing, providing all relevant documentation.[260] The Commission is expected to grant the State authorization to do so unless it concludes that doing so would conflict with EU law or fail to comport with the EU's external relations objectives, that the Commission itself intends to open negotiations with the third country concerned, or that the State's initiative would prejudice the EU's negotiation or conclusion of bilateral investment agreements with third countries.[261] However, the Commission may make its authorization dependent on the Member State's inclusion in or removal from any prospective agreement clauses that the Commission deems necessary for compliance with EU law or policy.[262] Finally, the Regulation entitles the Commission to participate in any such negotiations.[263]

Assuming that, following negotiations, a Member State intends to proceed to sign an **12.104** investment agreement with a third country, the Commission once again has a role to play. At this stage, the Commission makes a further assessment so as to satisfy itself that the agreement, as reached, neither fails to comply with EU law or policy nor prejudices the EU's own negotiation of international investment agreements. Absent a finding to that effect, authorization of the Member State to enter into the agreement is granted.[264]

The conduct of Member States under the Regulation varies widely. Some States continue **12.105** individually negotiating new extra-EU BITs with third countries, with the authorization of the Commission.[265] Malta, the Czech Republic and the Netherlands have taken the position that extra-EU BITs of Member States will remain in place and enforceable on a complementary basis as long as the EU fails to provide an equally high protection standard under its

---

257 Regulation (EU) No 1219/2012 of the European Parliament (n 48), Art 12(1), (2).
258 Ibid., Art 12(3).
259 Ibid., Art 12(5).
260 Ibid., Art 8.
261 Ibid., Art 9(1).
262 Ibid., Art 9(2)
263 Ibid., Art 10.
264 Ibid., Art 11(3), (4). For a critique of this approach see Nikos Lavranos, 'In Defence of Member States' BITs Gold Standard: The Regulation 1219/2012 Establishing a Transitional Regime for existing Extra-EU BITs – A Member States' Perspective' (2013)10(2) *Transnational Dispute Management*. See also August Reinisch, 'The EU on the Investment Path – Quo Vadis Europe? The Future of EU BITs and other Investment Agreements' (2014) 12(1) *Santa Clara Journal of International Law* 111,120; Juliane Kokott and Christoph Sobotta, 'Investment Arbitration and EU Law' (2016) 18 *Cambridge Yearbook of European Legal Studies* 3, 16.
265 For example, just within the last three years the following extra-EU BITs were concluded by Member States: Lithuania-Turkey BIT (signed in 2018), Ukraine-Turkey BIT (signed in 2017), Slovakia-United Arab Emirates BIT (signed in 2017, entered into force in 2018), Austria-Kyrgyzstan BIT (signed in 2016), Slovakia-Iran BIT (signed in 2016 and entered into force in 2017), Hungary-Cambodia BIT (signed in 2016). For further extra-EU BITs see: <http://investmentpolicyhub.unctad.org/IIA/AdvancedSearchBITResults> accessed 26 November 2018.

investment agreements. On the other hand, France and Greece support the view taken by the CJEU in its Opinion 2/15 to the effect that Member States must abstain from an investment agreement once the EU has started negotiating with the respective third state.[266]

12.106   The EU's exclusive competence under Article 207(1) TFEU is further complicated with respect to portfolio investments.[267] Since that competence by its terms is limited to direct investment, Member States presumably retain competence in connection with portfolio investments, and most BITs currently in force do in fact cover both forms of investment. Mixed agreements may on this account continue to play a central role.

12.107   A further regulation, EU Regulation No 912/2014, lays down principles for the allocation of liability between the EU and a Member State in consideration of their respective roles in taking the measure that an investment tribunal may have condemned.[268] This financial responsibility regulation (FRR) applies to any ISDS proceedings conducted under agreements to which the EU is a party. As investment agreements at the EU level could still, arguably, be described as in their nascency, mixed agreements providing for shared competencies between the EU and Member States therefore raise a number of unanswered liability issues. Under the FRR, both financial responsibility and respondent status are generally allocated to the entity responsible for the treatment that gives rise to compensation. The FRR also lay down procedures for Member States and the Commission to enter into arrangement to pay the costs of such proceedings, to ensure that the resources of the EU are not, even temporarily, unduly burdened, and establishes procedures and requirements for settling cases when this would be in the best interests of the EU. Throughout the various stages of a dispute, the Commission has information duties vis-à-vis the European Parliament and Council and the Member States have reporting and consulting obligations vis-à-vis the Commission. In November 2019, the Commission issued a Report to the European Parliament and Council on the operation of this regulation.[269]

b.   EU foreign investment protection standards

12.108   Understandably, the Commission has also turned its attention to standards of foreign investor protection. In 2013, the Commission officially called for clearer and better standards,[270] and the Council's 2013 mandate for the CETA negotiations called for maintaining 'the highest

---

266   José Luís da Cruz Vilaça and others (eds), 'The external dimension of the EU policies: horizontal issues; trade and investment; immigration and asylum' (Congress Proceedings Volume 3, XXVIII FIDE Congress, Lisbon/Estoril, 23–26 May 2018), 118; Opinion 2/15 (n 16).

267   Titi (n 232) 641; see also Hoffmeister and Ünüvar (n 256) 66.

268   Regulation (EU) 912/2014 of the European Parliament and of the Council establishing a framework for managing financial responsibility linked to investor-to-state dispute settlement tribunals established by international agreements to which the European Union is party [2014] OJ L257/121.

269   Commission, 'Report from the Commission to the European Parliament and the Council on the operation of Regulation (EU) No 912/2014 on the financial responsibility linked to investor-to-state dispute settlement under international agreements to which the European Union is party' COM(2019)597/F1 <https://ec.europa.eu/transparency/regdoc/rep/1/2019/EN/COM-2019-597-F1-EN-MAIN-PART-1.PDF> accessed 21 February 2020.

270   Commission, 'Fact Sheet – Investment Protection and Investor-to-State Dispute Settlement in EU Agreements', (November 2013) <https://www.italaw.com/sites/default/files/archive/Investment%20Protection%20and%20Investor-to-State%20Dispute%20Settlement%20in%20EU%20agreements_0.pdf> accessed 14 February 2019.

standards of protection'.[271] The EU has committed to clarifying the level of protection for investors by setting out 'precisely what elements are covered' under the FET standard pursuant to its agreements.[272] The current proposal for a Deep and Comprehensive Free Trade Agreement (DCFTA) between the EU and Tunisia, for instance, defines the 'obligation to grant [FET]' by 'an exhaustive list of fundamental rights, such as access to justice'.[273] The best indication of the EU's attitudes toward foreign investment protection, and the standards for ensuring protection, consists of the agreements into which the EU has entered pursuant to its authority under the Lisbon Treaty.

Taking the CETA,[274] by way of example, one sees how the EU has introduced certain limitations on investment protection as compared to then-prevailing standards.[275] **12.109**

From a substantive point of view, the key changes include: (a) limiting the bases on which a Contracting State may deny market access to nationals of the other State[276] or impose performance requirements;[277] (b) specific recognition of a State's right to regulate;[278] (c) limitation of the right to FET to a list of specific guarantees;[279] (d) confining 'full protection and security' to physical treatment;[280] (e) narrowing of the concept of 'legitimate expectations' **12.110**

---

271 Commission, 'Recommendation for a Council Decision authorizing the Opening of Negotiations on a Comprehensive Trade and Investment Agreement, called the Transatlantic Trade and Investment Partnership, between the European Union and the United States of America' COM (2013) 136 final.

272 Commission, Fact Sheet on ISDS (n 270), 2.

273 Commission, 'The European Union's Proposal for an Investment Protection Agreement – Explanatory Note' (January 2019), 2 <http://trade.ec.europa.eu/doclib/docs/2019/january/tradoc_157647.%2020190124%20-%20Factsheet%20on%20Investment%20Protection%20Agreement%20-%20EN.pdf> accessed 14 February 2019.

274 Comprehensive Economic and Trade Agreement (CETA) between Canada, of the one part, and the European Union and its Member States, of the other part [2017] OJ L11/23.

275 August Reinisch, 'The European Union and Investor-State Dispute Settlement: From Investor-State Dispute Arbitration to a Permanent Investment Court' (2016) CIGI Investor-State Arbitration Series Paper No 2, 14; see also Titi (n 232) 654–7.

276 Comprehensive Economic and Trade Agreement (CETA) between Canada, of the one part, and the European Union and its Member States, of the other part [2017] OJ L11/23, Art 8.4.

277 Ibid., Art 8.5.

278 Ibid., Art 8.9(1):

> For the purpose of this Chapter, the Parties reaffirm their right to regulate within their territories to achieve legitimate policy objectives, such as the protection of public health, safety, the environment or public morals, social or consumer protection or the promotion and protection of cultural diversity.

Moreover, Art 8.9(2) states:

> For greater certainty, the mere fact that a Party regulates, including through a modification to its laws, in a manner which negatively affects an investment or interferes with an investor's expectations, including its expectations of profits, does not amount to a breach of an obligation under this Section.

279 Ibid., Art 8.10(2). A State denies an investor FET if it commits:

> (a) denial of justice in criminal, civil or administrative proceedings;
> (b) fundamental breach of due process, including a fundamental breach of transparency, in judicial and administrative proceedings;
> (c) manifest arbitrariness;
> (d) targeted discrimination on manifestly wrongful grounds, such as gender, race or religious belief;
> (e) abusive treatment of investors, such as coercion, duress and harassment; or
> (f) a breach of any further elements of the fair and equitable treatment obligation adopted by the Parties … in accordance with paragraph 3 of this Article.

280 Ibid., Art 8.4.

to situations in which a specific promise or representation is made by the State;[281] and (f) reformulating in some detail the standard of indirect expropriation, requiring proof by an investor of substantial deprivation of its investment and specifying the factors to be taken into account in making a determination.[282] The Contracting States, borrowing from NAFTA, have reserved the right to issue authoritative treaty interpretations as a 'safety valve.'[283]

12.111 More generally, the EU consistently emphasizes in its negotiations respect for 'broader European values',[284] which are understood to include labour, consumer, environmental and social protection.[285] The EU also maintains a number of initiatives to increase investment in developing countries, particularly in the European Neighbourhood and Africa. Pursuant to Regulation (EU) 978/2012,[286] this includes a 'Generalized Scheme of Preferences',[287] which sets out a system of tariff preferences for the import of goods from less-developed and developing countries. Through multiple other projects carried out by the European Bank for Reconstruction and Development and the European Investment Bank, the EU also aims to boost foreign investment and sustainable development.[288]

c. The EU investment protection architecture

12.112 The most salient, and controversial, aspects of the EU's international investment agreements are their ISDS provisions. The EU's position on this has considerably evolved, as reflected in a succession of policy papers published by the EU institutions.[289] As a general matter, the EU finds itself in an unusual posture in entering the foreign investment law arena. It is neither a party to the ICSID Convention, nor can it access the ICSID Additional Facility, as these are

---

281 Ibid., Art 8.5.

282 CETA (n 276), annex 8-A, paragraph 1(b): 'Indirect expropriation occurs if a measure or series of measures ... substantially deprives the investor of the fundamental attributes of property in its investment, including the right to use, enjoy and dispose of its investment, without formal transfer of title or outright seizure.' Among the factors to be considered in making this determination are, as per CETA (n 276), annex 8-A, para 2(a), are:

the economic impact of the measure or series of measures, although the sole fact that a measure or series of measures of a Party has an adverse impact on the economic value of an investment does not establish that an indirect expropriation has occurred, (2) the duration of the measure or series of measures, (3) the extent to which the measure or series of measures interferes with distinct, reasonable investment-backed expectations; and (d) the character of the measure or series of measures, notably their object, context and intent.

283 Commission, 'Investment provisions in the EU-Canada free trade agreement (CETA)' (February 2016), 7 <https://trade.ec.europa.eu/doclib/docs/2013/november/tradoc_151918.pdf> accessed 25 May 2020; see also Reinisch (n 275) 19.

284 Commission, 'Communication from the Commission to The Council and The European Parliament - The Review of export control policy: ensuring security and competitiveness in a changing world' COM (2014) 244 final, 8.

285 Ibid, paras 12, 21.

286 Commission Regulation 978/2012 applying a scheme of generalized tariff preferences [2012] OJ L303/1; see also European Commission, The EU's new Generalised Scheme of Preferences <http://trade.ec.europa.eu/doclib/docs/2012/december/tradoc_150164.pdf> accessed 26 November 2018.

287 See generally Titi (n 232) 647–50.

288 Commission, 'Communication from The Commission to The European Parliament, The European Council, The Council and The European Investment Bank – Towards a more efficient financial architecture for investment outside the European Union' COM (2018) 644 final.

289 See Reinisch (n 275).

only open to States and EU accession would require amending the relevant provisions of the ICSID Convention, which in turn requires unanimity.[290]

Initially, the Commission announced that it would follow the available 'best practices' adopted by Member States in their previous negotiations with third countries.[291] The Commission accordingly voiced support for inclusion of an ISDS mechanism in future investment agreements, as it 'forms a key part of the inheritance that the Union receives from Member States BITs'.[292] To be sure, the EU had already subscribed to ISDS in connection with the Energy Charter Treaty to which it is a party.[293] In fact, the initial draft of CETA, produced at the EU-Canada Summit in Ottawa in 2014, provided for ISDS, albeit with some innovative elements such as a binding code of conduct for arbitrators.[294] **12.113**

However, in June 2013, when the Council formulated its negotiating mandate for TTIP, it specifically did so in the expectation that 'a satisfactory solution meeting the EU interests is achieved'.[295] Reactions among the Member States on ISDS were varied. Opposition to ISDS as then practised was most evident in Germany, where the German Federal Council expressly opposed the inclusion of ISDS in the TTIP.[296] The national reports collected for the XXVIII FIDE Congress[297] reveal a range of views among the other Member States on the institutional front. The Czech Republic and Poland tended to favour retaining the existing investor-State dispute settlement mechanism as a complementary option for investors. Other States, like Slovenia, favoured a dispute settlement mechanism with permanent arbitrators in place of party-appointed arbitrators.[298] Still other States such as Finland, France and the Netherlands, gravitated toward creation of an international court, with Finland expressly arguing that an international court system would enhance transparency, increase legitimacy of the investor-State-dispute-resolution system, while still providing some role for domestic courts.[299] Austria, **12.114**

---

290 Ibid.; see generally (on the diplomatic difficulties for the EU to join the ICSID Convention) August Reinisch, 'Will the EU's Proposal Concerning an Investment Court System for CETA and TTIP Lead to Enforceable Awards? – The Limits of Modifying the ICSID Convention and the Nature of Investment Arbitration' (2016) 19 *Journal of International Economic Law* 761; Francisco J Pascual Vives, 'Shaping the EU Investment Regime: Choice of Forum and Applicable Law in International Investment Agreements' (2014) 6 *Cuadernos Derecho Transnacional* 269, 293; Markus Burgstaller, 'Dispute Settlement in EU International Investment Agreements with Third States: Three Salient Problems' (2014) 15 *Journal of World Investment and Trade* 551.
291 Commission, Towards a Comprehensive European International Investment Policy (n 27), 11.
292 Ibid., 9.
293 Reinisch (n 275). See also Wybe Douma, 'Investor-state arbitration in the light of EU policy and law after the Lisbon Treaty' (EUSA Conference Papers EUSA, Fifteenth Biennial Conference, 2017), 20 and 25.
294 Elfriede Bierbrauer, 'Negotiations on the EU-Canada Comprehensive Economic and Trade Agreement (CETA) concluded' (2014) DG EXPO/B/PolDep/Note/2014_106, 9 <https://www.europarl.europa.eu/RegData/etudes/ID AN/2014/536410/EXPO_IDA(2014)536410_EN.pdf> accessed 25 May 2020.
295 Council, 'Directives for the negotiation on the Transatlantic Trade and Investment Partnership between the European Union and the United States of America' (11103/13 DCL 1, 2013), 8.
296 See Ralph Alexander Lorz, 'Germany, the Transatlantic Trade and Investment Partnership and investment-dispute settlement: Observations on a paradox', (2014) 132 Columbia FDI Perspectives.
297 da Cruz Vilaça and others (n 266).
298 Ibid., paras 120–121.
299 Ibid., para 121.

Hungary, Malta, Croatia, Portugal and Greece welcomed a full-fledged multilateral investment court similar to the CETA model.[300] The latter approach was also shared by France and the Netherlands.[301]

12.115 A grassroots backlash against ISDS gained political momentum, under the pressure of various civil society organizations in a number of EU Member States, deeply protective of a State's right to regulate in the public interest.[302] Critics also focused on the lack of transparency in arbitral proceedings and the alleged a pro-investor bias on the part of tribunals.[303] Anti-globalization movements became mobilized, joining forces with traditional euro-sceptics.[304] In the European Parliament, the Socialists and Democrats published a position paper in 2015 advocating the suppression of traditional ad hoc investment tribunals[305]

12.116 Perceiving the hostility, the Commission determined to make the negotiation process more transparent. It took its first major step by opening a public consultation in 2014, giving all stakeholders, which included the public, an opportunity to comment on a number of issues, but most prominently on ISDS. Following the consultation, the Commission reported wide opposition to the inclusion of ISDS, as it stood, in the EU's international investment agreements to come.[306]

12.117 The following year, in light of those results, the Commission published a concept paper proposing a 'path for reform' in the TTIP and beyond in which it acknowledged the need to 'ensure that the goal of protecting and encouraging investment does not affect the ability of the EU and its Member States to pursue public policy objectives'.[307] It highlighted four priority respects, both procedural and substantive, in which the Commission proposed to amend its negotiating position on investment provisions: protection of States' right to regulate, greater legitimacy in the formation and conduct of arbitral tribunals, introduction of an appellate mechanism, and a clearer articulation of tribunals' relationship with domestic courts.

12.118 The Commission then took a decisive step, publishing in September 2015 a draft text of a TTIP investment chapter entailing an 'Investment Court System' that moved ISDS in a distinctly more judicial direction.[308] Negotiations for the TTIP did not proceed, but by

---

300 Ibid., para 122.

301 Ibid., para 122.

302 Reinisch (n 275); see also Roland Klager, 'The Impact of the TTIP on Europe's Investment Arbitration Architecture' (2014) 39 *ZDAR* 70.

303 Group of the Progressive Alliance of Socialists and Democrats in the European Parliament, 'S&D Position Paper on Investor-state dispute settlement mechanisms in ongoing trade negotiations' (4 March 2015) <https://www.socialists anddemocrats.eu/sites/default/files/position_paper/ISDS_mechanisms_ongoing_trade_negotiations_en_150304.pdf> accessed 26 May 2020.

304 Ibid., para 8.

305 Ibid.

306 Commission, 'Online public consultation on investment protection and investor-to-state dispute settlement (ISDS) in the Transatlantic Trade and Investment Partnership Agreement (TTIP)' (Commission Staff Working Report) SWD (2015) 3 final, 134–40.

307 Commission, 'Investment in TTIP and beyond – the path for reform: Enhancing the right to regulate and moving from current ad hoc arbitration towards an Investment Court' (Commission TTIP Concept Paper 2015), 1 <https://trade. ec.europa.eu/doclib/docs/2015/may/tradoc_153408.PDF> accessed 26 May 2020.

308 Commission, 'Commission draft text TTIP – investment' (16 September 2015) <https://trade.ec.europa.eu/doclib/ docs/2015/september/tradoc_153807.pdf> accessed 26 May 2020.

February 2016, the main features of such a system already figured centrally in a revised version of the CETA.[309] The EU found in Canada a negotiating partner willing to embark on large-scale reform of international investment arbitration, that would not only address issues of substantive investor protection, but also institutional reform.

The investment chapter of the CETA currently offers the best expression of the new EU position on ISDS, as it is the first EU agreement including the so-called Investment Court System (ICS) that has entered into force.[310] This CETA ICS is discussed in detail in the Chapter by Dorieke Overduin.[311]   **12.119**

D. OUTLOOK

In the midst of the CETA negotiations, the Commission moved decisively in favour of a permanent multilateral court system in preference to individual investment courts for specific investment agreements. It urged what it called a Multilateral Investment Court (MIC) to be developed principally under the auspices of the United Nations Commission on International Trade Law (UNCITRAL). The system would 'apply to multiple agreements and between different trading partners, also on the basis of an opt-in system,' the ultimate goal being to 'multilateralise the court either as a self-standing international body or as a unit within an existing multilateral organization'.[312]   **12.120**

The MIC is discussed in detail in the chapter of Friedrich Rosenfeld.[313]   **12.121**

Ironically, the EU legal order itself presents a challenge to the Commission's ambitions and threatens its momentum. The challenge, put simply, is to reconcile the CJEU's longstanding assertion of the autonomy of the EU legal order and more particularly its exclusive right to interpret and apply EU law, on the one hand, and the reality that issues of EU law cannot help but arise in disputes before the eventual MIC, on the other.[314] The CJEU's *Achmea* judgment has already been discussed in some detail.[315] It will be recalled that the Court there found the ISDS system in intra-EU BITs to be incompatible with EU law, largely due to its threat to the autonomy of the EU legal order, which the CJEU defined as entailing a reservation to that   **12.122**

---

309   Commission, 'CETA: EU and Canada agree on new approach on investment in trade agreement' (Press Release IP/16/399, 29 February 2016).

310   CETA entered into force provisionally on 21 September 2017 following its approval by the EU Council and by the European Parliament. It will only enter into force fully and definitively when all EU Member States have ratified the Agreement. See Commission, 'EU-Canada trade agreement enters into force' (Press Release IP/17/3121, 17 September 10).

311   See Chapter 15.

312   Commission TTIP Concept Paper 2015 (n 307), 11.

313   See Chapter 19.

314   George A Bermann, 'Recalibrating the EU – International Arbitration Interface' (Lecture delivered at 4th Annual European Federation for Investment Law and Arbitration, 2018): 'It is no exaggeration to describe the relationship between the European Union and the international arbitration as the most dramatic confrontation between two international legal regimes seen in a great many years'. See *also* Gisèle Uwera, 'Investor-State Dispute Settlement (ISDS) in Future EU Investment-Related Agreements: Is the Autonomy of the EU Legal Order an Obstacle?' (2016) 15 *The Law and Practice of International Courts and Tribunals* 102.

315   *Achmea* (n 14).

Court (and Member State courts as well) of essentially a monopoly on the interpretation and application of EU law.[316] Of course, *Achmea* also raised larger issues, notably the potential impact of intra-EU BIT awards on governance of the EU internal market.

12.123   The EU sought to address the legal autonomy challenge in CETA, which of course raises the same spectre. As noted,[317] CETA provides that a tribunal may only consider the domestic law of the disputing party as a matter of fact and must abide by the prevailing interpretation given to domestic law by the court or authorities of that party, while stating that no interpretation of domestic law by a CETA Tribunal shall be binding upon the courts or other authorities of that party. As set out in its Opinion 1/17, the CJEU considers this set of precautions sufficient to protect the autonomy of EU law. Opinion 1/17 reflects the light at the end of the tunnel, restoring some clarity in this knotty area, where the EU regime and international investment arbitration laws uncertainly intertwine; prior to Opinion 1/17, there was some doubt as to whether the CJEU would deem CETA to be compatible with the EU legal order, in light of the proviso in paragraph 57 of the *Achmea* judgment itself, quoted earlier, making the EU's submission to rulings by international investment agreements to which it is a party contingent on respect for 'the autonomy of the EU and its legal order'.[318] This passage, while ostensibly meant, to reassure the EU's trading partners that it considers itself bound to comply with rulings of a tribunal established under an international investment agreement to which it is a party, nevertheless makes that commitment less than absolute.

12.124   In appreciating the full significance of Opinion 1/17, two important points should be borne in mind.

12.125   First, prior to Opinion 1/17, the *Achmea* ruling emphasized the inability of an intra-EU BIT tribunal to make preliminary references to the CJEU under Article 267 TFEU, and to receive preliminary rulings by which it would be bound, with consequent prejudice to EU law autonomy. In *Achmea*, Advocate-General Wathelet had forcefully argued that an intra-EU BIT tribunal should be considered as a court or tribunal of a Member State, within the meaning of Article 267,[319] but the Court flatly disagreed. On this basis, there was, initially, some uncertainty as to how a CETA tribunal or a panel of an eventual multilateral investment court would have any greater claim than a BIT tribunal to meet the Article 267 test. However, in Opinion 1/17, the CJEU reasoned that international agreements of CETA's variety were part of the EU legal order separate from other rules of EU law. The jurisdiction granted to EU-affiliated courts and tribunals is only exclusive to EU law *senso strictu*, rather than international law. As elucidated in Section B.2, *supra*, under the provisions of CETA, CETA Tribunals are only to interpret and apply CETA itself and international law, unlike the BIT in *Achmea* which invited tribunals to both interpret and apply EU law. Moreover, a dichotomy should be drawn between on the basis of the principles of 'mutual trust' and 'sincere cooperation' between domestic courts within EU Member States, which, as a matter of EU

---

316   Peter Pukan, 'Implications of the ECJ Achmea decision for CETA's Investment Court System' (Master Thesis, University of Amsterdam, 26 July 2018).
317   Opinion 1/17 (n 12), para 106, citing Opinion 2/13, para 182, Opinion 1/91, paras 40 and 70, and Opinion 1/09, para 74.
318   *Achmea* (n 14), para 57.
319   Case C-284/16 *Slowakische Republik v Achmea BV* [2017] ECLI:EU:C:2017:699, Opinion of A-G Wathelet, para 84.

law, are 'not applicable in relations between the Union and a non-Member State'.[320] While these principles governed intra-EU BITs, they did not apply to CETA, which involved Canada, a non-member State.

Second, CETA provides that a claim may be submitted under the ICSID Rules or the **12.126** UNCITRAL Arbitration Rules. Under the ICSID system, no EU Member State court (nor the CJEU) may entertain an action to annul an award, and it is open to question whether there are grounds on which a Member State court might deny an ICSID award recognition or enforcement due to its incompatibility with EU law. The uncertainty as to CETA's autonomy with the autonomy of EU law was, prior to Opinion 1/17, underscored by a Swedish court's earlier refusal to enforce the *Micula* award, which, as discussed in Section B.3, *supra*, serves as a useful foil to more recent national court and ICSID tribunal cases, which have upheld such awards by distinguishing the *Achmea* judgment. Despite *Micula* being an ICSID award, the Swedish court found that it had no choice but to respect the Commission's ruling that the award was contrary to EU law and therefore unenforceable:

> Enforcing the arbitral award would … mean that a Swedish public agency [i.e., the court itself] contributes to side-stepping the Commission's decision. As long as the Commission's decision is valid, the principle of sincere cooperation … prohibits an approval of the sought enforcement. The duty for domestic courts to refrain from issuing decisions that are not in conformity with decisions by the Commission is far-reaching. EU law bars applying the principle of res judicata, if such an application would result in disregarding EU State aid rules.

The court considered this outcome justified under Article 54 of the ICSID Convention, in **12.127** particular:

> The … Court notes that Article 54 of the [ICSID] Convention obligates Sweden to enforce the arbitral award in the same way as a final Swedish court decision. Such a Swedish decision whose enforcement violated EU law could not have been enforced either. Thus, there is no difference between the arbitral award and a Swedish final decision in this respect.[321]

Interestingly, the court relied entirely on its duty of 'sincere cooperation' with the Commis- **12.128** sion's understanding of EU law. The CJEU's *Achmea* judgment passed unmentioned. In this regard, it is relevant to briefly consider the procedural differences between the ICSID system and the UNCITRAL Arbitration Rules. In arbitration under the UNCITRAL Rules, the arbitral seat could well be outside the EU and, while a Member State court, if moved to do so, could deny the resulting award recognition or enforcement, it could not annul it.

ICSID tribunals appear to have disregarded the consequences of the *Achmea* judgment, even in **12.129** the context of intra-EU BITs. As described, both the tribunals in *United Utilities v Estonia*[322] and *Magyar Farming v Hungary*[323] held that, in line with the 'kompetenz-kompetenz' doctrine, they had jurisdiction to decide the matters before them, and that the *Achmea* judgment could

---

320 Opinion 1/17 (n 12), para 129.
321 *Micula v Romania*, Nacka District Court (n 111).
322 *United Utilities v Estonia* (n 121).
323 *Magyar Farming v Hungary* (n 122).

not be used to restrict their authority under the applicable BITs, which should be analysed under public international law, rather than the exclusively EU lens that the CJEU had adopted in *Achmea*.

12.130 In the wake of Opinion 1/17, it now appears, beyond a glimmer of doubt, that if the compatibility of a MCI were to come before the CJEU, the Court would find the mechanism to be compatible with the autonomy of the EU legal order, notwithstanding paragraph 57 of the *Achmea* judgment. The CJEU's willingness to find the CETA compatible with such autonomy bodes well not only for the EU's other bilateral investment agreements and FTAs with investment chapters, but also for the future of the MIC that the Commission so strongly favours. This would be in striking contrast with the CJEU's history of rejecting the EU's accession to any international agreement providing for a court whose decisions could bind the EU.[324] This development was necessary if, as was indisputably its intention, the EU was to pursue a strategy based on bilateral investment treaties in the short run and a MIC in the long run. It was also necessary in order to ensure the protection of EU investors abroad and extend the guarantees required to attract foreign investment in the EU.

---

324 See Opinion 1/17 (n 12), para 106, citing Opinion 2/13, para 182, Opinion 1/91, paras 40 and 70, and Opinion 1/09, para 74; see also Allan Rosas, 'The EU and international dispute settlement' (2017) 1 *Europe and the World* 3.

13

INVESTMENT ARBITRATION UNDER INTRA-EU BITS

Quentin Declève and Isabelle Van Damme[1]

A. INTRODUCTION AND HISTORY

Since the entry into force of the Lisbon Treaty and the conferral of exclusive competence in respect of foreign direct investment on the European Union ('EU'),[2] an important dialogue has started between the EU institutions and the Member States as well as between various EU institutions regarding the consequences of this newly acquired competence and the relationship between international investment law and EU law. That dialogue, and related litigation before the Court of Justice of the European Union ('CJEU'), has focused on (i) the competence of the EU to conclude investment agreements with third States (*Opinion 2/15*[3]), (ii) the compatibility of investment arbitration clauses contained in intra-EU investment agreements

13.01

---

1   The views expressed in this chapter are personal. The authors are grateful for the research assistance of Elyse Kneller, Rebecca Halbach and Brendan Rooney. Subject to limited updates made afterwards, this chapter covers developments as of 31 May 2020.
2   Consolidated version of the Treaty on the Functioning of the European Union (TFEU) [2008] OJ 115/13, Article 207(1).
3   Opinion 2/15 *Free Trade Agreement with Singapore* [2017] EU:C:2017:376.

with EU law (*Achmea*[4]), and (iii) the compatibility with EU law of the investment court mechanism currently being promoted by the EU, in bilateral agreements (but also at a multilateral level[5]) as a means for reforming the existing investor-State dispute settlement ('ISDS') model (*Opinion 1/17*[6]).

13.02 In *Opinion 2/15*, the CJEU confirmed that issues relating to ISDS fall within the EU's shared competences and can, consequently, only be dealt with by the European Union and its Member States acting together[7] – though it has since signalled that that position might need to be nuanced. In *Achmea*, the CJEU found that investment arbitration clauses contained in bilateral investment treaties concluded between two EU Member States, which envisage that the tribunal may apply EU law, are incompatible with EU law.[8] Finally, in *Opinion 1/17*, the CJEU expressly confirmed the compatibility of the investment court system in the Comprehensive and Economic Trade Agreement between Canada, of the one part, and the EU and its Member States, of the other part ('CETA')[9] with EU law.

13.03 One specific category of agreements affected by these developments are 'intra-EU BITs', meaning bilateral investment agreements between two EU Member States. These agreements were initially concluded between an EU Member State and a third State.[10] However, as a result of a series of accessions, some of those third States subsequently became EU Member States, thereby creating the situation in which investment relations could be covered both by EU law and intra-EU BITs, each providing for their own system of judicial remedies. This resulted in questions regarding the co-existence of those (judicial) protections as a matter of international law and EU law.

13.04 Although the EU initially supported the signing of such intra-EU BITs as means to catalyze the economic development of candidate countries prior to their accession to the EU,[11] the

---

4   Case C-284/16 *Achmea* [2018] EU:C:2018:158.
5   See European Union and its Member States, 'Establishing a standing mechanism for the settlement of international investment disputes' (Submission of the European Union and its Member States to UNCITRAL Working Group III, 18 January 2019) <https://trade.ec.europa.eu/doclib/docs/2019/january/tradoc_157631.pdf> accessed 31 May 2020; European Union and its Member States, 'Possible work plan for Working Group III' (Submission of the European Union and its Member States to UNCITRAL Working Group III, 18 January 2019) <https://trade.ec.europa.eu/doclib/docs/2019/january/tradoc_157632.pdf> accessed 31 May 2020; United Nations Commission on International Trade Law, 'Draft report of Working Group III (Investor-State Dispute Settlement Reform) on the work of its thirty-sixth session' (6 November 2018) <https://uncitral.un.org/sites/uncitral.un.org/files/draft_report_of_wg_iii_for_the_website.pdf> accessed 31 May 2020.
6   Opinion 1/17 *Comprehensive Economic and Trade Agreement with Canada* [2019] EU:C:2019:341.
7   Opinion 2/15, para 293.
8   Case C-284/16 *Achmea*, para 60.
9   Opinion 1/17, para 245.
10 For example, the first BIT ever signed was between Pakistan and Germany in 1959. See UNCTAD Investment Policy Hub, 'Most recent IIAs' <https://investmentpolicy.unctad.org/international-investment-agreements> accessed 31 May 2020, for a list of all International Investment Agreements.
11 N. Basener, *Investment Protection in the European Union: Considering EU law in investment arbitrations arising from intra-EU and extra-EU bilateral investment agreements* (Nomos Verlagsgesellschaft, 2017), 68; see also Case C-284/16 *Achmea* [2017] EU:C:2017:699, Opinion of Advocate General Wathelet, paras 40 and 41.

position expressed by the EU shifted once those third countries (mostly Central and Eastern European States) joined the EU without the termination of those intra-EU BITs.[12]

The European Union's position[13] is that those intra-EU BITs undermine the Single Market **13.05** and are contrary to the founding goals and principles of the EU which aim to maintain and develop an area of freedom, security and justice.[14] In particular, intra-EU BITs are deemed to discriminate between EU citizens by offering to an investor originating from one Member State the possibility to use judicial remedies that might not be available to other EU citizens originating from another EU Member State. Those judicial remedies are also considered to be incompatible with the system of judicial remedies for which EU law provides (mostly because there is a considerable risk that the fora used for adjudicating claims under the intra-EU BITs might decide on the interpretation of EU law in disregard of the exclusive competence of the CJEU to interpret EU law).

In the aftermath of the above-mentioned rulings, the current challenges relate primarily to the **13.06** management of the consequences in respect of existing investment agreements, in particular existing bilateral investment agreements to which only Member States are a party, investment agreements between a Member State and a third State and the Energy Charter Treaty. That management has taken the form of various agreements between and declarations of EU Member States and decisions at an EU institutional level and has resulted in further questions being (or that will be) referred to the CJEU.

The focus of this chapter is primarily on intra-EU BITs and less on so-called 'extra-EU BITs', **13.07** meaning investment agreements between EU Member States (or the European Union) and third States.

A difficulty arises in respect of one investment agreement, the Energy Charter Treaty, because **13.08** the European Union, all of its Member States and third States are parties to it. Concerns regarding both intra-EU BITs and extra-EU BITs might be relevant to that agreement. The Energy Charter Treaty is discussed in Chapter 14 of this volume.

Against that background, section B first discusses the allocation of competences in respect of **13.09** the negotiation and conclusion of investment agreements. Section C then considers the CJEU's judgment in *Achmea*, its consequences and the management of those consequences. Section D concludes.

---

12   B. Onica Jarka, 'The Decimation of the Intra EU BITS' (2018) 12 *Challenges of the Knowledge Society* 532, 536; see also, Commission, 'Protection of intra-EU investment' (Communication) COM (2018) 547 final, 2–3.

13   Communication, above n 12, 'Protection of intra-EU investment', 2; see also, D. Moskvan, 'Reforming Intra-EU Investment Protection: Amid a Running Battle of Interests' (2015) 22(5) *Maastricht Journal of European and Comparative Law* 732, 736–8.

14   See, e.g., Joined Cases C-411/10 and C-493/10 *NS* [2011] EU:C:2011:865, para 83.

B. THE COMPETENCE OF EU MEMBER STATES TO CONCLUDE BILATERAL INVESTMENT AGREEMENTS

13.10 The first type of question relating to the post-Lisbon status of investment agreements concerned the competence of the European Union to conclude investment agreements with a third State.[15] *Opinion 2/15* addressed the allocation of competences between the EU and the Member States in respect of the Free Trade Agreement envisaged between the European Union and the Republic of Singapore ('EUSFTA'),[16] which contained commitments in relation to both trade and investment. In particular, the Court was asked to resolve what parts of that agreement fell within the exclusive or shared competences of the European Union or the competence of the Member States alone. In respect of the investment chapter of the EUSFTA (Chapter Nine), this question required the CJEU to consider both the substantive obligations assumed under that chapter and the ISDS provisions. For the purposes of this contribution, the focus will be on the analysis in *Opinion 2/15* in respect of ISDS. Whilst that opinion relates to an extra-EU BIT, the reasoning of the CJEU nonetheless offered a first insight into how it understands ISDS to operate. It also signalled that, in considering questions relating to investment agreements, the CJEU appears to take into account the political aspects of the continuing tension between the EU and the Member States on this matter.

13.11 In *Opinion 2/15*, the CJEU found that the provisions regarding ISDS fall within the shared competences of the European Union.[17] That conclusion appeared to apply regardless of whether the dispute concerned foreign direct investment (falling within the EU's exclusive competence[18]) or portfolio investment (falling within the shared competence of the EU[19]).

13.12 The CJEU relied primarily on the fact that ISDS 'removes disputes from the jurisdiction of the courts of the Member States' to conclude that such provisions are not purely ancillary and thus require the consent of the Member States.[20] The criterion of removing a dispute from the courts of the Member States is taken from the case-law regarding the compatibility of international agreements with EU law.[21] It is not a criterion that finds a basis in the Treaty rules governing the allocation of competences. It is also not a criterion previously used by the CJEU to assess competence questions in respect of dispute settlement provisions in an international agreement.

13.13 Previously, the CJEU had consistently held that the material competence conferred upon the EU in the field of external relations as well as its treaty-making capacity entail, in principle, the

---

15 See further G. Kübek and I. Van Damme, 'Facultative Mixity and the European Union's Trade and Investment Agreements' in I. Govaere and M. Chamon (eds), *EU External Relations Law Post-Lisbon: The Law and Practice of Facultative Mixity* (Brill Publishing, 2020), Chapter 6.

16 Opinion 2/15, para 1.

17 Ibid., para 293.

18 Ibid., para 109.

19 Ibid., para 243.

20 Ibid., para 292.

21 See, by way of example, Opinion 1/09 *Draft agreement on the European and Community Patents Court* [2011] EU:C:2011:123, paras 66–89.

power to establish international courts and tribunals.[22] Thus, the general principle is that, as the CJEU confirmed at paragraph 267 of *Opinion 2/15*, institutional provisions on mediation and dispute settlement 'fall within the same competence as the substantive provisions which they accompany'. Such provisions are typically 'ancillary' to the substantive provisions, meaning also that the allocation of competences for the dispute settlement provisions mirrors that in respect of the substantive provisions. In *Opinion 2/15*, the CJEU did not depart from that general principle. Instead, it seemed to assume that ISDS is unlike other types of dispute settlement under international agreements, in respect of which it has previously established the allocation of competences. In particular, the CJEU found that the competence for ISDS 'cannot be of a purely ancillary nature [...] and cannot, therefore, be established without the Member States' consent'.[23]

The use of the criterion of 'removing disputes from Member State courts' in order to conclude **13.14** that treaty provisions regarding ISDS require the consent of Member States, in essence, means that the CJEU relied on the autonomy of the EU legal order as a basis for allocating competences. That criterion focuses on whether an international agreement has the effect of removing from Member State courts the power to request a preliminary ruling from the CJEU. It is taken from cases such as *Opinion 1/09*[24] and was used recently in *Achmea*[25] in which the CJEU examined the compatibility of international agreements with EU law. It is unclear on what basis the CJEU considered this criterion to be relevant for the distinct question of allocating competences between the EU and the Member States. The CJEU mentioned no basis in the Treaties.

Neither did the CJEU explain what disputes would necessarily be removed from the courts of **13.15** the Member States (and therefore from the CJEU) as a result of the conclusion of an agreement providing for ISDS. As Advocate General Bot observed in his Opinion regarding CETA, 'the establishment of the [investment court system] does not prevent foreign investors from seeking to protect their investments by bringing proceedings before the courts and tribunals of the Parties with a view to the domestic law of those Parties being applied'. He took the view that an action before a national court would be based on different rules (domestic law) and its subject matter would not necessarily be the same.[26] According to Advocate General Bot, Member States' courts and tribunals are 'not [...] deprived of their status of "general law" courts within the EU legal order, including their role in any making of references for a preliminary ruling'.[27] That reasoning, albeit indirectly, stands at odds with the criterion used in *Opinion 2/15*.

Putting aside the merits of the criterion on which the Court relied in *Opinion 2/15*, the fact **13.16** that the Court linked its conclusion that the ISDS provisions were not purely ancillary in

---

22 Opinion 1/91 *Draft Agreement relating to the creation of the European Economic Area* [1991] EU:C:1991:490, paras 40 and 70; Opinion 1/09, para 74; Opinion 2/13 *Draft Agreement on the European Union's Accession to the European Convention on Human Rights* [2014] EU:C:2014:2454, para 182.

23 Opinion 2/15, para 292.

24 Opinion 1/09, para 81.

25 Case C-284/16 *Achmea*, para 55.

26 Opinion 1/17 *Comprehensive Economic and Trade Agreement with Canada* [2019] EU:C:2019:72, Opinion of Advocate General Bot, para 168.

27 Ibid., para 172.

nature to its remark that Member States' consent is required for concluding an investment agreement between the EU and third States caused some concern regarding the legal basis in the EU Treaties and the Court's own case-law. The conclusion that the competence to conclude an international agreement is shared does not mean that there is an obligation to conclude a mixed agreement (meaning an agreement to which both the EU and the Member States are parties).

13.17   Although the CJEU remarked in *Opinion 2/15* that the consent of the Member States was required to conclude an international agreement because the area of foreign non-direct investment was found to fall within the European Union's shared competence, it corrected that apparent error in *COTIF*. In that subsequent judgment, the CJEU confirmed that Member States need not necessarily become a party to an agreement as a result of the fact that portfolio investment is a shared competence. In *COTIF*, the CJEU explained that, in *Opinion 2/15*, 'there was no possibility of the required majority being obtained within the Council for the Union to be able to exercise alone the external competence that it shares with the Member States in [the area of portfolio investment]'.[28] The CJEU thus expressly recognized the political discretion of the Council to choose for or against mixity in areas of shared competence. That clarification was limited to the part of *Opinion 2/15* which related to the shared competence in respect of the substantive obligations for portfolio investment. The Court did not, therefore, seek to correct the paragraph of *Opinion 2/15* where it concluded that the Member States' consent was required for the ISDS provisions.

13.18   However, some guidance may be found in public statements made by individual members of the Court. In particular, President Lenaerts has explained that the *COTIF* clarification in essence applies also in respect of ISDS because '[s]ince there is no qualified majority in the Council to decide that the EU should exercise that competence alone, ISDS mechanisms in recently negotiated trade and investment agreements have to be accepted by the Union and all Member States'.[29] This statement might suggest that, in a later case involving the question of the allocation of competences in respect of an international agreement envisaging the creation of a dispute settlement system, the Court will explain how *Opinion 2/15* should be read and fully restore the status quo in respect of the notion of facultative mixity.

13.19   As a result of these clarifications and as a matter of EU law, provisions regarding ISDS (and portfolio investment) fall within the European Union's shared competences but the agreements in which they are found need not be signed by both the European Union and the Member States because of those provisions. Thus, the status quo in terms of the circumstances in which a mixed agreement is either required or optional still applies. The fact that the Council (and, thus, in essence the Member States) wishes to prevent that the EU exercises the competence alone (which it lawfully may do) is a political consideration that arguably did not need to be addressed in the Court's response to the legal questions relating to the allocation of competences raised in *Opinion 2/15*.

---

28   Case C-600/14 *COTIF* [2017] EU:C:2017:935, para 68.
29   Speech by K. Lenaerts, 'Modernising trade whilst safeguarding the EU constitutional framework: an insight into the balanced approach of Opinion 1/17' (6 September 2019) <https://diplomatie.belgium.be/sites/default/files/downloads/presentation_lenaerts_opinion_1_17.pdf> accessed 31 May 2020.

C. THE COMPATIBILITY OF ISDS CLAUSES IN INTRA-EU BITS WITH EU LAW

1. Introduction

The question concerning the compatibility of ISDS provisions in intra-EU BITs and **13.20** extra-EU BITs with EU law was, shortly after *Opinion 2/15*, raised in *Achmea* (regarding intra-EU BITs) and *Opinion 1/17* (regarding extra-EU BITs), respectively. For the purposes of this contribution, the focus will be on *Achmea*, although the reasoning in that judgment must also be understood in light of *Opinion 1/17*. So far, the CJEU has not yet taken a position on the Energy Charter Treaty, which has features of both intra-EU BITs and extra-EU BITs, insofar as it applies between EU Member States.[30]

In the *Achmea* judgment, the CJEU found that ISDS clauses in intra-EU BITs were contrary **13.21** to EU law because such clauses provide for the possibility that an arbitral tribunal would rule on the interpretation and application of EU law without any means for the CJEU to control and review such decisions. As a result of that judgment, the EU and the Member States have chosen to terminate all intra-EU BITs.

However, the termination of international agreements that, in particular, establish individual **13.22** rights and pursuant to which arbitral awards have been issued or are pending at the time of termination taking effect, raises a number of transitional issues. While it appears that the EU and the Member States have adopted certain positions on how those issues should be managed, arbitral tribunals as well as courts of third States (which might be asked to recognise or enforce arbitral awards) might not share the same position. As the following sections will discuss, this has resulted in a situation of continued legal uncertainty regarding the full consequences of the judgment in *Achmea*.

The following sub-sections therefore discuss how the *Achmea* judgment has been received by **13.23** the European Union and the Member States (sub-section C.2) and how domestic courts (including courts of third States) and arbitral tribunals have responded to that judgment (sub-section C.3). Sub-section C.4 examines how the European Union and the Member States seek to manage the post-*Achmea* transition towards the settlement of future intra-EU investment disputes without recourse to ISDS.

2. ISDS clauses in intra-EU BITs and the need to protect the autonomy of EU law and the principle of mutual trust

a. The judgment in Achmea

In the *Achmea* judgment, the CJEU found that a clause contained in an intra-EU BIT allowing **13.24** investors originating from one EU Member State to initiate arbitral proceedings against another EU Member State and envisaging that the arbitral tribunal may apply EU law, was

---

30 On 24 September 2019, the Paris Court of Appeal decided to refer three questions for preliminary ruling to the CJEU regarding the definition of an 'investment' in the Energy Charter Treaty ('ECT'). The upcoming decision of the CJEU could potentially have a great impact on the scope of future ECT-based investment arbitration proceedings, which require, pursuant to Art 26(1) of the ECT, that the dispute relate to 'an investment' (Case C-741/19, *République de Moldavie*, still pending).

incompatible with EU law, in particular, the autonomy of the EU legal order. That judgment seemed, as a matter of EU law, understandable and not entirely unpredictable in light of past case-law of the CJEU.[31] In that case-law, the CJEU emphasised, in assessing whether the autonomy of EU law was preserved, the protection of the relationship and dialogue between national courts of the Member States and the CJEU through the preliminary ruling procedure. At the same time, the *Achmea* judgment caused a strong reaction from the arbitration community which expressed concerns about the implications of the judgment and considered that the CJEU had second-guessed ISDS as an appropriate remedy for resolving investment disputes and that the judgment unduly subjected the validity of ISDS clauses to EU primary law.[32]

13.25 In *Achmea*, the CJEU was responding to a request for a preliminary ruling from the German Federal Court (*Bundesgerichtshof*). Before the referring court, Slovakia had sought the annulment of an arbitral award in favour of Achmea, a Dutch insurance company. The arbitral tribunal, which had delivered the contested arbitral award, had been established pursuant to an intra-EU BIT concluded between the former Czechoslovakia and the Netherlands (the 'Czechoslovakia-Netherlands BIT').

13.26 The referring court asked the CJEU whether the application of the ISDS clause in the Czechoslovakia-Netherlands BIT was compatible with (i) Article 344 TFEU (which prohibits EU Member States from submitting a dispute concerning the interpretation or application of EU law to any method of settlement other than those for which the EU Treaties provide); (ii) Article 267 TFEU (which provides for a preliminary ruling mechanism that ensures that only the CJEU gives a final legally binding interpretation of EU law); and (iii) Article 18 TFEU (which prohibits discrimination on grounds of nationality).

13.27 The CJEU responded only to the questions in respect of Articles 267 and 344 TFEU. It held that those provisions must be understood as

> precluding a provision in an international agreement concluded between [EU] Member States [...] under which an investor from one of those Member States may, in the event of a dispute concerning investments in the other Member State, bring proceedings against the latter Member State before an arbitral tribunal whose jurisdiction that Member State has undertaken to accept.[33]

In light of that response, there was no need to consider the question relating to the discriminatory nature of intra-EU investment arbitration.[34] Advocate General Wathelet did, however, address the question of discrimination in his Opinion and concluded there that the

---

31 See, e.g., Opinion 1/91 *Draft agreement relating to the creation of the European Economic Area* [1991] EU:C:1991:490; Opinion 1/92 *Draft agreement relating to the creation of the European Economic Area* [1992] EU:C:1992:189; Opinion 1/00 *Proposed agreement on the establishment of a European Common Aviation Area* [2002] EU:C:2002:231; Case C-459/03 *Commission v Ireland* [2006] EU:C:2006:345; Opinion 1/09 *Agreement on the creation of a unified patent litigation system* [2011] EU:C:2011:123; Opinion 2/13 *Accession of the European Union to the ECHR* [2014] EU:C:2014:2454.

32 See, e.g., V. Kapoor, 'Slovak Republic v. Achmea: When Politics Came Out to Play' (Kluwer Arbitration Blog, 1 July 2018) <http://arbitrationblog.kluwerarbitration.com/2018/07/01/slovak-republic-v-achmea-politics-came-play/>; See also N. Lavranos, 'Black Tuesday: the end of intra-EU BITs' (Practical Law Blog, 7 March 2018) <http://arbitrationblog.practicallaw.com/black-tuesday-the-end-of-intra-eu-bits/> both accessed 21 November 2020.

33 Case C-284/16 *Achmea*, para 60.

34 Ibid., para 61.

ISDS clause was fully compatible with the general principle of EU law prohibiting discrimination on the ground of nationality.[35]

The CJEU had previously held that Articles 267 and 344 TFEU preserve the principle of the autonomy of the EU legal order.[36] This principle expresses the understanding that the EU has its own distinct legal system that is autonomous and independent from that of the Member States and that of international law.[37] One important feature of this autonomy is that the CJEU enjoys exclusive jurisdiction to interpret EU law and to decide on the validity of acts of the EU institutions.[38] The preliminary ruling procedure is a central element of the system of EU judicial remedies as it ensures that any questions regarding the interpretation and validity of EU law, arising before national courts of the EU Member States, may (and, in certain cases, must) be referred to the CJEU. **13.28**

The difficulty with the Czechoslovakia-Netherlands BIT was that Article 8.6 of that agreement envisaged that the applicable law to be applied by the arbitral tribunal included, apart from the agreement itself, the domestic law of the party concerned and other relevant agreements between the parties to the treaty. According to the CJEU, EU law is both part of the law of the EU Member States (and thus, the parties to the Czechoslovakia-Netherlands BIT) but is also derived from an international agreement between the Member States.[39] Thus, an arbitral tribunal established under the Czechoslovakia-Netherlands BIT might need to interpret and apply EU law and thereby potentially affect the autonomy of the EU legal order.[40] **13.29**

In light of that fact, the CJEU then examined whether the autonomy of the EU legal order could nonetheless be preserved in the event that an arbitral tribunal such as that established under the Czechoslovakia-Netherlands BIT could request a preliminary ruling from the CJEU.[41] In his Opinion, Advocate General Wathelet found that an arbitral tribunal established pursuant to Article 8 of the Czechoslovakia-Netherlands BIT was a court or tribunal within the meaning of Article 267 TFEU that could request a preliminary ruling from the CJEU because, taking into account the criteria developed in the CJEU's case-law, such a tribunal: (i) is established by law; (ii) is permanent; (iii) enjoys compulsory jurisdiction; (iv) hears disputes in *inter partes* proceedings, (v) applies rules of law in the settlement of disputes before them and (vi) consists of independent and impartial arbitrators.[42] **13.30**

However, contrary to what Advocate General Wathelet held, the CJEU found that arbitral tribunals of the type established under the Czechoslovakia-Netherlands BIT were not courts or tribunals of Member States within the meaning of Article 267 TFEU. It considered that a distinguishing feature of those tribunals is that they operate a form of remedy that is not part of **13.31**

---

35 Case C-284/16 *Achmea*, Opinion of Advocate General Wathelet, paras 59–82.
36 Opinion 2/13, paras 176 and 201; see also Opinion 1/17, paras 108–110.
37 Case 26/62 *Van Gend den Loos v Nederlandse Administratie Der Belastingen* [1963] EU:C:1963:1, p. 12; Case 6/64 *Costa v ENEL* [1964] EU:C:1964:66, p. 594; Opinion 2/13, para 210; Opinion 1/17, para 111.
38 Opinion 1/91, para 35; Opinion 2/13, para 234.
39 Case C-284/16 *Achmea*, para 41.
40 Ibid., paras 40–42.
41 Ibid., para 43.
42 Case C-284/16 *Achmea*, Opinion of Advocate General Wathelet, paras 85–131.

the judicial systems of the Member States (and thus of the parties to the Czechoslovakia-Netherlands BIT). As a result, it concluded that such tribunals may not request a preliminary ruling from the CJEU.[43] That arbitral tribunals operate a form of remedy that is not part of the judicial systems of the Member States was a line of reasoning that the CJEU already relied on in *Opinion 2/15*, namely the fact that ISDS results in removing disputes from the judicial systems of national courts for which national law provides. In this regard, the manner in which the CJEU had described ISDS, in *Opinion 2/15*, signalled that the CJEU viewed ISDS as a system of judicial remedies that is extraneous to that of the judicial remedies for which EU law and national laws of Member States provide. In *Achmea*, the CJEU also considered that this feature distinguished ISDS from, for example, the Benelux Court of Justice, which is a court comprising three Member States which have accepted jurisdiction in order to ensure the uniform application of common rules and has ties to the judicial systems of those Member States.[44]

13.32 The CJEU also recognised that there might be instances where arbitral awards are challenged before the national courts of the Member States. It was therefore necessary to consider whether, in the context of such a review, preliminary questions regarding the interpretation of EU law addressed in those awards may nonetheless be referred to the CJEU in such a manner so that the autonomy of EU law could be preserved.[45] The CJEU deemed it important that, in respect of the ISDS clause at issue, the arbitral tribunal could decide, in particular, its seat and therefore the law governing the procedure for judicial review of the validity of the award.[46] Implicitly, the CJEU seemed to find that – in the case of intra-EU BITs – there was no absolute guarantee of judicial review before a national court of a Member State. In any event, any judicial review would be circumscribed by national law which might limit the grounds for review.[47] In this regard, the CJEU considered that – unlike in a commercial arbitration context[48] – investment arbitration tribunals are not subject to sufficient judicial review in a manner that ensures the full effectiveness of EU law.[49] The CJEU emphasised that, unlike what is the case for commercial arbitration, ISDS 'derive[s] from a treaty by which Member States agree to remove from the jurisdiction of their own courts [...] disputes which may concern the application or interpretation of EU law'.[50]

13.33 Finally, the CJEU signalled that the reasoning in *Achmea* did not undermine the settled case-law according to which 'an international agreement providing for the establishment of a court responsible for the interpretation of its provisions and whose decisions are binding on the institutions, including the Court of Justice, is not in principle incompatible with EU law'.[51] However, the CJEU emphasised that the competence of the EU to conclude international agreements, which envisage the establishment of judicial remedies that enable parties to submit questions regarding the interpretation and application of those agreements to a third party

---

43   Case C-284/16 *Achmea*, paras 45–46 and 49.
44   Ibid., paras 47 and 48.
45   Ibid., para 50.
46   Ibid., para 51.
47   Ibid., para 53.
48   See for instance, Case C-126/97 *Eco Swiss* [1999] EU:C:1999:269.
49   Case C-284/16 *Achmea*, paras 54–58.
50   Ibid., para 55.
51   Ibid., para 57.

adjudicator, is subject to the condition that such judicial remedies respect the autonomy of the EU and its legal order.[52]

In any event, the settled case-law was not critical to the consideration of the questions referred to the CJEU because the Czechoslovakia-Netherlands BIT was not an agreement concluded by the EU. Rather, it was an agreement concluded between two Member States. As a matter of EU law, the principle of mutual trust applies to the relationship between Member States.[53] At paragraph 34 of its judgment, the CJEU explained that 'EU law is [...] based on the fundamental premise that each Member State shares with all the other Member States, and recognises that they share with it, a set of common values on which the EU is founded, as stated in Article 2 TEU'. The CJEU added that '[t]hat premiss implies and justifies the existence of mutual trust between the Member States that those values will be recognised, and therefore that the law of the EU that implements them will be respected'.[54] In addition, the CJEU referred notably to the principle of sincere cooperation, requiring the Member States to: **13.34**

> ensure in their respective territories the application of and respect for EU law, and to take for those purposes any appropriate measure, whether general or particular, to ensure fulfilment of the obligations arising out of the Treaties or resulting from the acts of the institutions of the EU.[55]

In light of those principles that apply specifically to the relationship between EU Member States, the CJEU found that Article 8 of the Czechoslovakia-Netherlands BIT risks undermining the principle of mutual trust between the Member States.[56] While it was not strictly necessary to refer to the principles of mutual trust and sincere cooperation in order to reach that conclusion, by emphasising the relevance of those principles, the CJEU was quite possibly stressing in indirect terms that the judgment in *Achmea* should be understood as being relevant specifically to intra-EU BITs insofar as to not prejudice the question of whether ISDS clauses in extra-EU BITs are likewise incompatible with EU law. It should be noted that at the time of delivering the judgment in *Achmea*, the Court had already been asked to consider the ISDS chapter in CETA. **13.35**

b. Clarifications of the Achmea judgment in Opinion 1/17

The judgment of the CJEU in *Achmea* must also be read in light of the subsequent *Opinion 1/17* regarding extra-EU BITs. While at the time when the *Achmea* judgment was handed down there was some discussion on whether the application of the criteria used in that judgment could mean that the ISDS system in CETA would also be declared incompatible with EU law, the CJEU in *Opinion 1/17* focused on the principle of mutual trust, applicable solely to the relations between EU Member States and signaled that the reasoning in *Achmea* was not intended to decide similar questions in respect of extra-EU BITs. In fact, by referring to the principle of mutual trust, the CJEU was cautious in laying down a basis (though there are also others) to distinguish the judgment in *Achmea* from any future decisions regarding extra-EU BITs. **13.36**

---

52   Ibid., para 57 and the case-law cited.
53   Ibid., para 58.
54   Ibid., para 34.
55   Ibid., para 34 and the case-law cited.
56   Ibid., para 58.

13.37   In *Opinion 1/17*, the CJEU elaborated on the importance of the principle of mutual trust based on its reasoning in the *Achmea* judgment. In particular, it explained that the principle of mutual trust 'obliges each of those States to consider, other than in exceptional circumstances, that all the other Member States comply with EU law, including fundamental rights, such as the right to an effective remedy before an independent tribunal laid down in Article 47 of the Charter'.[57] The same guarantees in respect of, notably, compliance with the right to an effective remedy before an independent tribunal, are not available in the relations between Member States or the European Union, on the one hand, and third States, on the other.[58]

13.38   In essence, the CJEU accepted that, in relations with third States, there is a rationale for resorting to ISDS because there are no guarantees that EU investors will benefit, in third States, from the right to an effective remedy before an independent tribunal in a manner that satisfies the standards of fundamental rights under EU law. However, in relations between Member States, that guarantee is enshrined in fundamental principles of EU law, which are subject to the scrutiny of the CJEU. As the CJEU in *Associação Sindical dos Juízes Portugueses* held (and to which the CJEU in *Opinion 1/17* expressly refers), the principle of sincere cooperation requires Member States 'to ensure, in their respective territories, the application of a respect for EU law' and, pursuant to Article 19(1) TEU, 'Member States are to provide remedies sufficient to ensure effective judicial protection for individual parties in the fields covered by EU law.'[59] This reasoning is also based on the CJEU's understanding that all the matters covered by intra-BITs are also covered by standards of protection under EU law, even if the CJEU has not specifically explained the extent to which that premise is justified.

13.39   When reading the judgment in *Achmea* in light of the further clarifications offered in *Opinion 1/17*, it becomes clear that the principles of mutual trust and sincere cooperation operate as a stand-alone reason for declaring intra-EU BITs to be incompatible with EU law, regardless of the specific details of the applicable law clause for which a particular intra-EU BIT provides.

c.   Reception of the Achmea judgment

13.40   The judgment in *Achmea* concerned specifically intra-EU BITs containing a clause similar to Article 8 of the Czechoslovakia-Netherlands BIT, according to which an arbitral tribunal may resolve disputes by applying EU law (whether as a part of the law of the Member States or as derived from an international agreement). However, in practice and taking into account the CJEU's emphasis on the principles of mutual trust and sincere cooperation in the judgment in *Achmea* and subsequently in *Opinion 1/17*, the result of the *Achmea* judgment is that intra-EU BITs are not compatible with EU law. In any event, most of the relevant clauses in intra-EU BITs envisage the possibility that EU law might be part of the law to be interpreted and applied by an arbitral tribunal (as distinct from the circumstances, as is the case for extra-EU BITs,[60] where EU law is a question of fact).

---

57   *Opinion 1/17*, para 128 and the case-law cited.
58   Ibid., para 129.
59   Case C-64/16 *Associação Sindical dos Juízes Portugueses* [2018] EU:C:2018:117, para 34 and the case-law cited.
60   *Opinion 1/17*, para. 76.

Furthermore, pursuant to the case-law of the CJEU, judgments of the CJEU handed down in preliminary ruling cases have retroactive effects.[61] Consequently, the findings of the CJEU in *Achmea* should (theoretically) apply retroactively, meaning that as of the moment that a Member State joined the EU, the arbitration clauses contained in its respective BITs that were concluded with other EU Member States, prior to accession, have become inapplicable. **13.41**

In an attempt to clarify the effects of these rulings, the European Commission issued on 19 July 2018 a Communication in which it described intra-EU BITs as having 'bec[o]me a parallel treaty system overlapping with single market rules, thereby preventing the full application of EU law'.[62] It also considered such agreements to conflict with the principle of non-discrimination and, in essence, to undermine the system of EU judicial remedies.[63] Specifically in respect of ISDS clauses in intra-EU BITs, the Commission took the position that, after the judgment in *Achmea*, 'all investor-State arbitration clauses in intra-EU BITS are inapplicable and that any arbitration tribunal established on the basis of such clauses lacks jurisdiction due to the absence of a valid arbitration agreement'. In respect of the specific obligations of Member States, the Commission stated that their national courts 'are under the obligation to annul any arbitral award rendered on that basis and to refuse to enforce it' (although the statement is broad enough to possibly cover national courts of third States) and that Member States 'are bound to formally terminate their intra-EU BITs'.[64] The remaining part of the Communication sought to explain what substantive rules of EU law and EU judicial remedies protect investments and investors. **13.42**

The Commission, thus, made no attempt at claiming any competence of the EU to terminate (parts of) those intra-EU BITs, despite the fact that in *Opinion 2/15* the CJEU had found that, when the EU acquires exclusive competence (such as in the field of foreign direct investment), it 'can succeed the Member States in their international commitments when the Member States have transferred to it, by one of its founding Treaties, their competences relating to those commitments and it exercises those competences'.[65] According to the CJEU, this includes also terminating agreements to which the EU was not initially a party.[66] Arguably, such a far-reaching competence must be exercised with due care, taking into account also the possible response of the Member States. **13.43**

Instead, the Commission preferred to fully put the burden on the Member States to terminate their intra-EU BITs. In response, the Member States produced in January 2019 three declarations regarding the consequences of the *Achmea* judgment. The need for three different declarations is explained by the fact that the Member States were not fully united in their understanding of those consequences. **13.44**

The first declaration, dated 15 January 2019, was adopted by 22 Member States. That declaration focuses on the primacy of EU law over intra-EU BITs and the fact that all ISDS **13.45**

---

61 Case 61/79 *Denkavit italiana* [1980] EU:C:1980:100, para 16; Case C-2/06 *Kempter* [2008] EU:C:2008:78, paras 35–36.

62 Communication, above n 12, 'Protection of intra-EU investment', 2.

63 Ibid.

64 Ibid., 3.

65 *Opinion 2/15*, para 248.

66 Ibid., para 249.

clauses in those agreements are contrary to EU law, making them, therefore, inapplicable.[67] It outlines the main actions to be taken, as follows: (i) Member States are to inform arbitral tribunals (in all pending intra-EU arbitrations, either under an intra-EU BIT or the Energy Charter Treaty) of the legal consequences of the *Achmea* judgment, particularly the fact that all ISDS clauses in intra-EU BITs should be considered as contrary to EU law and thus be declared inapplicable; (ii) defending Member States are to request that national courts of the Member States and of third States set aside intra-EU investment awards or do not enforce such awards; (iii) Member States are to inform investors that no new intra-EU arbitration proceedings may be initiated and seek to have undertakings withdraw from pending investment arbitration cases; (iv) Member States must terminate all intra-EU BITs through a plurilateral treaty (or a bilateral treaty, in case that would be faster) with the objective of ratification no later than 6 December 2019; and (v) intra-EU settlements and arbitral awards that were handed down before the *Achmea* judgment, should not be challenged if they can no longer be annulled or set aside and compliance has been achieved or enforcement has been completed.

13.46 The second declaration, dated 16 January 2019, was adopted solely by Hungary.[68] Its content is similar to the first declaration made by 22 Member States except for the fact that Hungary declares that the *Achmea* judgment is silent on the Energy Charter Treaty and, therefore, no consequences from that judgment should be attached to intra-EU Energy Charter Treaty arbitration.

13.47 The third declaration, also dated 16 January 2019, was signed by Finland, Luxembourg, Malta, Slovenia and Sweden.[69] Similar to the Hungarian declaration, it expresses a reservation as to what the consequences of the *Achmea* judgment are for the specific situation of the Energy Charter Treaty. It insists on the need to refrain from taking a position as to the compatibility of intra-EU application of the Energy Charter Treaty so long as the CJEU has not weighed in on the matter.[70]

13.48 These responses to the *Achmea* judgment thus signal that compliance with the interpretation of EU law require, according to the EU and the Member States, positive action in the form of, at least: (i) termination of the intra-EU BITs; (ii) asking arbitral tribunals in pending proceedings initiated under such agreements to cease the proceedings and declare that their jurisdiction was not properly established; (iii) not initiating new arbitral proceedings under such agreements; and (iv) in respect of the enforcement of arbitral awards that are already issued, asking courts (of Member States or third States) to set aside those awards or to refuse to enforce them.

---

67 Financial Stability, Financial Services and Capital Markets Union, 'Declaration of the Member States of 15 January 2019 on the legal consequences of the Achmea judgment and on investment protection' (European Commission, 17 January 2019) <https://ec.europa.eu/info/publications/190117-bilateral-investment-treaties_en> accessed 21 November 2020.

68 Declaration of the Representative of the Government of Hungary on the Legal Consequences of the Judgment of the Court of Justice in Achmea and on Investment Protection in the European Union (16 January 2019) <https://www.kormany.hu/download/5/1b/81000/Hungarys%20Declaration%20on%20Achmea.pdf> accessed 21 November 2020.

69 Declaration of the Member States of 16 January 2019 on the legal consequences of the Achmea judgment and on investment protection (adopted by Finland, Luxembourg, Malta, Slovenia and Sweden) <https://www.regeringen.se/48ee19/contentassets/d759689c0c804a9ea7af6b2de7320128/achmea-declaration.pdf> accessed 21 November 2020.

70 On 2 December 2020, Belgium filed a request to the CJEU for an opinion on the compatibility with EU law of the ISDS provisions of the modernized version of the Energy Charter Treaty.

The current challenge is how to manage all of these actions seeking to address the conse- **13.49** quences from the *Achmea* judgment as identified by the EU and the Member States. Certain of these actions are fully within the control of the EU and the Member States, and under the supervision of the CJEU, such as the termination of the intra-EU BITs and the obligations resting on national courts of Member States. Others are mostly outside their control, such as the responses of arbitral tribunals and courts of third States or the decision of an investor to nonetheless initiate new arbitral proceedings pursuant to an intra-EU BIT. In particular, with respect to courts of third States and arbitral tribunals, it must be noted that they are not bound by EU law, including the obligation to respect the primacy of EU law. From their perspective, the Member States and the EU are, in essence, asking them to set aside an award or to refuse exercising their jurisdiction because the parties to the intra-EU BITs allegedly did not validly consent to those agreements for reasons that EU law precludes agreements between Member States containing ISDS clauses. Thus, the result which the EU and the Member States seek to achieve, as elaborated in the three respective declarations, might result in questions regarding the application of the generally applicable principles laid down in the Vienna Convention on the Law of Treaties ('VCLT'),[71] in particular Articles 30 VCLT (application of successive treaties relating to the same subject matter), Article 31 VCLT (treaty interpretation) and Articles 54 and 59 VCLT (treaty termination).

3. Post-*Achmea* issues arising before national courts and arbitral tribunals

In essence, the *Achmea* judgment means that EU law should be interpreted as precluding an **13.50** ISDS clause in an intra-EU BIT regardless of when that BIT was concluded and entered into force. In accordance with established case-law, the provisions of bilateral agreements between two Member States cannot apply in the relations between those States if they are found to be contrary to the rules of the EU Treaties.[72] However, that does not necessarily mean that, as a matter of international law, an ISDS clause is to be declared invalid or inapplicable or that an arbitral tribunal or national court of a third State should give full effect to the *Achmea* judgment as though it expressed also a position on the agreement's validity under or compatibility with international law.

Since the *Achmea* judgment, arbitral tribunals and national courts have been asked to consider **13.51** the implications of that judgment for pending arbitral proceedings or awards already issued. So far, the EU and its Member States do not appear to have succeeded in advancing their position in respect of implementing the *Achmea* judgment. The debates before arbitral tribunals and national courts (of especially third States) expose the continuing unsettled interaction between international law and EU law. The CJEU has declared the EU legal order to be a separate legal order.[73] At the same time, from the perspective of international law, EU law is based on international treaties which are a source of international law. However, it also operates as (part of) the internal law of the parties (the Member States and/or the EU) to other international agreements. This hybrid character of EU law, when considered from both the perspective of

---

71 Vienna Convention on the Law of Treaties (VCLT) (adopted 23 May 1969, entered into force 27 January 1980) 1155 UNTS 331 <https://legal.un.org/ilc/texts/instruments/english/conventions/1_1_1969.pdf> accessed 21 November 2020.

72 Case C-478/07 *Budvar* [2009] EU:C:2009:521, para 98 and the case-law cited.

73 Case C-284/16 *Achmea*, para 35; *Opinion 2/13*, para 174; Case 26/62 *Van Gend den Loos v Nederlandse Administratie Der Belastingen* [1963] EU:C:1963:1, p. 12.

international law and EU law itself, means that it is difficult to apply general international law regarding, especially, the law of treaties. The latter is based on a dichotomy between national law and international law. The EU operates between those two sets of legal orders. This has resulted in particular challenges for arbitral tribunals and national courts of third States which are, unlike national courts of the Member States, not bound by the primacy of EU law or subject to the control of the CJEU (by means of, notably, the preliminary ruling procedure).

13.52 In essence, as a matter of international law, it is difficult to find bases for not applying valid intra-EU BITs. Either the relationship between EU law and international law is viewed in a vertical manner (i.e., EU law being considered as part of the laws of the Member States) but then the difficulty lies in the consideration that municipal law, including constitutional law, may not take precedence over international law.[74] Or, when viewed in a horizontal manner (i.e., EU law being considered as part of international law), tribunals have refused to consider that EU law concerns the same subject matter as intra-EU BITs.[75] In any event, both perspectives are possibly incomplete and imperfect conceptualizations of the relationship between EU law and international law.[76] In effect, international law, including the law of treaties, has so far not been designed to address the relationship between international law and a legal system, as described by the CJEU in *Achmea* as follows:[77]

> the autonomy of EU law with respect both to the law of the Member States and to international law is justified by the essential characteristics of the EU and its law, relating in particular to the constitutional structure of the EU and the very nature of that law. EU law is characterised by the fact that it stems from an independent source of law, the Treaties, by its primacy over the laws of the Member States, and by the direct effect of a whole series of provisions which are applicable to their nationals and to the Member States themselves. Those characteristics have given rise to a structured network of principles, rules and mutually interdependent legal relations binding the EU and its Member States reciprocally and binding its Member States to each other.

13.53 As a result, relying on so-called conflict of norms and principles under international law has not succeeded.

a. The position of national courts of the Member States after the Achmea *judgment*

13.54 National courts of the Member States must, like any other organs of a State, comply with EU law and respect the primacy of EU law.[78] They are also bound to respect the jurisdiction of the

---

74 See, e.g., VCLT, Art 27; International Law Commission (ILC) Articles on Responsibility of States for Internationally Wrongful Acts (adopted 23 April–1 June and 2 July–10 August 2001), Report on the work of its fifty-third session Supplement No. 10 (A/56/10) <https://legal.un.org/ilc/texts/instruments/english/draft_articles/9_6_2001.pdf> accessed 21 November 2020, Arts 3 and 32; *Elettronica Sicula SPA (ESLI) (United States of America v Italy)* [1989] ICJ Report, p. 15, paras 71 to 73; *Interpretation of the Convention between Greece and Bulgaria respecting reciprocal emigration*, Advisory Opinion [1930] PCIJ 17 Series B; *Treatment of Polish nationals and other persons of Polish origin or speech in the Danzig territory*, Advisory Opinion [1932] PCIJ 44 Series A/B.

75 See, section 3.c below.

76 See, generally, J. Wouters, C. Ryngaert, T. Ruys and G. De Baere, *International Law – A European Perspective* (Hart, 2018), Ch 4.

77 Case C-284/16 *Achmea*, para 33 and the case-law cited.

78 Joined Cases C-314/81 to 316/81 and C-83/82 *Waterkeyn* [1982] EU:C:1982:430, para 14; Case C-224/01 *Köbler* [2003] EU:C:2003:513; Case C-129/00 *Commission v. Italy* [2003] EU:C:2003:656, where Member States were found liable for their failure to comply with EU law, including the obligation to suspend proceedings and request a preliminary ruling from the CJEU.

CJEU in respect of the interpretation and application of EU law. Judicial remedies are available to maintain that allocation of powers between the Member States and the EU, and between the courts at both levels of power. Thus, national courts of the Member States may (and in certain circumstances, must) suspend proceedings and request a preliminary ruling from the CJEU.[79] The failure of Member States' courts to comply with EU law may also be the subject of infringement proceedings.

National courts of the Member States have been asked to consider the consequences of the **13.55** *Achmea* judgment, especially in the context of setting aside proceedings and enforcement proceedings.[80] Enforcement or setting aside of arbitral awards not subject to the ICSID Convention[81] must be sought pursuant to the grounds laid down in the United Nations Convention on the Recognition and Enforcement of Foreign Arbitral Awards (the 'New York Convention'). In light of the latter Convention, the fact that the *Achmea* judgment confirmed that ISDS clauses in intra-EU BITs were contrary to EU law has caused defendant Member States to seek the annulment and refusal of the enforcement of intra-EU arbitral awards on the grounds that there was no valid arbitration agreement,[82] the dispute was not arbitrable,[83] or the arbitral awards violated the public policy of that Member State.[84]

Despite the obligation of national courts of the Member States to comply with EU law, **13.56** including as interpreted by the judgment in *Achmea*, in the first setting aside case brought in respect of an intra-EU BIT award after that judgment, the Swedish Court of Appeal surprisingly rejected the jurisdictional challenge brought by Poland. That dispute related to an arbitral award against Poland, issued by a tribunal established pursuant to the Poland-Belgium/Luxembourg BIT, in favour of a Luxemburgish company.[85] Before the Swedish court, Poland argued that intra-EU investment disputes (such as the one at stake) were not arbitrable and could 'not be determined by arbitrators'. Poland also argued that given that Articles 267 and 344 TFEU precluded intra-EU ISDS arbitral proceedings, the ISDS clause

---

79 TFEU, Art 267.
80 In light of the CJEU judgment in *Achmea*, the German Federal Court (*Bundesgerichtshof*) (i.e., the court which referred the *Achmea* preliminary ruling to the CJEU) handed down a decision which set aside the award obtained by Achmea (Case No. I ZB 2/15). Achmea then submitted an extraordinary challenge before the German Federal Constitutional Court (*Bundesverfassungsgericht*) alleging that certain German constitutional law provisions had been violated (Case 2 BvR 557/19) – Still pending. In the same vein but in a different case, on 11 February 2021, the Frankfurt Court of Appeals (Oberlandesgericht Frankfurt am Main) relied on the judgment in *Achmea* in order to find that arbitral proceedings initiated by an Austrian Bank against Croatia were inadmissible (Case 26 SchH 2/20).
81 Convention on the Settlement of Investment Disputes between States and Nationals of Other States (the 'ICSID Convention'). Arbitral awards handed down pursuant to the ICSID Convention are subject to an ad hoc annulment mechanism governed by the ICSID Convention itself. Those awards are therefore not subject to domestic judicial review. Pursuant to Art 52 of the ICSID Convention, a party can request the annulment of an ICSID award if: (a) the tribunal was not properly constituted; (b) the tribunal had manifestly exceeded its powers; (c) there was corruption on the part of a member of the tribunal; (d) there has been a serious departure from a fundamental rule of procedure; or (e) the award has failed to state the reasons on which it is based.
     At the time of writing, a number of intra-EU ICSID awards handed down after the *Achmea* judgment were subject to annulment proceedings pursuant to Art 52 of the ICSID Convention. However, since none of those annulment proceedings had yet been concluded it is unknown (but nevertheless very likely) whether any of the alleged reasons for annulment relate to the issue raised by the *Achmea* judgment.
82 New York Convention, Art V(1)(a).
83 Ibid., Art V(2)(a).
84 Ibid., Art V(2)(b).
85 *PL Holdings S.à.r.l. v. Republic of Poland*, SCC Case No. V 2014/163, Final award of 28 September 2017.

in the Poland-Belgium/Luxembourg BIT was invalid and the arbitral awards handed down pursuant to that clause violated Swedish public order.[86]

13.57 However, the Swedish Court of Appeal understood the CJEU in *Achmea* to have ruled that:

> What the TFEU precludes is that Member States conclude agreements with each other meaning that one Member State is obligated to accept subsequent arbitral proceeding with an investor and that the Member States thereby establish a system where they have excluded disputes from the possibility of requesting a preliminary ruling, even though the disputes may involve interpretation and application of EU law.[87]

13.58 In light of this understanding, and although the ISDS clause in the Poland-Belgium/Luxembourg BIT was identical to the one at issue in *Achmea*, the Swedish Court found that Poland – unlike Slovakia in *Achmea* – had not raised any objection to the existence of an arbitration agreement in its statement of defence; Poland had only done so later in the proceeding. This absence of a timely objection resulted in Poland having entered into an implicit commercial arbitration agreement with the investor. Since the Swedish Court of Appeal had previously found that the *Achmea* judgment did not preclude a Member State from entering into an arbitration agreement with an investor from another Member State, the Court of Appeal confirmed the jurisdiction of the arbitral tribunal. Although the position expressed by the Swedish Court is legally creative, perhaps it too easily dismissed Poland's objection, which related to a public policy issue that could have been raised at any stage of the proceedings. The Swedish Court's decision also raises the question of whether the acceptance of such an implicit arbitration agreement complies with Article 2 of the New York Convention, which requires that arbitration agreements should be in writing. In any event, the judgment of the Swedish Court is currently subject to an appeal before the Swedish Supreme Court, which recently decided to refer the matter to the CJEU for a preliminary ruling.[88] The issue put before the CJEU relates specifically to the question of whether a Member State may tacitly accept an investor's request for arbitration by not objecting in due time to arbitration proceedings under an intra-EU BIT.[89] This preliminary ruling procedure will offer the CJEU a first opportunity to clarify the consequences to attach to its judgment in *Achmea*.

b. The position of non-EU national courts after the Achmea judgment

13.59 So far, a few national courts of third States, including those of the US, have been asked to consider whether the *Achmea* judgment has consequences for the applications pending before them. Notably, a recent decision of the US District Court for the District of Columbia addressed, for the first time, the question of whether intra-EU arbitral awards may be enforced in the United States. In that case, which related to the enforcement of the *Micula* award against Romania, the District Court found that the *Achmea* judgment was based on the premise that the arbitral tribunal had been called upon to interpret and apply EU law. However, according to the District Court, the *Micula* case was distinguishable from *Achmea* because the dispute in *Micula* did not relate to the interpretation or application of EU law. To

---

86 *Poland v PL Holding SARL*, Case No. T 8538-17 and T 12033-17, Judgment of the Svea Court of Appeal of 22 February 2019.

87 Ibid.

88 *Poland v PL Holdings SARL*, Case No. T 1569-19, decision of the Swedish Supreme Court of 12 December 2020.

89 Case C-109/20, *Poland v PL Holding SARL*, CJEU, [2020] OJ C 161/40 – still pending.

reach that conclusion, the District Court found that the *Micula* dispute before the arbitral tribunal was related to events that occurred before Romania acceded to the EU and, consequently, EU law was not the 'controlling law'.[90] Based on that distinction, the District Court was able to avoid dealing directly with the implications of the *Achmea* judgment.

c. The position of arbitral tribunals after the Achmea judgment

Following the judgment in *Achmea*, the Member States that are parties in proceedings before arbitral tribunals and the European Commission (where admitted as an *amicus curiae*), have sought, in pending arbitral proceedings, a declaration from arbitral tribunals that they lack jurisdiction to continue the proceedings. So far, the Member States and the European Commission have mostly failed in that quest. **13.60**

In general, the position of tribunals has been that the *Achmea* judgment operates so as to produce effects within the EU legal order whereas their jurisdiction is rooted in international law pursuant to which intra-EU BITs, including their ISDS clauses, remain valid.[91] More particularly, when asserting their jurisdiction, and despite the fact that the *Achmea* judgment had declared ISDS clauses in intra-EU BITs incompatible with EU law, arbitral tribunals have found that they derive their powers from international treaties and international law 'rather than directly from EU law'.[92] Whilst some arbitral tribunals have been cognizant of the fact that the EU legal order is based on international treaties, which are in a specific relationship to national law,[93] the operation of the primacy of EU law over the national laws of the Member States has been seen as distinct from how the relationship between international law and national law is typically perceived.[94] Consequently, arbitral tribunals have found that they were required to operate in the international legal framework, outside the boundaries of EU law.[95] **13.61**

---

90 *Micula v Romania*, United States District Court for the District of Columbia, Memorandum Opinion of 11 September 2019, Case No. 17-cv-02332 (APM), pp. 20 and 21. This decision is currently subject to an appeal before the US Court of Appeals for District of Columbia Circuit. Another case is currently pending before the District Court for the District of Columbia (*Eiser Infrastructure Ltd and Energia Solar Luxembourg S.A.R.L. v Kingdom of Spain*, case 18-1686 (CKK)). At the time of writing, however, the proceedings were stayed and the parties have been invited to inform the court of their position on whether the case should be dismissed).

91 *UP (formerly Le Chèque Déjeuner) and C.D Holding Internationale v Hungary*, ICSID Case No. ARB/13/35, Award 9 October 2018, para 253; *Foresight Luxembourg e.a. v Kingdom of Spain* (ECT) SCC Case No. 2015/150, Final award of 14 November 2018, paras 218–219; *Cube Infrastructure Fund v Kingdom of Spain* (ECT), ICSID Case No. ARB/15/20, Decision on Jurisdiction, Liability and Partial Decision on Quantum of 19 February 2019, paras 142 and following; *Landesbank Baden-Württemberg and others v Kingdom of Spain* (ECT), ICSID Case No. ARB/15/45, Decision on the Intra-EU Jurisdictional Objection of 25 February 2019, paras 177-178; *NextEra Energy Global Holdings BV and NextEra Energy Spain Holdings BV v Kingdom of Spain* (ECT), ICSID Case No. ARB/14/11, Decision on Jurisdiction, Liability and Quantum Principles of 12 March 2019, paras 350–351; *Eskosol v Italy* (ECT), ICSID Case No. ARB/15/50, Decision on Termination Request and Intra-EU Objection of 7 May 2019, paras 110–111.

92 *Eskosol v Italy*, ibid.

93 *Vattenfall AB and others v Federal Republic of Germany* (ECT), ICSID Case No. ARB/12/12, Decision on the Achmea Issue of 31 August 2018, para 146; *Cube Infrastructure Fund v Kingdom of Spain* (ECT), ICSID Case No. ARB/15/20, Decision on Jurisdiction, Liability and Partial Decision on Quantum of 19 February 2019, para 158.

94 *Eskosol v Italy* (ECT), ICSID Case No. ARB/15/50, Decision on Termination Request and Intra-EU Objection of 7 May 2019, para 182.

95 Ibid., para 186.

13.62   Notably, the tribunal in *Eskosol* appeared to focus on the essence of the problem following the *Achmea* judgment, namely that that judgment (i) may not automatically invalidate an international treaty or any individual provision of a treaty[96] and (ii), in any event, may not affect Member States' consent to arbitration prior to 6 March 2018.[97] According to the tribunal in *Eskosol*, '[i]t was not until the CJEU actually issued the *Achmea* Judgment that, at the very earliest, [...], it could be said that investors were placed on notice about the risks of relying on Member States' apparent consent to arbitration'.[98]

13.63   Arbitral tribunals have also refused to find that they lack jurisdiction based on an interpretation of the intra-EU BIT by taking into account EU law as a 'relevant [rule] of international law applicable in the relations between the parties' within the meaning of Article 31(3)(c) of the VCLT. According to arbitral tribunals, Article 31(3)(c) does not operate so as to have other 'relevant rules of international law applicable in the relations between the parties' prevail over the intra-EU BITs that are the subject of the interpretation. According to arbitral tribunals, Article 31(3)(c) of the VCLT simply directs tribunals, when interpreting intra-EU BITs, to 'take account' of those 'relevant rule[s] of international law applicable in the relations between the parties' together with the 'context' of the terms of the treaty and all other elements relevant to treaty interpretation.[99] In other words, they have focused on the fact that there are limits to what interpretation may achieve and that they consider that Article 31(3)(c) cannot operate so as to displace an intra-EU BIT to the benefit of the application of EU law.

13.64   The Member States and the European Commission have also argued that the EU Treaties have the same subject matter as intra-EU BITs and therefore are 'successive treaties' within the meaning of Article 30 VCLT. Pursuant to that provision, a treaty dealing with the same subject matter should prevail over a former treaty concluded between the same parties. Relying on that provision, the Member States have argued that their consent to arbitration initially expressed in an intra-EU BIT was revoked when they acceded to the EU. However, that argument has not succeeded because arbitral tribunals have taken the view that intra-EU BITs and the EU Treaties do not have the same subject matter[100] given that the subject matter

---

96   Ibid., para. 187. See also *Magyar Farming Company Ltd, Kintyre Kft and Inicia Zrt v Hungary*, ICSID Case No. ARB/17/27, Award of 13 November 2019, para 207.

97   *Eskosol v Italy*, ibid., paras 199 and 206. See also: *UP (formerly Le Chèque Déjeuner) and C.D Holding Internationale v Hungary*, ICSID Case No. ARB/13/35, Award 9 October 2018, para 264.

98   *Eskosol v Italy*, ibid., para 206.

99   *Vattenfall AB and others v Federal Republic of Germany* (ECT), ICSID Case No. ARB/12/12, Decision on the Achmea Issue of 31 August 2018, paras 154–155; *Landesbank Baden-Württemberg and others v Kingdom of Spain* (ECT), ICSID Case No. ARB/15/45, Decision on the Intra-EU Jurisdictional Objection of 25 February 2019, paras 163–164.

100   *Marfin Investment Group v The Republic of Cyprus*, ICSID Case No. ARB/13/27, Award of 26 July 2018, para 588; *Eskosol v Italy* (ECT), ICSID Case No. ARB/15/50, Decision on Termination Request and Intra-EU Objection of 7 May 2019, para 146; *United Utilities (Tallinn) BV and Aktsiaselts Tallinna Vesi v Republic of Estonia*, ICSID Case No. ARB/14/24, Award of 21 June 2019, paras 538 and following; *Belenergia SA v Italian Republic* (ECT), ICSID Case No. ARB/15/40, Award of 6 August 2019, paras 316 and following; *Magyar Farming Co Ltd, Kintyre Kft and Inicia Zrt v Hungary*, ICSID Case No. ARB/17/27, Award of 13 November 2019, paras 228–238. Some tribunals sitting in ECT-based intra-EU ISDS also found that the rule expressed in Art 30 VCLT was a 'subsidiary' rule and that when a treaty included specific provisions (such as Art 16 ECT) dealing with its relationship to other treaties, that specific provision applied as lex specialis (see *Vattenfall AB and others v Federal Republic of Germany* (ECT), ICSID Case No. ARB/12/12, Decision on the Achmea Issue of 31 August 2018, para 217: *Landesbank Baden-Württemberg and others v Kingdom of Spain* (ECT), ICSID Case No. ARB/15/45, Decision on the Intra-EU Jurisdictional Objection of 25 February 2019, paras 181–184).

of a BIT is the protection of foreign investment while the EU Treaties establish the free movement of capital.[101] Tribunals have also considered that the objective of the EU Treaties is to create a common market between the Member States, whereas the objective of BITs is to provide specific guarantees in order to encourage international flows of investment into particular States.[102]

Some arbitral tribunals have also addressed the status and value of the Member States' **13.65** post-*Achmea* declarations of January 2019. Perhaps unsurprisingly, the tribunals that addressed those declarations refused to consider that those declarations had any impact on their jurisdiction. According to the tribunal in *Magyar Farming*, those declarations 'are not an exclusive and dispositive method of treaty interpretation' and while they can help interpreting the treaty terms, they cannot change their meaning.[103] That same tribunal also found that the declarations were not the proper procedure for terminating or amending the intra-EU BIT at stake. According to that tribunal, '[t]he BIT is an international treaty that confers rights on private parties. While the Contracting States remain the masters of their treaty, their control is limited by the general principles of legal certainty and *res inter alios acta, aliis nec nocet nec prodest*'.[104] Furthermore, the tribunal in *Eskosol* noted that important language in the declarations was written in the future tense, thereby suggesting that the signatories of those declarations did not believe that their intra-EU BITs were already terminated.[105] In the same vein, the tribunal in *United Utilities* found that the fact that the declarations stated that the Member States will make their best efforts to terminate their BIT before 6 December 2019 necessarily implied that the intra-EU BIT at stake is still in force.[106]

Finally, some tribunals have adopted a specific (perhaps too narrow) reading of *Achmea* and **13.66** have found that the findings of the CJEU in that judgment only extend to intra-EU BITs of which the ISDS clause was similar to the one in the Czechoslovakia-Netherlands BIT[107] or did not extend to intra-EU ISDS disputes of which the place of arbitration is outside the European Union.[108]

---

101   *Eastern Sugar BV (Netherlands) v The Czech Republic*, SCC Case No. 088/2004, Partial award of 27 March 2007, paras 161–164.

102   *Marfin Investment Group v The Republic of Cyprus*, ICSID Case No. ARB/13/27, Award of 26 July 2018, para 589, quoting *Jan Oostergetel and Theodora Laurentius v The Slovak Republic*, UNCITRAL, Decision on jurisdiction of 30 April 2010, paras 74–79 and *European American Investment Bank AG (EURAM) v Slovak Republic*, UNCITRAL, Award on jurisdiction of 22 October 2012, paras 178–184.

103   *Magyar Farming Co Ltd, Kintyre Kft and Inicia Zrt v Hungary*, ICSID Case No. ARB/17/27, Award of 13 November 2019, para 218. On the same issue, see also, *Eskosol v Italy* (ECT), ICSID Case No. ARB/15/50, Decision on Termination Request and Intra-EU Objection of 7 May 2019, paras 223–224.

104   *Magyar Farming Co Ltd, Kintyre Kft and Inicia Zrt v Hungary*, ibid., para 222.

105   *Eskosol v Italy* (ECT), ICSID Case No. ARB/15/50, Decision on Termination Request and Intra-EU Objection of 7 May 2019, paras 216–217.

106   *United Utilities (Tallinn) BV and Aktsiaselts Tallinna Vesi v Republic of Estonia*, ICSID Case No. ARB/14/24, Award of 21 June 2019, paras 558–560.

107   *CEF Energia BV v Italian Republic* (ECT), SCC Case No. 158/2015, Award of 16 January 2019, para 96.

108   *WA Investments Europa Nova Ltd v Czech Republic*, PCA Case No. 2014-19, Award of 15 May 2019, paras 438 and following; *Photovoltaik Knopf Betriebs-GmbH (Germany) v Czech Republic*, PCA Case No. 2014-21, Award of 15 May 2019, paras 337 and following; *ICW Europe Investments Ltd v Czech Republic*, PCA Case No. 2014-22, Award of 15 May 2019, paras 396 and following.

13.67 Those are the main reasons that underlie the Member States' search for a more sustainable solution for managing the consequences resulting from the *Achmea* judgment.

4. Searching for a more sustainable management of the consequences of the *Achmea* judgment – the plurilateral agreement between the Member States

a. Introduction

13.68 Instead of the Member States agreeing, on a bilateral basis, to amend or terminate their respective intra-EU BITs, EU Member States have elected, as envisaged in their declarations of January 2019, to negotiate a single plurilateral agreement to which they are all party that will terminate all of the intra-EU BITs ('the plurilateral agreement'). That agreement received the political consensus of all EU Member States in October 2019 and 23 Member States (with the notable exceptions of Austria, Sweden, Finland, the UK[109] and Ireland)[110] signed the agreement on 5 May 2020.[111] This plurilateral agreement entered into force on 29 August 2020,[112] following its ratification by Hungary and Denmark.[113] Since then, and at the date of finalizing this chapter, Bulgaria, Croatia, Cyprus, Malta, Slovakia, Estonia, Latvia and Slovenia had also ratified this agreement while Luxembourg, the Netherlands and Portugal have made official declarations.[114]

13.69 The use of a plurilateral agreement to terminate, amend, interpret or complement a series of existing agreements is not novel. This method – which relies on Article 30(3) of the VCLT ('When all the parties to the earlier treaty are parties also to the later treaty but the earlier treaty is not terminated or suspended in operation under Article 59, the earlier treaty applies only to the extent that its provisions are compatible with those of the later treaty') – have been used in the past to, for example, modify bilateral tax treaties[115] and conclude the United Nations Convention on Transparency in Treaty-based Investor-State Arbitration (the 'Mauritius Convention on Transparency'). It is currently being contemplated within the UNCITRAL Working Group III as a preferable method for the creation of a Multilateral Investment

---

109   Under the Withdrawal Agreement, EU law continues to apply to the United Kingdom during the post-Brexit transition period.

110   On 14 May 2020, following the non-signature of the plurilateral agreement by those Member States, the European Commission sent letters of formal notice to Finland and the United Kingdom for failing to effectively remove intra-EU BITs from their legal orders, <https://ec.europa.eu/commission/presscorner/detail/en/INF_20_859> accessed 21 November 2020.

111   Financial Stability, Financial Services and Capital Markets Union, 'Agreement for the Termination of Bilateral Investment Treaties between the Member States of the European Union' (European Commission, 5 May 2020) <https://ec.europa.eu/info/sites/info/files/business_economy_euro/banking_and_finance/documents/200505-bilateral-investment-treaties-agreement_en.pdf> accessed 21 November 2020. Publication in the Official Journal of the European Union, [2020] OJ L 169/1.

112   OJ 2020 L 281, p. 1.

113   Pursuant to its Article 16(1), the plurilateral agreement entered into force 30 calendar days after the date on which the Depositary received the second instrument of ratification, approval or acceptance.

114   <https://www.consilium.europa.eu/en/documents-publications/treaties-agreements/agreement/?id=2019049&Doc Language=en#> accessed 17 December 2020. On 3 February 2021, the German Constitutional Court rejected an application submitted by Achmea aimed at preventing Germany's ratification of the plurilateral agreement. The German Constitutional Court dismissed the application noting the lack of relationship between the ratification of the plurilateral agreement and Achmea's pending claims (Case 2 BvQ 97/20).

115   OECD Study, 'Developing a Multilateral Instrument to Modify Bilateral Tax Treaties Action 15 – 2015 Final Report' (OECD/G20 Base Erosion and Profit Shifting Project, 2015), p. 31, para 14.

Court.[116] Such a method is typically preferred because, instead of concluding a high number of separate agreements whereby State parties amend or terminate existing agreements between themselves on a bilateral basis, it allows for the conclusion of a single multilateral agreement whereby the parties agree to amend all their respective (bilateral) treaties having the same subject matter at once.

The entire premise of the plurilateral agreement is that, as a result of the *Achmea* judgment, **13.70** intra-EU BITs, insofar as they have not yet been unilaterally or bilaterally terminated or their sunset clauses[117] have not yet expired,[118] may not be applied 'after the date on which the last of the Parties to an intra-EU bilateral investment treaty became a Member State of the European Union'.[119] The use of the date on which the last of the parties to an intra-EU BIT became Member States, can be explained by the fact that it enables the Member States to include all of the intra-EU BITs within the scope of the plurilateral agreement.

To that effect, the plurilateral agreement provides that intra-EU arbitral proceedings under the **13.71** Energy Charter Treaty are excluded from the scope of the agreement.[120] Taking into account the different declarations made by the Member States, it is clear that no consensus could be reached on the solution in respect of the Energy Charter Treaty.[121] Further intervention of the CJEU thus appears necessary to achieve convergence of the position of the Member States on that matter.

The plurilateral agreement is conceived as addressing only the consequences resulting from the **13.72** *Achmea* judgment and ISDS pursuant to intra-EU BITs. This is because the parties do not wish that the substantive provisions of intra-EU BITs are also necessarily incompatible with EU law.[122] At the same time, however, the agreement is based on the assumption that whatever protection is given to investors under intra-EU BITs, who exercise fundamental freedoms in the internal market, is equally guaranteed by EU law.[123]

Two annexes are attached to the plurilateral agreement. Annex A lists the intra-EU BITs that **13.73** will be terminated as a result of the agreement. Annex B lists intra-EU BITs that have already been terminated but contain sunset clauses that may still produce effects.

In essence, the plurilateral agreement serves three distinctive purposes: (i) it terminates all **13.74** intra-EU BITs (including their sunset clauses); (ii) it prohibits the initiation of new intra-EU ISDS cases and provides rules regarding the management of pending cases; and (iii) it provides alternatives to the recourse – by investors – to intra-EU ISDS arbitration proceedings.

---

116 See Ch 12, paras 12.120–12.131 and Ch 19, paras 19.61–19.65.
117 Plurilateral agreement, Art 1(7).
118 Ibid., recital VIII.
119 Ibid., recital V.
120 Ibid., recital X.
121 On 2 December 2020, Belgium submitted a request to the CJEU for an opinion on the compatibility with EU law of the ISDS provisions of the modernized version of the Energy Charter Treaty.
122 Plurilateral agreement, recital IX.
123 Ibid., recital XI.

b.   Termination of intra-EU BITs, including their sunset clauses

13.75   The plurilateral agreement terminates the intra-EU BITs, including the sunset clauses in those agreements, which are listed in Annex A to the agreement.[124] A sunset clause is defined as 'any provision in a Bilateral Investment Treaty which extends the protection of investments made prior to the date of termination of that Treaty for a further period of time'. Sunset clauses thus seek to protect rights acquired by investors prior to the termination of the BIT. Given that this type of clause presupposes the termination of the BITs while the clause remains effective, the termination of the sunset clause along with the BIT, as discerned in the plurilateral agreement, had to be made explicit so as to avoid that investors can continue to rely on their rights under the BITs despite its termination. Such rights include the right to resort to ISDS in respect of measures allegedly violating a BIT prior to its termination.[125] Otherwise, the BIT would continue to produce effects as if it was lawful prior to its termination.

13.76   A separate provision in the plurilateral agreement states that sunset clauses of the intra-EU BITs listed in Annex B are also terminated and may not produce any legal effects.[126] This termination will take effect on the date of the entry into force of the plurilateral agreement.[127] As of that time, there will no longer be any basis to initiate arbitral proceedings pursuant to any of the intra-EU BITs included in Annexes A and B. By terminating the sunset clauses along with the entire BIT, the Member States seek to avoid that an investor may still, nonetheless, initiate proceedings in respect of facts having taken place before the entry into force of the plurilateral agreement.

13.77   While States are normally in a position to terminate the international treaties to which they are party,[128] the fact that the plurilateral agreement also terminates the sunset clause in those intra-EU treaties might result in investors claiming that the plurilateral agreement deprives them of their rights acquired under the intra-EU BITs.[129] As the tribunal in *Magyar Farming* noted, the purpose of a sunset clause is to 'acknowledge that long-term interests of investors who have invested in the host State in reliance on the treaty guarantees must be respected'.[130] Given that the purpose of a sunset clause is precisely to prolong the protection granted to investors under a BIT following its termination, investors might argue that the termination of the sunset clauses contained in the intra-EU BITs violates the protection of their legitimate expectations.

13.78   This tension has resulted in some debate regarding the question of whether ISDS tribunals will give full effect to the termination of the sunset clauses in the intra-EU BITs. It has been

---

124   Ibid., Arts 2(1) and (2).

125   On the termination of BITs and sunset clauses, see *Eastern Sugar BV (Netherlands) v The Czech Republic*, SCC Case No. 088/2004, Partial award of 27 March 2007, paras 174 and following; and *Rupert Joseph Binder v Czech Republic*, UNCITRAL, Award on jurisdiction of 6 June 2007, paras 59 and following.

126   Plurilateral agreement, Art 3.

127   Ibid., Art 4(2).

128   VCLT, Arts 54 and 59.

129   On this question, see also, e.g., L. Halonen, 'Termination of Intra-EU BITs: Commission and Most Member States Testing the Principle of Good Faith under International Law' (Kluwer Arbitration Blog, 13 May 2020) <http://arbitrationblog.kluwerarbitration.com/2020/05/13/termination-of-intra-eu-bits-commission-and-most-member-states-testing-the-principle-of-good-faith-under-international-law/?doing_wp_cron=1590679658.9551689624786376953125> accessed 21 November 2020.

130   *Magyar Farming Co Ltd, Kintyre Kft and Inicia Zrt v Hungary*, ICSID Case No. ARB/17/27, Award of 13 November 2019, para 223.

argued that, irrespective of the benefits and legitimate expectations that investors derive from a treaty, the States parties to a treaty may terminate, taking into account Article 54 of the VCLT, a sunset clause, like any other clause of a treaty, by extinguishing this clause at the same time as they agree to terminate the rest of the treaty.[131] Based on that understanding, sunset clauses are intended to have effects especially where a party seeks to unilaterally withdraw from a bilateral investment agreement but not where both parties consent to terminate the entirety of the agreement. Others consider that a sunset clause results in acquired rights for investors which must survive the termination of the treaty. In part, this argument has been based on Article 37(2) VCLT (which provides that '[w]hen a right has arisen for a third state [...], the right may not be revoked or modified by the parties if it is established that the right was intended not to be revocable or subject to modification without the consent of the third State') and on the presumption that this provision reflects a general principle which is applicable to all third party right holders (and not solely third States), including investors.[132]

Overall, the debate suggests that investors are likely, following the entry into force of the **13.79** plurilateral agreement, to continue to rely on the sunset clauses in the terminated intra-EU BITs and to insist on the distinct function of such clauses (the effect of which depends on termination). At the same time, respondent States will have strong arguments based on the notion of consent in international law. Should this tension need to be resolved as a matter of EU law, it will also become necessary to take into account, in particular, the principle of legitimate expectations as established in the case-law of the CJEU.[133]

c. No new arbitral proceedings and the management of pending arbitral proceedings

The plurilateral agreement also envisages, as a general principle, that regardless of the date on **13.80** which those intra-EU BITs will be terminated, as of the date on which the last of the parties to an intra-EU BIT became an EU Member State (meaning, in essence, 2004, for intra-EU BITs to which Cyprus, Czech Republic, Estonia, Hungary, Latvia, Lithuania, Malta, Poland, Slovakia and Slovenia are parties; 2007, for intra-EU BITs to which Romania and Bulgaria are parties; and 2013, for intra-EU BITs to which Croatia is a party), the arbitration clauses in intra-EU BITs may no longer serve as a legal basis for arbitration proceedings.[134]

---

131   T. Voon and A.D. Mitchell, 'Denunciation, Termination and Survival: The Interplay of Treaty Law and International Investment Law' [2016] 31(2) *ICSID Review* 413, 430.

132   J. Harrison, 'The Life and Death of BITs: Legal Issues Concerning Survival Clauses and the Termination of Investment Treaties' [2012] 13(6) *The Journal of World Investment & Trade* 928, 944.

133   The CJEU has recognised that any trader who has justified hopes may rely on the principle of the protection of legitimate expectation (see: Case C-265/85 *Van den Bergh en Jurgens v Commission* [1987] EU:C:1987:121, para 44). See also Case T-203/96 *Embassy Limousines & Services v European Parliament* [1998] EU:T:1998:302, paras 74–76; Case T-106/13 *d.d. Synergy Hellas Anonymi Emporiki Etaireia Parochis Ypiresion Pliroforikis v European Commission* [2015] EU:T:2015:860, para 66; Case T-271/04 *Citymo SA v Commission of the European Communities* [2007] EU:T:2007:128, paras 138–155 Case C-153/10 *Staatssecretaris van Financiën v Sony Supply Chain Solutions (Europe) BV* [2011] EU:C:2011:224, para 47; Case C-349/17 *Eesti Pagar AS v Ettevõtluse Arendamise Sihtasutus and Majandus- ja Kommunikatsiooniministeerium* [2019] EU:C:2019:172, paras 96 and following and the case-law cited. In addition, the European Court of Human Rights has found that, in certain circumstances, a claimant could have a legitimate expectation that his claim would be determined in a certain manner (see: ECtHR, *Pressos Compania Naviera SA and Others v Belgium*, judgment of 20 November 1995, para 31 and ECtHR, *National & Provincial Building Society, Leeds Permanent Building Society and Yorkshire Building Society v the United Kingdom*, judgment of 23 October 1997, para 70).

134   Plurilateral agreement, Art 4(1).

13.81 This recognises the principle of retroactivity of CJEU rulings, which implies that the findings of the CJEU in the *Achmea* judgment regarding the invalidity of ISDS clauses in intra-EU BITs apply as of the moment that a Member State joined the EU. This inclusion in the plurilateral agreement is also a clear response to the position expressed so far by arbitral tribunals, which have refused to apply the *Achmea* judgment retroactively.[135]

13.82 Article 5 of the plurilateral agreement states that ISDS clauses may not serve as a legal basis for arbitral proceedings initiated on or after 6 March 2018, which is the date of the *Achmea* judgment. Thus, arbitration proceedings which have been concluded or settlements completed before 6 March 2018, but possibly after the date on which the ISDS clause became inapplicable, are not affected by the general principle expressed in Article 4(1).[136]

13.83 Those rules presuppose that investors having invested in another EU country after the accession of that country to the EU with the legitimate expectation that they would benefit from the protection under the intra-EU BIT (including, the ISDS clause in that BIT) would now, pursuant to Article 4(1) of the plurilateral treaty, need to accept that the host State never consented to intra-EU ISDS proceedings after it joined the EU. Likewise, where two (or more) investors initiated ISDS proceedings against the same Member State, pursuant to the same intra-EU BIT, at the same time or shortly after one another but one of these proceedings may have been concluded prior to 6 March 2018 whereas the other proceedings remained pending after that date, investors are to be treated differently.

13.84 Finally, Articles 4 and 5 of the plurilateral agreement apply together with certain obligations of conduct on Member States in respect of pending or new arbitration proceedings. Those obligations include informing arbitral tribunals of the consequences of the *Achmea* judgment and asking national courts (of a Member State or a third State) to set aside an existing arbitral award, annul it or refrain from recognising and enforcing it.[137] Whilst those obligations under Article 7 of the plurilateral agreement seek to ensure some degree of uniformity in the approach of the Member States, they do not include a commitment expressing a common position in respect of the legal arguments to be presented before arbitral tribunals or national courts. In respect of proceedings before national courts of the Member States, including such a commitment arguably is not required. The principles of EU law to be applied by those courts are settled. However, before arbitral proceedings and national courts of third States, the answer must be found in international law. The plurilateral agreement does not express a consensus between the Member States on what approach under international law is most likely to prevail.

d. Removing disputes from the jurisdiction of arbitral tribunals

13.85 The third purpose of the plurilateral agreement for seeking to manage the consequences of the *Achmea* judgment is, in essence, to seek to remove pending proceedings from the jurisdiction of arbitral tribunals by incentivising the use of either alternative methods of dispute resolution or the national courts of the Member States. Faced with the fact that, so far, arbitral tribunals

---

135 *Eskosol v Italy* (ECT), ICSID Case No. ARB/15/50, Decision on Termination Request and Intra-EU Objection of 7 May 2019, paras 199 and 206. See also: *UP (formerly Le Chèque Déjeuner) and CD Holding Internationale v Hungary*, ICSID Case No. ARB/13/35, Award 9 October 2018, para 264.

136 Plurilateral agreement, Art 6.

137 Ibid., Art 7.

have refused to give effect to the *Achmea* judgment and the position that ISDS clauses in intra-EU BITs have become inapplicable, the Member States are trying to remove disputes from arbitral tribunals which are seen as providing a type of judicial remedy that exists in parallel with those offered by national law of the Member States and falls outside the control of the CJEU.

The plurilateral agreement envisages two alternatives.   **13.86**

The first alternative is a settlement procedure in which an arbitral tribunal or national court is   **13.87** not to play any role. Article 9 describes a process through which pending proceedings might be taken away from arbitral tribunals and resolved amicably between the parties to the dispute, with the help of a facilitator. That process is, in essence, intended to operate as a form of mediation. The understanding is that, in using such a process, there is no longer a risk of a third party making a binding decision in which it might interpret and apply EU law and bypassing the role of the national courts of the Member States. Instead, the resolution of the dispute is placed within the control of the parties to the dispute, namely the investor and the Member State concerned.

The design and structure of the mechanism, as set out in Article 9, are based on the premise   **13.88** that both parties to the dispute have the right to propose to the other party to enter into a settlement procedure, implying that, during that procedure, the pending arbitration proceedings will be suspended and, where an award was already issued, no action will be taken in a national court in respect of that award.[138] Whether it is a requirement that the matter considered under the settlement procedure involves a measure that might violate EU law is unclear; in any event, Article 9(6) refers, in a permissive manner, to the scenario where the measure might be contrary to EU law. The option of entering into a settlement proceeding is limited in time: the procedure must be started within six months of the termination of the relevant intra-EU BIT.[139]

However, two exceptions apply to the right to enter into settlement procedures.   **13.89**

Where the measures at issue have been found in a final judgment, of either the CJEU or a   **13.90** national court, to violate EU law, the parties are obliged to enter into a settlement procedure. Whilst the Member States are free to accept such an obligation, it remains uncertain on what basis Article 9(3) of the plurilateral agreement may impose a similar obligation on individuals who might claim that, as a matter of international law, they continue to benefit from a right conferred by the earlier intra-EU BIT.

Where the measures at issue have been found in a final judgment, of either the CJEU or a   **13.91** national court, not to violate EU law, the parties are precluded from entering into a settlement procedure. That rule in Article 9(4) of the plurilateral agreement appears to be based on the understanding that, in such circumstances, an arbitral tribunal (assuming it finds that it has jurisdiction) will find that there is no violation of the intra-EU BIT. However, whether the understanding of equivalent protection under intra-EU BITs and EU law, which the Member

---

138 Ibid., Art 9(1).
139 Ibid., Art 9(2).

States seem to express in recital XI, will be shared by arbitral tribunals remains unresolved. At the same time, in the circumstance envisaged by Article 9(4), there might be fewer concerns about the arbitral tribunals interpreting or applying EU law in a manner that results in a favourable award for the investor.

13.92 Putting aside those exceptions, the parties are to participate in the settlement procedure with the help of the facilitator whose task is to oversee an impartial facilitation 'with a view to finding between the parties an amicable, lawful and fair out-of-court and out-of-arbitration settlement of the dispute which is the subject of the Arbitration Proceedings'.[140] The person appointed, (in principle) by common accord, as a facilitator must meet certain qualification requirements.[141] Where parties cannot agree on the facilitator, the Member States envisage that an appointing authority might be asked to intervene, namely a person appointed by a former Member of the CJEU who was asked by the Director General of the Legal Service of the Commission to make that appointment.[142] This mechanism avoids that either an investor or a respondent Member State might block the operation of the facilitation process by opposing the appointment of the facilitator. The design of this default mechanism appears to be directed at ensuring that the facilitator has a sufficient background in EU law. A considerable part of Article 9 is concerned with putting in place a procedural framework for the settlement procedure, in which the facilitator is to play a critical role and to indirectly seek to ensure that any solution found complies with EU law. The outcome of a successful settlement procedure will be an agreement binding on both parties, in which, notably, the investor must relinquish any rights derived from the ISDS clause under the intra-EU BIT.[143]

13.93 Although there is (obviously) no obligation for the parties to reach an amicable settlement, the facilitation process nevertheless seeks to safeguard the rights and interests of Member States and to mitigate the potential negative effects of decisions which may find that a Member State measure violated an investor's rights. To that effect, Article 9(3) and 9(4) identifies circumstances in which resort to the facilitation process (but without any guarantee of an effective outcome at the end of that process) is either excluded or required. If the Member State measure has previously been found to be incompatible with EU law, the parties must enter into a settlement procedure whereby the investor would seek a compromise with the Member State to obtain monetary compensation for the State's violation. However, if the State measure has been found to be compatible with EU law, the investor may not have recourse to the facilitation process.

13.94 The second alternative is removing a dispute from the jurisdiction of arbitral tribunals and placing it fully under the jurisdiction of the national courts of the Member States and thus also of the CJEU. To that effect, the Member States accept, in essence, to change their national laws so that time limits otherwise possibly barring investors' access to national remedies are no longer an obstacle.[144] This option is available where the investor seeks to make a claim based on either national law or EU law and not involving the application of the intra-EU BIT.[145]

---

140   Ibid., Art 9(7).
141   Ibid., Art 9(8).
142   Ibid., Art 9(8).
143   Ibid., Art 9(14)(a).
144   Ibid., Art 10(1).
145   Ibid., Arts 10(1)(b) and 10(3).

Accessing national courts on this basis also requires investors to relinquish rights derived from the ISDS clause under the intra-EU BIT and is subject to some time limits.[146] However, the plurilateral agreement does envisage that parties may first seek to use the first alternative (the settlement procedure) before resorting to the second alternative.[147]

D. CONCLUSION

Whilst the judgment in *Achmea* related to questions in respect of a particular arbitral clause in a specific intra-EU BIT, that judgment, read together with *Opinion 1/17*, means that EU law precludes the use of ISDS in resolving disputes between an investor and a Member State pursuant to an intra-EU BIT. As a matter of EU law, full effect can be given to that judgment by national courts of the Member States even if they might require further guidance from the CJEU on how to do so. However, as a matter of international law, it remains uncertain on what legal basis arbitral tribunals and national courts of third States, which are not bound by the primacy of EU law, would agree that no arbitration may be validly established pursuant to such an ISDS clause. This uncertainty results from the unresolved conceptualisation, in international law, of the relationship between international law, EU law and national law. Despite the EU having now considerable competences in the area of investment, the Member States prefer to assume the responsibility of seeking more sustainable solutions for managing the consequences resulting from the *Achmea* judgment. To that effect, they have negotiated a plurilateral agreement the objective of which is to terminate intra-EU BITs, set out general principles in respect of pending arbitral proceedings and to divert disputes from arbitration to settlement procedures and/or the jurisdiction of the national courts of the Member States.   **13.95**

Whilst it is generally accepted, under international law, that Member States are entitled to terminate their intra-EU BITs by mutual consent, the consequences of this termination on third parties (and in particular on investors' acquired rights and legitimate expectations) likely will be contested. It therefore cannot be excluded that further litigation regarding the consequences of the plurilateral agreement on investors' rights will take place before EU domestic courts based on a cause of action under EU law or domestic law.   **13.96**

---

146   Ibid., Art 10(1)(a).
147   Ibid., Arts 10(1)(a)(ii)–(iii) and 10(1)(c).

14

ARBITRATION UNDER THE ENERGY CHARTER TREATY: THE RELEVANCE OF EU LAW

Jeffrey Sullivan and David Ingle*

A. INTRODUCTION

14.01 This chapter examines the 'intra-EU' and 'extra-EU' disputes that have arisen under the Energy Charter Treaty (ECT). The ECT is an energy-specific multilateral agreement that covers all major aspects of international energy turnover: trade, transit, investment and energy efficiency. The ECT is the first and only multilateral investment treaty that contains binding provisions on the promotion and protection of investments specifically in relation to the energy sector.[1] The purpose of the ECT was to establish a new legal framework in the energy field, as confirmed by its Article 2: 'a legal framework in order to promote long-term co-operation in the energy field, based on complementarities and mutual benefits, in accordance with the objectives and principles of the [European Energy] Charter'.

14.02 According to the Energy Charter Secretariat's Reader's Guide to the ECT, the 'ECT's investment provisions build upon the content of bilateral investment treaties as they have developed during the last half-century.' As compared to typical bilateral investment treaties, however, the ECT has 'added value as compared to the bilateral investment treaties' given that the ECT 'is the first multilateral agreement on the promotion and protection of foreign investment, covering all important investment issues and providing *high standards of protection*'.[2] In other words, the ECT was intended by the Contracting Parties to provide investors stronger investment protection than that found in typical bilateral investment treaties.

---

* Date of submission: 14/2/2020.

1 Andrei Konoplyanik and Thomas Wälde, 'Energy Charter Treaty and its Role in International Energy' (2006) 24 *Journal of Energy and Natural Resources Law* 523.

2 Energy Charter Secretariat, *The Energy Charter Treaty: A Reader's Guide* (Energy Charter Secretariat 2002), 10 (emphasis added).

The ECT emerged from the 1991 European Energy Charter.[3] One of the original goals of the   **14.03** European Energy Charter was to enhance energy security and to facilitate investment and co-operation in the energy sector in the EU after the dissolution of the Soviet Union and the independence of the former Soviet Republics.[4] By providing contracting states and their investors certain standards of protection and mechanisms to resolve disputes relating to investments in the energy sector, the ECT sought to create more predictable legal frameworks that would foster the large international investments that are required in the energy sector.

The backdrop to this early 1990s initiative was the collapse of the Soviet Union and the desire   **14.04** of the Western European states at the time to have access to the energy-rich states in Eastern Europe.[5] As the late Professor Wälde explained: 'The overall background of the Treaty [the ECT] was the effort to help the transition economies of Eastern Europe to attract investment, mainly by helping to install a rule of law, safeguarding of property, respect for contracts and liberalisation of investment conditions in the model of Western market economies.'[6]

While the European Energy Charter was initially a European initiative, the scope expanded   **14.05** and the ECT itself of course goes far beyond Europe. It is true that, until recently, every EU Member State was a contracting party to the ECT, but this changed in 2016 when Italy gave its notice of withdrawal from the ECT. While 26 EU Member States remain party to the ECT,[7] there are 22 ECT contracting parties that come from outside of the EU.[8][9] The proportion of non-EU Member States in the ECT has increased in recent years, albeit at a slow pace. For example, Afghanistan ratified the ECT in January 2013,[10] Yemen ratified it in July 2018,[11] and Jordan ratified it in August 2018.[12]

---

3 According to the European Commission, 'Energy Charter Treaty – Background Note' (16 December 1994) <https://europa.eu/rapid/press-release_MEMO-94-75_en.htm?locale=EN> accessed 29 September 2019):

> The former Prime-Minister of the Netherlands, Mr Lubbers, launched his idea for a European Community for Energy at the European Council of 25th June 1990. Mr Lubbers and Mr Delors proposed a conference for the negotiations on an Energy Charter drafted by the European Commission in November 1990. In July 1991, the US and other non-European members of the OECD joined the negotiation process, as the EC had proposed to the EC Council of Ministers. On the 17th of December 1991, 48 States and the EC agreed on the principles set out in the Charter. After this political declaration of interest, the Contracting Parties undertook to negotiate the legally binding Treaty and three protocols on energy efficiency, hydrocarbons and nuclear safety.

4 Crina Baltag, *The Energy Charter Treaty: The Notion of Investor* (Kluwer Law International 2012) 1–25.

5 See Konoplyanik and Wälde (n 1), noting that the main appeal of the ECT for resource-rich countries in the East was to appear attractive to investors, to be seen to play the rules of the global economy, reduce their political risk perception and not to be left out of a possibly significant energy policy dialogue(s), and that:

> this was and is the more important aspect as most of the Eastern countries have problems in attracting (and keeping) foreign investment (which are needed both in order to bring innovations as well as for risk-mitigation and risk sharing in raising new projects), mainly in terms of legal and political instability and insecurity.

6 Ibid.

7 At the time of writing in February 2020, the UK had withdrawn from the EU but remained subject to EU law as part of the agreed transitory period.

8 Australia, Belarus, Norway, and Russia have signed but not ratified the ECT.

9 Afghanistan, Albania, Armenia, Azerbaijan, Georgia, Iceland, Japan, Jordan, Kazakhstan, Kyrgyzstan, Liechtenstein, Moldova, Mongolia, Montenegro, North Macedonia, Switzerland, Tajikistan, Turkey, Turkmenistan, the United Kingdom, Uzbekistan, and Yemen.

10 See <https://energycharter.org/who-we-are/members-observers/countries/afghanistan/> accessed 29 September 2019.

11 See <https://energycharter.org/who-we-are/members-observers/countries/yemen/> accessed 29 September 2019.

12 See <https://energycharter.org/who-we-are/members-observers/countries/jordan/> accessed 29 September 2019.

14.06   This chapter addresses the 'intra-EU' and 'extra-EU' disputes that have been brought under Article 26 of the Energy Charter Treaty. It first examines the cases that have arisen under the ECT between an EU Member State and an investor incorporated in another EU Member State. These so-called 'intra-EU' disputes are numerous; it has been observed that the ECT has more often than not been used as a tool to settle intra-EU controversies.[13] These disputes give rise to numerous legal issues regarding the relevance and status of EU law in the interpretation of the provisions of the ECT.

14.07   The chapter then considers so-called 'extra-EU' disputes. That is, disputes brought under the ECT by an investor from a non-EU Member State against the EU or an EU Member State. Although there is comparatively little jurisprudence considering the role EU law in these extra-EU disputes, this may be set to change with the resolution of inter alia disputes brought by Swiss and Japanese investors against Spain and a pending claim brought by a Swiss investor against the EU itself.

B. INTRA-EU DISPUTES

1.   EU law and tribunals' jurisdiction in intra-EU disputes under the ECT

14.08   Intra-EU disputes under the ECT have given rise to a number of jurisdictional objections founded on EU law. In particular, respondent States have argued that Article 26 of the ECT does not confer jurisdiction on tribunals to hear disputes between an EU Member State and an investor from another EU Member State. To date, no EU Member State has had any success when making this jurisdictional objection. In the words of the *RREEF* tribunal 'in all published or known investment treaty cases in which the intra-EU objection has been invoked by the Respondent, it has been rejected'.[14]

---

13   Graham Coop, former General Counsel to the ECT Secretariat, noted in 2014 that:

> something like half of all known ECT investor-State cases – and considerably more than half of the recent known ECT investor-State cases – concern disputes between an EU investor and another EU government. In other words, the ECT is invoked as an Intra-EU BIT more often than not.

Graham Coop, '20 Years of the Energy Charter Treaty (2014) 29 *ICSID Review – Foreign Investment Law Journal* 515, 523. More generally, 20 per cent of all known investment arbitration cases are intra-EU disputes (United Nations Conference on Trade and Development, 'Factsheet on Intra European Union Investor-State Arbitration Cases' (UNCTAD/DIAE/PCB/2018/7, December 2018):

> The overall number of known intra-EU cases (treaty-based arbitrations initiated by an investor from one EU member State against another EU member State) totalled 174 by 31 July 2018, which constitutes 20 per cent of the 904 known investor–State dispute settlement (ISDS) cases globally.

<https://unctad.org/en/PublicationsLibrary/diaepcb2018d7_en.pdf> accessed 14 May 2020).

14   *RREEF Infrastructure (GP) Ltd and RREEF Pan European Infrastructure Two Lux SARL v The Kingdom of Spain*, ICSID Case No ARB/13/30, Decision on Jurisdiction, 6 June 2016, para 89. In addition to the various decisions directly addressing the intra-EU objection, there have also been other investor-State arbitrations involving disputes between EU Member States and EU investors where no intra-EU objection was raised by the respondent State. For example, the respondent State did not raise an intra-EU objection in *AES Summit Generation Ltd v Hungary*. See *AES Summit Generation Ltd and AES-Tisza Erömü Kft v The Republic of Hungary*, ICSID Case No ARB/07/22, Award, 23 September 2010, section 6.

This should not be surprising in light of the text of Article 26 of the ECT.[15] In line with the **14.09** interpretive requirements of the Vienna Convention on the Law of Treaties, arbitral tribunals have routinely dismissed the intra-EU objection based on a plain reading of the ECT. The ordinary meaning of Article 26 of the ECT is clear:[16] it applies to disputes between any contracting party to the ECT and an investor of any other contracting party. Each EU Member State signed the ECT in its own capacity and became an ECT contracting party. Thus, an investor from one EU Member State that is an ECT contracting party can bring a dispute against another EU Member State that is a contracting party based on the plain language and ordinary meaning of Article 26.

There is no indication in the text of the ECT that any contracting parties limited their consent **14.10** to arbitration on the basis that some of the contracting parties are Member States of the EU.[17] On the contrary, Article 26(3) of the ECT specifically provides that the contracting parties' 'unconditional consent' to arbitration is 'subject only to subparagraphs (b) and (c)'. Those subparagraphs in turn refer to Annexes ID and IA of the ECT pursuant to which certain contracting parties have specifically narrowed their consent in respect of disputes previously submitted to another forum and to the umbrella clause contained in Article 10(1) of the ECT. The ECT provides no further exceptions to the contracting parties' 'unconditional' consent. In the absence of any provision to the contrary in the ECT, the dispute-settlement mechanism under Article 26 applies to 'disputes between a Contracting Party and an Investor of another Contracting Party', irrespective of whether the investor is an EU national and the ECT contracting party is also an EU Member State.

Respondent states raising the intra-EU objection have nevertheless argued that investors' **14.11** rights under the ECT are superseded by the investment protection provisions of the EU legal framework which, it is claimed, address the same subject matter.[18] According to this argument, Article 26 of the ECT is rendered invalid by EU law and, in particular, the 2009 Lisbon Treaty on the Functioning of the European Union (the TFEU). This argument is unconvincing for many reasons. First, the ECT and the TFEU do not address the same subject matter. The ECT grants investors rights that are additional to any other rights provided by the EU internal market. Investment protection under EU law is primarily focused on ensuring access to the market of another Member State.[19] Once an investment is made, EU law provides only limited investment protection, compared with the broad protection afforded by the ECT. For example, there is no obligation on the EU Member States to provide foreign investors or their

---

15 Art 26(1) of the ECT reads as follows:

> Disputes between a Contracting Party and an Investor of another Contracting Party relating to an Investment of the latter in the Area of the former, which concern an alleged breach of an obligation of the former under Part III shall, if possible, be settled amicably.

16 As Jan Paulsson has noted: 'Article 26 [of the ECT] is unambiguous, technical, and precise' (see Jan Paulsson, 'Arbitration Without Privity' (1995) 10 *ICSID Review – Foreign Investment Law Journal* 232, 249).

17 As noted in *Eiser*, 'treaty makers should be understood to carry out their function in good faith, and not to lay traps for the unwary with hidden meanings and sweeping implied exclusions' (see *Eiser Infrastructure Ltd and Energía Solar Luxembourg SARL v Kingdom of Spain*, ICSID Case No ARB/13/36, Final Award, 4 May 2017, para 186).

18 See e.g., *Vattenfall AB and others v Federal Republic of Germany*, ICSID Case No ARB/12/12, Decision on the *Achmea* Issue, 31 August 2018, para 215.

19 See, e.g., Catherine Barnard, *The Substantive Law of the EU: The Four Freedoms* (2nd edn, OUP 2007) 19.

investments with fair and equitable treatment.[20] As held in *Novenergia*, the FET standard is '*a legal notion which does not even exist, as such, in the EU legal order*'.[21] It should be further noted that, even if it were considered that EU law *does* cover the same subject matter as the ECT, Article 16 of the ECT provides that the provisions which are more favourable to the investor would prevail.[22] From an investor's prospective, recourse to international arbitration will almost certainly be more favourable than pursuing a claim in an EU national court.

14.12   EU law also does not enable an investor to bring claims in international arbitration proceedings for violation of any illegal governmental action taken against foreign investment. While it is possible for a private investor to claim damages from an EU Member State concerning a breach of the rights afforded to it under the rules of the internal market, for example on free movement of capital or freedom of establishment, such claims need to be brought before the domestic courts of the state where the investment is located. The ECT, however, is different in that (like other investment treaties) it allows investors direct recourse against the contracting states through international arbitration.

14.13   It has also been argued that intra-EU disputes brought under the ECT contravene Article 344 of the TFEU.[23] Although the Court of Justice of the European Union has considered that Article 344 was incompatible with a bilateral investment treaty entered into between The Netherlands and Slovakia in the *Achmea* judgment (discussed below), the same cannot be said of the ECT. Article 344 of the TFEU has limited application and provides that it applies only to disputes involving two or more EU Member States '*regarding the interpretation of EU law*'. Article 344 does not prohibit Member States from submitting disputes that are not related to EU law to other 'fora', nor does it prohibit the submission of disputes between other actors to a different method of settlement not contemplated in the EU treaties.[24] Nor does it apply to disputes between a Member State and a private investor. Given that there is no provision in any of the EU treaties dealing with investor-state arbitration, the principle set out in Article 344 of the TFEU does not apply to such a mechanism. This was confirmed by the tribunal in *Electrabel*, which held that Article 344 of the TFEU was not applicable in the context of investor-state arbitration.[25]

---

20   See Energy Charter Treaty (adopted 17 December 1994, entered into force 16 April 1998) 2080 UNTS 95 (ECT), Art 10(1).

21   *Novenergia II – Energy & Environment (SCA) (Grand Duchy of Luxembourg), SICAR v The Kingdom of Spain*, SCC Case No 2015/063, Award, 15 February 2018, para 465.

22   See ECT, Art 16.

23   See e.g., *RREEF Infrastructure v Spain* (n 14), paras 46ff.

24   Art 344 of the TFEU states the following: 'Member States undertake not to submit a dispute concerning the interpretation or application of the Treaties to any method of settlement other than those provided for therein.'

25   *Electrabel SA v The Republic of Hungary*, ICSID Case No ARB/07/19, Decision on Jurisdiction, Applicable Law and Liability, 30 November 2012, para 4.151. See also Christer Söderlund, 'Intra-EU BIT Investment Protection and the EC Treaty' (2007) 24 *Journal of International Arbitration* 455, 458:

  The investor-state dispute resolution mechanism contained in a BIT does not call into question the competence of the ECJ. The EC Treaty only imposes obligations on Member States in their dealings with each other, inter alia, by instituting an obligation to refer disputes within the exclusive remit of the EC Treaty to the ECJ for adjudication to the exclusion of any other procedural remedy. It does not commit any non-signatory – such as a private investor – to submit to ECJ jurisdiction. Hence, provisions of the EC Treaty cannot intrude on the BIT-based investor-state dispute resolution facility.

A further argument raised with respect to the ECT is that it contains an implicit disconnection **14.14** clause pursuant to which the ECT does not apply to intra-EU disputes.[26] Disconnection clauses are a well-known mechanism of public international law. The purpose of such a clause is to ensure that, as between those parties to a multilateral treaty that are also parties to another treaty, the rules of the other treaty will apply in their inter-se relations.[27] The ECT contains no express disconnection clause or declaration of competencies that would allow an ECT Tribunal to disregard its provisions in an intra-EU dispute. Although the ECT *travaux préparatoires* show that the EU had proposed the insertion of a disconnection clause, this was ultimately rejected from the draft treaty.[28] In the absence of such a disconnection clause, a multilateral treaty applies between all of its contracting parties.[29]

Given that there is no express disconnection clause, it has been argued by some states (and the **14.15** European Commission) that the ECT has an 'implicit' disconnection clause. However, the argument has been routinely rejected as flawed given that prior to the conclusion of the ECT, the EU had used disconnection clauses where they were intended to apply.[30] Moreover, the ECT does contain disconnection clauses where they are intended to apply.[31] Reading an

---

26 See e.g., *RREEF Infrastructure v Spain* (n 14), para 81.

27 As stated in Maja Smrkolj, 'The Use of the "Disconnection Clause" in International Treaties: What Does it Tell Us about the EC/EU as an Actor in the Sphere of Public International Law?' (GARNET Conference: 'The EU in International Affairs', Brussels, 24–26 April 2008) 5, this is also the purpose the European Commission ascribes to these clauses; namely, to: 'clarify relations between Community or EU rules, on the one hand, and the provisions of each of the conventions on the other hand' and 'to ensure the coexistence of this Convention with other (including existing) international legal instruments dealing with matters which are also dealt with in this Convention'. If Member States would be obliged to among themselves apply the law of a convention or a treaty instead of Community law these would, 'jeopardise the integrity and development of Community law in the area covered by the Convention, unless they are countered by a disconnection clause in the Convention itself'.
    See also 1988 Council of Europe/OECD Convention on Mutual Administrative Assistance in Tax Matters, Article 27, quoted in International Law Commission (ILC), 'Fragmentation of International Law: Difficulties Arising from the Diversification and Expansion of International Law, Report of the Study Group of the International Law Commission' finalised by Martti Koskenniemi, Fifty-Eighth Session (1 May–9 June and 3 July–11 August 2006), UN Document A/CN4/L682 (ILC Report on Fragmentation of International Law), para 289: '[t]he purpose of the clause is, according to the European Commission, to ensure the continuing application of Community rules between EC member States without any intent to affect the obligations between member States and other parties to treaties'; and Christian Tietje, 'The Applicability of the Energy Charter Treaty in ICSID Arbitration of EU Nationals vs. EU Member States' (Beiträge zum Transnationalen Wirtschaftsrecht, Martin-Luther-Universität Halle-Wittemberg No 78, 2008) 10–11.

28 *Vattenfall v Germany* (n 18), para 205.

29 Tietje, 'The Applicability of the Energy Charter Treaty in ICSID Arbitration of EU Nationals vs. EU Member States' (n 27), 11: '[t]he Energy Charter Treaty does not contain a "disconnection clause". From a public international law perspective, this again clearly indicates that the ECT establishes a comprehensive legally-binding effect, also with regard to the inter se relationship of the EU Member States.'

30 The first treaty to which the EU is a party that contains a disconnection clause is the 1988 Council of Europe/OECD Convention on Mutual Administrative Assistance in Tax Matters. This provides, in Art 27, as follows: 'Notwithstanding the rules of the present Convention, those Parties which are members of the European Economic Community shall apply in their mutual relations the common rules in force in that Community.' (see 1988 Council of Europe/OECD Convention on Mutual Administrative Assistance in Tax Matters, Article 27, quoted in ILC Report on Fragmentation of International Law (n 27), para 289).

31 Annex 2 to the Final Act of the European Energy Charter Conference thus contains a decision regarding the Svalbard Treaty as follows:
    In the event of a conflict between the treaty concerning Spitsbergen of 9 February 1920 (the Svalbard Treaty) and the Energy Charter Treaty, the treaty concerning Spitsbergen shall prevail to the extent of the conflict, without prejudice to the positions of the Contracting Parties in respect of the Svalbard Treaty. In the event of such conflict or a dispute

implicit intra-EU disconnection clause into the ECT is therefore irreconcilable with the ordinary meaning of the ECT and impermissible under the Vienna Convention.[32] Tribunals have thus found there to be no valid basis to contend that EU law deprives a tribunal of jurisdiction in an intra-EU dispute under the ECT.

2.   The status of EU law in intra-EU disputes under the ECT

14.16   Once it is clear that the intra-EU nature of a dispute is no bar to jurisdiction, the next question is to determine the proper status of EU law in the determination of the dispute. Article 26(6) of the ECT provides that '[a] tribunal established under [Article 26 of the ECT] shall decide the issues in dispute in accordance with this Treaty and applicable rules and principles of international law'. This has required ECT tribunals to consider whether EU law should be considered among the 'applicable rules and principles of international law' and thus form part of the governing law applicable to the dispute.

14.17   On this issue, some EU respondent states have argued that Article 26(6) of the ECT requires the application of EU law to the issue of the jurisdiction of the tribunal.[33] The correct view, however, is that the choice of law provision set out in Article 26(6) of the ECT applies only to the merits of the dispute and is, therefore, irrelevant to determine a tribunal's jurisdiction.

14.18   This should be uncontroversial. In investment treaty law, it is well established that questions of jurisdiction are not subject to the law applicable to the merits of the case. Questions of jurisdiction are governed by the instruments containing the parties' consent to jurisdiction. Given the doctrine of separability, the law applicable to the merits does not affect the tribunal's determination on its jurisdiction. As Professor Schreuer explains: 'Just as the basis of a tribunal's jurisdiction does not determine the law it has to apply, the law applicable in a case does not determine the tribunal's jurisdiction. The law governing jurisdictional issues is independent of the law applicable to the merits of a case.'[34]

14.19   This has been confirmed by the tribunals in *Vattenfall*, *Greentech* and *Eskosol*.[35] The *Vattenfall* tribunal explained that Article 26(6) of the ECT requires a tribunal to decide the '*issues in dispute*' in accordance with '*applicable rules and principles of international law*'.[36] These '*issues in dispute*' are those that concern Part III of the ECT, i.e., claims concerning the substantive

---

as to whether there is such conflict or as to its extent, Article 16 and Part V of the Energy Charter Treaty shall not apply.

32   See *RREEF Infrastructure v Spain* (n 14), paras 78–87.

33   *RREEF Infrastructure (GP) Limited and RREEF Pan European Infrastructure Two Lux SARL v The Kingdom of Spain*, ICSID Case No ARB/13/30, Reply on Jurisdiction, para 63.

34   Christoph Schreuer, 'Jurisdiction and Applicable Law in Investment Treaty Arbitration' (2014) 1(1) *McGill Journal of Dispute Resolution* 2.

35   *Vattenfall v Germany* (n 18), paras 114–116; *Foresight Luxembourg Solar 1 SÀRL, Foresight Luxembourg Solar 2 SÀRL, Greentech Energy Systems A/S, GWM Renewable Energy I SPA, GWM Renewable Energy II SPA v The Kingdom of Spain*, SCC Arbitration V (2015/150), Final Award, 14 November 2018, para 264; *Eskosol SpA in liquidazione v Italian Republic*, ICSID Case No ARB/15/50, Decision on Termination Request and Intra-EU Objection, 7 May 2019, paras 180 and 187–188.

36   *Vattenfall v Germany* (n 18), paras 114ff.

standards of protection of the ECT.[37] The provisions on dispute settlement appear in Part V of the ECT and are therefore not subject to the ECT's choice-of-law provision.[38] Therefore, the *Vattenfall* tribunal found that Article 26(6) of the ECT applies only to the merits of the dispute between the parties. It does not apply to issues or questions relating to the tribunal's jurisdiction.[39] The law applicable to the issue of the tribunal's jurisdiction is the ECT itself, and in particular, Article 26(4), which contains the parties' consent to arbitration.[40]

The tribunal in *Greentech* reached the same conclusion, finding that:　　　　　　　　　**14.20**

> Article 26(6) ECT applies to the merits of the case and not to jurisdiction. The Tribunal must determine its jurisdiction exclusively in accordance with the jurisdictional requirements of the ECT. [...] Accordingly, the Tribunal decides that EU law is not relevant to the question of the Tribunal's jurisdiction and the Respondent's jurisdictional objection based on the 'primacy' of EU law must be rejected.[41]

The issue of whether EU law should apply to the merits of an intra-EU dispute requires a more **14.21** complex analysis. A tribunal must determine whether EU law constitutes a fact to be taken into account as part of its fact-finding exercise when determining the merits of the dispute or whether EU law is a form of international law that falls within the applicable law clause in Article 26(6).

The *AES v Hungary* tribunal held, in light of the pleadings before it, that EU law should be **14.22** considered domestic law and thus as a fact in the dispute:

> Regarding the Community competition law regime, it has a dual nature: on the one hand, it is an international law regime, on the other hand, once introduced in the national legal orders, it is part of these legal orders. It is common ground that in an international arbitration, national laws are to be considered as facts. Both parties having pleaded that the Community competition law regime should be considered as a fact, it will be considered by this Tribunal as a fact, always taking into account that a state may not invoke its domestic law as an excuse for alleged breaches of its international obligations.[42]

The *Electrabel* tribunal considered EU law to have a '*multiple nature*'. In its view, EU law was 'a **14.23** *sui generis* legal order, presenting different facets depending on the perspective from where it is analysed'.[43] The tribunal found that 'on the one hand, it is an international legal regime; but on the other hand, once introduced in the national legal orders of EU Member States, it becomes also part of these national legal orders'.[44] It therefore held that EU law was both international and national law and thus was applicable under Article 26(6).

37　Ibid., paras 114–116.
38　Ibid., paras 115–116.
39　Ibid., paras 121–122.
40　Ibid., para 126.
41　*Foresight Luxembourg Solar v Spain* (n 35), paras 218–219.
42　*AES Summit v Hungary* (n 14), para 7.6.6.
43　*Electrabel v Hungary* (n 25), para 4.117.
44　Ibid., para 4.118.

14.24   The *Electrabel* Tribunal largely stands alone in this view and this is not surprising. If it were correct that EU law is part of the law applicable to the merits of the case, then *any* international treaty or agreement that is binding on an investor and an EU Member State involved in arbitration under the ECT would be part of the *"applicable rules and principles of international law"* under Article 26(6) of the ECT. This would include a broad range of international rules and treaties, such as the WTO Agreement, the European Convention on Human Rights, the UN Charter and many others. There is no valid legal basis to support this interpretation of Article 26(6) and subsequent ECT tribunals have rejected this suggestion.

The *Eskosol* tribunal also examined the relationship between EU law and the ECT and explained this as follows:

> It is useful to recall that the international legal system is a general system without any central authority from whom the entire system flows. It is composed of different legal sub-systems which have independent life, even if at times there may be interactions between them. As a whole, the international legal system is bound by general principles of international law, i.e., by customary international law, including norms such as *jus cogens* and *pacta sunt servanda* as discussed above. But below this level of general principles there exist various sub-systems of international law, with no precise hierarchy between the different norms established in each sub-system. Rather, each of these sub-systems is governed by its own applicable norms, and vests dispute resolution authority in particular bodies obligated to proceed under those norms. The EU Treaties are one such sub-system, vesting authority in various organs including the Commission, the CJEU, etc. But the EU Treaties are not general international law displacing all other sub-systems of international law; rather, they exist side-by-side with other sub-systems, including those created by various multilateral treaties. The ECT is one such other sub-system of law, and it vests authority in arbitral tribunals such as this one. Each authority is empowered in its sub-system to render decisions within its sphere, such as the CJEU's *Achmea* Judgment under the EU Treaties and the awards of various arbitral tribunals under the ECT. A given State may be subject to obligations arising from both types of decisions.[45]

14.25   The *Eskosol* tribunal thus found that 'EU law is different and separate not only from the national legal orders of its constituent States, but also from general international law, including other sub-systems of international law in the broader international legal order'.[46]

14.26   Some ECT tribunals have considered which law should prevail in the event of a conflict between EU law and the provisions of the ECT. The *RREEF* tribunal found that, in the event of an inconsistency with EU law and the ECT, it would have to apply the ECT:

> ... should it ever be determined that there existed an inconsistency between the ECT and EU law – *quod non* in the present case – and absent any possibility to reconcile both rules through interpretation, the unqualified obligation in public international law of any arbitration tribunal constituted under the ECT would be to apply the former. This would be the case even were this to be the source of possible detriment to EU law. EU law does not and cannot 'trump' public international law.[47]

---

45   *Eskosol v Italy* (n 35), para 181.
46   Ibid., para 182.
47   *RREEF Infrastructure v Spain* (n 14), para 87. See also *Electrabel v Hungary* (n 25), para 4.191.

The opposite conclusion was reached in *Electrabel*.[48] The reasoning of the *RREEF* tribunal **14.27** appears to be more compelling on this point. As noted above, an ECT Tribunal is bound, first and foremost, to apply the ECT. Moreover, Article 16 of the ECT provides in short that in the event of a conflicting provision in a prior or subsequent treaty of the same subject matter, the treaty with the provisions more favourable to the investor take precedence.[49] Article 26 of the ECT is more favourable to investors than the provisions of the EU treaties since the investor's right to bring a claim in arbitration against a Contracting Party under the ECT is an additional right not contained in the provisions of EU law.

That the investor-state dispute settlement mechanism is an additional and more favourable **14.28** right provided by the ECT has been confirmed, inter alia, by the tribunals in *Electrabel*,[50] *Blusun*,[51] *Eiser*,[52] *Novenergia*[53] and *Masdar*.[54] The tribunal in *Novenergia* held that:

> Depriving ECT-protected investors of their substantive and procedural rights under Parts III and V of the ECT would have a negative effect on these investors and their investments. Even though the EU may have an 'internal market', as asserted by the Respondent, any argument that EU law provides investors greater protection than the ECT is unsustainable. It is obvious that the ECT is more favourable, as it grants investors substantive and procedural rights that are neither covered nor regulated by EU law. Most notably, EU law does not grant investors a right of direct action to protect their interests against host States that have violated those interests. Investment treaty tribunals have consistently affirmed that pursuant to Article 16 ECT, the ECT prevails over EU law, as its protections, especially the right to arbitration, are more favourable to investors.[55]

The tribunal in *Masdar* confirmed that: **14.29**

> Article 16 of the ECT affords precedence to the more favourable investor-protection provisions of Article 26 of the ECT of which Claimant has availed itself over any conflicting provision of the EU treaties. They are more favourable, not least, because they obviate the need to bring the claim in the Spanish courts and Respondent cannot derogate from Article 26, pursuant to which it has given unconditional consent to arbitration.[56]

---

48   *Electrabel v Hungary* (n 25), para. 4.191.
49   Art 16 provides as follows:

> Where two or more Contracting Parties have entered into a prior international agreement, or enter into a subsequent international agreement, whose terms in either case concern the subject matter of Part III or V of this Treaty, (1) nothing in Part III or V of this Treaty shall be construed to derogate from any provision of such terms of the other agreement or from any right to dispute resolution with respect thereto under that agreement; and (2) nothing in such terms of the other agreement shall be construed to derogate from any provision of Part III or V of this Treaty or from any right to dispute resolution with respect thereto under this Treaty, where any such provision is more favourable to the Investor or Investment.

50   *Electrabel v Hungary* (n 25), para 4.175. See also Michele Potestà, 'Bilateral Investment Treaties and the European Union: Recent Developments in Arbitration and before the ECJ' (2009) 8 *The Law and Practice of International Courts and Tribunals* 225, 232–3.
51   *Blusun SA, Jean-Pierre Lecorcier and Michael Stein v The Italian Republic*, ICSID Case No ARB/14/3, Award, 27 December 2016, para 289.
52   *Eiser v Spain* (n 17), para 202.
53   *Novenergia II v Spain* (n 21), para 445.
54   *Masdar Solar & Wind Cooperatief U.A. v The Kingdom of Spain*, ICSID Case No ARB/14/1, Award, 16 May 2018, para 332.
55   *Novenergia II v Spain* (n 21), para 445.
56   *Masdar Solar v Spain* (n 54), para 332.

14.30 It has been argued, however, that the TFEU should prevail over the ECT under the *lex posterior* principle contained in Article 30(4)(a) of the Vienna Convention. This argument contends that Article 267 and 344 of the TFEU conflict with the investor-state provision of the ECT.[57] According to that argument, since these Articles were contained in the 2009 Lisbon Treaty, they are part of a subsequent treaty postdating the ECT and thus prevailing over it by dint of the *lex posterior* principle.

14.31 This contention is also flawed since, as regards these provisions, it is the ECT that is the subsequent treaty. Indeed, the 2009 Lisbon Treaty was not a *'subsequent treaty'* but rather an amendment to a pre-existing treaty. Article 267 of the TFEU was previously Article 234 of the Treaty of Functioning Establishing the European Community (TEC) of 1992; and originally Article 177 of the Treaty of Rome of 1957. Likewise, Article 344 TFEU was previously Article 292 of the TEC and Article 219 of the Treaty of Rome. The official name of the Treaty of Lisbon is 'Treaty of Lisbon *amending* the Treaty on European Union and the Treaty establishing the European Community', which confirms that the Lisbon Treaty was not a new treaty. Whilst it contained certain amendments, none of those amendments is of relevance to this issue. As the *Vattenfall* tribunal explained, Articles 267 and 344 of the TFEU 'have existed in substantively similar form since a time prior to the conclusion of the ECT, and have only been renumbered in the successive versions of the EU Treaties'.[58] Consequently, it is the ECT that prevails under the *lex posterior* principle.

14.32 It has also been alleged that the EU Treaties prevail over the ECT as a result of Declaration 17 of the Treaty of Lisbon, which records the doctrine of the primacy of EU law.[59] This suggestion does not stand scrutiny however as this Declaration 17 only provides for the primacy of EU law over the respective national laws of EU Member States. It states as follows:

> [t]he Conference recalls that, in accordance with well settled case law of the Court of Justice of the European Union, the Treaties and the law adopted by the Union on the basis of the Treaties have primacy over the law of Member States, under the conditions laid down by the said case law.

It does not provide that it applies with primacy over international law or an international treaty such as the ECT.

---

57 Art 267 TFEU provides as follows:

> The Court of Justice of the European Union shall have jurisdiction to give preliminary rulings concerning: (a) the interpretation of the Treaties; (b) the validity and interpretation of acts of the institutions, bodies, offices or agencies of the Union; Where such a question is raised before any court or tribunal of a Member State, that court or tribunal may, if it considers that a decision on the question is necessary to enable it to give judgment, request the Court to give a ruling thereon. Where any such question is raised in a case pending before a court or tribunal of a Member State against whose decisions there is no judicial remedy under national law, that court or tribunal shall bring the matter before the Court. If such a question is raised in a case pending before a court or tribunal of a Member State with regard to a person in custody, the Court of Justice of the European Union shall act with the minimum of delay.

> Art 344 TFEU provides as follows: 'Member States undertake not to submit a dispute concerning the interpretation or application of the Treaties to any method of settlement other than those provided for therein.'

58 *Vattenfall v Germany* (n 18), para 218.
59 See e.g., Commission, 'Declaration of the Representatives of the Governments of the Member States, of 15 January 2019, on the legal consequences of the Judgment of the Court of Justice in *Achmea* and on Investment Protection in the European Union' (17 January 2019) (Declaration) 1, n 1.

3. The impact of *Achmea* and subsequent developments on intra-EU disputes

The issue of whether the ECT should prevail over the EU Treaties has always been the subject **14.33** of academic interest and in 2018 and 2019 it assumed a degree of practical significance following the judgment of the Court of Justice of the European Union in *Achmea* and subsequent statements of the European Commission and EU Member States regarding the applicability of intra-EU bilateral investment treaties. These developments and their impact on intra-EU ECT disputes are considered here.

In the CJEU's *Achmea* judgment dated 6 March 2018, it found that the submission to **14.34** arbitration set forth in Article 8 of the BIT between the Netherlands and Slovakia was not compatible with EU law.[60] In *Achmea*, the Federal Supreme Court of Germany had made a request for a preliminary ruling concerning the interpretation of Articles 18, 267 and 344 TFEU. This request was made in the context of the annulment proceedings of an arbitral award, dated 7 December 2012, rendered pursuant to the Netherlands-Slovakia BIT.

Article 8(6) of the Netherlands-Slovakia BIT provides that: **14.35**

> 6. The arbitral tribunal shall decide on the basis of the law, taking into account in particular though not exclusively:
> - the law in force of the Contracting Party concerned;
> - the provisions of this Agreement, and other relevant agreements between the Contracting Parties …[61]

The CJEU reasoned that: '[in order to rule on possible infringements of the BIT, an arbitral **14.36** tribunal] must, in accordance with Article 8(6) of the BIT, take account in particular of *the law in force of the contracting party concerned and other relevant agreements between the contracting parties*'.[62]

The CJEU then established that EU law was both: (i) the law in force in every Member State; **14.37** and (ii) the law deriving from an agreement between the Member States. Framing EU law in this manner, the CJEU concluded that Article 8 of the Netherlands-Slovakia BIT determines that an arbitral tribunal 'may be called on to interpret or indeed to apply EU law'.[63] The CJEU found that because arbitral tribunals, which may be called on to apply or interpret EU law, are not entitled to raise preliminary questions to it, thereby ensuring the full effectiveness of EU law, Article 8 of the Netherlands-Slovakia BIT was incompatible with EU law.

Although the reasoning of the *Achmea* judgment is difficult to follow in some respects,[64] it **14.38** cannot be properly construed as a determination that the ECT is incompatible with EU law.

---

60   Case C-284/16 *Slowakische Republik v Achmea BV* [2018] ECLI:EU:C:2018:158, para 60.
61   Ibid., para 4.
62   Ibid., para 40 (emphasis added).
63   Ibid., para 42.
64   The tribunal in *9REN v Spain* made the following observation on this point: 'The Tribunal has attempted, with the Parties' assistance, to understand the truncated reasoning in the ECJ's decision in *Achmea*. There is much to understand.' (*9REN Holding SARL v. Kingdom of Spain*, ICSID Case No ARB/15/15, Award, 31 May 2019, para 150).

14.39   First, the dispute-resolution provision in the Netherlands-Slovakia BIT provides that the domestic law of the host state forms part of the law applicable to the dispute. Since EU law forms part of the domestic law of EU Member States, EU law was part of the applicable law in a dispute arising under that BIT. The *Achmea* judgment appears to have been motivated by the ECJ's concerns that 'questions of EU law which the tribunal may have to address' cannot be 'submitted to the Court by means of a reference for a preliminary ruling'.[65]

14.40   No such concern can arise with respect to an investor-state dispute under the ECT. Unlike the Netherlands-Slovakia BIT, as noted above Article 26(6) of the ECT provides that ECT tribunals must 'decide the issues in dispute in accordance with this Treaty [the ECT] and applicable rules and principles of international law'. Therefore, the investor-state arbitration mechanism under Article 26 of the ECT is not open to claims for breaches of EU law by a contracting party.

14.41   Secondly, the *Achmea* judgment cannot be said to apply to the ECT since *Achmea* did not concern a treaty to which the EU was a contracting party.[66] In the *Achmea* judgment, it was held that 'an international agreement providing for the establishment of a court responsible for the interpretation of its provisions and whose decisions are binding on the institutions, including the Court of Justice, is not in principle incompatible with EU law'.[67] One specific issue identified by the CJEU with the treaty in *Achmea* was that it was 'an agreement which was concluded not by the EU but by Member States'.[68] The EU, of course, is a contracting party to the ECT. Given this difference, the *Achmea* judgment cannot be applied to the ECT by its own terms. This was confirmed in *Masdar*: '[T] he *Achmea* Judgment does not take into consideration, and thus it cannot be applied to, multilateral treaties, such as the ECT, to which the EU itself is a party.'[69]

14.42   This is consistent with EU law. Article 216(2) of the TFEU expressly provides that '[a]greements concluded by the [EU] are binding on the institutions of the [EU] and on its Member States'. The ECJ has ruled that this has the effect that agreements concluded by the EU prevail over acts of the Union and that judgments of the CJEU are acts of the Union.[70] Since the ECT is an agreement concluded by the EU, it follows that it must prevail over acts of the Union, including the *Achmea* judgment.

14.43   In any event, even if one were to take that view that the *Achmea* judgment did apply to the ECT, thus creating a potential conflict between the TFEU and the ECT, the ECT would prevail for the reasons stated above. It is therefore not surprising that all intra-EU ECT

---

65   *Slovak Republic v Achmea* (n 60), para 50.
66   PCA Case No. 2008-13, *Achmea BV v The Slovak Republic*, Claimant's Counter-Memorial on the Intra-EU Jurisdictional Objection, dated 26 February 2010, paras 467–470.
67   *Slovak Republic v Achmea* (n 60), para 57.
68   Ibid., para 58.
69   *Masdar v Spain* (n 54), para 679.
70   Case C-366/10 *Air Transport Association of America v Secretary of State for Energy and Climate Change* [2001] ECLI:EU: C:2011:864, para 50.

decisions or awards emerging after the *Achmea* judgment have found that it has no impact on their jurisdiction.[71] For example, the *Vattenfall* tribunal found that:

> Article 26 ECT and the above-cited provisions must be read in the context of Article 16 ECT, which specifically and explicitly addresses this situation. The plain language of Article 16 speaks against Respondent's and the EC's proposed interpretation of the ECT.
>
> [...] assuming for the sake of argument that Articles 267 and 344 TFEU are understood to 'concern' investor State dispute settlement, this would necessarily bring Article 16 ECT into application. The Tribunal also considers that Article 26 ECT, granting the possibility to pursue arbitration, would be understood as 'more favourable to the Investor', insofar as the EU Treaties are interpreted to prohibit that avenue of dispute resolution.
>
> In this way, by the terms of Article 16 ECT itself, it would be prohibited for a Contracting Party to construe the EU Treaties so as to derogate from an Investor's right to dispute resolution under Article 26 ECT, to the extent that they are understood to concern the same subject matter.[72]

14.44 The *Eskosol* tribunal also concluded that *Achmea* did not affect its jurisdiction, finding that, in the event of contradiction, the ECT and EU treaties would co-exist in accordance with their own provisions:

> Ultimately, the bottom line is that in a case of contradiction, each legal order remains bound by its own rules, for purposes of its own judgments. The CJEU's conclusions regarding the EU legal order are addressed to EU Member States and European institutions, and they accordingly may have no choice but to take steps consistent with the CJEU's ruling, including submitting arguments to international tribunals based on the EU legal order. But the CJEU's conclusions derived from EU law do not alter this Tribunal's mandate to proceed under the legal order on which its jurisdiction is founded, namely the ECT. This means that an international investment tribunal empaneled under the ECT is not bound by the jurisprudence of the CJEU, just as the CJEU is not bound by decisions taken by ECT tribunals.[73]

14.45 The *Achmea* judgment was followed by the European Commission's Communication to the European Parliament and the Council of 19 July 2018 titled 'Protection of intra-EU investment'. The Communication stated as follows regarding the ECT and intra-EU disputes:

> The Achmea judgment is also relevant for the investor-State arbitration mechanism established in Article 26 of the Energy Charter Treaty as regards intra-EU relations. This provision, if interpreted correctly, does not provide for an investor-State arbitration clause applicable between investors from a Member States of the EU and another Member States of the EU. Given the primacy of Union law, that clause, if interpreted as applying intra-EU, is incompatible with EU primary law and thus inapplicable. Indeed, the reasoning of the Court in Achmea applies equally to the intra-EU

---

71 See e.g., *Stadtwerke München GmbH, RWE Innogy GmbH, and others v Kingdom of Spain*, ICSID Case No ARB/15/1, Award of 2 December 2019; *BayWa re Renewable Energy GmbH and BayWa re Asset Holding GmbH v Spain*, ICSID Case No ARB/15/16, Decision on Jurisdiction, Liability and Directions on Quantum of 2 December 2019; *RWE Innogy GmbH and RWE Innogy Aersa SAU v Kingdom of Spain*, ICSID Case No ARB/14/34, Decision on jurisdiction, liability and certain issues of quantum of 30 December 2019; *Watkins Holdings S à rl and others v Kingdom of Spain*, ICSID Case No ARB/15/44, Award of 21 January 2020; *Hydro Energy 1 S à rl and Hydroxana Sweden AB v Kingdom of Spain*, ICSID Case No ARB/15/42, Decision on Jurisdiction, Liability and Directions on Quantum of 9 March 2020.

72 *Vattenfall v Germany* (n 18), paras 192–195.

73 *Eskosol v Italy* (n 35), para 185.

application of such a clause which, just like the clauses of intra-EU BITs, opens the possibility of submitting those disputes to a body which is not part of the judicial system of the EU. The fact that the EU is also a party to the Energy Charter Treaty does not affect this conclusion: the participation of the EU in that Treaty has only created rights and obligations between the EU and third countries and has not affected the relations between the EU Member States.

14.46   This view announced by the European Commission is difficult to reconcile with both EU and international law. First, as noted above, there is no 'primacy of Union law' over the ECT or international law. Secondly, contrary to the European Commission's assertion, the fact that the EU is also a contracting party to the ECT is a key distinction between the ECT and Netherlands-Slovakia BIT. Indeed, Advocate General Wathelet in his 19 September 2017 opinion on *Achmea* found that:

> That multilateral treaty on investment in the field of energy [the ECT] operates even between Member States, since it was concluded not as an agreement between the Union and its Member States, of the one part, and third countries, of the other part, but as an ordinary multilateral treaty in which all the Contracting Parties participate on an equal footing. In that sense, the material provisions for the protection of investments provided for in that Treaty and the ISDS mechanism also operate between Member States. I note that if no EU institution and no Member State sought an opinion from the Court on the compatibility of that treaty with the EU and FEU Treaties, that is because none of them had the slightest suspicion that it might be incompatible.[74]

14.47   The CJEU's judgment in *Achmea* made no observation in respect of Advocate General Wathelet's finding on this point. This prompted the *Masdar* tribunal to find that:

> Had the CJEU seen it necessary to address the distinction drawn by the Advocate General between the ISDS provisions of the ECT and the investment protection mechanisms to be found in bilateral investment treaties made between Member States within the ambit of its ruling, it had the opportunity to do so. In fact, the Tribunal notes that the CJEU did not address this part of the Advocate General's Opinion, much less depart from, or reject, it. The Achmea Judgment is simply silent on the subject of the ECT. The Tribunal respectfully adopts the Advocate General's reasoning on this matter, and it relies in particular upon the observation in the final sentence cited above from his Opinion.[75]

14.48   Since the *Achmea* judgment pointedly refused to comment on the ECT and given that its reasoning concerning the Netherlands-Slovakia bilateral investment treaty cannot apply to the ECT, the European Commission's statements concerning the *Achmea* judgment and the ECT have no sound legal basis. Rather, those statements appear to be statements of the Commission's policy position (i.e., what the Commission would like the law to be) rather than the Commission's understanding of existing law.

14.49   On this point it must be recalled that the European Commission cannot offer any authoritative interpretation of the ECT and thus its Communication cannot have any legal force with regard to the correct interpretation of Article 26 of the ECT. The stated aim of the EC Communication is to: (i) provide guidance on existing EU rules for the treatment of cross-border EU

---

74   Case C-284/16 *Slowakische Republik v Achmea BV* [2017] ECLI:EU:C:2017:699, Opinion of AG Wathelet.
75   *Masdar v Spain* (n 54), para 682.

investments;[76] and to (ii) seek to reassure investors that the absence of intra-EU investment treaties does not mean that investors within the EU are not protected.[77] Thus, it does not have any bearing on the correct interpretation of Article 26 of the ECT or the proper conclusions to be drawn from the *Achmea* judgment.

Subsequent to the EC Communication, in January 2019, EU Member States issued three **14.50** separate declarations addressing the issue of intra-EU disputes: 22 EU Member States issued a declaration on 15 January 2019 (the Declaration);[78] Finland, Luxembourg, Malta, Slovenia and Sweden issued a second declaration of their own on 16 January 2019 (the Additional Declaration);[79] and Hungary also issued its own declaration on 16 January 2019 (the Hungary Declaration).[80]

Of particular relevance to intra-EU disputes under the ECT, the Declaration draws a **14.51** distinction between the legal consequences of *Achmea* for bilateral investment treaties and the ECT. It states that, in the light of the *Achmea* judgment, 'all investor-State arbitration clauses contained in *bilateral* investment treaties concluded between Member States are contrary to Union law and thus inapplicable'.[81] For this reason, the 22 Member States signatories to the Declaration have agreed to use their best efforts to terminate intra-EU bilateral investment treaties by the end of 2019.[82] In contrast, with respect to the ECT, the 22 Member States only announce that they 'will discuss without undue delay whether any additional steps are necessary to draw all the consequences from the *Achmea* judgment in relation to the intra-EU application of the Energy Charter Treaty'.[83]

The Declaration also states that 'Union law takes precedence over *bilateral* investment treaties **14.52** concluded between Member States'.[84] The Declaration does not, however, express the same view with respect to the ECT; and rightly so as the ECT is a multilateral treaty to which both the EU and the Member States are parties.

In the Additional Declaration, the five signatory Member States note that the *Achmea* **14.53** judgment: (i) only 'concerns the interpretation of EU law' (i.e., not public international law); and (ii) 'is silent on the investor-state arbitration clause in the Energy Charter Treaty'.[85] The Additional Declaration also observes that whether the ECT contains an arbitration clause

---

76 Commission, 'Communication from The European Commission to The European Parliament and The Council on the Protection of intra-EU investment. COM (2018) 547/2 (the EC Communication), 19 July 2018, pp 1–3.

77 Ibid.

78 Declaration (n 59).

79 Representatives of the Governments of Finland, Luxembourg, Malta, Slovenia and Sweden, 'Declaration of the Representatives of the Governments of the Member States, of 16 January 2019, on the enforcement of the Judgment of the Court of Justice in *Achmea* and on Investment Protection in the European' (January 2019) (Additional Declaration).

80 Representative of the Government of Hungary, 'Declaration of the Representative of the Government of Hungary, of 16 January 2019, on the legal consequences of the Judgment of the Court of Justice in *Achmea* and on Investment Protection in the European Union' (January 2019) (Hungary Declaration).

81 Declaration (n 59), 1 (emphasis added).

82 Ibid., 4.

83 Ibid.

84 Ibid., 1 (emphasis added).

85 Additional Declaration (n 79), 3.

applicable between EU Member States is 'currently contested before a national court in a Member State' and stresses the 'importance of allowing for due process and consider that it would be inappropriate, in the absence of a specific judgment on this matter, to express views as regards the compatibility with Union law of the intra-EU application of the Energy Charter Treaty'.[86] Hungary's Declaration unambiguously declares that 'the *Achmea* judgment concerns only the intra-EU bilateral investment treaties' and 'does not concern any pending or prospective arbitration proceedings initiated under the ECT'.[87]

C. EXTRA-EU DISPUTES

14.54 In contrast to the numerous decisions and awards considering intra-EU disputes and the relevance of EU law in this context, there has to date been scant assessment of the relevance of EU law under the ECT in extra-EU disputes (i.e., disputes brought by non-EU investors against an EU Member State). Although Spain is currently facing claims brought by Swiss and Japanese investors which may raise issues of the relevance of EU law in extra-EU disputes,[88] at the time of writing no decision or award has been issued in these cases.

14.55 Separately, the EU itself now faces its first ECT claim. On 12 April 2019 *Nord Stream 2 AG* notified the President of the European Commission, as representative of the EU, of a dispute and requested that the EU attempted to reach an amicable settlement pursuant to Article 26 of the ECT.[89] *Nord Stream 2 AG* is a Swiss company which, according to press reports, has invested over €5.8 billion in the construction of a 1,200-kilometre pipeline to transport natural gas from Russia to Germany via the Baltic Sea.[90] This dispute arises from amendments to the EU's 2009 Gas Directive which, in the opinion of *Nord Stream 2 AG*, unfairly targets the pipeline.

14.56 It is possible that these cases brought by Swiss and Japanese investors against the EU and one of its Member States will provide further commentary on the relevance of EU law in ECT disputes that involve investors from non-EU Member States. If, as noted above, EU law cannot deprive an ECT tribunal of its jurisdiction in an intra-EU dispute, it applies *a fortiori* that EU law should have no bearing on a tribunal's jurisdiction in an extra-EU context. It may also be difficult to contend that EU law should have any special status when it comes to the determination of the merits to an extra-EU dispute. To the extent that EU law is viewed as the

---

86 Ibid., 3.
87 Hungary Declaration (n 80), 3.
88 See *EBL (Genossenschaft Elektra Baselland) and Tubo Sol PE2 SL v Kingdom of Spain*, ICSID Case No ARB/18/42; *Itochu Corporation v Kingdom of Spain*, ICSID Case No ARB/18/25; *DCM Energy GmbH & Co Solar 1 KG and others v Kingdom of Spain*, ICSID Case No ARB/17/41; *Eurus Energy Holdings Corporation v Kingdom of Spain*, ICSID Case No ARB/16/4; *OperaFund Eco-Invest SICAV PLC and Schwab Holding AG v Kingdom of Spain*, ICSID Case No ARB/15/36; *JGC Corporation v Kingdom of Spain*, ICSID Case No ARB/15/27.
89 Letter from Nord Stream 2 AG to Mr Jean-Claude Juncker, President of the European Commission (12 April 2019) <https://trade.ec.europa.eu/doclib/docs/2019/july/tradoc_158069.pd_Redacted.pdf> accessed 30 September 2019; EU's Response dated 13 May 2019 to letter from Nord Stream AG dated 12 April <https://trade.ec.europa.eu/doclib/docs/2019/july/tradoc_158070.pdf> accessed 30 September 2019.
90 See Sebastian Perry, 'Pipeline developer launches ECT claim against EU' (2019) <https://globalarbitrationreview.com/article/1200602/pipeline-developer-launches-ect-claim-against-eu> accessed 30 September 2019.

internal law of the Member State, as with the domestic law of any State, compliance with that law could not be a defence to a claim brought under international law.[91] It would, however, be considered as a relevant fact for purposes of the dispute. Whether a Member State is able successfully to argue that it should take on more significance remains to be seen.

---

91   See International Law Commission 'Articles on Responsibility of States for Internationally Wrongful Acts', UNGA Res 56/83, 12 December 2001, UN Doc A/RES/56/83, Annex, Art 3: 'The characterization of an act of a State as internationally wrongful is governed by international law. Such characterization is not affected by the characterization of the same act as lawful by internal law.'

15

INVESTMENT CHAPTER IN CETA: GROUNDBREAKING OR MUCH ADO ABOUT NOTHING?

Dorieke Overduin[*]

A. INTRODUCTION

15.01 Following years of talks, the European Union (EU) and Canada officially launched negotiations for a Comprehensive Economic and Trade Agreement (CETA) on 6 May 2009 at the Canada-EU Summit in Prague. During the global economic downturn that followed the 2008 financial crisis and amidst a sentiment of trade protectionism, the EU and Canada clearly signalled their joint ambition of concluding an agreement that aimed to liberalize trade in goods and services, remove tariff and non-tariff barriers, create market access opportunities and introduce new rules for trade-related issues, such as the promotion and protection of investments.[1]

15.02 The launch of CETA was not only an external landmark, it was for both parties also historical for internal reasons. For Canada, the United States has remained its key trade and investment partner, but the EU as a bloc has since long been its second trading partner.[2] Hence, CETA is Canada's biggest bilateral initiative since NAFTA came into force in 1994 and was meant to result in at least an equivalent amount of ambition and success. For the EU, CETA was one of the first agreements the EU negotiated since the entry into force of the Treaty of Lisbon on

---

[*] All opinions expressed in this chapter are personal to the author and are not to be attributed to the position of the Dutch government. Date of submission: 22/05/02020.

[1] Canada-EU Summit Joint Statement (2009), 'Canada-EU Summit Declaration – May 6, 2009', <http://www.sice.oas.org/TPD/CAN_EU/Negotiations/Dec2009_Prague_e.pdf> accessed May 3, 2020.

[2] Government of Canada, 'Trade and Investment Agreements', <https://www.international.gc.ca/trade-commerce/trade-agreements-accords-commerciaux/agr-acc/index.aspx?lang=eng> accessed May 3, 2020.

1 January 2009.[3] Whereas the EU has always had competences to conclude trade treaties aiming to remove tariff and non-tariff barriers, the Treaty of Lisbon expanded the scope of competences to a whole new area of trade-related issues, such as intellectual property, foreign direct investments and sustainable development.[4] As a result, CETA was meant to become the most far-reaching bilateral agreement that the EU has negotiated with any non-EU nation and to be more comprehensive than any of the agreements in place at that time.[5]

After more than five years of negotiations, CETA indeed became the EU's most ambitious **15.03** and liberal trade agreement to date, removing 98 per cent of custom duties and import tariffs upon ratification and removing up to 100 per cent of the tariffs within the next seven years.[6] However, after conclusion of the negotiations CETA became particularly (in)famous for the inclusion of exactly these new areas of trade-related issues. Specifically CETA's Investment Chapter became heavily contested and subject of heated political debates in Parliaments of EU Member States. At the time of writing, CETA is still undergoing a bumpy ratification ride in EU Member States.[7] However, in contrast to traditional older generation Bilateral Investment Treaties (BITs) that EU Member States still maintain, CETA's Investment Chapter goes a long way to address public concerns about the legitimacy of CETA's investment protection regime.

Therefore, this chapter aims to assess in detail whether CETA's Investment Chapter is **15.04** groundbreaking or much ado about nothing from an EU perspective. Without aspiring to provide a conclusive overview of CETA's Investment Chapter, this contribution will first provide historical context to one of the EU's most ambitious and comprehensive trade agreements. The coming of age of CETA's Investment Chapter should be assessed against the background of the entry into force of the Treaty of Lisbon, that changed the landscape of EU competences and switched the power to conclude international treaties in the field of Foreign Direct Investment (FDI) from the EU Member States to the EU. This seismic shift did influence the CETA negotiations at more than one occasion. After setting the scene, the remaining part of this contribution will be dedicated to a detailed analysis of substantial and procedural innovations introduced in CETA's Investment Chapter. In assessing those changes, it will compare CETA's Investment Chapter to the traditional older-generation BITs of EU Member States. After all, when the EU assumed competences in the field of FDI right after the entry into force of the Treaty of Lisbon, the EU Member States' BITs explicitly served as a template for future EU agreements. However, at the end of this contribution, one must conclude that CETA clearly differs from the substantive and procedural provisions included in older-generation BITs of EU Member States. And while one can still debate the

---

3   Commission, 'Trade, Growth and World Affairs: Trade Policy as a Core Component of the EU's 2020 Strategy', COM (2010) 612 final <https://eur-lex.europa.eu/LexUriServ/LexUriServ.do?uri=COM:2010:0612:FIN:EN:PDF> accessed May 3, 2020.

4   Consolidated version of the Treaty on the Functioning of the European Union [2008] OJ 115/13 (TFEU), article 207.

5   Commission, 'EU-Canada: Green light for the Commission to negotiate new free trade and economic agreement' (27 April 2009) <http://www.sice.oas.org/TPD/CAN_EU/Negotiations/Initiate_Neg_e.pdf> accessed May 4, 2020.

6   Commission, 'EU-Canada trade agreement enters into force' (Press Release IP/17/3121, 20 September 2017) <https://ec.europa.eu/commission/presscorner/detail/en/IP_17_3121> accessed May 4, 2020.

7   European Parliament, 'Legislative Train Schedule – A Balanced and Progressive Trade Policy to Harness Globalisation-EU-Canada Comprehensive Economic and Trade Agreement (CETA)' (20 November 2019) <https://www.europarl. europa.eu/legislative-train/theme-a-balanced-and-progressive-trade-policy-to-harness-globalisation/file-ceta> accessed May 19, 2020.

legitimacy of treaties offering protection to investors by linking certain rule of law standards to an effective enforcement mechanism, in the land of investment treaties, CETA is certainly a *primus inter pares*.

B. COMING OF AGE OF CETA'S INVESTMENT CHAPTER

15.05 Over the course of the negotiations, CETA's Investment Chapter underwent a radical transformation. When the EU and Canada launched their negotiations in 2009, the EU as a bloc was Canada's second largest source of incoming FDI and vice versa, Canada was the EU's fourth largest source of incoming FDI.[8] Ten years later this relationship has only intensified. Despite a global decline of investments in developed economies, the EU has remained the second largest investor in Canada and Canada has climbed to rank the second largest investor in the EU.[9]

15.06 The most important component of the EU-Canada investment relationship are so-called 'mode 3' investments, meaning investments to establish a commercial presence in a country to realize sale of goods or services.[10] The Joint Study that was produced by the EU and Canada prior to the start of negotiations showed that finance, telecommunications, transport and electricity were amongst the most restricted 'mode 3' sectors in both territories[11] and hence, the EU and Canada would both particularly benefit from enhanced market access for investments in those sectors.[12] Therefore, while FDI had become a competence of the EU's exclusive competence as a result of the Treaty of Lisbon, EU Member States initially only agreed for the EU to negotiate a treaty that would result in market access for FDI.

15.07 Investment protection, including dispute settlement provisions, were not included in the EU's negotiating objectives, as this competency had remained within the realm of EU Member States ever since the first BIT was concluded. Germany was the first nation in the world to conclude a bilateral investment treaty in 1959 with Pakistan, but many countries around the world, including all but one EU Member State, followed suit.[13] So, while traditionally, the EU has been equipped with the competence to conclude so-called 'pre-establishment' agreements with third countries covering market access for investments, EU Member States individually

---

8   Government of Canada, 'Assessing the costs and benefits of a closer EU-Canada economic partnership – A Joint Study by the European Commission and Government of Canada' (EU-Canada Joint Study) (15 May 2007) <https://www.international.gc.ca/trade-agreements-accords-commerciaux/agr-acc/eu-ue/study-etude.aspx?lang=eng> accessed May 4, 2020.

9   Eurostat, 'EU Foreign Direct Investment flows in 2018' (17 July 2019) <https://ec.europa.eu/eurostat/web/products-eurostat-news/-/DDN-20190717-1> accessed May 21, 2020.

10   General Agreement on Tariffs and Trade 1994 (adopted 15 April 1994, Marrakesh Agreement Establishing the World Trade Organization, Annex 1A (adopted 15 April 1994, entered into force 1 January 1995) 1867 UNTS 187 (GATT), art I:2 defines services supplied in so-called 4 modes of supply. According to art I:2(c), mode 3 means trade in services is defined as the supply of a service by a service supplier of one Member, through commercial presence, in the territory of any other Member.

11   EU-Canada Joint Study (n 8).

12   Ibid., 9.

13   See Bilateral Investment Treaty between Germany and the Islamic Republic of Pakistan, 1959 via United Nations Conference on Trade and Development's Investment Policy Hub <https://investmentpolicy.unctad.org>, accessed May 4, 2020. Ireland is the only EU Member State that does not maintain any Bilateral Investment Treaty with a third country.

concluded a spaghetti-bowl of almost 1200 BITs with third countries covering so-called 'post-establishment' standards of treatment and dispute settlement provisions. Prior to the start of the CETA negotiations, Canada had seven BITs in place with EU Member States.[14] At the commencement of the CETA negotiations, these EU Member States were working with Canada to finalize those respective texts, outside the context of CETA.

However, after the Treaty of Lisbon endowed the EU with the competence to also conclude **15.08** post-establishment provisions in negotiations with third countries, the EU now sought to establish a comprehensive trade policy that would integrate investment liberalization, investment protection and related dispute settlement mechanisms in one single investment policy. To that end, in 2010, the European Commission presented its new strategy in which it announced that EU Member States' BITs with third countries would gradually be superseded by EU agreements covering investment protection provisions, starting with the negotiations with Canada.[15] With regard to substantive investment protection rules, the European Commission promised in its 2010 Communication that the new legal framework should not negatively affect the level of investment protection granted to investors under the 1200 EU Member States' BITs. To foster that objective, EU Member States amended the negotiation directives for CETA in July 2011. The mandate was amended to not only contain market access provisions for FDI, but also include investment protection and dispute resolution that 'provide[s] for the highest possible level of legal protection and certainty for European investors in Canada' and 'be built upon the Member States' experience and best practice regarding their bilateral investment agreements'.[16]

In addition, the new mandate required CETA's Investment Chapter to include 'an effective **15.09** and state-of-the-art investor-to-state-dispute settlement mechanism'[17] and a 'wide range of arbitration fora for investors as currently available under the Member States' BITs.[18] So, while EU Member States were still a bit sour about the transfer of competences after the Treaty of Lisbon, they quickly came around for a new objective for CETA and pushed for substantive protection for investors and their investments and dispute settlement mechanisms in line with their own BITs. The mandate shows no sign of a wish by EU Member States to limit the scope of these treaties, apart from the fact that CETA's Investment Chapter should preserve the right of the EU and its Member States to adopt and enforce measures necessary to pursue legitimate public policy objectives such as social, environmental, security, public health and safety in a non-discriminatory manner.[19]

---

14 Croatia, Czech Republic, Hungary, Latvia, Poland, Romania and Slovakia have investment treaties with Canada in force. See Government of Canada, 'Trade and investment agreements', <https://www.international.gc.ca/trade-agreements-accords-commerciaux/agr-acc/eu-ue/study-etude.aspx?lang=eng> accessed May 4, 2020.

15 Commission, 'Trade, Growth and World Affairs: Trade Policy as a Core Component of the EU's 2020 Strategy' COM(2010) 612 final <https://eur-lex.europa.eu/LexUriServ/LexUriServ.do?uri=COM:2010:0612:FIN:EN:PDF> accessed May 3, 2020.

16 Council, 'Recommendation from the Commission to the Council on the modification of the negotiating directives for an Economic Integration Agreement with Canada in order to authorize the Commission to negotiate, on behalf of the Union, on investment' (WTO 270 FDI 19 CDN 5 Services 79 Restreint UE, 2011), 2 <http://data.consilium.europa.eu/doc/document/ST-12838-2011-EXT-2/en/pdf> accessed May 21, 2020.

17 Ibid., 4.

18 Ibid.

19 Ibid., 2.

15.10   However, soon enough this new mandate also became abundant. Catching wind in relation to the proposed Investment Chapter in the Transatlantic Trade and Investment Partnership Agreement (TTIP), a vast storm of public criticism arose in relation to the inclusion of investment protection and ISDS in general in all EU trade agreements.[20] While the critique seemed to concentrate on proposed investment protection in TTIP and CETA, it is in fact much more systemic in nature and questions the fundamental role of investment protection and ISDS in international investment agreements (IIAs) in general.

15.11   Broadly speaking, and without any attempt to minimize the scope or legitimacy of the critique, the concerns fall into two categories. First, in terms of substance, investment treaties and particularly, investment protection is by some perceived to significantly limit the policy space of governments. Critics fear that as a result of these treaties, governments will be reluctant to introduce or maintain regulations necessary to achieve public policy objectives. Well-known and often-cited cases in this respect are *Vattenfall v Germany* and *Phillip Morris v Australia*.[21] Second, in terms of procedure, the traditional Investor-State Dispute Settlement (ISDS)-system has been under attack, because according to some it facilitates a way for investors to sue governments in ad hoc arbitration, in non-transparent ways, with no democratic control and no way to correct legal errors.[22]

15.12   In an effort to address this criticism, the European Commission presented a new proposal for investment protection and dispute settlement in the context of TTIP after more than a year of extensive consultations.[23] This had severe consequences for the CETA negotiations as well. By then, the EU and Canada had already concluded the CETA negotiations and included an Investment Chapter in line with the 2011 mandate. However, during the legal scrubbing of the agreement, then EU Commissioner for Trade Cecilia Malmström and the Honourable Chrystia Freeland, Minister of International Trade of Canada agreed to make modifications to the Investment Chapter, in line with the EU's new approach.[24] With these modifications, CETA became the first investment agreement that includes the new EU approach towards investment protection and signalled a clear, new direction for investment protection and dispute resolution for future EU agreements. In doing so, CETA's Investment Chapter clearly deviates from the 2011 mandate and fundamentally differs from the older generation BITs held by EU Member States.

---

20   See, e.g., European Parliament, 'TTIP Negotiations on Investment Protection: Investor-State Dispute Settlement (ISDS), (Legislative Train, June 2020), 2: 'to replace the ISDS-system with a new system for resolving disputes between investors and states which is subject to democratic principles and scrutiny.'

21   See *Vattenfall AB and others v Federal Republic of Germany*, ICSID Case No ARB/12/12, and *Philip Morris Asia Ltd v The Commonwealth of Australia*, UNCITRAL, PCA Case No 2012-12.

22   Marco Bronckers, 'Is Investor–State Dispute Settlement (ISDS) Superior to Litigation Before Domestic Courts? An EU View on Bilateral Trade Agreements' (2015) 18(3) *Journal of International Economic Law* 655.

23   The European Commission held debates with Member States, the European Parliament, stakeholders and citizens and launched an online public consultation on investment protection and investor-to-state dispute settlement (ISDS) in the Transatlantic Trade and Investment Partnership Agreement (TTIP) on 27 March 2014, to whom it received almost 150,000 replies. See Commission, 'Report on the online consultation on investment protection and investor-to-state dispute settlement in the Transatlantic Trade and Investment Partnership Agreement (13 January 2015) <https://ec.europa.eu/commission/presscorner/detail/en/MEMO_15_3202> accessed May 4, 2020.

24   Commission, 'Joint statement Canada-EU Comprehensive Economic and Trade Agreement (CETA)' (29 February 2016) <https://trade.ec.europa.eu/doclib/docs/2016/february/tradoc_154330.pdf> accessed May 4, 2020.

Yet, this outcome did not at all pave the way for a swift ratification of CETA in the EU. On **15.13** the contrary, on 16 May 2017, the Court of Justice of the European Union (CJEU) ruled in *Opinion 2/15* that while the EU has exclusive competence with regard to the provisions concerning substantive protection of incoming and outgoing FDI, according to the Court, the EU is not endowed with exclusive competences in the field of so-called indirect foreign investments, or 'portfolio' investments,[25] and the regime governing dispute settlement between investors and States.[26] Those regimes, and only those, remain shared competences between the EU and the Member States in the field of FDI. As a result, EU agreements that contain those provisions, must be concluded and ratified with the participation of the Member States. As ratification of EU Member States was now required,[27] CETA was left to the mercy of Member States' internal political debates.

Soon, as a consequence of such internal deliberations with its Walloon region, Belgium **15.14** requested the opinion of the European Court of Justice concerning the legality of the new Investment Court System in CETA with EU primary law. In short, Belgium expressed doubts as to the effects of that mechanism on the exclusive jurisdiction of the Court over the definitive interpretation of EU law, as well as to its compatibility with the general principle of equal treatment and requirements of access to an independent and impartial tribunal.[28] Finally, on 30 April 2019, the CJEU confirmed CETA's Investment Chapter, including its new approach to dispute settlement through an Investment Court System (ICS), is compatible with EU law and is now awaiting ratification and implementation. The remaining sections of this contribution will provide a detailed, but non-conclusive analysis of substantial and procedural innovations introduced in CETA's Investment Chapter in comparison to older-generation BITs of EU Member States, that served as point of departure for the new EU's investment policy.

C. SUBSTANTIVE RULES

Most of all 1200+ EU Member States' BITs follow a similar model that has not changed much **15.15** in terms of substance since the 1990s. While Germany was the first EU Member State to conclude a BIT, the Dutch investment treaties were generally considered the 'gold standard'[29] as far as investment protection is concerned.[30] This model is used by most EU Member

---

25   I.e., investments made without any intention to influence the management and control of an undertaking. See definition used by United Nations Conference on Trade and Development (1999) in UNCTAD, 'Comprehensive Study of the Interrelationship between Foreign Direct Investment (FDI) and Foreign Portfolio Investment (FPI)' (UNCTAD/GDS/DFSB/5, Staff Paper by UNCTAD Secretariat, 23 June 1999) <https://unctad.org/en/Docs/pogdsdfsbd5.pdf> accessed May 21, 2020.

26   *Opinion 2/15 (Competence of the EU to sign the EU–Singapore FTA)* [2018] ECLI:EU:C:2017:376.

27   Pursuant to Treaty on Functioning of the European Union, art 218, a qualified majority officially suffices.

28   *Opinion 1/17 (Compatibility of the ISDS mechanism under CETA with EU Law)* [2019] ECLI:EU:C:2019:341.

29   Nikos Lavranos 'The New EU Investment Treaties: Convergence towards the NAFTA model as the new Plurilateral Model BIT text?' (Social Science Research Network, 29 March 2013).

30   The Netherlands presented a new Model BIT in 2019, denouncing the 'gold standard', inspired by the EU's new approach, but it has not yet signed any treaty. For the new Model BIT, see Dutch government 'Nieuwe modeltekst investeringsakkoorden', <https://www.rijksoverheid.nl/documenten/publicaties/2019/03/22/nieuwe-modeltekst-investeringsakkoorden> 22 March, 2019. Accessed May 3, 2020.

States[31] and offers the highest level of protection for investors. Amongst all, it features broad-based definitions for investors and investment; broadly and mostly undefined standards of treatment for national treatment, most-favoured nation (MFN) treatment, Fair and Equitable Treatment (FET), full compensation for direct and indirect expropriation, full protection and security, a broad umbrella clause, no exceptions for certain sectors and a broad choice of access to remedies under ISDS mechanisms.[32] As the European Commission made clear that the EU's new investment policy would not limit investment protection provided for in existing EU Member States' BITs, this 'gold standard' will serve as baseline scenario for a more detailed analysis of new provisions introduced in CETA.

15.16 Starting with the substantial provisions, CETA departs from older-generation EU Member States' BITs in two ways. Firstly, it introduces an explicit reference to the right of governments to regulate in the public interest. Secondly, it contains more limited definitions of investment protection standards, for example in the provisions on FET and indirect expropriation. A closer look to CETA's new provisions will be provided in the following section.

1.   Introduction of a right to regulate

15.17 The right to regulate has always been assumed in EU Member States' BITs. The 'Dutch gold standard' refers to this right in the preamble, underlining 'the desire to achieve intensification of investment relations without compromising health, safety and environmental measures of general application'.[33] In addition, the right to regulate is included in treaty provisions itself, for example as justification for State conduct resulting in expropriation.[34] However, the right to regulate has never been included in a BIT as an independent legal standard per se. CETA's Investment Chapter is the first to introduce a 'reaffirmation' of this right to regulate.

15.18 While the right to regulate is stressed throughout the agreement, Article 8.9 CETA specifically includes this right per se. It says that 'the Parties reaffirm their right to regulate within their territories to achieve legitimate policy objectives, such as the protection of public health, safety, the environment or public morals, social or consumer protection or the promotion and protection of cultural diversity'. The remaining provisions of Article 8.9 CETA clarify that 'for greater certainty' the mere fact that if a party regulates, including through a modification of its laws, in a manner which negatively affects an investment or interferes with an investor's expectations including its expectations of profits, that does not amount to a breach of an obligation under CETA. Also, a Party's decision not to issue, renew or maintain a subsidy or to discontinue a subsidy or request a reimbursement where such measure is necessary in order to comply with European Union law, does not constitute a breach of the provisions of CETA.

---

31   Joachim Pohl (2013), 'Temporal Validity of International Investment Agreements: A Large Sample Survey of Treaty Provisions' (OECD Working Papers on International Investment No 2013/04, OECD Publishing, 2013) <https://doi.org/10.1787/5k3tsjsl5fvh-en> accessed May 21, 2020.

32   Lavranos (n 29), 1.

33   Netherlands Model BIT (1997), preamble no 4. Available through UNCTAD's Investment Policy Hub <https://investmentpolicy.unctad.org/international-investment-agreements/treaty-files/2857/download> accessed May 4, 2020.

34   Christian Tietje and Kevin Crow, 'The Reform of Investment Protection Rules in CETA, TTIP and other Recent EU-FTAs: Convincing?' (Social Science Research Network, 12 December 2016), 4.

A number of observations can be made to this new text. First, the first paragraph reads as an **15.19** interpretive statement, by reiterating declarations already made in the preamble, and by doing so, it seems to function like a recital.[35] After all, even inserted in the body of the treaty, the text does not confer a concrete actionable right to investors or States, but merely reads as an open list of acceptable objectives for States to justify any regulatory behaviour. According to the European Commission, the right to regulate in CETA's Investment Chapter is meant to 'recognize the right of domestic authorities to regulate matters within their own borders which exists already under international law. It allows setting the right context in which investment protection standards are applied.'[36] Hence, it seems that the Article is indeed meant to function like a recital. This becomes particularly clear when compared to the World Trade Organization's general exceptions under Article XX of the GATT.[37] That article is also a stand-alone article, allowing States to invoke a limited list of public interest exceptions to justify a violation of treaty provisions, but clearly limits that freedom of states by ensuring that these measures are non-discriminatory, necessary and proportionate. Such clarification lacks in Article 8.9 CETA.

Second, it can be observed that while this provision is particularly relevant in a political **15.20** context, it carries less importance from a legal perspective. After all, as touched upon above, the principle that investment treatment standards that favour the investor must be balanced against the legitimate regulatory interests of the host State were already assumed to be included in the substantive standards. For example, Tietje and Crow underline that the 'right to regulate' can be found in factors determining a non-compensable expropriation.[38] Therefore, they conclude that the new provisions on the right to regulate that appear in CETA have at least the potential of being tautologies, at least in relation to the notion of indirect expropriation.[39]

Third, really new in CETA is the 'for greater certainty' provision providing freedom for host **15.21** States not to issue, renew or maintain a subsidy or to withdraw an existing subsidy based on a respective decision of a court, tribunal or other competent authority. This provision seems to be a direct response to cases like *Micula v Romania*[40] and the numerous cases against Spain concerning the withdrawal of subsidies in the renewable energy sector. While some cases have been decided and some of them are still pending, these new provisions might at least become

---

35   Catharine Titi, 'The Right to Regulate', in Mbengue MM and Schacherer S (eds), *Foreign Investment Under the Comprehensive Economic and Trade Agreement (CETA)*, Studies in European Economic Law and Regulation (Springer 2019) 159.

36   Commission, 'Investment in TTIP and beyond – the path for reform: Enhancing the right to regulate and moving from current ad hoc arbitration towards an Investment Court' (Concept Paper, May 2015) <https://trade.ec.europa.eu/doclib/docs/2015/may/tradoc_153408.PDF> accessed May 4, 2020.

37   Note that Art 28.3 CETA provides general exceptions for the purposes of sections B (Establishment of investments) and C (Non-discriminatory treatment), but not for section C on Investment protection.

38   Tietje and Crow (n 34), 12 where it is explained that Art 8.12 (1)(a) CETA codifies this practice, but the prerequisite is already well-established. See, e.g., *Tidewater Investment SRL and Tidewater Caribe CA v The Bolivarian Republic of Venezuela*, ICSID Case No ARB/10/5, Award, 13 March 2015; *Saipem SpA v The Peoples Republic of Bangladesh*, ICSID Case No ARB/05/7, Award, 30 June 2009; *Marvin Feldman v Mexico*, ICSID Case No ARB(AF)/99/1, Award, 16 December 2002.

39   Tietje and Crow (n 34), 12.

40   *Ioan Micula, Viorel Micula, SC European Food SA, SC Starmill SRL and SC Multipack SRL v Romania*, ICSID Case No ARB/05/20, Final Award, 11 December 2013.

relevant for future disputes as they will restrict the flexibility of tribunals to apply investment protection to subsidy disputes.[41]

15.22 Hence, even though the stand-alone provision of the right to regulate in CETA seems to be a reaffirmation of existing treaty practice and does not constitute a right per se, the inclusion of this right is important for interpretative reasons and provides a clear political signal. Moreover, the right to regulate is firmly established in CETA's substantive provisions, such as the FET standard and provisions relating to indirect expropriation.

2. Narrower definition of substantive standards

a. *Fair and equitable treatment*

i. *CETA's substantive standard*

15.23 Most EU Member States' BITs simply offer 'fair and equitable treatment'[42] to investments of nationals of contracting States. This open-ended, unqualified FET standard plays a crucial role in investment arbitration. As this standard is found in the vast majority of bilateral investment treaties,[43] it has proven to be the most frequently invoked provision in ISDS-cases.[44] An open-ended, unqualified FET standard was originally meant to 'fill the gaps' that might occur should the other substantive investment protection standards not be applicable.[45] Hence, traditionally, the FET was purposely meant to be a vague standard in order to leave room for changing circumstances and situations.[46] However, this flexible approach has left room for interpretation to arbitral tribunals, resulting in much discretion and different approaches by arbitral tribunals, sometimes even in almost identical cases.[47]

---

41 Tietje and Crow (n 34), 13.

42 E.g., Netherlands Model BIT (1997) art 3(1) provides: 'Each Contracting Party shall ensure fair and equitable treatment of the investments of nationals of the other Contracting Party'. Available through UNCTAD's Investment Policy Hub <https://investmentpolicy.unctad.org/international-investment-agreements/treaty-files/2857/download> accessed May 4, 2020.

43 Patrick Dumberry, 'The Prohibition against Arbitrary Conduct and the Fair and Equitable Treatment Standard under NAFTA Article 1105' (2014) 15 *The Journal of World Investment & Trade* 117.

44 UNCTAD, 'Expropriation-UNCTAD Series on Issues in International Investment Agreements II' (United Nations, 2012) (UNCTAD Series on IIAs-Expropriation), 1 <https://unctad.org/en/Docs/unctaddiaeia2011d7_en.pdf> accessed May 21, 2020.

45 See Sabrina A Bandali, 'Understanding FET: The Case for Protecting Contract-Based Legitimate Expectations', in Ian A Laird, Borzu Sabahi, Frédéric G Sourgens and Todd J Weiler (eds), *Investment Treaty Arbitration and Arbitration Law* (Vol 7, Juris 2014) 133.

46 Tietje and Crow (n 34), 5.

47 For example, the tribunal in *CME Czech Republic BV v Czech Republic, UNCITRAL, Partial Award, 13 September 2001*, decided that 'the broad concept of fair and equitable treatment imposes obligations beyond customary international requirements of good faith treatment', and therefore found a breach of the FET standard under the Dutch–Czech Republic BIT. But in an almost identical case under a United States–Czech Republic BIT, the arbitral Tribunal held in *Ronald S Lauder v The Czech Republic, UNCITRAL, Final Award, 3 September 2001* that there was no violation of the FET standard as 'the Claimant has not identified any specific obligation of international law which would provide the foreign investor with a broader protection than the other Treaty obligations on which he otherwise relies'.

The three parties to The North American Free Trade Agreement (NAFTA) that includes **15.24**
Canada, were amongst the first to realize the impact of leaving it to arbitral tribunals to
interpret the FET standard widely. As a result, they made successful attempts to limit the
scope of discretion to arbitral tribunals.[48] Research by UNCTAD shows that limiting the
scope of the standard results in a significantly lower number of claims. Only 22 per cent of
claims based on the FET-provision in NAFTA litigation after 2001 have been accepted (four
out of 18); while claims based on open-ended FET-provisions as included in other investment
treaties result in acceptance of 62 per cent (41 out of 66).[49] UNCTAD concludes:

> these statistics suggest that it is more difficult for a claimant to establish a violation of FET under
> NAFTA than under a BIT. In cases under NAFTA that links the FET standard to Minimum
> Standard of Treatment, the claimants' success rate is much lower than in cases under traditional BITS
> and the ECT […].[50]

Hence, given Canada's prior experiences it is not surprising that CETA's FET provision **15.25**
closely mirrors the much narrower interpretation given by NAFTA parties that linked the
standard to a closed list of conduct that constitutes such a breach. Article 8.10 CETA clarifies
that a breach of the FET can only occur in situations where a government denies justice in
criminal, civil or administrative proceedings; does fundamentally breach due process; exposes
manifest arbitrariness; displays targeted discrimination on manifestly wrongful grounds, such
as gender, race or religious belief; or exercises abusive treatment of investors, such as coercion,
duress and harassment. By linking the behaviour to a closed-list of conduct, the scope of
application of the FET provision is significantly limited. However, these elements are not set
in stone. Pursuant to Article 8.10 (3) CETA the closed list will be reviewed regularly, or upon
request of a party. In addition, the Committee on Services and Investment, may develop
recommendations in this regard and submit them to the CETA Joint Committee for decision,
which mirrors Canada's NAFTA practice.

ii. Compromise on legitimate expectations

A particularly contested element of the FET standard is the question whether and to what **15.26**
extent legitimate expectations of investors are part of the FET standard. Claims involving a
breach of legitimate expectations particularly arise in situations where an investor has suffered
damages due to a change of laws and regulations of a host state.[51] Moreover, the number of
cases in which claimants base themselves on this argument, has significantly increased over
time and to such extent that investor's legitimate expectations might be seen as the most
important aspect of the FET standard.[52]

---

48 NAFTA Free Trade Commission, 'North American Free Trade Agreement – Notes of Interpretation of Certain
    Chapter 11 Provisions' (31 July 2001) <http://www.sice.oas.org/tpd/nafta/Commission/CH11understanding_e.asp?>
    Accessed May 4, 2020.
49 UNCTAD Series on IIAs-Expropriation (n 44), 61.
50 Ibid., 60.
51 Ibid., 64.
52 For example, the tribunal in *Electrabel SA v Republic of Hungary*, ICSID Case No ARB/07/19, Decision on Jurisdiction,
    30 November 2012, highlighted that '*the most important function of the FET standard is the protection of the investor's
    legitimate expectations*'. See also Thomas Westcott, 'Recent Practice on Fair and Equitable Treatment' (2007) 8 *Journal
    of World Investment & Trade* 409.

15.27 It is generally understood that the concept of legitimate expectations consists of three elements: a focus on a stable and predictable business and regulatory environment; a focus on transparency of governmental regulations towards a foreign investor and assurances by government officials in the form of specific representations.[53] Many national legal systems place similar emphasis on legal certainty and legal security, in German law known as 'Rechtssicherheit' or in Dutch law known as a general law principle of 'rechtszekerheid'. Yet, despite the emphasis on legal stability, this does and should not mean that the legal framework will never change. Such outcome would be, to paraphrase UNCTAD, 'unjustified, as it would potentially prevent the host State from introducing any legitimate regulatory change'.[54]

15.28 In response to public concerns 'that such an explicit reference to a stable business environment has been interpreted by some arbitral tribunals as offering a general guarantee against repeated legislative changes',[55] an important part of the reform introduced by the EU was to clarify that EU investment protection standards do not offer such a guarantee. Therefore, in assessing a breach of legitimate expectations as part of the FET standard, Article 8.10(4) CETA specifically provides that in assessing a FET claim:

> a Tribunal may take into account whether a Party made a *specific representation* to an investor to induce a covered investment, that created a legitimate expectation, and upon which the investor relied in deciding to make or maintain the covered investment, but that the Party subsequently frustrated.

15.29 This means that whereas legitimate expectations in EU Member States' BITs could be seen as a stand-alone element of the FET standard, a breach of legitimate expectations in CETA is no longer a breach of the FET standard in itself.[56] In CETA, legitimate expectations may only be taken into account in the context of the categories mentioned in Article 8.10 (2) CETA. Thus, compared to EU Member States' BITs, in order to preserve governments' right to regulate, CETA provides a much narrower definition of the FET standard due to a clear limitation of the concept of legitimate expectations.[57] Another big reform took place to clarify the parameters of indirect expropriation.

b. *Indirect expropriation*

15.30 A core provision in EU Member States' BITs is the obligation to provide safeguards to investors in case of expropriation. These older-generation BITs protect investors against *any* government measure depriving their investments, *directly or indirectly*, unless the following three cumulative conditions are met. Firstly, the measures must be taken in the public interest

---

53 Benedict Kingsbury and Stephan Schill (2009), 'Investor-State Arbitration as Governance: Fair and Equitable Treatment, Proportionality and the Emerging Global Administrative Law' (IILJ Working Paper 2009/6, New York University School of Law, 2009).

54 UNCTAD, 'Fair and Equitable Treatment – UNCTAD Series on Issues in International Investment Agreements II' (United Nations, 2012) (UNCTAD Series on IIAs-FET) 67 <https://unctad.org/en/Docs/unctaddiaeia2011d5_en.pdf> accessed May 21, 2020.

55 Concept Paper (n 36), 5.

56 See Steffen Hindelang and Carl-Philipp Sassenrath, *The Investment Chapters of the EU's International Trade and Investment Agreements – In a Comparative Perspective*' (Study, European Parliament, September 2015), 141.

57 European Parliament, 'EU investment protection after the ECJ opinion on Singapore: Questions of Competence and Coherence' (Study, PE 603.476, March 2019), <https://www.europarl.europa.eu/RegData/etudes/STUD/2019/603476/EXPO_STU(2019)603476_EN.pdf> accessed May 4, 2020.

and with due process of law; secondly, the measures must not be applied in a discriminatory manner; and thirdly, the investors are awarded just compensation.[58]

In determining a breach of an older-generation expropriation provision, arbitral tribunals have conducted a two-step analysis. First, on the basis of the above-mentioned factors, it must be determined whether a direct or indirect expropriation took place or whether the conduct qualifies as the State's non-compensable exercise of police powers and regulatory prerogatives.[59] Second, if it is confirmed that the case constitutes direct or indirect expropriation, the analysis turns to matters of its lawfulness or unlawfulness and the question of compensation or reparation. In CETA, the second step of the analysis has not been changed, but a tribunal is given much more guidance in the first step of the analysis.   **15.31**

After all, none of the older-generation BITs of EU Member States offers any guidance as to what constitutes direct or indirect expropriation, leaving much discretion to arbitral tribunals to decide this issue.[60] And while disputes regarding direct expropriations have become rare,[61] the concept of indirect expropriation is increasingly popular in recent ISDS-cases and has led to different and diverging interpretations of tribunals. Hence, research from UNCTAD shows that cases involving a breach of (in)direct expropriation stem from BITs that do not include clarifications or additional guidance to the meaning of indirect expropriation.[62]   **15.32**

Therefore, considerable efforts were taken by Canada and the EU to clarify the definition of 'indirect expropriation' in CETA.   **15.33**

At first sight, Article 8.12 CETA includes traditional treaty language regarding conditions for expropriation. However, the real ground-breaking element is found in Annex 8-A, that includes an interpretive Annex drawing a distinction between direct and indirect expropriation. Significantly for the present discussion, CETA's Annex on Expropriation defines indirect expropriation very narrowly as a measure or series of measures of the host State that has an *effect equivalent* to direct expropriation. In addition, Annex 8-A(3) CETA includes a specific provision that aims at preserving the regulatory autonomy of the host State. Measures taken by a government to protect health, safety or the environment are presumed not to amount to indirect expropriation. Only measures that are manifestly excessive in light of their objective might amount to indirect expropriation pursuant to Annex 8-A(3) CETA. So, arbitral tribunals are clearly instructed to preserve the right to regulate for States in cases of indirect expropriation. Together with the FET provision, these two provisions mark a clear departure   **15.34**

---

58 E.g., Netherlands Model BIT (1997), art 6. Available through UNCTAD's Investment Policy Hub <https://investmentpolicy.unctad.org/international-investment-agreements/treaty-files/2857/download> accessed May 4, 2020.

59 UNCTAD Series on IIAs – Expropriation (n 44), 10.

60 Ibid., 12.

61 In the first part of the twentieth century, the first major phase of mass expropriations (nationalizations) occurred during revolutionary movements in Russia and Mexico. A second wave of nationalizations and expropriations followed the period of decolonization that took place after the Second World War. See OECD, "'Indirect Expropriation' and the 'Right to Regulate' in International Investment Law" (OECD Working Papers on International Investment No 2004/04, OECD Publishing) <http://dx.doi.org/10.1787/780155872321> accessed May 21, 2020.

62 UNCTAD, 'Review of ISDS Decisions in 2018: Selected IIA Reform Issues' (IIA Issues Note – International Investment Agreements, Vol 4, July 2019) (UNCTAD Series on IIAs – Vol 4) <https://unctad.org/en/Publications Library/diaepcbinf2019d6_en.pdf> accessed May 4, 2020.

from the 'Dutch gold standard.' In both provisions, the scope of application is limited and arbitral tribunals are given clear guidance in order to preserve policy space for governments.

c.   *Other substantive changes in light of the right to regulate*

15.35 While CETA introduces two clear-cut innovations to preserve the right to regulate through the FET-standard and provisions of indirect expropriation, the right to regulate is also found in other provisions. And also in relation to these provisions, CETA introduces some new elements to prevent abuse. The following section will shortly address these innovations below.

15.36 First, CETA limits the definition of 'investment' as well as the definition of 'investor'. Articles 8.2(2) and (3) CETA contain sectorial carve-outs that deny investments in certain sectors investment protection under CETA.[63] Such sectorial carve-outs are alien in EU Member States' BITs. In addition, the term 'investment' in CETA explicitly incorporates three of four elements identified in *Salini v Morocco*[64] as part of the definition of an investment, namely contributions, and other criteria such as a certain duration of performance of the contract and participation in the risks of the transaction. This should limit the scope of protection to 'genuine' investments only. In addition, the definition of investor has changed. Pursuant to Article 8.1 CETA, the term 'investor' is drafted in such way that it explicitly only offers protection to genuine investors, being a natural person or legal person that is 'an enterprise constituted or organised under the laws of that Party and has substantial business activities in the territory of that Party'. This last clarification is particularly important in relation to the older-generation Dutch BITs, that traditionally and purposely lacked such a definition. As a result, these BITs have been widely used by legal persons without substantial business activities, so called 'shell companies'[65] to benefit from investment protection under Dutch BITs.[66] CETA specifically excludes these companies from protection under CETA.

15.37 Second, CETA limits the MFN standard in Article 8.7 only to future, forward-looking situations. The purpose of this new provision is to avoid that the MFN clause can be used as a way to import a 'better' ISDS provision from another treaty in a current treaty, as done in the infamous *Maffezini* case.[67] On this basis, MFN clauses could be used to modify any provision of a BIT in terms of substance of procedure. CETA prevents such abuse by preventing incorporation of the open-ended MFN-definition of older-generation BITs.[68]

15.38 Third, with regard to the standard of full protection and security, one of the outstanding issues in investment law has for long been the question whether the standard covers physical *and* legal

---

63   For example, Art 8.2(2) excludes air services and related services and audiovisual services from the scope of application.

64   *Salini Costruttori SpA and Italstrade SpA v Morocco*, ICSID Case No ARB/00/4, Decision on Jurisdiction, 23 July 2001.

65   Some figures even estimate that 75 per cent of the claims brought under Dutch treaties were initiated by mailbox companies, see SOMO, 'Socializing Losses, Privatizing Gains – How Dutch investment treaties harm the public interest' (Briefing, January 2015) <https://www.somo.nl/wp-content/uploads/2015/01/Socialising-losses-privatising-gains.pdf> accessed May 21, 2020.

66   One of the important features of the 2019 Model BIT of the Netherlands corrects this definition and requires a substantial business interest in the Netherlands as a prerequisite for treaty protection.

67   *Emilio Agustín Maffezini v The Kingdom of Spain*, ICSID Case No ARB/97/7, Decision on Objections to Jurisdiction, 25 January 2000.

68   Titi (n 35), 171.

security, or whether this standard is limited to cover physical security only.[69] Now, Article 8.10(5) CETA provides 'for greater certainty', that full protection and security only relates to the Party's obligations to guarantee the physical security of investors and covered investments, limiting the scope of application severely compared to older-generation BITs of EU Member States.

Fourth, older-generation EU Member States' BITs guarantee free transfer of payments **15.39** relating to an investment, in a freely convertible currency and without restriction or delay. CETA introduces a couple of exceptions to this rule by introducing in Article 8.13(3) CETA a safeguard provision that allows governments to restrict transfers of capital in emergency situations, provided these measures are applied in an equitable and non-discriminatory manner and are not construed as a disguised restriction on transfer.[70] Moreover, CETA's Chapter 13 on Financial Services applies to investment in financial institutions in the territory of the host State and Article 13.16 CETA incorporates a so-called 'prudential carve-out' which allows parties to adopt measures in order to protect the integrity and stability of a party's financial system. Together with Articles 28.4 CETA and 28.5 CETA, these provisions offer a robust framework for Parties to take temporary safeguard measures in case of balance of payments deficits and external financial difficulties.[71]

Lastly, most BITs of EU Member States include a so-called 'umbrella-clause' that allows a **15.40** foreign investor to bring a breach of *any* obligation it may have received from a State with regard to its investments, under the scope of the BIT.[72] This could be any legislative, contractual and/or other treaty-based obligation. To avoid such extensive scope of application, Article 8.18(1) CETA explicitly limits the jurisdiction of the CETA Investment Tribunal to the examination of breaches of the CETA provisions only. Also, pursuant to Article 8.18(5) CETA: 'The Tribunal constituted under this Section shall not decide claims that fall outside of the scope of this [Agreement].' So, claims for breaches of contracts alone or for breaches of the domestic law of the host country are not admissible under CETA and remain subject to the exclusive jurisdiction of the domestic courts of the parties.

As shown in the aforementioned analysis, CETA's new approach to investment protection **15.41** builds upon traditional elements found in older-generation BITs of EU Member States, but clearly focusses on strengthening the right to regulate. In doing so, CETA clearly deviates from the 2011 mandate that instructed the EU to negotiate a chapter that would provide for the highest possible level of investment protection and was to be built upon best practices of BITs of EU Member States. However, by inserting a stand-alone provision to preserve the right to regulate and in addition, impose limitations to substantive investment protection

---

69   E.g., *Compañía de Aguas del Aconquija, SA and Vivendi Universal SA v Argentina*, Award, 20 August 2007, para 7.4.16; *AES Summit Generation Ltd and AES-Tisza Erömü Kft v The Republic of Hungary*, ICSID Case No ARB/07/22, Award, 23 September 2010, para 13.3.2 and 343; *Spyridon Roussalis v Romania*, ICSID Case No ARB/06/1, Award, 7 December 2011, para 321.

70   The article allows room for governments that may restrict transfers in case of (a) bankruptcy, insolvency or the protection of the rights of creditors; (b) issuing, trading or dealing in securities; (c) criminal or penal offences; (d) financial reporting or record keeping of transfers when necessary to assist law enforcement or financial regulatory authorities; and (e) the satisfaction of judgments in adjudicatory proceedings.

71   Titi (n 35), 177.

72   See, e.g., Art 3(4) Model BIT 1997: 'Each Contracting Party shall observe any obligation it may have entered into with regard to investments of nationals of the other Contracting Party.'

standards, CETA's Investment Chapter offers less protection to investors compared to older-generation BITs. In doing so, the EU seems to get in line with Canada's Model BIT. As a result of being at the wrong end of several NAFTA arbitrations, that model has been re-calibrated since 2004 in the direction of narrowing investors' rights[73] and preserving the right to regulate by states.[74] Hence, CETA's Investment Chapter contains some new elements in terms of substance compared to older-generation BITs of EU Member States. However, real ground-breaking innovations of CETA are to be found in its new regime for dispute settlement.

D. PROCEDURAL RULES

1. Point of departure: arbitration

15.42 The most fundamental change in CETA's Investment Chapter is the introduction of a completely new, unprecedented mechanism to resolve disputes between investors and states. The older-generation EU Member States BITs include an investor-state dispute settlement mechanism (ISDS) to settle disputes between states and investors of the other Party. ISDS has always been a rare animal in international law. From the start, it was designed as a hybrid mechanism creating access to effective judicial protection and remedies for natural and legal persons in disputes with states based on a combination of international private and public law. At its core, ISDS is a form of international arbitration. Arbitration is by far the most common way to resolve international disputes, either in State-to-State disputes[75] or between private parties acting internationally.[76] Arbitration is an alternative dispute settlement procedure in which a dispute is submitted, by agreement of the parties, to one or more arbitrators who make legally binding decisions to resolve the dispute. ISDS adds a new element to this traditional system, by creating an opportunity for private parties to settle disputes with States by using international private law instruments to solve international public law disputes.[77] To date, it is the only mechanism known in international law that gives direct legal standing to individuals

---

73 José Alvarez, 'Why Are We "Re-Calibrating" Our Investment Treaties?', (2010) 4(2) *World Arbitration and Mediation Review* 143.

74 Lavranos (n 29), 4.

75 Founded in 1899, the PCA was the first permanent intergovernmental organization to provide a forum for the resolution of international disputes through arbitration and other peaceful means that provides administrative support in international arbitrations involving various combinations of states, state entities, international organizations and private parties. Permanent Court of Arbitration, 'History' <https://pca-cpa.org/en/about/introduction/history/> accessed May 4, 2020

76 The use of international commercial arbitration has particularly been spurred by the success of the Convention on the Recognition and Enforcement of Foreign Arbitral Awards, commonly known as the New York Convention, which was adopted by a United Nations diplomatic conference on 10 June 1958 and entered into force on 7 June 1959. With an almost universal membership of 163 States, the Convention requires courts of contracting States to give effect to private agreements to arbitrate and to recognize and enforce arbitration awards made in other contracting States. It is widely considered the foundational instrument for international arbitration and applies to arbitrations that are not considered as domestic awards in the state where recognition and enforcement is sought. See United Nations, Enforcing Arbitration Awards under the New York Convention; Experience and Prospects (United Nations Publications, 1998) <https://www.uncitral.org/pdf/english/texts/arbitration/NY-conv/NYCDay-e.pdf> accessed May 4, 2020.

77 Muthucumaraswamy Sornarajah, *The International Law on Foreign Investment* (CUP 2010), 324–57.

in international public law to challenge government measures that harmed them and gives them an opportunity to seek redress.[78]

Commercial arbitration is based on the consent of parties in a contract. In the case of ISDS, **15.43** this contract is concluded between the investor and the host State in the form of an investment treaty. Among other distinct features, ISDS follows international commercial arbitration practice, by using either ad hoc or institutional arbitration tribunals to settle disputes between investors and States. In this process, parties enjoy a great deal of party autonomy and procedural flexibility, as to choose the seat or forum and appoint arbitrators. Moreover, as commercial arbitration usually takes place in relation to performance of commercial contracts, by default, the proceedings are confidential. Thanks to the widely recognized stature of the New York Convention,[79] that ensures effective enforcement of international commercial arbitral awards and investor-State arbitral awards as well as through an almost universal ratification of the ICSID Convention, arbitral awards can be enforced throughout the world.

While ISDS is a relatively new concept in international law, over time it has become a **15.44** frequently-used legal instrument for Claimants, resulting in a total number of over 1,000 publicly known ISDS claims by the end of 2019.[80] In comparison, 'only' a number of 177 cases have been brought for consideration before the International Court of Justice.[81] On the other hand, the average annual administrative court case load in the Netherlands consists of over 100,000 cases.[82]

2. Investment court system

In CETA, the ISDS provision found in older-generation BITs of EU Member States has been **15.45** replaced by a court-like system that functions on two levels. First, pursuant to Article 8.27 CETA, cases will be brought to a Tribunal of First Instance, composed of 15 members: five members will be nationals of Canada, five will be nationals of the EU and the remaining five will be third-country nationals.[83] The members of the tribunal will be appointed by Canada and the EU to serve on a pre-established roster of arbitrators. Like most domestic courts, the tribunal will hear cases in divisions consisting of three members, respecting the tripartite balance of nationalities and chaired by the third-country national. The appointment of arbitrators and allocation of cases significantly differ from the current arbitration practice, in

---

78 Only the European Court of Human Rights is praised as the other forum that gives direct standing to individuals, but only after exhaustion of national legal remedies. See Convention for the Protection of Human Rights and Fundamental Freedoms (European Convention on Human Rights, as amended), art 35.

79 Ibid., 76.

80 UNCTAD Series on IIAs – Vol 2 (2020).

81 United Nations, 'Report of the International Court of Justice (1 August 2018–31 July 2019)' UN Doc Supp No 4 (A/74/4) <https://www.icj-cij.org/files/annual-reports/2018-2019-en.pdf> accessed 4 May 2020.

82 See Dutch Research and Documentation Center for annual statistics 2017 and 2018 regarding use of civil and administrative procedures in the Netherlands: 'Rechtspleging Civiel en Bestuur' (Scientific Research and Documentation Center) <https://www.wodc.nl/cijfers-en-prognoses/rechtspleging-civiel-en-bestuur/> accessed May 4, 2020.

83 Note that the CETA Joint Committee has the power to increase or decrease the number of adjudicators by multiples of three, see art 8.27 (3) CETA.

which disputing parties are free to select 'their' arbitrators,[84] partly subject to the condition that they should not be nationals of disputing parties.[85] Instead, pursuant to Article 8.27(6) CETA, the tribunal will always consist of a member who will have the nationality of a Member State of the EU and one, having the nationality of its treaty partner.

15.46 Second, Article 8.28 CETA introduces the establishment of an Appellate Tribunal to review awards rendered by the Tribunal of First Instance. The aim of the Appellate Tribunal is to contribute to the creation of a more coherent and harmonious set of case law as well as to ensure the legal correctness of decisions and awards.[86] After all, while the opportunity for judicial review is a central element in most domestic legal systems, the introduction of an appeal mechanism is a novel element in the field of ISDS.[87] Pursuant to Article 8.28(9) CETA, awards rendered by the Tribunal of First Instance can be appealed to the Appellate Tribunal within 90 days of their issuance. An appeal must be submitted based on the grounds listed in Article 8.28(2) CETA, that expands the scope of the review to errors in application of the law; manifest errors in the appreciation of the facts and the grounds for annulment set out in Article 52(1) of the ICSID Convention.[88] Based on these grounds, the Appellate Tribunal may uphold, modify, or reverse the Tribunal's award. However, the Appeal/Appellate Tribunal does not itself render a modified final award. Instead, the First Instance Tribunal subsequently has to issue a revised award within 90 days of receiving the report of the Appeal Tribunal.

15.47 The establishment of an appellate mechanism is one of the most important features of the proposed ICS, yet also one of its most contested elements. On the one hand, an appeal mechanism can be seen as a way to channel divergent interpretations into a more harmonious body of law. In doing so, CETA's appeal mechanism seems to be inspired by the crucial role that the WTO Appellate Body has played in developing a *jurisprudence constante* in international economic law by following the reasoning developed in its previous decisions and providing useful guidance to panels in subsequent cases involving the same legal questions.[89] Precisely because this case law has become coherent through repetition, the Appellate Body has established itself as a natural authority and has been able to influence and contribute to the

---

84 E.g., Convention on the Settlement of Investment Disputes between States and Nationals of Other States (adopted 18 March 1965, entered into force 14 October 1966), 575 UNTS 159 (ICSID Convention), Art 37(2)(b) and UNCITRAL, 'UNCITRAL Arbitration Rules (with new article 1, paragraph 4, as adopted in 2013)' (United Nations, 2013), Art 9.

85 E.g., ICSID Convention (n 84), Arts 38 and 39 particularly provide that the majority of the arbitrators shall be nationals of States other than the contracting State party to the dispute and the contracting State whose national is a party to the dispute; provided, however, that the foregoing provisions of this Article shall not apply if the sole arbitrator or each individual member of the tribunal has been appointed by agreement of the parties.

86 André von Walter and Maria Luisa Andrisani, 'Resolution of Investment Disputes', in Makane Moïse Mbengue and Stefanie Schacherer (eds) *Foreign Investment Under the Comprehensive Economic and Trade Agreement (CETA)* (Studies in European Economic Law and Regulation vol 15. Springer 2018) 185, 190.

87 ICSID's Secretariat explored possibilities for the creation of an appeal mechanism within ICSID already back in 2004; see ICSID Secretariat Discussion Paper, 'Possible Improvements of the Framework for ICSID Arbitration' (October 22, 2004).

88 ICSID Convention (n 84), Art 52(1) provides for limited grounds for annulment. The Convention on the Recognition and Enforcement of Foreign Arbitral Awards (opened for signature 10 June 1958, entered into force 7 June 1959) 330 UNTS 3 (New York Convention), Art 5 provides limited grounds to set an award aside, see Art 5 and below.

89 See Joost Pauwelyn, 'Foreword', in Graham Cook, *A Digest of WTO Jurisprudence on Public International Law Concepts and Principles* (CUP 2015) xiii, xxvii, referring to AV Lowe and A Tzanakopoulos, 'Economic Warfare' in R Wolfrum (ed) *Max Planck Encyclopaedia of Public International Law* (Oxford University Press 2012), 186.

key objective of enhancing the security and predictability of the multilateral trading system. However, by including a possibility to appeal a decision, the system also runs risks of attempts to create 'another bite of the apple'. This might have particular negative consequences for states in ISDS procedures, as tribunals have increasingly decided in favour of States over the years.[90]

In addition, the appeal facility in CETA's Investment Chapter is empowered to not only annul **15.48** an award, but also to review errors in law and, to a more limited extent, the assessment of facts.[91] However, by breaking through the traditional limited scope of review for annulment of awards, either through limited review through Article 52 of ICSID or through annulment proceedings in domestic courts based on Article V of the New York Convention, the appeal mechanism in CETA is faced with some practical obstacles. In the eyes of some, the new system is either inconsistent with the ICSID Convention or a deviation of the specifically narrowly designed grounds for review of arbitral awards under Article V of the New York Convention.[92] Hence, the introduction of an appeal mechanism in CETA might lead to practical difficulties with respect to the enforcement of awards.

3. Enforcement of awards

After all, while ICS clearly shifts to a 'public law' approach for the conduct of the proceedings, **15.49** it remains dependent on 'private law' instruments for the effective enforcement of the awards. Article 8.41(1) CETA underlines that an award issued under CETA shall be binding between the disputing parties and in respect of that particular case. In addition, Article 8.41 CETA underlines that a final award is enforceable pursuant to provisions of the ICSID Convention or the New York Convention. However, some scholars question the compatibility of CETA's ICS with the functioning of existing mechanisms.

Starting with an assessment in the context of ICSID, ICS features a system that deviates in **15.50** many aspects from the arbitration procedures provided for under the ICSID Convention, that is a closed and independent system. Article 53(1) ICSID Convention specifically provides for awards to be binding upon its members and requires that the parties 'shall abide by and comply with the terms of the award'. The Convention specifically prohibits opportunities for 'any appeal or to any other remedy except those provided for in this Convention'.[93] In this regard it must be noted that the EU itself is not a contracting party to the ICSID Convention.[94]

Since the ICSID Convention does not offer an opportunity of appeal, the question is if **15.51** contracting parties themselves can change rules between themselves. While Article 41 of the 1969 Vienna Convention on the Law of Treaties (VCLT)[95] foresees a possibility for so-called *inter se* amendments of applicable treaties between parties, the question remains whether such a

---

90 UNCTAD Series on IIAs – Vol 4 (n 62).
91 August Reinisch, 'Will the EU's Proposal Concerning an Investment Court System for CETA and TTIP Lead to Enforceable Awards? – The Limits of Modifying the ICSID Convention and the Nature of Investment Arbitration' (2016) 19 *Journal of International Economic Law* 761, 777.
92 Ibid.
93 Reinisch (n 91), 780.
94 Except for Poland, all EU Member States are also Contracting Parties of the ICSID Convention to date. See <https://icsid.worldbank.org/apps/ICSIDWEB/about/Pages/Database-of-Member-States> accessed May 21 2020.
95 Vienna Convention on the Law of Treaties (adopted 23 May 1969, entered into force 27 January 1980) 1155 UNTS 331.

change between contracting parties would be enforceable in other ICSID States.[96] Therefore, some argue that an 'ICS' award cannot be treated as 'an award rendered pursuant to this Convention' within the meaning of Article 54 ICSID. Reinisch observes that even though CETA negotiators tried to craft the final ICS awards as if it were ICSID awards, this does not guarantee that other ICSID Contracting Parties will also recognize them as ICSID awards enforceable under the specific rules of the ICSID Convention. Permissible *inter se* agreements under general treaty law remain *inter se* agreements, meaning that agreements modifications will only bind the modifying partners. While questions remain as to compatibility with the ICSID Convention, the issue seems less complex for UNCITRAL-awards that will be enforced through the New York Convention.

15.52　The New York Convention has been essential to ensure the effective enforcement of international commercial arbitral awards as well as for ISDS-arbitral awards. The main objective of the New York Convention is to provide common legislative standards for the recognition of arbitration agreements and court recognition and enforcement of foreign and non-domestic arbitral awards.[97] In order to effectively enforce an award under the New York Convention, an award must be an 'arbitral award'. The question arises whether a ruling of an Investment Court in CETA qualifies as an 'arbitral award' if they are rendered by a permanent institution instead of ad hoc arbitration tribunals. However, pursuant to Article I(2) of the New York Convention, '[t]he term "arbitral awards" shall include *not only* awards made by arbitrators appointed for each case but also those made by permanent arbitral bodies to which the parties have submitted. [...]'. Also, while the New York Convention does not define the notion of 'permanent arbitral bodies', there is judicial practice that semi-permanent institutions like the Iran–US Claims Tribunal can qualify as a permanent arbitration body.[98]

15.53　Ultimately, the *travaux preparatoires* of the New York Convention indicate that the application of the New York Convention to enforce and recognize awards really depends on the crucial question whether the arbitration proceeding is conducted '*voluntarily*', based on the free 'will' or 'agreement' of the parties, as opposed to any type of 'compulsory', or 'mandatory' adjudication, imposed on the parties 'regardless of their will'.[99] Therefore, Reinisch concludes that while ICS has lost many of its arbitration features, for application of the New York Convention, the only relevant question is whether parties freely consent to such dispute settlement. Otherwise, a ruling would lose its character as an arbitration award and would not be enforceable under the New York Convention. Since investors will still be accepting the contracting parties' offer for arbitration on a voluntary basis and can still submit their disputes to domestic litigation, it seems that this requirement is fulfilled. As outlined above, there are compelling arguments to believe that ICS awards could qualify as award under the New York Convention, but it is up for national courts to recognize them as enforceable awards under the New York Convention.

96　Reinisch (n 91), 771.

97　See New York Convention (n 88), Objective.

98　Reinisch (n 91), 767.

99　Gabriel Kaufmann-Kohler and Michele Potestà, 'Can the Mauritius Convention serve as a model for the reform of Investor-State arbitration in connection with the introduction of a permanent investment tribunal or an appeal mechanism? – Analysis and roadmap' (Geneva Centre for International Dispute Settlement, 2016) <https://lk-k.com/wp-content/uploads/2016/05/KAUFMANN-KOHLER-POTESTA-CIDS-Research-Paper-Reform-of-Investor-State-Arbitration-2016.pdf> accessed May 3, 2020.

4. Related procedural innovations

To facilitate the implementation of the 'Court system,' other procedural innovations have been **15.54** made in CETA. For purposes of this discussion, only the most important new features will be highlighted in the next section. Firstly, CETA introduces specific requirements for Members of the Tribunal to possess qualifications required in their respective countries for appointment to judicial office and to have demonstrated expertise in the field.[100] Also, CETA aims to include stricter ethical rules for adjudicators in order to ensure their independence and impartiality, the absence of conflict of interest, bias or appearance of bias, coupled with its own procedure for potential disqualifications of adjudicators. To that end, Article 8.30 CETA provides that Members of the Tribunals cannot be affiliated with any government, nor take instructions from any organization or government related to the matters of the dispute, nor hear any dispute that would create a direct or indirect conflict of interest. They shall comply with the International Bar Association's (IBA) Guidelines on Conflicts of Interest in International Arbitration or other professional ethics rules adopted by the CETA Committee on Services and Investment. Lastly, Article 8.30(1) CETA requires adjudicators under CETA to refrain, upon appointment, from acting as legal counsel or as party-appointed expert or witness in any pending or new investment dispute under CETA or under any other international agreement.

Secondly, in the majority of ICSID proceedings to date, tribunals ordered the parties to equally **15.55** share costs of the proceedings (i.e., arbitrators' fees and costs incurred by the Centre) and for each party to bear their own expenses.[101] However, CETA's Investment Chapter explicitly tackles the issue of cost allocation, providing for application of a 'loser pays principle'. Article 8.39(5) CETA explicitly provides as a general rule that the costs of the proceedings shall be borne by the unsuccessful disputing party. The tribunal can depart from this rule only in 'exceptional circumstances'. The costs incurred by the losing party can also include other reasonable costs, such as the costs of legal representation and assistance, unless such costs would be considered unreasonable in the circumstances of the case.

Third, in contrast to traditional arbitration that is confidential by default, CETA enhances **15.56** transparency in proceedings in two ways. Article 8.39 CETA ensures that both contracting parties are kept fully informed of all cases and procedural steps that may arise under the CETA investment provisions. Consequently, whenever dispute settlement proceedings are initiated under CETA, the non-disputing party (i.e., the home party of the investor who initiated the dispute) is entitled to receive all documents submitted in the dispute (including evidence), to make written and oral submissions on issues of treaty interpretation and to attend the hearings. This procedure ensures that the non-disputing party is given an adequate voice in the conduct of the proceedings and ensures that the tribunal can have the full picture of the parties' joint intentions when making its decision.

In addition, CETA probably provides for the highest standards of transparency in investment **15.57** dispute settlement provisions.[102] Article 8.36 CETA incorporates by cross-reference the

---

100 Reinisch (n 91), 764.
101 Shaheeza Lalani and Rodrigo Polanco Lazzo, *The Role of the State in Investor-State Arbitration* (Brill 2015).
102 von Walter and Maria Luisa Andrisani (n 86), 198.

UNCITRAL Rules on Transparency in Treaty-based Investor-State Arbitration that came into force on 18 October 2017 and states in Article 8.36(5) CETA as a principle that all hearings shall be open to the public.[103] However, on several occasions it goes beyond the UNCITRAL standards, for example by requiring the publication of documents before the constitution of the arbitral tribunal and by systematically publishing the request for consultations, the determination of the respondent, the agreement to mediate, the request for and the decisions on arbitrator challenges, as well as the request for consolidation among the list of documents to be systematically published. Through the incorporation of Article 4 of the UNCITRAL Transparency Rules, CETA also allows interested third persons (such as individuals or civil society organizations) to make submissions, also known as *amicus curiae* briefs, to the tribunal. This allows 'any natural or legal person which can establish a direct and present interest in the result of the dispute (the intervener) to intervene as a third party'.[104] Further, tribunals may allow NGOs to submit *amicus curiae* briefs.

5. Preventing potential misuse

15.58 In order to prevent abuse of the procedures enshrined in the Agreement, CETA introduces a couple of new elements. First, Article 8.18(3) CETA introduces a general prohibition of submitting a claim if the investment was made through fraud, misrepresentation, concealment, corruption, or conduct amounting to an abuse of process. Also, 'forum shopping' or 'treaty-shopping', i.e., the practice of choosing the most favourable dispute settlement mechanism under which a claim might be heard is excluded in Article 8.18 CETA.[105] Second, Articles 8.32 and 8.33 CETA provide for two different procedures allowing the expeditious dismissal of unfounded or abusive claims. It incorporates provisions of the ICSID Arbitration Rules and UNCITRAL Arbitration Rules that allow claims that are manifestly without legal merit to be dismissed at the very beginning of the proceedings. Third, CETA follows a so-called 'no-U-turn'-approach, stipulated in Article 8.22 CETA under which investors are incentivized to first seek redress in domestic courts before turning to the CETA Investment Tribunal. In other words, by encouraging domestic proceedings first, CETA's ICS will function as a means of last resort.

15.59 Lastly, CETA's Investment Chapter flashes out in some more detail the, still problematic, relationship of the ICS and domestic law, seeking to address in detail the boundaries between the domestic and the international legal orders. As most EU Member States' BITs do not limit the scope of applicable law, arbitral tribunals might have been free to take elements of domestic law into account. Article 8.31 CETA clarifies that if such interpretation is necessary, the Court only use the elements of domestic law as a matter of fact, i.e., by following strictly the interpretation given to the domestic law by the competent domestic courts or authorities of the parties. For greater certainty, Article 8.31(2) CETA also explicitly states that any meaning given to the domestic law by the CETA Investment Tribunal can never be considered to be binding on the domestic courts or authorities of the parties. Conversely, Article 30.6 CETA explicitly excludes the invocation of the CETA investment protection rules before the domestic courts of the parties. In *Opinion 1/17*, the European Court of Justice explicitly confirmed that because the specific characteristics and autonomy of the EU legal order are

---

103   Ibid., 190.
104   Hindelang and Sassenrath (n 56).
105   von Walter and Maria Luisa Andrisani (n 86), 198.

preserved, the EU can enter into international agreements providing for the creation of a court.[106] Hence, CETA's Investment Chapter, including its new approach to dispute settlement through ICS, is compatible with EU law and is now awaiting ratification and implementation.

'With our proposals for a new Investment Court System, we are breaking new ground',[107] said **15.60** EU Vice-President Frans Timmermans proudly when presenting the EU's new investment policy. As shown above, in relation to the procedural rules of dispute settlement, CETA fundamentally shifts from a 'private law' approach in BITs of EU Member States to a more 'public law' approach, inspired by proceedings in domestic courts and international Courts. Main features of this new Court system are a composition of pre-appointed judges appointed in divisions, a possibility for review by an appeal tribunal, other fixed procedural rules, including enhanced transparency and detailed guidance as to avoid interference with domestic law and prevent procedural abuse. While some doubts remain with regard to the enforceability of the awards, the Court system as included in CETA clearly deviates from the scope of ambition of the 2011 EU-mandate. After all, back then, EU Member States wanted to include 'an effective and state-of-the-art investor-to-state-dispute settlement mechanism' based on a 'wide range of arbitration fora for investors as currently available under the Member States' bilateral investment agreements (BIT's)'.[108] Ceta's ICS shifts from a 'private law' approach to a more 'public law' approach for the settlement of disputes. In doing so, CETA's Investment Court is a truly ground-breaking and systemic change compared to the older-generation BITs that simply provide for ISDS.

E. CONCLUSION

CETA was the first agreement that included a detailed chapter on investment promotion and **15.61** protection, including an investor-State dispute resolution mechanism, since the EU assumed exclusive competence in matters of FDI under the Lisbon Treaty. Against this background, CETA's Investment Chapter underwent a significant transformation. From the absence of investment protection to the integration of the 'Dutch gold standard', CETA's Investment Chapter ultimately emerged as the guinea pig of the new EU's investment policies. Ultimately, it can be concluded that CETA's Investment Chapter signals a ground-breaking change compared to older-generation BITs of EU Member States both in terms of substance and procedure. It is the first EU investment agreement that explicitly aims to safeguard the right to regulate, limits the scope of substantive provisions and beyond everything else, creates a fundamentally new approach towards dispute settlement resolution through an ICS with an appeal mechanism based on predetermined rules, with appointed judges and more transparent proceedings. CETA breaks away from the traditional system of investment protection and dispute settlement. It rebalances the right to regulate and in doing so, offers less substantive protection for investors. Moreover, CETA shifts from a 'private law' approach to a more 'public law' approach for the settlement of disputes. Therefore, in the land of investment treaties, CETA is certainly ground-breaking and a *primus inter pares*.

---

106   *Opinion 1/17* (n 28).
107   Commission, 'Commission draft text TTIP – investment' (2015) <https://trade.ec.europa.eu/doclib/docs/2015/september/tradoc_153807.pdf> accessed May 3, 2020.
108   Ibid., 4.

16

PROCEDURAL ISSUES: ANNULMENT, RECOGNITION AND ENFORCEMENT OF INVESTMENT TREATY AWARDS (ICSID AND NON-ICSID)

Olivier van der Haegen and Maria-Clara Van den Bossche [*]

A. INTRODUCTION

16.01 In investor-state arbitration, like in any other proceedings, victory is often claimed once a favourable final award is issued: on behalf of the investor if the award entitles him/her to all or an important part of the relief requested; on behalf of the State if the award rejected all or most of the claims brought against it. This is understandable, especially in view of the enormous time and costs spent in investor-state arbitration proceedings to arrive at a final award. Yet, the truth is that the issuance of the final award often constitutes only a step in the proceedings and certainly not the end of the matter. For the road to effective payment can still be a long and difficult one: setting aside or annulment proceedings can be initiated, a stay of enforcement can be ordered and, more generally, multiple hurdles may have to be tackled in cross-border

---

[*] Date of submission: 9/3/2020.

enforcement proceedings (including challenges based on sovereign immunities) if the losing party – particularly when it is a sovereign State – refuses to voluntarily satisfy the award.

Whilst investor-state arbitration has sparked many criticisms over the last years from politi- **16.02** cians, NGOs, the European Commission and other stakeholders, the public debate did not shed light on what we believe is one of the core issues faced by investor-state arbitration in recent years, namely the increasing tendency of States to refuse voluntary payment of awards issued against them, although they participated in the arbitration proceedings which were based on multilateral or bilateral investment treaties that States have voluntarily entered into and largely benefitted from (notably because they attracted foreign investments on their territories). Much more systematically than before, States oppose the award's finality in setting aside proceedings and/or their enforcement before national courts. It may well be that the criticisms levied in recent years against investor-state arbitration, especially within the European Union,[1] while they have nothing to do with the binding and final nature of investor-treaty awards, have given States support in their increasing attempts to refuse compliance with these awards.

The subject of the chapter is therefore topical: we will focus on what happens after the issuance **16.03** of an investment-treaty award, in case the losing party refuses to voluntarily/immediately comply with the outcome. We will address both annulment and recognition/enforcement of investment-treaty awards in the European Union, putting the emphasis on the procedural issues. In doing so, we will focus on the cohabitation – at times difficult – between, on the one hand, the international treaties and national arbitration laws applicable to these proceedings and, on the other hand, European Union law ('EU law').

We will first summarize the fundamental differences between the annulment and enforcement **16.04** regimes of investment-treaty awards rendered on the basis of the Convention on the Settlement of Investment Disputes between States and Nationals of Other States (the 'ICSID Convention')[2] under the auspices of the International Centre for Settlement of Investment Disputes ('ICSID' and 'ICSID awards') and the investment-treaty awards issued under other international arbitration rules, either *ad hoc* or under the auspices of other international institutions administering investor-state arbitrations (ICC, SCC, the PCA in The Hague, etc.). We will analyse, on the basis of some recent cases brought before courts of EU Member States, the difficulties that may arise when different EU Member State courts are seized of annulment and enforcement proceedings in relation to the same investment-treaty award (Section B).

In turn, we will focus on two landmark cases that have spurred the controversies in relation to **16.05** the validity of so-called 'intra-EU' investment-treaty awards (awards issued in investor-state arbitrations (ICSID or non-ICSID) on the basis of a treaty entered into between two EU Member States), namely the *Micula versus Romania* and *Achmea versus Slovakia* cases (Section C). In the latter section, we will focus on the national proceedings brought in these cases before

---

1 Lack of publicity, private nature of tribunals composed of individuals not elected or appointed through democratic instances, important costs involved, imbalance created between EU investors benefitting from intra-EU bilateral investment treaties and those who do not benefit from the same protections, etc.

2 The ICSID Convention was proposed for signature in Washington on 19 March 1965. To date it has been ratified by 154 States.

some of the Member State courts, as opposed to the decision issued by the General Court or the Court of Justice of the European Union, which will be the focus of another chapter of this book.

16.06 Finally, in the last section of our chapter, we will review some salient rules on State immunities, for virtually all enforcement proceedings of investor-state arbitral awards against States (also within the EU) naturally raise complex immunity issues (Section D).

B. THE ICSID VERSUS NON-ICSID ANNULMENT AND ENFORCEMENT REGIMES

16.07 As is well known, the regime applicable to annulment and enforcement of investment-treaty awards issued under the auspices of the ICSID is very different to the one applicable for other investment-treaty awards.[3] All EU Member States – with the notable exception of Poland – are parties to the ICSID Convention, which will therefore govern annulment and enforcement of ICSID awards throughout the EU. In substance, ICSID awards (i) may not be subject to setting aside proceedings before the national courts at the seat of the arbitration but instead may be reviewed on a number of limited grounds by an *ad hoc* Committee appointed under the ICSID Rules and (ii) ICSID awards shall not be reviewed in recognition and enforcement proceedings in the States party to the ICSID Convention (26 out of the 27 EU Member States), which are bound to recognize and enforce all ICSID awards on their respective territory as if they were judgments issued by their own national courts.

1. The ICSID annulment regime

16.08 Aside from requesting either the interpretation of an ICSID award (art 50) or its revision on the basis of the *'discovery of some fact of such a nature as to decisively affect the award'* (art 51) – which recourses shall, if possible, be submitted (by the ICSID Secretary-General) to the same arbitral tribunal – parties to an ICSID arbitration may request the 'annulment' of the award by an *ad hoc* Committee pursuant to Article 52(1) of the ICSID Convention. Annulment is only possible on the basis of five distinct grounds, namely (a) the tribunal was not properly constituted, (b) the tribunal manifestly exceeded its power, (c) there was corruption on the part of a member of the tribunal, (d) there has been a serious departure from a fundamental rule of procedure or (e) the award has failed to state the reasons on which it is based.

16.09 Similarly to setting aside proceedings of non-ICSID awards, the ICSID annulment procedure is not an appeal: it is, and must be interpreted as, an *'extraordinary and narrowly circumscribed remedy'*.[4] Also, ICSID *ad hoc* Committees may annul ICSID awards either in whole or in part, but in no instance can they decide the underlying dispute. In case of annulment, the dispute will have to be submitted by either party to a new ICSID arbitral tribunal.[5]

---

3 In the present contribution, ICSID awards does not encompass awards issued under the ICSID Additional Facility mechanism, which are not governed by the ICSID Convention.

4 Claudia Annacker, Laurie Achtouk-Spivak, Zeïneb Bouraoui, 'ICSID Awards' in Emmanuel Gaillard and Gordon E Kaiser (eds), *The Guide to Challenging and Enforcing Arbitration Awards* (Law Business Research 2019) 137.

5 Partial annulment may raise complex issues on the *res judicata* of unannulled sections of a previous award. In the *Pey Casado v Chile* case, initially brought in 1997, an ad hoc committee recently rejected a claim from the investor that the

The grounds for annulment under Article 52(1) differ from – and are more limited than – **16.10** those in Article 34 of the UNCITRAL[6] Model Law on International Commercial Arbitration (of 1985 and amended in 2006), which is copied in, or has influenced, many of the national arbitration rules applicable to setting aside proceedings of non-ICSID awards before national courts.[7] The most salient difference of the ICSID annulment regime is that it is a self-standing or self-contained arbitral regime without intervention of national courts. An ICSID award is reviewed (and may be annulled in certain limited circumstances), not by a State court, but by another arbitral tribunal, namely the *ad hoc* Committee. Once an ICSID award is annulled, it will not be enforceable anymore. This contrasts with the regime applicable to non-ICSID awards, for non-ICSID awards will usually be enforced by national courts on the basis of the New York Convention of 1985 on the Recognition and Enforcement of Foreign Arbitral Awards (the 'New York Convention'), which has been interpreted in certain jurisdictions (France, for instance) as permitting enforcement of arbitral awards despite their annulment by the national courts at the seat of the arbitration.[8]

Pursuant to Article 52(3) of the ICSID Convention, the *ad hoc* Committee is composed of **16.11** three arbitrators chosen from the ICSID Panel of Arbitrators: none of the members of the Committee shall have been a member of the arbitral tribunal having issued the award, be of the same nationality of any such member or be a national of the State party to the arbitration or have been designated to the Panel of Arbitrators by either of those States.

As recently shown by C. Anacker, L. Achtouk-Spivak and Z. Bouraoui, while some *ad hoc* **16.12** Committees have been criticized in the past for having interpreted their powers too broadly, the recent trend at ICSID is a narrow interpretation of the annulment grounds, with an annulment rate of 8 per cent for the years 2001–10 and 3 per cent for the years 2011–18.[9]

Despite this low rate of annulment, yet in line with the general trend referred to in the **16.13** introduction of the present chapter, parties to ICSID arbitration continue to try their luck and often seek annulment. One of the reasons is that, under Article 52(5) of the ICSID Convention, a party applying for annulment may, together with its application for annulment, request a stay of enforcement of the award pending the annulment proceedings before the *ad hoc* Committee. Such a stay may be ordered by the *ad hoc* Committee only in exceptional circumstances.[10] However, when a request for stay is made by the applicant, enforcement will

---

second ICSID arbitral tribunal, which decided the case in 2016, had exceeded its powers by giving effect to un-annulled parts of the original ICSID award issued in 2008. See *Pey Casado v Chile*, ICSID Case No ARB 98/2.

6   United Nations Commission on International Trade Law.

7   Importantly, under the ICSID regime, there is no possibility to annul the award on the basis of (substantive) public policy. Moreover, an annulment on the basis of a lack of jurisdiction of the Arbitral Tribunal, although possible under the ICSID regime either for excess of power or serious departure from a fundamental rule of procedure, will be reviewed more strictly than under the jurisdiction ground of the Model Law, which usually allows for a *de novo* review of jurisdiction by the national courts seized of a setting aside application against a non-ICSID award.

8   Carlo de Stefano, 'The Circulation of Investment Awards under the New York Convention' in Katia Fach Gómez and Ana Mercedes López Rodríguez (eds), *60 Years of the New York Convention: Key Issues and Future Challenges* (Kluwer Law 2019) 445–6.

9   Annacker, Achtouk-Spivak and Bouraoui (n 4) 137.

10   For a review of ICSID *ad hoc* committees' case-law on requests for stay, see Andrea K Bjorklund and Lukas Vanhonnaeker 'Stays of enforcement pending annulment and set-aside proceedings in investment arbitration' in Julien Fouret (ed) *Enforcement of Investment Treaty Arbitration Awards* (Globe Law and Business 2021) 49–55.

in any case be stayed '*provisionally*' as long as the *ad hoc* Committee has not ruled upon the request for stay (Article 51(4)). In the authors' view, this rule may encourage unjustified annulment applications. Indeed, knowing that the appointment of an *ad hoc* Committee may take between a few weeks and a couple of months (which is understandable in view of the strict nationality criteria imposed on the members of the *ad hoc* Committee), a losing party may want to file a setting aside application and a request for stay with the sole purpose of obtaining the provisional stay and thereby winning time. This delay may be used by the debtor under the award (including States) to remove assets out of certain enforcement-friendly jurisdictions, thereby undermining the efficiency of the system.

2. The ICSID recognition and enforcement regime

16.14 Following the same spirit as the self-contained annulment proceedings, the ICSID Convention provides for a specific enforcement regime which also intends to avoid – as much as possible – interferences from national courts. Article 53(1) of the ICSID Convention provides that the award shall be 'binding on the parties' and that 'each party shall abide by and comply with the terms of the award'. Article 54(1), in turn, provides that 'each Contracting State shall recognize an award rendered pursuant to this Convention as binding and enforce the pecuniary obligations imposed by that award within its territories as if it were a final judgment of a court in that State'. Article 52(2) adds that the recognition shall be granted, either by a court or a State authority, upon presentation of a certified copy of the ICSID award. In other words, in all States party to the ICSID Convention, an ICSID award will not have to be recognized by a national court pursuant to the New York Convention and/or the national law applicable to the enforcement of (foreign) arbitral awards, before it can actually be enforced on assets located on the relevant State's territory.

16.15 It is interesting to note that this specific recognition and enforcement regime, strongly debated when the ICSID Convention was negotiated in the early 60s (at a time when the New York Convention had just entered into force) was principally justified to avoid non-compliance by investors.[11] Today, the regime is mainly used to the advantage of investors in their attempts to enforce ICSID awards against recalcitrant States.

16.16 During the preparatory works of the ICSID Convention, it had been proposed to leave the possibility open for national courts to review whether the ICSID awards complied with public policy before recognizing and/or enforcing the awards on their territory. This public policy exception was eventually not retained, which increases the finality of the award.[12]

16.17 In the authors' experience, the ICSID regime strongly facilitates enforcement of awards against States, including in the EU Member States party to the ICSID Convention. In Belgium, for example, a request for recognition of an ICSID award must be submitted to the

---

11 Ruqiya BH Musa and Martina Polasek 'The Origins and Specificities of the ICSID Enforcement Mechanism' in Fouret (n 10) 16–17.

12 Ibid., 20.

Belgian Ministry of Foreign Affairs.[13] If the latter is satisfied that the award's copy is duly certified by the ICSID Secretary-General, it will request a stamp from the Brussels Court of appeal, which will not review the award's content. The procedure takes a couple of weeks, while recognition and enforcement proceedings of non-ICSID awards based on the New York Convention and/or Belgian law may lead to lengthy recognition proceedings, with the State often invoking various grounds for refusal of recognition.[14]

That being said, the advantages of the ICSID regime cannot be overestimated either. Article **16.18** 54(3) of the ICSID Convention provides that 'execution of the awards shall be governed by the laws concerning the execution of judgments in force in the States in whose territories such execution is sought'. As shown by the *Micula* case – which will be analysed below – the ICSID recognition regime does not avoid challenges being brought before national courts. This is because, even though an ICSID award has to be recognized by a State party to the ICSID Convention as if it were a judgment issued by the national courts of that State, once recognized, it will form the basis for enforcement measures taken on the relevant State's territory (attachments, garnishments of bank accounts, etc.). In turn, those enforcement measures will be challenged by the party opposing enforcement of the ICSID award before the national courts where enforcement takes place. It is frequent – and indeed an increasing trend – that, in the course of those challenges against enforcement measures, the opposing party invokes breaches of public policy, a lack of jurisdiction of the arbitral tribunal or procedural irregularities during the arbitration proceedings, i.e., the type of challenges that the drafters of the ICSID Convention sought to avoid.

3.   The setting aside and enforcement regime of non-ICSID awards

a.   *Setting aside of non-ICSID awards*

In contrast to the ICSID self-contained and centralized annulment and recognition regime, **16.19** setting aside claims of non-ICSID investment treaty awards in the EU will be brought before the national courts at the seat of the investment-treaty arbitration and will be governed by that State's national provisions.

National arbitration laws in EU Member States are either based on the UNCITRAL Model **16.20** Law on International Commercial Arbitration (the 'Model Law') (Germany, for instance) or provide for a comparable regime (France, for instance). The grounds allowing for setting aside of an arbitral award are contained in Article 34 of the Model Law. They cover the most important issues that can occur in the arbitral proceedings (violation of due process and rights of defence, arbitral tribunal not properly constituted) or the main defects that can affect an arbitral award (inarbitrability, invalidity of the arbitration clause, incapacity of the signatories, absence of jurisdiction, breach of public policy). National laws that have not copied the Model Law (in all or in part) provide for largely similar grounds.

---

13   Act of 17 July 1970 approving the ICSID Convention, art 3 (BE). It provides that an ICSID award can be enforced in Belgium once it has been (i) authenticated by the Belgian MFA and, subsequently (ii) transmitted by the Belgian MFA to the chief clerk of the Brussels Court of Appeal who will issue a recognition order.

14   The Belgian recognition regime, like the French one, provides that recognition is granted on an ex-parte basis, which means that the challenge will be brought in adversarial proceedings only after recognition has been granted.

b. Recognition and enforcement of non-ICSID awards

16.21 Recognition and enforcement of non-ICSID investment-treaty awards in the EU will be governed by the New York Convention and/or the national laws of the EU Member States where enforcement is sought. All EU Member States (including Poland) are parties to the New York Convention (to date, the Convention is applicable in 166 contracting States worldwide). National laws may still play a role for three notable reasons. First, under Article VII(1) of the Convention, international treaties or national laws that are more favourable to the recognition or enforcement of an award may be invoked by the award's creditor and may take precedence over the New York Convention. Second, the procedure to obtain recognition is still largely governed by national law (Article III of the Convention).[15] Third, the New York Convention only applies to foreign awards. Obviously, like all arbitral awards, an investment-treaty award can be enforced in the country where the arbitration was seated and, for the sake of enforcement in that country, the New York Convention will not apply.

16.22 A question which, to the authors' knowledge, has not attracted many commentaries concerns the possibility to enforce investment-treaty awards under the New York Convention also in States (including some EU Member States) that have made the so-called 'commercial reservation' under Article I(3) of the New York Convention. These States have limited the scope of the New York Convention in their country to arbitral awards (and arbitration agreements) relating to 'differences arising out of a legal relationship, whether contractual or not, which are considered as commercial under the State making such declaration'. Many investment-treaty awards concern mixed commercial and non-commercial issues and often imply the use, or actually the misuse, of public policy measures or public law powers by States. Some multilateral or bilateral investment treaties expressly provide that the awards issued on their basis shall be considered 'commercial' for the purposes of enforcement under the New York Convention (including in States having made the 'commercial' reservation under the Convention). For example, Article 26.5 (b) of the Energy Charter Treaty (the 'ECT') provides that 'claims submitted to arbitration hereunder shall be considered to arise out of a commercial relationship or transaction for the purposes of Article I of that Convention'. In the absence of such provision, it may well be that, in certain countries, the New York Convention will not apply to recognition and enforcement of foreign investment-treaty awards, in which case national law will enter into play.

16.23 A stay of enforcement can be granted by a national court under Article VI of the New York Convention pending setting aside proceedings before the courts at the seat of the arbitration. The regime is however entirely different from the ICSID regime summarized above because a request for a stay of enforcement under the New York Convention will have to be brought before the national courts where enforcement is sought and, if granted, the stay will only apply to the enforcement of the award on the territory of that country (and should not have extraterritorial effects). Moreover, and importantly, a stay is not automatic and may not be

---

15   Art III of the New York Convention provides that, 'Each Contracting State shall recognize arbitral awards as binding and enforce them in accordance with the rules of procedure of the territory where the award is relied upon, under the conditions laid down in the following articles.'

granted for the sole reason that setting aside proceedings have been initiated before the courts of the seat.[16] This follows from Article VI of the New York Convention which provides that:

'the authority before which the award is sought to be relied upon *may, if it considers it proper*, adjourn the decision on the enforcement of the award and may also, on the application of the party claiming enforcement of the award, order the other party to give suitable security (emphasis added).

c. *The absence of an autonomous EU law regime governing recognition and enforcement of investment-treaty awards*

The grounds to refuse recognition and enforcement are enumerated in Article V of the New York Convention. They have been copied (almost verbatim) in the grounds justifying setting aside and refusal of recognition under Articles 34 and 36 of the Model Law (which was finalized in 1985). Because of this similarity, the review of (investment-treaty) arbitral awards by national courts throughout the EU, both in setting aside and recognition and enforcement proceedings is, if not harmonized, at least largely coherent.[17]   **16.24**

Similarity between national arbitration laws throughout the European Union and a coherent interpretation of the New York Convention by all (or most of the) EU Member States courts does not, and it is submitted that it should not, lead to a system in which EU Member States courts are bound to adopt the same approach towards identical or similar challenges brought to the same (investment-treaty) arbitral award.   **16.25**

This was made clear in the framework of the drafting of the Brussels Recast Regulation. Arbitration is excluded from the scope *ratione materiae* of the Brussels Recast Regulation (art 1(2)(d)),[18] as it was under its predecessors, the Brussels I Regulation and the Brussels Convention. Recital 12 of the Brussels Recast Regulation clarifies that 'rules on recognition and enforcement of EU judgments shall not apply to judgments issued by Member State courts ruling on the validity, or invalidity, of arbitral awards' and further stressed that the Regulation 'should not apply (…) to any action or judgment concerning the annulment, review, appeal, recognition or enforcement of an arbitral award'. In addition, Article 73(2) of the Regulation provides that the 'Regulation shall not affect the application of the 1958 New York Convention'.   **16.26**

Therefore, there is no EU law obligation imposed on EU Member States courts to recognize and enforce judgments issued by other Member State courts in relation to setting aside or recognition and enforcement of arbitral awards.[19]   **16.27**

---

16 As has been observed by others, a stay appears to be more rarely granted by national courts under the New York Convention than by *ad hoc* committees under the ICSID Convention: see Musa and Polasek (n 11) 60.

17 Emmanuel Gaillard and Benjamin Siino, 'Enforcement under the New York Convention' in Emmanuel Gaillard and Gordon E Kaiser (eds), *The Guide to Challenging and Enforcing Arbitration Awards* (Law Business Research 2019) 87.

18 Regulation (EU) 1215/2012 of the European Parliament and of the Council on jurisdiction and the recognition and enforcement of judgments in civil and commercial matters [2012] OJ L351/1.

19 In the *Gazprom* judgment of 13 May 2015 (C-536/13, *Gazprom OAO v Lietuvos Respublika* [2015] EU:C:2015:316) – which concerned the question whether an arbitral award ordering a party to refrain from pursuing court proceedings in violation of an arbitration clause could be recognized and enforced under the New York Convention even if it had the effect of potentially depriving European nationals from their right to seize an EU Member State court on the basis of the Brussels Regulation – the Court of Justice of the European Union (CJEU) confirmed that the recognition and enforcement of an arbitral award, 'are covered by the national and international law applicable in the Member States in

16.28   The question whether an award (including an investment-treaty award) that has been set aside by the courts at the seat of the arbitration may still be enforced in other countries under their national laws and/or the New York Convention has brought and continues to bring important controversies, which are not only academic but have actually been the object of diverging decisions from State courts, including within the EU (where courts like France and Germany, for instance, have taken opposite views).

16.29   It would go beyond the scope of this chapter to come back on the many arguments that have been raised by both sides in this long-standing controversy. We want to stress that, both under Article 36 of the Model law (which enumerates the grounds for refusal of recognition and enforcement of arbitral awards and has been implemented in many national arbitration laws) as under Article V of the New York Convention, the drafters have used the verb '*may*' instead of '*shall*': this is generally interpreted as granting a margin of discretion to national courts when applying the grounds for refusal of recognition and enforcement, including the New York Convention ground provided in Article V(2)(e), namely that recognition and enforcement '*may*' be refused when the award 'has been set aside or suspended by a competent authority of the country in which, or under the law of which, that award was made'.[20]

16.30   French courts take the view that international arbitral awards (including investment-treaty awards)[21] are transnational or international by nature and, therefore, that a decision from a national court, be it the court at the seat of the arbitration which is exclusively competent to rule on setting aside claims, remains a *national* decision. This decision does not imply that other national courts are prevented from recognizing and enforcing, on their territory, the same international arbitral award (under the New York Convention or under their national law) if they consider the award to be valid.[22]

16.31   The French position is predicated on different legal grounds: the discretion granted to national courts by the New York Convention but also (and predominantly) the possibility to apply a more favourable national (in this case French) regime to enforcement, as is allowed under Article VII of the New York Convention.

16.32   Prominent French scholars have stressed that parties to an international arbitration agreement are not always and necessarily in a position to choose the seat of the arbitration, and when the choice is made, it is not (often) made with the aim to grant the national courts at the seat an overarching power to have the last word on the validity of an international arbitral award; to the contrary, parties resort to arbitration – including in investor-state arbitration – to avoid

---

which recognition and enforcement is sought, and not by Regulation 44/2001' (para 41). For a commentary of the *Gazprom* decision, see Olivier van der Haegen, 'Back to the CJEU's Gazprom judgment: anti-suit injunctions, arbitration and Brussels I' (2016) 2 *b-Arbitra* 151.

20   Jan Paulsson, 'May or Must under the New York Convention: An exercise in Syntax and Linguistics' (1998) 14(2) *Arbitration International* 299.

21   de Stefano (n 8) 4456.

22   See, amongst others, Berthold Goldman, '*Société Pabalk Ticaret Ltd Sirketi v Norsolor S.A.*' (1985) *Revue de l'arbitrage* 433 (note); Charles Jarrosson, '*Société Hilmarton v Société Omnium de traitement et de valorisation*' (1994) vol 2 *Revue de l'arbitrage* 327 (note); Philippe Fouchard '*République Arabe d'Egypte v Société Chromalloy Aéro Services*' (1997) *Revue de l'arbitrage* 395 (note); Emmanuel Gaillard, '*Société PT Putrabali Adyamulia v Rena Holding et Société Mnogutia Est Épices*' (2007) *Revue de l'arbitrage* 507 (note).

national courts' interference.[23] In the authors' view, this may be especially relevant in investment-treaty arbitration where the seat is often imposed by the institution administering the proceedings or by the arbitral tribunal itself. Interestingly, while the debate on the possibility to recognize and enforce arbitral awards annulled by the courts at the seat of the arbitration have attracted much attention, the related and broader question of the influence that the findings of one national court may or may not have on other national courts, seized of identical or similar challenges against the same (investment-treaty) award, did not attract the same attention so far.[24]

In the authors' home jurisdiction, Belgium, the question has been at issue in two recent **16.33** enforcement proceedings brought in relation to non-ICSID investment-treaty awards, namely the *Yukos v Russian Federation*[25] and the *Stati v Republic of Kazakhstan*[26] enforcement proceedings.

In the *Yukos* case, the former Yukos shareholders[27] sought to enforce in Belgium one of the **16.34** landmark ECT awards issued against the Russian Federation in 2014. The arbitration proceedings were governed by the UNCITRAL Rules of Arbitration and held under the auspices of the Permanent Court of Arbitration in The Hague. The Hague had been chosen as seat of the arbitration. During the course of the Belgian recognition proceedings, which were subject to the New York Convention and Belgian law, the ECT awards were set aside by a first instance court in The Hague. Despite the setting aside, the Belgian court seized of the recognition proceedings decided to uphold the validity of the Belgian recognition order, dismissing the Russian Federation's challenge for procedural reasons.[28]

However, since enforcement measures (attachment of assets and garnishment of bank **16.35** accounts) had been carried out on the basis of the recognized award, challenges were also brought by the Russian Federation before the Belgian court supervising enforcement (*Juge des saisies/Beslagrechter*). The latter court rejected the Russian Federation's argument that the judgment of the first instance court in The Hague had to be recognized in Belgium on the basis of the Brussels Recast Regulation, which was rightfully considered as not applicable.[29] However, the Belgian court upheld an alternative private international law argument based on a bilateral treaty on the recognition and enforcement of judgments in civil and commercial matters signed in 1925 between Belgium and The Netherlands, which, unlike the Brussels Recast Regulation, did not exclude 'arbitration' from its scope. The Belgian court decided that it was bound to recognize the judgment of the first instance court in The Hague and, for that reason, lifted the enforcement measures, considering that they were based on a foreign award that had been annulled in a foreign (first instance) judgment, which (according to the Belgian

---

23 Jarrosson, ibid., 331 para 10 (note); Emmanuel Gaillard, 'L'exécution des sentences annulées dans leur pays d'origine' (1998) 3 *Journal du droit International* 49–50.

24 For an analysis of some recent cases where this issue was raised in the US, the Netherlands and the UK, see Emmanuel Gaillard, 'Dialogue des ordres juridiques: ordre juridique arbitral et ordres juridiques étatiques' (2018) 3 *Revue de l'arbitrage* 511–12.

25 'Civ Bruxelles, 8 juin 2017 (chambre de saisies)' (2017) vol 2 *b-Arbitra*, 301ff; Alexander Hansebout, 'De actualiteit van de arbitrale uitspraak: een conflict tussen het exequaturvonnis en het vernietigingsvonnis' (2018) vol 1 *b-Arbitra* 93-105.

26 Belgium, Court of first instance of Brussels, 20 December 2019, Case 18/1312/A, unpublished.

27 The authors disclose that their firm represented the former *Yukos* shareholders in the Belgian proceedings.

28 'Civ Bruxelles, 9 décembre 2016 '(2017) vol 2 *b-Arbitra* 287.

29 'Civ Bruxelles, 8 June 2017(chambre des saisies)' (2017) vol 2 *b-Arbitra*, 301, 309–10.

court) had to be recognized in Belgium. The Belgian court considered that the act (or the 'title', referring to the award) at the basis of the enforcement measures had lost its 'topicality' (*actualité/actualiteit*), thus its enforceable nature.[30]

16.36 In the second case, *Stati v Republic of Kazakhstan*,[31] the ECT award was issued against the Republic of Kazakhstan by an arbitral tribunal seated in Stockholm and operating under the auspices of the Stockholm Chamber of Commerce (SCC). The Belgian court before which the challenge against the Belgian recognition order was brought (which recognition order had been issued pursuant to the New York Convention and Belgian law) was asked by the investors to recognize the Swedish judgment (issued this time in last instance) which had *dismissed* the Republic of Kazakhstan's request for setting aside the award in Sweden. Here again, though the Belgian court rightly confirmed that the Brussels Recast Regulation did not apply, it decided that it was bound to recognize the Swedish judgment based on the provisions of the Belgian Code of private international law. On that ground, the Belgian court decided that some of the challenges brought by the Republic of Kazakhstan against the recognition of the award in Belgium, which were similar to those already raised in the Swedish setting aside proceedings and which had been dismissed by the Swedish courts, enjoyed *res judicata* and could not be reviewed differently in Belgium.[32]

16.37 In the authors' view, these decisions entail a fundamental departure from the traditional operation of the New York Convention. Indeed, under the New York Convention, it should be upon each national court, seized of a request for recognition and enforcement of a foreign award, to review whether the award can be incorporated *in that court's national legal order* and form the basis of enforcement measures performed *on that country's territory*.[33] This is the essence of recognition and enforcement proceedings. As explained by E. Gaillard, the aim of the New York Convention is to favour circulation of foreign arbitral awards, not arbitration-related national courts decisions.[34]

16.38 Nothing in the New York Convention imposes on a court that is asked to recognize a foreign arbitral award to abide by (and agree with) findings made by another national court in relation to the same arbitral award, including findings of the court located at the seat of the arbitration. The reasoning of the Belgian court in the *Stati v Republic of Kazakhstan* matter implies that, as soon as the courts at the seat of the arbitration have upheld an arbitral award, recognition and enforcement shall be granted automatically in all other countries where enforcement is sought except if other arguments are found or may be invoked that have not been reviewed during the setting aside proceedings. From the rule enshrined in Article V(1)(e) – which provides that a national court '*may*' refuse recognition and enforcement of a foreign award that has been '*set aside by a competent authority of the country in which (...) that award was made*', a shift has been made in the aforementioned decisions of the Belgian courts to a rule (which in our view has no

---

30 Ibid., 311–12.
31 The authors disclose that their firm represents the National Bank of Kazakhstan in parallel proceedings before the Belgian courts.
32 Belgium, Court of first instance of Brussels, Case 18/1312/A, 20 December 2019, unpublished.
33 Ibid.
34 Gaillard (n 24), 510. See also Philippe Colle and Hakim Boularbah, '*De invloed van het bestaan van mogelijke nietigheidsgronden op het exequatur van een buitenlandse scheidsrechterlijke uitspraak*' in Jozef Van Den Heuvel (ed), *Liber amicorum* (Kluwer 1999).

legal basis in the New York Convention) under which a national court '*shall not*' refuse recognition and enforcement of an award on the basis of any of the grounds listed under Article V of the New York Convention if those grounds have been dismissed by '*the competent authority of the country in which (…) that award was made*'.

C. ENFORCEMENT OF INTRA-EU INVESTMENT-TREATY AWARDS BEFORE NATIONAL COURTS: THE *MICULA* AND *ACHMEA* CASES

When reviewing the question of setting aside and enforcement of investment-treaty awards in the EU, one cannot but address the difficulties created in recent years by the so-called intra-EU investment-treaty awards, namely investment-treaty awards issued in arbitrations based on bilateral (or multilateral) treaties signed between Member States. This issue was central in the landmark *Micula* and *Achmea* cases. In the following sections of this chapter, we will focus on the various national court proceedings as opposed to the judgments issued by the ECJ (General Court and Court of Justice).   **16.39**

1. The *Micula* case

a. Case background

In 2005, the brothers Ioan and Viorel Micula and three companies owned by them (the 'Micula claimants') commenced ICSID arbitration proceedings against Romania on the basis of the 2002 Sweden-Romania bilateral investment treaty (BIT), seeking compensation for Romania's premature repeal of a number of tax incentives that had been previously granted to promote investment in underdeveloped regions of the country. The incentives were meant to stay in place for ten years, but Romania prematurely withdrew them in 2005 in preparation for its accession to the EU, in order to eliminate domestic measures that could constitute State aid incompatible with the *acquis communautaire*. Romania subsequently acceded to the EU on 1 January 2007.   **16.40**

In the award dated 11 December 2013, an ICSID tribunal ruled that the withdrawal of the incentives by Romania was undertaken in a way that breached the fair and equitable treatment standard imposed by the BIT and ordered Romania to pay EUR 178 million in compensation (the 'Award'). The tribunal did not uphold the position of the European Commission, which intervened in the proceedings as *amicus curiae* and argued that the tribunal should not award damages to the Micula claimants because the payment of any such damages would be contrary to EU State aid rules and render the Award unenforceable in the EU. Romania's application for the annulment of the Award before an ICSID *ad hoc* Committee was rejected on 26 February 2016.   **16.41**

On 26 May 2014, the Commission adopted an injunction decision ordering Romania to suspend execution or implementation of the Award (the 'Injunction Decision').[35] By letter dated 1 October 2014, the Commission informed Romania that it had decided to initiate a   **16.42**

---

35   *Micula v Romania* (Case State aid SA.38517) Commission Decision of 26 May 2014 ordering Romania to suspend any action which may lead to the execution or implementation of the *Ioan Micula, Viorel Micula and others v Romania* ICSID Case No ARB/05/20 Award of 11 December 2013.

State aid investigation pursuant to Article 108(2) TFEU in respect of the implementation or execution of the Award by Romania (the 'Opening Decision').[36]

16.43 On 30 March 2015, following partial payment of the Award by Romania, the European Commission adopted a decision finding that the payment of the compensation awarded by the ICSID arbitral tribunal to the claimants constituted incompatible State aid (the 'State Aid Decision').[37] The decision precluded any further payment by Romania and ordered it to recover the partial payment that had already been made.

16.44 The Micula claimants filed an appeal for annulment of the State Aid Decision before the General Court of the European Union. In its judgment dated 18 June 2019, the General Court annulled the State Aid Decision.[38] The European Commission filed an appeal against the judgment of the General Court, which is still pending before the Court of Justice.[39]

16.45 In the meantime, the Micula claimants lodged proceedings to enforce the Award in various jurisdictions, including within the EU, namely in Belgium, the UK, Romania, France, Luxembourg and Sweden. They also pursued enforcement in the US. Most national courts (with the notable exception of the Brussels enforcement court in first instance and the UK Supreme Court, albeit for totally different reasons) decided to stay enforcement proceedings pending the decision of the European courts. The *Micula* case illustrates that, although Article 54 of the ICSID Convention requires a contracting State to the Convention to enforce an ICSID award as if it were a final judgment of a court in that State, EU Member State courts generally do not interpret this provision as allowing enforcement of an ICSID award whose validity under EU law is put into question.

b. National enforcement decisions

i. Belgium

16.46 In a decision dated 25 January 2016, the Brussels enforcement court (*juge des saisies/beslagrechter*) had to rule on the question whether the Award – which had been recognized in Belgium following an ex-parte request under the ICSID Convention – could be enforced on assets of the Romanian State in Belgium despite the State Aid Decision.[40] Importantly, the Brussels court issued its decision before the General Court ruled on the request for annulment of the State Aid Decision.

16.47 The Brussels court ordered a garnishment to be lifted because it considered that it had been levied based on an award that was no longer enforceable following the State Aid Decision. In

---

36 *Micula v Romania* (Case State aid SA.38517) Commission Decision of 1 October 2014 to initiate the formal investigation procedure; Commission (Letter to Romania) C(2014) 6848 final <https://ec.europa.eu/competition/state_aid/cases/254586/254586_1595781_31_11.pdf> accessed 21 April 2020.

37 *Micula v Romania* (Case State aid SA.38517) Commission Decision 2015/1470 [2015] OJ L232/43.

38 Joined Cases (T-624/15, T-694/15 and T-704/15) ECLI:EU:T:2019:423 *European Food SA and Others v European Commission* [2019] OJ C295/19.

39 Case C-638/19 P *Commission v European Food and Others* [2019] OJ C348/14.

40 Belgium, Brussels enforcement court (*juge des saisies/beslagrechter*), 25 January 2016, cases 15/7241/A and 15/7242/A; Michael De Boeck, 'Brussels Court of First Instance Acknowledges EU Law over ICSID: Intra-EU BIT ICSID awards not so "Benvenuti" in Belgium' (2016) vol 1 *b-Arbitra* 35. The authors disclose that their firm represented M. Viorel Micula before the Belgian courts.

the opinion of the Belgian court, the State Aid Decision – which decided that payment by Romania of the Award would amount to illegal State aid – had affected the enforceable nature of the 'title' (the Award) which was at the basis of the garnishment. More specifically, the court held that 'the [State Aid] decision of the European Commission – as long as it continues to exist – justifies *the failure to comply with this arbitral award, thus depriving it of its topicality and, consequently, of its enforceability. It therefore renders its enforcement unlawful'.*[41] The court held that this conclusion applied irrespective of the correctness of the State Aid Decision (subject to annulment proceedings before the General Court).

The subsidiary request of the Micula claimants for suspension of the proceedings pending the outcome of the proceedings before the General Court was rejected on the ground that there was no risk of contradiction between the decision of the Belgian court (which concerned the validity and 'topicality' of the enforcement in Belgium at the time the court issued its judgment) and the future decision of the General Court.   **16.48**

The Brussels enforcement court issued a decision comparable to the one issued in the *Yukos* enforcement case referred to above, namely that enforcement measures had to be lifted because the awards lost their enforceable nature. Interestingly, in both cases, this was grounded on decisions which were not final, namely the set aside judgment of the first instance court in The Hague (under appeal before The Hague Court of Appeal) and the State Aid Decision from the European Commission (subject to annulment proceedings before the General Court). In both cases, those decisions were eventually reversed: the *Yukos* first instance judgment was over-turned by The Hague Court of Appeal[42] and the State Aid Decision was annulled by the General Court. In both cases, the judgment of the Brussels enforcement court had important adverse consequences for the investors who lost the benefit of attachments and garnishments carried out on the Belgian territory, allowing the relevant sovereign debtors to remove assets out of Belgium.   **16.49**

The Micula claimants appealed the Brussels enforcement court's decision before the Brussels Court of Appeal. During the Brussels appeal proceedings, the proceedings before the General Court were still pending.   **16.50**

In a decision dated 12 March 2019, the Brussels Court of Appeal referred three questions to the Court of Justice for a preliminary ruling regarding the interplay between the Member States' obligations under EU State Aid Rules and the ICSID Convention, and more specifically regarding the impact of the State Aid Decision on the enforceability of the Award.[43] The Court of Appeal decided to suspend the proceedings until (1) a final decision of the European courts on the validity of the State Aid Decision and (2) the preliminary ruling of the Court of Justice on the referred questions.[44]   **16.51**

---

41 Free English translation of the French original text.
42 Netherlands, The Hague Court of Appeal, 18 February 2010, case number 200.197.079/01.
43 Case C-333/19 *DV v Romatsa* [2019] OJ C 220/24.
44 Belgium, Brussels Court of Appeal, decision of 12 March 2019 in cases 2016/AR/393 and 2016/AR/394.

16.52 On 5 September 2019, the Court of Justice suspended the preliminary ruling procedure on the questions referred to it by the Brussels Court of Appeal until it has ruled on the European Commission's appeal against the judgment of the General Court rendered in the meantime.

ii. United Kingdom

16.53 In 2014, the claimants sought the registration of the Award in England and Wales, which was confirmed by a Court Order dated 17 October 2014. Romania subsequently applied to the High Court in London to have that registration set aside inter alia because the State Aid Decision required the High Court to refuse registration of the Award. Alternatively, the High Court was asked to stay the proceedings pending the proceedings before the General Court on the State Aid Decision or, in the further alternative, pending a reference by the High Court to the Court of Justice for a preliminary ruling on the enforceability of the Award.

16.54 The High Court ruled on these requests in a judgment dated 20 January 2017.[45] Like the Brussels Court of Appeal, the High Court considered that it could not rule on a number of issues without creating a possible conflict with questions currently pending before the General Court.

16.55 The first issue submitted by the parties was the question whether the Award has the status of *res judicata*, and if so, whether the Injunction Decision and the State Aid Decision (which postdate the Award) could prevent enforcement thereof.[46]

16.56 The High Court agreed with the Micula claimants that, as a matter of English law, the Award became *res judicata* in the sense of acquiring finality from the time it was rendered on 11 December 2013 (and not only after the *ad hoc* Committee had rejected the request for annulment on 26 February 2016, as submitted by Romania).[47] The High Court however accepted Romania's submission that it could not determine the consequences of this for the enforcement of the Award in the UK without risking a conflict on the interpretation of certain principles of EU law raised before the General Court.[48] The High Court therefore stayed the final determination of this issue pending the decision of the General Court.[49]

16.57 The second issue for the High Court to consider was whether that Court had a duty to register/enforce the Award under the English Arbitration Act 1996. The High Court ruled on two distinct issues in this regard.

16.58 First, on the registration of the Award, the High Court decided that there was no reason to set aside the Order registering the Award, as was requested by Romania and by the Commission. The Court noted that the Injunction Decision was addressed to Romania only and required it to 'immediately suspend any action which may lead to the execution or implementation or execution of the Award', while the registration of the Award was upon request of the Micula

---

45 *Micula v Romania* [2017] EWHC 31 (Comm), [2017] Bus LR 1147, [2017] WLR (D) 35.
46 Ibid., [90ff].
47 Ibid., [108].
48 Kai Struckmann, Genevra Forwood, Aqeel Kadri and Adam Wallin 'Enforcement of Investor-State Arbitral Awards: More Questions than Answers' (2017) 16(2) *European State Aid Law Quarterly* 318.
49 *Micula* (n 45) [112].

claimants as holders of the Award and Romania played no part in that process.[50] The Court therefore decided that 'the registration of the Award did not place Romania in breach of the Injunction Decision, and the claimants were not in breach by registering the Award'.[51] Furthermore, the State Aid Decision prohibited payment of the Award, whether by implementation or execution, and registration of the Award does not constitute such 'payment' (although it was a necessary step towards enforcement).[52] In the view of the Court, '[r]egistration in itself does not create a risk of conflict between decisions of domestic and EU institutions in the sense established in the case law'.[53]

Second, as to the enforcement of the Award, the High Court noted that ICSID awards are **16.59** only required to be treated in the same way as final judgments of the English courts, which themselves are subject to EU State aid rules.[54] The High Court further noted that, pursuant to the principle of legal certainty, which underpins the duty of sincere cooperation, Member States must refrain from taking a decision which conflicts with a decision of the Commission, and that this applies to the High Court itself, as was confirmed in *Deutsche Lufthansa* by the CJEU.[55] The High Court therefore held that it was appropriate to stay the proceedings pending the outcome of the appeal for annulment of the State Aid Decision.[56] The High Court thereby accepted Romania's position that the State Aid Decision prohibited Romania from making any payment under the Award.[57]

The third issue submitted for consideration was whether the UK and the High Court were **16.60** obliged to enforce the Award under the ICSID Convention, and if so, if that obligation was affected by EU law, by reason of Article 351 TFEU, which provides that:

> the rights and obligations arising from agreements concluded (…), for acceding States, before the date of their accession, between one or more Member States on the one hand, and one or more third countries on the other, shall not be affected by the provisions of the Treaties.[58]

The High Court again found that, since the General Court would be considering the same cases and the same principles decided under Article 351 TFEU as the High Court was asked to consider, there was sufficient risk of conflict with a later judgment of the General Court. The High Court therefore decided to stay the determination of this issue pending the outcome of the annulment proceedings.[59]

The final EU law issue for the High Court to consider was whether EU law imposed duties **16.61** precluding the registration and enforcement of the Award. More specifically, the High Court was asked whether Article 4(3) TEU (the principle of sincere cooperation), Article 19 TEU

---

50 Ibid., [121–122].
51 Ibid., [123].
52 Ibid., [124–126].
53 Ibid., [126].
54 Ibid., [128–131].
55 Ibid., [131] referring to (C-284/12) ECLI:EU:C:2013:755 *Deutsche Lufthansa AG v Flughafen Frankfurt-Hahn GmbH* [2014] OJ C39/5, para 41.
56 Ibid., [127–135].
57 Struckmann, Forwood, Kadri and Wallin (n 48) 319 referring to *Micula* [131–132].
58 *Micula* (n 45) [136–152].
59 Ibid., [152].

(the obligation to ensure effective judicial protection) and/or the EU law principle of effectiveness require the Court not to recognize/enforce the Award.[60] The High Court held that there was no need to deal separately with Article 19 TEU, *'which does not add to Article 4(3) in this context'* and only dealt with the parties' arguments on the issue whether payment by Romania following forced execution of the Award in the UK would be imputable to Romania.[61]

16.62   On imputability, the Micula claimants argued that payment of the Award as a consequence of forced execution would not amount to an act imputable to Romania because it would be involuntary, and not pursuant to an autonomous decision by Romania.[62] Romania and the Commission argued that there was no need to show that payment pursuant to an order of a UK court would be 'imputable' to Romania because cooperation and effectiveness are standalone principles of EU law that can be breached independently by a UK court, and that any 'imputability' requirement is in any event satisfied by Romania entering into the BIT and creating the conditions for payment of compensation.[63] They contended that the latter issue, which relates to the meaning and scope of the State Aid Decision, was pending before the General Court.

16.63   The High Court agreed that the issue of imputability was under consideration by the General Court so that it could not render a decision on this issue without a risk of conflict with the General Court's decision; accordingly it also stayed the determination of this issue. The High Court added that allowing the enforcement of the Award would in any event conflict with the State Aid Decision, on the basis that it prohibited any kind of payment of the Award by Romania.[64]

16.64   As a result, the High Court dismissed the set aside application of Romania but granted a stay of enforcement pending the outcome of the annulment proceedings before the General Court.[65] The Micula claimants' cross-application for security was dismissed in a later judgment dated 15 June 2017.[66]

16.65   The High Court's judgment of 20 January 2017 accepts the position of Romania and the Commission that essentially any substantive finding of EU law would give rise to a significant risk of conflict with the upcoming decision of the General Court.[67] As a result, the High Court reached few firm conclusions in its judgment. The judgment illustrates the tension between international obligations under the ICSID Convention (including the finality of ICSID awards) and EU law, and the issues resulting from those tensions in enforcement proceedings brought before Member State courts.

---

60   Ibid., [161–172].
61   Ibid., [166–172].
62   Ibid., [162–163], [168].
63   Ibid., [164].
64   Ibid., [172].
65   Ibid., [203].
66   *Micula v Romania* [2017] EWHC 1430 (Comm).
67   Struckmann, Forwood, Kadri and Wallin (n 48) 320.

The Micula claimants appealed both the grant of the stay and the dismissal of their application **16.66** for security. On 27 July 2018, the UK Court of Appeal dismissed the Micula claimants' appeal against the stay, but granted the requested security and ordered Romania to provide GBP 150 million as a condition of the stay.[68]

The three Court of Appeal justices had different views on the interplay of the enforcement **16.67** regime under the ICSID Convention, the UK's obligations under EU law and the UK courts' powers under the 1966 Arbitration Act. However, the majority held that there was a potential conflict between the international obligations of the UK under the ICSID Convention and the English courts' EU law duties, the resolution of which would involve issues as to whether enforcement of the Convention is a pre-accession treaty obligation of the UK which is not displaced by entering into the EU treaties, requiring consideration in particular on Article 351 TFEU.[69]

The Court of Appeal did not decide that issue, but held that, even if obligations under the **16.68** ICSID Convention prevailed, it was within the powers of the English courts to temporarily stay the execution of the Award pending the proceedings before the General Court, not least in view of the risk of conflicting decisions if the court was to proceed to decide on the issue, and that such stay is consistent with the ICSID Convention's object and purpose.[70]

The Court of Appeal indicated that, if the General Court did decide to annul the State Aid **16.69** Decision and if that decision would be appealed before the CJEU, there would need to be a further application to the High Court for a further stay.[71] As to the legal framework for granting such further stay, the Court of Appeal noted that such stay 'could only be for a temporary purpose if the Award is enforceable under the ICSID Convention'.[72]

Since the General Court's decision annulling the State Aid Decision was indeed appealed **16.70** before the CJEU, Romania applied for a further stay of enforcement with the High Court. The Micula claimants again cross-applied for security. The High Court issued a further order extending the stay pending the appeal proceedings before the CJEU on the basis that:

> as held by the Court of Appeal, there is power to grant such a temporary stay, whether the governing obligation is that recognised by the 1966 [Arbitration] Act or that imposed by the duty of sincere co-operation under the court's EU Treaty obligations, and that such power should be exercised given the risk of conflicting decisions, given the recognition that there is a real prospect that the CJEU will reverse the decision of the GCEU and uphold the validity of the Decision, and that at some stage the European Courts will determine the conflict issue, including the effect of Article 351 of the TFEU.[73]

The High Court further ordered Romania to provide GBP 150 million security by 17 October 2019.[74]

---

68   *Micula v Romania* [2018] EWCA Civ 1801, [2019] Bus LR 1394; [2018] WLR (D) 496, [249–52].

69   *Micula* (n 68) [103–203], summarized in *Micula v Romania* [2019] EWHC 2401 (Comm) [6].

70   *Micula* (n 68) [103–203], summarized in *Micula v Romania* [2019] EWHC 2401 (Comm) [7].

71   *Micula* (n 68) [250].

72   Ibid., [251].

73   *Micula v Romania* [2019] EWHC 2401 (Comm) [14].

74   Ibid., [15–16].

16.71 Romania appealed the order for security before the UK Supreme Court, following which the Micula claimants cross-appealed the grant of a stay.[75] In its decision of 19 February 2020, the Supreme Court first considered whether the High Court has the power to stay the enforcement of an ICSID award, and decided to lift the stay.[76] Although the Supreme Court agreed with the majority in the Court of Appeal that UK courts indeed have the power to stay enforcement of an ICSID award in limited circumstances, it held that staying enforcement until a final decision of the CJEU exceeds the proper limits of that power and is not consistent with the ICSID Convention because 'the Court of Appeal made use of powers to stay execution granted by domestic law in order to thwart enforcement of an award which had become enforceable under the ICSID Convention'.[77]

16.72 The Supreme Court held that this conclusion was not affected by the EU duty of sincere cooperation enshrined in Article 4(3) TEU, as it was inapplicable by virtue of Article 351 TFEU.[78] The latter provision is an express provision of EU law regulating priority where there are potentially conflicting obligations, 'which is intended to establish (…) that the application of the EU Treaties does not affect the duty of a member state to respect the rights of non-member states under a prior agreement and to perform its obligations thereunder'.[79] In the opinion of the Court, the specific duties in Articles 54 and 69 of the ICSID Convention are owed to all other Contracting States, including non-Member States.[80] Since the UK joined and implemented the ICSID Convention before its accession to the EU, the duty of sincere cooperation could not affect the UK's obligation to enforce the award under Article 54 of the ICSID Convention.[81]

iii. US

16.73 In April 2014, Viorel Micula filed a petition before the District Court of Columbia for confirmation of the Award through ex parte and summary proceedings. After the court refused to confirm the Award ex-parte, the Micula claimants filed another ex-parte petition for confirmation in the Southern District of New York. They initially found success,[82] but the judgment was eventually vacated inter alia because it was considered that it should not have been granted on an ex-parte basis and because the District of Columbia was the only proper venue.[83]

---

75 The claimants appealed the stay on five grounds, *Micula v Romania* [2020] UKSC 5, [2020] WLR(D) 115 [38–39].

76 *Micula v Romania* [2020] UKSC 5, [2020] WLR(D) 115.

77 Ibid., [84].

78 See Guillaume Croisant, 'Micula Case: The UK Supreme Court Rules That The EU Duty Of Sincere Co-operation Does Not Affect The UK's International Obligations Under The ICSID Convention' (*Kluwer Arbitration Blog*, 20 February 2020) <http://arbitrationblog.kluwerarbitration.com/2020/02/20/micula-case-the-uk-supreme-court-rules-that-the-eu-duty-of-sincere-co-operation-does-not-affect-the-uks-international-obligations-under-the-icsid-convention/> accessed 27 April 2020.

79 *Micula* (n 75) [97].

80 Ibid., [107–108].

81 Ibid., [101–118].

82 *Micula v Romania*, No 15 Misc 107 (Part I), 2015 WL 4643180 (SDNY 5 August 2015) (allowing proceeding to move forward ex-parte); *Micula v Romania*, No 15 Misc 107 (LGS), 2015 WL 5257013 (SDNY 3 September 2015) (rejecting the second motion for reconsideration by Romania).

83 *Micula v Romania*, 714 Fed App'x 18, 21–22 (2d Cir 2017).

On 6 November 2017, the Micula claimants filed another petition for confirmation of the **16.74** Award and for entering judgment before the District Court of Columbia. On 6 November 2018, Romania filed a lengthy memorandum of law in 'opposition' to the petition and moved to stay the proceedings inter alia because of the pending request for annulment of the State Aid Decision before the General Court. Again, the European Commission intervened in the proceedings as amicus curiae to support Romania's position.

As a result of the General Court's decision of 18 June 2019, the District Court considered as **16.75** moot Romania's request for a stay and ordered additional briefing on the impact of the General Court's annulment of the State Aid Decision and the Commission's subsequent appeal before the CJEU.

On 11 September 2019, the District Court granted enforcement of the Award and ordered **16.76** judgment against Romania in the amount of USD 331,557,687.[84] The District Court rejected all four challenges raised by Romania against the enforcement of the Award, three of which related to EU law and will be discussed hereafter.[85]

The first argument related to the arbitration exception to sovereign immunity under the **16.77** Foreign Sovereign Immunities Act (FSIA), regarding which US courts have consistently held that it confers subject matter jurisdiction over petitions to enforce ICSID awards. Romania argued that the arbitration exception did not apply because the arbitration clause in the Sweden-Romania BIT had been rendered invalid by the *Achmea* decision (as to which see below).[86]

The District Court found it had jurisdiction under the FSIA's arbitration exception.[87] The **16.78** District Court held that Romania failed to carry its burden to show that 'the concern that animated Achmea – the un-reviewability of an arbitral tribunal's determination of EU law by an EU court – is present in this case'.[88] The District Court based its decision on the following three reasons. First, where in *Achmea* all material facts occurred *after* the Slovak Republic entered the EU and EU law was clearly applicable, all key events of the *Micula* case occurred *before* Romania acceded to the EU.[89] Second, since all key events took place *before* Romania became an EU Member State, the District Court held that 'EU law was not directly applicable to Romania' and the tribunal did not interpret or apply EU law 'in a way that implicates the core rationale of *Achmea*'.[90] Third, the District Court found support in the General Court's decision, which itself explicitly distinguished the present case from *Achmea* in para 87 of the decision of 18 June 2019: '[I]t must be pointed out that, in the present case, the arbitral

---

84 *Micula v Romania*, No 17-cv-02332 (APM), at 31. In a later decision dated 20 September 2019, the Court entered judgment against Romania in the amount of USD 356,439,727.

85 Romania raised four challenges to enforcement of the Award, '(1) the court lacks subject matter jurisdiction under the [Foreign Sovereign Immunities Act ('FSIA')], (2) it has fully satisfied the Award, (3) the act of State doctrine prohibits the Award's enforcement, and (4) so, too, does the foreign sovereign compulsion doctrine'. The Commission joined these arguments, except Romania's contention that it had satisfied the Award. See *Micula v Romania*, No 17-cv-02332 (APM), at 14.

86 Ibid., at 16–17.

87 Ibid., at 22.

88 Ibid., at 19.

89 Ibid., at 19–20.

90 Ibid., at 20–21.

tribunal was not bound to apply EU law to events occurring prior to the accession before it, unlike the situation in the case which gave rise to the [*Achmea* judgment].'[91]

16.79   Under the second and third challenges, Romania argued that the act of State and foreign sovereign compulsion doctrines prohibit enforcement of the Award.[92]

16.80   The District Court held that the 'original rationale for invoking [the act of state and foreign sovereign compulsion] doctrines has been overtaken by events' – namely the General Court's decision.[93] The District Court found that, pursuant to EU law, after the General Court's decision, the Commission could no longer 'take any steps that would be incompatible with the Court's findings'.[94]

16.81   Importantly, the District Court noted that while the Commission had appealed the General Court's decision before the CJEU, it did not seek to suspend the decision pending appeal, and the court was not willing to further delay the enforcement proceedings 'based on the mere possibility that the CJEU (…) might reverse the General Court's decision'.[95]

16.82   On 9 October 2019, Romania filed a notice of appeal against the District Court's 11 September 2019 decision granting enforcement of the Award. The appeal is pending before the US Court of Appeals for the District of Columbia Circuit.

iv.   Sweden

16.83   While the Brussels Court of Appeal and the High Court in London decided to stay the enforcement pending the annulment proceedings before the General Court, the Swedish Nacka District Court ruled in its decision dated 23 January 2019 that pursuant to the EU law principle of sincere cooperation it was compelled to implement the State Aid Decision, under which the European Commission considered that enforcement of the Award would constitute illegal State aid.[96]

16.84   Interestingly, although the Swedish court recognized that under the ICSID Convention it is required to enforce ICSID awards in the same way as a legally enforceable Swedish judgment, it observed that such a judgment would not be executed either since its enforcement would also be considered contrary to EU law.[97]

---

91   Ibid., at 21–2.
92   Ibid., at 22–6.
93   Ibid., at 22.
94   Ibid., at 23–6.
95   Ibid., at 26.
96   Decision of the Nacka District Court dated 23 January 2019 in case 2550-17, discussed in Tom Jones, 'Miculas suffer setback in Sweden' (*Global Arbitration Review*, 4 February 2019) <https://globalarbitrationreview.com/article/1179932/miculas-suffer-setback-in-sweden> accessed 28 April 2020.
97   Ibid. Following the State Aid Decision, Romania initiated its own enforcement proceedings against the Micula claimants in Sweden, alleging that as a result of the State Aid Decision they had an obligation to repay amounts Romania claimed to have paid under the Award. However, in 2016, the Swedish Enforcement Authority decided to discontinue all enforcement measures against the Micula claimants until similar proceedings that had been initiated in Romania had been settled.

v. Luxembourg

In May 2015, the Micula claimants obtained ex parte an order permitting enforcement of the Award from the Luxembourg District Court. The issuance of the order enabled the service on 28 and 29 July 2015 of garnishment orders on 61 banks based in Luxembourg, which required them to freeze (in the full amount of the award) any Romanian State account they held. **16.85**

Romania's subsequent request to order the lifting of the garnishments was dismissed by the Luxembourg District Court in a decision dated 10 May 2017.[98] The Luxembourg Court held that Romania did not demonstrate that: **16.86**

> by initiating a purely conservatory measure on the basis of the valid and final act which is the Arbitral Award (…), despite the existence of the [State Aid Decision], which generates a conflict between [European] Community law and a final decision on the enforceable nature of the Arbitral Award (…), took a manifestly illicit action (…).[99]

This judgment was however overruled on appeal by the Luxembourg Supreme Court of Justice, which decided to lift the attachment in a decision of 21 March 2018.[100] Like the Belgian enforcement court (in first instance), the Supreme Court held that the act (the 'title') underlying the attachments (i.e. the Award) had lost its effectiveness and therefore its enforceable nature (its 'topicality') as a result of the State Aid Decision.[101] **16.87**

The Luxembourg Court held that, even if Article 5 of the State Aid Decision provides that '[t]his decision is addressed to Romania' and Article 288 TFEU provides that '[a] decision which specifies those to whom it is addressed shall be binding only on them', the State Aid Decision has to be complied with in all Member States where the claimants initiate enforcement proceedings, even pending the appeal before the General Court (which had no suspensive effect).[102] In the Luxembourg Court's view, the State Aid Decision prohibited it from validating the garnishments since '(i) the law on State aid, which is part of public policy, must prevail over national law and (ii) the Arbitral Award is contrary to European public policy and therefore Luxembourg public policy'.[103] **16.88**

---

98 Grand Duchy of Luxembourg, Luxembourg District Court, Decision No 272/2017 of 10 May 2017, docket number 179517.

99 Ibid., at 32 free translation of:

[Q]u'en initiant une mesure purement conservatoire sur base du titre valable et définitif que constitue la Sentence Arbitrale du 1, nonobstant l'existence de la Décision (UE) 2015/1470, génératrice d'un conflit entre une norme communautaire et une décision définitive au niveau du caractère purement exécutoire de la Sentence Arbitrale, X.1.) a commis un acte manifestement illicite susceptible d'être constitutif d'une voie de fait.

100 Grand Duchy of Luxembourg, Supreme Court of Justice, Decision No 71/18 – VII – REF of 21 March 2018, docket number 45337.

101 Ibid., at 12.

102 Ibid., at 10–11.

103 Ibid., at 11–12 free translation of, '(i) le droit des aides d'Etat, qui fait partie de l'ordre public, doit prévaloir sur le droit national et (ii) la Sentence arbitrale est contraire à l'ordre public communautaire et donc luxembourgeois' and referring to Case (C-119/05) ECLI:EU:C:2007:434 *Ministero dell'Industria, del Commercio e dell'Artigianato v Lucchini SpA* [2007] OJ C 211/3; Case (C-505/14) ECLI:EU:C:2015:742 *Klausner Holz Niedersachsen GmbH v Land Nordrhein-Westfalen* [2016] OJ C 016/14 and C-40/08 *Asturcom Telecomunicaciones SL v Rodríguez Nogueira* [2009] OJ C 282/12. Referring to Case (C-284/12) ECLI:EU:C:2013:755 *Deutsche Lufthansa AG v Flughafen Frankfurt-Hahn GmbH* [2014] OJ C 39/08, the Luxembourg Court also noted that the primacy of EU law requires national courts to refrain from

vi. Conclusion

16.89 The Luxembourg decision is expressly based on a review of the Award based on EU and Luxembourg (international) public policy, i.e. a ground which exists under the New York Convention or the Model Law but was, according to the preparatory works of the ICSID Convention, not supposed to apply in the self-contained ICSID regime. As mentioned above, the ICSID Convention did not succeed in avoiding that challenges be brought before national courts. This is because – as was made clear in the Swedish judgment – imposing upon contracting States to enforce ICSID awards as if they were final judgments from their countries (art 54(1) of the ICSID Convention) is not the same as prohibiting any form of review of the ICSID awards by national courts. The *Micula* case shows that this review by national courts is applied without a coherent applicable legal regime across jurisdictions. Moreover, as is also illustrated in the *Micula* case, by providing under Article 54(3) that 'execution of the [ICSID] awards shall be governed by the laws concerning the execution of judgments in force in the States in whose territories such execution is sought' (see para 16.17 above), the ICSID Convention in fact shifts the control over the award later in time, when enforcement measures have taken place or are under way, rather than before they are carried out.

2. The *Achmea* case and its consequences in setting aside and enforcement proceedings before EU Member States courts

16.90 Achmea B.V. ('Achmea'), a Dutch insurance company which set up a subsidiary in Slovakia, challenged legislative measures taken in 2006 and 2007 by the Slovak Republic to reverse the liberalization of the private health insurance market and prevent the distribution of profits to foreign shareholders. For this reason, Achmea brought investment-treaty arbitration proceedings against the Slovak Republic in October 2018 under the Netherlands-Slovakia BIT, claiming EUR 65 million in damages. The seat of the arbitration was in Germany and the arbitration was held in accordance with the UNCITRAL Rules.[104] During the arbitration proceedings, the Slovak Republic raised an objection of lack of jurisdiction, on the basis that the arbitration clause in Article 8(2) of the BIT was incompatible with EU law. The arbitral tribunal rejected the objection and ordered the Slovak Republic to pay Achmea EUR 22,1 million in damages.

16.91 Consequently, the Slovak Republic filed setting aside proceedings before the German courts. After considering that the BIT constitutes an agreement between EU Member States, over which EU law takes precedence, the German Federal Court of Justice referred a series of questions to the CJEU for a preliminary ruling, including whether Article 344 TFEU[105] (or art

---

applying any provision that may call into question the exclusive competence of the Commission to rule on the compatibility of State aid with the common market.

104 For commentaries on the *Achmea* judgment, see the other relevant chapters of this book; Jacob Grierson, 'The Court of Justice of the European Union and International Arbitration' (2018) vol 2 *b-Arbitra* 309-30; Nicolas de Sadeleer, 'Le contentieux du droit des investissements dans tous ses états – De la disparition des tribunaux d'investissement intra-UE à l'avènement d'une Cour multilatérale d'investissement' (2019) vol 6 *Revue de droit commercial belge* 742–69.

105 Article 344 of the Consolidated version of the Treaty on the Functioning of the European Union (TFEU) [2016] OJ C 202/1 provides, 'Member States undertake not to submit a dispute concerning the interpretation or application of the Treaties to any method of settlement other than those provided for therein.'

267 TFEU[106] or art 18 TFEU)[107] preclude the application of a provision in a bilateral investment protection agreement between Member States of the EU, under which an investor of a contracting State, in the event of a dispute concerning investments in the other contracting State, may bring proceedings against the latter State before an arbitration tribunal, in a case where the investment protection agreement was concluded before one of the contracting States acceded to the European Union but the arbitration proceedings are brought after that date.

In its judgment dated 6 March 2018, the CJEU ruled – opposite to the, in the authors' view, well-articulated and thought-through opinion of AG Wathelet[108] – that the arbitration clause included in the BIT was indeed incompatible with EU law because it establishes a mechanism that prevents disputes over the application or interpretation of EU law from being decided by Member State courts. The CJEU found that: **16.92**

> Articles 267 and 344 TFEU must be interpreted as precluding a provision in an international agreement concluded between Member States, such as Article 8 of the BIT, under which an investor from one of those Member States may, in the event of a dispute concerning investments in the other Member State, bring proceedings against the latter Member State before an arbitral tribunal whose jurisdiction that Member State has undertaken to accept.[109]

On 31 October 2018, the German *Bundesgerichtshof* followed that CJEU's reasoning and set aside the award in favour of the Dutch insurer in light of the CJEU's ruling that the arbitration provisions of such treaties are incompatible with EU law.[110] **16.93**

The *Achmea* judgment – decided several months before the General Court ruled on the State Aid Decision in *Micula* – was the first opportunity for the CJEU to rule on the issue of the **16.94**

---

106   Article 267 TFEU provides:

> The Court of Justice of the European Union shall have jurisdiction to give preliminary rulings concerning:
>
> (a) the interpretation of the Treaties;
> (b) the validity and interpretation of acts of the institutions, bodies, offices or agencies of the Union;
>
> Where such a question is raised before any court or tribunal of a Member State, that court or tribunal may, if it considers that a decision on the question is necessary to enable it to give judgment, request the Court to give a ruling thereon.
>
> Where any such question is raised in a case pending before a court or tribunal of a Member State against whose decisions there is no judicial remedy under national law, that court or tribunal shall bring the matter before the Court.
>
> If such a question is raised in a case pending before a court or tribunal of a Member State with regard to a person in custody, the Court of Justice of the European Union shall act with the minimum of delay.

107   Article 18 TFEU provides:

> Within the scope of application of the Treaties, and without prejudice to any special provisions contained therein, any discrimination on grounds of nationality shall be prohibited.
>
> The European Parliament and the Council, acting in accordance with the ordinary legislative procedure, may adopt rules designed to prohibit such discrimination.

108   Case (C-284/16) ECLI:EU:C:2017:699 *Slowakische Republik v Achmea BV*, Opinion of AG Wathelet, para 126ff.
109   Case (C-284/16) ECLI:EU:C:2018:158, *Slowakische Republik v Achmea BV* [2018] OJ C 161/7, para 60.
110   Germany, Federal Court of Justice, decision of 31 October 2018, I ZB 2/15, OLG Frankfurt am Main <https://www.italaw.com/sites/default/files/case-documents/italaw10114.pdf> accessed 29 April 2020.

compatibility of this type of ISDS provision with EU law.[111] Since similar arbitration clauses are included in most of the intra-EU BITs, the *Achmea* decision causes great concern for the future of investment arbitration in the EU.[112]

16.95 So far, however, arbitral tribunals have generally refused to give effect to the *Achmea* decision in ongoing investment-treaty arbitration proceedings.[113]

16.96 For example, in a decision dated 13 June 2018, the Svea Court of Appeal in Sweden has granted Poland a stay of enforcement of an SCC award rendered in favour of the Luxembourgish subsidiary PL Holdings pending set-aside proceedings (also brought before the Swedish courts), after Poland argued that the award should be set aside on the basis of the *Achmea* ruling of the CJEU.[114]

16.97 Subsequently, in a decision dated 22 February 2019, the Svea Court of Appeal partly upheld the SCC awards rendered in favour of PL Holdings against Poland, ruling that the State had left it too late to raise objections based on the incompatibility of intra-EU BITs with EU law.[115] The Court held that under the applicable SCC Rules as well as under the Swedish Arbitration Act, Poland had raised the jurisdictional objection based on EU law too late and was therefore precluded from raising the objection at the post-award stage.[116]

16.98 Despite that conclusion, the Svea Court also addressed the merits of the objection, ruling that 'neither general EU law nor the *Achmea* judgment, in principle, means that arbitration between EU states and investors of EU nationality is prohibited as such'.[117] It concluded that the underlying dispute was arbitrable and that the CJEU ruling in *Achmea* did not render the award clearly incompatible with Swedish public policy. The Svea Court further found that the *Achmea* ruling did not prevent Poland and PL Holdings from entering into an implicit or express arbitration agreement regarding the specific dispute.[118]

---

111   Grierson (n 104) 309, 323.

112   Ibid.

113   See e.g., *Masdar Solar v Kingdom of Spain* ICSID Case No ARB/14/1 Award 16 May 2018; *Infrastructure Services Luxembourg SARL v Kingdom of Spain*, ICSID Case No ARB/13/31 Award 15 June 2018; *A11Y Ltd v Czech Republic*, ICSID Case No UNCT/15/1 Award 29 June 2018; *Vattenfall AB v Federal Republic of Germany II*, ICSID Case No ARB/12/12 Decision on the Achmea Issue, 31 August 2018; *Eskosol SpA v Italian Republic*, ICSID Case No ARB/15/50 Decision on Respondent Request for Immediate Termination and Respondent Jurisdictional Objection based on Inapplicability of the Energy Charter Treaty to Intra-EU Disputes, 7 May 2019; Grierson (n 104) 309, 325, n 55.

114   See 'Enforcement against Poland stayed in light of Achmea' (*Global Arbitration Review*, 15 June 2018) <https://globalarbitrationreview.com/article/1170617/enforcement-against-poland-stayed-in-light-of-achmea> accessed 29 April 2020. Two weeks earlier, in an ex-parte ruling on an application filed by Spain to set aside an ECT award against Spain rendered in favour of the Luxembourg investment fund Novenergia, the same Swedish Court had already stayed enforcement of the award on the same basis. See Sweden, Svea Court of Appeal, 16 May 2018, No T 4658-18 <https://www.italaw.com/sites/default/files/case-documents/italaw9746.pdf> accessed 29 April 2020.

115   Sweden, Svea Court of Appeal, 22 February 2019, Nos T 8538-17 and T 12033-17, English translation available at <https://www.italaw.com/sites/default/files/case-documents/italaw10447.pdf> accessed 29 April 2020.

116   Ibid., para 56. See also Joel Dahlquist Cullborg, 'The role of the Swedish Supreme Court in International Arbitration' (2019) vol 2 *b-Arbitra* 469, 479.

117   Dahlquist Cullborg, ibid.

118   Ibid.

The Svea Court partially set aside the award on another ground, finding that the arbitral **16.99** tribunal had amended its decision on post-award interests after exceeding the deadline for making such a decision.[119]

The Svea Court of Appeal allowed for its judgment to be appealed to the Swedish Supreme **16.100** Court, which, according to some authors, 'indicate[s] that the Court of Appeal potentially saw some precedential value in the jurisdictional objections, should the Supreme Court find them to be admissible'.[120] In a decision of 12 December 2019, the Supreme Court referred the following question to the CJEU for a preliminary ruling:

> Do Articles 267 and 344 TFEU, as interpreted in Achmea, mean that an arbitration agreement is invalid if it has been concluded between a Member State and an investor – where an investment agreement contains an arbitration clause that is invalid because the agreement was concluded between two Member States – the Member State, since the investor called for arbitration, as a result of the state's free will through passivity refrain from making any objections to the jurisdiction?[121]

Although the tribunals ruling on the basis of intra-EU BIT or multilateral treaties may have **16.101** valid reasons not to abide by the *Achmea* ruling of the CJEU, their awards will inevitably lead to recurring difficulties if and when setting aside and recognition and enforcement proceedings will be brought before EU Member State courts.

D. STATE IMMUNITY

1. Introduction and sources

An important hurdle in the enforcement of investment-treaty awards is State immunity. **16.102** Fortunately for investors prevailing in investment-treaty arbitrations, over the past decades States have become increasingly active beyond their traditional prerogatives *de iure imperii*, which resulted in an important trend towards a more restrictive approach to State immunity (immunity which does not extend to States' activities *de jure gestionis*).[122] This general trend towards more restrictive immunity is not unanimous and, as will be explained below, some national laws, including within the EU, have recently enacted new procedural rules making enforcement of awards against States or sovereign entities' assets more difficult.

The rules on State immunity can be found in the classic sources of international public law, i.e., **16.103** international conventions, customary international law (State practice and *opinio juris* in judicial, executive and legislative actions), general principles of law and – in subsidiary order – case law and legal doctrine. There is no EU law regime applicable to immunities.

---

119   Sweden, Svea Court of Appeal, 22 February 2019, Nos T 8538-17 and T 12033-17 (n 115) 88.

120   Dahlquist Cullborg (n 116) 469, 479.

121   Swedish Supreme Court, case No T 1569-19, decision of 12 April 2019 <https://www.italaw.com/sites/default/files/case-documents/italaw11099.pdf> accessed 29 April 2020. See also Joel Dahlquist, 'Swedish Supreme Court to send Achmea-related question to European Court of Justice' *(Investment Arbitration Reporter, 14 December 2019)* <https://www.iareporter.com/articles/swedish-supreme-court-sends-achmea-related-issue-to-european-court-of-justice/> accessed 29 April 2020.

122   Tom Ruys, Nicolas Angelet, Luca Ferro, 'International Immunities in a State of Flux?' in Tom Ruys, Nicolas Angelet, Luca Ferro (eds), *The Cambridge Handbook of Immunities and International Law* (Cambridge University Press 2019) 1, 4.

16.104   The first main international instrument pertaining to State immunity is the European Convention on State Immunity (the 'ECSI') which was adopted by the Council of Europe in 1972.[123] The ECSI was the most advanced of the three instruments adopted in the 1970s which introduced a more restrictive approach to State Immunity.[124] The Convention was ratified by eight Member States of the Council of Europe, all of them also Member States of the European Union (including Germany and the UK). The ECSI entered into force in 1976.[125] It sets out in five chapters the rules of immunity under two heads: jurisdiction and enforcement. The weakness of the ECSI is that, short of general ratification, it was easily overtaken by subsequent developments in the law, in particular by the work of the Committee on the Jurisdictional Immunities of States and their Property set up by the International Law Commission (the 'ILC').[126]

16.105   The work of the ILC Committee resulted in the second main international instrument pertaining to State Immunity, i.e. the UN Convention on Jurisdictional Immunities of States and Their Property of 2004 (the 'UNCSI').[127] In the absence of sufficient ratifications, the UNCSI has not yet entered into force at the time of writing.[128] Nevertheless, its provisions already have a high impact on the regime of sovereign immunity law.[129] The International Court of Justice (the 'ICJ') and the European Court of Human Rights (the 'ECtHR') have indicated that at least some provisions of the UNCSI reflect customary international law.[130] Some domestic courts within the EU have ruled in the same sense.[131] Furthermore, some national legislations have been directly inspired by the UNCSI.

16.106   Immunity law is further impacted by European human rights law. The ECtHR has on several occasions addressed the compatibility of domestic court decisions upholding the immunity of States with human rights, in particular the right to access to court enshrined in Article 6

---

123   European Convention on State Immunity (adopted 16 May 1972, entered into force 11 June 1976) 1495 UNTS 181 (ECSI).

124   The other instruments are the UK State Immunity Act of 1978 and the US Foreign Sovereign Immunities Act of 1976.

125   Austria, Belgium, Cyprus, Germany, Luxembourg, the Netherlands, Switzerland and the UK, with Portugal signing as well.

126   Hazel Fox, 'The Restrictive Rule of State Immunity' in Ruys, Angelet, Ferro (n 122), 21, 27.

127   United Nations Convention on Jurisdictional Immunities of States and Their Property (adopted 2 December 2004) UNGA A/RES/59/38 (UNCSI).

128   At the time of writing, the UNCSI has 28 signatories and 22 parties. Pursuant to art 30(1) UNCSI, it will enter into force following the deposit of the thirtieth instrument of ratification, acceptance, approval or accession with the UN Secretary-General.

129   Mathias Audit, Nicolas Angelet, Maria-Clara Van den Bossche, 'Immunity from Execution and Domestic Procedural Rules – Preventive Control, Burden of Proof and Discovery' in Ruys, Angelet, Ferro (n 122), 379.

130   *Jurisdictional Immunities of the State (Germany v Italy: Greece intervening)*, Judgment [2012] ICJ Rep 99, para 56; *Cudak v Lithuania* No 15869/02 ECHR 2010-III 370, para 66; *Sabeh El Leil v France* No 34869/05 (ECtHR 29 June 2011) para 54.

131   France, Court of Cassation, *Société NML Capital v Argentina and Total Austral*, Case No 10-25.938, 28 March 2013, 2013 Bulletin I No 62; France, Court of Cassation, *Société NML Capital v Argentina*, Case No 11-10.450, 28 March 2013, 2013 Bulletin I No 62; France, Court of Cassation, *Société NML Capital v Argentina and Air France*, Case No 11-13.323, 28 March 2013, 2013 Bulletin I No 64; Belgium, Constitutional Court, 27 April 2017, Case No 48/2017, B 13.3, B 26.1; Belgium, Court of Cassation, Opinion of AG Leclercq in *Société NML Capital v Argentina*, Case No C.13.0537.F, 11 December 2014, para 11; The Netherlands, Supreme Court, 28 June 2013, ECLI:NL:HR:2013:45, 3.6.2

ECHR, which implicitly encompasses the right to enforcement of judicial decisions.[132] Generally, the ECtHR holds that immunities granted to foreign States are a lawful exception to the right to a fair trial if, and only if, such immunities correspond to the legal norm under international law.[133]

2. State immunity from jurisdiction

The ECSI confirms as a general principle the foreign State's immunity from jurisdiction in respect of (civil) proceedings in the courts of another State (the forum State) (art 15), which does not apply in case of an express waiver of that immunity by the foreign State (art 2). At the same time, the ECSI provides a significant list of exceptions to that immunity: employment (art 5); companies (art 6); patents, trademarks and similar rights (art 8); rights over, or possession of, immovable property (art 9); personal injury and damage to tangible property (art 11); and, importantly for our purposes, arbitration (art 12).[134] **16.107**

Already from the adoption of the ECSI, the abovementioned provisions governing immunity from jurisdiction were of limited importance since Article 24(1) ECSI allows any Contracting State to declare that 'in cases not falling within Articles 1 to 13, its courts shall be entitled to entertain proceedings against another Contracting State to the extent that its courts are entitled to entertain proceedings against States not party to the present Convention', and therefore to apply its own domestic rules in many instances.[135] **16.108**

The UNCSI equally confirms as a general principle that 'a State enjoys immunity, in respect of itself and its property, from the jurisdiction of the courts of another State' (art 5). Article 6 UNCSI sets out the modalities for giving effect to that State immunity from jurisdiction. Article 7 UNCSI provides for an exception to that immunity in case the State has expressly waived its immunity from jurisdiction. Article 8 UNCSI provides a further exception to immunity from jurisdiction in case of participation by the foreign State in the proceedings before the court of the forum State. Article 9 UNCSI stipulates that immunity from jurisdiction cannot be relied upon in respect of counterclaims filed against the foreign State who filed or intervened in proceedings before the forum State. Finally, and most importantly, Articles 10–17 UNCSI list a number of private law exceptions to the immunity from jurisdiction similar to the ECSI, including, again, arbitration (see art 17). **16.109**

Be it based on the latter provisions or on general principles of international (customary) law, it is commonly accepted that, by entering into bilateral or multilateral investment treaties allowing foreign investors to resort to international arbitration against them, States have **16.110**

---

132 See e.g., *Waite and Kennedy v Germany* No 26083/94 ECHR 1999-I 13; *Beer and Regan v Germany* No 28934/95 (ECtHR 18 February 1999); *Al-Adsani v The United Kingdom* No 35763/97 ECHR 2001-XI 761; *Stichting Mothers of Srebrenica v the Netherlands* No 65542/12 (ECtHR 11 June 2013).

133 See e.g., *Cudak v Lithuania* No 15869/02 ECHR 2010-III 370, paras 57–67.

134 Fox (n 126) 21, 23.

135 European Treaty Series – No. 74, 'Explanatory Report to the European Convention on State Immunity' (*Council of Europe*, 16 May 1972) <https://www.coe.int/en/web/conventions/full-list/-/conventions/treaty/074> accessed 29 April 2020.

waived their immunity from jurisdiction, also for the purpose of setting aside or enforcement proceedings in relation to investment-treaty awards based on those treaties.[136]

3. State immunity from enforcement

16.111 While immunity from jurisdiction was restricted under the ECSI, immunity from enforcement has long remained absolute, subject only to an express waiver in writing. This followed from Article 23 ECSI.[137] However, as a substitute for generally non-available enforcement measures, Article 20(1) ECSI stipulated that the contracting States shall give effect to judgments delivered against them in accordance with the provisions of the Convention.[138] In addition, the absolute immunity was mitigated by Article 26 ECSI which stipulates that, between States who have made optional declarations under Article 24 ECSI and with respect to judgments (and awards) concerning industrial or commercial activities, enforcement measures remained possible against property 'used exclusively in connection with such an activity'.

16.112 In the decades following the adoption of the ECSI, a closer correspondence grew between the rules of immunity from jurisdiction and immunity from enforcement, at least as they relate to States' commercial activities, and immunity from enforcement became more restrictive, as reflected in the 2004 UNCSI.

16.113 Article 18 UNCSI provides that State-owned property is immune from prejudgment measures of constraint (such as attachments) except in limited circumstances, i.e., if the State has expressly consented to such measures or has allocated or earmarked specific property for the satisfaction of the particular claim. Regarding post-judgment measures of constraint, Article 19 UNCSI provides that:

> No post-judgment measures of constraint, such as attachment, arrest or execution, against property of a State may be taken in connection with a proceeding before a court of another State unless and except to the extent that:
>
> (a) the State has expressly consented to the taking of such measures as indicated:
>   (i) by international agreement;
>   (ii) by an arbitration agreement or in a written contract; or
>   (iii) by a declaration before the court or by a written communication after a dispute between the parties has arisen; or
> (b) the State has allocated or earmarked property for the satisfaction of the claim which is the object of that proceeding; or
> (c) it has been established that the property is specifically in use or intended for use by the State for other than government non-commercial purposes and is in the territory of the State of the forum, provided that post-judgment measures of constraint may only be taken against property that has a connection with the entity against which the proceeding was directed.

---

136   *Re* ICSID arbitration, see Musa, Polasek (n 11) 28.

137   Art 23 ECSI provides, 'No measures of execution or preventive measures against the property of a Contracting State may be taken in the territory of another Contracting State except where and to the extent that the State has expressly consented thereto in writing in any particular case.'

138   August Reinisch, 'European Court Practice Concerning State Immunity from Enforcement Measures' (2006) 17(4) *European Journal of International Law* 803, 805.

Article 21 UNCSI further lists four categories of State property that are presumed not to be **16.114** 'property specifically in use or intended for use by the State for other than government non-commercial purposes' under Article 19(c), i.e., diplomatic assets, military property, central bank assets and cultural property. In order to enforce against such property, a judgment or award creditor thus needs to demonstrate either the existence of a valid waiver of immunity from enforcement (art 19(a)) or that the particular property was allocated or earmarked for the satisfaction of the judgment debt (art 19(b)).

4. Belgian and French regimes of pre-authorization

Some States, including within the EU, have recently adopted specific immunity legislation **16.115** introducing preventive control regimes, which make enforcement measures against property of foreign States subject to preventive control by a competent national authority.[139]

For instance, both the Belgian and the French legislator have introduced a judicial preventive **16.116** control regime under which creditors wishing to attach assets of foreign States on Belgian or French territory must first obtain judicial authorization to attach such assets through an ex-parte request before the court competent in attachment matters.

The Belgian regime is laid down in Article 1412*quinquies*, paragraph 2 of the Judicial Code **16.117** which provides: 'A creditor with an enforceable title or an authentic or private title which, as the case may be, grounds the attachment may apply to the judge of attachments for authorization to attach the assets of a foreign State'.[140] The French rules can be found in Article L. 111-1-1 of the Code of Civil Enforcement Procedure which provides: 'Provisional measures or enforcement measures may be executed on property belonging to a foreign State only with the prior authorization of the judge by order issued on request.'[141]

Under both provisions, the attachment of foreign State property may be authorized only if one **16.118** of the following conditions is met:

(1)   the Foreign State has expressly consented to the taking of such measure; or
(2)   the Foreign State has reserved or earmarked property to the satisfaction of the claim which is the object of the proceeding; or
(3)   a judgment or an arbitral award has sentenced the foreign State and the property which the creditor seeks to attach is specifically used or intended for use by that State for other than non-commercial public service purposes, and has a link with the entity against which the proceeding was directed.

Although these conditions were copied from Article 19 UNCSI, the latter provision signifi- **16.119** cantly differs from the Belgian and French rules in that it does not provide for the prior judicial authorization mechanism.

---

139   See more extensively, Audit, Angelet, Van den Bossche (n 129) 379, 380ff.
140   French original text, 'Le créancier muni d'un titre exécutoire ou d'un titre authentique ou privé qui, selon le cas, fonde la saisie, peut introduire une requête auprès du juge des saisies afin de demander l'autorisation de saisir les avoirs d'une puissance étrangère.'
141   French original text, 'Des mesures conservatoires ou des mesures d'exécution forcée ne peuvent être mises en œuvre sur un bien appartenant à un Etat étranger que sur autorisation préalable du juge par ordonnance rendue sur requête.'

16.120 In the authors' view, the prior authorization requirement constitutes a further impediment to enforcement on property of foreign States, since – as the conditions (1) and (2) will be difficult to meet – creditors will have to meet the burden of proving the existence and use (for other than non-commercial public purposes) of a foreign State's assets. Such proof will have to be delivered in ex-parte proceedings, which have the advantage of preventing the foreign State from removing its assets from the territory of the forum State before the attachment measures, but at the same time exclude the foreign State's cooperation in the establishment of evidence with respect to the nature of the (intended) use of the envisaged assets. By their implications for the burden of proof of creditors, these prior authorization regimes – which are not provided under international law – *de facto* grant broader immunity to foreign State property than the immunity which results from the limited exceptions (derived from international law) in which such property can be attached. They result in immunity which does not correspond to a legal norm under international law and constitute a limitation of the right to a fair trial (which encompasses the right to enforcement).[142]

16.121 Yet, the Belgian Constitutional Court upheld the Belgian authorization regime, finding that it does not violate the right to a fair trial on the ground that it is not, in the Court's view, impossible *in all cases* for creditors to adduce evidence of the existence and use of State property for non-governmental purposes.[143] Similarly, the French constitutional court upheld the French authorization regime in a decision dated 8 December 2016.[144]

16.122 Since the enactment of the new Belgian law regime, the practice in Belgium has shown that the enforcement courts grant the requested authorization for attachment of foreign State property in Belgium on the basis of evidence submitted by the creditor in ex-parte applications,[145] probably encouraged by the fact that the foreign State keeps the opportunity to prove any potential immunity of the attached assets in subsequent (adversarial) proceedings challenging the attachment after it has been carried out.

---

142 See in more detail, Audit, Angelet, Van den Bossche (n 129) 379, 383ff.

143 Belgium, Constitutional Court, *NML Capital Ltd and Yukos Universal Limited*, Case No 48/2017, 27 April 2018, B.25.2, B.27.2. This decision was criticized for the reason that, 'its reasoning was uninformed by the practicalities of enforcing judgments and awards against foreign States' and because the Court did not make a proper distinction between bank accounts held by a foreign State and embassy bank accounts, which are subject to a specific protective regime. See also Audit, Angelet, Van den Bossche (n 129) 379, 384.

144 France, Constitutional Court, Decision No 2016-741 of 8 December 2016 <https://www.conseil-constitutionnel.fr/decision/2016/2016741DC.htm> accessed 29 April 2020.

145 See for instance the *Stati v Kazakstan* case referred to in para 16.36.

17

DAMAGES IN INVESTMENT TREATY ARBITRATION

Herfried Wöss and Adriana San Román Rivera[*]

A. INTRODUCTION

This chapter will briefly discuss the function and role of international damages law. It will also **17.01** refer to its historic development in order to find out whether Chorzów may be explained only from its particular historical circumstances or if it plays a relevant role today apart from being cited in most investment arbitrations. This chapter will also examine discrete aspects of international damages law such as the full reparation principle and what it means in the light of the Chorzów formula. Particular attention will be given to the elements of the Chorzów formula as the measure of damages in investment arbitration, the need to define the illegality threshold in indirect expropriation and fair and equitable treatment (FET) violation for the purpose of the application of the but-for premise, the implications of the difference between legal and illegal expropriation when valuating damages, and the notion of the contract as investment under a recent landmark case.

---

[*] Date of submission: 15/1/2020.

17.02 Furthermore, the elements of the Chorzów formula such as the Fair Market Value (FMV) and the date of valuation will be analysed together with their implications when quantifying damages. In this respect, the notion of FMV has a predominant role and will be compared with the market value. Other aspects of damages valuation will be considered such as the use of hindsight information and what interests intend to represent when updating or discounting cash flows in order to valuate damages.

17.03 This chapter also focuses on damages analysis and quantification of recent landmark cases such as *Burlington v Ecuador*,[1] *Murphy v Ecuador*,[2] *Crystallex v Venezuela*,[3] *Mobil v Venezuela*,[4] and recent Spanish renewable energy cases, where aspects of such as the FMV, the role of the contract as investment and the determination of the illegality threshold, are dealt with.

B. THE ROLE AND FUNCTION OF DAMAGES LAW IN INVESTMENT ARBITRATION

17.04 The principal function of damages law in investment arbitration is the compensation of loss caused by an illegal measure affecting an investment. The payment of an amount of money should place the injured party in the economic position it would be in if the damaging act had not occurred, that is, to wipe out all the consequences of the violation as established in the well-known *Factory at Chorzów* formula.[5] Compensation has to be in accordance with the full reparation principle, which is a general principle of international law and the customary law standard.[6] This principle is achieved through the so-called but-for premise or differential hypothesis, which determines the economic difference between the actual situation as a consequence of the illegal measure and the hypothetical situation without such measure.

17.05 International damages law aims to bring balance to the economic relation between investors and States and to give legal certainty to investors by protecting their legitimate expectations. The relevant issue is that by protecting legitimate expectations or honouring the general principle of law of full reparation, economies would be more efficient as this protection would avoid unnecessary transaction cost. It is precisely the role of damages law to promote economic efficiency through the avoidance of waste of resources. According to Ottho Heldring:

> There is an economic reason for the ethical and legal framework of economic life. ... Efficient economic life assumes a broadly-based legal certainty and predictability. Where mutual trust is

---

1   *Burlington Resources Inc v Republic of Ecuador*, ICSID Case No ARB/08/5, Decision on Reconsideration and Award, 7 February 2017.

2   *Murphy Exploration & Production Company – International v The Republic of Ecuador*, PCA, Partial Final Award, 6 May 2016.

3   *Crystallex International Corporation v Bolivarian Republic of Venezuela*, ICSID Case No ARB(AF)/11/2, Award, 4 April 2016.

4   *Venezuela Holdings, BV, Mobil Cerro Negro Holding, Ltd, Mobil Venezolana de Petróleos Holdings, Inc, Mobil Cerro Negro, Ltd and Mobil Venezolana de Petróleos, Inc v The Bolivarian Republic of Venezuela*, ICSID Case No ARB/07/27, Award, 9 October 2014 and Decision on Annulment, 9 March 2017.

5   Herfried Wöss and others, *Damages in International Arbitration under Complex Long-term Contracts* (Oxford International Arbitration Series, Oxford University Press 2014), Chapter 2.

6   Irmgard Marboe, *Calculation of Compensation and Damages in International Investment Law* (2nd edn, Oxford University Press 2017), para 2.78.

lacking, transaction costs increase for the economic actors, which makes trading with countries lacking a trustworthy legal system so difficult.[7]

According to Austrian economists Ludwig von Mises and Nobel laureate Friedrich August von Hayek, the institution of private property and the rule of law provide legal certainty, which encourages investment – a motivation for responsible decision-making on behalf of owners, the background for social experimentation – which spurs progress.[8]

Damages law plays a major role in this context. If damages are not properly analysed and awarded, leading to less than full reparation, fewer people would be willing to invest as the risk that they will lose their investment is higher. This would negatively affect the economy. In addition, investors will ask for a higher rate of return and creditors will increase their interest rates. If the risk is increased by legal uncertainty, projects become more expensive in accordance with the risk. The higher the risk, the higher the price. Wasting resources is called economic inefficiency and causes great harm to the economy.[9] **17.06**

The full reparation principle is essential for the legitimacy of international law and an important element of fairness and justice. According to Thomas M Franck: **17.07**

> [H]umanity wants to be reassured that the ... legal system is capable of ensuring stability and progressive change ... only a system which is perceived as legitimate can contain within its framework the tensions between stability and change. Legitimacy thus is the first aspect of fairness to which we must turn our attention.[10]

As stated in the monograph *Damages in International Arbitration under Complex Long-term Contracts*, which also refers to investment arbitration: **17.08**

> The adequate and fair compensation of damages is a fundamental element of any legal system. In the light of the compensation and prevention principles, damages law has an important economic and social role. It provides stability in [legal] relationships and prevents opportunistic behaviour, which in turn results in legal certainty and predictability. This has a positive effect on the perception of risk, which is reflected in lower transaction costs and a more efficient economy. An efficient economy creates welfare. Not granting damages [when all the legal requirements have been met] or granting them deficiently in particular when disregarding fundamental issues of due process and the principle of full reparation adds further grievance to loss with the corresponding social and economic implications. The same happens in case of overcompensation due to the application of inadequate measures of damages or the lack of legal and economic knowledge.[11]

---

7   Ottho Heldring, 'Business Administration and Concept Formation' in Christian Krijnen and Bas Kee (eds), *Philosophy of Economics and Management and Organization Studies: A Critical Introduction* (Kluwer 2009) 165, cited in Wöss and others (n 5), para. 2.29.

8   John M Cobin, *A Primer on Modern Themes in Free Market Economics and Policy* (2nd edn, Universal Publishers 2009) 246, with further references; Hans-Herrmann Hoppe, *The Economics and Ethics of Private Property, Studies in Political Economy and Philosophy* (2nd edn, Ludwig van Mises Institute 2006), cited in Wöss and others, ibid, para. 2.30.

9   Wöss and others (n 5) para. 2.31.

10 Thomas M Franck, 'Fairness in the International Legal and Institutional System: General Course on Public International Law' (1993) 240 *Recueil des cours* 26.

11 Wöss and others (n 5), para. 2.33.

C. THE FULL REPARATION PRINCIPLE IN INVESTMENT ARBITRATION

17.09 The full reparation principle has its origins in the PCIJ *Factory at Chorzów* case. As observed by Professor Hersch Lauterpacht, 'states were originally reluctant to provide full compensation, however, at the beginning of the twentieth century, both the award of lost profits and the full compensation principle were already duly recognized, as shown by the well-known *Factory at Chorzów* case', which reflects contemporary State practice.[12]

17.10 The full reparation principle is recognized in the *Chorzów* formula when it refers to the obligation to 'wipe out all consequences of the illegal act', and in Article 31 (Reparation), paragraph 1, of the Draft Articles on State Responsibility for Internationally Wrongful Acts, which states that '[t]he responsible State is under an obligation to make full reparation for the injury caused by the internationally wrongful act'. Article 36 of the Draft Articles refers to 'any assessable damage including loss of profits insofar as it is established'. Both articles refer to the *Factory in Chorzów* case in their comments.

17.11 However, the full compensation principle does not arise in 1927 out of a legal vacuum. It is the result of a long-lasting legal development that commenced with Aristotle and culminated with the formulation of the but-for premise in English and German law and its particular formulation precisely in the *Factory at Chorzów* case. In order to understand the foundations of modern international damages law, it is, therefore, necessary to look back at its historical development.

17.12 The compensation function of damages law[13] has its origins in Greek philosophy. Aristotle (384–322 BC) dealt with compensation under the notion of 'corrective or commutative justice'. Commutative justice treats the wrong and the transfer of resources that undoes it, as a link between the injured party and the wrongdoer. Corrective and commutative justice seeks to subtract the unjust gain of one party to make up for the loss of the other party. In his Nicomachean ethics, Aristotle states that 'the law has regards only to the difference made by the harm done; they are on the same footing, apart from the fact that one has perpetrated and the other suffered the harm'.[14] Roman law settled the focus on the interest of the claimant to give him the value what he was expected to receive which leads to the formula *'id quod interest'*.[15] A prominent member of the scholastics, Thomas Aquinas (1225–1274) said that a person might violate commutative justice either by interfering with another's property in a wrongful manner or simply by taking what belongs to another.[16]

---

[12] Hersch Lauterpacht, *The Development of International Law by the International Court* (Cambridge University Press 1958) 315–16; see analysis in Wöss and others (n 5), paras 5.163–206; 6.24–34; 6.65–83; 6.92 and 6.121–2.

[13] Herfried Wöss and Adriana San Román, 'Full Compensation, Full Reparation and the But-for Premise', in John A Trenor (ed), *GAR Guide to Damages in International Arbitration* (3rd edn GAR 2019) 113.

[14] Wöss and others (n 5) paras 2.1–2 and 2.17–8; Gerard J Hughes, *The Routledge Guidebook to Aristotle's Nicomachean Ethics* (Taylor & Francis Group 2013).

[15] Borzu Sabahi, *Compensation and Restitution in Investor-State Arbitration* (International Economic Law Series, Oxford University Press 2011) 21.

[16] James Gordley, *Foundations of Private Law: Property, Tort, Contract, Unjust Enrichment* (Oxford University Press 2006) 423–34.

The underlying notion of Aristotle, the scholastics and post-scholastics was full compensation **17.13** and total reparation, whereby at that time both terms were used synonymously. Hugo Grotius (1583–1645) established the leading natural law damages doctrine in Chapter 17 of his master work *'De iure belli ac pacis'* based on total reparation and the compensation of damages and lost profits, which comprises the violation of legal positions including property, contract and the law.[17] Grotius' doctrine was further developed by another natural law scholar, Samuel Pufendorf (1632–1694) who was heavily influenced by Thomas Hobbes. Damages law was understood as a defence against the absolute prohibition of *'neminem laedere'* (not to hurt anybody).[18] At that time, damages law focused on the position of the injured party, though notions such as the requirement of culpability exclude the damaging party's liability according to the principle of 'everything or nothing'. This principle means that if the injured party does not prove culpability of the party in breach or other conditions it would not receive anything.

In 1848, the leading English case *Robinson v Harman* established that the aim of damages is to **17.14** give the injured party the necessary amount of money to put him 'so far as money can do it, in the same position as he would have been in had the contract been performed'.[19] In 1855 Friedrich Mommsen developed his *'Doctrine of Interest'* which states that the interest to be compensated is the economic difference between two situations: the actual situation affected by the breach of contract or violation of an international law standard, and the hypothetical situation but-for the breach or illegal act, which is the so-called expectation interest. The application of the but-for premise is the means to achieve full compensation or total reparation.[20]

The development of international damages law went in parallel with private law. As mentioned **17.15** by Professor Hersch Lauterpacht, private law sources and analogies are found in international law, in particular, in the areas of 'international law of tort and the problems of State responsibility, the measure of damages; the question of interest, moratory or compensatory'.[21] The full reparation principle in international law started to differentiate itself from the private law full compensation principle only at the beginning of the 20th century precisely with the *Factory at Chorzów* case that replicates the but-for premise already recognized in private law, stating that 'reparation must, as far as possible wipe out all the consequences of the illegal act and re-establish the situation which would, in all probability, have existed if that act had not been committed'.[22] According to Professor Irmgard Marboe, '[t]he principle of full reparation

---

17 Hugo Grotius, *De iure, lib.* II, *cap.* XVII, §§IV f, cited in Feras Gisawi, *Der Grundsatz der Totalreparation*, Gundlagen der Rechtswissenschaft 25 (Mohr Siebeck 2015), 28–9.

18 Samuel Pufendorf, 'Ut nemo laedatur, et si quod damnum fuit datum, reparetur', title to *De iure belli ac pacis, lib.* III, *cap.* I, §2, cited in Feras Gisawi, *Der Grundsatz der Totalreparation* (n 17), 44.

19 *Robinson v Harman* (1848) 13 P.D. 191 (CA), 200.

20 Friedrich Mommsen, *Beiträge zum Obligationenrecht: Abth. Zur Lehre von dem Interesse* (E.U. Schwetschke und Sohn 1855), 27: 'Das Interesse ist allerdings ein Schadenersatz; und sofern man den Ausdruck Schadenersatz allein auf die vollständige Entschädigung bezieht, treffen beide Ausdrücke in ihrer Bedeutung zusammen' ('Interest means, however, damages; and if the expression damages is exclusively understood as full compensation, both terms coincide in their meaning').

21 Hersch Lauterpacht, *Private Law Sources and Analogies of Law* (Longmans, Green & Co Ltd 1927) 6; Hersch Lauterpacht, *The Development of International Law by the International Court* (n 12), 32.

22 *Case Concerning the Factory at Chorzów (Claim for Indemnity)*, Judgment, 13 September 1928, PCIJ Series A, No 17, 47.

has been recognized in international judicial practice not only in the context of international investment but also in cases of other violations of international law'.[23]

17.16 The application of the but-for premise under the Chorzów formula, when ordering to 're-establish the situation which would, in all probability, have existed if that act had not been committed' leads to full reparation.

D. THE CHORZÓW FORMULA

1. The Chorzów formula as the measure of damages in investment arbitration

17.17 The measure of damages is what the applicable law allows to be compensated which means it is a normative notion. In investment arbitration the measure of damages is the Chorzów formula. The Chorzów formula states that 'Reparation must, so far as possible, wipe out all the circumstances of the *illegal act* and re-establish the situation which would, in all probability, have existed if that act had not been committed...'.[24] The measure of damages in international law is in essence defined by the Chorzów dictum which is cited in nearly all leading investment arbitration cases[25] (emphasis added).

17.18 This refers to the total reparation principle and it is not limited to illegal expropriation but it refers to any illegal act, which is then further defined though the measure of damages established by the arbitral tribunal though the questions that it posed to the experts:

- Question IA asked the experts to compute the FMV of the factory at the time of expropriation, updated to the time of indemnification (i.e., the date of the award).[26]
- Question IB asked the experts to value the *lucrum cessans* between the interim period of the date of the expropriation and the date of the indemnification. This means that the injured party has to be compensated for the lost profits between the date of the expropriation and the date of indemnification.[27]
- Question II asked the experts to compute the FMV of the factory as of the date of indemnification or the date of the award. This question 'leaves aside the situation as of the time of expropriation, and instead focuses on a valuation of assets as of the time of the experts' assessment. Observe, that Question II allows for the reasonable development

---

23 Marboe (n 6), para 2.78.
24 *Factory at Chorzow* (n 22), 47.
25 Marboe (n 6), paras 2.78, 3.104–106; Wöss and others (n 5), paras 1.08–09, 3.41–61, 5.175–206 with further references; Mark W Friedman and Floriane Lavaud, 'Damages Principles in Investment Arbitration' in John A Trenor (ed) (n 13) 96; Timothy G Nelson, 'A Factory in Chorzów: The Silesian Dispute that Continues to Influence International Law and Expropriation Damages Almost a Century Later' (2014) 1 *The Journal of Damages in International Arbitration* 77; Manuel A Abdala and Pablo T Spiller, 'Chorzów's Standard Rejuvenated: Assessing Damages in Investment Treaty Arbitrations' (2008) 25 *Journal of International Arbitration* 1.
26 *Factory at Chorzow* (n 22), 51; Pablo T Spiller and Santiago Dellepiane, 'Valuation of Damages', in Wöss and others, (n 5), para 6.72.
27 Adriana San Román and Herfried Wöss, 'Damages in International Arbitration with Respect to Income Generating Assets or Investments in Commercial and Investment Arbitration' (2015) 2(1) *Journal of Damages in International Arbitration* 37; also published in (2015) 5 *Transnational Dispute Management*.

of the undertaking, not just maintaining the assets as they were as of the time of expropriation, but also including a reasonable investment programme'.[28]

17.19 From the Chorzów formula it can be seen that 'wiping out all the effects of the illegal act' through monetary compensation can be achieved by two means:

> Granting the Fair Market Value as of the date of the expropriation brought forward and expressed in current currency; or granting the sum of the Fair Market Value as of the date of the award, plus the profits that the investor would have probably obtained in the interim period, between the date of the expropriation and the date of the award.

Therefore, it is reasonable to interpret from the Chorzów tribunal's questions damages as the highest value between the answer to question IA, that is the value of the undertaking at the time of the expropriation updated to the date of the award, and the answer to questions II and IB, that is the FMV of the undertaking as of the date of the award plus the lost profits between the date of the expropriation and the date of the award.

17.20 Some professionals argue that the Chorzów case is outdated and has lost its relevance as it happened such a long time ago and that it should not be discussed nowadays. In that respect, it must be said that the full reparation principle contained in Chorzów is international customary law duly recognized in Article 31 of the Draft Articles of the International Law Commission (ILC) on the Responsibility of States for Unlawful Acts, that reads that '[t]he responsible State is under an obligation to make full reparation for the injury caused by the internationally wrongful act', that in turn refers to the Chorzów case in its comment (1). Article 36 of the Draft Articles refers to 'any assessable damage including loss of profits insofar as it is established' and to the *Factory in Chorzów* case in its comment (27) and (30).[29] It is well-established that the Draft Articles are also applicable by analogy to investor-State arbitrations.

17.21 The Chorzów formula refers to the FMV as the measure of damages in order to achieve full reparation without, however, using this term, as explained further below. What is also very interesting about the Chorzów formula is that even at that time, that is nearly 100 years ago, the tribunal recognized that in order to make the injured party whole, it was necessary that if the damages were valued at the date of the legal measures, interest should be awarded till the date of the payment and if the selected date was the date of the award, lost profits between the date of the illegal measures and the date of award should be added. The PCIJ understood the financial logic in order to avoid under compensation which is why it arrived at that formula. This represents the standard of compensation to achieve full reparation whose function is to 'wipe out all the consequences of the illegal act'. It is important to underline that this measure refers to an illegal act. If there were no illegal act there would be no damages but only compensation in case there is an expropriation as established under the applicable International Investment Agreement (IIA).

---

28 Spiller and Dellepiane (n 26), paras 6.73, 6.76–77.
29 Ibid., para 5.178.

17.22 The key legal principle for damages compensation in the *Factory at Chorzów* is that compensation 'should wipe out all the consequences of the illegal act and re-establish the situation which would, in all probability, have existed if that act had not been committed'.[30] In order to achieve this purpose, the Chorzów formula uses the higher FMV at either the date of the violation or illegal expropriation or the date of the award. In case of the latter lost profits from the date of the illegal act to the date of the award have to be added.

17.23 If there is total destruction of the investment due to an illegal act, the calculation of the FMV of the whole investment suffices under Chorzów formula. However, if the investment is not totally destroyed the but-for premise is the tool to calculate the effect of the illegal act on the income stream or the value of the investment under the Chorzów formula in order to achieve total reparation.

17.24 In the recent landmark case *Burlington v Ecuador*,[31] Ecuador illegally expropriated Blocks 7 and 21 which takeover became permanent on 30 August 2009 preceded by tax increases on profits from the proceeds of the sale of oil to 50 per cent, and later on to 99 per cent. The arbitral tribunal found that the standard of compensation was full reparation set out in Article 31 of the ILC Articles, applied by analogy which leads to the application of the Chorzów formula.[32] In order to determine the value of the operating assets which is the lost profits under the Production Sharing Contracts (PSCs) the issue was the calculation of the expected free cash flows generated under the PCS, absent (that is: but-for) unlawful government conduct.[33]

17.25 In the majority's views, the full reparation standard requires that the damages resulting from the unlawful act be valued on the date of the award, using information available at that point of time, which derives from the Chorzów case, according to which wiping out all the consequences of the illegal act 'involves the obligation to restore the undertaking and, if this be not possible, to be its value at the time of the indemnification, which value is designed to take the place instead of restitution which has become impossible'.[34] The arbitral tribunal states that its task is to place Burlington in the situation it would have been had Ecuador not expropriated the PSCs. For this, the tribunal stated that it must assess what the PSC's value would have been in real life on the date of the award. The date of valuation was 31 August 2016.[35]

17.26 With respect to quantification, the tribunal found that:

> its task is to place Burlington in the position in which it would have been but for the expropriation. ... The question here is whether, when assessing the value of PSCs' revenue stream, the Tribunal should assume that extraordinary revenues are taxed at 99% (as mandated by Law 42) or that Ecuador absorbs the impact of this tax.[36]

---

30   *Factory at Chorzow* (n 22), 27.
31   *Burlington v Ecuador* (n 1).
32   Ibid., para 177.
33   Ibid., para 225.
34   Ibid., para 326.
35   Ibid., paras 332 and 337.
36   Ibid., para 357.

The tribunal further stated that '[w]hen building the counterfactual scenario in which the expropriation has not occurred, the Tribunal states that it must assume that Burlington holds the rights that made up the expropriated assets and that those rights are respected'.[37]

The arbitral tribunal found: 'When quantifying the value of a going concern, the Tribunal **17.27** must disregard the effects of value-depressing measures taken by the State related to the investments.'[38]

> Under the standard of full reparation, the Tribunal must value what Burlington lost as a result of the expropriation. When determining the FMV, the tribunal is not bound by the 'willing buyer-willing seller' analogy. What Burlington lost was a contract with a full set of rights, each of which must be given its value. Burlington did not lose an opportunity to sell its contract rights, it lost an opportunity to exercise them. The relevant question is thus not whether a hypothetical buyer would have paid full value for the PSCs, it is what value would have derived from exercising the rights under the PSCs, but for their expropriation.[39]

2. Elements of the Chorzów formula

a. Fair market value

The reference to the 'value of the undertaking' under the *Factory at Chorzów* has been **17.28** considered to refer to the notion of FMV,[40] although the case does not expressly refer to this term. The notion of FMV in the Chorzów formula derives from German private law, in particular, the notion of the hypothetical normal course of events according to which extraordinary economic circumstances which would affect the hypothetical course of events used to calculate the expectation interest should be ignored.[41] According to the Court, the reference to the value at the date of the award supposes:

> that the factory had remained essentially in the state in which it was on the date of expropriation, and secondly, the factory is to be considered in the state in which it would (hypothetically but probably) have in the hands of Oberschlesische and Bayerische, if, instead of being taken in 1922 by Poland, it had been able to continue its supposedly normal development from that time onwards.[42]

The PCIJ states that: **17.29**

> It has already been pointed out ... that the value of the undertaking of the moment of dispossession does not necessarily indicate the criterion for the fixing of compensation. Now it is certain that the moment of the contract of sale and that of the negotiations with the Genevese company belong to a period of serious economic and monetary crisis; the difference between the value which the undertaking then had and that which it would have had at present may therefore be considerable. And further it must be considered that the price stipulated in the contract of 1919 was determined by circumstances and accompanied by clauses which in reality seem hardly to admit of its being considered as a true indication of the value which the Parties placed on the factory; and that the offer

---

37 Ibid., para 358.
38 Ibid., para 362.
39 Ibid., para 366.
40 Abdala and Spiller (n 25), 108.
41 Wolfgang Fikentscher and Andreas Heinemann, *Schuldrecht* (10th edn, De Gruyter 2006), para 701.
42 *Factory at Chorzów* (n 22), 52.

to the Genevese company is probably to be explained by the fear of measures such as those which the Polish government adopted afterwards against the Chorzów undertaking and which the Court has judged not to be in conformity with the Geneva convention.[43]

17.30   Therefore, it may be clearly seen that the FMV measure of damages appears in the Chorzów formula. The rationale behind it is to avoid opportunistic behaviour of the State, as it would be cheaper to expropriate investments at market values that take into consideration the imminent threat of expropriation or potential violations of international law standards on the value of the investment. When applying the FMV the distress caused by the imminent threat of expropriation should be not be taken into consideration.

17.31   The notion of FMV was first used by the Iran-US Claims Tribunal in *American International Group v The Islamic Republic of Iran* in 1983, which stated that 'the valuation should be made on the basis of the FMV of the shares'[44] and in *Starrett Housing Corporation v Government of the Islamic Republic of Iran* in 1987.[45] In *Starrett* the expert defined the FMV 'as the price that a willing buyer would pay to a willing seller in circumstances in which each had good information, each desired to maximize his financial gain and neither was under duress or threat.'[46] The commentaries (21) and (22) of the Article 36 of the Draft Articles on Responsibility of States for Internationally Wrongful Acts state that compensation reflecting the capital of the property taken or destroyed is generally assessed on the basis of the FMV of the property lost.

17.32   This is reflected in the FMV formula originally developed in the US, when referring to situations 'without duress or threat'. The US Supreme Court classic definition of the FMV reads: 'The Fair Market Value is the price at which the property would change hands between a willing buyer and a willing seller, neither being under any compulsion to buy or to sell and both having reasonable knowledge of relevant facts.'[47] This formula is also referred to in the World Bank 'Guidelines on the Treatment of Foreign Direct Investment' 1992. A fair market valuation must assume that neither party to the transaction is under compulsion to buy or sell, therefore, it is standard to exclude distress when assessing fair market value.[48] The terms 'duress' or 'threat' are particularly important in economic crises where there are normally no willing buyers. The fair market value ignores such duress or threat to a certain extent.

17.33   With respect to economic distress, in modern investment arbitration practice, however, economic circumstances are taken into consideration when calculating the cash flows of the company, which could mean that the cash flows are considerably diminished during an economic crisis. Therefore, the economic crisis is being taken into consideration when preparing the economic scenarios, but as the crisis is not going to last forever, the discount rate would have to be adjusted and reflect that it will tend to normalize in time. This issue is relevant with respect to the country risk, as adding additional country risk at the moment of valuation because of the risk that expropriation or an illegal measure would take place, would

---

43   Ibid., 50.
44   *American International Group v Islamic Republic of Iran* (1983) 4 Iran-USCTR 106.
45   *Starrett Housing Corporation v Islamic Republic of Iran* (1987) 16 Iran-USCTR 112.
46   Ibid., 201.
47   *United States v Cartwright*, 411 US 546 (1973).
48   Spiller and Dellepiane (n 26), para 6.39.

mean taking distress into consideration, which would lead to market value instead of FMV and might not be the proper approach.[49]

b. Date of valuation of damages: date of the breach and date of the award

With respect to the date of valuation of damages, the rationale in the Chorzów formula behind **17.34** using the higher of the FMV at the date of the illegal act and the date of the award is that the State should not obtain windfall profits from the illegal expropriation. As stated by Professor Pablo T Spiller and Santiago Dellepiane:

> [t]he Chorzów standard, however, has a powerful economic logic. It is equivalent to transferring to the expropriating state the ex-post risks (up to the time of the award) associated with the expropriated asset. In other words, if the asset has increased in value in the absence of the measures, the state ought not to benefit from its expropriating actions, and thus, the windfall ought to belong to the investor.[50]

In the *Factory at Chorzów* case, it is clear that wiping out all effects of the measures through **17.35** monetary compensation can be achieved by two alternative means: Granting the FMV as of the date of the expropriation brought forward to the date of the award and expressed in current currency; or granting the sum of the FMV as of the date of the award plus the lost profits that the investor would have probably obtained in the interim period between the date of expropriation and the date of the award. Thus, it is reasonable to interpret from the Chorzów tribunal's questions, damages as the highest value between the date of the breach and the date of the award, and the lost profits between the date of the breach and the date of the award, in case the latter is chosen.[51]

Nowadays, there is a discussion between damages professionals in international arbitration **17.36** whether it is appropriate to use the date of award as the valuation date when the company stopped operations due to the illegal measures. This situation can be solved by using the but-for premise. The question to answer is: 'What would be the economic position of the injured party but for the illegal measure?' In order to answer this question, the hypothetical course of events has to be re-constructed to the date of the award. The economic difference between the actual situation subject to the illegal measure and the situation that would have existed if the illegal measure had not taken place is what has to be compensated. As the injured party would receive the money at the date of the award, in order to achieve the full reparation principle, this date should be used for compensation purposes. If the date of the illegal measure is the valuation date, the but-for premise should also be used, that is the economic difference between the undertaking between the actual situation and the situation but for the illegal measure and this economic difference has to be updated till the date of the award or the date of the indemnification to achieve full reparation, that is to place the injured party in the position it would be but for the illegal measure.

---

49   See also James Searby, 'Measuring Country Risk in International Arbitration', in Christina L Beharry (ed), *Contemporary and Emerging Issues on the Law of Damages and Valuation in International Investment Arbitration* (Brill Nijhoff 2018), 231.

50   Spiller and Dellepiane (n 26), para 6.69.

51   Ibid., paras 6.78–79.

3. Difference between fair market value and market value

17.37 The difference between FMV and market value may be significant. Market value is the result of considering the prevailing economic circumstances affecting the business including situations of distress and economic crisis, while the FMV is the result of the considering distress, threat or economic crises in the cash flows but not necessarily in the discount rate because crises do not last forever and, therefore, risks tend to normalize over time.

17.38 The application of the Chorzów formula applying the FMV leads to full reparation in investment arbitration which is likely to be higher than the market value corresponding to full compensation in commercial arbitration. However, in many investment arbitrations, the only reference to Chorzów is to the 'wipe-out' formulation, without actually applying the Chorzów measure of damages which leads to rather diverse results that are difficult to verify.[52]

17.39 In *Sempra v Argentina*,[53] the Tribunal was confronted with two conflicting assessments of the discount rate: (i) one relied on a long-term view of the cost of capital, and (ii) was based on the prevalent market conditions circa end of 2001 in Argentina, assessing country risk based on the yield of the government's debt. Based on the concept of FMV, the Tribunal held that the appropriate discount rate was the cost of capital proposed by the Claimant's experts. In doing so, the Tribunal recognized the difference between FMV and market value at which Sempra may have been able to dispose of its Argentina assets as of 2002 in what might have been characterized as a distress sale.

17.40 *Enron v Argentina*[54] and *LG&E v Argentina*[55] are examples of the no compulsion to buy or sell. In these cases, the tribunal determined that the discount rate should reflect neither the risks of the measures themselves, nor the financial dislocation that preceded the measures.[56]

4. Different opinions with respect to the Chorzów formula

17.41 The *Factory at Chorzów* case has to be seen in the context of the 1919 Treaty of Versailles. Bayerische Stickstoffwerke AG had a long-term contract with the German government to establish and build a nitrates factory at Chorzów on land to be acquired and owned by the German government. The Treaty of Versailles provided for various cessions of German territory to Poland and the right of Poland to confiscate German-owned assets. However, the destiny of Upper Silesia was not clear by that time. In order to bring equilibrium to the region and avoid conflicts, the Geneva Convention of 15 May 1922 was signed and established that

---

52 Marboe (n 6), para 3.163; Diora Ziyaeva, 'Arbitral Tribunals Tend to Pay Lip Service to the Chorzów Factory Full Reparation Principle, This Regarding the Context and Full Implication of the Dictum' (2015) 2(2) *Journal of Damages in International Arbitration* 121, 124 et seq.

53 Professor Pablo T Spiller, Presentation at the 'DC Bar Advanced Seminar on Damages in International Arbitration' (23 January 2019) (Presentation at DC Bar Seminar); *Sempra Energy International v The Argentine Republic*, ICSID Case No ARB/02/16, Award, 28 September 2007.

54 *Enron Corporation and Ponderosa Assets LP v The Argentine Republic*, ICSID Case No ARB/01/13, Award, 22 May 2007, paras 387, 411–12.

55 *LG&E Energy Corp., LG&E Capital Corp., and LG&E International Inc v The Argentine Republic*, ICSID Case No ARB/02/01, Award, 25 July 2007, para 52.

56 Spiller, Presentation at DC Bar Seminar (n 53).

Upper Silesia was supposed to continue as a single economic entity, under which Poland was precluded from conducting seizures of property owned by German nationals. Article 23 further provided that the PCIJ would have jurisdiction over certain disputes. However, Poland expropriated the factory at Chorzów which the German government had previously sold to Oberschlesische Stickstoffwerke and which was managed by Bayerische under a long-term contract, against the outright prohibition of expropriation contained in the Geneva Convention putting in danger the peace in the region.[57]

The arguments against the Chorzów formula are based on the fact that the Geneva treaty established a particular legal regime to protect German interests in Upper Silesia, which was the reason why the Chorzów formula established a high measure of damages, aiming to create balance in the region and avoid possible future World conflicts. Accordingly, such measure of damages is only justified among States that pursue the interest of the international legal order but not for investors who pursue individual commercial interests.[58] However, this argument overlooks that international trade and investment is precisely an important part of the international legal order. Even if the Chorzów dictum was formulated under specific political circumstances, it must be observed that the Chorzów formula follows the development of comparative damages law of that time as confirmed by Professor Hersch Lauterpacht in his work on analogy and his comments on the Chorzów case already mentioned. **17.42**

It has been argued that the Chorzów formula requires to pay the value of the investment at the moment of the award.[59] This is, however, not correct, because as it has been explained in this chapter, the value that has to be taken under the Chorzów formula is the higher between the value as of date of the illegal measure updated to the date of the award, and the value at the date of the award plus the lost profits between the date of the illegal measure and the date of the award, this is in order to place the injured party in the economic position it would be but for the illegal measure, which is in accordance with the full reparation principle. However, it must be observed that taking the date of the award as the date for valuating damages is nothing exceptional, as the valuation of damages at the date of the award is the prevailing standard under comparative law, with even English law moving in that direction.[60] **17.43**

Nearly all investment arbitration cases pay at least 'lip-service' to the *Factory at Chorzów*. The authority of Chorzów not only derives from being authored by the most important tribunal of its time but because of its detailed reasoning and sophistication as regards the formulation of the measure of damages or standard of compensation. It is a matter of its contents and the conclusiveness of the arguments in the Chorzów formula that make it so authoritative. What the Chorzów formula actually establishes without expressly saying so, is that the compensation for legal expropriation is the benchmark value that has to be paid in any case and only if there is reasonable certainty that the investment would have produced a higher value at the date of the award, and there is clear evidence of an illegal measure, then the investor may claim such **17.44**

---

57 Nelson (n 25), 77–80.
58 Amongst others, Ronald EM Goodman and Yuri Parkhomenko, 'Does the Chorzów Factory Standard Apply in Investment Arbitration? A Contextual Reappraisal' (2017) 32 *ICSID Review* 304, 319.
59 Ibid., 320.
60 See the comparative law analysis in: Wöss and others (n 5), Chapter 4 and Chapter 7 of this book.

higher value as has happened in the *ADC v Hungary*,[61] *ConocoPhilipps v Venezuela*[62] and *Yukos v Russia*[63] cases, amongst others. What Chorzów is actually adding is not the fact that damages are being valued at the date of the award, which has been known under many jurisdictions for quite some time, but that the minimum compensation is the one applicable to legal expropriation as the State shall not benefit from the downside in value of an investment that it has expropriated. Under Chorzów, the expropriating State may not argue that the investor would not have recovered its investment. That is one of the novelties introduced by Chorzów.

17.45   Chorzów intends to have a preventive function, establishing a balance between States and investors in order to avoid opportunistic behaviour of States. Without the Chorzów formula the risk of illegal measures would increase, which would make projects more expensive. That would consequently diminish or bar investments which are the engine of economies as already explained in detail at the beginning of this chapter.

17.46   Another criticism of the Chorzów formula is that it is a rigid measure which is limited to the value of the expropriated investment. However, as shown in *Murphy v Ecuador* below, the but-for premise under the Chorzów formula allows targeting the causal effect of the illegal measure in a precise manner and it is not limited to the value of the whole expropriated investment but is equally applicable to partial effects on the investment's value such as in case of indirect expropriation or FET violations. What happens is that in case of expropriation or total destruction of property the actual situation is a zero value of the investment and the hypothetical situation is the total value, which means that the calculation of the FMV of the undertaking suffices. However, in case of FET, indirect or partial expropriation, what is being determined through the but-for premise is precisely the economic difference between the legal situation and the situation under the illegal measure which is often an issue of the intensity of the measure exceeding the illegality threshold as explained below.

17.47   In *El Paso v Argentina*:[64]

> Argentina asserted that there is no causal connection between the GOA [Government of Argentina] measures and the damages allegedly suffered by the Claimant since the latter decided to sell at the worst possible time of the financial crisis, the country's macroeconomic conditions at that time being the cause of the reduced value of its investment.

The tribunal upheld the claimant's expert's but-for approach stating that it was 'satisfied that [the Claimant's expert] has calculated the Claimant's damage under its DCF valuation method by considering only damage directly attributable to the [Government of Argentina] measures, to the exclusion of damage which might be attributable to the financial crisis'. This shows that

---

61   *ADC Affiliate Ltd and ADC & ADMC Management Ltd v The Republic of Hungary*, ICSID Case No ARB/03/6, Award of the Tribunal, 2 October 2006.

62   *ConocoPhillips Petrozuata BV, ConocoPhillips Mamaca BV and ConocoPhillips Gulf of Paria BV v Bolivarian Republic of Venezuela*, ICSID Case No ARB/07/30, Decision on Jurisdiction and the Merits, Award, 3 September 2013, paras 343, 401.

63   *Yukos Universal Ltd (Isle of Man) v Russian Federation*, PCA Case No AA 227, Final Award, 18 July 2014, para 1763.

64   *El Paso Energy International Company v The Argentine Republic*, ICSID Case No ARB/03/15, Award, 31 October 2011.

an experienced and well-qualified expert can only take into consideration the effects of the measure that caused the damages but not the effects of an economic crisis in general.[65]

E. VALUATION APPROACHES TO CALCULATE THE FMV

The value of an undertaking is what it generates or the market pays for it. In case of **17.48** income-generating contracts, assets or investments what is normally lost though the illegal measure are precisely the cash flows as eloquently stated in *Burlington v Ecuador*.[66] The most suitable valuation method depends on the kind of assets being valued. The following methods are frequently used when valuating damages:[67]

(i)   Income approach (DCF): the value of an asset is calculated as the present value of the future cash flows it is expected to generate, discounted to reflect time value of money and riskiness;

(ii)   Relative valuation (Multiples): the value of an asset is calculated based on the price of comparable companies observed through either transaction or stock market multiples;

(iii) Stock Market approach (Market Capitalization): the price of a publicly traded company is estimated in a counter-factual scenario, by assuming prices would have followed a benchmark index;

(iv)   ABV: value is calculated on the company's audited financial statements;

(v)   NCC (Non-Cash Charge): the value of an asset is estimated based on historic investments net of historic distributions updated to a current date to reflect a reasonable rate of return.

With respect to the income-approach, in *Occidental v Ecuador*,[68] the tribunal described the **17.49** DCF as the 'standard economic approach to measuring the fair market value today of a stream of net revenues'. In *Novenergia II v Spain*[69] the tribunal opted for a DCF noting that 'the DCF method is widely supported in professional literature, but more importantly, the method has been broadly accepted by numerous arbitral tribunals'. The tribunal in *Enron v Argentina*[70] noted that

> since DCF reflects the company's capacity to generate positive returns in the future, it appears as the appropriate method to value a 'going concern' as [Transportadora de Gas del Sur/TGS]. Moreover, there is convincing evidence that the DCF is a sound tool used internationally to value companies, albeit, that it is to be used with caution as it can give rise to speculation. It has also been constantly used by Tribunals in establishing the fair market value of assets to determine compensation of breaches of international law.

---

65   Ibid., paras 683, 685.
66   *Burlington v Ecuador* (n 1), para 366.
67   The following paragraphs and case references with regard to the different valuation methods currently used in investment arbitration are taken from Spiller, Presentation at DC Bar Seminar (n 53).
68   *Occidental Petroleum Corporation and Occidental Exploration and Production Company v The Republic of Ecuador*, ICSID Case No ARB/06/11, Award, 5 October 2012, para 708.
69   *Novenergia II – Energy & Environment (SCA) (Grand Duchy of Luxembourg), SICAR v The Kingdom of Spain*, SCC Case No 2015/063, Final Award, 15 February 2018, para 818.
70   *Enron v Argentina* (n 54), para 17.

17.50 In *Tza Yap Shum v Peru*,[71] Tza based its request for damages on the discounted cash flow of TSG, while Peru argued that appropriate standard was the company's adjusted book value. The tribunal rejected Tza's requested damages, which were based on the discounted cash flow of TSG. The tribunal noted that TSG had been operation for only two years during which its cash flow was negative. TGS was also highly leveraged, operated in the high-risk fishing industry and had already begun to lose market share in the industry when SUNNAT imposed its interim measures.

17.51 In relation with the multiple methods, in *Crystallex v Venezuela*,[72]

> the tribunal found that the application of forward-looking methodologies is appropriate to assess the fair market value of Crystallex's investment ... and has come to the conclusion that ... the stock market and the market multiples approaches provide reliable bases upon which to value the Claimant's loss.

In *Windstream v Canada*,[73] 'the Tribunal considers that in the circumstances the Project can be best valued, and the damage to it quantified, on the basis of the comparable transactions methodology'. In *Tenaris & Talta v Venezuela*:[74]

> [t]he methodology and logic of this 'market multiples' analysis is certainly sound in principle, but the Tribunal considers that this approach as applies to Matesi does not adequately take account of the unique market circumstances. ... The Tribunal is not persuaded that the five companies by Claimants' experts provide reliable guidance on the bases of which it might proceed to achieve a satisfactory finding of value in this case.

In *Occidental v Ecuador*,[75] '[t]he Tribunal rejected the use of multiples on the basis of lack of comparability agreeing with Claimant that each oil and gas property presents a unique set of value parameters'.

17.52 With respect to the stock market approach, in *Crystallex v Venezuela*,[76] 'the Tribunal found in this particular case, the stock market approach is a particular appropriate and reliable valuation method, amongst others, because it was a one asset company'. In *Quasar v Russia*,[77] the tribunal adjusted claimant's expert valuation downward by 23 per cent. The Tribunal stated that 'it is the Tribunal's view that this downward adjustment more properly represents the actual value of the Claimant's shares but for the Respondent's expropriatory measures'.

17.53 With respect to the asset approach using Book Value and Adjusted Book Value, in *Tza Yap Shum v Peru*, the tribunal stated that '[i]n light of this, the Tribunal adopted Respondent's position that proper compensation should be based on the TSG's adjusted book value'. In

---

71 *Señor Tza Yap Shum v The Republic of Peru*, ICSID Case No ARB/07/6, Award, 7 July 2011.
72 *Crystallex v Venezuela* (n 3), para 916.
73 *Windstream Energy LLC v Government of Canada*, PCA, Award, 27 September 2016, para 476.
74 *Tenaris SA and Talta-Trading E Marketing Sociedade Unipessoal LDA v Boliviarian Republic of Venezuela*, ICSID Case No ARB/11/26, Award, 29 January 2016, paras 529, 532.
75 *Occidental v Ecuador* (n 68), para 787.
76 *Crystallex v Venezuela* (n 3), paras 889, 895.
77 *Quasar de Valores SCAV SA, Orgor de Valores SICAV SA, GBI 9000 SCAV SA and ALOS 34 SL v The Russian Federation*, SCC Case No 24/2007, Award, 20 July 2012, paras 209–18.

Rusoro v Venezuela[78] the tribunal found that the 'genuine value' of the expropriated investment was a weighted combination of the Book Valuation as a number that derives directly from Rusoro's audited balance sheet, which is frequently found in the valuation of enterprises, however, the downside is that it does not reflect 'the increase in the price of gold and gold mining companies between investment and expropriation, nor the development of mining properties carried out under Rusoro's watch; setting off pros and cons the Tribunal gives it a weighting of 25 per cent'. Another 25 per cent of the weight value was given to the Stock Market Valuation and 50 per cent to the Adjusted Investment Valuation. In *Novoenergia v Spain*[79] the tribunal was not convinced by the argument of an asset-based approach, and instead awarded damages based on a DCF. In *Enron v Argentina*[80] the tribunal was not persuaded by the use of book value or unjust enrichment, because in this case the methodologies did not provide an adequate tool for estimating the market value of TGS' stake. 'The book value of TGS stake is by definition valid for accounting purposes but, as noted by LEGG, fails to incorporate the expected performance of the firm in the future.'

Regarding the cost approach, in *Bear Creek v Peru*[81] the tribunal considered that it was **17.54** not possible to calculate the damages by relying on the expected profitability and the DCF-method.

> [T]he Tribunal concludes that the calculation of Claimant's damages in the present case cannot be carried out by reference to the potential expected profitability of the Santa Ana Project and the DCF method. The Project remained too speculative and uncertain to allow such a method to be utilized. Instead the Tribunal concludes that the measure of damages should be made by reference to the amounts actually invested by Claimant.

In *Caratube v Kazakhstan*[82] the majority of the tribunal considered that claimants did not prove **17.55** with sufficient certainty the damages based on the valuation methods proposed by the claimants:

> ... a majority of the Tribunal agrees that, in the present case, the issue of whether CIOC's damages should be assessed using the FMV standard or a full reparation standard without FMV is in any event of little practical relevance, given that CIOC's claim for compensatory damages is exclusively for lost profits or, alternatively, lost opportunity. A majority of the Tribunal considers that the Claimants have not sufficiently and convincingly established either of these claims. In other words ..., a majority of the Tribunal finds that the valuation methods proposed by the Claimants to determine CIOC's FMV, in any event, do not provide a basis for damages that are sufficiently certain. Therefore, ..., in these circumstances, CIOC's sunk investment cost best express in monetary terms the damages incurred by CIOC as a result of the unlawful expropriation.

---

78   *Rusoro Mining Ltd v The Bolivarian Republic of Venezuela*, ICSID Case No ARB(AF)/12/5, Award, 22 August 2016, paras 771–790.

79   *Novenergia II v Spain* (n 69), paras 775, 837.

80   *Enron v Argentina* (n 54), para 382.

81   *Bear Creek Mining Corporation v Republic of Peru*, ICSID Case No ARB/14/21, Award, 30 November 2017, paras 598–604, 656.

82   *Caratube International Oil Company LLP and Devincci Salah Hourani v Republic of Kazakhstan*, ICSID Case No ARB/13/13, Award, 27 September 2017, para 1087.

17.56 In *Crystallex v Venezuela*[83] the tribunal disregarded the cost approach and focused on forward-looking methodologies.

> The Tribunal considers that in this case only forward-looking methodologies aimed at calculating lost profits are appropriate in order to determine the fair market value of Crystallex' investment. By contrast, a backward-looking methodology such as the cost approach, while susceptible to being utilized in certain circumstances where there is no record of profitability, and while other methodologies would lead to excessively speculative and uncertain results cannot be resorted in this case. The cost approach method would not reflect the fair market value of the investment, as by definition it only assesses what has been expended into the project rather than what the market value of the investment is at the relevant time.

In this case it is important to notice that the tribunal recognized the Chorzów measure of damages as the FMV of the investment. It also recognized the full compensation principle which is also established in the Chorzów formula:[84] which in essence corresponds to the Chorzów formula according to which 'reparation must, as far as possible wipe out all the consequences of the illegal act and re-establish the situation which would, in all probability, have existed if that act had not been committed'[85] which reflects the but-for formula as in order to wipe out all the consequences of the illegal measure it is necessary to calculate the economic difference between the actual economic situation and the economic situation of the injured party but for the illegal measure.

F. THE DISTINCTION BETWEEN LEGAL AND ILLEGAL EXPROPRIATION

17.57 For an expropriation to be considered legal, international law demands: (1) the existence of public interest; (2) the interest is protected in a non-discriminatory manner; (3) in accordance with due process of law; and (4) against the payment of prompt and adequate compensation. The compensation for legal expropriation is normally the FMV of the property before the date of the expropriation or the last 'clean date' updated to the date of the payment of the compensation.[86] The need for a distinction between the compensation for legal and illegal expropriation has been recognized in the *Factory at Chorzów* case, according to which treating legal and illegal expropriation alike:

> would not only be unjust, but also and above all incompatible with the aim of Article 6 [of the Geneva Convention] – that is to say, the prohibition, in principle, of the liquidation of the property – since it would be tantamount to rendering lawful liquidation and unlawful dispossession indistinguishable in so far as their financial results are concerned.[87]

17.58 As shown by Professor Irmgard Marboe there are convincing arguments that there should be a difference between compensation for legal expropriation and damages for illegal expropriation, however, international practice and scholarly writing has not provided a clear answer as to what

---

83 *Crystallex v Venezuela* (n 3), para 882.
84 Ibid., para 849.
85 *Factory at Chorzow* (n 22), 47.
86 Christoph Schreuer, 'The Concept of Expropriation under ECT and other Investment Protection Treaties', in Clarisse Ribeiro (ed), *Investment Arbitration and the Energy Charter Treaty* (Juris Publishing 2006), 108.
87 *Factory at Chorzow* (n 22), 47.

the difference should be and how it should be calculated.[88] For example, Judge Brower at the Iran-US Claims Tribunal argued in his Separate Opinion in *Sedco v NIOC* that the distinction between lawful and unlawful expropriation was necessary, otherwise 'the injured party would receive nothing additional for the enhanced wrong done and the offending State would experience no disincentive to repetition of unlawful conduct'.[89] In this respect modern economic theory and valuation expertise is of relevance according to which the value 'must be assessed with reference to expectations regarding the revenues that the property would have generated in the future. To award the former owner anything less would, in effect, be to confiscate a portion of his property without compensation'.[90]

As regards the argument that the mere failure to pay compensation does not justify the application of the Chorzów formula,[91] as a general rule, there is a requirement that the payment of the compensation for expropriation be made promptly under most IIAs and the Hull formula. Some authors argue that in case all requirements for legal expropriation are met and only the payment is late, the compensation for expropriation and not damages under the Chorzów formula should apply which is reflected in some arbitral awards.[92] Therefore, the question whether the violation of the prompt payment obligation renders an expropriation unlawful is a matter of definition of the international law standard, and not a matter of international damages law. The question arises whether customary international law has changed with respect to the requirement of prompt payment or not. **17.59**

In this respect, it has to be mentioned that in at least three decisions where expropriation was found in awards published in 2018, the tribunal decided that the respondent's failure to pay compensation rendered the expropriation unlawful, regardless of whether such expropriation was direct or indirect. In *Olin v Lybia*,[93] the tribunal stated that the failure to pay adequate, prompt and effective compensation would render any expropriation unlawful and would give rise to international liability. In *South American Silver v Bolivia*,[94] the State argued that its participation in the arbitration fulfils the compensation requirement, which was rejected by the tribunal, which held that Bolivia did not fulfil its compensation requirement under the Treaty. Furthermore, the tribunal held that customary international law applied as compensation standard for unlawful expropriation.[95] In *UP and CD Holding v Hungary*,[96] the tribunal stated that '[a]lthough it can be argued that the failure to pay compensation should not render an otherwise lawful expropriation unlawful, Respondent has never even offered Claimants **17.60**

---

88 Marboe (n 6), paras 3.81–96 with further references.
89 *Sedco Inc v NIOC*, Second Interlocutory Award, Separate Opinion Brower, (1986) 10 Iran-USCTR 189, footnote 40, cited in Marboe (n 6), para 3.82.
90 William C Lieblich, 'Determinations by International Tribunals of the Economic Value of Expropriated Enterprises' (1990) 7 *Journal of International Arbitration* 37, 47–8.
91 David Kachavani, 'Compensation for Unlawful Expropriation: Targeting the Illegality' (2017) 32 *ICSID Review* 385.
92 August Reinisch, 'Legality of Expropriations', in August Reinisch (ed), *Standards of Investment Protection* (Oxford University Press 2008), 199; Audley Sheppard, 'The Distinction between Lawful and Unlawful Expropriation', in Ribeiro (n 86), 171.
93 *Olin Holdings Ltd v State of Libya* (ICC Case No 20355/MCP), Final Award, 25 May 2018, para 135.
94 *South American Silver Limited v The Plurinational State of Bolivia*, PCA Case No 2013-15, Award, 30 August 2018, paras 608, 610.
95 Ibid., para 801.
96 *UP and CD Holding International v Hungary*, ICSID Case No ARB/13/35, Award, 9 October 2018, paras 410, 419.

compensation. Accordingly, Respondent committed an unlawful expropriation contrary to Art. 5(2) of the BIT'.

17.61 The damages case should be a mirror-image of the liability case and the question whether damages are due for the violation of the prompt payment obligation is not a matter of damages but of the determination of liability. When all the requirements for legal expropriation but the prompt payment of compensation have been met, one solution in search of fairness could be to value the expropriated undertaking at the date of expropriation and then update it till the payment date at a reasonable rate which should not be lower than the discount rate, otherwise, this would result in considerable under compensation.

G. CONSIDERATIONS WHEN CALCULATING DAMAGES

1. The role of interest rates as a means to achieve full reparation

17.62 The value of any good depends on the price given by the market or by the cash flows it generates. This means that the future cash flows generated by the good should be discounted at a reasonable interest rate at a certain date in order to obtain the present value of that good. The same applies with respect to the value of an undertaking, whose value depends on the cash flows it generates. In this sense, if valuation is made before the award, for example, the date of the illegal measure, that value has to be updated till the date of payment. In order to meet the full reparation principle, the interest rate used for updating the discounted cash flows should be the same or very similar to the one used when discounting the cash flows. If the interest rate used to update the cash flows was lower than the discount rate, it would result in under compensation.

17.63 If the date of the award is the date chosen to value the undertaking, the future cash flows till the end of the project should be considered and should be discounted at a reasonable interest rate as of the date of the award, and the cash flows between the date of the breach and the date of the award should be updated to the date of the award at a reasonable interest rate. The total amount of the discounted and updated cash flows would be the value of the undertaking. Even if under both scenarios the cash flows are the basis for the valuation of the undertaking, these can vary depending on the information and assumptions used in order to calculate them, which must in any case be reasonable and in accordance with the evidence available.

2. The use of hindsight information

17.64 If the date of valuation is the date of the illegal measure but calculations are being made some time after that date, and the use of hindsight information between the date of the illegal measure and the date of the calculation of damages results in a higher value than the one that would have been obtained without considering such information, not considering hindsight information would result in unfairness against the injured party as the State would obtain windfall profits. On the other hand, if the use of hindsight information would lower the value of the undertaking and this information is not being taken into consideration, it would result in unfairness against the State as the injured party would get the windfall profits. If there is hindsight information it has to be used so it avoids uncertainty and places the injured party in the position it would be in but for the illegal measure which would bring balance, certainty and fairness to both sides at least during the period of time that hindsight information is available. The use of hindsight information when the valuation is the date of the illegal measure and calculations are made after that date, could increase or decrease the value of the undertaking. Both scenarios could happen, but using hindsight information reduces speculation.[97]

If the decision is to use hindsight information, then it should be used in both, the actual and **17.65** the but-for scenarios, in order to obtain consistency. If the decision is not to use hindsight information, then it should not be used in the actual nor in the but-for scenario, again for the sake of consistency. Not using hindsight information in the actual scenario would bring unrealistic results, which would add speculation. It has to be noted, that the rejection of hindsight information in the US derives from criminal law and refers to ex-post qualification of a crime, that is criminal liability.[98] In this respect it has to be observed, that in the context of damages valuation, hindsight refers to the consideration of the economic circumstances between the date of the illegal measure and the date of valuation, it does not apply to the determination of liability and the arguments against hindsight in criminal law are not applicable to the determination of damages.

3. The Chorzów formula together with the but-for premise serve to calculate damages caused by the violation of the FET standard and indirect expropriation

The but-for premise referred to in the Chorzów formula applies to all kinds of illegal measures **17.66** and is not limited to illegal expropriation or the determination of the value of the whole undertaking. In case of indirect expropriation or violation of FET, multiple measures may take place. Each of these measures has a different economic impact on the investment and this increases the complexity of valuating damages. The Chorzów formula together with the but-for method serves to identify the impact of the different measures and to quantify the effect of those measures that constitute indirect expropriation or a violation of FET. Comparing the situation taking into consideration the effects of those measures and the situation without the measures under indirect expropriation or violation of FET through the but-for premise, allows to determine causation of damages and experienced experts should be able to quantify the respective effects.

This is illustrated in cases such as *Murphy v Ecuador* where the tribunal found that the first tax **17.67** increase to 50 per cent was legal and the second increase to 99 per cent was violating the FET standard. Therefore, the quantification of damages was only the difference between the illegality threshold and the illegal tax. A similar situation applies in the Spanish energy cases whereby the first government decrees were considered legal and subsequent measures illegal which has a direct effect on damages. These cases will be analysed in detail further below.

97   See also Manuel A Abdala, 'Damages in Energy and Natural Resources Arbitration', in Trenor (n 13), 351.
98   See, amongst many, Megan E Giroux and others, 'Hindsight Bias and Law' (2016) 224(3) *Zeitschrift für Psychologie* 190 <https://www.researchgate.net/publication/309539553_Hindsight_Bias_and_Law> accessed 21 July 2019.

4. Do early investments have a value?

17.68 With respect to the question whether early investments have a value, in particular, investments that were frustrated at a pre-operative stage, the point is that the risk of a project certainly increases, or, in other words, there are additional contingencies that may bar the success of the investment. This situation has to be considered when calculating future cash flows, determining the corresponding discount rate or when comparing the investment to similar undertakings. However, it is not enough reason to discard the value of an investment simply because it is an early investment. As shown in *Crystallex v Venezuela*,[99] where a so-called event study was used, early investments may have a value.[100]

17.69 Sometimes illegal expropriation or illegal measures take place at an early stage of investment. In that respect, some tribunals see problems in granting compensation due to the uncertainty involved with respect to the generation of future cash flows,[101] while others consider this as part of the opportunity recognized in the contract. The fundamental point, however, in early investments is whether there was a probability that the early investment would have been successful without the illegal measure and what would have been the value without the illegal measure. In other words, absent any illegal measure, would the owner of the project sell the project to a third party, and in that case what price would it be able to obtain?[102] What is important to consider is that there are methods and experts capable of dealing with uncertainty. In these cases the challenge for the arbitral tribunal is to be able to analyse these scenarios, to ask the right questions of the experts and to assess the value of an early investment, because it is important to bear in mind that not because it is an early stage investment it would not have any possibilities of success and any value at all. In this respect, claimants should prove with reasonable certainty that without the illegal measure the investment would generate an income stream of cash flow, and, therefore, it would have had a value. This may require the use of econometric methods such as the Monte Carlo method.[103]

17.70 *Crystallex v Venezuela* is an example of damages valuation through stock market valuation, where the tribunal accepted the 'build up' of the stock market price performed by claimant's experts, which tracked Crystallex' actual stock market price movement up to the last trading date free of any threat of the unlawful act, known as the 'last clean date', which was some days after the company announced that it had complied with all the requirements to obtain the permit to exploit the gold mine (2007), and then make it evolve according to the relevant industry index till the date of the announcement from the government of Venezuela that Crystallex would not get the permit to operate. For the arbitral tribunal such a build-up is appropriate to reflect a but-for scenario. This scenario was compared with the actual market capitalization of Crystallex and the economic difference calculated by the experts. The arbitral

---

99   *Crystallex v Venezuela* (n 3).

100   With respect to new valuation methods such as events studies, see Spiller and Dellepiane (n 26), paras 6.197–213.

101   For example, *PSEG Global Inc v Republic of Turkey*, ICSID Case No ARB/02/5, Award, 19 January 2007.

102   Spiller and Dellepiane (n 26), para 6.121.

103   For the use of novel valuation approaches including econometric methods such as the Monte Carlo method and its application in *Turkmenistan v Bridas* (n 105 below), see: Wöss and others (n 5), paras 5.46–5.56; Garrett Rush, Kiran Sequeira and Matthew Shopp, 'Valuation for Early-Stage Businesses in Investor-State Arbitration', in Beharry (n 49), 262, and Noah Rubins, Vasuda Sinha and Baxter Roberts, 'Approaches to Valuation in Investment Treaty Arbitration' in Beharry, ibid., 171, 202–4.

tribunal considered that in this particular case, the stock market approach reflects the market's assessment of the present value of future profits discounted for all publicly known or unknown risks. It also considered this method appropriate because Crystallex was a one-asset company and the right to extract gold was the single asset and thus any buyer would have acquired the entire value of Crystallex to exploit the gold mine and would be interested exclusively on the basis of that single asset. Furthermore, Crystallex' stock was actively traded on two main stock exchanges for mining companies, so there were enough transactions to provide sufficient pricing information.[104]

In this respect, it is important to underline that in case of natural resources the mere fact of their existence indicates a value as shown in Crystallex. However, this has to be analysed on a case-by-case basis. For example, in *Bridas v Turkmenistan*,[105] which is not investment arbitration, but a good example of an investment related to gas reserves, no expectation interest was granted although it was proved with reasonable certainty that there were gas reserves. No expectation interest was granted because it was not proved with reasonable certainty that this gas could be sold to Western Europe due to lack of access to gas pipelines. Still in *Bridas* the reliance interest in form of the sunk investment was granted which was also the case with *PSEG Global v the Republic of Turkey*.[106] **17.71**

5. What interest is intended to represent

According to the full reparation principle, the appropriate interest rate is the one that would place the injured party in the economic position it would be but for the illegal measure at the moment of the award.[107] As stated by leading economists: **17.72**

> when a valuation date is chosen at a date that is far apart in time from the date of the award, the selection of the pre-judgment [interest] plays a central role in the amount of compensation. A wrong interest rate could result in a monetary award that does not fully restore the position of the damaged party in the absence of the measures.[108]

In many cases, the injured party has operated a business:

> which has been deprived of some or all of its cash flows. Any company borrows money at any time to operate, either from the shareholders or from the bank. Money is never provided for free. This means that the injured party has a financing cost equivalent to the cost of capital of the affected business or WACC.[109]

The WACC that should be used is the one of a similar and efficiently managed company in the same sector. The WACC has both the cost of borrowing money from the bank, as well as

---

104 *Crystallex v Venezuela* (n 3), paras 889–895.
105 *Joint Venture Yashlar (Turkmenistan), Bridas SAPIC (Argentina) v The Government of Turkmenistan (or Turkmenistan, or the State of Turkmenistan and/or The Ministry of Oil and Gas of Turkmenistan)*, ICC Case 9151/FMS/KGA, Final Award, 18 May 2000, paras 174, 176–178; 151, 359.
106 *PSEG v Turkey* (n 101), paras 317–337.
107 Wöss and others (n 5), para 7.11.
108 Manuel A Abdala, 'Key Damage Compensation Issues in Oil and Gas Arbitration Cases' (2009) 24(3) *American University International Law Review* 540.
109 Ibid., 566.

from the shareholders and as it is the weighted average of both of them that will be considered as the source of financing. The application of the WACC makes the injured party whole and is an instrument commonly used in finance. When the full reparation principle is used to guide the award of compensation in investment arbitration, the arbitral tribunal must think about the capital supplied from the moment of investment to the time of the award.[110] This requires considering pre-award interest as part of the damages analysis using a common approach to the cost of capital.[111]

H. THE BUT-FOR PREMISE, CAUSATION AND THE ILLEGALITY THRESHOLD

17.73 The objective of the but-for method is to build a scenario that takes into account the world as it is, except for the economic and financial implications that could arise from a hypothetical circumstance where the illegal measure had not occurred and to compare with actual scenario affected by the illegal measure. However, the application may not be that simple, in particular, because of lack of information and the inability to disentangle the effects of specific illegal measures from other forces affecting the business.[112]

17.74 Under the but-for premise, the question to be asked is what would have happened in the absence of the breach which refers to causality. If the claimant would be in the same economic situation without the breach, there would be no causation. The loss must be properly attributable to the illegal measure. Liability is to the extent that losses would have been avoided in the absence of the illegal measure. If the loss would have occurred even in the absence of the illegal measure then there is no damage to be compensated.[113]

17.75 Causation is not only a requirement for the recovery of damages but has also implications on the amount or extent of damages to be recovered. If through the application of the but-for premise only partial causation is proved, this may lead to the substantial reduction of the damages claim. This situation is intimately related to contributory negligence of the injured party, where the difficulty lies in the construction by the State of hypothetical concurrent causation situations in order to prove that the injured party caused its own loss. For example, in the case of a badly managed company, where even in the absence of the illegal measure there would have been no cash flows.[114] Once the hypothetical situation has been reconstructed and compared to the actual situation, if there is a difference, there is a loss. That is why the but-for premise serves as a means to determine whether there is an actual loss caused by the illegal measure and to which extent.

17.76 Damages are a mirror image of the liability case. They not only depend on the finding of illegality, but in some cases also on the determination of the illegality threshold by the arbitral tribunal. Temporal and subject matter limitations of the liability findings have a direct impact on damages due to the causality requirement applied through the but-for premise.

---

110   Wöss and others (n 5), para 7.12.
111   Mick Smith and Romans Vikis, 'Whose Money is it and Should it Matter? An Essay on the Cost of Capital in International Arbitration' (2014) 1(2) *Journal of Damages in International Arbitration* 77.
112   Spiller and Dellepiane (n 26), paras 6.29–30.
113   Wöss and others (n 5), para 5.61, footnotes omitted.
114   Ibid., para 5.63.

The illegality of a measure under the indirect expropriation and FET standards depends to a **17.77** large extent on the intensity of the measure. Only when a certain intensity threshold is reached will the arbitral tribunal make a finding of violation which raises the question of the determination of a legal threshold measure that would not be considered a violation, and the moment when such illegality threshold has been surpassed which defines the date of the illegal measure. The first aspect has been illustrated by one of the authors as follows: in a telecommunications investment arbitration case (*Telefónica v Mexico*[115]), the issue at stake is the considerable and discriminatory reduction of interconnection tariffs for market participants of 70 per cent. If the arbitral tribunal would find a 70 per cent discriminatory tariff reduction to represent a violation of the FET Standard, the question arises where to set the benchmark for illegality. If set at 50 per cent, would the damages be in the amount corresponding to the 70 per cent price reduction, or just 20 per cent (the difference between 50 and 70 per cent). The choice between the two approaches is certainly significant. According to a proper application of the but-for premise, the result would be that the damages correspond to the 20 per cent differential.[116]

This approach has been espoused in the landmark case *Murphy v Ecuador*[117] where the measure **17.78** at stake was legislation enacted by the Ecuadoran government known as Law 42 that provided that Ecuador would participate in the Consortiums' profits from the sale of crude oil if the market value of oil exceeded a reference price. Under the Participation Contract, the Consortium would receive a share of the production calculated on the basis of the volume of production and without regard to oil prices. Initially the government set the level of its participation at a minimum of 50 per cent. Several months later the government raised the level of its participation to 99 per cent.[118]

Murphy argued that Law 42 constituted a unilateral and unlawful modification of the **17.79** Participation Contract by Ecuador and had a significantly detrimental effect on the financial performance of claimant's investment. It sold its investment in March 2009 to a third party. Murphy claimed that Law 42 breached Ecuador's obligations under the Treaty and sought reparation in the form of compensation for (1) the payments Murphy Ecuador made to Ecuador under Law 42, (2) the cash flows it would have received through Murphy Ecuador from the date of its sale through the end of the Participation Contract's term, and (3) interest.[119]

The arbitral tribunal found that Murphy had a legitimate expectation to full ownership of a **17.80** percentage of its production through participation. Claimant would assume any decrease in the price of crude oil as well as the benefit of any increase. It further stated that following the enactment of Law 42 and Decree No. 1672 as of 25 April 2006, the Consortium was entitled to only 50 per cent of the 'extraordinary' income generated from sales of its production share, which does not fundamentally change the operation of the Participation Contract. The Consortium was still able to earn more revenue with Law 42 at 50 per cent than it did before

---

115 *Telefónica SA v United Mexican States*, ICSID Case No. ARB(AF)/12/4.
116 Herfried Wöss, 'Systemic Aspects and the Need for Codification of International Tort Law Standards in Investment Arbitration' (2016) 1 *TDM* (CETA Special Volume), 1, 3, 4–5, 10.
117 *Murphy v Ecuador* (n 2).
118 Ibid., paras 82–112.
119 Ibid., para 415.

the oil price rise. The tribunal, therefore, did not consider that the enactment of Law 42 at 50 per cent breached claimant's legitimate expectations.[120]

17.81 The arbitral tribunal, however, found that Law 42 and Decree 662 issued in October 2007 raised the State's participation in the extraordinary income to 99 per cent, which fundamentally changed the nature of the Participation Contract and occurred within the context of an increasingly hostile and coercive investment environment. Law 42 at 99 per cent breached clause 10.1 of the Participation Contract pursuant to which claimant had the right to 'freely dispose of the Crude Oil that corresponds to it', subject to domestic supply needs, and clause 10.23 which guaranteed claimant the full value of its share of production. It also ran afoul of the domestic legal regime, as well as the promise under Article II (3) of the Treaty to accord claimant's investment fair and equitable treatment. The tribunal found that Ecuador breached the FET standard under said article with the Law 42 at 99 per cent.[121]

17.82 When determining damages, the tribunal finds that the applicable standard for compensation is the *Factory at Chorzów* case citing Article 31 of the ILC Articles, which means it applied the but-for premise comparing the economic situation of Murphy in the absence of a violation of the FET Standard with the Law 42 at 50 per cent (but-for situation) and the Law 42 at 99 per cent (actual situation). This also means that the arbitral tribunal determined as but-for situation from a legal point of view the Law 42 at 50 per cent and not the situation without the law imposing a participation of Ecuador in the Consortium's profits from the sale of crude oil.[122] As regards the moment of the illegal act, the tribunal did not take into consideration any government measures that pre-dated the second tax increase and, therefore, fixed the illegality threshold as regards the intensity of the measure and its time aspect.

17.83 This approach of determining a legal threshold scenario has also been applied in some of the Spanish renewable energy cases, whereas only measures that exceeded the illegality threshold would give rise to damages. The issue is that different arbitral tribunals determined the legal threshold situation in a different way. In *Eiser v Spain* the arbitral tribunal stated that:

> the Respondent 'crossed the line' and violated the obligation to accord fair and equitable treatment at the point in June 2014 when the prior regulatory regime was definitely replaced by an entirely new regime. The Tribunal had not found that the several piecemeal changes made by the Respondent prior to that time, individually or collectively, violated the ECT.[123]

In *Novoenergía*, the arbitral tribunal found that the pre-2014 measures did not 'fall outside the acceptable range of legislative and regulatory behaviour' and did not violate the FET standard.[124] In *Masdar*, the tribunal considered some of the pre-2014 measures exceeding the illegality threshold which led to a considerably higher award, which confirms that the raising

---

120 Ibid., paras 273, 278.
121 Ibid., paras 281–282.
122 Ibid., para 423.
123 *Eiser Infrastructure Ltd and Energía Solar Luxembourg Sàrl v Kindom of Spain*, ICSID Case No ARB/13/36, para 458.
124 *Novenergia II v Spain* (n 69), paras 685–689.

or lowering of the illegality threshold reduces or increases damages. This also confirms that the damages case is a 'mirror-image' of the liability case in the context of a tort-law system.[125]

In this respect the tribunal finds that as regards the restitution of the Law 42 payments up to the sale of the company in 2009, Murphy would receive the differential amount it had overpaid less adjustments for taxes. As regards the lost cash flows from March 2009 to January 2012, the arbitral tribunal found that the valuation at the date of the award is not appropriate in this case because the *ex-post data* does not reflect what the situation would have been in a but-for scenario, due to the sale of Murphy Ecuador on 12 March 2009 and would determine the market value as of that date. However, the Tribunal admits that it has considered the information that became known after the valuation date (*ex-post* data), in particular, as regards the development of oil prices and oil production levels.[126] **17.84**

The arbitral tribunal further considers that the fair market value approach values an asset by considering its ability to generate future economic benefits, which allows to determine the 'free cash flows' generated by the asset. The arbitral tribunal found it then appropriate to determine the fair market value of Murphy Ecuador on 12 March 2009 and then compare it with the actual sales prices for the company. The arbitral tribunal found the respondent's expert calculation of the 'but-for' value of Murphy Ecuador in the absence of Law 42 is reasonable and convincing. The value-drivers considered in this case are (i) the expected production of crude oil, (ii) the expected oil-market prices, (iii) the expected capital expenditures ('Capex') and operating expenses ('Opex'); and (iv) taxes, levies and other liabilities.[127] **17.85**

I. CONTRACT AS INVESTMENT

Income-generating contracts are investments.[128] Their scope and contents determine the extent and limitation of property in international investment law. In particular the underlying contractual risk allocation may not be ignored by an arbitral tribunal. The violation of an international law standard leads to a reduction or the elimination of the income stream of the investment. What has to be analysed in the context of investment contracts with respect to damages, is the effect of the illegal measure on the investment that is represented by an income generating contract. This issue is different from the question whether the violation of a contractual right may lead to a violation of an international law standard, which is a liability issue beyond the scope of this chapter.[129] **17.86**

---

125 Wöss and others (n 5), 1, 5–6, 8; see also: Sergey Ripinsky, 'Damages Assessment in the Spanish Renewable Energy Arbitrations: First Awards and Alternative Compensation Approach Proposal' (2018) *TDM* (provisional), subsequently published in (2020) 2 *TDM*.

126 *Murphy v Ecuador* (n 2), paras 484, 487.

127 Ibid., para 494.

128 San Román and Wöss (n 27), 37–9; Herfried Wöss and Devin Bray, 'Investment Protection and the Mexican Energy Reform' (2018) 12(1) *Dispute Resolution International*, 49; See also Wöss and others (n 5), Chs 3 and 5, which develop an international damages doctrine for income-generating investments.

129 Stanimir Alexandrov, 'Breach of Treaty Claims and Breach of Contract Claims, When Can an International Tribunal Exercise Jurisdiction?' in Katia Yannaca-Small (ed), *Arbitration under International Investment Agreements – A Guide to Key Issues* (2nd edn, Oxford University Press 2018) 370.

17.87   This has recently been illustrated in the landmark *Mobil v Venezuela* case,[130] in particular, in its Decision on Annulment, which will be analysed in detail in this section due to its importance for damages analysis. The recognition by the Annulment Committee of the contents of the contract as the scope and limits of the investment and property has a direct effect on compensation as only rights that were duly granted may be expropriated.

17.88   In *Mobil v Venezuela*, claimants submitted that the series of production and export curtailments imposed by the respondent on the Cerro Negro Project from late 2006 through the first part of 2007 reduced its production by approximately 560,000 barrels of extra-heavy crude oil in 2006, as compared with the production target for 2006 and reduced its exports by about 5.5 million barrels of synthetic crude oil by the end of June 2007 when compared with the export target for the first half of 2007. Claimants contended that these production and export cuts violated both the Framework of Conditions of the Cerro Negro Project and the Association Agreement, which permitted production cuts only if they were necessary to comply with Venezuela's international commitments, and only if they were applicable on a *pro rata* basis to all producers in Venezuela. Claimants argued that they were in breach of FET as well as arbitrary and discriminatory treatment violating Article 3(1) of the BIT.[131]

17.89   In its analysis of whether legitimate expectations of the investor might have been violated, the tribunal refers to the Framework of Conditions of the Association Agreement for the exploitation, upgrading and marketing of extra-heavy crude oil to be produced in the Cerro Negro area of the Orinoco Oil Belt as approved by the Congress of Venezuela on 24 April 1997. According to clause 8 of the Association Agreement, the level of production was fixed at 120,000 barrels per day. The tribunal concluded that, when making their investment, the claimant could reasonably and legitimately have expected to produce at least 120,000 barrels per day of extra-heavy crude oil and that their production would not be unilaterally reduced at a lower level except as provided for in condition thirteen of the Framework of Conditions. It found that the November 2006 production curtailment and the January 2007 and March 2007 export curtailments were not shared on a *pro rata* basis as required by condition thirteen of the Framework of Conditions and were incompatible with the claimant's reasonable and legitimate expectations, and breached the FET standard contained in Article 3(1) of the BIT which made respondent liable for the damages resulting from such breach.[132] The tribunal also found that respondent's conduct was arbitrary and discriminatory which is an additional ground of violation of Article 3(1) of the BIT, which, however, does not give rise to additional damages.[133]

17.90   The damages were calculated applying the but-for premise whereby '[t]he expert calculates the volume of extra-heavy oil that the Cerro Negro project would have produced between October 2006 and June 2007 had the curtailment not been imposed, and determines the corresponding curtailed SCO sales'. The tribunal made adjustments to the experts' calculations in particular as regards to the hypothetical situation in the absence of the illegal measure which would not be a production of 120,000 barrels per day of EHCO, but the lower *pro rata* production cut legally

---

130   *Mobil v Venezuela* (n 4).
131   Award of the Tribunal in *Mobil v Venezuela* (n 4), paras 249–50.
132   Ibid., paras 258, 260, 263–264.
133   Ibid., para 272.

imposed in accordance with condition thirteen of the Framework of Conditions as a result of an OPEC decision. The resulting lost SCO sales of US$30,781,144 were adjusted to production cost, taxes, co-production royalties and extraction tax, as well as the income tax.[134]

The claimants further submit that Venezuela breached Article 6 of the BIT by wrongfully **17.91** expropriating its investment in the Cerro Negro and La Ceiba Projects through Decree-Law 5200 in June 2007. Respondent argues that the expropriation was lawful.[135] The tribunal finds that claimants did not receive compensation and that Venezuela did not fulfil its obligation to pay compensation in accordance with Article 6(c) of the BIT. Nevertheless, it considers that:

> the mere fact that an investor has not received compensation does not in itself render an expropriation unlawful. An offer of compensation may have been made to the investor and, in such a case, the legality of the expropriation will depend on the terms of the offer. In order to decide whether an expropriation is lawful or not in the absence of payment of compensation, a tribunal must consider the facts of the case.[136]

Decree-Law 5200 did not envisage compensation but discussions took place between the parties on the compensation that was due to the claimants on account of the expropriation which led the tribunal to consider the expropriation as legal.[137]

As regards damages, finding the expropriation lawful, the tribunal did not have to engage in an **17.92** analysis of the *Factory at Chorzów* measure of damages relied on by claimants,[138] but applied the compensation for lawful expropriation established in Article 6 of the BIT which must 'represent the market value of the investment affected immediately before the measures were taken or the impending measures became public knowledge, whichever is the earlier'. This was to be determined immediately after the failure of the negotiations between the parties and before the expropriation, that is on 27 June 2007, which requires to calculate the net cash flows in form of the future revenues and expenses of the Cerro Negro Project, which are determined by the volume of the production of oil and by the oil price level, the cost of the operations, the capital investment, if any, and the royalties and taxes to be paid to the government.[139]

The net cash flows had to be discounted to its value in June 2007. In this respect, the expert of **17.93** the claimants argued that the appropriate discount rate is the cost of capital which is defined as the expected rate of return with the same risk as the project to be determined using the capital asset pricing model (CAPM), which depends upon three components: the ratio of return for risk free investments, the market risk premium that is generally expected by investors and a measure of a particular investment's contribution to the risk of a diversified portfolio, which is known as the beta value and arrived at a discount rate in June 2007 of 8.7 per cent.[140] The

---

134 Ibid., paras 266–270.
135 Ibid., para 279.
136 Ibid., para 301.
137 Ibid., paras 288–306.
138 Ibid., para 288, footnote 348.
139 Ibid., paras 307–359.
140 Ibid., paras 360–361.

respondents arrived at a discount rate of 19.8 per cent by considering the country risk as a particular risk issue, which is the risk of uncompensated expropriation.[141]

17.94 In this respect the tribunal observed that applying the willing buyer–willing seller formula, at the time before the expropriation had happened or before it had become public that it would occur 'that the risk of a potential expropriation would exist and this hypothetical buyer would take it into account when determining the amount he would be willing to pay in that moment'. It considers that the confiscation risk remains part of the country risk and must be taken into account in the determination of the discount rate and arrives at a discount rate of 18 per cent arriving to a discounted net cash flow of US$1,411.7 million, and US$179 million for the La Ceiba project.[142]

17.95 In this respect, it is interesting to observe that in *Mobil v Venezuela* the tribunal mentioned that the FMV had to be calculated. However, FMV was in fact not calculated, because the tribunal stated that the value should be what a willing buyer and a willing seller would pay under expropriation risk. This is contradictory, as under the FMV any economic distress situation including imminent expropriation risk should not be considered. Therefore, what the tribunal determined was the market value and not the FMV.

17.96 The key issue in the *Mobil v Venezuela* case was, however, the importance and effect of the price cap established in the Cerro Negro Association Agreement which had the effect of a liquidated damages clause. In this respect, the respondent argues that the price cap set forth in the Cerro Negro Association Agreement in implementation of the twentieth condition of the Cerro Negro Congressional Authorization is applicable in this case. The eighteenth condition of the Association Agreement establishes that:

> it shall not be considered that a Party has suffered an adverse and significant economic consequence as a result of any said decisions or changes in legislation, at any time when the Party is receiving income from THE ASSOCIATION equal to a price of crude oil above a maximum price that shall be specified in the Association Agreement.

According to respondent, this limitation was embodied in clause 15(2)(a) of the Agreement, which establishes that, under certain conditions, 'compensation would not be granted for any fiscal year if the price of the benchmark crude oil (Brent) has exceeded US$27 per barrel in 1996 dollars (corresponding to US$25.07 in 2007 dollars)' and should apply to compensation.[143]

17.97 Claimants submit that respondent was not a party to the Cerro Negro Association Agreement and that his case does not involve a claim under clause 15 of the Association Agreement which means that the price cap is not applicable. According to respondent the issue is not one of enforcing a contract but a question of respecting the terms and conditions under which the project was authorized. This would also certainly affect the value of the interest in the Mobil Cerro Negro project.[144]

---

141   Ibid., para 362.
142   Ibid., para 365.
143   Ibid., para 369.
144   Ibid., para 370.

The tribunal acknowledges that the twentieth condition of the Congressional Authorization **17.98** refers to the income to be provided to the parties by the association and to a price cap to be established in the Association Agreement. Clause 15(1) of the Association Agreement makes a clear distinction between the action that the foreign party may initiate against Lagoven CN on the one hand, and the action that it may initiate against the government on the other. It observes that the price cap contained in clause 15(2)(a) is applicable only to the compensation payable to Lagoven CN. Since the respondent in this proceeding is the Bolivarian Republic of Venezuela, not Lagoven CN, the tribunal concludes that it may not oppose this price cap to the claimants and maintains the compensation to be paid by the respondent for the expropriation of the Cerro Negro Project which is US$1,411.7 million.[145]

As regards Venezuela's argument, that the Cerro Negro Conditions 'import the contractual **17.99** limitations to PDVSA-CN'2 indemnity obligations under clause 15 of the CNAA into the State's responsibility for breach of the Treaty', the tribunal concludes:

> The Tribunal recalls that it is a fundamental principle of international law that a party may not invoke the provisions of its internal law as justification for its failure to perform a treaty. Under this principle, international obligations arising from a treaty cannot be discarded on the grounds of national law. Among the legal systems on which the Award shall be based pursuant to Article 9(5) of the Treaty, ... the Tribunal has no doubt in concluding that this issue must be governed by international law. Consequently, the Eighteenth and Twentieth Conditions cannot exempt or excuse the Respondent from its obligations under the Treaty or under customary international law.[146]

The Decision on Annulment in *Mobil v Venezuela* made important findings with respect to the **17.100** effect of contractual price caps and similar clauses such as liquidated damages formulas, as well as the scope and content of income-generating investments in form of contracts which espouses the doctrine established by the authors in previous publications, according to which the scope and limits of income generating contracts also represent the scope of limits of the investment.

Respondent argues in the annulment procedure that the tribunal did not apply the applicable **17.101** law and the special agreement relating to the investment of the Mobil Parties in the Cerro Negro Project, thereby disregarding the basic terms and conditions on which that investment was authorized.[147] According to the applicant, Article 9(5) of the Dutch Treaty required that the Award be based 'not only on the provisions of the Dutch Treaty and international law', but also on Venezuelan law and 'the provisions of special agreements relating to the investments'. The tribunal disregarded the compensation structure for the Cerro Negro Project applicable under Venezuelan law and the special agreement on compensation for the Cerro Negro Project, namely the Cerro Negro Association Agreement, as authorized by the Cerro Negro Congressional Authorization.

In particular, respondent alleges that '[a] party cannot claim compensation for the expropri- **17.102** ation of rights it never had'. In this respect, the relevant enquiry is not 'whether a particular asset qualifies as an investment under the Treaty but rather what that asset consists of'. It

---

145 Ibid., paras 373, 404.
146 Ibid., para 225.
147 Decision on Annulment *in Mobil v Venezuela* (n 4), para 36.

further states that '[w]hat the asset consists of (or the scope of the rights attached to it) is determined by national law, not international law. International law can only provide protection for rights recognized by domestic law, but not create new property rights or expand existing property rights'. It argues further that the tribunal 'determined the extent of compensation due for the expropriation of the respondents' rights under international law, in reliance on the fundamental but irrelevant principle that a State may not invoke its internal law as an excuse to escape international obligations'[148] that an investor's property rights are defined by local law or its corollary and that an investment treaty merely protects these rights but does not create or expand them.

17.103 According to respondent, the Cerro Negro Congressional Authorization and the Cerro Negro Association Agreement establish the terms and conditions of the Cerro Negro Project, including its compensation structure and the price cap on compensation for governmental action affecting the project. The issue to be decided by the Annulment Committee is 'whether there was any basis for the tribunal to disregard the terms and conditions established for the Cerro Negro Project pursuant to the Cerro Negro Congressional Authorization'.[149]

17.104 In its deliberations, the Annulment Committee acknowledges that the issue of the 'Tribunal's flawed approach to the assessment of compensation for expropriation' which is over 'the nature and magnitude of the compensation due'. The Committee considers that the project was subject to certain legal provisions, that is the Cerro Negro Congressional Authorization (a formal decision by which the Venezuelan legislature approved the project, as required by Venezuelan law) and the Cerro Negro Association Agreement (the contractual agreement under which the Mobil Parties and the Venezuelan State entity Lagoven CN entered into and undertook the project). The latter:

> required the parties to that Agreement to carry out the Project 'under the terms ... and in accordance with the requirements set forth in the Venezuelan nationalization law of 1975, and the Conditions ... defined in terms as those set forth in the decision of 2 October 1997 by which the Venezuelan Congress approved the Agreement and authorized Lagoven to enter into it (the Cerro Negro Congressional Authorization).[150]

17.105 According to the Committee, the key issue to be considered is 'what exactly was the investment that had been expropriated and how was it to be valued for compensation purposes'. It takes as a 'starting point that the classification of an investment as a form of property is indisputably correct. Even if the property is incorporeal or intangible, and consists merely of a collection of rights, the proposition remains unaffected'. In particular, the Committee 'does not see that there can be any reasonable basis for contesting that the bundle of rights constituting the Cerro Negro investment was created by or under Venezuelan law and, having been so created, was then a type of property recognized and protected by international law in the form of the BIT'. It accepts the reasoning of Venezuela according to which an investment is of its very nature, an item of property and the definition of the scope and contents of such property is an 'inescapable precondition to any assessment of its value, and specifically of its "market value" under Article 6(c) of the BIT'. Moreover, property is not created by international law but the role of

---

148   Ibid., paras 43–45, 47.
149   Ibid., paras 46–48.
150   Ibid., paras 137–139.

international law is to recognize property created and defined by national law. This has consequences with respect to compensation,[151] which was reduced to some US$200 million.

The Committee finds that the portions of the Award dealing with the compensation due for **17.106** the admitted (and lawful) expropriation of the Cerro Negro Project are so seriously deficient in both their reasoning and in the choice of the appropriate resources of law under the BIT as to give rise to grounds for annulment.

This ruling of the Annulment Committee is highly important. First, it recognizes the effect of **17.107** the scope of contractual limitations on damages. Second, it considers that the bundle of contractual rights and obligations on which the investment is based represents property and defines the scope, contents and limits of property and the investment. Income-generating contracts are recognized as income-generating assets or investments. This also establishes a precedent for the limitation of damages in investment arbitration through sophisticated liquidated damages formulas contained in investment contracts.

The creation of property rights through contracts is recognized in international law amongst **17.108** others in *Company General of the Orinoco*, where the French-Venezuelan Mixed Claims Commission determined that the government of Venezuela owed compensation for its unilateral repudiation of a concession agreement, which was to be 'commensurate to the damages caused by the act of the respondent government in denying efficacy to the contract.' In *Shufelt*, the government of Guatemala nullified a concession agreement that it had concluded with a US investor. In considering whether Shufeldt has 'acquire[d] any rights of property under the contract' for the purposes of pecuniary indemnification, the tribunal found that '[t]here can not be any doubt that property rights are created under and by virtue of a contract'. In *SPP v Egypt* an ICSID tribunal found that it has 'long been recognized that contractual rights may be indirectly expropriated'.[152]

The Annulment Committee decision in *Mobil v Venezuela* seems to be the first decision where **17.109** the contents, scope and limits are considered in a comprehensive form as understood by project finance lawyers, banks and infrastructure project specialists and represents a significant progress with respect to the analysis of investment contracts and project agreements in investment arbitration.

J. CONCLUSIONS

The role and function of international damages law in investment arbitration is bringing **17.110** balance between the State and investors which in turn protects the economy. The mere fact of establishing legal certainty and predictability with respect to damages avoids transaction costs and leads to a more efficient economy. The Chorzów formula is not just the result of a certain historical situation that aimed at preventing conflicts in Upper Silesia but is the result of the

---

151 Ibid., paras 163, 168, 172–173.
152 Cases cited in this paragraph: *Opinion of the Umpire, Company General of the Orinoco Case (France v Venezuela)* (1906) 10 *Reports of International Arbitral Awards* 250, 282; *Shufeldt Claim* (US v Guatemala) (1930) 2 Reports of International Arbitral Awards 1081, 1097; *Southern Pacific Properties (Middle East) Ltd v Arab Republic of Egypt*, ICSID Case No ARB/84/3, Award, 20 May 1990; cited in Alexandrov (n 129), paras 15.08–15.09.

development of damages law throughout history that serves to prevent opportunistic behaviour of the State that would prejudice investments and economies. In this regard, the measure of damages established by the landmark *Factory at Chorzów* case maintains its authority and usefulness. The particularity of Chorzów is not that it allows valuation of damages on the date of the award, which is known under many applicable laws, but that the compensation for expropriation is the benchmark value that has to be paid in any case.

17.111   The Chorzów formula as the measure of damages in investment arbitration has two main elements: FMV and the date of valuation. With respect to the first, the FMV is implicit in Chorzów through the use of the hypothetical normal course of events originally developed under German law and which means that distress situations that negatively affect the value of the investment are not going to be taken into consideration when valuating damages in unlawful expropriations and other illegal measures. The modern notion of FMV first appeared in 1980 in *American International Group v Iran* and *Starrett Housing v Iran* and derives from US legal practice. In leading investment arbitration cases distress is considered when projecting future cash flows, but not in the discount rate as economic crises or situations of distress do not last forever and, therefore, it is considered that the discount rate should be normalized in the long run. This means that the FMV would be the price between a willing buyer and a willing seller both under no distress and without the need to sell or buy, while the market value, on the other hand, would fully consider economic distress.

17.112   With respect to the date of valuation, the Chorzów formula does not establish that the only date for valuing damages is the date of the award but the higher value between the date of the illegal measure updated till the date of the award and the date of the award plus lost cash flows between the date of the illegal measure and the date of the award. It goes without saying that the post-award interest should apply in order to make the injured party whole.

17.113   The full reparation principle which applies through the but-for premise is contained in the Chorzów formula when stating that the aim of damages compensation is to wipe out all the consequences of the illegal act, which, in other words means, to place the injured party in the economic position it would be but for the illegal measure. This is achieved by the application of the but-for method which compares the actual economic situation of the injured party taking into consideration the illegal measure, and its economic situation without the illegal measure. Chorzów is not a rigid method that only serves to calculate the value of the undertaking at the moment of the award or the moment of the illegal measure, but together with the but-for premise, as explained in detail in this chapter and as applied by leading cases, allows to quantify only the effects of indirect expropriation and FET violations. However, in the latter situations it will be important to establish the illegality threshold as was first suggested by one of the authors for *Telefónica v México*, applied in *Murphy v Ecuador* and the Spanish renewable energy cases.

17.114   The use of hindsight information may increase or decrease the value of an investment. There is no obligation nor restriction to use hindsight information or not to omit it. However, the use of hindsight information would reduce speculation when calculating the cash flows[153] in case it is available. Whatever the decision made, the use or rejection of hindsight information must be

---

153   Abdala (n 97).

consistent, that is, if it is used it has to be taken into consideration in both scenarios, the but-for and actual scenarios, and if it is decided not to take it into consideration, it should be avoided in both.

The purpose of interest rates is to make the injured party whole. Any investment or company **17.115** has a cost of capital which means that money is borrowed from the banks or from the shareholders but is not given for free. The WACC represents the cost of operating any company and in this sense the WACC of an efficient company in the same sector is a reasonable interest rate to be used when trying to place the injured in the economic position it would be in but for the illegal act.

With respect to a newly established company, econometric methods may be used in order to **17.116** determine if the investment is likely to produce an income stream with reasonable certainty which would show whether the investment has a value or not.

The requirements for legal expropriation are mentioned in this chapter and in case that only **17.117** the payment of the compensation is being late a potential solution is being suggested, which could be to calculate the FMV at the date of the illegal measure updated at an appropriate interest rate till the date of its payment.

As regards the notion of contract as investment, this chapter contains an extensive analysis of **17.118** the landmark *Mobil v Venezuela* case that espouses prior publications of the authors and confirms that the bundle of rights and obligations, as well as the content and limitations of income-generating contracts represent the property or investment in investment arbitration. This also means that the arbitral tribunal has to deal with contractual risk allocation and limitations when making the damages analysis and should not ignore those elements and factors. This also means that contractual liquidated damages formulas are relevant in investment arbitration.

Finally, this chapter contains a reference to valuation methods being used in recent leading **17.119** investment arbitrations as presented by Professor Pablo T Spiller at a recent advanced seminar on damages held by the authors in Washington DC, which shows that the most suitable valuation method depends on the kind of asset being valued and the particular economic circumstances surrounding the valuation.

18

ESSENTIAL ELEMENTS OF TAXATION – INVESTMENT PROTECTION AND DISPUTE SETTLEMENT

Stefano Castagna[*]

A. INTRODUCTION

18.01 When matters of investment and international operations are intertwined with elements of taxation, thorny issues tend to present themselves at the practitioner's doorstep. Investment arbitration is sufficiently complex by itself, as are international tax arbitration cases. The reciprocal impact and potential interactions between international investment arbitration and international taxation is a topic where one must humbly[1] acknowledge that there will never be a hard drive large enough to store all solutions to all issues that might arise.[2] It might be difficult even for the best practitioner to anticipate how the tax liability in relation to the damages awarded to a claimant by an investment tribunal will be treated by the jurisdictions involved, or how a tax administration will address the taxation of a given operation between multiple related entities. One should therefore be particularly careful in managing risk. On the other hand, investment tribunals have struggled to juggle maintaining equilibrium between the rights of claimants and respondents in various instances, including tax audits and indirect

---

[*] Date of submission: 25/05/2020.

[1] For a discussion on humility, knowledge and deficiency, see Thomas Aquinas, *Summa Theologiae* (New York: Benziger Brothers 1911–1925) IIa-IIae Q 161.

[2] Just for the record, the OECD has specifically addressed possible overlaps in relation to international taxation and the international trade regime. See OECD, *Model Tax Convention on Income and on Capital* (OECD Publishing 2017), Commentary to art 25 paras 88–94.

expropriation cases. It is striking, however, that only in the recent past has academia begun to recognize the importance of knowing the main aspects of and interplay between taxation and investment arbitration. Relevant sums of money are at stake when taxation issues are argued in investment cases, and there is much that the dispute settlement regimes of both specialties of law may benefit from considering the best practices adopted by the other.

This chapter will focus first on providing an introduction to the most relevant issues that could **18.02** arise in relation to tax and international investment, giving particular weight to investment protection standards. It will then turn to consider international tax dispute resolution, and thirdly how the particular characteristics of this latter regime may be helpful in the context of the international investment arena.

B. TAX WITHIN INTERNATIONAL INVESTMENT PROTECTION

1. Protection of investment and taxation in international investment agreements

a. *Jurisdiction of investment tribunals over tax matters and topical exclusions of jurisdiction*

In investment arbitration, host States are generally held accountable for measures taken against **18.03** a foreign investor whose rights were guaranteed through a promise of the host government, either through local legislation, international treaty or contract. Any contested measure falling within the scope of an IIA, will likely be subject to the scrutiny of an international arbitral tribunal or court having jurisdiction over the matter, including tax measures, in the absence of a specific carve-out.

There is however no uniform definition of 'tax' nor 'tax measure' within the realm of **18.04** international investment law.[3] Some instruments provide for a limited definition. An example is given by the Energy Charter Treaty (ECT) at Article 21.7 for the very purpose of a tax carve-out, which states:

> (a) The term 'Taxation Measure' includes: (i) any provision relating to taxes of the domestic law of the Contracting Party or of a political subdivision thereof or a local authority therein; and (ii) any provision relating to taxes of any convention for the avoidance of double taxation or of any other international agreement or arrangement by which the Contracting Party is bound.[4]

It is even harder to find a definition of what is 'tax'. This might be problematic in cases where **18.05** one has to distinguish between what is 'tax', what is a 'fee' and other financial disbursements, such as special levies (often known as 'royalties').[5] To distinguish what is a tax from what is not a tax, one should look at the substance of the measure itself[6] and not formal labels, especially considering the scope and the aim of the protections accorded to the investor by parties to the

---

3   Paul HM Simonis, 'BITs and Taxes' (2014) 42 *Intertax* 234, 240.
4   Energy Charter Treaty (adopted 17 December 1994, entered into force 16 April 1998) 2080 UNTS 95, art 21.
5   Thomas Wälde and Abba Kolo, 'Coverage of Taxation Under Modern Investment Treaties', in Peter Muchlinski, Federico Ortino and Christoph Schreuer (eds), *The Oxford Handbook of Investment Law* (OUP 2008) 317.
6   Ibid., 319.

agreement. In addressing the matter, tribunals and courts have also resorted to the host State's definition of tax, even through the analysis of use of characterizations by local courts.[7]

18.06 A substantive analysis should be not only necessary when deciding whether a given measure is a tax measure and has impacted the operations of an investor in violation of its rights,[8] but also when assessing whether a given tax-related item in a balance sheet can be deemed an investment. *Per se* tax advantages, credits and other rights should ordinarily not be considered 'investments' under an International Investment Agreement (IIA): these are not part of the operations of an investor, but impact on it only. Therefore, there should generally be no jurisdiction of an investment tribunal in case the issue relates to tax liabilities, credits or advantages *per se*, meaning deemed by themselves *as a protected investment*. This especially if one considers the objective and purpose of the agreement as part of the interpretative process of a treaty.[9] IIAs aim at promoting investment which parties expect will (potentially) generate value, and they usually state in the agreement that such aims are the reasons for which the agreement has been signed. Obtaining or using tax benefits should not be sole or near-exclusive purpose of a protected investment. This notion might be relevant in peculiar, but possible circumstances. In the Republic of Italy, as in many other jurisdictions, there have been cases where the value of a company was essentially the tax-loss carryforward that it had (so-called 'tax coffins', or *bare fiscali* in Italian). This carryforward could not be used, because the company was constantly operating at loss and often had no expectation of improvement. Corporations generating a high amount of taxable revenue would merge with such a company to gain a tax advantage paying a portion of the tax loss carryforward to the owner of the 'coffin', being able to use the rest to abate their own taxable income. The tax regime has changed with the introduction of what is now Article 172.7 of Presidential Decree n. 917 of 1986 to avoid such use of M&A operations.

18.07 Investments on essentially valueless companies, but for the possible connected tax benefits for which they could be used, should not be ordinarily considered falling within the notion of 'investment' unless there are other material reasons for the 'investment' to have taken place. In fact, as noted in the case of Value Added Tax (VAT) refunds, the OEPC tribunal found, amongst other VAT related decisions, that:

> [i]t is not tenable to argue that there can be 'no doubt that under the Treaty the Refund Claim is an investment per se'. However broad the definition of investment might be under the Treaty it would be quite extraordinary for a company to invest in a refund claim.[10]

---

7 *Antaris Solar GmbH and Dr Michael Göde v Czech Republic*, PCA Case No 2014-01, Award, 2 May 2018, para 242. The tribunal has also found that while the contested measure was a tax under local law, it was not a tax under the ECT, since it had not the aim to collect revenue but reduce the level of Feed-in Tariffs that were payable to the investor (see para 253). Available at: <https://www.italaw.com/cases/2080> accessed 15 May 2020.

8 See as e.g., *Occidental Exploration and Production Company (OEPC) v The Republic of Ecuador* LCIA Case No UN3467, Final Award, 1 July 2004 (*OEPC v Ecuador*), paras 86–88, available at: <https://www.italaw.com/sites/default/files/case-documents/ita0571.pdf> accessed 15 May 2020.

9 In this regard see, consider Tarcisio Gazzini, 'Objects(s) and Purpose(s)', in Tarcisio Gazzini (ed) *Interpretation of International Investment Treaties* (Hart Publishing 2016) 157.

10 *OEPC v Ecuador* (n 8), para 86. The tribunal found, however, that there had been other kinds of breaches in relation to the VAT refund scheme.

One might say that this view was confirmed by the *EnCana* tribunal, which too ruled over whether Ecuadorian VAT refunds fell within the scope of the relevant Bilateral Investment Treaty (BIT), when it stated that 'the corresponding right to be paid is capable of falling within the broad scope of "amounts yielded by an investment"'.[11] Therefore, the general key element to consider with regard to questions that are clearly pertaining to tax-related rights only, is whether the tax-related issues have a direct link to the operations of the protected investment and impact its (expected) cash flows owed to the investor. This of course unless the IIA, the applicable law and/or other applicable agreement state, or can be interpreted to mean, otherwise.

As noted above, States may exclude taxation issues from the scope of the protection of IIAs or the jurisdiction of any tribunal. States may also decide to expressly bind themselves to given tax-related commitments, such as the stabilization of their tax regime vis-à-vis an international investor. Therefore, the definition of 'tax' will be relevant only if an exception applies. **18.08**

There may be several types of exclusions of tax matters within an IIA. There may be general exclusions, such as that present in the Cambodia-Singapore BIT[12] ('[t]he provisions of this Agreement shall not apply to matters of taxation in the territory of either Contracting Party. Such matters shall be governed by any Avoidance of Double Taxation Treaty between the two Contracting Parties and the domestic laws of each Contracting Party'), specifications as to what treaty will prevail (e.g., India-Iceland BIT,[13] which reads '[n]othing in this Agreement shall affect the rights and obligations of either Contracting Party derived from any tax convention. In the event of any inconsistency between the provisions of this Agreement and any tax convention, the provisions of the latter shall prevail'), specific exclusions based on the type of tax or protection (e.g., Canada-Tanzania BIT,[14] which reads at Article 14.4 'the provisions of Articles 4 (National Treatment) and 5 (Most Favoured Nation Treatment) shall apply to all taxation measures, other than taxation measures on income, capital gains or on the taxable capital of corporations'), and the combination of exceptions within exclusions. **18.09**

An additional limitation often found is a tax veto, also referred to as 'joined tax consultation'.[15] This is typically not present to limit the substantive rights of an investor, but to impede or limit the investor's ability to file a claim through investment arbitration. An example of such provision can be found in the Japan-Peru BIT of 2008 at Article 23.5(b):[16] **18.10**

---

11 *EnCana Corporation v Republic of Ecuador* LCIA Case No UN3481, Award 3 February 2006, paras 180–183, available at: <https://www.italaw.com/sites/default/files/case-documents/ita0285_0.pdf> accessed 15 May 2020.

12 Agreement between the Government of the Kingdom of Cambodia and the Government of the Republic of Singapore on the Promotion and Protection of Investments (adopted 4 November 1996, entered into force 24 February 2000), art 5.2.

13 Agreement between the Government of the Republic of India and the Government of the Republic of Iceland for the Promotion and Protection of Investments (adopted 29 June 2007, entered into force 16 December 2008), art 4.4.

14 Agreement between the Government of Canada and the Government of the United Republic of Tanzania for the Promotion and Reciprocal Protection of Investments (adopted 17 May 2013, entered into force 9 December 2013), art 14.4.

15 Stefano Castagna, 'ICSID Arbitration: BITs, Buts and Taxation: An Introductory Guide' (2016) 7 *Bulletin for Internal Taxation* 375.

16 Agreement Between Japan and the Republic of Peru for The Promotion, Protection and Liberalisation of Investment (adopted 21 November 2008, entered into force 10 December 2009), available at: <https://investmentpolicy.unctad.org/international-investment-agreements/treaty-files/1733/download> accessed 15 May 2020.

[t]he investor shall refer the issue, at the time that it delivers the notice of intent under Article 18, to the competent authorities of both Contracting Parties to determine whether such [tax] measure is not an expropriation. If the competent authorities of both Contracting Parties do not consider the issue or, having considered it, fail to determine, within a period of 180 days of such referral, that the measure is not an expropriation, the investor may submit its claim to arbitration under Article 18. (c) For the purposes of subparagraph (b), the term "competent authorities" means: (i) with respect to Japan, the Minister of Finance or his or her authorised representatives, who shall consider the issue in consultation with the Minister for Foreign Affairs or his or her authorised representatives; and (ii) with respect to the Republic of Peru, the Minister of Economy and Finance (el Ministro de Economía y Finanzas), or his or her authorised representatives.

18.11   Finally, it should be noted that often IIAs guarantee the right to transfer capital, profits, interests and other type of financial flows to ensure the effectiveness of the rights of the investor. Such right, however, is at times expressly subject to the previous satisfaction of all tax liabilities to be borne by the investor itself.[17]

18.12   When no exception applies, other sources of law which relate to tax – other than the BIT – may also be applicable to interpret the standards of investment protection under the IIA. This means that even tax treaties will be considered part of the law applicable to the investment.[18] In such cases, tax disputes of foreign investors may be decided not only within the dispute resolution tools proper of Double Tax Treaties (DTTs), but through those of IIAs. It might also be possible, even with the presence of fork in the road provisions,[19] that the investor/ taxpayer may have the possibility to try and obtain relief through the use of both regimes, since it is likely that there will not be any specific exclusion addressing the reciprocal use of the two tools, and surely dispute resolution tools under DTTs are not domestic remedies.

b.   Consequences of the jurisdiction of international investment arbitral tribunals

18.13   Often, State 'measures' from which investors are protected in BITs and other IIAs include procedures and practices of the contracting parties.[20] Tax imposition alone may be considered

---

17   As an e.g., see the Agreement between the Government of the Republic of Azerbaijan and the Government of the Syrian Arab Republic on the Promotion and Reciprocal Protection of Investments (adopted 8 July 2009, entered into force 4 January 2010), art 8.3(a).

18   Arno E Gildemeister, 'Chapter 12: Germany', in Michael Lang et al (eds) *The Impact of Bilateral Investment Treaties on Taxation* (IBFD 2017) 309.

19   These clauses provide that if the investor chooses to settle its claims through local court proceedings, the choice is final. See Christoph Schreuer, 'Travelling the BIT Route: Of waiting periods, Umbrella Clauses and Forks in the Road' (2004) 5 *Journal of World Investment and Trade* 240. One should note that fork in the road provisions may vary widely in terms of language, and therefore a thorough case-by-case analysis should be considered.

20   See, e.g., Agreement between Canada and the Slovak Republic on the Promotion and Protection of Investments (adopted 20 July 2010, entered into force 14 March 2012) art I (f); The Comprehensive Economic and Trade Agreement between the EU and Canada (CETA) [2017] OJ L11/23, art 1.1 'measure', available at: <http:// trade.ec.europa.eu/doclib/docs/2014/september/tradoc_152806.pdf> accessed 15 May 2020; Agreement for the Promotion and Protection of Investment between the Republic of Austria and the Federal Republic of Nigeria (adopted 8 April 2013), art 1 (f)7, available at: <https://investmentpolicy.unctad.org/international-investment-agreements/ treaty-files/2972/download> accessed 15 May 2020.

tantamount to expropriation, with the condition that there is proof that 'as a direct consequence of the measures complained of [,] Claimant was deprived of its investment'.[21] In
addition, issues can arise when the government or parliament takes action in passing a bill or
law, or in relation to the behaviour of the tax authorities or tax tribunals.[22] This was the case of
Mr Tza Yap Shum against Peru. In this particular case, the local tax authority, named
Superintendencia Nacional de Aduanas y de Administración Tributaria (SUNAT) found irregularities during a tax audit, and as a consequence had *de facto* caused the interruption of
the operations of the business of Mr Sum. The tribunal found that jointly to the violations of
the investors' rights by the SUNAT, the tax tribunal called to decide on the appeal against the
measures of the tax authority had failed to perform a substantive review of the SUNAT's
actions and had not provided a truly reasoned decision on the matter. Consequently, there had
also been a violation of the right of access to courts granted under the relevant BIT.[23] There
have also been instances in which a breach of National Treatment standards occurred due to
tax imposition, such as the presence of excise taxes that could not be rebated – a possibility
instead granted to national comparable operators.[24] Tribunals have also found that Fair and
Equitable Treatment (FET) clauses in BITs can be breached through the imposition of tax
measures or the denial of certain tax benefits, such as in the case of withdrawal of a VAT
certificate.[25]

Practices in tax assessment and tax valuation may put a contracting party in the position of **18.14**
having violated the rights of an investor. This especially if there is a deviation from binding
standards that have been codified and are routine in procedures such as tax audits. In addition,
institutions such as the EU Joint Transfer Pricing Forum, which assists and advises the
European Commission on transfer pricing matters, regularly issue documents on standards of
treatment of assessment in international and domestic taxation, promoting best practices
which are *per se* non-binding, however.[26]

Another institution that has drafted soft law guidelines is the Organisation for Economic **18.15**
Cooperation and Development (OECD). For example, in its latest version of the Transfer

---

21 Denying the presence of indirect expropriation measures, *Link-Trading Joint Stack Company v Department for Customs Control of the Republic of Moldova*, UNCITRAL, Final Award, 18 April 2002, para 91, available at: <https://www.italaw.com/sites/default/files/case-documents/ita0468_0.pdf> accessed 15 May 2020.

22 See *CMS Gas Transmission Company v The Republic of Argentina* ICSID Case No ARB/01/8, Decision of the Tribunal on Objections to Jurisdiction, 17 July 2003, para 108:

> In so far as the international liability of Argentina under the Treaty is concerned, it also does not matter whether some actions were taken by the judiciary and others by an administrative agency, the executive or the legislative branch of the State. Article 4 of the Articles on State Responsibility adopted by the International Law Commission is abundantly clear on this point. Unless a specific reservation is made in accordance with Articles 19, 20 and 23 of the Vienna Convention on the Law of Treaties, the responsibility of the State can be engaged and the fact that some actions were taken by the judiciary and others by other state institutions does not necessarily make them separate disputes. No such reservation took place in connection with the BIT.

Available at: <https://www.italaw.com/cases/288> accessed 15 May 2020.

23 *Mr Tza Yap Shum v Republic of Peru* ICSID Case No ARB/07/6, Award (Spanish), 7 July 2011, para 238.

24 See *Marvin Feldman v Mexico* ICSID Case No ARB (AF)/99/1, Award (English), 16 December 2002, para 173.

25 This was one of the elements through which the tribunal found a breach FET clause in *Biwater Gauff (Tanzania) Ltd v United Republic of Tanzania*, ICSID Case No ARB/05/22, Award, 24 July 2008, para 814; for denial of tax benefits, see *OEPC v Ecuador* (n 8).

26 EU, 'EU Joint Transfer Pricing Forum: Report on the Use of Comparables in the EU' (JTPF/007/2016/FINAL/EN, 2016) 3.

Pricing Guidelines (TPG), the OECD highlights that even when cooperation of the taxpayer during an audit is necessary, in any event the tax administration should not 'seek to impose such a high level of cooperation that would make it too difficult for reasonable taxpayers to comply'.[27] If it is up to the taxpayer to prove that there has been tax compliance, tax administrations can raise assessments only when these are soundly grounded in law.[28] The OECD further notes that good faith principles should guide both tax administrations and taxpayers in assessing tax issues during audits.[29]

18.16 Similar, but more detailed standards have been codified in non-binding instruments by the European Commission itself, such as the Guidelines for a Model for a European Taxpayers' Code, which are considered an aspiration to follow and provide 'a core of principles, which compiles the main existing rights and obligations that govern the relationships between taxpayers and tax administrations' and are an instrument that 'expects to provide European citizens with a convenient source of knowledge on the main rights and obligations they can expect when dealing with a tax administration in a Member State other than their State of residence'.[30] The guidelines include, inter alia, model standards of conduct for audits and court and tribunal review. Although not part of a treaty or binding instrument, these principles might be of interest to an international tribunal for comparison between the actual treatment of an investor-taxpayer and what treatment should be expected by international standards for the purpose of ascertaining violation of rights such as FET standards.[31]

18.17 In addition, it should be noted that concepts related to FET and issues that are connected to investor expectations may arise from the complex structure of the multi-layered relationship of Member States of the European Union and the Union itself. This is the case of a recent State aid decision of the General Court of the European Union following the submission by the investor affected by the European Commission decision on the Fiat Finance and Trade (FFT) case, where the company now known as Fiat Chrysler Finance Europe, member of the FIAT Group, had reached an Advanced Pricing Arrangement (or 'APA', which will be addressed in section C.1) with Luxembourg.[32] The agreement ascertained the taxable base for some operations of the group, but was found in violation of EU law by the Commission. The Commission's decision, according to the Court, did not violate the party's

---

27 OECD, *OECD Transfer Pricing Guidelines for Multinational Enterprises and Tax Administrations* (OECD Publishing 2017), chapter IV section B2 paras 4.11–14.

28 Ibid.

29 Ibid.

30 Commission, 'Guidelines for a Model for A European Taxpayers Code' Ref Ares (2016) 6598744, available at: <https://ec.europa.eu/taxation_customs/business/tax-cooperation-control/guidelines-model-european-taxpayers-code_en> accessed 15 May 2020.

31 As soft law practices and documents, at least under the definition of Marc Jacob and Stephan Schill. For a discussion on the role of such type of uses see José Enrique Alvarez, 'Reviewing the Use of "Soft Law" in Investment Arbitration' (NYU School of Law, Public Law Research Paper No 18-46, 2018), available at: <https://ssrn.com/abstract=3258737> accessed 15 May 2020.

32 See State aid SA.38375 (2014/C ex 2014/NN) which Luxembourg granted to Fiat (notified under document C (2015) 7152) Commission Decision 2016/2326 [2015] OJ L351/1, available at: <http://ec.europa.eu/competition/state_aid/cases/253203/253203_1757564_318_2.pdf> accessed 15 May 2020; the judgment of the General Court (Seventh Chamber, Extended Composition) in Cases T-755/15 and T-759/15 *Grand Duchy of Luxembourg and Fiat Chrysler Finance Europe v Commission* [2019] ECLI:EU:T:2019:670, available at <http://curia.europa.eu/juris/document/document.jsf?text=&docid=218102&pageIndex=0&doclang=EN&mode=lst&dir=&occ=first&part=1&cid=362281> accessed 9 May 2020.

rights. In its suit, claimant argued, amongst other things, that its legitimate expectations had been violated by the European Commission, since the APA had been agreed upon under the best practices of the OECD which had been allegedly adhered to by the Commission until then ('the contested decision breaches the principle of legitimate expectations since the Commission has created a legitimate expectation that for State aid purposes it assesses transfer pricing arrangements on the basis of the OECD Guidelines and its sudden departure from this has breached the principle of legitimate expectations'[33]). This obviously does not mean that a 'legitimate expectation' standard under EU State aid[34] when applied in the context of tax law is equivalent to that of international investment law, but it must be noted that there can be significant amount of interplay between the various specialities, as noted in the introduction.

2. The effect of tax liability on full compensation and damages valuation

Taxation is not just a matter of substantive rights in investment arbitration. It also impacts on **18.18** the worth of the damages provision of an award. This is particularly relevant since investment arbitration is used as a means to make up for a financial loss. If a claimant is to be successful in obtaining an award on damages, the tribunal will have typically ruled on the *an* (whether damages are due) and the *quantum* (amount) due. However, taxes will typically be owed on the damages awarded, and if full compensation must be accorded to the investor, such tax liability must be considered when rendering an award.[35] This with the view that the claimant will be compensated for any additional tax that it will have to pay due to the award, versus what it would have paid had the violation not occurred.

The quantification of such additional tax liability may be complex to calculate, as taxation **18.19** typically is connected to a given local territorial reality[36] and the type of investment structure might have changed over time and be quite articulated,[37] which might entail issues of double-taxation, often governed by DTTs. Article 13 of the Model Tax Convention regulates

---

33 Case T-759/15 *Fiat Chrysler Finance Europe v Commission* [2015] OJ C 59/49, available at: <https://eur-lex.europa.eu/legal-content/EN/TXT/PDF/?uri=CELEX:62015TN0759&from=EN> accessed 15 May 2020.

34 See for a brief analysis Commission (EU), 'Notice from the Commission – Towards an effective implementation of Commission decisions ordering Member States to recover unlawful and incompatible State aid' [2007] OJ C272/4, para 17, available at: <https://eur-lex.europa.eu/legal-content/EN/TXT/PDF/?uri=CELEX:52007XC1115(01)&from=EN> accessed 15 May 2020.

35 Eddie Tobis, 'Avoiding Double Taxation on International Arbitration Awards' (2017) 4 *Journal of Damages in International Arbitration* 16.

36 Edoardo Traversa and Alice Pirlot, 'Chapter 6: Tax Sovereignty and Territoriality under Siege: How Far Should the EU Freedoms of Movement Impact on the Territorial Allocation of Taxing Powers between Member States?' in Cécile Brokelind (ed) *Principles of Law: Function, Status and Impact in EU Tax Law* (IBFD 2014) 125.

37 Tobis (n 35) 18.

the right to tax capital gains, including those deriving from expropriation.[38] However, arbitral tribunals appear to neglect an analysis of the role of possibly applicable DTTs.[39]

18.20   The issue pertains not just as to which jurisdiction will have the right to tax (or claims to have such right), but also as to which entity will ultimately bear the tax liability on the damages awarded. An additional matter to consider in quantifying the amount of damages suffered might be whether there has been a mitigation of losses from a tax perspective within the overall multinational group to which a claimant might belong. As an example, some jurisdictions enable the deduction of the losses incurred by subsidiaries from the calculation of taxable profits of the mother company.[40]

18.21   Another additional issue that could be relevant is how the jurisdiction having the right to tax the amount awarded will treat the damages granted: whether as income, capital gain or other category,[41] or whether the investor will have the right to a rollover, and thus subject to tax liability further in the future.[42]

18.22   Consequently, tax liability must always be assessed, if necessary, on a case-by-case basis, with particular prudence as to the use to adequate counsel and expert opinion in understanding the interplay between the structure of the investment and the liability arising upon claimants.[43] There is no general rule to answer what amount of tax will be due and by whom. It is necessary to understand how the consideration of the potential tax treatment will affect the net amount of compensation of final award rendered by the tribunal on a case-by-case basis. This safeguards both the host state and the claimant's rights. One should also note that tribunals have at times not accepted the idea that one should take into consideration the impact of tax

---

38   OECD Model Tax Convention (n 2), Commentary to Article 13, para 5 reads:

> [t]he Article does not give a detailed definition of capital gains. This is not necessary for the reasons mentioned above. The words 'alienation of property' are used to cover in particular capital gains resulting from the sale or exchange of property and also from a partial alienation, the expropriation, the transfer to a company in exchange for stock, the sale of a right, the gift and even the passing of property on death.

39   Consider the position of claimant in the annulled award *Occidental Petroleum Corporation Occidental Exploration and Production Company v The Republic of Ecuador*, ICSID Case No ARB/06/11, Award, 5 October 2012, paras 850–853 (*Occidental v Ecuador*), available at: <https://www.italaw.com/sites/default/files/case-documents/italaw1094.pdf> accessed 15 May 2020; *Mobil Investments Canada Inc & Murphy Oil Corp v Government of Canada*, ICSID Case No ARB(AF)/07/4, Decision on Liability and on Principles of Quantum (redacted), 22 May 2012, available at: <https://www.italaw.com/sites/default/files/case-documents/italaw1145.pdf> accessed 15 May 2019.

40   Consider a related issue from a tax perspective addressed in Case C-446/03 *Marks & Spencer plc v David Halsey (Her Majesty's Inspector of Taxes)* [2005] ECLI:EU:C:2005:763 available at <http://curia.europa.eu/juris/showPdf.jsf?text= &docid=57067&pageIndex=0&doclang=en&mode=lst&dir=&occ=first&part=1&cid=15639586> accessed 25 May 2020. See also for a discussion of the Marks & Spencer case, Michael Lang, 'Has the Case Law of the ECJ on Final Losses Reached the End of the Line?' in Madalina Cotrut (ed) *ECJ direct tax compass 2014* (IBFD tax travel companions 2014) 530.

41   Adam Scherer and Shane Rayman, 'Tax Implications of Expropriation' (2008) 56 *Canadian Tax Journal/Revenue Fiscale Canadienne* 870, 883.

42   As in the case of South Africa. See South African Revenue Service, Guide to Capital Gains Tax (2000), 13. Available at: <http://www.treasury.gov.za/documents/national%20budget/2000/cgt/cgt.pdf> accessed 15 May 2020; South African Revenue Service, Exclusions and Roll-Overs <https://www.sars.gov.za/TaxTypes/CGT/Exclusions/Pages/default. aspx> accessed 25 May 2020.

43   As done in *PSEG Global, Inc, The North American Coal Corporation, and Konya Ingin Electrik Üretim ve Ticaret Ltd Sirketi v Republic of Turkey*, ICSID Case No ARB/02/5, Award, 19 January 2007, paras 338–339.

liability on an award of damages, and have also requested a detailed explanation of the justification of the reason as to why and how a tax liability should arise.[44]

In addressing the potential impact of tax liability on the amount awarded, tribunals have used **18.23** two different approaches in dealing with the issue: calculating the damages owed on the basis of the pre-tax counterfactual cash flows of the investment, or taking into consideration a gross-up after calculating the liability due on an after-tax basis. In addition, the tribunal may resort to a further complementing option, which does not constitute a method of calculation of damages to be awarded, but consists in ensuring through the power of the tribunal that local tax liability owed to respondent will be fully satisfied by the respondent itself[45] or ask respondent to agree to ensure in the payment of a certain precise amount as tax liability (or grant no tax liability). While the best applicable approach may vary from case to case, the only constraint upon the arbitral tribunal seems to be to make a coherent decision as to the data and values judged appropriate in assessing what is due by respondent.[46]

In the first case, there must be an equivalence, on paper or as hypothesis, between the amount **18.24** of tax that would have been owed if the investor had not suffered the loss (a counterfactual situation) and the tax liability arisen from the amount awarded.[47] This, however, means that there must be a clear understanding of how the award of damages will be considered by the tax administration(s) involved, in order to ensure the rights of claimant to full compensation. As mentioned above, this may by no means be an easy task, especially taking into consideration that the damages awarded may be considered to have a different taxable nature than the counterfactual cash flows, and therefore be taxed differently.

The second possible way of taking into account tax liability consists in calculating damages on **18.25** an after-tax basis with a gross-up to account for payable tax. This seems to be easier when considering issues of both valuation and legal analysis.[48] However, there are still issues with the application of this methodology, since there must be a relative certainty as to the burden of the tax liability and who has the right to be paid by respondent. This is particularly true if a tribunal might wish to grant claimant and its parent company, unlike the *Mobil* tribunal did, to order respondent to pay the extra taxes that would be allegedly be owed consequent to a transfer of the amount of the awarded sum from the liable host State to the State of origin of the original investment.[49]

---

44 See *Mobil v Canada* (n 39), para 485.
45 Tobis (n 35), 19.
46 Mark Kantor, 'Chapter 4: Important Components of DCF Valuations', in Mark Kantor (ed) *Valuation for Arbitration* (Wolters Kluwer 2008) 131, 192–3.
47 This type of valuation is probably easier for States such as the Republic of Italy, where tax liability on damages awarded is calculated on the basis of the nature of the loss suffered based on the categories that the law establishes for different type of profits. See Article 6, para 2 of Presidential Decree no 917 of 22 December 1986 (so-called 'TUIR').
48 Tobis (n 35), 29.
49 For example, see *Mobil v Canada* (n 39) para 485:

> The Majority sees little basis for incorporating the Claimants' request for a 38 per cent 'gross up' for tax reasons. The Claimants did not justify why compensation could not remain with the Canadian enterprises, nor why it had to be taxed in the United States, nor what the tax rate was, nor why this is a necessary part of any resulting compensation. Moreover, we are not aware of a requirement under international law to gross up compensation as a result of tax considerations.

18.26 A complementing option to the ones above that the tribunal might choose to adopt is to ensure that claimant will be paid net of all taxes due to respondent, be liable for a precise given amount equal to what would have paid if there had not been any infringement or that the State will avoid imposing any tax at all (in these last two cases if it is respondent itself to offer such possibility through agreeing on taxing in a given way the amounts awarded). There have been cases where tribunals decided how the compensation will be provided (net instead of gross of local taxes)[50] or to whom (if there are different claimants with the same mother company or claimants are a subsidiary and the mother, and one of them will not be subject to the taxing power of the respondent)[51] with the view of impeding abuses of the respondent state (such as taxing the award with a 99 per cent tax rate on 100 per cent of the amount awarded). If a tribunal found to have the power to ensure the amount of net compensation owed versus the respondent and through the aid of applicable DTTs determined whether and how the amounts will be taxed in other jurisdictions, this would already constitute a step forward in ensuring full compensation with a greater certainty.

C. INTERNATIONAL TAX DISPUTE SETTLEMENT

18.27 Rights under IIAs will not always be affected by DDTs, but there might indeed be such circumstances. When IIAs do not have specific carve-outs, but are sufficiently broad as to cover violations of FET or any other investment right impacting tax matters, or any agreement between a foreign investor and the host State in matters of tax such as APAs, then there might be an overlap between different international dispute settlement mechanisms. One might also endeavour to ascertain whether failing to agree to start a Mutual Agreement Procedure (MAP, see para 18.34 below), failing to implement a MAP agreement or an arbitral decision under DTTs or the EU tax dispute settlement mechanism might constitute a violation of FET or other provisions in applicable IIAs. When this is the case, addressing international taxation concerns is not easy, especially in the case of complex multinational transactions, as above noted. This is why it is important to understand the context of international taxation disputes and what are the main standards of treatment of taxpayers internationally in this regard.

1. The OECD approach to dispute settlement in international tax law

18.28 Dispute settlement mechanisms within the international tax law arena are key elements which ensure the taxpayers' rights to fair and legitimate taxation. Tax litigation and connected issues typically arise from an audit. This is an assessment of whether the correct tax has been paid at the right time in accordance with the applicable domestic tax legislation.[52] Due to the fact that international taxation matters typically have a complex factual background, there might be legitimate reasons for which a taxpayer might have a different understanding of its situation

---

50 *Tenaris SA & Talta – Trading e Marketing Sociedade Unipessoal Lda v Bolivarian Republic of Venezuela*, ICSID Case No ARB/12/23, Award (Spanish), 12 November 2016, para 790 available at: <https://www.italaw.com/sites/default/files/case-documents/italaw8137_0.pdf> accessed 15 May 2020.

51 See, e.g., *PSEG Global v Turkey* (n 43), para 338.

52 Centre for Tax Policy and Administration, 'Forum on Tax Administration – Guidance Note: Guidance on Test Procedures for Tax Audit Assurance' (April 2010) 7, available at: <http://www.oecd.org/tax/administration/45045414.pdf> accessed 15 May 2020.

with regards to its duties towards the local tax administration.[53] At times, international standards will accept that there will be a range of correct results within which a taxpayer will be able to claim to have paid the amount due. This is the case of transfer pricing valuation.[54]

18.29 In accounting, transfer pricing has been defined as: 'the price one segment, of an organization (subunit, department, division and so on) charges for a product or service supplied to another segment of the same organization [...] [and] intercompany transfers between affiliates'.[55]

18.30 It may be noted that 'transfer price' is a neutral concept.[56] In assessing the transfer price between affiliated entities, the most popular standard which has been used as the primary method of valuation is the arm's length principle.[57] This principle is incorporated within the OECD framework (and art 9 of the 2017 Model Convention), and is defined in the following terms in relation to the powers of the tax administration to adjust multinational transfer price:

> [Where] conditions are made or imposed between the two [associated] enterprises in their commercial or financial relations which differ from those which would be made between independent enterprises, then any profits which would, but for those conditions, have accrued to one of the enterprises, but, by reason of those conditions, have not so accrued, may be included in the profits of that enterprise and taxed accordingly.[58]

18.31 The arm's length principle has been frequently adopted even amongst non-OECD economies[59] for several reasons, one of which is the fact that multinational enterprises and independent entities are treated equally before the tax administrations.[60] If the arm's length principle were correctly applied, ideally independent entities and multinational enterprises would suffer neither advantages nor disadvantages.[61] To ascertain the arm's length value of a controlled transaction, the OECD has identified a series of methods which use comparable transactions or data of comparable companies in its TPG. The OECD TPG, although not specifically designed for matters other than transfer pricing[62] have also been used by tax authorities to evaluate the revenue and worth generated by intangibles in patent box regimes.[63]

---

53 OECD Transfer Pricing Guidelines (n 27), chapter IV section A.

54 Ibid.

55 Elaboration of a definition given by Horngren and Foster in 1991 (Charles Horngren and George Foster, *Cost Accounting: A Managerial Emphasis* (Prentice Hall 1991, 7th edn) 855). See Shirin Rathore, *International Accounting* (PHI Learning 2009) 287.

56 Ad Hoc Group of Experts on International Cooperation in Tax Matters, 'Transfer Pricing: History, State of the Art, Perspectives' (2001) UN Doc ST/SG/AC.8/2001/CRP.6 2.

57 Ibid.

58 OECD Model Tax Convention (n 2), art 9; OECD Transfer Pricing Guidelines (n 27), chapter I, section B1, para 1.6.

59 OECD Transfer Pricing Guidelines (n 27), chapter I, section B1, para 1.6

60 Ibid., chapter I, section B1, para 1.8.

61 Ibid.

62 For example, note the observation at Ibid., chapter VI, section A.2, para 6.13.

63 For example, the Italian Patent Box regime. See for guidance Agenzia delle Entrate, 'Circolare N. 11/E. Chiarimenti in tema di Patent Box – Articolo 1, commi da 37 a 45, della legge 23 dicembre 2014, n.190 e successive modificazioni e Decreto del Ministro dello Sviluppo Economico di concerto con il Ministro dell'Economia e delle Finanze del 30 luglio 2015' (7 April 2016), available at: <https://www.agenziaentrate.gov.it/portale/documents/20143/239558/Circolare +11e+7+aprile+2016_AGE.AGEDC001.REGISTRO+BOZZE.0003638.06-04-2016-B_Circolare+11_sostituita.pdf/ 521608a1-41d9-c00b-faeb-0419fabd1557> accessed 15 May 2020.

18.32 The application of such standard, however, may be difficult. This is why the OECD recommends the use of APAs which determine, before a transaction is made, 'an appropriate set of criteria (e.g., method, comparables and appropriate adjustments thereto, critical assumptions as to future events) for the determination of the transfer pricing for those transactions over a fixed period of time'.[64]

18.33 APAs aim at providing a way to supplement traditional tax mechanisms in order to resolve in a more efficient manner transfer pricing issues, amongst other tax-related problematics.[65] However, APAs with one jurisdiction only may not be sufficient. The absence of an agreement between more than one State can lead to tax controversy and double taxation. A bilateral APA process, where at least two jurisdictions discuss and approve an APA, is possible thanks to Article 25 of the OECD Model Convention,[66] and should prevent such conflict. As noted with the FFT case mentioned above, having negotiated a multilateral APA in the EU may not be enough to prevent controversies due to state aid issues. The understanding of all the complexities and implications in play is a key aspect in securing the certainty which APAs strive to achieve.

18.34 This particular Article of the 2017 OECD Model provides for a mechanism called Mutual Agreement Procedure (MAP) through which tax authorities can agree on the tax base allocated to each jurisdiction, and for the taxpayer to request the start of arbitration if the tax authorities do not agree on the allocation of the tax base within two years, in a fashion similar to the arbitration procedure provided by the earlier Multilateral Instrument (or MLI) of 2016, although regulated in less detail.[67] It must be noted that the arbitration proceeding can be initiated also for specific issues only. According to the OECD, this would distinguish international tax arbitration proceedings from other commercial or 'government-private party' arbitrations which instead aim at resolving 'the whole case'.[68] Another possibility that this Article imposes on state parties is to endeavour to resolve through mutual agreement disputes concerning 'any difficulty or doubts arising as to the interpretation or application of the [c]onvention'.[69] Both types of mutual agreement procedure may be carried out by communicating with each other directly, 'including through a joint commission consisting of themselves or their representatives'.[70]

18.35 The MAP procedure found at Article 25.1 of the Model Convention gives the possibility to taxpayers to request a MAP in parallel with domestic tax litigation.[71] The procedure may start even when the taxpayer will be charged only in the future by a party to the Convention, as long as such a possibility arises out of a present action of one or both or the contracting States.[72]

---

64   OECD Transfer Pricing Guidelines (n 27), Chapter IV, section F.1, para 4.134.

65   Ibid.

66   Ibid., F.2.

67   OECD Model Tax Convention (n 2), art 25.5(b). See also OECD, Multilateral Instrument (MLI) and its Explanatory Statement (adopted on 24 November 2016 and entered into force on 1 July 2018), available at: <https://www.oecd.org/tax/treaties/multilateral-convention-to-implement-tax-treaty-related-measures-to-prevent-beps.htm> accessed 15 May 2020.

68   Ibid., commentary to art 25.5 para 64.

69   Ibid., art 25.3.

70   Ibid., art 25.4.

71   Ibid., commentary to art 25 para 70.2.

72   Ibid., commentary to art 25 para 13.

This applies also to newly enacted laws regardless of whether they are of general or individual application, as long as their direct and necessary consequence is a violation of the Convention.[73] To exercise such a right, the taxpayer must 'present his case' to the authority of either contracting State that is competent on the matter within three years 'from the first notification of the action' contested.[74] However, the competent authorities may require the taxpayer to abide by any special procedure for filing that they deem appropriate, obliging the taxpayer to follow certain additional provided standards.[75] For the competent authorities to accept a case, it should not be necessary for the taxpayer to have proven that there will be an infringement of its rights, but that the taxpayer has presented a reasonable case based on facts that can be established.[76]

Due to the right of the taxpayer to start the procedure at such an early stage where there has **18.36** not yet been a damage or formal notification, the expiration date of three years' time within which tax authorities can be requested to settle the case might depend on the relevant circumstances.[77] As mentioned above, if one or both authorities have found that there has been a violation of the Convention, they have received all sufficient information to make a decision on the matter, and if in two years' time they have not yet reached an agreement, the taxpayer may request in writing for arbitration to commence.[78] This is possible only if no tribunal or court of one of the States has ruled on the matter.[79]

If arbitration has started, taxpayers may be required to sign a confidentiality agreement. In fact, **18.37** the OECD suggests the implementation of the following provision in tax conventions, which is drafted on the basis of the MLI:

> Prior to the beginning of arbitration proceedings, the competent authorities of the Contracting States shall ensure that each person that presented the case and their advisors agree in writing not to disclose to any other person any information received during the course of the arbitration proceedings from either competent authority or the arbitration panel. The mutual agreement procedure and the arbitration proceedings related to the case shall terminate if, at any time after a request for arbitration has been made and before the arbitration panel has delivered its decision to the competent authorities, a person that presented the case or one of that person's advisors materially breaches that agreement.[80]

Interestingly, while within the investment arbitration context there has been a push for **18.38** transparency of the proceedings, it is the OECD itself that acknowledges that States may want *all* information provided to be kept private.[81]

The commentary on Article 25 also provides in an Annex a sample agreement that States may **18.39** use to bilaterally bind themselves, in order to implement what may be considered the

---

73   Ibid., commentary to art 25 para 14.
74   Ibid., art 25.1.
75   Ibid., commentary to art 25 para 16.
76   Ibid., commentary to art 25 para 14.
77   Ibid., commentary to art 25 paras 21–24.
78   Ibid., art 25.5.
79   Ibid.
80   Ibid., commentary to art 25 para 80.1.
81   Ibid.

'Arbitration Rules' that will be used in case of arbitration. In any event, the participation of the taxpayer is generally viewed as at times helpful, but always optional.

18.40 As will certainly be noted, international tax dispute settlement is a very peculiar mechanism which has developed in recent times to address concerns of transparency and taxpayer participation. The system has many similarities with some recent Brazilian IIAs. These treaties were signed with Mozambique and Angola, and do not provide for investor-state arbitration, but State-to-State arbitration only.[82] At Article 4, both agreements constitute a Joint Committee, which aims to 'seek consensus and resolve amicably any questions or conflicts regarding the investments of the Parties'.[83]

18.41 Both agreements provide for the resort to the same mechanisms in case of dispute. It is possible for a party to the bilateral agreement to submit a question 'of interest of an investor [...] specifying the name of the interested investor and the challenges or difficulties faced'.[84] Such a request will trigger the institution of a bilateral meeting, where, whenever possible, the representatives of the interested investor will participate at least in part.[85] Nongovernmental entities may also participate if 'involved in the measure or situation that is the object of the consultation'.[86] In case of dissatisfaction and inability to reach an agreement, parties may resort to state-to-state arbitration.[87] As one can note, this type of system resembles a softer version of MAP procedures coupled to a form of arbitration in case of dispute.

2. International tax dispute settlement in the European Union

18.42 While the OECD has its own standard in terms of MAP and arbitration proceedings, it is probably the European Union that has implemented the most detailed binding and uniform protocol with the highest number of Member States parties to it so far, through the publication of a recent Directive of the Council (2017/1852), which allows for so-called 'final offer', 'last best offer' or 'baseball' arbitration, in additional to the more conventional method illustrated below.[88]

18.43 This Directive was issued to implement interpretative provisions to the previous Convention on the Elimination of Double Taxation in Connection with the Adjustment of Profits of Associated Enterprises of 1990, and broaden the number of cases and persons falling within

---

82 Martin Dietrich Brauch, 'Side-by-side Comparison of the Brazil-Mozambique and Brazil-Angola Cooperation and Investment Facilitation Agreements' (International Institute for Sustainable Development, 2015) <http://www.iisd.org/sites/default/files/publications/comparison-cooperation-investment-facilitation-agreements.pdf> accessed 15 May 2020.

83 Ibid., art 4.

84 Ibid., art 15.3.

85 Ibid.

86 Ibid., art 15. The agreement with Angola at art 15.6 reads instead: '6. If it is not possible to resolve the dispute in the terms of paragraph 2 of this article by a recommendation of the Joint Committee, the Parties may resort to mechanisms of arbitration between States to resolve the abovementioned dispute.'

87 Ibid., art 15.3.

88 Council Directive (EU) 2017/1852 of 10 October 2017 on tax dispute resolution mechanisms in the European Union [2017] OJ L265/1, preamble paras 2–6. The MLI too allows for such type of arbitration. This method of dispute resolution obliges the tribunal to choose between the two last offers provided by one party to the other, without explaining why, after parties have concluded their submissions.

scope of the dispute resolution mechanism.[89] The Directive was thought to help the reduction of time and resources necessary to solve cases of double taxation and to render them 'comprehensive, effective and sustainable'.[90]

A further aim of the measures implemented is to 'introduce an effective and efficient **18.44** framework for the resolution of tax disputes which ensures legal certainty and a business-friendly environment for investments in order to achieve fair and efficient tax systems in the Union' and to 'create a harmonised and transparent framework for solving disputes and thereby provide benefits to all taxpayers'.[91] Interestingly, the Directive expressly indicates rules of transparency as the main means to create a fairer tax environment, jointly with anti-avoidance measures.[92]

In the Directive, arbitration is considered a useful tool only once there is an absence of **18.45** agreement after a prolonged period of time, as a last resort mechanism.[93] Similarly to the Investor-State Dispute Settlement (ISDS), the Directive envisages a system where the 'choice of the method for dispute resolution should be flexible, which could be either through ad hoc structures or through more permanent structures'.[94]

The Directive lays down some innovative methods to ensure that disputes will be solved. This **18.46** is accomplished through the use of multiple layers and options for protection. The affected person[95] has the opportunity and right to recourse to national courts to protect his interests in various circumstances. The Directive does not address exactly which are the 'Arbitration Rules' for each of the various mechanisms involved in the dispute resolution process, but is concerned more with providing for the protection of the affected person and the Member States involved. This is why it has only 24 articles.

Under the Directive, an affected person has the right to file a complaint. Following the **18.47** complaint, the tax authorities will evaluate whether or not the complaint should be accepted. One of the Member States affected may also decide to unilaterally resolve the question submitted within six months of filing the complaint or the receipt of any necessary information requested.[96] If the complaint is not accepted by all States, the affected person may, under certain conditions, ask for the institution of an Advisory Commission or may appeal at a national level under the law of the single Member State(s) rejecting the complaint.[97] If any controversy on admissibility is solved in favour of the affected taxpayer, the matter will be subject to a MAP. If the MAP is successful, there will be implementation of the agreement, while if there is no agreement within the States affected, the matter can be resolved through arbitration. This can be made via an Advisory Commission or an Alternative Dispute

---

89   Ibid.: '[f]or this reason, it is necessary that there are mechanisms in the Union that ensure the effective resolution of disputes concerning the interpretation and application of such bilateral tax treaties and the Union Arbitration Convention, in particular disputes leading to double taxation'. See also preambles 6 and 7 of the same Directive.
90   Ibid., preambles 3–4.
91   Ibid., preamble 4.
92   Ibid.
93   Ibid.
94   Ibid.
95   Ibid., art 2.
96   Ibid., art 3.5.
97   Ibid., arts 5.3, 6.1.

Resolution Commission, and with a flexible approach (including the use of 'last best offer' arbitration). States may implement the decisions taken by the Commission, or solve the matter differently through an agreement. In case of non-agreement, the decision of the Commission becomes binding. The details of the procedure are explained below.

18.48 As mentioned, the Directive grants to taxpayers the possibility of furthering a complaint due to the arising of double taxation on matters covered by its scope, and it is subject to certain formal requirements[98] which are more extensive than the OECD proposed standards of the Annex to the Commentary on Article 25. Having received the necessary documentation, Tax Authorities have the opportunity to reject the application for a MAP if:

> (a) the complaint lacks information required under Article 3(3) [...] including any information requested under Article 3(3)(f) that was not submitted within the deadline specified in Article 3(4));
> (b) there is no question in dispute; or (c) the complaint was not submitted within the three-year period set out in Article 3(1).[99]

18.49 If one or more of the competent authorities does reject the application for the MAP,[100] the taxpayer should not despair: the Directive grants the possibility to appeal in front of an Advisory Commission within 50 days of notification of the decision.[101] This recourse is possible only if the rejection was not unanimous. If so, the affected person can always appeal in front of competent organs identified by the national rules of each Member State involved.

18.50 If States have accepted or have been compelled to start a MAP, they have to do so within two years from the last notification of acceptance given to the affected person by one of the states concerned, save for a possible one-year extension. The affected taxpayer has the right to be notified both of the decision or of the reasons for the failure to reach a decision.

18.51 In cases where Member States cannot reach an agreement, they can be compelled by the taxpayer to settle the controversy through the establishment of the Advisory Commission. The panel of the Advisory Commission, nominated by the States involved in the failed MAP, may be constituted by a minimum of five members (in a bilateral MAP), with each State involved

---

98 See ibid., art 3.3(e):

> (i) an explanation of why the affected person considers that there is a question in dispute; (ii) the details of any appeals and litigation initiated by the affected person regarding the relevant transactions and of any court decisions concerning the question in dispute; (iii) a commitment by the affected person to respond as completely and quickly as possible to all appropriate requests made by a competent authority and to provide any documentation at the request of the competent authorities; (iv) a copy of the final tax assessment decision in the form of a final tax assessment notice, tax audit report or other equivalent document leading to the question in dispute and a copy of any other documents issued by the tax authorities with regard to the question in dispute where relevant; (v) information on any complaint submitted by the affected person under another mutual agreement procedure or under another dispute resolution procedure as defined in Article 16(5) and an express commitment by the affected person that he will abide by the provisions of Article 16(5), if applicable;

> see also, art 3.3(f): 'any specific additional information requested by the competent authorities that is considered necessary to undertake the substantive consideration of the particular case'.

99   Tax Dispute Resolution Directive (n 88), art 5.1.
100 Ibid., art 6.1.
101 Ibid.

being able to appoint at least one representative and one independent person of standing.[102] The independent person may be challenged only on a limited number of grounds.[103]

18.52 Even when the concerned States do not appoint members to the commission, the taxpayer has the right to compel the States to do so by bringing the matter to the national court of the State identified in the respective national law, or other body.[104]

18.53 Therefore, the mechanism devised guarantees in any case a solution of the problems of the taxpayer.

18.54 The EU regime also allows for the possibility of the creation of another type of entity to rule over the matter, the 'Alternative Dispute Resolution Commission' instead of an Advisory Commission.[105] Its institution is based on the agreement of the tax authorities involved, and imposes in any event the observance of the impartiality of the independent person of standing of the panel in the Advisory Commission.[106] The Alternative Dispute Resolution Commission might be of a permanent nature (a 'Standing Committee').

18.55 Once the request by the taxpayer to set up an Advisory Commission has been filed, the tax authorities have the duty to provide the taxpayer with the following documents within 120 days:

(a) the Rules of Functioning for the Advisory Commission or Alternative Dispute Resolution Commission;

(b) the date by which the opinion on the resolution of the question in dispute shall be adopted;

(c) references to any applicable legal provisions in national law of the Member States and to any applicable agreements or conventions.[107]

18.56 The regulation of the details of the management of the proceedings are dictated through the 'Rules of Functioning' of the Commission, which will have to contain several details on the procedure, with some limited exceptions for the Commissions established for an opinion with respect to a rejection of the complaint.[108]

---

102 Ibid., art 8.1.
103 Ibid., art 8.4.
104 Ibid., art 7.
105 Ibid., art 10.
106 Ibid.
107 Ibid., art 11.
108 Ibid., art 11.2:

> (a) the description and the characteristics of the question in dispute; (b) the terms of reference on which the competent authorities of the Member States agree as regards the legal and factual questions to be resolved; (c) the form of the dispute resolution body, which shall be either an Advisory Commission or an Alternative Dispute Resolution Commission, as well as the type of process for any Alternative Dispute Resolution, if the process differs from the independent opinion process applied by an Advisory Commission; (d) the time frame for the dispute resolution procedure; (e) the composition of the Advisory Commission or Alternative Dispute Resolution Commission (including the number and names of the members, details of their competence and qualifications, and disclosing any conflicts of interest of the members); (f) the rules governing the participation of the affected person(s) and third parties in the proceedings, exchanges of memoranda, information and evidence, the costs, the type of dispute

18.57   It is mandatory for tax authorities and affected persons to cooperate with the panel upon request, save for limited exceptions.[109] In particular, tax authorities may refuse to cooperate if:

(a)   obtaining the information requires carrying out administrative measures that are against national law;

(b)   the information cannot be obtained under the national law of the Member State concerned;

(c)   the information concerns trade secrets, business secrets, industrial secrets, professional secrets or trade processes;

(d)   the disclosure of the information is contrary to public policy.[110]

18.58   Persons affected by the panel's decision have the possibility, under limited circumstances, to appear in front of the panel to present their case, with the possibility of being represented.[111]

18.59   In any event, proceedings will terminate with an 'opinion' of the Commission within six months from the start at the latest through a majority vote, save for a possible three months' extension.[112] Once the opinion has been rendered, the Member States will have the possibility within six months to agree on different terms for the solution of the case.[113] Such a decision is final and binding, but does not constitute precedent, and will be implemented, save for the refusal of the affected person to renounce to any domestic remedy within 60 days from the notification of the decision.[114]

18.60   The decision rendered 'shall be implemented under the national law of the Member States concerned which as a result of the final decision shall amend their taxation, irrespective of any time limits prescribed by the national law'.[115] Therefore, it cleanses of any error the previous determinations of the local tax authorities.

18.61   In addition, the competent authorities, with the consent of the affected person, may decide to publish the decision in its entirety through procedures identified in implementing acts.[116] In any case, it will be necessary to publish an abstract with 'a description of the issue and the subject matter, the date, the tax periods involved, the legal basis, the industry sector, and a short description of the final outcome'.[117] The decision will also have to contain a description of the type of arbitration used,[118] and the taxpayer will have the right to see redacted any information which 'concerns any trade, business, industrial or professional secret or trade process, or that is contrary to public policy'.[119]

---

resolution process to be used, and any other relevant procedural or organisational matters; (g) the logistical arrangements for the Advisory Commission's proceedings and delivery of its opinion.

109   Ibid., art 13.1.
110   Ibid.
111   Ibid., art 13.2.
112   Ibid., art 14.
113   Ibid., art 15 paras 1–2.
114   Ibid., art 15.4.
115   Ibid.
116   Ibid., art 18.
117   Ibid., art 18.3.
118   Ibid.
119   Ibid.

As one will note, more sophisticated provisions in relation to disclosure and transparency can be found in the Investment Arbitration field, in particular where the United Nations Commission on International Trade Law (UNCITRAL) Rules on Transparency in Treaty-based Investor-State Arbitration are used within proceedings. **18.62**

D. SOFT LAW STANDARDS IN TAXATION AND THEIR POTENTIAL PRACTICAL USES IN INVESTMENT ARBITRATION

As has been noted above, in international taxation there are harmonized and systematic procedures of treaty interpretation and dispute prevention and resolution. In addition, States often use the OECD Model[120] when they enter into bilateral DTT's, and may end up with near to verbatim adoptions of the model. In addition to the Model, the OECD has issued interpretative guidelines. States and taxpayers can reasonably rely on these soft law instruments.[121] This helps to limit in a systematic way the risk of unpredictable results in judgments of local courts in a system where there is no court having the ultimate word on the uniform interpretation of international tax provisions. **18.63**

In investment arbitration, uncertainty on the strength of a claim has been found to lead to settlements only once arbitration proceedings have started, albeit at an early stage.[122] This is why in international investment arbitration, it might be useful to look at international tax dispute settlement mechanisms to understand how to improve a system which has been deemed struggling to provide uniform interpretations to provisions.[123] **18.64**

Notwithstanding its defects, international tax law may be useful for professionals operating in the international investment arena in limiting risks and uncertainty. Naturally, this will depend on the type of instrument (treaty, investment agreement or other) with which these will be negotiated and the actual circumstances of the matter at hand and the context of the application (with contracts or whether there are applicable umbrella clauses or not, for example). The use of instruments deriving from established tax practice might be considered favourably by the local government, since its own tax authority is used to implement these or similar practices already. **18.65**

Several non-tax related matters in investment deals or arbitrations can be solved at least in part through the use of international tax standards. This might be done by States at international level or through international investment contracts by States and investors. **18.66**

---

120   Commission, 'Guidelines for a Model for a European Taxpayers' Code' (2017), available at: <https:// un.org/esa/ffd/wp-content/uploads/2018/05/MDT_2017.pdf> accessed 15 May 2020.

121   Brian J Arnold, 'An Introduction to Tax Treaties', 1 <https:// un.org/esa/ffd/wp-content/uploads/2015/10/TT_Introduction_Eng.pdf> accessed 15 May 2020.

122   Roberto Echandi and Priyanka Kher, 'Can International Investor–State Disputes be Prevented? Empirical Evidence from Settlements in ICSID Arbitration' (2014) 29 ICSID Review 41, 56.

123   UNCITRAL, 'Report of Working Group III (Investor-State Dispute Settlement Reform) on the work of its thirty-sixth session (Vienna, 29 October–2 November 2018)' (A/CN9/964, 6 November 2018), paras 27–38, available at: <https://undocs.org/en/A/CN.9/964> accessed 15 May 2020.

18.67   Naturally, it might be more useful for States themselves to reform international investment law on the basis of the opportunities offered by practices in the international tax regime. Although in the past it has been impossible for States to come to an agreement, and it seems impossible to find a unique type of treaty standard to fit all needs, it might still be possible to consider also the drafting of model clauses regarding the protection of substantive rights for an *à la carte* use, to compose a bilateral treaty according to the needs of the contracting parties.

18.68   Each type of provision and model would be accompanied with relevant comments, examples and instruction as to their interpretation and implementation, similarly as done by the OECD with DTTs. Comments might include reference to the relevant case law that has interpreted the relevant provisions. States might then decide to negotiate bilaterally or in a multilateral fashion changes to treaties already in existence, ensuring certainty in the application of the investment protection standards. This might be a solution which would have a certain appeal, since it would enable both investors and States alike to consider their positions with respect to a baseline which would be considered authoritative for all tribunals, unifying interpretation according to the type of clause chosen while ensuring that the choice in the wording used by each contracting State is respected. Similar instruments are already drafted by UNCITRAL with respect to the implementation of its model laws, where several drafting options are provided jointly with comments to the model provisions.[124]

18.69   In a way similar to how the OECD has drafted model guidelines with respect to the valuation of transfer pricing transactions, States may draft through international institutions one common document providing with step-by-step guidelines for experts in valuation of damages, in order to ensure the uniform application of valuation standards to the smallest possible detail. This would obviously not limit the role of experts and tribunals. However, it would enable parties to arising disputes to consider issues of valuation with more certainty. The project could build from the current World Bank Guidelines on the Treatment of Foreign Direct Investment to a much more detailed manual on valuation.

18.70   States may also consider implementing guidelines to direct tribunals on how comparable circumstances should be assessed in cases of application of, for example, the national treatment standard, just as in the TPG there is an indication as to how comparable transactions have to be identified.

18.71   In the alternative, investors may also contract some special provisions or regimes with host States.[125] In international investment arbitration, it is possible for a tribunal to calculate damages on the basis of a contract provision.[126] Although transfer pricing issues are still a matter of complex cases of valuation, transparent and predefined methods of calculation and choices of methodologies for valuation are of great aid to courts in tax matters, which may refer

---

124   See, e.g., the case of UNCITRAL, 'UNCITRAL Model Law on Secured Transactions – Guide to Enactment (2017) <https://www.uncitral.org/pdf/english/texts/security/MLST_Guide_to_enactment_E.pdf> accessed 30 May 2020; OECD Model Tax Convention (n 2), para 216.

125   See, for a complete discussion on responsibility for breaches of investment contracts and their legal framework, Jean Ho, *State Responsibility for Breaches of Investment Contracts* (CUP 2018).

126   Irmgard Marboe, 'Chapter 5: Methods of Valuations in International Practice' in Irmgard Marboe (ed) *Calculation of Compensation and Damages in International Investment Law* (OUP 2009) 213, 301–4.

to predefined standards to make an accurate ruling.[127] International investment practice has shown that including in contracts provisions for the calculation of damages may be helpful.[128] In any case, tax law practice too shows that reference to specific best practices in choosing what is the most suitable methodology to apply in a given instance and how the method of valuation used should be used, greatly aid individuals called to judge on valuation matters, especially those lacking a specific quantitative background.[129]

In particular, even though the TPG have not been created for other regimes but for transfer **18.72** pricing valuation only, parties may want to consider using or adapting the valuation methodologies therein for the estimation of the worth of intangible or tangible assets.

In addition, it would be useful to ensure through a provision that in cases where a tribunal or a **18.73** judicial authority has the duty to evaluate the worth of the investment and award damages, it should apply Article 13 of the applicable DTT if relevant to the situation, if this has been drafted under the OECD Model, to ensure more certainty as to the tax treatment of the award. In any case, it should be good practice to ensure that such matter is addressed in an agreement. This provision would be useful also to avoid asking the tribunal for measures to avoid double taxation of the award.[130]

Another possible instrument useful in the prevention of litigation may be inspired by the **18.74** possibility that taxpayers have to start a MAP even before any actual double taxation has taken place. To avoid potential costly litigation, the investor may contract with the State a clause according to which, if any measure is taken by the State or its organs which has violated or if applied might directly violate the investor's rights, it may ask the entity and the central government to avoid taking action, giving a preliminary statement of facts and rights. Such clause could also oblige the organ or central government to provide an explanation to its decision and as to why the investor's concerns are not justified. This might help the local authorities to understand the validity of the investor's claims and to assess before any liability is due whether the measure should or could be changed obtaining the same scope. This without violating the rights and limiting damages to the investor. It might also help the State entity to consider consequences not addressed when evaluating policy decisions. This type of approach may only work if there is a duty of the investor to signal the violation within a given timeframe to access directly investment arbitration, and if the exchange of opinions between the investor and the State entity is done in good faith. This type of clause would be particularly useful to avoid the need, whether present, for the investor to exhaust available local remedies and save time, while in the meantime giving the chance to the state entity to avoid liability.[131]

---

127 See as e.g., the use of the OECD guidelines imposed by the Court of Cassation of the Republic of Italy, 5th section, Judgment no 17953 of 19 October 2012.

128 Marboe (n 126), 301–4.

129 Demonstrated by the amount of references to the OECD Transfer Pricing Guidelines (n 27).

130 As happened in *Occidental v Ecuador* (n 39), para 851: 'During the quantum phase of this proceeding, the Claimants have sought confirmation on the part of the Respondent that it will not seek to collect taxes on any award that the Claimants may receive.'

131 Which is the *ratio* of a local remedies provision. See Martin Dietrich Brauch, 'Exhaustion of Local Remedies in International Investment Law' (International Institute for Sustainable Development, IISD Best Practices Series, 2017) 2, available at: <https://www.iisd.org/sites/default/files/publications/best-practices-exhaustion-local-remedies-law-investment-en.pdf> accessed 15 May 2020.

18.75 Finally, one could consider explicating in the arbitration agreement an actual statute of limitations or other clause indicating until when the claimant has the right to claim damages against respondent. Issues of statute of limitations are not addressed in the vast majority of IIAs.[132] In international tax law, instead, taxpayers have a given limited timeframe in which they can start MAP procedures. Whether statues of limitations or similar provisions would be more useful to claimant or respondent depends on the actual amount of time accorded to start proceedings. A long period of time would favour claimant, a very short one respondent.

E. CONCLUSION

18.76 The interplay between international investment provisions and the local or international tax regime may have profound implications on the rights of an investor and their assessment. In the context of complex international transactions and structured investment, the impact of the applicable tax regime on investor rights should be carefully analysed by the tribunal called to solve an international investment dispute, and by the investor planning its operations.

18.77 This in particular when considering the valuation of damages and the consequences of the tax treatment of the amounts awarded on the investor. Since it is of primary importance to balance the rights of the respondent and of claimant, it is imperative to aim at understanding what are claimant's possibilities with respect to avoid, defer or limit tax liability on the amount awarded, and whether there are any ways to ensure that respondent will not overcompensate the claimant.

18.78 At the same time, it is necessary to ascertain how the single tax controversy should be settled. If it is possible for it to be done through a very early MAP process before the tax measure becomes definitive, this could avoid the potential costs of commencing an international Investment Arbitration claim, if both mechanisms of dispute resolution are accessible to the investor. The taxpayer/investor might also wish to consider the filing of both type of proceedings, if all legal requirements are met.

18.79 Most importantly, if there is the possibility, the investor should assess whether a cost/benefit analysis and the applicable legal framework enable a negotiation of some provisions within an investment contract inspired by the international tax regime to ensure more stability and certainty to the treatment of its investments.

---

132 See, for a deep analysis, Pedro J Martinez-Fraga and Joaquin Moreno Pampin, 'Reconceptualising the Statute of Limitations Doctrine in the International Law of Foreign Investment Protection: Reform beyond Historical Legacies' (2018) 50 *NYU Journal of International Law and Politics* 789.

19

THE MULTILATERAL INVESTMENT COURT

Friedrich Rosenfeld*

A. INTRODUCTION

On 20 March 2018, the General Secretariat of the Council of the European Union issued **19.01** negotiating directives for a Convention establishing a multilateral court for the settlement of investment disputes.[1] This permanent court is intended to replace the existing system of

---

* Date of submission: 09/02/2020.

1 Negotiating directives for a Convention establishing a multilateral court for the settlement of investment disputes, 12981/17 Add 1 ('Negotiating Directives') <http://data.consilium.europa.eu/doc/document/ST-12981-2017-ADD-1-DCL-1/en/pdf> accessed 3 October 2018. See also Commission Staff Working Document Impact Assessment – Multilateral reform of investment dispute resolution, 13.9.2017, SWD(2017) 302 final and M. Bungenberg and A. Reinisch, *From Bilateral Arbitral Tribunals and Investment Courts to a Multilateral Investment Court, European Yearbook of International Economic Law* (Springer 2018). For more general literature on the proposal to create a court system for the resolution of investor-State disputes, see A. Reinisch, 'The EU and Investor-State Dispute Settlement: WTO Litigators Going "Investor-State Arbitration" and Back to a Permanent "Investment Court"' in M. Bungenberg et al. (eds), *European Yearbook of International Economic Law 2017* (Springer 2017) 247; P. Bernardini, 'The European Union's Investment Court System – A Critical Analysis' (2017) 35(4) *ASA Bulletin* 812; N. van den Broek and D. Morris, 'The EU's Proposed Investment Court and WTO Dispute Settlement: A Comparison and Lessons Learned', (2017) 2(1) *European Investment Law and Arbitration Review Online* 35; H. Lenk, 'Something Borrowed, Something New: The TTIP Investment Court: How to Fit Old Procedures into New Institutional Design' in E. Fahey (ed) *Institutionalisation beyond the Nation State* (Springer 2018) 129; S. Heppner, 'A Critical Appraisal of the Investment

international arbitration for the resolution of investor-State disputes. It is projected to have jurisdiction over claims arising not only under one but under multiple investment treaties.[2]

19.02 For some stakeholders, this proposal marks a critical milestone in the process towards a better system of investor-State dispute settlement ('ISDS').[3] Others are concerned, fearing that the hallmarks of international arbitration will be sacrificed without any valid reason.[4] Irrespective of which camp one favors, there is no doubt that ISDS is at a critical juncture that will determine its future. Against this background, this chapter will examine what triggered the proposal to create a multilateral investment court (see B.), what the court could look like (see C.) and what challenges lie ahead of the European Union when attempting to implement its proposal (see D.).

B. THE ORIGINS OF THE PROPOSAL TO CREATE A MULTILATERAL INVESTMENT COURT

19.03 To place the proposal to create a multilateral investment court in context, it is helpful to start by examining how ISDS has developed over the last two centuries.

1. Nineteenth century

19.04 In the nineteenth century, investment protection was still to a considerable extent a power-based regime,[5] and investor-State dispute resolution as we know it today did not yet exist. When an investor was injured by acts contrary to international law, its home State was responsible for exercising diplomatic protection.[6] It was not uncommon for diplomatic

---

Court System Proposed by the European Commission' (2017) *Dispute Resolution Journal* 93; J.G. Coyne, 'The TTIP Investment Court System: An Evolution of Investor-State Dispute Settlement' (2016) *European International Arbitration Review* 1; C. Titi, 'Procedural Multilateralism and Multilateral Investment Court: Discussion in light of Increased Institutionalism in Transatlantic Relations' in E. Fahey (ed), *Institutionalisation beyond the Nation State* (Springer 2018) 149.

2 For details, see below.

3 See, e.g., R. Howse, 'Designing a Multilateral Investment Court: Issues and Options' (2017) 36 *Yearbook of European Law 209.*

4 See, e.g., C.N. Brower and J. Ahmad, 'From the Two-Headed Nightingale to the Fifteen-Headed Hydra: The Many Follies of the Proposed International Investment Court' (2018) 41 *Fordham International Law Journal* 791; J.B. Simmons, 'The Misdiagnosed Investment Court: The Wrong Remedy for the Right Problem' (2016) *European International Arbitration Review* 23.

5 On the development of international investment law, see C. Brown, 'The Evolution of the Regime of International Investment Agreements – History, Economics and Politics' in M. Bungenberg et al. (eds), *International Investment Law – A Handbook* (Hart Publishing 2015) 153; K. Vandevelde, *Bilateral Investment Treaties – History, Policy and Interpretation* (OUP 2010); T. Johnson and J. Gimblett, 'From Gunboats to BITs – The Evolution of International Investment Law' in K. Sauvant (ed), *Yearbook on International Investment Law & Policy 2010 – 2011* (OUP 2012) 649.

6 On the role of diplomatic protection, see K. Parlett, 'Diplomatic Protection and Investment Arbitration' in R. Hofmann and C.J. Tams (eds), *International Investment Law and General International Law – From Clinical Isolation to Systemic Integration?* (Nomos 2011) 211; J. Dugard, 'Diplomatic Protection' in J. Crawford et al. (eds), *The Law of International Responsibility* (OUP 2010) 1051.

protection to be accompanied by military force – a phenomenon that has been characterized as 'gunboat diplomacy'.[7]

This power-based approach to international investment protection at the inter-State level was **19.05** not only a threat to the development of peaceful relations, it also left investors at the mercy of their home States. As such, it reflected the Westphalian conceptualization of public international law as a system limited to regulating legal relations between sovereign States. It was at odds with the ideals of liberalism, which acknowledge individuals as holders of individual rights and freedoms.

2. Mid-twentieth century

The mid-twentieth century was marked by a shift away from this power-based approach **19.06** towards a treaty-based approach of investment protection. In these treaties, States did not only grant substantive protections to individual investors, they also made offers to arbitrate investor disputes and thereby empowered individual investors to assert their rights in a judicial procedure outside the realm of State courts.

Being a form of dispute resolution with a long tradition – predecessors already existed under **19.07** Roman and Greek law – arbitration has significant advantages compared to other forms of dispute resolution.[8] Among others, it offers a fair procedure resulting in a final, binding and enforceable award. Parties have the possibility to select experienced decision-makers as arbitrators who do not owe any allegiance to a State that could have interests in the outcome of the case. This has been a significant legitimizing factor and one of the main reasons for the success of international arbitration as a mechanism to resolve international investment disputes.

Throughout the twentieth century, arbitration was never seriously put into question as a means **19.08** for the resolution of investment disputes. While investment protection suffered significant backlash up until the late twentieth century, the criticism focused on the substantive rather than the procedural guarantees of protection.[9] The fierce debates between capital exporting and capital importing States as to how the substantive guarantees of investment protection

---

7   See, e.g., the comments of Lord Palmerston on the Don Pacifico Affair:

> [A]s the Roman, in days of old, held himself free from indignity, when he could say Civis Romanus sum, so also a British subject, in whatever land he may be, shall feel confident that the watchful eye and the strong arm of English will protect him against injustice and wrong.

House of Commons Debates, June 25, 1980, vol. 112 (3rd Ser.), c.444 (statement of Lord Palmerston).

8   See only G. Born, *International Commercial Arbitration – Volume I* (2nd edn Wolters Kluwer 2014) pp. 7 et seq, 73 et seq.

9   Capital importing States invoked the doctrine of the Argentine jurist Carlos Calvo who had argued that foreign investors should not receive better treatment than nationals of the host State and that the claims of foreign investors should be resolved in domestic courts on the basis of domestic law. See W. Shan, 'Calvo Doctrine, State Sovereignty and the Changing Landscape of International Investment Law' in W. Shan et al. (eds), *Redefining Sovereignty in International Economic Law* (Hart Publishing 2008) 247; C. Calvo, *Le Droit International Théorique et Pratique*, Vol. VI, 1896, 231. Capital exporting States fought for a robust regime of investment protection that included prompt, adequate and effective compensation in case of expropriation. See 'Mexico-United States: Expropriation by Mexico of Agrarian Properties Owned by American Citizens' (1938) 32(4) *Am. J. Int'l L.* 191. For further reference, see A. Kaushal, 'Revisiting History: How the Past Matters for the Present Backlash against the Foreign Investment Regime' (2009) 50 *Harv. Int'l L.J.* 491, 499; J.W. Salacuse, *The Foundations of International Investment Law* (OUP 2010) 65; D. Vagts,

should be designed are testament to this. However, they did not prevent States from concluding the ICSID Convention, which offers a procedural framework for the resolution of investor-State disputes by arbitration.[10]

3. Twenty-first century

19.09 Today, at the beginning of the twenty-first century, the conflict between capital importing and capital exporting States has dissipated.[11] A tight-knit network of international investment treaties spans the globe and investment cases are brought against developed and developing States alike.[12] Nevertheless, international investment law is now subject to a new form of backlash that has not spared ISDS.[13] As far as the procedural guarantees are concerned, which are the focus of this chapter, the main points of criticism include the following:

a. Transparency

19.10 First, certain stakeholders have voiced their concern that arbitration proceedings are not sufficiently transparent.[14] It has been argued that principles of privacy and confidentiality, which apply in most commercial arbitration proceedings, are not appropriate for investment arbitration proceedings.[15]

'Foreword to the Backlash Against Investment Arbitration' in M. Waibel and A. Kaushal (eds), *The Backlash Against Investment Arbitration* (Wolters Kluwer 2010) xiii.

10 Convention on the Settlement of Investment Disputes between States and Nationals of Other States (adopted 18 March 1965, entered into force 14 October 1966), 575 UNTS 159 ('ICSID Convention').

11 UNCTAD World Investment Report 2016, Investor Nationality: Policy Challenges, p. 2 et seq.

12 ICSID Caseload, Statistics 2018-2 <https://icsid.worldbank.org/en/Documents/resources/ICSID%20Web%20Stats %202018-2%20(English).pdf> accessed 3 November 2018, p. 11. See also the database <http://mappinginvestment treaties.com> accessed 3 November 2018.

13 On the backlash against investment arbitration, see M. Waibel, *The Backlash against Investment Arbitration – Perceptions and Reality* (Wolters Kluwer 2010); Kaushal (n 9). See also J. Kalicki and A. Joubin-Bret (eds), *Reshaping the Investor-State Dispute Settlement System – Journeys for the 21st Century* (Martinus Nijhoff 2015); S. Hindelang and M. Krajewski, *Shifting Paradigms in International Investment Law – More Balanced, Less Isolated, Increasingly Diversified* (OUP 2016); C. Schreuer, 'The Future of International Investment Law' in M. Bungenberg et al. (eds), *International Investment Law – A Handbook* (Hart Publishing 2015) 1904; K.H. Böckstiegel, 'The Future of International Investment Law – Substantive Protection and Dispute Settlement' in M. Bungenberg et al. (eds), *International Investment Law – A Handbook* (Hart Publishing 2015) 1863; A. Reinisch, 'The Future of Investment Arbitration' in C. Binder et al. (eds) *International Investment Law for the 21ˢᵗ Century* (OUP 2009) 894; C. Schreuer, 'The Future of Investment Arbitration' in M.H. Arsanjani et al. (eds), *Looking to the Future – Essays on International Law in Honor of W. Michael Reisman* (Martinus Nijhoff 2011) 787; T. Johnson and C. Gibson, 'The Objections of Developed and Developing States to Investor-State Arbitration and what They are Doing about Them' in A. Rovine (ed), *The Fordham Papers 2013 – Contemporary Issues in International Arbitration and Mediation* (Martinus Nijhoff 2014) 253; D. Ma, 'A Bit Unfair? An Illustration of the Backlash against Arbitration in Latin America' (2012) *J. Disp. Res.* 571.

14 Report of Working Group III (Investor-State Dispute Settlement Reform) on the work of its thirty-fourth session (Vienna, 27 November – 1 December 2017), UN Doc. A/CN.9/930/Rev.1, para. 79.

15 On transparency in investment arbitration, see, e.g., L. Malintoppi and N. Limbasan, 'Living in Glass Houses? The Debate on Transparency in International Investment Arbitration' (2015) 2 *BCDR Int'l Arb. Rev.* 31; J.A. Maupin, 'Transparency in International Investment Law – The Good, the Bad and the Murky' in A. Bianchi and A. Peters (eds), *Transparency in International Law* (CUP 2013) 142; J. Nakagawa (ed), *Transparency in International Trade and Investment Dispute Settlement* (Routledge 2013); M. Zachariasiewicz, 'Amicus Curiae in International Investment Arbitration – Can it Enhance the Transparency of Investment Dispute Resolution' (2012) 29 *J. Int'l Arb.* 205; A. Asteriti and C.J. Tams, 'Transparency and Representation of the Public Interest in Investment Treaty Arbitration', in S. Schill (ed), *International Investment Law and Comparative Public Law* (OUP 2010) 787; I. Maxwell, 'Transparency in Investment Arbitration – Are Amici Curiae the Solution?' (2007) 3 *Asia Int'l Arb. J.* 159; M.A. Orellana, 'The Right

An often-propounded argument in support of demands for transparency is the fact that **19.11** treaty-based investment arbitration proceedings typically impact upon the public interest.[16] On the one hand, this may arise from the subject matter of investment arbitration proceedings, which have covered a wide array of fields such as sovereign debt,[17] water services,[18] and the operation of hazardous waste landfills.[19] On the other hand, the participation of State actors may in itself trigger a public interest. After all, arbitrations involving State actors may lead to liability for public treasuries. States may also be obliged to provide access to information of general interest under international human rights law (or under their domestic laws).[20]

b. Coherence and consistency

The second area of concern relates to the perceived lack of coherence and consistency. As an **19.12** example of such inconsistent decision-making, reference is often made to the parallel cases of *Ronald Lauder v. Czech Republic*[21] and *CME v. Czech Republic*,[22] where claims based on nearly identical fact patterns were decided in opposite ways. Another frequently cited example of inconsistency is offered by the cases of *SGS v. Islamic Republic of Pakistan*[23] and *SGS v. Republic of Philippines*,[24] in which two arbitral tribunals reached different decisions as to the scope of umbrella clauses. More recently, tribunals have reached different conclusions in assessing the compatibility of changes in the Spanish regulatory regime on solar energy under the Energy Charter Treaty. While the fact patterns of many cases were similar, the tribunals took different approaches in their assessments.[25]

Various factors have been identified as possible reasons for the perceived lack of consistency **19.13** and coherence. They include the fact that substantive standards of protection are often phrased

---

of Access to Information and Investment Arbitration' (2011) 26 No. 2 *ICSID Rev.* 59; H. Mann, 'Transparency and Consistency in International Investment Law – Can the Problems be fixed by Tinkering?' in K. Sauvant and M. Chiswick-Patterson (eds), *Appeals Mechanism in International Investment Disputes* (OUP 2008) 213; C. Knahr and A. Reinisch, 'Transparency in International Investment Arbitration – The Biwater Gauff Compromise' (2007–2008) 6 *Law & Prac. Int'l Cts. & Tribunals* 97.

16 See, *e.g.*, *Methanex v. US*, UNCITRAL, Decision of the Tribunal on Petitions from Third Persons to Intervene as 'Amici Curiae' in the Matter of an Arbitration under Chapter 11 of the North American Free Trade Agreement and the UNCITRAL Arbitration Rules, para. 49 (Jan. 15, 2001):

> There is undoubtedly public interest in this arbitration. The substantive issues extend far beyond those by the usual transnational arbitration between private parties. This is not merely because one of the Disputing Parties is a State. ... The public interest in this arbitration arises from its subject matter as powerfully suggested in the petitions.

17 See, e.g., *Abaclat et al. v. Arg. Rep.*, ICSID Case No. ARB/07/5, Decision on Jurisdiction and Admissibility (Aug. 4, 2011).
18 *Biwater Gauff (Tanzania) Ltd. v. United Rep. of Tanz.*, ICSID Case No. ARB/05/22, Award (July 4, 2008).
19 See, e.g., *Metalclad Corporation v. Mex.*, ICSID Case No. ARB (AF)/97/1, Award (Aug. 30, 2000).
20 Reference to the right of access to information was also made during the negotiations of the UNCITRAL Transparency Rules. See A/CN.9/717, 25 February 2011, para. 16, with reference to *Claude Reyes et al. v. Chile*, Inter-Am. Ct. H.R. (ser. C) No. 151, 19 September 2006 and *Társág a Szabadságjogokért v. Hungary*, App. No. 37374/05, Eur. Ct. H.R., 14 April 2009.
21 *Ronald S. Lauder v. Czech Rep.*, Final Award, UNCITRAL (Sep. 3, 2001).
22 *CME v. Czech Rep.*, Final Award, UNCITRAL (Mar. 14, 2003).
23 *SGS Société Générale de Surveillance S.A. v. Islamic Rep. of Pak.*, ICSID Case No. ARB/01/13, Decision of the Tribunal on Objections to Jurisdiction (Aug. 6, 2003).
24 *SGS Société Générale de Surveillance S.A. v. Rep. of the Phil.*, ICSID Case No. ARB/02/6, Decision of the Tribunal on Objections to Jurisdiction (Jan. 29, 2004).
25 Possible reform of investor-State dispute settlement (ISDS), Note by the Secretariat, UN Doc. A/CN.9/WG.III.150, para. 13.

as vague standards and not as detailed rules. Tribunals may have a considerable degree of discretion when they determine the meaning of these broad standards. Moreover, arbitration is a decentralized system of dispute resolution. Tribunals are established for each and every case and decide without being bound by previous decisions. This harbours the risk of inconsistent and incoherent decisions.[26] The existing review mechanisms do not help to overcome this risk, as they mainly address the integrity and fairness of the proceedings, but do not allow for a systemic check for correctness and consistency.[27]

19.14   While the lack of consistency and coherence is less prominent than one would expect it to be,[28] it nevertheless represents a problem. Legal norms are a form of social control, which only functions when said norms are intelligible. As far as guarantees of investment protection are concerned, States can only align their investment policies with treaty obligations when they know their content.[29] A coherent and consistent body of case law is also necessary in order to build up the trust and confidence in the system of investment protection.

c.   Decision-makers

19.15   The third area of concern relates to the decision-makers. Various stakeholders have complained about the fact that arbitrators are selected on an ex post basis, i.e., once a dispute has arisen.[30] This, it is argued, implies the risk that arbitrators are selected on the basis that they are known for favouring either States or investors.[31] The concern has been raised that these arbitrators would perpetuate their respective investor- or State-friendly positions to secure reappointment in future cases.[32]

19.16   Critics have also taken issue with the appointment process for arbitrators,[33] which is at times characterized as being overly intransparent.[34] The suspicion has been voiced that some arbitrators might have a commercial mindset and not be in the position to sufficiently consider public interest concerns.[35] The possibility of certain individuals acting as counsel and arbitrator

---

26   S.D. Franck, 'The Legitimacy Crisis in Investment Treaty Arbitration: Privatizing Public International Law Through Inconsistent Decisions' (2005) 73 *Fordham L. Rev.* 1521; L.T. Wells, 'Backlash to Investment Arbitration: Three Causes' in M. Waibel and A. Kaushal et al. (eds), *The Backlash against Investment Arbitration* (Kluwer Law International 2010) 341; Ma (n 13) 576. See, however, also T. Schultz, 'Against Consistency in Investment Arbitration' in Z. Douglas et al. (eds), *The Foundations of International Investment Law* (OUP 2014) 297; A. Joubin-Bret, 'The Growing Diversity and Inconsistency in the IIA System' in K.P. Sauvant and M. Chiswick-Patterson (n 15) 137.

27   Possible reform of investor-State dispute settlement (ISDS), Submission from the European Union, UN Doc. A/CN:9/WG.III/WP.145, para. 28.

28   S.W. Schilll, 'System-Building in Investment Treaty Arbitration and Lawmaking' in A. von Bogdandy and I. Venzke (eds), *International Judicial Lawmaking – On Public Authority and Democratic Legitimation in Global Governance* (Springer 2012) 133.

29   Report of Working Group III (n 14) para. 15.

30   Submission from the European Union (n 27) para. 32.

31   Report of Working Group III (Investor-State Dispute Settlement Reform) on the work of its thirty-fifth session (New York, 23–27 April 2018), UN Doc. A/CN.9/935, 14 May 2018, para. 54; Impact Assessment – Multilateral reform of Investment Dispute Resolution (n 1) p. 11.

32   Report of Working Group III, ibid., para. 56.

33   Ibid., para. 73.

34   Ibid., para. 76.

35   Ibid., para. 82.

has also sparked criticism. Some stakeholders see a risk that these individuals might take positions as arbitrators that are influenced by their interests when acting as counsel to parties.[36]

d. Duration and costs

The fourth aspect of the backlash against ISDS relates to the time and costs of investment arbitration proceedings.[37] Investment arbitrations have often lasted for years and required significant expenditures by the litigants. Statistics indicate that the combined legal and arbitration costs for claimants and respondents averaged USD 8 million in recent years.[38] The average duration of arbitration proceedings has been 3.63 years from the filing of the request for arbitration until the date of the final award.[39] **19.17**

The time and costs pose a challenge for States and investors alike: States criticize the expenditures that are necessary to defend against investment claims, irrespective of whether they are meritorious or frivolous. This is particularly burdensome for developing States whose financial resources are limited. States may also be put at a disadvantage if investors initiate proceedings through corporate vehicles without assets, as this limits States' prospects to seek recovery.[40] Investors, in contrast, may consider the time and costs of arbitration proceedings to be prohibitive. This holds true, in particular, for small- and medium-sized companies with limited resources. **19.18**

C. THE PROPOSED MULTILATERAL INVESTMENT COURT

Against this background, the EU has proposed the establishment of a multilateral investment court. The EU's ambition to create such a court system has its origins in 2015. After an online consultation had revealed significant criticism against ISDS, commissioner Malstrom announced the establishment of a court system as an alternative to arbitration.[41] Various investment treaties negotiated in the years following introduced such an investment court as a mechanism to resolve investor-State disputes. Examples include the Comprehensive and Economic Trade Agreement ('CETA') between the EU and Canada,[42] the EU-Vietnam Free **19.19**

---

36   Ibid., para. 78; Possible reform of investor-State dispute settlement (ISDS), Ensuring independence and impartiality on the part of arbitrators and decision makers in ISDS, note by the Secretariat, UN Doc. A/CN.9/WG.III/WP.151, 30 August 2018, para. 25. For a discussion of this topic, see also F. Dias Simoes, 'Hold on to Your Hat! Issue Conflicts in the Investment Court System' (2018) *The Law and Practice of International Courts and Tribunals*, 98.

37   A. Raviv, 'Achieving a Faster ICSID' in Kalicki and Joubin-Bret (n 13) 653; M. Hodgson, 'Costs in Investment Treaty Arbitration – The Case for Reform' in Kalicki and Joubin-Bret (n 13) 748; Report of Working Group III (n 14) para. 35.

38   Possible reform of investor-State dispute settlement (ISDS) – cost and duration, UN Doc. A/CN.9/WG.III/WP.153, para. 42.

39   Ibid., para. 54.

40   Report of Working Group III (n 14) para. 56.

41   See Commission, 'Concept Paper, Investment in TTIP and beyond – the path for reform'; 'Report containing the European Parliament's recommendations to the European Commission on the negotiations for the Transatlantic Trade and Investment Partnership (TTIP)' (1 June 2015) <http://www.europarl.europa.eu/sides/getDoc.do?pubRef=-//EP//NONSGML+REPORT+A8-2015-0175+0+DOC+PDF+V0//EN> accessed 12 September 2016.

42   Comprehensive Economic and Trade Agreement (CETA) between Canada, of the one part, and the European Union and its Member States, of the other part, Official Journal of the European Union, L 11/23, 14 January 2017.

Trade Agreement[43] and the draft EU-Mexican Trade Agreement,[44] all of which provide for the creation of a two-tiered structure of permanent tribunals to resolve disputes under the pertinent investment agreements.

19.20 All these agreements already anticipate the option that a multilateral investment court might replace them in the future. With the adoption of the negotiating directives on the multilateral investment court on 20 March 2018, the EU has taken further steps to attain this goal. It lies in the nature of such a document that it describes the proposed investment court only in rudimentary form. Yet, it allows for some conclusions to be drawn as to how the European Union conceives the creation of the multilateral investment court.

1. Key features of the institutional and jurisdictional set-up

a. Creation of permanent decision-making bodies

19.21 The main institutional reform consists of the envisaged creation of a permanent tribunal of first instance as well as a permanent appellate tribunal that shall be competent to review decisions for errors of law, manifest errors in the appreciation of facts or, where appropriate, serious procedural shortcomings.[45] The creation of such permanent bodies is based upon the expectation that permanent bodies can 'deliver predictability and consistency' and ensure 'effective and consistent application' of investment treaties when multiple disputes arise.[46]

19.22 The tribunals shall be composed of permanent members who shall be subject to stringent requirements of independence and impartiality as well as to ethical obligations set forth in a code of conduct. This marks a shift from a disputing party framework to a contracting party framework concerning the appointment of the decision-makers.[47] In other words: the decision-makers are not selected by the parties to the dispute ex post but by the parties to the treaty ex ante. The EU expects that permanent decision-makers will be to a lesser extent subject to impartiality concerns.[48] Two reasons are adduced in support of this assumption. First, it is argued that there will be fewer incentives to select predisposed decision-makers at a time when it cannot yet be determined whether the decision-maker will decide in cases in which the respective State is a respondent or in cases in which its investors act as claimant.[49] Second, it is asserted that the decision-makers would not have any incentives to render decisions with a view to being reappointed since they would be appointed for a non-renewable period of time and receive a permanent remuneration.[50]

---

43   EU-Vietnam Free Trade Agreement, available at <http://trade.ec.europa.eu/doclib/press/index.cfm?id=1437>, accessed 21 November 2020.

44   EU-Mexico Trade Agreement, available at <http://trade.ec.europa.eu/doclib/docs/2018/april/tradoc_156791.pdf>, accessed 21 November 2020.

45   Negotiating Directives, para. 10.

46   Submission from the European Union (n 27) para. 7. See also D.M. Howard, 'Creating Consistency Through a World Investment Court' (2017) 41 *Fordham Int'l L.J.* 1.

47   CIDS Research Paper, available at <https://www.cids.ch/news/isds-project-cids-supplemental-report>, p. 14. See also Anthea Roberts (2017), Would a Multilateral Investment Court be Biased? Shifting to a treaty party framework of analysis, EJIL:Talk!, 28 April 2017 available at: <https://www.ejiltalk.org/would-a-multilateral-investment-court-be-biased-shifting-to-a-treaty-party-framework-of-analysis/>.

48   Submission from the European Union (n 27) para. 7.

49   Ibid., para. 32.

50   Negotiating directives, para. 11.

The negotiating directives leave open whether the multilateral investment court will be **19.23** supported by the secretariat of an existing institution such as the International Centre for Settlement of Investment Disputes or the Permanent Court of Arbitration or whether a new administrative structure will be established.[51] This decision will not only heavily influence the efficiency of the proceedings but will also have significant cost implications. International courts such as the International Court of Justice create significant costs. For example, the budget of the International Court of Justice for the biennium 2016–2017 exceeded USD 45 million, out of which more than two-thirds was reserved for costs other than the remuneration of the judges.[52] The negotiating directives of the EU do not yet address these financial implications in detail. They merely provide that the fixed costs shall be covered by the Contracting Parties to the Convention and by the disputing parties.[53] The share of the Contracting Parties shall be allocated based on fair standards that take into consideration the Parties' level of economic development.[54]

The institutional set-up envisaged under the negotiating directives very much resembles the **19.24** investment court system that is currently foreseen under recent investment treaties concluded by the EU. For example, CETA provides for the creation of a Tribunal of First Instance composed of 15 members, out of which five members shall be nationals of a Member State of the European Union, five shall be nationals of Canada and five shall be nationals of third countries.[55] The members shall possess the qualifications required for appointment to judicial office or be jurists of recognized competence. They must have 'demonstrated experience in public international law' and preferably 'expertise in particular, in international investment law, in international trade law and the resolution of disputes arising under international investment or international trade agreements'.[56]

The CETA Tribunal of First Instance shall usually hear cases in divisions of three members, **19.25** out of which one shall be a national of the EU, one a national of Canada and the chair a national of a third country.[57] The assignment of cases to a division shall be made on a 'random and unpredictable' basis, which nevertheless ensures that equal opportunity is given to all members of the Tribunal. Similar requirements apply to the members of the Appellate Tribunal.[58]

While the members of the permanent tribunals established under CETA are foreseen as being **19.26** selected by the so-called CETA joint committee – a political organ established under CETA – it is as of today unclear how the members of the proposed multilateral investment court will be selected. The negotiating directives are rather vague on this point. One option referred to in the negotiating directives is that all parties to the convention establishing the multilateral

---

51 Ibid., para. 12.
52 Report of the International Court of Justice, General Assembly, Official Records, Seventy-second Session, Supplement No. 4, UN Doc. A/72/4, para. 334.
53 Negotiating directives, para. 15.
54 Ibid. On this aspect, see also Settlement of commercial disputes, Investor-State Dispute Settlement Framework, UN Doc. A/CN.9/918/Add 4, 31 January 2017, p. 12 (Comments from Thailand).
55 Art. 8.27 (4) CETA.
56 Ibid.
57 Art. 8.27 (5) CETA.
58 Art. 8.28 (4) and (5) CETA.

investment court are entitled to appoint one member.[59] This modality of full representation would have the downside that the number of members would constantly fluctuate depending on which States have become party to the convention establishing the multilateral investment court. Alternatively, the negotiating directives envisage that a selective group of members will be appointed through methods that currently apply for the selection of judges at international courts such as the International Court of Justice or the International Criminal Court. The judges of the International Court of Justice are elected by the members of the United Nations General Assembly and by the Security Council.[60] At the International Criminal Court, the Assembly of States Parties votes on the bench of judges with a view to their legal expertise, region and gender.[61] It remains to be seen whether similar methods will ultimately apply for the selection of the members of a multilateral investment court. One thing, however, is already certain today. The appointment of a balanced pool of first-class decision-makers will be critical for the success and legitimacy of a future multilateral investment court.[62]

b. Jurisdiction

19.27 The jurisdiction of the multilateral investment court shall cover all investment agreements to which the European Union is or will be a party.[63] Members States of the European Union and third countries shall all be put into the position to bring agreements to which they are or will be parties under the jurisdiction of the court.[64]

19.28 In principle, this presupposes that the relevant parties to an investment agreement have agreed to submit disputes to the multilateral investment court. However, the negotiating directives provide that it shall be explored whether the convention establishing the multilateral investment court could also be utilized if only the respondent state is party to the convention.[65]

19.29 The main precedent for this approach is the opt-in mechanism foreseen under the Mauritius Convention on Transparency.[66] The Mauritius Convention governs the application of the UNCITRAL Transparency Rules, which are a set of procedural rules geared at enhancing transparency and accessibility to the public of treaty-based investor-State arbitrations.[67] The

---

59   Negotiating directives, para. 11.
60   Art. 4 Statute of the International Court of Justice.
61   Art. 36 Rome Statute of the International Criminal Court.
62   On this challenge, see <https://www.cids.ch/images/Documents/CIDS_Supplemental_Report_ISDS_2016.pdf>. See also K. Fach Gómez, 'Diversity and the Principle of Independence and Impartiality in the Future Multilateral Investment Court' (2018) 17 *The Law and Practice of International Courts and Tribunals* 78; C.N. Brower and J. Ahmad (n 4) 793 (arguing that appointment of the judges will involve 'a political scrum').
63   Negotiating directives, para. 6.
64   Ibid., para. 7.
65   Ibid., para. 8.
66   See G. Kaufmann-Kohler and M. Potestà, 'Can the Mauritius Convention serve as a model for the reform of investor-State arbitration in connection with the introduction of a permanent investment tribunal or an appeal mechanism?', available at <https://www.cids.ch/images/Documents/CIDS_First_Report_ISDS_2015.pdf>.
67   See D. Euler, *Transparency in International Investment Arbitration – A Guide to the UNCITRAL Rules on Transparency in Treaty-Based Investor-State Arbitration* (CUP 2015); P. Coates, 'The UNCITRAL Rules on Transparency in Treaty-Based Investor State Arbitration – Continuing the Evolution of Investment Treaty Arbitration' (2014) 17 *Int'l Arb. L. Rev.* 113; F. Rosenfeld and J.H. Nedden, 'The New UNCITRAL Transparency Rules – How the Trend towards Transparency Differs in Investment and Commercial Arbitration' in C. Müller and A. Rigozzi (eds), *New Developments in International Commercial Arbitration 2013* (Schulthess Juristische Medien 2013) 41.

Mauritius Convention provides that the Transparency Rules apply under the following conditions to existing treaties:

- First, the UNCITRAL Transparency Rules apply to an investor-State arbitration if the home State of the claimant and respondent are a party to the Mauritius Convention and they have not made relevant reservations as specified thereunder.[68]
- Second, the UNCITRAL Transparency Rules apply where the respondent is a party to the Mauritius Convention and has not made a relevant reservation, and the claimant agrees to the application of the UNCITRAL Transparency Rules.[69]

19.30 The Mauritius Convention thereby extends the scope of application *ratione temporis* of the Transparency Rules, which would otherwise only apply to investment arbitrations initiated under the UNCITRAL Arbitration Rules pursuant to a treaty adopted on or after 1 April 2014 (unless opted out by the parties).

19.31 As compelling as this approach may sound at first glance, it is likely to create problems at the transitional stage. Specifically, this solution could have the effect that the investor's right to arbitrate is taken away without the consent of the investor where the investor's home State and the host State become a party to the convention establishing the multilateral investment court. Depending on how one conceptualizes the position of investors under investment treaties,[70] this solution could trigger criticism. Those proponents who argue that investors enjoy independent rights under investment treaties are likely to demand safeguards for investors' rights.

2. Key features of the procedure

19.32 Various reform proposals have been made for the procedure before the multilateral investment court. Five aspects stand out in this respect.

a. Transparency

19.33 First, the procedure is envisaged to be conducted based on rules that allow for the transparency of the proceedings. On this point, the negotiating directives explicitly reference the above-mentioned UNCITRAL Transparency Rules.[71] These rules require the publication of certain information and documents, public hearings, and the possibility of submissions by non-disputing parties.[72]

b. Applicability of the arbitration framework

19.34 Second, it remains unclear whether this reference to the UNCITRAL Transparency Rules implies that the entire proceedings before the multilateral investment court will be conducted based on arbitration rules.

---

68 Art. 2 (1) Mauritius Convention.
69 Ibid., Art. 2 (2).
70 For a discussion, see T. Braun, 'Globalization-Driven Innovation: The Investor as a Partial Subject in Public International Law – An Inquiry into the Nature and Limits of Investor Rights', *Jean Monnet Working Paper 04/13 (2013)*.
71 Negotiating directives, para. 13.
72 UNCITRAL Transparency Rules, Arts. 2, 3, 4, 5, 6, 8.

19.35   The court system foreseen under CETA is a precedent for this approach. CETA provides that proceedings before the investment court remain consent-based[73] and will be conducted based on arbitration rules.[74] The outcome of the proceedings under CETA shall be an award,[75] which is deemed to qualify as an award under the ICSID Convention or to satisfy the commerciality criterion set forth in Article I of the New York Convention.[76] The EU thereby hopes to ensure the enforceability of the decision under the New York Convention or the ICSID Convention.

19.36   In consultations on the reform of ISDS, certain States have already voiced a similar desire. Germany, for example, underlined that a future convention on a multilateral investment court should be designed in a way that awards can be reliably executed also in States that are not signatory to the Convention establishing the multilateral investment court, but which are a party to the ICSID Convention and the New York Convention.[77]

19.37   As much as this petitum is understandable from a policy perspective, it is very unclear how it can be implemented in practice. After all, the multilateral investment court is intended to mark a turn away from international arbitration. Without doubt, it does not suffice to merely include a provision pursuant to which the outcome of the proceedings is deemed to qualify as an award under the New York Convention or the ICSID Convention.[78] Such a provision will not have any effects upon third States that have not signed the convention establishing the multilateral investment court.

19.38   In relation to those third States, it will matter whether the decision rendered by the multilateral investment court will qualify as an award under the ICSID Convention or the New York Convention. There is no authority for the former proposition. The main precedent for the latter proposition are the awards rendered by the Iran-United States Claims Tribunal, which is a permanent arbitral body created in 1981 after the Iranian hostage crisis between the United States of America and the Islamic Republic of Iran. The Iran-United States Claims Tribunal was formed to resolve certain claims by nationals of one State Party against the other State Party and certain claims between the two State Parties.[79] Some courts have considered the Iran-United States Claims Tribunal to be a permanent arbitral body. These courts found that an individual voluntarily submits to arbitration by starting proceedings before the Iran-United States Claims Tribunal or that its consent can be replaced through that of its home State.[80] Accordingly, they have enforced awards of the Iran-United States Claims Tribunal under the New York Convention. However, this position has remained controversial.

---

73   Art. 8.25 CETA.

74   Ibid., Art. 8.23 (7).

75   Ibid., Art. 8.39.

76   Ibid., Art. 8.41 (5) and (6).

77   Settlement of commercial disputes, Investor-State Dispute Settlement Framework, UN Doc. A/CN.9/918/Add 3, 31 January 2017, p. 12 (Comments from Germany).

78   N.J. Calamita, 'The (In)Compatibility of Appellate Mechanisms with Existing Instruments of the Investment Treaty Regime' (2017) 18 *Journal of World Investment & Trade* 585.

79   Declaration of the Government of the Democratic and Popular Republic of Algeria Concerning the Settlement of Claims by the Government of the United States of America and the Government of the Islamic Republic of Iran [hereinafter Claims Settlement Declaration], Jan. 19, 1981, 75 *A.J.I.L.* 418.

80   *Ministry of Def. of the Islamic Republic of Iran v. Gould Inc.*, 887 F.2d 1357 (9th Cir. 1989). See also *Abrahim Rahman Golshani v. The Government of the Islamic Republic of Iran*, Cour d'Appel de Paris, Decision of 28 June 2001.

The English High Court, for example, ruled in an obiter in *Mark Dallal v. Bank Mellat* that an award of the Iran-United States Claims Tribunal would not be based on an arbitration agreement that is valid under Dutch law.[81] According to the English High Court, the award could not be enforced under the New York Convention.

In light of the aforesaid, uncertainty remains as to whether decisions rendered by a multilateral investment court will be enforceable in third States that have not signed the future convention establishing the multilateral investment court. While the proposal has been made to create a fund to overcome this enforcement deficit,[82] it is unlikely that this option will be realized. States have no incentive to fund compensation claims that are directed against other States. **19.39**

c. Mechanisms to reduce time and costs

Third, the negotiating directives provide for various mechanisms that are geared at reducing the time and costs of the proceedings notwithstanding the establishment of a second instance, which bears the potential to significantly prolong their duration and to increase costs. Among others, the EU intends to create mechanisms that allow for the early dismissal of frivolous claims.[83] Such mechanisms are already foreseen under various arbitration rules. ICSID Arbitration Rule 41 (5) stands as an example.[84] The text of CETA likewise contains provisions allowing for the early dismissal of claims that are manifestly without legal merit[85] or unfounded as a matter of law.[86] Such mechanisms have increasingly been used in recent practice.[87] **19.40**

---

81 United Kingdom, No. 20. High Court, 26 July 1985, *Mark Dallal v. Bank Mellat*, in 11 *Y.B. Com. Arb.* 547, 547 (Albert Jan van den Berg ed., 1986).

82 Bungenberg and Reinisch (n 1) 163.

83 Negotiating directives, para. 9.

84 See F. Rosenfeld, 'Early Dismissal of Claims in Investment Arbitration' in A. Kulick (ed), *Reassertion of Control over the Investment Treaty* Regime (CUP 2016) 83; C. Puig and C. Brown, 'The Power of ICSID Tribunals to Dismiss Proceedings Summarily: An Analysis of Rule 41(5) of the ICSID Arbitration Rules' (2011) *Sydney Law School, Legal Studies Research Paper No. 11/33*, 3; E. De Brabandere, 'The ICSID Rule on Early Dismissal of Unmeritorious Treaty Claims: Preserving the Integrity of ICSID Arbitration' (2012) 9 (1) *Manchester Journal of International Economic Law* 23; M. Potestà and M. Sobat, 'Frivolous claims in international adjudication: a study of ICSID Rule 41(5) and of procedures of other courts and tribunals to dismiss claims summarily' (2012) 3 *J. Int'l Disp. Settl.* 137; A. Goldsmith, 'Trans-Global Petroleum: "Rare Bird" or Significant Step in the Development of Early Merits-Based Claim-Vetting?' (2008) 26 *ASA Bulletin* 667; L. Markert, 'Preliminary Objections pursuant to ICSID Arbitration Rule 41(5) – Soon to Become the Preliminary Objection of Choice?' (2012) 9 *TDM* 1.

85 Art. 8.32 CETA.

86 Ibid., Art. 8.33.

87 Jurisprudence on ICSID Arbitration Rule 41(5) includes: *MOL Hungarian Oil and Gas Company plc v. Republic of Croatia*, ICSID Case No. ARB/13/32, Decision on Respondent's Application under ICSID Arbitration Rule 41(5), 2 December 2014; *PNG Sustainable Development Program Ltd. v. Independent State of Papua New Guinea*, ICSID Case No. ARB/13/33, The Tribunal's Decision on the Respondent's Objections under Rule 41(5) of the ICSID Arbitration Rules, 28 October 2014; *Elsamex S.A. v. República de Honduras, Decisión sobre la Excepción de Elsamex S.A. contra la Solicitud de Anulación del Laudo presentada por la República de Honduras*, ICSID Case No. ARB/09/4, 7 January 2014; *Emmis International Holding B.V., Emmis Radio Operating, B.V., Mem Magyar Electronic Media Kereskedelmi És Szolgáltató KFT v. Hungary*, ICSID Case No. ARB/12/2, Decision on Respondent's Objection under ICSID Arbitration Rule 41(5), 11 March 2013; *Accession Mezzanine Capital L.P. and Danubius Kereskedõház Vagyonkezelõ Zrt v. Hungary*, ICSID Case No. ARB/12/3, Decision on Respondent's Objection under Arbitration Rule 41(5), 16 January 2013; *Vattenfall AB and others v. Federal Republic of Germany*, ICSID Case No. ARB/12/12, Decision of 2 July 2013, reported in: IAreporter, 4 July 2013; *Rafat Ali Rizvi v. The Republic of Indonesia*, ICSID Case No. ARB/11/13, Award on Jurisdiction, 16 July 2013, para. 20; *Global Trading Resource Corp. and Global International, Inc. v. Ukraine*, ICSID Case No. ARB/09/11, Award, 1 December 2010; *Brandes Investment Partners, LP v. Bolivarian Republic of Venezuela*, ICSID Case No. ARB/08/3, Decision on the Respondent's Objection under Rule 41(5) of the ICSID Arbitration

19.41 CETA also envisages the adoption of supplemental rules aimed at reducing the financial burden on claimants who are natural persons or small- or medium-sized enterprises.[88] A similar goal is reflected in the EU-Vietnam FTA, which sets limits to the costs that may be awarded against specific categories of unsuccessful parties.[89] While such a mechanism may indeed alleviate the financial risks of smaller investors who initiate investment arbitration proceedings, it places an additional burden on States, who are limited in their ability to recover their costs of legal assistance and representation if they prevail.

d. Amicable dispute resolution mechanisms

19.42 Fourth, the EU intends to foster the use of amicable dispute resolution mechanisms.[90] The negotiating directives do not specify any details in this respect. Possibly, the amicable dispute resolution mechanisms foreseen under CETA will serve as guidance.

19.43 Pursuant to Art. 8.19 CETA, a dispute should as far as possible be settled amicably. A request for consultations must be submitted within three years after the date on which the investor or the locally established enterprise first acquired or should have acquired knowledge of the alleged breach and the loss or damage incurred thereby or two years after the investor or, as applicable, the locally established enterprise ceases to pursue claims or proceedings before a tribunal or court under the law of the party or when such proceedings have otherwise ended. In any event, the request for consultations must be submitted no later than ten years after the date on which the investor or the locally established enterprise first acquired or should have first acquired knowledge of the alleged breach and the loss or damage incurred thereby.[91] CETA thereby introduces a statute of limitations for investment claims.

19.44 Unless agreed otherwise, consultations shall be held within 60 days of the submission of the request for consultations.[92] If the dispute cannot be settled within 90 days of the submission of the request for consultations, the respondent shall be determined if the request concerns an alleged breach of the CETA by the EU or a Member State of the EU.[93] The determination shall be made by the EU. Absent such a determination within 50 days, the Member State shall be the respondent if the measures are exclusively measures of the Member State; otherwise the EU shall be respondent.[94]

Rules, 2 February 2009; *Trans-Global Petroleum Inc. v. The Hashemite Kingdom of Jordan*, ICSID Case No. Arb/07/25, The Tribunal's Decision on the Respondent's Objection under Rule 41(5) of the ICSID Arbitration Rules, 12 May 2008; *Rachel S. Grynberg, Stephen M. Grynberg, Miriam Z. Grynberg, and RSM Production Corporation v. Grenada*, ICSID Case No. ARB/10/6, Award, 10 December 2010. Additional cases without public decision include *CEAC Holdings Limited v. Montenegro*, ICSID Case No. ARB/14/8, Decision of 27 January 2015; *Transglobal Green Energy, LLC and Transglobal Green Panama, S.A. v. Republic of Panama*, Decision of 17 March 2015; *Edenred S.A. v. Hungary*, ICSID Case No. ARB/13/21, Decision of 6 June 2014.

88   Art. 8.39 CETA. On this issue, see also K. Boon, 'Investment Treaty Arbitration: Making a Place for Small Claims' (2018) 19 *Journal of World Investment & Trade* 667.

89   EU-Vietnam FTA, Chapter 8, Section 3, Art. 27.

90   Negotiating directives, para. 9.

91   Art. 8.19(6) CETA.

92   Ibid., Art. 8.19.

93   Ibid., Art. 8.21.

94   Ibid., Art. 8.21 (4).

The conduct of consultations is a requirement for the eventual submission of the claim to the **19.45** tribunal. Pursuant to Article 8.22 CETA, an investor may only submit a claim to the tribunal if 180 days have elapsed from the submission of the request for consultations and, if applicable, at least 90 days have elapsed from the submission of the notice requesting a determination of the respondent. The proceedings before the tribunal of first instance are limited to those measures that were already identified in the request for consultations.[95] It remains to be seen whether a similar regime will be created for the multilateral investment court.

e. Provisions regulating parallel claims

Fifth, the EU intends to create provisions governing parallel claims.[96] Such provisions are **19.46** already contained in the CETA text, pursuant to which the investor is required to withdraw or discontinue any existing proceeding before a tribunal or court under domestic or international law with respect to a measure that is alleged to constitute a breach referred to in its claim.[97] The investor must also waive its right to initiate any claim or proceeding before a tribunal or court under domestic or international law with respect to a measure that is alleged to constitute such a breach.[98]

A further mechanism to coordinate parallel claims is set forth in Article 8.24 CETA. This **19.47** provision applies where a parallel claim is brought pursuant to another international agreement and where there is a potential for overlapping compensation or where the other international claim could otherwise have a significant impact on the resolution of the claim. Article 8.24 CETA directs the tribunal to stay its proceedings or otherwise to ensure that proceedings brought pursuant to another international agreement are taken into account in its decision, order or award.

In addition, Article 8.43 CETA allows for the consolidation of two or more claims that have a **19.48** question of law or fact in common and arise out of the same events or circumstances.[99]

3. Conclusion

Overall, it hence appears that the EU is striving to create a dispute resolution system that very **19.49** much resembles the court system foreseen under recent investment treaties such as CETA. One key difference will consist of the multilateral character of the new court system to be established.

D. CHALLENGES WHEN IMPLEMENTING THE MULTILATERAL COURT SYSTEM

As of today, it remains very much unclear whether the EU will succeed in its endeavours to **19.50** establish such a multilateral court system. The EU is likely to face challenges at multiple levels.

---

95   Ibid., Art. 8.22 (1) lit. e.
96   Negotiating directives, para. 9.
97   Art. 8.22 (1) lit. f CETA.
98   Ibid., Art. 8.22 (1) lit. g.
99   Ibid., Art. 8.43.

1. Challenges at the level of EU Member States

19.51 To begin with, the EU will have to convince its Member States of the need for a multilateral investment court. This is because the EU does not have the exclusive competence to sign a convention establishing a multilateral investment court.

19.52 The Court of Justice of the European Union ('CJEU') clarified this in its *Opinion 2/15*. In this opinion, the CJEU had to assess whether the EU had exclusive competence to conclude the Singapore-EU Free Trade Agreement. The CJEU denied this, among others, on the grounds that the EU-Singapore FTA provided for arbitration. Arbitration entails, as the CJEU correctly noted, that disputes are 'removed from the jurisdiction of the courts of the Member States'.[100] This, the CJEU held, would not merely be an ancillary aspect that falls 'within the same competence as the substantive provisions which they accompany'.[101] Accordingly, the consent of the Member States is necessary to conclude the Singapore-EU FTA.[102]

19.53 The same reasoning can also be applied to the multilateral investment court. As the establishment of the multilateral investment court would likewise remove the settlement of investor-state disputes from the realm of State courts, it would equally require the consent of the Member States.

2. Challenges at the EU level

19.54 At the EU level, the main challenge will consist in ensuring the compatibility of the investment court with EU law. In this respect, important lessons can be learnt from *Opinion 1/17* of the CJEU.[103] This opinion concerned the question of whether the CETA court system is compatible with EU law. The CJEU ruled that it is, but it did so in view of specific features of CETA's institutional set-up.

19.55 As a starting point for its analysis, and in line with existing case law,[104] the CJEU confirmed that the EU may conclude international agreements and submit to a court system to resolve disputes regarding the interpretation and application of such agreements.[105] That said, the CJEU emphasized that the establishment of such a court system may not have any adverse effect on the autonomy of the EU legal order.[106] According to the CJEU, this presupposes two things:

---

100 *Opinion 2/15 (Free Trade Agreement between the European Union and the Republic of Singapore)* of 16 May 2017, ECLI:EU:C:2017:376, para. 292.

101 Ibid., para. 276. The EU further lacked exclusive competence on the ground that the EU-Singapore FTA also covered portfolio investments, while the EU's competence is restricted to direct investment.

102 See also N. Lavranos, 'Mixed Exclusivity: The CJEU's Opinion on the EU-Singapore FTA' (2017) 2(1) *European Investment Law and Arbitration Review* 1.

103 *Opinion 1/17* of the Court of 30 April 2019, ECLI:EU:C:2019:341.

104 *Opinion 1/91 (EEA Agreement – I)* of 14 December 1991, EU:C:1991:490, paras. 40 and 70; Opinion 1/09 (Agreement creating a unified patent litigation system) of 8 March 2011, EU:C:2011:123, paras. 74 and 76; *Opinion 2/13 (Accession of the EU to the ECHR)* of 18 December 2014, EU:C:2014:2453, paras. 182 and 183; *Slovak Republic v. Achmea B.V.*, EU:C:284/16, 6 March 2018, para. 57.

105 Ibid., para. 106.

106 *Opinion 1/17* of the Court of 30 April 2019, ECLI:EU:C:2019:341, para. 208.

First, the CETA tribunals may not have the authority to interpret or apply rules of EU law **19.56** other than the provisions of CETA.[107] The CJEU found that they do not and noted that the CETA tribunals may consider, where appropriate, the domestic law of a party merely as a 'matter of fact' and 'in doing so [...] shall follow the prevailing interpretation given to the domestic law by the courts or authorities of that Party'.[108] The CJEU further noted that CETA tribunals will not have any jurisdiction to give rulings on the division of powers between the Union and the Member States.[109]

Second, the CJEU ruled that the CETA tribunal may not 'issue awards which have the effect **19.57** of preventing the EU operations from operating in accordance with the EU constitutional framework'.[110] The CJEU found that this requirement was complied with. It noted that the CETA tribunals will not have the power to 'call into question the level of protection of public interest determined by the Union following a democratic process'.[111] The CJEU based its opinion on the CETA's provisions on the right to regulate.

Having found that the CETA court system is compatible with the autonomy of the EU legal **19.58** order, the CJEU proceeded by finding that it is compatible with the general principle of equal treatment and the requirement of effectiveness.[112]

The CJEU finally ruled that the CETA court system does not violate the right of access to an **19.59** independent tribunal, either.[113] In reaching this conclusion, it emphasized the need to ensure that the CETA Tribunal of First Instance and the CETA Appellate Tribunal are financially accessible also for small- and medium-sized enterprises and private individuals. The CJEU therefore attributed much weight to the commitment of the CETA Joint Committee in Article 8.39.6 to 'consider supplemental rules aimed at reducing the financial burden on claimants who are natural persons or small and medium-sized enterprises'.[114] With respect to the requirement of independence, the CJEU made a distinction between its external and internal aspects. The external aspect of the requirement of independence means that tribunals must exercise their functions wholly autonomously.[115] The CJEU noted that measures such as an appointment of the court's members for a fixed term, a requirement of specific expertise and a level of remuneration commensurate with the importance of their duties would ensure such external independence.[116] The internal dimension of the requirement of independence, in contrast, presupposes an equal distance from the parties and the absence of any personal interest of the members in the outcome of the proceedings. The CJEU noted that measures

---

107   Ibid., paras. 120 et seq.
108   Ibid., para. 130.
109   Ibid., para. 132.
110   Ibid., para. 119.
111   Ibid., para. 156.
112   Ibid., para. 162.
113   Ibid., paras. 189 et seq.
114   Ibid., paras. 207, 218 et seq.
115   Ibid., para. 223.
116   Ibid.

such as the random and unpredictable composition of the division, the nationality require-ments for the members of a division as well as the reference to the IBA Guidelines on Conflicts of Interest would ensure compliance with this requirement.[117]

19.60 It is very likely that this decision will influence the way in which EU will tailor its proposal for a multilateral investment court and the fact is that the CJEU made express reference to a future multilateral investment tribunal in its opinion.[118] Key factors to be taken into consideration in the future set-up of a multilateral investment court include that (1) such court may not have jurisdiction to apply and interpret EU law, (2) the court may not have jurisdiction for disputes between Member States or between Member States and their investors, (3) there must be institutional guarantees of independence for the court members, (4) the court must be financially accessible also for small- and medium-sized enterprises and private individuals.

3. Challenges at the international level in relation to third States

19.61 The EU will also face challenges in relation to third States. After all, it is unlikely that third States that have not been involved in the hitherto negotiations of EU investment treaties will accept the court system negotiated under those treaties as a blueprint for a multilateral investment court system.

19.62 In an attempt to alleviate this problem, it has been proposed to negotiate the multilateral convention on the establishment of the investment court under the auspices of UNCITRAL. While UNCITRAL's Working Group III has embarked on a project on the reform of ISDS, it is as of today very unclear whether the outcome of its work will be a convention on a multilateral court system as per the EU's proposal. For the time being, UNCITRAL is still discussing various alternative reform proposals, which include:

- A combination of arbitration on an ad hoc basis and a standing appellate mechanism.[119]
- The adoption of rules fostering consolidation of similar cases and the exchange of information among tribunals.[120]
- The introduction of a system of prior scrutiny of arbitral awards as foreseen under the ICC Rules.[121]

---

117 Ibid., para. 238.
118 Ibid., para. 108.
119 Article 9.23 of Chapter 9 (Investment) of the Free Trade Agreement between the Government of the People's Republic of China and the Government of Australia. Art. 9.23 (Chapter 9) of the Transpacific Partnership Agreement (TPP), in Art. 10.19 of the United States-Chile Free Trade Agreement, Article 10.20 of the Additional Protocol to the Pacific Alliance or Article 29 of India's model BIT as well as various FTAs concluded by Korea (US, Australia, Canada, New Zealand). On the proposal to create an appellate mechanism more generally, see also K. Yannaca-Small, 'Improving the System of Investor-State Dispute Settlement: The OECD Governments' Perspective' in K.P. Sauvant and M. Chiswick-Patterson (n 15) 223; B. Legum, 'Appellate Mechanisms for Investment Arbitration: Worth a Second Look for the Trans-Pacific Partnership and the Proposed EU-US FTA?' in Kalicki and Joubin-Bret (n 13) 437; G. Bottini, 'Reform of the Investor-State Arbitration Regime – the Appeal Proposal' in Kalicki and Joubin-Bret (n 13) 455; J. Lee, 'Introduction of an Appellate Review Mechanism for International Investment Disputes – Expected Benefits and Remaining Tasks' in Kalicki and Joubin-Bret (n 13) 474; K. Andelic, 'Why ICSID Doesn't Need an Appellate Procedure and What to Do Instead' in Kalicki and Joubin-Bret (n 13) 496.
120 Possible reform of investor-State dispute settlement (ISDS), Note by the Secretariat, UN Doc. A/CN.9/WG.III.149, para. 34.
121 Ibid., para. 35.

- The introduction of a system of 'preliminary rulings' similar to the one carried out at the Court of Justice of the European Union.[122]
- The development of a code of conduct for arbitrators and the further elaboration of relevant challenge mechanisms.[123]
- An alternative appointment process for arbitrators, which gives a greater role to arbitral institutions or independent bodies equivalent to the WTO Dispute Settlement Body.[124]
- The introduction of tools to manage costs,[125] such as setting up a budget for costs at the initiation of the process and offering real-time information about the status of the case.[126]
- The use of dispute prevention mechanisms.[127]
- The establishment of an advisory centre to complement other reform options.[128]

19.63 One could certainly continue to list such examples and the fact remains that the multilateral investment court is not the only possible reform option. In an attempt to bridge these different reform options, it has been proposed to create a multilateral instrument with built-in flexibility to choose between options such as:

(i) only investor-State arbitration as reformed; (ii) only certain aspects of a reform investor-State arbitration (for instance, a code of conduct, or certain new mechanisms for the selection and appointment of arbitrators, their challenge, or certain procedures, such as on dismissal of frivolous claims or expedited proceedings), (iii) only a multilateral standing mechanism; (iv) only inter-State dispute settlement; (iv) only inter-State dispute settlement; (v) a multilateral standing mechanism, or certain elements thereof, and investor-State arbitration, or certain elements thereof, mixing various reform options.[129]

19.64 Critics might observe that this proposal will not create more than an institutional framework for a 'spaghetti bowl' of various dispute resolution options. But the drafters of this proposal seem to take comfort in the fact that other international instruments such as the United Nations Convention on the Law of the Sea ('UNCLOS') do likewise offer a menu of various dispute resolution options.

E. CONCLUSION

19.65 In conclusion, the future fate of the multilateral investment court is far from certain at the time of writing this chapter. While it is likely that the EU and several of its partners will continue their endeavours to establish such an institution, major jurisdictions such as the United States of America and Japan have been hesitant to support this initiative. Possibly, a multi-track

---

122 Ibid., para. 39.
123 Ibid., para. 51. See also Report of Working Group III (Investor-State Dispute Settlement Reform) on the work of its thirty-eighth session (Vienna, 14–18 October 2019), UN Doc. A/CN.9/1004, paras. 51 et seq.
124 Possible reform of investor-State dispute settlement (ISDS), Note by the Secretariat (n 120) para. 53.
125 Ibid., para. 65.
126 Ibid., para. 66.
127 Possible reform of investor-State dispute settlement (ISDS) (n 38) para. 101.
128 Report of Working Group III (n 123) paras. 28 et seq.
129 Possible reform of investor-State dispute settlement (ISDS), Multilateral instrument on ISDS reform, 16 January 2020, UN DOC A/CN.9/WG.III/WP.194.

system of ISDS will evolve in this situation with some States accepting the multilateral investment court whilst others take advantage of alternatives such as a reformed arbitration regime with its benefit of a universal enforcement mechanism. This would create a new form of fragmentation with its own challenges and problems.

20

THE IMPACT OF EU LAW ON INTERNATIONAL COMMERCIAL MEDIATION

Anne-Karin Grill and Emanuela Martin[1]

A. INTRODUCTION

Alternative dispute resolution is as relevant as ever and, particularly in Europe, parties in dispute are increasingly relying on mediation as the preferred tool to resolve conflict. This trend is further accentuated by the cost and duration of adversarial dispute resolution processes and the general disenchantment of the international corporate community with arbitration in particular.[2] Indeed, mediation has a lot to offer: flexibility, both in terms of timeframes and procedure, privacy, affordability, and the benefit of full party autonomy, from the initiation of the process up until its termination, ideally by an amicable solution crafted by the parties themselves. With notable multinational corporations and intergovernmental actors endorsing mediation as a standard tool to be used early on in the dispute resolution process, mediation will likely continue its rise.[3] **20.01**

This chapter sets out to scrutinize the impact of European law on international mediation with a particular focus on the commercial context. It explores the existing legal framework of mediation by taking Directive 2008/52/EC on certain aspects of mediation in civil and commercial matters (the 'European Mediation Directive') as the relevant starting point. As an example of the implementation of the European Mediation Directive, it further highlights the **20.02**

---

1 We are most grateful to Dr Georg Adler for his helpful comments and to Fabian Kissenkoetter for his excellent research assistance. Date of submission: 21/12/2020.
2 Stacie I Strong, 'Beyond International Commercial Arbitration? The Promise of International Commercial Mediation' (2014) 45 *Washington University Journal of Law and Policy* 11.
3 Stacie I Strong, 'Applying the Lessons of International Commercial Arbitration to International Commercial Mediation: A Dispute System Design Analysis' in Catharine Titi and Katia Fach Gomez (eds), *Mediation in International Commercial and Investment Disputes* (OUP 2019) 39.

intricacies of the legal framework for mediation in Austria. Finally, it describes the most recent efforts to harmonize the legal framework for commercial mediation and the enforcement of mediation outcomes on the international stage, most notably through the UNCITRAL Model Law on International Commercial Mediation and International Settlement Agreements Resulting from Mediation and the United Nations Convention on International Settlement Agreements Resulting from Mediation. The chapter concludes with a brief outlook on what to expect in the not-so-distant future.

B. LEGAL FRAMEWORK AND IMPLEMENTATION

1. The European Mediation Directive

20.03 The process of developing and eventually enacting Directive 2008/52/EC of the European Parliament and of the Council on certain aspects of mediation in civil and commercial matters (the 'European Mediation Directive') was marked by several milestones. Already in 1968, the Brussels Convention[4] undertook to facilitate the formalities governing the reciprocal recognition and enforcement of judgments and to introduce an expeditious procedure for enforcement. A further step forward was taken through the adoption of Recommendation 98/257/EEC[5] on the principles applicable to the bodies responsible for out-of-court settlement of consumer disputes by the European Commission on 30 March 1998. Recommendation 98/257/EE, however, was not yet focused on mediation *per se*.

20.04 A more decisive step was taken in Finland in 1999 during the Tampere European Council. There, the political leaders of Europe called for better access to justice and to this end decided that the Member States of the European Union (the 'EU') should endeavour to create alternative, extrajudicial procedures.[6] Further, in 2002, the European Commission published its Green Paper on Alternative Dispute Resolution in Civil and Commercial Law[7], which drew on the development of alternative dispute resolution ('ADR') up until that point. The Green Paper was followed by a broadly based consultation concerning the use of ADR in civil and commercial matters. The EU was finally showing serious interest in ADR. In the same year, a recommendation of the Committee of Ministers of the Council of Europe on mediation in civil matters[8] reiterated the potential of mediation in cross-border disputes and underlined the need to make continuous efforts to improve existing methods of dispute resolution with the

---

4 1968 Brussels Convention on jurisdiction and the enforcement of judgments in civil and commercial matters [1979] OJ L299/32.

5 Commission, 'Commission Recommendation of 30 March 1998 on the principles applicable to the bodies responsible for out-of-court settlement of consumer disputes' [1998] OJ L115/31.

6 Tampere European Council, 'Presidency conclusions' (15–16 October 1999) 29, 30, referenced in the EU Mediation Directive (n 12), Recital 2.

7 Commission, 'Green Paper on alternative dispute resolution in civil and commercial law' COM/2002/ 0196 final, referenced in EU Mediation Directive (n 12), Recital 4.

8 Council, 'Recommendation of the Committee of Ministers to Member States on mediation in civil matters (adopted at the 808th meeting of the Ministers' Deputies)' Recommendation Rec (2002) 10.

particular aim of facilitating mediation in civil matters. Subsequently, the European Commission elaborated a first Code of Conduct for Mediation[9] and, in 2004, put forward a first proposal for a directive on mediation in civil and commercial matters.[10]

The pivotal step was made in 2008. After years of negotiations and the introduction of amendments,[11] the European Mediation Directive was adopted on 21 May 2008 and finally entered into force on 13 June 2008. The EU Member States[12] were required to transpose its content into national law within a period of three years, i.e., until 20 May 2011. **20.05**

a. The fundamentals of the European Mediation Directive

The European Mediation Directive strives to create a reliable and predictable cross-border legal framework for mediation by addressing, in particular, key aspects of civil procedure in order to promote its further use. Quite notably, the European Mediation Directive does not create a uniform mediation law that applies directly throughout the territory of the EU. Rather, it is a legal act that defines a number of principles with the goal of promoting harmonization in the broader European context. Such harmonization is to be achieved through uniform implementation, which remains the inherent obligation of each individual EU Member State. **20.06**

i. Purpose and scope of application

As set forth in paragraph 5 of its Preamble, the core objective of the European Mediation Directive is to secure better access to justice. Concretely, it aims at ensuring a balanced relationship between judicial and extrajudicial dispute resolution methods and to alleviate the burden of over-crowded court systems. Ultimately, in a broader context, the availability of mediation services is thought of as contributing to the proper functioning of the internal market of the EU. **20.07**

The scope of application of the European Mediation Directive is confined to mediation as defined in Article 3, namely: **20.08**

> a structured process, however named or referred to, whereby two or more parties to a dispute attempt by themselves, on a voluntary basis, to reach an agreement on the settlement of their dispute with the assistance of a mediator. This process may be initiated by the parties or suggested or ordered by a court or prescribed by the law of a Member State. It includes mediation conducted by a judge who is not responsible for any judicial proceedings concerning the dispute in question. It excludes attempts made by the court or the judge seized to settle a dispute in the course of judicial proceedings concerning the dispute in question.

---

9   EuroMed Justice, European Code of Conduct for Mediators <https://euromed-justice.eu/en/system/files/20090128130552_adr_ec_code_conduct_en.pdf> accessed 21 December 2020.

10   Commission, 'Proposal for a Directive of the European Parliament and of the Council on certain aspects of mediation in civil and commercial matters' COM (2004) 718 final.

11   Opinion of the European Economic and Social Committee on the Proposal for a Directive of the European Parliament and of the Council on certain aspects of mediation in civil and commercial matters [2005] OJ C 286/1.

12   Council Directive 2008/52/EC of the European Parliament and of the Council of 21 May 2008 on certain aspects of mediation in civil and commercial matters [2008] OJ L 136/3 (EU Mediation Directive), Art 1(3) (with the exception of Denmark).

20.09   Further, the European Mediation Directive covers civil and commercial matters only, and as stressed in Article 1(2), it does not extend to rights and obligations that are not at the parties' disposal under the relevant law, such as revenue, customs or administrative matters or to the liability of the State for acts and omissions in the exercise of State authority.

20.10   Finally, the European Mediation Directive applies to cross-border disputes, broadly defined in Article 2 as disputes in which at least one of the parties is domiciled or habitually resident in a Member State other than that of any other party. This requirement must be fulfilled on the date on which: (a) the parties agree to use mediation after the dispute has arisen; (b) mediation is ordered by a court; (c) an obligation to use mediation arises under national law; or (d) for the purpose of recourse to mediation an invitation is made to the parties. For example, matters arising between two companies with the same nationality remain unaffected by the Directive.[13] This, of course, does not limit the freedom of EU Member States to enact mediation legislation that covers both cross-border and domestic dispute scenarios.

ii.   Quality control

20.11   Article 4 of the European Mediation Directive emphasizes the importance of ensuring that any mediation process is conducted such that it serves the parties' interests and needs in an effective and professional manner. EU Member States are to encourage, by any means which they consider appropriate, the development of, and adherence to, voluntary codes of conduct by mediators and organizations providing mediation services, as well as other effective control mechanisms concerning the provision of mediation services.

20.12   In this respect, the European Mediation Directive does not prescribe any concrete measures, but offers quality control guidance in the form of the European Code of Conduct for Mediators, a document that was developed by a group of stakeholders with the assistance of the European Commission and launched at a conference held in Brussels in 2004.[14] The European Code of Conduct for Mediators describes proper mediator conduct and lists principles which individual mediators may subscribe to voluntarily and on their own responsibility. Concretely, it touches upon crucial issues such as mediator competence, independence and impartiality, confidentiality, and fairness of process. The European Code of Conduct for Mediators has received wide recognition not only amongst mediation professionals but also amongst mediation organizations throughout Europe who commit themselves by calling upon the mediators acting on their behalf to comply with its principles.[15]

iii.   Recourse to mediation

20.13   Article 5 of the European Mediation Directive tackles the relationship between mediation and court proceedings. A court before which an action is brought may, when appropriate and having regard to all the circumstances of the case, invite the parties to use mediation in order to settle their dispute. The court may also invite the parties to attend an information session on

---

13   Peter F Phillips, 'The European Directive on Commercial Mediation: What it Provides and What it Doesn't (Business Conflict Management, 2008) <https://businessconflictmanagement.com/pdf/BCMpress_EUDirective.pdf> accessed 21 December 2020.

14   European Code of Conduct for Mediators (n 9).

15   Commission, 'European Code of Conduct for Mediators – List of Organisations' <https://kmfcr.cz/download/adr_ec_list_org_en.pdf> accessed 21 December 2020.

the use of mediation if such sessions are held and are easily available. This provision reflects the parties' autonomy as to the tool they want to rely on to resolve their dispute. Also, it prominently highlights that mediation is an entirely voluntary process. Still, the provision does not prevent EU Member States from making the use of mediation compulsory or subject to incentives or sanctions in their domestic mediation legislation. However, such legislation may never cut parties short from exercising their right to access to the judicial system.

iv. Enforcement

In accordance with Article 6 of the European Mediation Directive, Member States are **20.14** required to provide mechanisms through which to ensure that it is possible for parties in dispute, or for one of them with the explicit consent of the other(s), to request that the content of a written agreement resulting from mediation be made enforceable. A limit is set as to the content of such agreement. An agreement resulting from mediation may only be made enforceable unless, in the case in question, either the content of that agreement is contrary to the law of the Member State where the enforcement request is made or the law of that Member State does not provide for its enforceability.

As to the institutions competent for enforcement, the European Mediation Directive provides **20.15** two alternatives, namely State courts or other competent authorities. As to form, it stipulates that agreements resulting from mediation may be made enforceable in a judgment, a decision, or an authentic instrument in accordance with the law of the Member State where the request in made. Indeed, enforcement practice in the various EU Member States is diverse and examples of the instruments available for making a mediation settlement enforceable are as well, ranging from notarial deeds, declaratory settlement deeds, arbitral awards by consent to agreements co-signed by legal counsel. An obvious option reflecting the principle of party autonomy and contractual liberty is the incorporation of the mediation settlement in a new contract between the parties.[16] Overall, such new contracts generated by the parties themselves at the end of an ADR process will enjoy a higher degree of voluntary compliance vis-à-vis court or tribunal-imposed decisions.

v. Confidentiality

Confidentiality is a key principle of mediation. Article 7 of the European Mediation Directive **20.16** emphasizes that EU Member States shall ensure that, unless the parties agree otherwise, neither mediators nor those involved in the administration of the mediation process shall be compelled to give evidence in judicial proceedings or arbitration regarding information arising out of or in connection with the mediation process. The same provision also sets out two exceptions to this rule, namely (a) where it is necessary for overriding considerations of public policy of the Member State concerned, in particular when required to ensure the protection of the best interests of children or to prevent harm to the physical or psychological integrity of a person, or (b) where disclosure of the content of the agreement resulting from mediation is

---

16 European Parliament, 'Rebooting the Mediation Directive: Assessing the Limited Impact of Its Implementation and Proposing Measures to Increase the Number of Mediations in the EU' (PE 493.042, Study, 2014) (EU Study on Rebooting Mediation Directive); John M Bosnack, 'The European Mediation Directive: More Questions Than Answers' in Arnold Ingen-Housz (ed), *ADR in Business, Practice and Issues Across Countries and Cultures* (Wolters Kluwer Law and Business 2011) 625, 647–50; Nadja Alexander, 'Harmonization and Diversity in the Private International Law of Mediation: the Rhythms of Regulatory Reform' in Klaus J Hopt and Felix Steffek (eds), *Mediation, Principles and Regulations in Comparative Perspective* (OUP 2013) 131, 179.

necessary in order to implement or enforce that agreement. Again, EU Member States are free to enact even stricter measures to protect the confidentiality of mediation.

vi. Limitation and prescription periods

20.17 According to Article 8 of the European Mediation Directive, EU Member States shall design their national mediation frameworks such that parties who choose mediation in an attempt to settle a dispute amicably are not subsequently prevented from initiating judicial or arbitral proceedings in relation to that dispute due to the expiry of limitation or prescription periods during the mediation process. The purpose of this provision is to ensure that parties in dispute have a range of options at their disposal when it comes to resolving their differences and that they may make their choice without having to fear prejudice if their choice falls on mediation.

b. Practical relevance of the European Mediation Directive

20.18 The European Mediation Directive laid the groundwork for unifying the standards for civil and commercial mediation across EU jurisdictions. As such, this supranational legal instrument is very concretely aimed at increasing the use of mediation and to promote it as a standard tool of commercial dispute resolution.

i. Statistical findings

20.19 International surveys document impressive successes. In cases of court-ordered mediation, parties in dispute reached settlement in about 70 per cent of the cases.[17] The success rate was even up to 80 per cent where the parties committed to mediation on an entirely voluntary basis.[18] Recently, the figures have become even more pronounced. According to Dispute Resolution Data (the first and only global database pertaining to international commercial arbitration and mediation), mediations conducted within the territory of the EU between 2005 and 2020 showed an 83 per cent success rate.[19]

20.20 Despite these considerably positive outcomes, mediation still does not live up to its full potential.[20] Until 2014, only one EU Member State, namely Italy, exceeded 200,000 (civil and commercial) mediations per year. Three other countries[21] exceeded 10,000 mediations per year, whereas most of the remaining EU Member States each reported less than 500 mediation cases per year.[22] Overall, the available statistics show that, on average, mediation is used in less than 1 per cent of the cases that are brought before EU civil and commercial courts.[23]

---

17 ADR Center, 'The Cost of Non-ADR – Surveying and Showing the Actual Costs of Intra-Community Commercial Litigation' (Survey Data Report, 2010), 42 <https://www.adrcenterfordevelopment.com/wp-content/uploads/2018/06/Survey-Data-Report.pdf> accessed 21 December 2020 (Survey Data Report).
18 Ibid.
19 Dispute Resolution Data, LLC (DRD) <www.disputeresolutiondata.com> accessed 21 December 2020.
20 EU Study on Rebooting Mediation Directive (n 16), 6.
21 Germany, Netherlands and the United Kingdom.
22 The survey took into consideration civil and commercial mediation.
23 European Parliament, 'Resolution of 12 September 2017 on the implementation of Directive 2008/52/EC of the European Parliament and of the Council of 21 May 2008 on certain aspects of mediation in civil and commercial matters (the 'Mediation Directive') (2016/2066(INI))' [2018] OJ C337/01, 3; European Parliament, 'The Implementation of the Mediation Directive' (PE 571.395, Workshop, 29 November 2016), 25.

However, also on a broader international level, it seems that recourse to mediation as a tool to resolve commercial disputes remains relatively scarce.[24]

There are also reliable studies covering the territory of the EU that look at the costs of not **20.21** using mediation. These studies allow compelling conclusions as regards the economic advantages of mediation as an effective dispute resolution tool that also takes into account individual and societal values.[25] According to the 2011 study 'Quantifying the cost of not using mediation – a data analysis', which focused on commercial mediation, the average cost to litigate in the EU was EUR 10,449, while the average cost to mediate was EUR 2,497. Concerning time spent on dispute resolution, the average duration of regular court proceedings at first instance in the EU ranged from 275 days (in Lithuania) to 1,210 days (in Italy) and 1,290 days (in Slovenia), compared to only 46 days for mediation.[26]

ii.   Conclusions and rebooting ideas

The conundrum presented by the well-documented benefits of mediation on one hand, and **20.22** the low percentage of mediation use throughout the EU Member States on the other, is commonly known as the 'EU Mediation Paradox'.[27] A panoply of factors are thought to have contributed to it, but key explanations center around the structure of the regulatory framework, the lack of a strong incentive scheme, and persistently low levels of awareness about the benefits of mediation. It is against this background that parties in dispute continue to rely upon traditional adjudicative processes when it comes to resolving their disputes.

In this respect, behavioural science provides further useful insights. In 2017, the Nobel Prize in **20.23** Economics was awarded to Professor Richard Thaler for his theory of 'nudging'.[28] Professor Thaler had demonstrated how people can be 'nudged' in a certain direction through choice architecture, notably through the use of opt-out models as opposed to opt-in models. The staggering impact of the concept was observed, for example, in the organ donation policies in Austria and Germany.[29] In 2003, with an opt-in (meaning that people had to register to be donors) policy in place, Germany had a 12 per cent organ donation consent rate, whereas Austria, with an opt-out (meaning that people were by default considered donors and had the possibility to deregister in case they did not wish to donate) system in place, had a 99 per cent organ donation consent rate. Very evidently, opt-out policies increase take-up rates.

With regards to mediation, Italy is the only EU Member State that has implemented an **20.24** opt-out mediation model. All other EU Member States follow a voluntary (opt-in) model approach to mediation. This difference in the systematic approach to mediation presents itself

---

24   Stacy I Strong, 'Realizing Rationality: An Empirical Assessment of International Commercial Mediation' (2016) 73 *Washington and Lee Law Review* 1973 <https://scholarlycommons.law.wlu.edu/wlulr/vol73/iss4/7/> accessed 21 December 2020.

25   European Parliament, 'Quantifying the cost of not using mediation – a data analysis' (PE 453.180, Note, 2011) (Note on the Cost of Not Using Mediation) 14; Survey Data Report (n 17), 22.

26   Note on the Cost of Not Using Mediation (n 25), 4 and 12–13.

27   European Parliament, 'A ten-year-long "EU Mediation Paradox" when an EU Directive needs to be more … Directive' (PE 608.847, Briefing, November 2018), 2.

28   Richard H Thaler and Cass R Sunstein, *Nudge: Improving Decisions about Health, Wealth and Happiness* (Penguin Books 2008).

29   Eric J Johnson and Daniel Goldstein, 'Do Defaults Save Lives?' (2003) 302 *Science* 1338 <https://papers.ssrn.com/abstract=1324774> accessed 21 December 2020.

as a plausible factor when it comes to explaining Italy's remarkable mediation records in the EU and can be considered a best practice model. European policy makers seem to have taken on board such considerations as well.

20.25 In 2014, the European Parliament published a 'rebooting' study in which experts recommended that 'the legislators in the EU should consider requiring mandatory mediation in certain categories of cases with the ability to opt out'.[30] Furthermore, it was emphasized that 'there is evidence that the single regulatory feature likely to produce a significant increase in the use of mediation is the introduction of "mandatory mediation elements" in the legal systems of the Member States'.[31] While building consensus on this vital point seems to still require time, non-legislative measures are all the more important to boost the visibility of mediation. Dispute resolution professionals and institutions alike are particularly called upon when it comes to advocating the use of mediation as an effective dispute resolution tool.

2. Successful implementation: The example of Austria

20.26 When it comes to ADR, Austria can rightly be considered a true pioneer country. Mediation was first introduced as a method of dispute resolution in 1994/1995, when pilot projects were set up at certain courts in Vienna and Salzburg. Married couples seeking divorce were invited, on an entirely voluntary basis, to settle both legal and economic aspects of the divorce with the support of a neutral third party. The objective was to conclude a consensual agreement regarding the divorcees' future role as parents and the wellbeing of their children. Given the success of the pilot projects, mediation proceedings were formally introduced in the context of family law shortly thereafter. The Austrian Mediation Act (*Zivilrechts-Mediations-Gesetz – ZivMediatG*) was passed in 2003,[32] opening up the possibility of resolving disputes by way of mediation in all civil law matters. It was one of the first codifications of mediation laws in Europe and served as a model for other European jurisdictions. The UNCITRAL Model Law on International Commercial Conciliation was not enacted by Austria since the Austrian mediation approach seeks to be predominantly interest-based with the mediator's role being limited to the facilitation of negotiations between the parties. The UNCITRAL Model Law, by contrast, promotes a more evaluative style of mediation. Furthermore, Austria was also the first of the European civil law jurisdictions to enact legislation regulating the obligatory qualifications and training of mediators in the By-Law on Training for Mediation in Civil Matters (*Zivilrechts-Mediations-Ausbildungsverordnung – ZivMediatAV*). More generally, also the Austrian Code of Civil Procedure (*Zivilprozessordnung – ZPO*) and the Austrian Code of Criminal Procedure (*Strafprozessordnung – StPO*) contain mediation related provisions, most notably as regards the right of mediators to refuse to give evidence.

a. The Austrian Mediation Act

20.27 In Austria, mediation is an entirely voluntary process. Section 1 of the Austrian Mediation Act provides the following definition: 'Mediation is a process in which, based on the parties'

---

30 EU Study on Rebooting Mediation Directive (n 16), 164.
31 Ibid., 163.
32 BGBl 2003/29 (2003) <https://www.ris.bka.gv.at/Dokumente/BgblPdf/2003_29_1/2003_29_1.pdf> accessed 21 December 2020.

voluntariness, a professionally trained neutral (mediator) uses recognised methods to systematically stimulate communication between the parties in order to facilitate the resolution of their dispute in a mutually beneficial manner.' There are no statutory provisions that would make mediation a mandatory requirement before a case can move to the courts. The Austrian mediation legislation does not provide parties with any incentives whatsoever – neither positive nor negative – to attempt mediation. The recent rise in commercial mediation cases in Austria can be attributed to both the open-mindedness of the Austrian courts as well as Austrian dispute resolution professionals who actively integrate alternative methods of dispute resolution into their service portfolio.

The Austrian Mediation Act is the primary source of legislation on mediation for all disputes that fall within the jurisdiction of the Austrian civil and commercial courts. It regulates the profession of so-called 'listed' mediators in civil and commercial matters and sets out certain procedural benefits for parties who chose to mediate rather than litigate their case. Mediators trained in accordance with the requirements set out in the Austrian Mediation Act can apply to be listed on the roster of mediators administered by the Austrian Ministry of Justice. It is not compulsory to be listed on the roster to be a mediator in Austria. However, non-listed mediators do not enjoy the benefits expressly granted under the Austrian Mediation Act (e.g., automatic interruption of prescription periods,[33] protection of confidentiality beyond the scope of the mediation[34]). In order to be listed on the roster of mediators administered by the Austrian Ministry of Justice, candidates must fulfil the following criteria: **20.28**

- written application
- minimum age: 28 years
- qualification as mediator
- extract from police records/disclosure
- professional liability insurance (min. coverage: EUR 400 000)
- information as to where the mediator will offer his/her services.

Candidates will be considered qualified if they

- have completed relevant training
- display knowledge and skills in mediation
- have completed basic legal and psycho-social training.

Training is considered 'relevant' if completed with registered training institutions, including universities. The Austrian Ministry of Justice keeps a list of those training institutions. The content of the training is laid down in Section 29 of the Austrian Mediation Act and in the respective By-Law. By international standards, the training requirements laid down in the Austrian Mediation Act are quite rigorous. This is owed to the fact that mediation is not a regulated profession in Austria and that the Austrian Mediation Act was implemented to introduce uniform quality standards for individuals coming from diverse professional backgrounds who seek to qualify as mediators. Any listing on the roster is limited to a period of five years. Listed mediators may apply for the extension of their listing for a period of a maximum of ten additional years.   **20.29**

---

33   The Austrian Mediation Act 2003, pt V s 22(1) (Austrian Mediation Act).
34   Ibid., pt IV s 18.

b. The Austrian EU-Mediation Act

20.30 Complying with the obligation incumbent on Member States to transpose EU Directives into national law, Austria enacted the EU-Mediation Act in 2011 while maintaining the Austrian Mediation Act as a distinct legal instrument.

20.31 The Austrian Mediation Act exclusively governs mediations conducted by 'listed' mediators, whereas the Austrian EU-Mediation Act applies to EU-cross-border mediation scenarios in general and subscribes to a wider, less formalistic approach. Austria thus upholds a dual system in mediation[35] which has contributed to a somewhat confusing ADR landscape overall. There are essentially four ways in which mediations can be conducted: (i) with a mediator who is listed on the roster of mediators administered by the Austrian Ministry of Justice (enjoying the privileges granted under the Austrian Mediation Act); (ii) with a mediator who is not listed on the roster of mediators administered by the Austrian Ministry of Justice; (iii) with a mediator that falls under the provisions of the Austrian EU-Mediation Act, and finally (iv) with a (dispute resolution or other) professional who may not even be qualified as a mediator but who enjoys the trust of the parties.

i. Purpose and scope of application

20.32 The legal definition of 'mediation' given in the Austrian EU-Mediation Act closely follows the one set out in the EU Mediation Directive.[36] As such, the scope of application of the Austrian EU-Mediation Act encompasses mediation as defined in the underlying legal instrument, namely with a view to cross-border disputes in civil law matters. The subsection in the EU Mediation Directive referring to mediations conducted by judges was not implemented in Austria as this type of mediation is not firmly established here.[37] Furthermore, the Austrian EU-Mediation Act covers only mediations relating to civil law disputes and matters within the

---

35 Ulrike Frauenberger-Pfeiler, 'Austria' in Carlos Esplugues, Jose Iglesias and Guillermo Palao (eds), *Civil and Commercial Mediation in Europe: National Mediation Rules and Procedures* (Intersentia 2013) 7.

36 Christina Lenz and Martin Risak, 'Austria' in Nadja Alexander, Sabine Walsh and Martin Svatos (eds), *EU Mediation Law Handbook, Regulatory Robustness Rating for Mediation Regimes* (Wolters Kluwer 2017) 39; Section 2 (1) of the the Austrian EU-Mediation Act defines mediation as:

> a structured process, however named or referred to, whereby two or more parties to a dispute attempt by themselves, on a voluntary basis, to reach an agreement on the settlement of their dispute with the assistance of a mediator, no matter whether the procedure was initiated by the parties, suggested by a court or ordered or is mandatory according to the national regulations of a member state.

37 Lenz and Risak, ibid., 40; Some Austrian civil courts have started a pilot project for a so called 'conciliation procedure' (*Einigungsverfahren*). In this procedure, which is entirely voluntary and not open to the public, alternative dispute resolution methods, in particular mediation, are employed to deal with the parties' dispute and help them resolve it. The conciliation procedure is conducted by specifically trained judges who support the parties in finding an amicable solution to their problem without any competence to decide the dispute. Quite importantly, the judge in the conciliation procedure is not the same judge as in the regular civil proceedings originally initiated by the parties. The conciliation procedure usually spans two session with the conciliation judge (*Einigungsrichter*) and can be concluded by signing a written agreement. In order to turn such agreement into an enforceable legal title, the parties need to make an appointment with the judge hearing their case in the regular civil proceedings. If it is the wish of the parties, the conciliation judge may refer them to mediators outside the court setting, in order to deal with more complex issues in a different forum. If the conciliation procedure is unsuccessful, the regular civil proceedings will continue. No additional registration and court fees are charged if the parties decide to try out a conciliation procedure. Information (in German) can be found at <www.einigungsverfahren.at> accessed 21 December 2020.

competence of the civil courts, including contentious and non-contentious commercial and employment matters.[38]

ii. Mediator qualifications

Article 3(b) of the European Mediation Directive defines a mediator as 'a third person who is   **20.33**
asked to conduct a mediation in an effective, impartial and competent way and who has residence in a Member State'.[39] The Austrian EU-Mediation Act incorporates this very definition and does not set forth any formal accreditation, registration or even training requirements. Hence, under the framework of the Austrian EU-Mediation Act, cross-border disputes may be mediated by any neutral third party chosen or accepted by the parties in dispute. Nevertheless, as expressly set out in Article 5(2) of the Austrian EU-Mediation Act, and mindful of the dual system that is characteristic for Austria, mediators are under an obligation to inform the parties that the mediation is conducted outside the scope of the Austrian Mediation Act and that therefore certain privileges afforded under the latter do not apply.[40]

iii. Confidentiality

Article 7 of the EU Mediation Directive stipulates that neither mediators nor those involved in   **20.34**
the administration of the mediation process shall be compelled to give evidence in civil and commercial judicial proceedings or arbitration regarding information arising out of or in connection with a mediation process, except (a) where this is necessary for overriding considerations of public policy of the Member State concerned, in particular when require to ensure the protection of the best interests of children or to prevent harm to the physical or psychological integrity of a person, or (b) where disclosure of the content of the agreement resulting from mediation is necessary in order to implement or enforce the agreement. The Austrian EU-Mediation Act reflects the core of said provision in its Section 3. Concretely, insofar as the parties in dispute do not agree otherwise, it establishes an obligation for the mediator and any other person involved in the mediation proceedings to refuse to testify.[41] In accordance with the provisions of the Austrian Code of Civil Procedure (*Zivilprozessordnung – ZPO*) and the Austrian Code of Criminal Procedure (*Strafprozessordnung – StPO*) mediators may, under certain circumstances, not be heard as witnesses in court proceedings. Under the dual system that is characteristic for Austria, the confidentiality rules are not the same for 'listed' mediators that enjoy the privileges granted by the Austrian Mediation Act and all 'other' mediators. The Austrian Mediation Act imposes an absolute duty of confidentiality that must be observed by 'listed' mediators at all times.[42] They are thus under an obligation to keep confidential all facts revealed by the parties. In case of a breach of such obligation, the 'listed' mediator may be subject to prosecution and punishment by imprisonment of up to six months or a fine of up to 360 daily fine rates.[43] Non-listed mediators who otherwise practise a profession that does not include elements of mediation are solely bound to confidentiality by the terms of the written mediation agreement entered into with the parties. They may not

---

38   Ibid.
39   EU Mediation Directive (n 12).
40   Austrian Mediation Act (n 33), s 5(2).
41   Lenz and Risak (n 36), 51.
42   Austrian Mediation Act (n 33), s 18.
43   Ibid., s 31.

refuse to give testimony in court. Non-listed mediators who otherwise practise a profession that does include elements of mediation (e.g., lawyers), may refuse to testify in court by reference to professional privilege and the relevant deontological rules.

iv. Neutrality

20.35 The European Mediation Directive states the obligation for mediators to be impartial.[44] The Austrian EU-Mediation Act, however, does not contain any express provisions relating to mediator neutrality, independence and impartiality. Quite generally, there is no legal (mediation specific) rule under Austrian law, that obliges mediators to disclose possible conflicts of interest. However, disclosure is regularly a necessity that flows from the requirement that mediators must be independent and assist the parties in a neutral manner. Professionals listed on the roster of mediators administered by the Austrian Ministry of Justice must not act as mediator in any dispute in which they are or were involved as a party, a party representative, a third-party advisor or decision maker.[45] Despite this narrow rule, mediators in Austria are allowed to assist with the implementation of the outcome of the mediation proceedings as long as the parties agree.

20.36 In this regard it is well worth mentioning the Austrian Ethical Guidelines for Mediators (*Ethikrichtlinien für MediatorInnen*, the 'Guidelines'). The Guidelines are based on the considerations of the working group 'Quality in Mediation' initiated by ÖNM, the Austrian Mediation Network (*Österreichisches Netzwerk Mediation*), the umbrella organization for mediation and ADR associations in Austria.[46] The Guidelines were revised in 2017 with an express reference to the European Code of Conduct for Mediators. Overall, their purpose is to provide all Austrian mediators with a generally acceptable deontological framework for their professional activities that they may adopt on a voluntary basis (the standards defined in the Guidelines are, however, binding for mediations conducted in accordance with the Austrian Mediation Act by 'listed' mediators). Besides providing rules concerning appointment and fees of mediators, the Guidelines stress principles of what constitutes a fair procedure and emphasize independence, impartiality and confidentiality as express duties of a mediator.

v. Enforcement

20.37 Once a mediation has come to a successful end, the question of enforceability in respect of its outcome arises. The European Mediation Directive requires Member States to ensure that it is possible for the parties, or for one of them with the explicit consent of the other, to request that the content of a written agreement resulting from mediation be made enforceable.[47] The Austrian EU-Mediation Act, however, does not contain any specific provisions in this respect. Yet, under the Austrian Mediation Act, mediators are expressly instructed to direct the parties towards seeking legal assistance in ensuring that the mediation settlement is recorded in such form that secures enforceability.[48]

---

44   EU Mediation Directive (n 12), art 3(b).
45   Austrian Mediation Act (n 33), s 16(1).
46   Umbrella Organization for Out-Of-Court Conflict Resolution in Austria, 'Ethics Guidelines' (2017) <https://www.netzwerk-mediation.at/content/ethikrichtlinien> accessed 21 December 2020.
47   EU Mediation Directive (n 12), art 6(1).
48   Austrian Mediation Act (n 33), s 16(3).

Overall, there are no specific legal requirements in Austria as to what form a mediation **20.38** settlement agreement must take. Such settlement agreements are essentially civil law contracts between the parties and reflect the terms of how the parties intend to solve their dispute. Whether the mediation settlement agreement will be directly enforceable or not, mainly depends on the legal form chosen by the parties. Unless the mediation settlement agreement is concluded before a competent Austrian court[49] or integrated in a notarial deed, it will not be directly enforceable. In the context of arbitration, settlements agreed by the parties in mediation are regularly issued (by the separately constituted arbitral tribunal) in the form of an award on agreed terms.[50] That said, mediation settlement agreements that stand at the end of a mediation process conducted in Austria will only have *res judicata* effect if they take one of the aforementioned forms. If this is not the case, the only way to hold a non-compliant party to its obligations is to file a claim before the competent State court or arbitral tribunal.

vi.   Limitation and prescription periods

In mediations that fall within the scope of application of the Austrian EU-Mediation Act, the **20.39** initiation of the mediation leads to a suspension of the expiration of the limitation period as regards the rights and obligations that are subject to the mediation proceeding.[51] The commencement and continuation of a mediation that is conducted by a mediator listed on the roster of mediators administered by the Austrian Ministry of Justice interrupts the limitation period such that it will not continue to run for the duration of the mediation and only resume (where it has left off) once the mediation has ended.[52] Finally, as a matter of general principle under Austrian law, the conduct of settlement negotiations *per se* leads to the suspension of the expiration of a limitation period.[53]

vii.   Practical relevance

As is the case with most EU countries, statistical data on the use of commercial mediation as a **20.40** tool for dispute resolution is scarce. Informal records kept at the Commercial Court of Vienna indicate that about 20 cases per year are diverted to mediation. More reliable data exists, however, in respect of government-funded mediation cases (which constitute only mediations concerning custody and visitation rights, alimony disputes and separation of property after divorce). According to the European Parliament's 'rebooting' study, during the comparative period beginning 1 May 2005 and ending 1 April 2012, i.e., during a period of seven years, a total of 2,504 government-funded mediations took place in Austria.[54]

While the current legal framework in Austria was created with the intention of setting a very **20.41** high bar in terms of quality and professionalism in the mediation process, commercial

---

49   Austrian Code of Civil Procedure 1983, s 433a.
50   An increasingly followed practice in Austria is the synergetic approach of mediation embedded in (usually institutional) arbitration settings known as Arb-Med-Arb. The parties in dispute first initiate arbitral proceedings, then the arbitration is suspended and mediation is initiated with the purpose of conducting settlement negotiations. If the parties succeed in settling their dispute, the arbitration is resumed upon their request and their settlement is recorded as an award on agreed terms with the benefit of enforceability under the Convention on the Recognition and Enforcement of Foreign Arbitral Awards (adopted 19 June 1958, entered into force 7 June 1959) 330 UNTS 3 (New York Convention).
51   Austrian Mediation Act (n 33), s 4 (*Ablaufshemmung*).
52   Ibid., s 22 (*Fortlaufshemmung*).
53   Austrian Civil Code 1811, s 1497 (*Ablaufshemmung*).
54   EU Study on Rebooting Meditation Directive (n 16), 20.

mediation practice in Austria has not quite lived up to the expectations. Access to justice in Austria is guaranteed by comparatively low court fees and a functioning system of legal aid available to impecunious parties (*Verfahrenshilfe*). Litigation is thus a truly affordable option with no immediate pressure to take recourse to cost and time-saving alternatives such as mediation. That being so, one of the key challenges in terms of policy remains that the Austrian mediation legislation does still not provide parties with any incentives to refer their cases to mediation. Also, quite to the chagrin of the users of alternative dispute resolution services, the Austrian tax authorities continue to collect a contract levy (*Rechtsgeschäftsgebühr*) in the amount of 1 per cent of the settlement volume if the settlement concerns a litigious matter pending in court and 2 per cent of the settlement volume if the latter is not the case.[55]

3. Attempts at unification on the international stage

20.42 To maximize the utility of mediation as an efficient dispute resolution tool, robust legal frameworks are a vital precondition. This goes for both the domestic and international levels. Especially in cross-border disputes, the issue of enforcement can be prohibitive to effective ADR solutions if the jurisdictions where the enforcement of the agreements resulting from the process is likely to be sought are perceived as unsophisticated and weak.

20.43 It is against this background that attempts have been made, on the international stage, to unify the standards for the enforcement of settlement agreements resulting from mediation. In this respect, two international instruments stand out and have gained considerable practical relevance: the UNCITRAL Model Law on International Commercial Mediation and International Settlement Agreements Resulting from Mediation (amending the Model Law on International Commercial Conciliation 2002)[56] (the 'UNCITRAL Model Law on International Commercial Mediation') and the United Nations Convention on International Settlement Agreements Resulting from Mediation[57] (the 'Singapore Convention on Mediation').

a. The UNCITRAL Model Law on International Commercial Mediation

20.44 Recognizing the potential and value of conciliation as a method of amicably settling disputes arising in the context of international commercial relations, the UN General Assembly recommended the adoption of a comprehensive set of procedural rules that parties may agree on for the conduct of conciliation proceedings arising out of their commercial relationship. The United Nations Commission on International Trade Law adopted the UNCITRAL Conciliation Rules on 23 July 1980.[58] They covered all aspects of the conciliation process,

---

55   Austrian Fees Act, s 33 tariff item 20(1).

56   UNCITRAL, 'Model Law on International Commercial Mediation and International Settlement Agreements Resulting from Mediation, 2018 (amending the UNCITRAL Model Law on International Commercial Conciliation 2002)' A//73/17 <https://uncitral.un.org/sites/uncitral.un.org/files/media-documents/uncitral/en/annex_ii.pdf> accessed 21 December 2020 (UNCITRAL Model Law on Mediation).

57   United Nations Convention on International Settlement Agreements Resulting from Mediation (New York, 2018) (adopted 20 December 2018, entered into force on 12 September 2020) <https://undocs.org/en/A/RES/73/198> accessed 21 December 2020 (UN Convention on Mediation).

58   UNCITRAL, 'UNCITRAL Conciliation Rules' (1980) <https://www.uncitral.org/pdf/english/texts/arbitration/conc-rules/conc-rules-e.pdf> accessed 21 December 2020.

provided a model conciliation clause, defined when conciliation was deemed to have commenced and terminated and addressed procedural aspects relating to the appointment and role of conciliators and the general conduct of proceedings.

In 2002, the United Nations Commission on International Trade Law adopted the **20.45** UNCITRAL Model Law on International Commercial Conciliation,[59] which was also accompanied by a guide to their enactment and use. The Model Law on International Commercial Conciliation established model legislation on conciliation with the aim of assisting States in enhancing or formulating legislation governing the use of conciliation techniques so as to contribute to the development of harmonious international economic relations. Its adoption highlighted the desirability of uniformity in the law and practice of dispute settlement procedures and the establishment of a harmonized legal framework for the fair and efficient settlement of disputes arising in international commercial relations.

With the swift growth of international trade and e-commerce, cross-border transactions in the **20.46** years to come, the need for effective (international) dispute resolution grew ever more accentuated. Against this background, the UNCITRAL Model Law on International Commercial Conciliation was amended in 2018 and reissued as the UNCITRAL Model Law on International Commercial Mediation and International Settlement Agreements Resulting from Mediation.

i. Scope of application

The revised Model Law covers both international commercial mediation and international **20.47** settlement agreements.[60] The term 'commercial' is interpreted rather broadly, covering matters arising from all relationships of a commercial nature, whether contractual or not. Such relationships include, but are not limited to the following transactions: any trade transaction for the supply or exchange of goods or services, distribution agreements, commercial representation or agency, factoring, leasing, construction of works, consulting, engineering, licensing, investment, financing, banking, insurance, exploitation agreement or concession, joint venture and other forms of industrial or business cooperation, and carriage of goods or passengers by air, sea, rail or road.[61] As such, personal, family, inheritance and employment matters do not fall within the scope of application of the Model Law on International Commercial Mediation.

In previously adopted texts and relevant documents, UNCITRAL had used the term **20.48** 'conciliation' with the understanding that it was interchangeable with the term 'mediation'. In amending the Model Law, UNCITRAL decided to switch to the term 'mediation' in an effort to adapt to the actual and practical use of the term and with the expectation that this change would facilitate the promotion and heighten the visibility of the Model Law. This change in

---

59   UNCITRAL, 'UNCITRAL Model Law on International Commercial Conciliation with Guide to Enactment and Use' (2002) <https://www.uncitral.org/pdf/english/texts/arbitration/ml-conc/03-90953_Ebook.pdf> accessed 21 December 2020 (UNCITRAL Model Law on Conciliation).
60   UNCITRAL Model Law on Mediation (n 56), art 1(1).
61   Ibid.

terminology does not have any substantive or conceptual implications.[62] The definition of 'mediation' given in the Model Law is the following:

> a process, whether referred to by the expression mediation, conciliation or an expression of similar import, whereby parties request a third person or persons ('the mediator') to assist them in their attempt to reach an amicable settlement of their dispute arising out of or relating to a contractual or other legal relationship.[63]

20.49 Under the terms of the UNCITRAL Model Law on International Commercial Mediation, a mediation is considered 'international' if (a) the parties to an agreement to mediate have, at the time of the conclusion of that agreement, their places of business in different States, or (b) the State in which the parties have their places of business is different from either: (i) the State in which a substantial part of the obligations of the commercial relationship is to be performed; or (ii) the State with which the subject matter of the dispute is most closely connected.[64] If a party has more than one place of business, the place of business is that which has the closest relationship to the agreement to mediate.[65] If a party does not have a place of business, reference is to be made to the party's habitual residence.[66] Moreover, the parties have the possibility to agree that the mediation is international.[67]

ii.   Pertinent provisions

20.50 To avoid uncertainty resulting from an absence of statutory provisions, the UNCITRAL Model Law on International Commercial Mediation addresses the full range of procedural aspects of mediation, such as rules for the commencement (art 5) and termination (art 12) of the mediation, the appointment of neutrals (art 6), the conduct of the mediation (art 7), the communication between the mediator and the parties (art 8), disclosure of information (art 9), confidentiality (art 10), and the admissibility of evidence in other proceedings (art 11). It also addresses post-mediation issues, such as the mediator acting as arbitrator (art 13), resort to arbitral or judicial proceedings (art 14), and the binding and enforceable nature of settlement agreements (art 15). Thus, the UNCITRAL Model Law on International Commercial Mediation may be used as a basis for the enactment of legislation on mediation, included, where needed, for implementing the Singapore Convention on Mediation.

20.51 As an important new feature, the UNCITRAL Model Law on International Commercial Mediation addresses general principles relating to the enforcement of international settlement agreements resulting from mediation and concluded in writing by parties to resolve a commercial dispute.[68] It provides uniform rules on enforcement (art 17) and addresses the right of a party to invoke a settlement agreement in any relevant procedure in accordance with the relevant rules of the State in which enforcement is sought (art 18). Also, it contains an

---

62   UNCITRAL, 'Report of Working Group II (Dispute Settlement) on the work of its sixty-seventh session (Vienna, 2–6 October 2017)' (A/CN9/929, 11 October 2017), paras 102–104 <https://undocs.org/en/A/CN.9/929> accessed 21 December 2020.
63   UNCITRAL Model Law on Mediation (n 56), art 1(3).
64   Ibid., art 3(2).
65   Ibid., art 3(3)(a).
66   Ibid., art 3(3)(b).
67   Ibid., art 3(4) and (5).
68   Ibid., s 3.

exhaustive list of grounds that a party against whom the relief is sought may invoke so that the competent authority of the State may refuse enforcement (art 19).

iii.   *Status quo*

On 16 April 2019, the UNCITRAL Secretariat tabled a note concerning draft UNCITRAL **20.52** Mediation Rules. This occurred against the background that, at its fifty-first session, in 2018, the United Nations Commission on International Trade Law had noted that the UNCITRAL Secretariat would undertake work on updating the UNCITRAL Conciliation Rules (1980) to both reflect current practice and ensure consistency with the contents of the UNCITRAL Model Law on International Commercial Mediation finalized by the Commission at that very same session and the Singapore Convention on Mediation.

The draft UNCITRAL Mediation Rules were prepared with a view to take account of **20.53** developments in the field of alternative dispute resolution since the introduction of the initial UNCITRAL Conciliation Rules 40 years ago, including the developments regarding court-ordered mediation in some jurisdictions. The draft UNCITRAL Mediation Rules emphasize that mediation is an interest-based process. Therefore, terms that are normally used in connection with adversarial proceedings are avoided. Further, the text includes gender neutral language. The draft Rules span a total of 13 provisions that cover all relevant procedural aspects in mediation, such as, besides the scope of application (art 1), the commencement of the mediation (art 2), the number and appointment of mediators (art 3), the conduct of mediation (art 4), communication between the parties and the mediator (art 5), confidentiality (art 6), the introduction of evidence in other proceedings (art 7), settlement agreements (art 8), the termination of mediation (art 9), arbitral judicial or other dispute settlement proceedings (art 10), costs and deposit of costs (art 11), the role of the mediator in other proceedings (art 12), and exclusion of liability (art 13). In an annex, the draft UNCITRAL Mediation Rules offer model mediation clauses including variants, from a simple clause to a multi-tiered provision.

On 18 April 2019, the UNCITRAL Secretariat further tabled a note concerning draft **20.54** UNCITRAL Notes on Mediation.[69] The draft Notes list and briefly describe matters relevant to mediation. Prepared with a focus on international mediation, they are intended to be used in a general and universal manner by mediation practitioners and parties to a dispute. Given the flexibility that characterizes mediation, they take account of the fact that procedural styles, practices and methods to foster a settlement between parties may and do vary substantially. Each approach has its own merit. Therefore, the draft Notes do not seek to promote any particular practice as best practice. Rather, they seek to assist parties in better understanding mediation including the wide and flexible range of possible outcomes. The parties and the mediator may use or refer to them at their discretion and to the extent they see fit and need not adopt or provide reasons for not adopting any particular element contained therein. As such, the draft Notes do not impose any legal requirements binding upon the parties or the mediator and are not suitable to be used as mediation rules.

---

69   UNCITRAL, 'Settlement of Commercial Disputes – International Commercial Mediation: Draft UNCITRAL Notes on Mediation – Note by the Secretariat' (A/CN9/987, 18 April 2019) <https://undocs.org/en/A/CN.9/987> accessed 21 December 2020.

20.55 In terms of content, the Notes address main features of mediation (non-adjudicatory, flexible, and voluntary nature of a process that is based on party autonomy) and even provide a flow chart that gives an overview of the various steps usually followed in mediation. Further, the draft Notes address the existing legal framework for mediation provided under the auspices of UNCITRAL (the Singapore Convention on Mediation, the UNCITRAL Model Laws and Rules). The draft Notes also provide an overview of matters for possible consideration in organizing a mediation with concise annotations under various headers (commencement of the mediation, selection and appointment of a mediator, preparatory steps, conduct of the mediation, settlement agreement, termination of the mediation). Finally, they also expressly address mediation as a valuable tool in the settlement of investor-State disputes, recognizing that mediation is increasingly provided for in investment treaties as a step or condition precedent to the filing of a court action or arbitration in investor-State dispute settlement. Mediation can be efficiently used during the 'cooling-off period'[70] or as a parallel track during or even after arbitral, judicial or similar proceedings have been commenced or concluded. Particular issues addressed in the context of investor-State mediation are the selection and appointment of a mediator, confidentiality and transparency, third parties (civil society and/or other interested stakeholders such as third-party funders), and the pertinent issue of authority to settle.

20.56 At its seventy-fourth session, by reference to the Report of the United Nations Commission on International Trade Law on the work of its fifty-second session, the United Nations General Assembly noted that it will further consider the draft UNCITRAL Mediation Rules and the draft UNCITRAL Notes on Mediation at its next session in 2020, following further comments and considerations from States and other interested relevant organization, and any appropriate revisions to the draft texts.[71] The seventy-fifth session of the United Nations General Assembly took place on 14 – 18 September 2020 and UNCITRAL reported on the work of its fifty-third session. The report noted that UNCITRAL had requested Working Group II to review the revised mediation texts to be prepared by the Secretariat prior to their finalization and adoption by UNCITRAL in 2021.[72]

b. The Singapore Convention on Mediation

20.57 UNCITRAL's Guide to Enactment and Use of the Model Law 2002 had already highlighted the view taken by many practitioners that the attractiveness of alternative dispute resolution would be increased if settlements reached through a process of alternative dispute resolution enjoyed a regime of expedited enforcement or would, for the purposes of

---

70 A 'cooling-off period' in investment treaties is usually a period between the notification of the claim to the opposing party and the initiation of the dispute resolution proceedings, either before an arbitral tribunal or a domestic court. Negotiations usually take place during this period with a view to reaching an amicable settlement.

71 UNGA Res 74/182, Report of the UNCITRAL work of its fifty-second session (adopted on 18 December 2019), para 8 <https://undocs.org/en/A/RES/74/182> accessed 21 December 2020.

72 The UNCITRAL Secretariat has noted that comments were received on both the draft UNCITRAL Mediation Rules (A/CN.9/1026) and the draft UNCITRAL Notes on Mediation (A/CN.9/1025). The comments will be incorporated into the revised drafts, then to be considered by the Working Group prior to their finalization and adoption by UNCITRAL in 2021. Meetings of Working Group II are currently postponed until March 2021. The preparatory documents for the seventy-third session of Working Group II show that comments on the draft Mediation Rules and Notes were received from Italy, Poland, Thailand, Iraq and China.

enforcement, be treated as or similarly to an arbitral award.[73] UNCITRAL was in support of 'the general policy that easy and fast enforcement of settlement agreements should be promoted'.[74]

Bolstering enforceability across borders also helps promote finality in settlement of cross-border disputes, as it reduces the possibility of parties pursuing duplicative litigation in other jurisdictions. For these reasons, initial consultations with the private sector indicated strong support for further efforts by UNCITRAL to facilitate the enforceability of conciliated settlement agreements. To further these goals, the United States proposed in 2014 that UNCITRAL Working Group II should develop a multilateral convention on the enforceability of international commercial settlement agreements reached through 'conciliation' (used synonymously with the term 'mediation'), with the goal of encouraging 'conciliation' in the same way that the New York Convention (1958) had facilitated the growth of arbitration.[75] At its forty-eighth session, UNCITRAL mandated Working Group II to elaborate an instrument for the enforcement of international commercial settlement agreements reached through mediation.[76] In 2015, Working Group II commenced deliberations for the preparation of such instrument.[77] **20.58**

i. Genesis and recent developments

As per the mandate given to it by UNCITRAL, Working Group II set out to boost international mediation in the same way that the New York Convention (1958) had succeeded in facilitating the international growth and success of arbitration.[78] It concluded its work in February 2018 with consensus on not one, but two instruments: the Singapore Convention on Mediation and the UNCITRAL Model Law on International Commercial Mediation.[79] **20.59**

The Singapore Convention on Mediation was adopted by the United Nations General Assembly on 20 December 2018[80] and has been open for signature since 7 August 2019.[81] The Convention will enter into force six months after deposit of the third instrument of ratification, **20.60**

---

73 UNCITRAL Model Law on Conciliation (n 59), para 87.

74 Ibid., para 88.

75 UNCITRAL, 'Planned and possible future work – Part III – Proposal by the Government of the United States of America: future work for Working Group II' (A/CN9/822, 2 June 2014) <https://undocs.org/en/A/CN.9/822> accessed 21 December 2020.

76 UNCITRAL, 'Report on the work of its forty-eighth session (29 June–16 July 2015)' (A/70/17), paras 135–142 <https://undocs.org/en/A/70/17> accessed 21 December 2020.

77 UNCITRAL, 'Report of the Working Group II (Arbitration and Conciliation) on the work of its sixty-third session (Vienna, 7–11 September 2015)' (A/CN9/861, 17 September 2015), para 15 <https://undocs.org/en/A/CN.9/861> accessed 21 December 2020.

78 Jan O'Neill, 'The new Singapore Convention: will it be the New York Convention for Mediation?' (Dispute Resolution Blog, 19 November 2018) <http://disputeresolutionblog.practicallaw.com/the-new-singapore-convention-will-it-be-the-new-york-convention-for-mediation/> accessed 21 December 2020; Eunice Chua, 'The Singapore Convention on Mediation – A Brighter Future for Asian Dispute Resolution' (2019) *9 Asian Journal of International Law* 195 < https://ssrn.com/abstract=3309433> accessed 21 December 2020.

79 UNCITRAL, 'Report of Working Group II (Dispute Settlement) on the work of its sixty-eighth session (5–9 February 2018)' (A/CN9/934, 19 February 2018), para 18 <https://undocs.org/A/CN.9/934> accessed 21 December 2020.

80 UN Convention on Mediation (n 57).

81 For details on the status of the UN Convention on Mediation, see <https://treaties.un.org/pages/ViewDetails.aspx?src=TREATY&mtdsg_no=XXII-4&chapter=22&clang=_en> accessed 21 December 2020.

acceptance, approval or accession.[82] Singapore and Fiji were the first countries to ratify the Convention on 25 February 2020. Currently, 53 countries have signed the Convention[83] and on 12 March 2020, Qatar was the third state to ratify the Convention. Thus, by virtue of its Article 14, the Singapore Convention on Mediation entered into force upon expiry of a period of six months following the deposit of the third instrument of ratification, i.e., on 12 September 2020. The current number of Parties to the Singapore Convention on Mediation is six (Belarus, Ecuador, Fiji, Qatar, Saudi Arabia, Singapore).

ii. Purpose and structure

20.61   The purpose of the Singapore Convention on Mediation is to establish an expedited legal mechanism for the enforcement of settlement agreements resulting from mediation in terms of a contribution to the development of harmonious international economic relations.[84] In the context of cross-border commercial disputes, unified enforcement standards are expected to foster confidence in the mediation process and to elevate the status of mediation to that of a reliable alternative dispute resolution tool.[85] In that sense, the Singapore Convention on Mediation goes beyond enhancing the current global use of mediation by establishing a new and additional source of international law – an internationally binding and inclusive stand-alone legal framework.[86]

20.62   The Singapore Convention on Mediation is a relatively short instrument. Following the obligatory clarifications as regards its scope of application (art 1), it provides definitions (art 2) and addresses general principles of enforcement such as the obligation of each party to the Convention to enforce a settlement agreement in accordance with its rules of procedure and under the conditions laid down in the Convention (art 3). It further deals with the requirements for reliance on settlement agreements (art 4) and, in its core – most controversial – part, lists grounds on the basis of which a competent enforcement authority may refuse to grant the relief at the request of the party against whom the relief is sought (art 5). Article 6 deals with the issue of parallel applications or claims and Article 7 explains how the Convention relates to other laws or treaties. The Convention further addresses the issue of reservations (art 8) and its effect on settlement agreements (art 9). The remaining provisions address technicalities such as the designation of a depository, signature, ratification, acceptance, approval and accession, and entry into force.

20.63   The Singapore Convention on Mediation is consistent with the UNCITRAL Model Law on International Commercial Mediation. This approach is intended to provide States with the flexibility to adopt either the Convention or the Model Law as a standalone text or both the

---

82   UN Convention on Mediation (n 57), art 14(1).
83   For details of the status of the UN Convention on Mediation, see: <https://uncitral.un.org/en/texts/mediation/conventions/international_settlement_agreements/status> accessed 21 December 2020.
84   UN Convention on Mediation (n 57), preamble.
85   Shouyu Chong and Felix Steffek, 'Enforcement of International Settlement Agreements resulting from Mediation under the Singapore Convention: Private international law issues in perspective' (2019) 31 (special issue) *Singapore Academy of Law Journal* 448, 450.
86   Piotr Wojtowicz and Franco Gevaerd, 'A New Global ADR Star is Born: The Singapore Convention on Mediation' (Wiley Online Library, 7 October 2019) <https://onlinelibrary.wiley.com/doi/abs/10.1002/alt.21810> accessed 21 December 2020.

Convention and the Model Law as complementary instruments for a comprehensive legal framework on mediation.

iii. Scope of application

The Singapore Convention on Mediation applies to international agreements resulting from mediation concluded in writing by parties to resolve a commercial dispute.[87] **20.64**

Thus, as a first requirement in order to be enforceable under the Convention, an agreement **20.65** must be the outcome of a successful mediation. Evidence that the settlement agreement resulted from mediation may be provided in the form of (i) the mediator's signature on the settlement agreement; (ii) a document signed by the mediator indicating that the mediation was carried out; (iii) an attestation by the institution that administered the mediation; or (iv) in the absence of the above, any other evidence acceptable to the authority competent to enforce the settlement agreement.[88] 'Mediation' in the context of the Convention means:

> a process, irrespective of the expression used or the basis upon which the process is carried out, whereby parties attempt to reach an amicable settlement of their dispute with the assistance of a third person or persons ('the mediator') lacking the authority to impose a solution upon the parties to the dispute.[89]

The definition provided in the Convention echoes the definitions put forward in the UNCITRAL Model Law on International Commercial Mediation and the European Mediation Directive. A common element in all these legal instruments is that they do not afford any relevance to giving a specific denomination to the procedure that is followed in the amicable dispute resolution process. This underlines quite clearly that what really matters is the involvement of a third neutral person who supports the resolution of the parties' dispute with his or her skilled interventions.[90] It is a distinct feature of the Singapore Convention on Mediation, however, that it does not set out any specific trigger mechanism for the procedure. The parties may decide voluntarily to resort to mediation, or it can be mandatory, ordered by law or by a court or tribunal. By contrast, the EU Mediation Directive advocates that the parties to a dispute attempt by themselves, on a voluntary basis, to reach an agreement on the settlement of their dispute.[91] The Directive is, however, without prejudice to national legislation making the use of mediation compulsory or subject to incentives or sanctions, whether before or after judicial proceedings have started, provided that such legislation does not prevent the parties from exercising their right of access to the judicial system.[92] This very point has sparked considerable debate within the context of the EU. Some Member States, such as Italy, propagate that the most efficient – and in fact only – way to increase recourse to mediation is to make it mandatory.[93]

---

87   UN Convention on Mediation (n 57), art 1(1).
88   Ibid., art 4(1)(b).
89   Ibid., art 2(3).
90   Elisabetta Silvestri, 'The Singapore Convention on Mediated Settlement Agreements: A New String to the Bow of International Mediation?' (2019) 2(3) *Access to Justice in Eastern Europe* 5, 7.
91   EU Mediation Directive (n 12), art 3(a).
92   Ibid., art 5(2).
93   Silvestri (n 90), 7.

20.66 As regards the requirement that the agreement resulting from mediation must be international, the Convention relies on the parties' places of business, which they must have in different States.[94] This approach is based on Article 1(4) of the UNCITRAL Model Law on International Commercial Mediation. The Convention, however, sets out an alternative for the requirement of internationality. The requirement is also fulfilled if the State in which the parties to the settlement agreement have their places of business is different from either: (i) the State in which a substantial part of the obligations under the settlement agreement is performed; or (ii) the State with which the subject matter of the settlement agreement is most closely connected.[95] A further particularity of the Convention that has been underlined is that it does not invoke the notion of 'State of Origin'. This circumstance essentially renders settlement agreements Stateless instruments.[96] Nevertheless, according to Article 3(1) of the Convention, which stipulates the obligation for each party to the Convention to enforce a settlement agreement in accordance with its rules of procedure and under the conditions laid down in the Convention, domestic law may very well interfere when it comes to the determination, by the competent authority seized with the enforcement of the settlement agreement, as to whether enforcement shall be granted or refused.[97]

20.67 The notion of the commercial nature of the settlement agreement as a requirement for international enforceability becomes clear by reference to the UNCITRAL Model Law on International Commercial Mediation, more concretely the footnote to its Article 3(1).[98] Further clarification may also be derived from the exclusions from the scope of the Convention listed in its Article 1, namely settlement agreements concluded by a consumer for personal, family or household purposes, or relating to family, inheritance or employment law.[99] A settlement agreement that is enforceable as a judgment or as an arbitral award is also excluded from the scope of the Convention in order to avoid possible overlap with existing and future conventions, namely the New York Convention (1958), the Convention on Choice of Court Agreements (2005) and the Convention on the Recognition and Enforcement of Foreign Judgments in Civil or Commercial Matters (2019). These exclusions must be read in light of the Convention's role to serve as a gap filler in the cross-border enforcement of international mediated settlement agreements.[100]

---

94 UN Convention on Mediation (n 57), art 1(1)(a).

95 Ibid., art 1(1)(b).

96 Timothy Schnabel, 'The Singapore Convention on Mediation: A Framework for the Cross-Border Recognition and Enforcement of Mediated Settlements' (2019) 19 *Pepperdine Dispute Resolution Law Journal* 1, 22; Chong and Steffek (n 85), 456.

97 Silvestri (n 90), 8.

98 UNCITRAL Model Law on Mediation (n 56), art 3(1), footnote 3:

> The term 'commercial' should be given a wide interpretation so as to cover matters arising from all relationships of a commercial nature, whether contractual or not. Relationships of a commercial nature include, but are not limited to, the following transactions: any trade transaction for the supply or exchange of goods or services; distribution agreement; commercial representation or agency; factoring; leasing; construction of works; consulting; engineering; licensing; investment; financing; banking; insurance; exploitation agreement or concession; joint venture and other forms of industrial or business cooperation; and carriage of goods or passengers by air, sea, rail or road.

> see <https://uncitral.un.org/sites/uncitral.un.org/files/media-documents/uncitral/en/annex_ii.pdf> accessed 21 December 2020.

99 UN Convention on Mediation (n 57), arts 1(2) and (3).

100 Chong and Steffek (n 85), 459; Nadja Alexander and Shouyu Chong, 'The New UN Convention on Mediation (aka the 'Singapore Convention') – Why It's Important for Hong Kong' (April 2019) *Hong Kong Lawyer* 26.

Finally, the 'in writing' requirement set out in Article 1(1) of the Singapore Convention on **20.68**
Mediation concerns the necessary formal features of the agreement. According to Article 2(2)
of the Convention:

> a settlement agreement is 'in writing' if its content is recorded in any form. The requirement that a
> settlement agreement must be in writing is met by an electronic communication if the information
> contained therein is accessible so as to be useable for subsequent reference.[101]

What is required in any case is that the settlement bears the signatures of all parties.[102]

iv. Enforcement

In order to enforce an international settlement agreement falling within the scope of **20.69**
application of the Singapore Convention on Mediation, the party seeking relief must supply
the authority competent to enforce the settlement with the agreement, signed by the parties,
and provide evidence that the settlement agreement resulted from mediation.[103]

Procedural aspects and requirements

The Singapore Convention on Mediation does not impose a specific procedure for enforce- **20.70**
ment. Article 3(1) sets out that each 'State party shall enforce the settlement agreement in
accordance with its rules of procedure and under the conditions laid down in the Convention.'[104] Just as under the European Mediation Directive, under the Singapore Convention on
Mediation, States are free in the way they adapt their domestic legal frameworks to provide
consistent enforcement mechanisms.[105]

Furthermore, Article 3(2) stipulates that: **20.71**

> a State shall allow a party to invoke the settlement agreement in accordance with its rules of procedure
> and under the conditions laid down in the Convention, in order to prove that the matter has been
> already resolved.

This provision essentially allows that a settlement agreement resulting from mediation may be
used as a defence. The provision encapsulates the practical effect of recognition without
explicitly using the term as it holds different meanings under domestic and international
law.[106] Metaphorically speaking, the mechanism provided under Article 3(1) is a 'sword' that
may be used to initiate enforcement proceedings, while the mechanism provided under Article
3(2) is a 'shield' that may be used to protect against dismissal (or striking out) proceedings.[107]
Upon the provision of the required evidence that the settlement agreement indeed resulted

---

101 UN Convention on Mediation (n 57), art 2(2).

102 Ibid., art 4(1)(a).

103 Ibid., art 4(1)(a) and (b).

104 Ibid., art 3(1).

105 Chong and Steffek (n 85), 464.

106 Anna KC Koo, 'Enforcing International Mediated Settlement Agreements' in Muruga Perumal Ramaswamy and João
     Ribeiro (eds), *Harmonizing Trade Law to Enable Private Sector Regional Development* (UNCITRAL Regional Centre for
     Asia and the Pacific 2017) 91–2.

107 Lucy Reed, 'Ultima Thule: Prospects for International Commercial Mediation' (NUS Centre for International Law
     Research Paper 19/03, 18 January 2019) <https://papers.ssrn.com/sol3/papers.cfm?abstract_id=3339788> accessed
     21 December 2020; Chong and Steffek (n 85), 466; Silvestri (n 90), 8.

from mediation,[108] the authority competent to enforce the settlement agreement shall act expeditiously.[109] It may require any necessary document in order to verify that the requirements of the Convention have been complied with.[110]

20.72   At the request of the party against whom the relief is sought, the authority competent to enforce the settlement agreement may refuse to enforce it even if the conditions set out under Article 4 of the Convention are fulfilled. This is the case if proof of one or more of the grounds for refusal is presented in accordance with Article 5 of the Singapore Convention on Mediation.

Grounds for refusing to grant relief

20.73   Article 5 of the Singapore Convention on Mediation defines, in an exhaustive manner, the grounds upon which the authority competent to enforce settlement agreements resulting from mediation may refuse to grant relief under the terms of the Convention at the request of the disputing party against whom it is invoked. These grounds can be grouped into three main categories, namely in relation to the disputing parties, the settlement agreement and the mediation procedure. Other grounds for refusal relate to public policy and the fact that the subject matter of the dispute cannot be settled by mediation.

20.74   Under the concrete terms of Article 5, proof must be furnished that a party to the settlement agreement was under some incapacity,[111] the settlement agreement sought to be relied upon is null and void, inoperative or incapable of being performed under the law to which the parties have validly subjected it,[112] is not binding or final according to its terms,[113] or has been subsequently modified.[114] Furthermore, the party against whom the relief is sought may invoke that the obligations in the settlement agreement have been performed,[115] or that they are not clear or comprehensible.[116] Further grounds for the refusal to grant relief are that granting relief would be contrary to the terms of the settlement agreement,[117] that there was a serious breach by the mediator of standards applicable to the mediator or the mediation without which breach that party would not have entered into the settlement agreement,[118] or that there was a failure by the mediator to disclose to the parties circumstances that raise justifiable doubts as to the mediator's impartiality or independence and such failure to disclose had a material impact or undue influence on a party without which failure that party would not have entered into the settlement agreement.[119]

20.75   The refusal grounds dealing with mediator misconduct were the subject of considerable debate in Working Group II. An initial draft of the two provisions addressed mediators' failures to

---

108   UN Convention on Mediation (n 57), art 4(1) (b).
109   Ibid., art 4(5).
110   Ibid., art 4(4).
111   Ibid., art 4(4).
112   Ibid., art 5(1)(b)(i).
113   Ibid., art 5(1)(b)(ii).
114   Ibid., art 5(1)(b)(iii).
115   Ibid., art 5(1)(c)(i).
116   Ibid., art 5(1)(c)(ii).
117   Ibid., art 5(1)(d).
118   Ibid., art 5(1)(e).
119   Ibid., art 5(1)(f).

'maintain fair treatment of the parties' or to disclose circumstances 'likely to give rise to justifiable doubts as to its impartiality or independence'.[120] Some delegates preferred a broader exception allowing courts to refuse to grant relief based on unfair treatment of the parties by the mediator. Others opposed the inclusion of such exception altogether, referring to codes of conduct and the terms usually laid down jointly by the mediator and the parties in agreements to mediate.[121] The differences between mediation and arbitration were also emphasized.[122] The version of Article 5 that was ultimately adopted represents a still controversial compromise. Parties seeking to avoid the enforcement of a settlement under the Convention must demonstrate that the mediator's breach of best practice standards was serious. Also, under both clauses (e) and (f) of Article 5, parties resisting enforcement must demonstrate a causal link between the mediator's transgressions and the resisting party's consent to settlement. The element of causation is crucial in the administration of this refusal ground, and is to be regarded as an objective test.[123]

20.76 Finally, the authority competent to enforce a settlement agreement under the Singapore Convention on Mediation may also refuse to grant relief if it finds that (a) granting relief would be contrary to the public policy of the party where relief is sought, or (b) the subject matter of the dispute is not capable of settlement by mediation under the law of that party.[124]

20.77 With an expedited enforcement mechanism for international settlement agreements resulting from mediation available under an internationally binding legal instrument, the Singapore Convention on Mediation is a vigorous step forward towards transforming commercial mediation into a truly effective dispute resolution tool. The hope is that the Convention will make mediation more appealing and promote a wider use of cross-border mediation.

C. OUTLOOK

20.78 As has been highlighted throughout this chapter, the advantages of mediation are evident and also recognized not only by dispute resolution professionals, but also, to a significantly increasing degree, by the users of alternative dispute resolution services. Empirical data, however scarce it may still be, shows that compared to adversarial dispute resolution methods such as litigation or arbitration, mediation offers genuine time and cost effectiveness. In terms of the value and sustainability of the outcome that stands at the end of the mediation process, success rates of well above 50 per cent are also compelling. However, despite the undeniably attractive features of the tool, mediation – at least within the territory of the EU – remains strikingly underused.

---

120 UNCITRAL, 'Settlement of Commercial Disputes – International Commercial Conciliation: preparation of an instrument on enforcement of international commercial settlement agreements resulting from conciliation – Note by the Secretariat (12-23 September 2016)' (A/CN9/WGII/WP198, 30 June 2016), para 35 <https://undocs.org/en/A/CN.9/WG.II/WP.198> accessed 21 December 2020.

121 Chua (n 78), 201–2.

122 Schnabel (n 96), 49–50.

123 Ibid., 51.

124 UN Convention on Mediation (n 57), art 5(2).

20.79   By way of the European Mediation Directive, the EU catalyzed a process for the harmon-ization of mediation legislation throughout its territory. It also set the groundwork for a unified standard of quality in mediation through the European Code of Conduct for Mediators. The particular case of Austria evidences that certain European jurisdictions have gone above and beyond the black letter of the European Mediation Directive in their ambition to strive for a true 'gold standard' in mediation, be it in domestic mediation or in processes that happen in a cross-border international context.

20.80   Under the Singapore Convention on Mediation, which entered into force on 12 September 2020, States are held to the commitment to enforce international settlement agreements resulting from mediation in a unified expedited procedure that echoes the principles of the New York Convention (1958). Hand in hand with other international instruments negotiated under the auspices of the United Nations Commission on International Trade Law, in particular the UNCITRAL Model Law on International Commercial Mediation, it contrib-utes to the further harmonization and development of best practices in alternative dispute resolution in a world of strongly entwined commercial relations. 2021 will also likely see the adoption of further momentous instruments, namely the UNCITRAL Mediation Rules and the UNCITRAL Notes on Mediation. Taken together, these instruments establish a well-rounded, strong and legally binding international framework for commercial mediation. However, also each instrument on its own is a pivotal element when it comes to bolstering the role of mediation as an effective alternative dispute resolution tool for resolving cross-border commercial disputes. With these new instruments in place and a new awareness and openness towards the use of consensual methods in professional dispute resolution processes, commer-cial mediation will flourish further and show its full potential in the years to come, not only in Europe but throughout the world.

BIBLIOGRAPHY

CHAPTER 1

Books

Born G, *International Commercial Arbitration* (Kluwer Law International 2014).

Blackaby N and others, *Redfern and Hunter on International Commercial Arbitration* (OUP 2015).

Blanke G and Landolt P (eds), *EU and US Antitrust Arbitration: A Handbook for Practitioners* (Kluwer Law International 2011).

Ferrari F (ed), *Limits to Party Autonomy in International Commercial Arbitration* (Juris 2016).

Ferrari F, *The Impact of EU Law on Commercial Arbitration* (Juris 2017).

Gaillard E and Domenico Di Pietro (eds), *Enforcement of Arbitration Agreements and International Arbitral Awards: The New York Convention in Practice* (Cameron May 2008).

Kronke H and others (eds), *Recognition and Enforcement of Foreign Arbitral Awards: A Global Commentary on the New York Convention* (Kluwer Law International 2010).

Paulsson J, *The Idea of Arbitration* (OUP 2013).

Wiliński P, *Excess of Powers in International Commercial Arbitration* (Eleven International Publishing 2021) (forthcoming).

Journal articles

Babić D, 'Rome I Regulation: binding authority for arbitral tribunals in the European Union?' (2017) 13(1) *Journal of Private International Law* 71.

Basedow J, 'EU Law in International Arbitration: Referrals to the European Court of Justice' (2015) 32(4) *Journal of International Arbitration* 367.

Bensaude D, 'Thalès Air Defence BV v GIE Euromissiles: Defining the Limits of Scrutiny of Awards Based on Alleged Violations of European Competition Law' (2005) 22(3) *Journal of International Arbitration* 239.

Bermann GA, 'Navigating EU Law and the Law of International Arbitration' (2012) 28(3) *Arbitration International* 397.

Betancourt JC, 'International Commercial Arbitration and Private Agreement to Abide under Recital 12, Paragraph 2, of the Recast Brussels Regulation' (2018) 33 *Spain Arbitration Review* 69.

Blanke G, 'Defining the Limits of Scrutiny of Awards Based on Alleged Violations of European Competition Law' (2006) 23(3) *Journal of International Arbitration* 249.

Brokelmann H, 'The Rail Track Judgement of the LG Dortmunt: Are Cartel Damages Claims Arbitrable?' (2018) 31 *Spain Arbitration Review* 9.

De Ly F, 'The Interface Between Arbitration and the Brussels Regulation' (2016) 5(3) *American University Business Law Review* 485.

Grierson J, 'The Court of Justice of the European Union and International Arbitration' (2019) 2 *b-Arbitra (Belgian Review of Arbitration)* 309.

Hanotiau B, 'What Law Governs the Issue of Arbitrability?' (1996) 12(4) *Arbitration International* 391.

Hascher D, 'Recognition and Enforcement of Judgments on the Existence and Validity of an Arbitration Clause under the Brussels Convention' (1997) 13(1) *Arbitration International* 33.

Kleinheisterkamp J, 'The Impact of Internationally Mandatory Laws on the Enforceability of Arbitration Agreements' (2009) 3 *World Arbitration & Mediation Review* 119.

Kramer X, 'Cross-Border Enforcement and the Brussels I-bis Regulation: Towards a New Balance between Mutual Trust and National Control over Fundamental Rights' (2013) 60(3) *Netherlands International Law Review* (NILR) 343.

Paschalidis P, 'Arbitral Tribunals and Preliminary References to the EU Court of Justice' (2017) 33(4) *Arbitration International* 663.

Paschalidis P, 'Genetech: EU Law Confronted with International Arbitration' (2016) 5(1) *European International Arbitration Review* 59.

Wiliński P, 'Emergence of Lis Pendens Arbitralis in Europe' (2011) 15(3) *Kwartalnik ADR* 135.

Yüksel B, 'The Relevance of the Rome I Regulation to International Commercial Arbitration in the European Union' (2011) 7(1) *Journal of Private International Law* 149.

CHAPTER 2

Books

'Legal Instruments and Practice of Arbitration in the EU: Study for the Juri Committee' (European Parliament 2014).

Blackaby N, Partasides C and others, *Redfern and Hunter on International Arbitration* (6th edn, OUP 2015).

Born GB, *International Arbitration: Law and Practice* (2nd edn, Kluwer Law International 2015).

Bosman L (ed), *ICCA International Handbook on Commercial Arbitration* (Kluwer 2020, Suppl 104, February 2019).

Bosman L (ed), *ICCA International Handbook on Commercial Arbitration* (Kluwer Law International 2020, Suppl 109, February 2020).

Bosman L (ed), *ICCA International Handbook on Commercial Arbitration* (ICCA & Kluwer Law International 2020, Suppl 110, April 2020).

Cole T and others, *Legal Instruments and Practice of Arbitration in the EU* (EU Directorate General for Internal Policies 2014).

Franke U, Magnusson A and others (eds), *International Arbitration in Sweden: A Practitioner's Guide* (Kluwer Law International 2013).

Leaua C and Baias F (eds), *Arbitration in Romania: A Practitioner's Guide* (Kluwer Law International 2016).

Meijer GJ and van Mierlo A, *Parlementaire Geschiedenis Arbitragewet* (Wolters Kluwer 2015).

Meijer GJ, *Tekst & Commentaar Burgerlijke Rechtsvordering* (Wolters Kluwer 2018).

Paulsson M, *The 1958 New York Convention in Action* (Kluwer Law International 2016).

van den Berg AJ, *The New York Arbitration Convention of 1958* (Kluwer Law International 1981).

Zeiler G and Siwy A, *The European Convention on International Commercial Arbitration: A Commentary* (Kluwer Law International 2018).

Journal articles

DCCP, Art 1058 note 1c, cf Amsterdam District Court 19 November 2019, ECLI:NL: GHAMS:2019:4121, *Korbusiness BV* (2020) 19 *Tijdschrift voor Arbitrage*.

Arnhem-Leeuwarden Court of Appeal 8 October 2019, ECLI:NL:GHARL:2019:8203, *Stichting Amphia* (2020) 13 *Tijdschrift voor Arbitrage*.

Report on the Accession of the Hellenic Republic to the Community Convention on Jurisdiction and the Enforcement of Judgments in Civil and Commercial Matters (1986) C 298/1 OJ.

Bensaude D, 'Thalès Air Defence BV v. GIE Euromissile: Defining the Limits of Scrutiny of Awards Based on Alleged Violations of European Competition Law' (2005) 22(3) *Journal of International Arbitration* 243.

de Groot D, 'Arbitrage en Europees mededingingsrecht – een voorlopige balans dertien jaar na Eco Swiss/Benetton' (2012) 64 *Tijdschrift voor Arbitrage*.

Graf BU and Appleton AE, 'ECJ Case C 40/08 Asturcom – EU Unfair Terms Law Confirmed as a Matter of Public Policy' (2010) 28 issue 2 *ASA Bulletin* (*Association Suisse de l'Arbitrage*) 417.

Jenard P, Report on the Convention of 27 September 1968 on jurisdiction and the enforcement of judgments in civil and commercial matters (1979) C 59/13 Official Journal of the European Community.

Konrad CW and Peters PA, 'Challenging and Enforcing Arbitration Awards 2019' (*Global Arbitration Review*, 15th May 2019).

Markus AR and Giroud S, 'A Swiss Perspective on West Tankers and Its Aftermath: What about the Lugano Convention?' (2010) vol 28 issue 2 *ASA Bulletin* (*Association Suisse de l'Arbitrage*) 233.

Paulsson J, 'May or must under the New York Convention: An exercise in syntax and linguistics' (1998) 14 *Arbitration International* 227.

Piers M, 'Consumer Arbitration in the EU: A Forced Marriage with Incompatible Expectations' (2011) 2(1) *Journal of International Dispute Settlement* 209.

Schlosser P, Report on the Convention of October 9, 1978, signed in Luxembourg, on the accession of the Kingdom of Denmark, Ireland and the United Kingdom to the Convention on Jurisdiction and the Enforcement of Judgments in Civil and Commercial Matters and to the Protocol on its interpretation by the Court of Justice (1979) C 59/71 OJ.

Toms Krūmiņš, 'Arbitration in Latvia: A cautionary tale?' (2017) 34(2) *Journal of International Arbitration* 327.

Blogs

Goldsmith A and Nettlau H, 'The Revised Swedish Arbitration Act: Some Noteworthy Developments' (Kluwer Arbitration Blog, 19 May 2019) <http://arbitrationblog.kluwerarbitration.com/2019/05/19/the-revised-swedish-arbitration-act-some-noteworthy-developments/> accessed 24 June 2020.

CHAPTER 3

Books

Briggs A, *Civil Jurisdiction and Judgments* (6th edn, Routledge 2015).

van den Berg AJ (ed), *Yearbook Commercial Arbitration 2000* (Volume XXV, Kluwer Law International 2000).

van den Berg AJ (ed), *Yearbook Commercial Arbitration 2003* (Volume XXVIII, Kluwer Law International 2003).

Journal articles

Camilleri S, 'Recital 12 of the Recast Regulation: A New Hope' (2013) 62 *ICLQ* 899.

Cuniberti G, 'The International Market for Contracts: The Most Attractive Contract Laws' (2014) 34 *NWJILB* 455.

Jones T, 'Lithuania fails to revive US$2 billion claim against Gazprom' (*Global Arbitration Review*, 5 July 2019) <https://globalarbitrationreview.com/article/1194864/lithuania-fails-to-revive-ususd2-billion-claim-against-gazprom> accessed on 8 January 2020.

Lat Am courts clash over gas exports award' (*Global Arbitration Review*, 11 March 2016) <https://globalarbitrationreview.com/article/1035336/lat-am-courts-clash-over-gas-exports-award> accessed 8 January 2020.

Peel E, 'Arbitration and Anti-Suit Injunctions in the European Union' (2009) 125 *LQR* 365.

Scherer M and Jahnel W, 'Anti-suit and Anti-arbitration Injunctions in International Arbitration: A Swiss Perspective' (2009) 12 *International Arbitration Law Review* 66.

Commission documents

Commission, 'EU Member States agree on a plurilateral treaty to terminate bilateral investment treaties' (24 October 2019).

Other secondary resources

Departmental Advisory Committee on Arbitration Law, *Report on the Arbitration Bill* (HL 1996).

International Law Association, Report of the Seventy-Second Conference (Toronto): Final Report on Lis Pendens and Arbitration (2006).

Jenard P, 'Report on the Convention on jurisdiction and the enforcement of judgments in civil and commercial matters' [1979] OJ C 59/1 13.

Kaufmann-Kohler G, 'Multiple Proceedings in International Arbitration: Blessing or Plague?' (Herbert Smith Freehills and Singapore Management University School of Law Asian Arbitration Lecture, 24 November 2015).

Rapport de la Commission des affaires juridiques du Conseil national, *Initiative parlementaire Modification de l'art. 186 de la loi fédérale sur le droit international privé* (17 February 2006, 02.415).

Representative of the Government of Hungary, 'Declaration of the Representative of the Government of Hungary, of 16 January 2019, on the legal consequences of the Judgment of the Court of Justice in Achmea and on Investment Protection in the European Union' (January 2019) (Hungary Declaration) <http://www.kormany.hu/download/5/1b/81000/Hungarys%20Declaration%20on%20Achmea.pdf> accessed 8 January 2020.

Representatives of the Governments of Finland, Luxembourg, Malta, Slovenia and Sweden, 'Declaration of the Representatives of the Governments of the Member States, of 16 January 2019, on the enforcement of the Judgment of the Court of Justice in Achmea and on Investment Protection in the European' (January 2019) (Second Declaration) <https://

www.regeringen.se/48ee19/contentassets/d759689c0c804a9ea7af6b2de7320128/achmea-declaration.pdf> accessed 8 January 2020.

Representatives of the Governments of the Member States of Belgium, Czech Republic, Germany, Ireland, Spain, Croatia, Cyprus, Bulgaria, Denmark, Estonia, Greece, France, Italy, Latvia, Lithuania, Austria, Portugal, Slovenia, Netherlands, Poland, Romania and United Kingdom, 'Declaration of Declaration of the Representatives of The Governments of The Member States, of 15 January 2019, on the legal consequences of the judgment of the Court of Justice In Achmea and on Investment Protection In The European Union' (January 2019) (Declaration) <https://ec.europa.eu/info/sites/info/files/business_economy_euro/banking_and_finance/documents/190117-bilateral-investment-treaties_en.pdf> 8 January 2020.

Schlosser P, 'Report on the Convention on the Association of the Kingdom of Denmark, Ireland and the United Kingdom of Great Britain and Northern Ireland to the Convention on jurisdiction and the enforcement of judgments in civil and commercial matters and to the Protocol on its interpretation by the Court of Justice' (European Council, 1979) OJ C59/71.

Blogs

Gonin E, 'How Effective are ICSID Provisional Measures at Suspending Criminal Proceedings before Domestic Courts: The English Example?' (Wolters Kluwer, 30 September 2017) <http://arbitrationblog.kluwerarbitration.com/2017/09/30/effective-icsid-provisional-measures-suspending-criminal-proceedings-domestic-courts-english-example/> accessed 8 January 2020.

CHAPTER 4

Books

Emberland M, *The Human Rights of Companies: Exploring the Structure of ECHR Protection* (OUP 2006).

Ferrari F (ed), *The Impact of EU Law on Commercial Law* (Jurisnet LLC 2017).

Frumer P, *La renunciation aux droits et libertés, La Convention européenne des droits de l'homme á l'épreuve de la volonté individuelle* (Bruylant 2001).

Mustill MJ and Boyd SC, *The Law and Practice of Commercial Arbitration in England* (2001 companion volume) (2nd edn, Butterworths 2009).

Poncet D and Cambi A, *Mélanges en l'honneur de Pierre Lambert* (Bruylant 2000).

Yearbook of the European Convention on Human Rights 1987 (Martinus Nijoff Publishers).

Journal articles

Besson S, 'Arbitration and Human Rights' (2006) 24 *ASA Bulletin* 395.

Fietta S and Upcher J, 'Public International Law, Investment Treaties and Commercial Arbitration: an emerging system of complementarity?' (2013) 29 *Arbitration International* 187.

Samuel A, 'Arbitration, Alternative Dispute Resolution Generally and the European Convention on Human Rights, An Anglo-Centric View' (2004) 21 *Journal of International Arbitration* 413–38.

Other secondary sources

Ringquist F, 'Do Procedural Human Rights Requirements Apply to Arbitration – A Study of Article 6 (1) of the European Convention on Human Rights and its Bearing upon Arbitration' (Master Thesis, University of Lund 2005).

Blogs

Voser N and Gottlieb B, 'How the European Court of Human Rights Interferes in (Sports) Arbitration' (Kluwer Arbitration Blog, 19 December 2018) <http://arbitrationblog.kluwerarbitration.com/2018/12/19/how-the-european-court-for-human-rights-interferes-in-sports-arbitration/ > accessed 12 June 2020.

CHAPTER 5

Books

Clay T, 'L'Arbitre' (Dalloz 2001).
Courbe P, 'L'ordre public de proximité, Mélanges offertes à Paul Lagarde' (Dalloz 2005).
Lalive P, 'Sur l'irresponsabilité arbitrale, Etudes de Procédure et d'arbitrage en l'honneur de J.-F. Poudret' (Faculté de Droit de l'Université de Lausanne 1999).

Journal articles

Azzi T, 'Précisions sur l'Ordre Public de Proximité' (2006) *La Semaine Juridique – Édition Générale* 10165.
Mouralis D, 'Conformité des sentences internationales à l'ordre public : la Cour de cassation maintient le principe d'un contrôle limité' (2014) 16–21 *La Semaine Juridique – Édition Générale* 782.
Paisley K, 'It's All About the Data: The Impact of the EU General Data Protection Regulation on International Arbitration' (2018) 41 *Fordham International Law Journal* 841.

Commission documents

Article 29 Data Protection Working Party, 'Working Document 1/2009 on pre-trial discovery for cross border civil Litigation' WP 158 <https://ec.europa.eu/justice/article-29/documentation/opinion-recommendation/files/2009/wp158_en.pdf> accessed 8 June 2020.
Commission Implementing Decision (EU) 2016/1250 of 12 July 2016 pursuant to Directive 95/46/EC of the European Parliament and of the Council on the adequacy of the protection provided by the EU-U.S. Privacy Shield [2016] OJ L 207/1.
The Working Party on the Protection of Individuals with regard to the processing of personal data set up by Directive 95/46/EC of the European Parliament and of the Council of 24 October 1995 (Article 29 Data Protection Working Party), 'Opinion 1/2010 on the concepts of "controller" and "processor"' WP 169 adopted on 16 February 2010 <https://

ec.europa.eu/justice/article-29/documentation/opinion-recommendation/files/2010/wp169_en.pdf> accessed 8 June 2020.

Other secondary sources

ICC, 'Note to the Parties and Arbitral Tribunals on the conduct of Arbitration', 1 January 2019.

ICCA, International Institute for Conflict Prevention and Resolution (CPR) and the New York City Bar Association, 'Cybersecurity Protocol for International Arbitration – Consultation Draft' (2018) <https://www.arbitration-icca.org/media/10/43322709923070/draft_cybersecurity_protocol_final_10_april.pdf> accessed 8 June 2020.

International Council for Commercial Arbitration, International Bar Association, 'The ICCA-IBA Roadmap to Data Protection in International Arbitration' (Public Consultation Draft, 28 February 2020).

The European Data Protection Board guidelines 3/2018 on the territorial scope of the GDPR, Art 3 (Version 2.1, 12 November 2019) <https://edpb.europa.eu/our-work-tools/our-documents/guidelines/guidelines-32018-territorial-scope-gdpr-article-3-version_fr> accessed 8 June 2020.

Blogs and websites

Baxi B, 'Tennant Energy v. Canada, diluting the impact of GDPR in International Treaty Arbitration' (KSLR EU Law Blog, 15 October 2019) <https://blogs.kcl.ac.uk/kslreuropeanlawblog/?p=1415#.Xt4y4OexXb0> accessed 8 June 2020.

Botts B, 'Foreign Data Protection Laws in U.S. Litigation and International Arbitration' (Insights, 6 February 2020) <https://www.bakerbotts.com/insights/publications/2020/february/foreign-data-protection-laws-in-us-litigation-and-international-arbitrationcapabilities/cybersecurity/protocol_cybersecurity_intl_arb_july2017.pdf> accessed 8 June 2020.

Commission Nationale de l'Informatique et des Libertés, French criminal law protections of data privacy <https://www.cnil.fr/fr/les-sanctions-penales> accessed 8 June 2020.

Debevoise and Plimpton, 'Protocol to Promote Cybersecurity in International Arbitration, 2017'<https://www.debevoise.com/~/media/files/capabilities/cybersecurity/protocol_cybersecurity_intl_arb_july2017.pdf> accessed 8 June 2020.

European Commission, 'What is personal data?' <https://ec.europa.eu/info/law/law-topic/data-protection/reform/what-personal-data_en> accessed 8 June 2020.

European Commission, 'What is the European Data Protection Board (EDPB)?' <https://ec.europa.eu/info/law/law-topic/data-protection/reform/rules-business-and-organisations/enforcement-and-sanctions/enforcement/what-european-data-protection-board-edpb_en> accessed 8 June 2020.

Hay E, 'The Invisible Arm of GDPR in International Treaty Arbitration: Can't We Make It Go Away?' (Kluwer Arbitration Blog, 29 August 2019) <http://arbitrationblog.kluwerarbitration.com/2019/08/29/the-invisible-arm-of-gdpr-in-international-treaty-arbitration-cant-we-make-it-go-away/> accessed 8 June 2020.

International Centre for Dispute Resolution (ICDR) – American Arbitration Association (AAA) EU-US Privacy Shield Program – Independent Recourse Mechanism (IRM) <https://go.adr.org/privacyshield.html> accessed 8 June 2020.

Stockholm Chamber of Commerce Platform <https://sccinstitute.com/scc-platform/> accessed 8 June 2020.

Szlarb NM, 'European Union: GDPR And International Arbitration at a Crossroad' (Sheppard Mullin Richter & Hampton, 5 December 2019) <https://www.mondaq.com/unitedstates/arbitration-dispute-resolution/871962/gdpr-and-international-arbitration-at-a-crossroad> accessed 8 June 2020.

Zahariev M, 'GDPR issues in commercial arbitration and how to mitigate them' (Kluwer Arbitration Blog, 7 September 2019) <http://arbitrationblog.kluwerarbitration.com/2019/09/07/gdpr-issues-in-commercial-arbitration-and-how-to-mitigate-them/> accessed 8 June 2020.

CHAPTER 6

Books

Aksen G and others (eds), *Global Reflections on International Law, Commerce and Dispute Resolution: Liber Amoricum in honour of Robert Briner* (ICC 2005).

Bassiri N and Draye M (eds), *Arbitration in Belgium: A Practitioner's Guide* (Kluwer 2016).

Bělohlávek AJ, *B2C Arbitration: Consumer Protection in Arbitration* (Juris Net 2012).

Born GB, *International Commercial Arbitration* (2nd ed, Kluwer 2014).

Kaufmann-Kohler G and Schultz T, *Online Dispute Resolution: Challenges for Contemporary Justice* (Kluwer 2004).

Kronke H and others (eds), *Recognition and Enforcement of Foreign Arbitral Awards: A Global Commentary on the New York Convention* (Kluwer 2010).

Meeusen J, Pertegás M and Straetmans G (eds), *Enforcement of International Contracts in the European Union* (Intersentia 2004).

Piers M and Aschauer C (eds), *Arbitration in the Digital Age – The Brave New World of Arbitration* (CUP 2018).

Journal articles

de Ly P, 'The Interface Between Arbitration and The Brussels Regulation' (2015) 5 *American University Business Law Review* 485.

Dowers N and Tang ZS, 'Arbitration in EU Jurisdiction Regulation: Brussels I Recast and a New Proposal' (2015) 3 *Groningen Journal of International Law* 125.

Gibbons LJ, 'Creating a Market for Justice; a Market Incentive Solution to Regulating the Playing Field: Judicial Deference, Judicial Review, Due Process, and Fair Play in Online Consumer Arbitration' (2002–2003) 23 *Northwestern Journal of International Law and Business* 1.

Gilliéron P, 'From Face-to-Face to Screen-to-Screen: Real Hope or True Fallacy?' (2008) 23 *Ohio State Journal on Dispute Resolution* 301.

Mania K, 'American and European Perspectives on Arbitration Agreement in Online Consumer Contracts' (2019) 36 *Journal of International Arbitration* 659.

Philippe M, 'ODR Redress System for Consumer Disputes: Clarifications, UNCITRAL Works & EU Regulation on ODR' (2014) 1 *Journal of Online Dispute Resolution* 57.

Piers M, 'Consumer Arbitration in the EU' (2011) 2 *Journal of International Dispute Settlement* 209.

Sewart K and Matthews J, 'Online Arbitration of Cross-border, Business To Consumer Disputes' (2002) 56 *University of Miami Law Review* 1111.

Sovern J and others, '"Whimsy Little Contracts" with Unexpected Consequences: An Empirical Analysis of Consumer Understanding of Arbitration Agreements' (2015) 75 *Maryland
Law Review* 1.

Szalai IS and Judge Wessel JD, 'The Prevalence of Consumer Arbitration Agreements by
America's Top Companies' (2019) 522 *UC Davis Law Review Online* 233.

Commission documents

Commission, 'A European Consumer Agenda – Boosting confidence and growth' (Communication from the European Commission to the European Parliament, the Council, the
Economic and Social Committee and the Committee of the Regions) COM (2012) 225
final, <https://eur-lex.europa.eu/legal-content/EN/TXT/PDF/?uri=CELEX:52012DC02
25&from=EN> accessed 1 June 2020.

Commission, 'A New Deal for Consumers' (Communication from the Commission to the
European Parliament, the Council and the European Economic and Social Committee)
COM (2018) 183 final, <https://eur-lex.europa.eu/legal-content/EN/TXT/PDF/?uri=
CELEX:52018DC0183&from=EN> accessed 1 June 2020.

Commission, 'Letter by President Barroso to the Members of the European Parliament'
(Memo/11/645, 28 September 2011) <http://europa.eu/rapid/press-release_MEMO-11-
645_en.htm> accessed 1 June 2020.

Commission, 'Online Dispute Resolution Platform', <https://ec.europa.eu/consumers/odr/
resources/public2/documents/trader_info_stats/ODR_Trader_Info_stat_EN.pdf> accessed
1 June 2020.

Commission, 'Online Dispute Resolution', <https://ec.europa.eu/consumers/odr/main/
index.cfm?event=main.home2.show&lng=EN> accessed 1 June 2020.

Commission, 'Reports and Statistics', <https://ec.europa.eu/consumers/odr/main/?event=
main.statistics.show> accessed 1 June 2020.

Other EU documents

EU Council Resolution of 14 April 1975 on a preliminary programme of the European
Economic Community for a consumer protection and information policy [1975] OJ C 92/1.

European Parliament, Motion for a Resolution, 6 February 2020, B9-0094/2020, <https://
www.europarl.europa.eu/doceo/document/B-9-2020-0094_EN.pdf> accessed 1 June 2020.

Position of the Council at first reading with a view to the adoption of a Directive of the
European Parliament and of the Council on representative actions for the protection of
the collective interests of consumers and repealing Directive 2009/22/EC, adopted by the
Council on 4 November 2020, Interinstitutional File: 2018/0089(COD).

Preliminary programme of the European Economic Community for a consumer protection
and information policy [1975] OJ C 92/2.

Other secondary sources

UNCITRAL, 'Online Dispute Resolution (2010-2016)' <https://uncitral.un.org/en/working_
groups/3/online_dispute> accessed 1 June 2020.

UNCITRAL, 'Report of Working Group III (Online Dispute Resolution) on the work of its
thirty-third session (New York, 29 February-4 March 2016)' (A/CN9/868, 11 March
2016), available at <https://undocs.org/en/a/cn.9/868> accessed 1 June 2020.

UNCITRAL, 'Technical Notes on Online Dispute Resolution' <https://www.uncitral.org/pdf/english/texts/odr/V1700382_English_Technical_Notes_on_ODR.pdf> accessed 1 June 2020.

Blogs and websites

Kuner C, 'Legal Obstacles to ADR in European Business-to-Consumer Electronic Commerce', <http://www.kuner.com/data/pay/adr.html> accessed 1 June 2020.

Lederer N, 'The UNCITRAL Technical Notes on Online Dispute Resolution – Paper Tiger or Game Changer?' (Kluwer Arbitration Blog, 11 January 2018) <http://arbitrationblog.kluwerarbitration.com/2018/01/11/new-found-emphasis-institutional-arbitration-india/> accessed 1 June 2020.

Schultz T, 'Online Arbitration: Binding or Non-Binding?' (ADR Online Monthly, November 2002) available at <https://papers.ssrn.com/sol3/papers.cfm?abstract_id=898622> accessed 1 June 2020.

CHAPTER 7

Books

Brieskorn K, *Vertragshaftung und responsabilité contractuelle, Ein Vergleich zwischen deutschem und französischem Recht mit Blick auf das Vertragsrecht in Europa* (Mohr Siebeck 2010).

Cohen N and McKendrick E (eds), *Comparative Remedies for Breach of Contract* (Hart Publishing 2005).

Fannon NJ (ed), *The Comprehensive Guide to Lost Profits Damages for Experts and Attorneys* (BVR 2011).

Farnsworth EA, *Contracts* (4th edn, Aspen Publishers 2004).

Fikentscher W and Heinemann A, *Schuldrecht* (10th edn, De Gruyter 2006).

Fontaine M and G Viney (eds), *Les sanctions de l'inexécution des obligations contractuelles, Estudes de droit comparé* (Bruylant 2001).

Gisawi F, *Der Grundsatz der Totalreparation*, Gundlagen der Rechtswissenschaft 25 (Mohr Siebeck 2015).

Gordley J, *Foundations of Private Law: Property, Tort, Contract, Unjust Enrichment* (OUP 2006).

Grotius H, *De iure*, lib II, cap XVII, §§IV f.

Gschnitzer F, *Österreichisches Schuldrecht, Besonderer Teil und Schadenersatz* (2nd revised edn by Faistenberger C, Barta H, Eccher B, Springer Verlag 1988).

Hughes GJ, *The Routledge Guidebook to Aristotle's Nicomachean Ethics* (Taylor & Francis Group 2013).

Jud B, *Schadenersatz bei mangelhafter Leistung* (Manzsche Verlags- und Universitätsbuchhandlung 2003).

McGregor H, *McGregor on Damages* (16th edn, Sweet & Maxwell 1997).

Mommsen F, *Beiträge zum Obligationenrecht: Abth. Zur Lehre von dem Interesse* (EU Schwetschke und Sohn 1855).

Nueber M (ed), *Handbuch Schiedsgerichtsbarkeit und ADR* (1st edn, LexisNexis ARD ORAC, 2021)

Pinna A, *La mesure du préjudice contractuel* (LGDJ, Université Panthéon-Assas Paris II 2007).

Pufendorf S, 'Ut nemo laedatur, et si quod damnum fuit datum, reparetur', title to *De iure belli ac pacis*, lib III.

Restatement (Second) of Contracts (American Law Institute 2013).

Rowan S, *Remedies for Breach of Contract: A Comparative Analysis of the Protection of Performance* (OUP 2012).

Sabahi B, *Compensation and Restitution in Investor-State Arbitration* (OUP, International Economic Law Series).

Saidov D and Cunnington R (eds), *Contract Damages* (Hart Publishing 2008).

Schwenzer I, Hachem P and Kee C, *Global Sales and Contract Law* (OUP 2012).

Simpson AWB, *The History of the Common Law of Contract, The Rise of the Question of Assumpsit* (OUP 1975).

Vogenauer S and Kleinheisterkamp J (eds), *Commentary on the UNIDROIT Principles of International Commercial Contracts (PICC)* (OUP 2009).

von Ihering R, *Culpa in contrahendo oder Schadenersatz bei nichtigen oder nicht zur Perfektion gelangten Verträgen* (Jahrbücher für die Dogmatik des heutigen römischen und deutschen Privaterechts IV, Jena: Friedrich Mauke, 1861).

Wächter GH, *M&A Litigation M&A Recht im Streit* (3rd rev edn, RWS Verlag Kommunikationsformum 2017).

Wöss H and others, *Damages in International Arbitration under Complex Long-term Contracts* (OUP 2014).

Zimmermann R, *The Law of Obligations – Roman Foundations of the Civilian Tradition* (OUP 1996).

Journal articles

Abdala MA, López Zadicoff PD and Spiller PT, 'Invalid Round Trips in Setting Pre-Judgment Interest in International Arbitration' (2011) 5(1) *World Arbitration and Mediation Review* 1.

Fisher FM and Romaine RC, 'Janis Joplin's Yearbook and the Theory of Damages' (1990) 5(3) *Journal of Accounting, Auditing and Finance* 149.

Fuller LL and Perdue WR, 'The Reliance Interest in Contract Damages' (1937) 46 *Yale Law Journal* 373.

Giroux ME and others, 'Hindsight Bias and Law' (2016) 224(3) *Zeitschrift für Psychologie* 190.

Gotanda JY, 'Damages in Private International Law' (2007) 326 *Recueil de cours* 209-12.

Kantor M, 'Editorial Yukos Special' (2015) 5 *Transnational Dispute Management*.

Koziol H, 'Grundfragen des Schadenersatzrechts (Jan Sramek Verlag, 2010)' (2011) 2(3) *Journal of European Tort Law* 336.

Neumann M, 'Geschichte des Wuchers in Deutschland bis zum Jahre 1654', *Zeitschrift für Kirchenrecht*, V Jahrgang (Laupp & Siebeck 1865) 49.

San Román A and Wöss H, 'Damages in International Arbitration with respect to Income Generating Assets or Investments in Commercial and Investment Arbitration' (2015) 2(1) *Journal of Damages in International Arbitration* 37.

Triebel V, 'Awarding Interest in International Arbitration' (1989) 6 *Journal of International Arbitration* 18.

Wöss H, 'Damages and Loss of a Change or Loss of Opportunity' 13 (2020) 1 *New York Dispute Resolution Lawyer* 33.

Other secondary resources

O'Reilly M, '13th Annual Review of the Arbitration Act 1996, Time to Review the Arbitration Act 1996? Provision on Costs and Appeals: An Assessment from an International Perspective' (British Institute of International and Comparative Law, 2010) <https://www.biicl.org/files/4936_biicl_13th_annual_mor.pdf> accessed 5 March 2019.

The Law Commission (Law Com no 287), Pre-judgment interest on debts and damages – Item 4 of the Eighth Programme of Law Reform: Compound Interest (2004) <http://www.lawcom.gov.uk> accessed 15 January 2020.

UNIDROIT, 'Principles of International Commercial Contracts' (International Institute for Unification of Private Law, 2016).

World Bank, 'Guidelines on the Treatment of Foreign Direct Investment' (1992).

Blogs and websites

Godek PE, 'Ex Ante vs. Ex Post: Janis Joplin's Yearbook Revisited' (Law 360, 22 July 2015) <https://www.law360.com/articles/681155/ex-ante-vs-ex-post-janis-joplin-s-yearbook-revisited> accessed 15 January 2020.

Hodgson M and Campbell A, 'Damages and Cost in Investment Treaty Arbitration Revised' (GAR News, 14 December 2017) <https://globalarbitrationreview.com/article/1151755/damages-and-costs-in-investment-treaty-arbitration-revisited> accessed 15 January 2020.

CHAPTER 8

Books

Ashton D, *Competition Damages Actions in the EU: Law and Practice* (2nd edn, Edward Elgar Publishing Ltd 2018).

Bergström M, Iacovides M and Strand M (eds), *Harmonising EU Competition Litigation: The New Directive and Beyond* (Hart Publishing 2016).

Blackaby N and others, *Redfern and Hunter on International Arbitration* (6th edn, OUP 2015).

Blanke G and Landolt P (eds), *EU and US Antitrust Arbitration: A Handbook for Practitioners* (Kluwer Law International 2011).

Born G, *International Commercial Arbitration* (2nd edn, Kluwer Law International 2014).

Journal articles

Elgueta GR, 'Understanding Discovery in International Commercial Arbitration Through Behavioral Law and Economics: A Journey Inside the Minds of Parties and Arbitrators' (2011) 16 *Harvard Negotiation Law Review* 165.

Geradin D, 'Collective Redress for Antitrust Damages in the European Union: Is This a Reality Now?' (2015) 22 *George Mason Law Review* 1079.

Schwarz D, 'Understanding Remedy-Stripping Arbitration Clauses: Validity, Arbitrability and Preclusion Principles' (2003) 38 *University of San Francisco Law Review* 49.

Laborde JF, 'Cartel damages actions in Europe: How courts have assessed cartel overcharges' (2019) 4 *Concurrences* 1.

Woods D, Sinclair A and Ashton D, 'Private enforcement of Community competition law: modernisation and the road ahead' (2004) 2 *Competition Policy Newsletter* 34.

Other secondary sources

International Court of Arbitration of the International Chamber of Commerce, Rules of Arbitration (in force as from 1 March 2017).
Singapore International Arbitration Centre, Arbitration Rules (in force as from 1 August 2016).
Vienna International Arbitration Centre, Vienna Arbitration Rules (in force as from 1 January 2018).

CHAPTER 9

Books

Billiet P and others (eds), *Class Actions and Arbitration in the European Union* (Maklu Publishers 2012).
Born GB, *International Commercial Arbitration* (Kluwer Law International 2014).
Bosman L (ed), *ICCA Congress Series No 20, Evolution and Adaptation: The Future of International Arbitration* (Wolters Kluwer, 2019).
Derains Y and Schwartz EA, *Guide to the ICC Rules of Arbitration* (Kluwer Law International 2005).
García AM (ed), *La Tutela de los Derechos e Intereses Colectivos en la Justicia del Siglo XXI* (Tirant Lo Blanch 2019).
Hanotiau B and Schwartz EA (eds), *Dossier VII: Arbitration and Multiparty Contracts* (ICC Institute of World Business Law 2010).
Hensler DR and others, *Class Action Dilemmas: Public Goals for Private Gain* (Rand Corporation 2004).
Hill J, *Cross-Border Consumer Contracts* (Oxford University Press 2008).
Klaassen CJM and others (eds), *Onderneming en ADR* (Kluwer 2011).
Lein E and others (eds), *Collective Redress in Europe: Why and How?* (British Institute of International and Comparative Law 2015).
Mistelis LA and Lew JDM (eds), *Pervasive Problems in International Arbitration* (Wolters Kluwer 2006).
Rovine AW (ed), *Contemporary Issues in International Arbitration and Mediation: The Fordham Papers 2013* (Brill 2014).
Strong SI, *Class, Mass, and Collective Arbitration in National and International Law* (Oxford University Press 2013).

Journal articles

'The Decision, Judgment of the Swiss Federal Court' (1999) 10 *American Review of International Arbitration* 559.
Burch EC, 'Securities Class Actions as Pragmatic *Ex Post* Regulation' (2008) 43 *Georgia Law Review* 63.

Gaboardi M, 'New Ways of Protection of Collective Interests: The Italian Class Litigation and Arbitration Through a Comparative Analysis' 2020 *Journal of Dispute Resolution* 61.

King AS, 'Too Much Power and Not Enough: Arbitrators Face the Class Dilemma' (2018) 21 *Lewis and Clark Law Review* 1031.

Luff P, 'Risk Regulation and Regulatory Litigation' (2011) 64 *Rutgers Law Review* 73.

Ostrager BR and others, '*Andersen v Andersen:* The Claimants' Perspective' (1999) 10 *American Review of International Arbitration* 443.

Resnik J, 'Fairness in Numbers: A Comment on *AT&T v Concepcion, Walmart v Dukes,* and *Turner v Rogers*' (2011) 125 *Harvard Law Review* 78.

Rutledge PB and Drahozal CR, '"Sticky" Arbitration Clauses? The Use of Arbitration Clauses After *Concepcion* and *Amex*' (2014) 67 *Vanderbilt Law Review* 955.

Schnabel T, 'The Singapore Convention on Mediation: A Framework for the Cross-Border Recognition and Enforcement of Mediated Settlements' (2019) 19 *Pepperdine Dispute Resolution Law Journal* 1.

Sternlight JR and Jensen EJ, 'Using Arbitration to Eliminate Consumer Class Actions: Efficient Business Practice or Unconscionable Abuse?' (2004) 67 *Law and Contemporary Problems* 75.

Strong SI, 'From Class to Collective: The De-Americanization of Class Arbitration' (2010) 26 *Arbitration International* 493.

Strong SI, 'Mandatory Arbitration of Internal Trust Disputes: Improving Arbitrability and Enforceability Through Proper Procedural Choices' (2012) 28 *Arbitration International* 591.

Strong SI, 'Regulatory Litigation in the European Union: Does the U.S. Class Action Have a New Analogue?' (2012) 88 *Notre Dame Law Review* 899.

Strong SI, 'Collective Consumer Arbitration in Spain: A Civil Law Response to U.S.-Style Class Arbitration' (2013) 30 *Journal of International Arbitration* 495.

Strong SI, 'Mass Procedures as a Form of "Regulatory Arbitration" – *Abaclat v Argentine Republic* and the International Investment Regime' (2013) 38 *Journal of Corporation Law* 259.

Strong SI, 'Beyond International Commercial Arbitration? The Promise of International Commercial Mediation' (2014) 45 *Washington University Journal of Law and Policy* 11.

Strong SI, 'Heir of *Abaclat*? Mass and Multiparty Proceedings: Ambiente Ufficio SpA v Argentine Republic' (2014) 29 *ICSID Review–Foreign Investment Law Journal* 149.

Strong SI, 'Large-Scale Dispute Resolution in Jurisdictions Without Judicial Class Actions: Learning from the Irish Experience' (2016) 22 *ILSA Journal of International & Comparative Law* 341.

Strong SI, 'Realizing Rationality: An Empirical Assessment of International Commercial Mediation' (2016) 73 *Washington and Lee Law Review* 1973, 2053.

Strong SI, 'Truth in a Post-Truth Society: How Sticky Defaults, Status Quo Bias and the Sovereign Prerogative Influence the Perceived Legitimacy of International Arbitration' (2018) *University of Illinois Law Review* 533.

Commission documents

Commission Recommendation of 11 June 2013 on common principles for injunctive and compensatory collective redress mechanisms in the Member States concerning violations of rights granted under Union Law [2013] OJ L201/60.

Communication from the Commission to the European Parliament, the Council, the European Economic and Social Committee and the Committee of the Regions, 'Towards a European Horizontal Framework for Collective Redress' COM (2013) 401 final.

Commission, 'Public Consultation: Towards a Coherent European Approach to Collective Redress' (Brussels, 4 February 2011).

Other secondary sources

Amaro R and others, *Collective Redress in the Member States of the European Union* (Study commissioned by the European Parliament) <http://www.europarl.europa.eu/RegData/etudes/STUD/2018/608829/IPOL_STU(2018)608829_EN.pdf> accessed 12 February 2019.

American Arbitration Association, Supplementary Rules for Class Arbitration, effective 8 October 2003 <https://www.adr.org/ClassArbitration> accessed 12 February 2019.

Cole T and others, *Legal Instruments and Practice of Arbitration in the EU* (2014) 41–42 (commissioned by the European Parliament Directorate-General for Internal Policies, Policy Department C – Citizens' Rights and Constitutional Affairs) <http://www.europarl.europa.eu/RegData/etudes/STUD/2015/509988/IPOL_STU%282015%29509988_EN.pdf> accessed 12 February 2019.

DIS Supplementary Rules for Corporate Law Disputes effective 15 September 2009 <http://www.dis-arb.de/download/DIS_SRCoLD_%202009_Download.pdf> accessed 12 February 2019.

DIS, Statistics <http://www.dis-arb.de/en/39/content/statistics-id54> accessed 12 February 2019.

European Parliament resolution of 2 February 2012 on 'Towards a Coherent European Approach to Collective Redress' (2011/2089(INI)) [2013] OJ C239 E/05.

'ICC Arbitration Clause for Trust Disputes' (2018) 29 *ICC International Court of Arbitration Bulletin* 92, 94 <https://iccwbo.org/publication/icc-arbitration-clause-trust-disputes-explanatory-note/> accessed 12 February 2019.

ICC Arbitration Rules (effective 1 March 2017) <https://iccwbo.org/publication/arbitration-rules-and-mediation-rules/> accessed 12 February 2019.

LCIA Arbitration Rules (effective 1 October 2014) <http://www.lcia.org/Dispute_Resolution_Services/lcia-arbitration-rules-2014.aspx> accessed 12 February 2019.

Lein E and others, *State of Collective Redress in the EU in the Context of the Implementation of the Commission Recommendation* (British Institute of International and Comparative Law 2018) <https://www.biicl.org/documents/1881_StudyontheStateofCollectiveRedress.pdf?showdocument=1> accessed 12 February 2019.

Letter from Skadden, Arps, Slate, Meagher & Flom LLP on behalf of Johnson & Johnson to the US Securities and Exchange Commission dated 11 December 2018 (including the shareholder proposal containing the waiver of class suits) <https://www.sec.gov/divisions/corpfin/cf-noaction/14a-8/2018/dorisbehr121118-14a8-incoming.pdf> accessed 12 February 2019.

Lindblom PH, 'National Report: Group Litigation in Sweden' (Global Class Actions Conference, Oxford, December 2007) <http://globalclassactions.stanford.edu/sites/default/files/documents/Sweden_National_Report.pdf> accessed 12 February 2019.

Personal Injuries Assessment Board <https://www.piab.ie/eng/> accessed 10 May 2020.

Personal Injuries Board FAQs <https://www.piab.ie/eng/help-support/faqs/> accessed 12 February 2019.

Public Statement on Shareholder Proposals Seeking to Require Mandatory Arbitration Bylaw Provisions, Jay Clayton, Chair of the US Securities and Exchange Commission <https://www.sec.gov/news/public-statement/clayton-statement-mandatory-arbitration-bylaw-provisions> accessed 12 February 2019.

UNCITRAL, 'Report of the United Nations Commission on International Trade Law-Fifty-first session (25 June-13 July 2018)' (UN Doc A/73/17, 31 July 2018).

Websites

Keena C, 'Court Due to Hear Six Cases Against Artificial Hip Maker' Irish Times (4 January 2019) <https://www.irishtimes.com/news/crime-and-law/court-due-to-hear-six-cases-against-artificial-hip-maker-1.3746887> accessed 12 February 2019.

Michaels D and Rubin GT, 'SEC Rejects Proposal for Mandatory Shareholder Action' Wall Street Journal (11 February 2019) <https://www.wsj.com/articles/sec-rejects-proposal-for-mandatory-shareholder-arbitration-11549927631> accessed 12 February 2019.

O'Faolain A, 'Woman (81) with DePuy Hip Replacement Awarded €321k by High Court' Independent (1 December 2017) <https://www.independent.ie/irish-news/courts/woman-81-with-depuy-hip-replacement-awarded-321k-by-high-court-36370366.html> accessed 12 February 2019.

CHAPTER 10

Books

Bassiri N and Draye M (eds), *Arbitration in Belgium, A Practitioner's Guide* (Wolters Kluwer 2016).

Busch D, Macgregor L and Watts P (eds), *Agency Law in Commercial Practice* (OUP 2016).

Delforge C (coord), *Actualités en matière de rédaction des contrats de distribution* (Bruylant 2014).

Engelmann J, *International Commercial Arbitration and the Commercial Agency Directive: A Perspective from Law and Economics* (Springer 2017).

Erauw J, *Arbitration and Commercial Distribution: Reports of the Colloquium of CEPANI, November 17th, 2005* (Bruylant 2005).

Erauw, Jardin A, Keutgen G, *L'arbitrage et la distribution commerciale* (Bruylant 2005).

Hollander P (ed), *Le droit de la distribution* (Anthemis 2009).

Hollander P, *Les pièges de la procédure civile et arbitrale dans la pratique* (Larcier 2019).

Karpenshif M and Nourissat C, *Les grands arrêts de la jurisprudence de l'Union européenne* (2nd edn, Presses Universitaires de France 2014).

Keutgen G and Albert Dal G, *L'arbitrage en droit belge et international, Tome I – Le droit belge* (3rd edn, Bruylant 2015).

Niboyer M and de la Pradelle GG, *Droit international privé* (4th edn, LGDJ 2013).

Nuyts A, *La concession de vente exclusive, l'agence commerciale et l'arbitrage* (Bruylant 1996).

Struyven D (ed), *Bestendig Handboek Distributierecht* (Kluwer 2002).

van Calster G, *European Private International Law* (2nd edn, Bloomsbury 2016).

Van de Casteele LB, *Les principes fondamentaux de l'arbitrage*, Francarbi (Bruylant 2012).

Verbraeken C, de Schoutheete A and Stuyck J, *Manuel des contrats de distribution commerciale* (Kluwer éditions juridiques 1997).

Willemart M and Willemart S, *Le contrat d'agence commerciale (loi du 13 avril 1995 modifiée par celles des 4 mai 1999, 1er juin 1999 et 21 février 2005)* (Larcier 2005).

Journal articles

Caprasse O, 'Les grands arrêts de la cour de cassation belge en droit de l'arbitrage' (2013) 1 *b-Arbitra* 142.

Cnudde S, 'Het arrest *Unamar*: op weg naar een spaarzamer gebruik door de forumrechter van de eigen voorrangsregels om het door partijen gekozen recht van een andere EU-lidstaat opzij te schuiven?' (2015) 9 *Rechtspraak Antwerpen Brussel Gent* (*RABG*) 663.

D'Avout L, 'Les directives européennes, les lois de police de transposition et leur application aux contrats internationaux' (2014) 1 *Recueil Dalloz* 60.

de Schoutheete A and Vandepitte P, 'Le caractère autolimité de la loi du 13 avril 1995 relative au contrat d'agence commerciale' (2012) 3 *Revue de Droit Commercial* 241.

Haugaard AM and Faelli, T, 'Chronique de jurisprudence relative à la loi du 13 avril 1995 sur le contrat d'agence (1995–2004)' (2005) 3 *Le droit des affaires – Het ondernemingsrecht* (*DAOR*) 241.

Hollander P, 'L'arrêt Unamar de la Cour de justice: une bombe atomique sur le droit belge de la distribution commerciale ?' (2014) *JT* 297.

Idot L, 'Des droits de l'agent commercial qui exerce son activité dans un Etat membre alors que son commettant est établi dans un pays tiers' (2001) *Rev crit DIP* 107.

International Court of Arbitration of the ICC, Decision of 15 February 2020 (2012) 3 *Revue de Droit Commercial Belge – Tijdschrift voor Belgisch Handelsrecht* (*RDC-TBH*) 238–41.

Kileste P and Staudt C, 'Jurisprudence récente relative aux règles de droit international privé applicable aux contrats de distribution: arrêts *Corman-Collins* et *Unamar*' (2015) 9 *Revue de Jurisprudence de Liège, Mons et Bruxelles* (*JLMB*) 403.

Lüttringhaus J, 'Eingriffsnormen im internationalen Unionsprivat- und Prozessrecht: Von Ingmar zu Unamar' (2014) 34 *IPRax* 150.

Mary J, 'Suite, et non fin, de la jurisprudence sur le contrat d'agence commerciale en Europe face aux lois de police' (2015) 1 *RDC-TBH* 74.

Mehmeti E and Verhellen J, 'Wilsautonomie en dwingend recht in het Europees contracten-recht: hoe dwingend is dwingend recht wanneer partijen kiezen?' (2014) 1 *b-Arbitra* 199.

Mertens D, 'Handelsagentuur en arbitrage' (note under Cass. 3 November 2011) (2011–12) *RW* 1646.

Mertens D, 'Over de arbitreerbaarheid van concessiegeschillen. Eindelijk een uitgemaakte zaak?' (noot onder Cass. 14 januari 2010) (2010–11) *Rechtskundig weekblad* (*RW*) 1087.

Nourissat C, 'De l'art délicat de manier les lois de police en présence d'un contrat d'agence commerciale intra-européen...' (2013) 49 *La Semaine Juridique Edition générale* 2222.

Nourissat C, 'Le contrat d'agence commercial en droit international privé. Retour sur quelques apports récents' (2014) *AJCA* 366.

Nourissat C, 'Loi applicable au contrat d'agent commercial: rappels et précisions' (2016) Actualité juridique Contrats d'affaires (*AJCA*) 162–3.

Nourissat C, 'La directive sur les agents commerciaux ne saurait bénéficier à un agent exerçant hors de l'Union européenne même si la loi applicable au contrat est d'un Etat member' (2017) 4 *AJ Contrat*, 186 ff.

Nuyts A, 'Les lois de police et dispositions impératives dans le règlement Rome I' (2009) 6 *RDC-TBH* 553.

Poillot-Peruzzetto S, 'L'impérativité européenne, du malaise du mouvement à la solidité du fondement' (2019) *Recueil Dalloz* 448–52.

Romain Dupeyré, 'Rupture de relations commerciales établies : la Cour de cassation confirme la priorité de la compétence arbitrale en dépit du caractère d'ordre public des textes invoqués et de la nature contestée de l'action, note sous Cass. com., 8 juillet 2010' (2010) 3 *Rev arb* 513.

Rühl G, 'Commercial Agents, Minimum Harmonization and Overriding Mandatory Provisions in the European Union: The Unamar Case (Case C 184/12, Unamar, ECLI:EU:2013:663)' (2016) 53 *Common Market Law Review* 209.

Schilling J, 'Eingriffsnormen im europäischen Richtlinienrecht - Anmerkung zu EuGH, 17.10.2013 – C-184/12, EU:C:2013:663 – Unamar' (2014) *Zeitschrift für Europäisches Privatrecht* 850.

Swerts K, 'Het internationaal dwingendrechtelijk karakter van de Belgisch agentuurwet' (2014) 12 *RABG* 826.

Traest M, 'Encore … un arrêt de la Cour de cassation sur l'arbitrabilité des litiges relatifs à la résiliation, sous l'empire de la loi du 27 juillet 1961, des concessions de vente exclusive' (note sous Cass., 14 janvier 2010) (2013) *Revue critique de jurisprudence belge* 255.

Verbist H and Erauw J, 'Arbitrability of Exclusive Distributorship Agreements with Application of Foreign Law Confirmed by Belgian Courts after the Reform of the Belgian Arbitration Law of 2013' (2019) 1 *b-Arbitra* 278.

Verbraeken C and De Schoutheete A, 'La loi du 13 avril 1995 relative au contrat d'agence commerciale' (1995) *Journal des tribunaux* (*JT*) 461.

von Bochove LM, 'Overriding Mandatory Rules as a Vehicle for Weaker Party Protection in European Private International Law' (2014) 7(3) *Erasmus Law Review* 155.

Wim Wijsmans and Van Gompel H, 'Het bijzonder dwingend recht van artikel 9.3 Rome I-Verordening toegepast op een de beëindiging van een handelsagentuur' (2019) 17 *RABG* 1486.

Other secondary sources

Van Couter Y, Van Parys E and Driesen G, 'Artikel 27 Handelsagentuurwet' in Handels-en Economisch Recht. Commentaar met overzicht van rechtspraak en rechtsleer, Kluwer 13–24.

Blogs and websites

De Meulemeester D, 'Unamar: Arbitration clause drowned by gold plated provision in Belgian law on commercial agency?' (Kluwer Arbitration Blog, 3 December 2013) <http://arbitrationblog.kluwerarbitration.com/2013/12/03/unamar-arbitration-clause-drowned-by-gold-plated-provision-in-belgian-law-on-commercial-agency/> accessed 16 April 2020.

Gosch T, 'Another Win for European Commercial Agents: Overriding Mandatory Austrian Law Provisions to Supersede Arbitration Agreement' (Kluwer Arbitration Blog 2017) <http://arbitrationblog.kluwerarbitration.com/2017/08/10/another-win-european-commercial-agents-overriding-mandatory-austrian-law-provisions-supersede-arbitration-agreement/> accessed 16 April 2020.

van Calster G, 'Belgian supreme court holds on gold-plated provisions in Unamar. Appeal judgment annulled, case to be revisited' <https://gavclaw.com/2014/09/26/belgian-supreme-court-holds-on-gold-plated-provisions-in-unamar-appeal-judgment-annulled-case-to-be-revisited/> accessed 16 April 2020.

CHAPTER 11

Books

Blackaby N and others, *Redfern and Hunter on International Arbitration* (6th edn, OUP 2015).
Born G, *International Commercial Arbitration* (Kluwer Law International 2014).
Lew JDM, Mistelis LA, and Kröll SM, *Comparative International Commercial Arbitration* (Wolters Kluwer Law & Business 2003).
Sanders P (ed), *Comparative Arbitration Practice and Public Policy in Arbitration* (Kluwer Law International 1987).
Tavares LV, Medeiros R, and Coelho D (eds), *The New Directive 2014/24/EU on Public Procurement* (OPET 2014).

Journal articles

Arias D, 'El Arbitraje Internacional' (2013) 29 *Revista Jurídica de Castilla y León* 3.
Devolvé JL and others, 'Final Report on Multi-Party Arbitrations' (1995) 6(1) *ICC International Court of Arbitration Bulletin*, para 113.
Leboulanger P, 'Multi-Contract Arbitration' (1996) 13(4) *Journal of International Arbitration* 43.
Schwartz E, 'Multi-Party Arbitration and the ICC' (1993) 10(3) *Journal of International Arbitration* 5.

Other secondary sources

Club Español del Arbitraje [Spanish Arbitration Club] (CEA), *Code of Good Practices* (2019).
ICC Arbitration Rules (in force as from 1 January 2021).
ICC Arbitration Rules (in force as from 1 March 2017).
ICC Rules (in force as from 1 January 1998).
ICC Rules (in force as from 1 January 1988).
LCIA Rules (effective 1 October 2020).
Vienna (VIAC) Arbitration Rules (in force as from 1 January 2018).
QMUL, SIA and PwC, 2013 International Arbitration Survey: Corporate choices in International Arbitration. Industry perspectives (2013) <http://www.arbitration.qmul.ac.uk/media/arbitration/docs/pwc-international-arbitration-study2013.pdf> accessed 26 June 2019.
QMUL, SIA and White & Case, 2018 International Arbitration Survey: The Evolution of International Arbitration (2018) 29 ('QMUL, SIA and White & Case, The Evolution of International Arbitration') <http://www.arbitration.qmul.ac.uk/media/arbitration/docs/2018-International-Arbitration-Survey—The-Evolution-of-International-Arbitration-(2).PDF> accessed 26 June 2019.

SIAC, 'Proposal on Cross-Institution Consolidation Protocol' (19 December 2017) <http://siac.org.sg/69-siac-news/551-proposal-on-cross-institution-consolidation-protocol> accessed 26 June 2019.

CHAPTER 12

Books

Barnard C, *The Substantive Law of the EU: The Four Freedoms* (OUP 2016).

Basener N, *Investment Protection in the European Union* (Nomos Verlagsgesellschaft 2017).

Biondi A, Eeckhout P and Ripley S (eds), *EU Law After Lisbon* (OUP 2012).

Bungenberg M, Griebel J and Hindelang S (eds), *European Yearbook of International Economic Law – International Investment Law and EU Law* (Springer 2011).

Bungenberg M, Reinisch A and Tietje C (eds), *EU and investment agreements: Open Questions and Remaining Challenges* (Nomos 2013).

Cardwell PJ (ed), *EU External Relations Law and Policy in the Post-Lisbon Era* (T.M.C Asser Press 2012).

Dashwood A and Maresceau M (eds), *Law and Practice of EU External Relations* (CUP 2008).

Dimopoulos A, *EU Foreign Investment Law* (OUP 2011).

Strik Philip FJS, *Shaping the Single European Market in the Field of Foreign Direct Investment* (Hart Publishing 2016).

Trackman L and Ranieri N (eds), *Regionalism in International Investment Law* (OUP 2013).

Weiss F and Kaupa C, *European Union Internal Market Law* (CUP 2014).

Journal articles

Basedow J, 'A Legal History of the EU's International Investment Policy' (2016) 17 *Journal of World Investment and Trade* 743.

Basedow J, 'The European Union's New International Investment Policy: Product of Commission Entrepreneurship or Business Lobbying?' (2016) 21 *European Foreign Affairs Review* 469.

Burgstaller M, 'Dispute Settlement in EU International Investment Agreements with Third States: Three Salient Problems' (2014) 15 *Journal of World Investment and Trade* 551.

Geraets D, 'Changes in EU Trade Policy After Opinion 2/15' (2018) 13 *Global Trade and Customs Journal* 13.

Gruni G, 'Towards a Sustainable World Trade Law? The Commercial Policy of the European Union After Opinion 2/15 ECJ' (2018) 13 *Global Trade and Customs Journal* 4.

Hartge C, 'China's National Security Review: Motivations and the Implications for Investors' (2013) 49 *Stanford Journal of International Law* 239.

Karl J, 'The Competence for Foreign Direct Investment – New Powers for the European Union?' (2006) 5 *Journal of World Investment and Trade* 413.

Klager R, 'The Impact of the TTIP on Europe's Investment Arbitration Architecture' (2014) 39 *ZDAR* 70.

Kleimann D and Kübek G, 'The Signing, Provisional Application, and Conclusion of Trade and Investment Agreements in the EU: The Case of CETA and Opinion 2/15' (2018) 45 *Legal Issues of Economic Integration* 13.

Kokott J and Sobotta C, 'Investment Arbitration and EU Law' (2016) 18 *Cambridge Yearbook of European Legal Studies* 3.

Lavranos N, 'CJEU Opinion 1/17: Keeping International Law and EU Law Strictly Apart' (2019) 4 *European Investment Law and Arbitration Review* 240.

Lavranos N, 'In Defence of Member States' BITs Gold Standard: The Regulation 1219/2012 Establishing a Transitional Regime for existing Extra-EU BITs – A Member States' Perspective' (2013) 10(2) *Transnational Dispute Management*.

Lavranos N, 'Mixed Exclusivity: The CJEU's Opinion on the EU-Singapore FTA' (2017) 2 *European Investment Law and Arbitration Review* 3.

Lenk H, 'More Trade and Less Investment for Future EU Trade and Investment Policy' (2018) 19 *Journal of World Investment & Trade* 305.

Meunier S, 'Integration by Stealth: How the European Union Gained Competence over Foreign Direct Investment' (2017) 55 *Journal of Common Market Studies* 593.

Moskvan D, 'The European Union's Competence on Foreign Investment: "New and Improved"?' (2017) 18 *San Diego International Law Journal* 241.

Pascual Vives FJ, 'Shaping the EU Investment Regime: Choice of Forum and Applicable Law in International Investment Agreements' (2014) 6 *Cuadernos Derecho Transnacional* 269, 293.

Reinisch A, 'The EU on the Investment Path – Quo Vadis Europe? The Future of EU BITs and other Investment Agreements' (2014) 12(1) S*anta Clara Journal of International Law* 111.

Reinisch A, 'Will the EU's Proposal Concerning an Investment Court System for CETA and TTIP Lead to Enforceable Awards? – The Limits of Modifying the ICSID Convention and the Nature of Investment Arbitration' (2016) 19 *Journal of International Economic Law* 761.

Riffel C, 'The CETA Opinion of the European Court of Justice and its Implications – Not That Selfish After All' (2019) 22(3) *Journal of International Economic Law* 503.

Rosas A, 'The EU and international dispute settlement' (2017) 1 *Europe and the World* 3.

Ross A, 'Achmea: Where Do We Stand Now?' 13 Global *Arbitration Review* 12.

Sattorova M, 'Investor Rights under EU law and International Investment Law' (2016) *Journal of World Investment and Trade* 899.

Titi C, 'International Investment Law and the European Union: Towards a New Generation of International Investment Agreements' (2015) 26 *EJIL* 639.

Tonsgaard T and Hindelang S, 'The Day After: Alternatives to Intra-EU BITs' (2016) 17(6) *Journal of World Investment and Trade* 984.

Uwera G, 'Investor-State Dispute Settlement (ISDS) in Future EU Investment-Related Agreements: Is the Autonomy of the EU Legal Order an Obstacle?' (2016) 15 *The Law and Practice of International Courts and Tribunals* 102.

Wehland H, 'Intra-EU Investment Agreements and Arbitration: Is European Community Law an Obstacle?' (2009) 58 *International and Comparative Law Quarterly* 297.

Working/conference/position papers

Douma W, 'Investor-state arbitration in the light of EU policy and law after the Lisbon Treaty' (EUSA Conference Papers EUSA, Fifteenth Biennial Conference, 2017).

Group of the Progressive Alliance of Socialists and Democrats in the European Parliament, 'S&D Position Paper on Investor-state dispute settlement mechanisms in ongoing trade negotiations' (4 March 2015) <https://www.socialistsanddemocrats.eu/sites/default/files/

position_paper/ISDS_mechanisms_ongoing_trade_negotiations_en_150304.pdf> accessed 26 May 2020.

Hanemann T and Huotari M, 'Record Flows and Global Imbalances – Chinese Investment in Europe in 2016' (Merics Paper on China Update No 3 January 2017, Mercator Institute for China Studies) 4 <http://rhg.com/wp-content/uploads/2017/01/RHG_Merics_COFDI_EU_2016.pdf> accessed 26 November 2018.

Lorz RA, 'Germany, the Transatlantic Trade and Investment Partnership and investment-dispute settlement: Observations on a paradox' (2014) 132 Columbia FDI Perspectives.

Non-paper from Austria, Finland, France, Germany and the Netherlands (7 April 2016), available at: <https://www.tni.org/files/article-downloads/intra-eu-bits2-18-05_0.pdf> accessed 24 May 2020.

Reinisch A, 'The European Union and Investor-State Dispute Settlement: From Investor-State Dispute Arbitration to a Permanent Investment Court' (2016) CIGI Investor-State Arbitration Series Paper No 2, 14.

Titi C, 'A stronger role for the European Parliament in the design of the EU's investment policy as a legitimacy safeguard' (2017) 209 Columbia FDI Perspectives – Perspectives on topical foreign direct investment issues 1.

Commission documents

Commission Regulation 978/2012 applying a scheme of generalized tariff preferences [2012] OJ L303/1.

Commission, 'CETA: EU and Canada agree on new approach on investment in trade agreement' (Press Release IP/16/399, 29 February 2016).

Commission, 'Commission asks Member States to terminate their Intra-EU bilateral investment treaties' (Press Release IP/15/5198, 18 June 2015) <http://europa.eu/rapid/press-release_IP-15-5198_en.htm> accessed 29 November 2018.

Commission, 'Commission draft text TTIP – investment' (16 September 2015) <https://trade.ec.europa.eu/doclib/docs/2015/september/tradoc_153807.pdf> accessed 26 May 2020.

Commission, 'Commission presents procedural proposals for the Investment Court System in CETA' (11 October 2019) (News Archive) <https://trade.ec.europa.eu/doclib/press/index.cfm?id=2070> accessed 22 February 2020.

Commission, 'Commission provides guidance on protection of cross-border EU investments' (Press Release IP/18/4528, 19 July 2018) <http://europa.eu/rapid/press-release_IP-18-4528_en.htm> accessed 29 November 2018.

Commission, 'Communication from the Commission to The Council and The European Parliament – The Review of export control policy: ensuring security and competitiveness in a changing world' COM (2014) 244 final.

Commission, 'Communication from The Commission to The Council, The European Parliament, The European Economic and Social Committee and The Committee of the Regions Towards a Comprehensive European International Investment Policy' COM (2010) 343 final.

Commission, 'Communication from the Commission to the European Parliament, the Council, the European Economic and Social Committee and the Committee of the Regions – Towards a Comprehensive European International Investment Policy' COM (2010) 343 final.

Commission, 'Communication from the Commission to the European Parliament and the Council- Protection of intra-EU investment' COM/2018/547 final <https://eur-lex.europa.eu/legal-content/EN/TXT/PDF/?uri=CELEX:52018DC0547&rid=8> accessed 10 February 2018.

Commission, 'Communication from The Commission to The European Parliament, The European Council, The Council and The European Investment Bank – Towards a more efficient financial architecture for investment outside the European Union' COM (2018) 644 final.

Commission, 'EU-Canada trade agreement enters into force' (Press Release IP/17/3121, 17 September 10).

Commission, 'European Commission services' Position Paper on the Sustainability Impact Assessment in support of negotiations of an Investment Agreement between the European Union and the People's Republic of China' (May 2018), 6-7 <http://trade.ec.europa.eu/doclib/docs/2018/may/tradoc_156863.pdf> accessed 26 November 2018.

Commission, 'Fact Sheet – Investment Protection and Investor-to-State Dispute Settlement in EU Agreements' (November 2013) <https://www.italaw.com/sites/default/files/archive/Investment%20Protection%20and%20Investor-to-State%20Dispute%20Settlement%20in%20EU%20agreements_0.pdf> accessed 14 February 2019.

Commission, 'Global Europe: Competing in the World – A Contribution to EU's Growth and Jobs Strategy' (Communication) COM (2006) 567 final.

Commission, 'Inception Impact Assessment – Prevention and amicable resolution of investment disputes within the single market' Ref Ares (2017) 3735364.

Commission, 'Investment in TTIP and beyond – the path for reform: Enhancing the right to regulate and moving from current ad hoc arbitration towards an Investment Court' (Commission TTIP Concept Paper 2015), 1 <https://trade.ec.europa.eu/doclib/docs/2015/may/tradoc_153408.PDF> accessed 26 May 2020.

Commission, 'Investment provisions in the EU-Canada free trade agreement (CETA)' (February 2016), 7 <https://trade.ec.europa.eu/doclib/docs/2013/november/tradoc_151918.pdf> accessed 25 May 2020.

Commission, 'Negotiations and Agreements' <http://ec.europa.eu/trade/policy/countries-and-regions/negotiations-and-agreements/> accessed 14 February 2019.

Commission, 'Online public consultation on investment protection and investor-to-state dispute settlement (ISDS) in the Transatlantic Trade and Investment Partnership Agreement (TTIP)' (Commission Staff Working Report) SWD (2015) 3 final.

Commission, 'Proposal for a Council Decision on the position to be taken on behalf of the European Union in the Committee on Services and Investment established under the Comprehensive Economic and Trade Agreement (CETA) between Canada, of the one part, and the European Union and its Member States, of the other part as regards the adoption of rules for mediation for use by disputing parties in investment disputes' COM/2019/460 final.

Commission, 'Report from the Commission to the European Parliament and the Council on the operation of Regulation (EU) No 912/2014 on the financial responsibility linked to investor-to-state dispute settlement under international agreements to which the European Union is party' COM(2019)597/F1<https://ec.europa.eu/transparency/regdoc/rep/1/2019/EN/COM-2019-597-F1-EN-MAIN-PART-1.PDF> accessed 21 February 2020.

Commission, 'State aid SA 38517(2014/C) (ex 2014/NN) – Implementation of Arbitral award Micula v Romania of 11 December 2013 – Invitation to submit comments pursuant to

Article 108(2) of the Treaty on the Functioning of the European Union Text with EEA relevance' (2014) OJ C393/27 <https://eur-lex.europa.eu/legal-content/EN/TXT/?uri=uriserv:OJ.C_.2014.393.01.0027.01.ENG&toc=OJ:C:2014:393:TOC> accessed 29 November 2018.

Commission, 'State aid SA 38517(2014/C) (ex 2014/NN) – Implementation of Arbitral award Micula v Romania of 11 December 2013.

Commission, 'State aid SA.40348 (2015/NN) – Spain Support for electricity generation from renewable energy sources, cogeneration and waste' C(2017) 7384 final <http://ec.europa.eu/competition/state_aid/cases/258770/258770_1945237_333_2.pdf>.

Commission, 'State aid: Commission orders Romania to recover incompatible state aid granted in compensation for abolished investment aid scheme' Press Release IP/15/4725 (2015) <http://europa.eu/rapid/press-release_IP-15-4725_en.htm> accessed 29 November 2018.

Commission, 'State of the Union 2017 – Trade Package: Commission unveils initiatives for a balanced and progressive trade policy' (Press Release IP/17/3182, 14 September 2017) <https://trade.ec.europa.eu/doclib/press/index.cfm?id=1715&title=State-of-the-Union-2017-Trade-Package-Commission-unveils-initiatives-for-a-balanced-and-progressive-trade-policy> accessed 24 May 2020.

Commission, 'The European Union's Proposal for an Investment Protection Agreement – Explanatory Note' (January 2019), 2 <http://trade.ec.europa.eu/doclib/docs/2019/january/tradoc_157647.%2020190124%20-%20Factsheet%20on%20Investment%20Protection%20Agreement%20-%20EN.pdf> accessed 14 February 2019.

Commission, e-Justice portal, available at: <https://e-justice.europa.eu/content_mediation_in_member_states-64-en.do> accessed 22 November 2018.

Commission, EU Member States agree on a plurilateral treaty to terminate bilateral investment treaties (Statement) (2019) <https://ec.europa.eu/info/sites/info/files/business_economy_euro/banking_and_finance/documents/191024-bilateral-investment-treaties_en.pdf> accessed 22 February 2020.

Commission, Proposal for a Regulation of the European Parliament and of the Council establishing a framework for screening of foreign direct investments into the European Union COM (2017) 487 final.

Commission, The EU's new Generalised Scheme of Preferences <http://trade.ec.europa.eu/doclib/docs/2012/december/tradoc_150164.pdf> accessed 26 November 2018.

Other secondary sources

Bermann GA, 'Recalibrating the EU – International Arbitration Interface' (Lecture delivered at 4th Annual European Federation for Investment Law and Arbitration, 2018).

Bierbrauer E, 'Negotiations on the EU-Canada Comprehensive Economic and Trade Agreement (CETA) concluded' (2014) DG EXPO/B/PolDep/Note/2014_106, 9 <https://www.europarl.europa.eu/RegData/etudes/IDAN/2014/536410/EXPO_IDA(2014)536410_EN.pdf> accessed 25 May 2020.

Council, 'Directives for the negotiation on the Transatlantic Trade and Investment Partnership between the European Union and the United States of America' (11103/13 DCL 1, 2013).

Council, 'Negotiating directives for a Convention establishing a multilateral court for the settlement of investment disputes' (12981/17 ADD 1 DCL 1, 2018), footnote 1 <http://

data.consilium.europa.eu/doc/document/ST-12981-2017-ADD-1-DCL-1/en/pdf> accessed 29 November 2018.

Council, 'Statement to be entered in Council Minutes – Statement by the Commission and the Council on investment protection and the Investment Court System (ICS)' [2017] OJ L11/20

da Cruz Vilaça JL and others (eds), 'The external dimension of the EU policies: horizontal issues; trade and investment; immigration and asylum' (Congress Proceedings Volume 3, XXVIII FIDE Congress, Lisbon/Estoril, 23-26 May 2018).

Déclaration du Royaume de Belgique relative aux conditions de pleins pouvoirs par l'Etat fédéral et les Entités fédérées pour la signature du CETA <http://liege.mpoc.be/doc/europe/-AECG-CETA/Belgique_Declarationpour-la-signature-du-CETA_27-oct-2016.pdf> accessed 29 November 2018.

EU, 'Council Decision on the Provisional Application of the Comprehensive Economic and Trade Agreement (CETA) Between Canada, of the One Part, and the European Union and Its Member States, of the Other Part' (10974/16, 5 October 2016) <http://data.consilium.europa.eu/doc/document/ST-10974-2016-INIT/en/pdf> accessed 29 November 2018.

European Council on Foreign Relations, Germany's turnabout on Chinese takeovers <https://www.ecfr.eu/Art./commentary_germanys_turnabout_on_chinese_takeovers_725> accessed 26 November 2018.

European Parliament resolution of 24 April 2008 on the free trade agreement between the EC and the Gulf Cooperation Council (2009/C 259 E/15) [2008] OJ C259 E/83.

European Parliament, 'Agreement reached on screening of foreign direct investment for EU security' <http://www.europarl.europa.eu/news/en/press-room/20181120IPR19506/agreement-reached-on-screening-of-foreign-direct-investment-for-eu-security> accessed 26 November 2018.

Pukan P, 'Implications of the ECJ Achmea decision for CETA's Investment Court System' (Master Thesis, University of Amsterdam, 26 July 2018).

Representative of the Government of Hungary, 'Declaration of the Representative of the Government of Hungary, of 16 January 2019, on the legal consequences of the Judgment of the Court of Justice in Achmea and on Investment Protection in the European Union' (January 2019) (Hungary Declaration) <http://www.kormany.hu/download/5/1b/81000/Hungarys%20Declaration%20on%20Achmea.pdf> accessed 10 February 2019.

Representatives of the Governments of Finland, Luxembourg, Malta, Slovenia and Sweden, 'Declaration of the Representatives of the Governments of the Member States, of 16 January 2019, on the enforcement of the Judgment of the Court of Justice in Achmea and on Investment Protection in the European' (January 2019) (Second Declaration) <https://www.regeringen.se/48ee19/contentassets/d759689c0c804a9ea7af6b2de7320128/achmea-declaration.pdf> accessed 10 February 2019.

Representatives of the Governments of the Member States of Belgium, Czech Republic, Germany, Ireland, Spain, Croatia, Cyprus, Bulgaria, Denmark, Estonia, Greece, France, Italy, Latvia, Lithuania, Austria, Portugal, Slovenia, Netherlands, Poland, Romania and United Kingdom, 'Declaration of the Representatives of The Governments of The Member States, of 15 January 2019, on the legal consequences of the judgment of the Court of Justice In Achmea and on Investment Protection In The European Union' (January 2019)

(Declaration) <https://ec.europa.eu/info/sites/info/files/business_economy_euro/banking_and_finance/documents/190117-bilateral-investment-treaties_en.pdf> accessed 10 February 2019.

UNCTAD, International Investment Agreements Navigator <http://investmentpolicyhub.unctad.org/IIA/AdvancedSearchBITResults> accessed 26 November 2018.

UNCTAD, 'World Investment Report 2019, Country fact sheet: Developed economies' <https://unctad.org/Sections/dite_dir/docs/WIR2019/wir19_fs_dvd_en.pdf> accessed 21 February 2020.

Blogs and websites

Ballantyne J, 'Romania to pay out on Micula award?' (Global Arbitration Review, 16 December 2019) <https://globalarbitrationreview.com/article/1212205/romania-to-pay-out-on-micula-award> accessed 21 February 2020.

Banila N, 'Romanian gov to pay 912.5 mln lei (191 mln euro) as compensation in Micula state aid case' (SeeNews.com, 13 December 2019) <https://seenews.com/news/romanian-govt-to-pay-9125-mln-lei-191-mln-euro-as-compensation-in-micula-state-aid-case-680232> accessed 21 February 2020.

Ilie L, 'What is the Future of Intra-EU BITs?' (Kluwer Arbitration Blog, 21 January 2018) <http://arbitrationblog.kluwerarbitration.com/2018/01/21/future-intra-eu-bits/> accessed 29 November 2018.

Kleimann D and Kübek G, 'The Future of EU External Trade Policy – Opinion 2/15: Report from the Hearing' (EU Law Analysis, 4 October 2016) <www.eulawanalysis.blogspot.co.uk> accessed 29 November 2018.

Lavranos N, 'Comment: When 23 EU member states terminate their intra EU BITs' (Borderlex, 6 May 2020) <https://borderlex.eu/2020/05/06/comment-when-23-eu-member-states-terminate-their-intra-eu-bits/> accessed 7 May 2020.

Lavranos N, 'After Achmea: The Need for an EU Investment Protection Regulation' (Kluwer Arbitration Blog, 17 March 2018) <http://arbitrationblog.kluwerarbitration.com/2018/03/17/achmea-need-eu-investment-protection-regulation/> accessed 29 November 2018.

Orecki M, 'Foreign Investments in Poland in Light of the Achmea Case and "Reform" of Polish Judicial System – Catch 22 Situation?', (Kluwer Arbitration Blog, 22 April 2018) <http://arbitrationblog.kluwerarbitration.com/2018/04/22/foreign-investments-poland-light-achmea-case-reform-polish-judicial-system-catch-22-situation/> accessed 28 November 2018.

CHAPTER 13

Books

Basener N, *Investment Protection in the European Union: Considering EU law in investment arbitrations arising from intra-EU and extra-EU bilateral investment agreements* (Nomos Verlagsgesellschaft 2017).

Govaere I and Chamon M (eds), *EU External Relations Post-Lisbon: The Law and Practice of Facultative Mixity* (Brill Publishing 2020).

Wouters J and others, *International Law – A European Perspective* (Hart Publishing 2018).

Journal articles

Harrison J, 'The Life and Death of BITs: Legal Issues Concerning Survival Clauses and the Termination of Investment Treaties' (2012) 13(6) *The Journal of World Investment & Trade* 928.

Jarka BO, 'The Decimation of the Intra EU BITS' (2018) 12 *Challenges of the Knowledge Society Public Law* 532.

Moskvan D, 'Reforming Intra-EU Investment Protection: Amid a Running Battle of Interests' (2015) 22(5) *Maastricht Journal of European and Comparative Law* 732.

Voon T and Mitchell AD, 'Denunciation, Termination and Survival: The Interplay of Treaty Law and International Investment Law' (2016) 31(2) *ICSID Rev* 413.

Commission documents

Commission, 'Agreement for the Termination of Bilateral Investment Treaties between the Member States of the European Union' (5 May 2020) <https://ec.europa.eu/info/sites/info/files/business_economy_euro/banking_and_finance/documents/200505-bilateral-investment-treaties-agreement_en.pdf> accessed 21 November 2020.

Commission, 'Protection of intra-EU investment' (Communication) COM (2018) 547 final.

Other secondary resources

Declaration of the Member States of 15 January 2019 on the legal consequences of the Achmea judgment and on investment protection (European Commission, 17 January 2019) <https://ec.europa.eu/info/publications/190117-bilateral-investment-treaties_en> accessed 21 November 2020.

Declaration of the Member States of 16 January 2019 on the legal consequences of the Achmea judgment and on investment protection (adopted by Finland, Luxembourg, Malta, Slovenia and Sweden) <https://www.regeringen.se/48ee19/contentassets/d759689c0c804a9ea7af6b2de7320128/achmea-declaration.pdf> accessed 21 November 2020.

Declaration of the Representative of the Government of Hungary on the Legal Consequences of the Judgment of the Court of Justice in Achmea and on Investment Protection in the European Union' (16 January 2019) <https://www.kormany.hu/download/5/1b/81000/Hungarys%20Declaration%20on%20Achmea.pdf> accessed 21 November 2020.

EU, 'Submission of the European Union and its Member States to UNCITRAL Working Group III, 18 January 2019 – Establishing a standing mechanism for the settlement of international investment disputes' <https://trade.ec.europa.eu/doclib/docs/2019/january/tradoc_157631.pdf> accessed 31 May 2020.

EU, 'Submission of the European Union and its Member States to UNCITRAL Working Group III, 18 January 2019 – Possible work plan for Working Group III' <https://trade.ec.europa.eu/doclib/docs/2019/january/tradoc_157632.pdf> accessed 31 May 2020.

International Law Commission (ILC), 'Articles on Responsibility of States for Internationally Wrongful Acts, Report on the work of its fifty-third session, Supplement No 10' (23 April–1 June and 2 July–10 August 2001) UN Doc A/56/10.

OECD Study, 'Developing a Multilateral Instrument to Modify Bilateral Tax Treaties Action 15 – 2015 Final Report' (OECD/G20 Base Erosion and Profit Shifting Project, 2015).

Speech by Lenaerts K, 'Modernising trade whilst safeguarding the EU constitutional framework: an insight into the balanced approach of Opinion 1/17' (6 September 2019)

<https://diplomatie.belgium.be/sites/default/files/downloads/presentation_lenaerts_opinion _1_17.pdf> accessed 31 May 2020.

UNCTAD Investment Policy Hub, 'Most recent IIAs' <https://investmentpolicy.unctad.org/ international-investment-agreements> accessed 31 May 2020.

United Nations Commission on International Trade Law, 'Draft report of Working Group III (Investor-State Dispute Settlement Reform) on the work of its thirty-sixth session', (6 November 2018) <https://uncitral.un.org/sites/uncitral.un.org/files/draft_report_of_wg_ iii_for_the_website.pdf> accessed 31 May 2020.

Blogs and websites

Halonen L, 'Termination of Intra-EU BITs: Commission and Most Member States Testing the Principle of Good Faith under International Law' (Kluwer Arbitration Blog, 13 May 2020) <http://arbitrationblog.kluwerarbitration.com/2020/05/13/termination-of-intra-eu-bits-commission-and-most-member-states-testing-the-principle-of-good-faith-under-international-law/?doing_wp_cron=1590679658.9551689624786376953125> accessed 21 November 2020.

Kapoor V, 'Slovak Republic v. Achmea: When Politics Came Out to Play' (Kluwer Arbitration Blog, 1 July 2018) <http://arbitrationblog.kluwerarbitration.com/2018/07/01/slovak-republic-v-achmea-politics-came-play/> accessed 21 November 2020.

Lavranos N, 'Black Tuesday: the end of intra-EU BITs' (Practical Law Blog, 7 March 2018) <http://arbitrationblog.practicallaw.com/black-tuesday-the-end-of-intra-eu-bits/> accessed 21 November 2020.

CHAPTER 14

Books

Baltag C, *The Energy Charter Treaty: The Notion of Investor* (Kluwer Law International 2012).

Barnard C, *The Substantive Law of the EU: The Four Freedoms* (2nd edn, OUP 2007).

Journal articles

Andrei Konoplyanik A and Wälde T, 'Energy Charter Treaty and its Role in International Energy' (2006) 24 *Journal of Energy and Natural Resources Law* 523.

Coop G, '20 Years of the Energy Charter Treaty' (2014) 29 *ICSID Review – Foreign Investment Law Journal* 515.

Paulsson J, 'Arbitration Without Privity' (1995) 10 *ICSID Review – Foreign Investment Law Journal* 232.

Perry S, 'Pipeline developer launches ECT claim against EU' (2019) <https://global arbitrationreview.com/article/1200602/pipeline-developer-launches-ect-claim-against-eu> accessed 30 September 2019.

Potestà M, 'Bilateral Investment Treaties and the European Union: Recent Developments in Arbitration and before the ECJ' (2009) 8 *The Law & Practice of International Courts and Tribunals* 225.

Schreuer C, 'Jurisdiction and Applicable Law in Investment Treaty Arbitration' (2014) 1(1:1) *McGill Journal of Dispute Resolution* 2.

Söderlund C, 'Intra-EU BIT Investment Protection and the EC Treaty' (2007) 24 *Journal of International Arbitration* 455.

Conference papers

Smrkolj M, 'The Use of the "Disconnection Clause" in International Treaties: What Does it Tell Us about the EC/EU as an Actor in the Sphere of Public International Law?' (GARNET Conference: 'The EU in International Affairs', Brussels, 24–26 April 2008).

Other secondary sources

Commission, 'Communication from The European Commission to The European Parliament and The Council on the Protection of intra-EU investment. COM (2018) 547/2, 19 July 2018.

Commission, 'Declaration of the Representatives of the Governments of the Member States, of 15 January 2019, on the legal consequences of the Judgment of the Court of Justice in Achmea and on Investment Protection in the European Union' (17 January 2019).

Energy Charter Secretariat, *The Energy Charter Treaty: A Reader's Guide* (Energy Charter Secretariat 2002).

European Commission, 'Energy Charter Treaty- Background Note' (16 December 1994) <https://europa.eu/rapid/press-release_MEMO-94-75_en.htm?locale=EN> accessed 29 September 2019.

EU's Response dated 13 May 2019 to letter from Nord Stream AG dated 12 April <https://trade.ec.europa.eu/doclib/docs/2019/july/tradoc_158070.pdf> accessed 30 September 2019.

International Law Commission (ILC), 'Fragmentation of International Law: Difficulties Arising from the Diversification and Expansion of International Law, Report of the Study Group of the International Law Commission' finalised by Martti Koskenniemi, Fifty-Eighth Session (1 May–9 June and 3 July–11 August 2006), UN Document A/CN4/L682.

Letter from Nord Stream 2 AG to Mr. Jean-Claude Juncker, President of the European Commission (12 April 2019) <https://trade.ec.europa.eu/doclib/docs/2019/july/tradoc_158069.pd_Redacted.pdf> accessed 30 September 2019.

Representative of the Government of Hungary, 'Declaration of the Representative of the Government of Hungary, of 16 January 2019, on the legal consequences of the Judgment of the Court of Justice in Achmea and on Investment Protection in the European Union' (January 2019) (Hungary Declaration).

Representatives of the Governments of Finland, Luxembourg, Malta, Slovenia and Sweden, 'Declaration of the Representatives of the Governments of the Member States, of 16 January 2019, on the enforcement of the Judgment of the Court of Justice in Achmea and on Investment Protection in the European Union' (January 2019) (Additional Declaration).

Tietje C, 'The Applicability of the Energy Charter Treaty in ICSID Arbitration of EU Nationals vs. EU Member States' (Beiträge zum Transnationalen Wirtschaftsrecht, Martin-Luther-Universität Halle-Wittemberg No 78, 2008).

United Nations Conference on Trade and Development 'Factsheet on Intra European Union Investor-State Arbitration Cases' IIA Issues Note Issue 3 (December 2018) UNCTAD/DIAE/PCB/2018/7<https://unctad.org/en/PublicationsLibrary/diaepcb2018d7_en.pdf> accessed 14 May 2020.

CHAPTER 15

Books

Cook G, *A Digest of WTO Jurisprudence on Public International Law Concepts and Principles* (CUP 2015).

Laird IA and others (eds), *Investment Treaty Arbitration and Arbitration Law* (Vol 7, Juris 2014).

Lalani S and Lazzo R, *The Role of the State in Investor-State Arbitration* (Brill 2015).

Mbengue MM and Schacherer S (eds), *Foreign Investment Under the Comprehensive Economic and Trade Agreement (CETA), Studies in European Economic Law and Regulation* (Springer 2019).

Sornarajah M, *The International Law on Foreign Investment* (CUP 2010).

Wolfrum R (ed), *Max Planck Encyclopaedia of Public International Law* (Oxford University Press 2012).

Journal articles

Alvarez J, 'Why Are We "Re-Calibrating Our Investment Treaties?' (2010) 4(2) *World Arbitration and Mediation Review* 143.

Bronckers M, 'Is Investor–State Dispute Settlement (ISDS) Superior to Litigation Before Domestic Courts? An EU View on Bilateral Trade Agreements' (2015) 18(3) *Journal of International Economic Law* 655.

Dorieke O, 'Turning Tides: The Landmark Decision in the Achmea Case – The Ecosystem of EU Law Means the End of Intra-EU BITS' (2018) 3(1) *European Investment Law and Arbitration Review* 242.

Dumberry P, 'The Prohibition against Arbitrary Conduct and the Fair and Equitable Treatment Standard under NAFTA Article 1105' (2014) 15 *The Journal of World Investment and Trade* 117.

Kriebaum U, 'Regulatory Takings: Balancing the Interests of the Investor and the State' (2007) 8 *Journal of World Investment & Trade* 717.

Reinisch A, 'Will the EU's Proposal Concerning an Investment Court System for CETA and TTIP Lead to Enforceable Awards? – The Limits of Modifying the ICSID Convention and the Nature of Investment Arbitration' (2016) 19 *Journal of International Economic Law* 761.

Westcott T, 'Recent Practice on Fair and Equitable Treatment' (2007) 8 *Journal of World Investment & Trade* 409.

Commission documents

Commission, 'Commission draft text TTIP – investment' (2015) <https://trade.ec.europa.eu/doclib/docs/2015/september/tradoc_153807.pdf> accessed 3 May 2020.

Commission, 'EU finalizes proposal for investment protection and Court System for TTIP' (Press Release IP/15/6059, 12 November 2015) <https://ec.europa.eu/commission/presscorner/detail/en/IP_15_6059> accessed 3 May 2020.

Commission, 'EU-Canada trade agreement enters into force' (Press Release IP/17/3121, 20 September 2017) <https://ec.europa.eu/commission/presscorner/detail/en/IP_17_3121> accessed 4 May 2020.

Commission, 'EU-Canada: Green light for the Commission to negotiate new free trade and economic agreement' (27 April 2009) <http://www.sice.oas.org/TPD/CAN_EU/Negotiations/Initiate_Neg_e.pdf> accessed 4 May 2020.

Commission, 'Investment in TTIP and beyond – the path for reform: Enhancing the right to regulate and moving from current ad hoc arbitration towards an Investment Court' (Concept Paper, May 2015) <https://trade.ec.europa.eu/doclib/docs/2015/may/tradoc_153408.PDF> accessed 4 May 2020.

Commission, 'Joint statement Canada-EU Comprehensive Economic and Trade Agreement (CETA)' (29 February 2016) <https://trade.ec.europa.eu/doclib/docs/2016/february/tradoc_154330.pdf> accessed 4 May 2020.

Commission, 'Report on the online consultation on investment protection and investor-to-state dispute settlement in the Transatlantic Trade and Investment Partnership Agreement (13 January 2015) <https://ec.europa.eu/commission/presscorner/detail/en/MEMO_15_3202> accessed 4 May 2020.

Commission, 'Trade, Growth and World Affairs: Trade Policy as a Core Component of the EU's 2020 Strategy' COM(2010) 612 final <https://eur-lex.europa.eu/LexUriServ/LexUriServ.do?uri=COM:2010:0612:FIN:EN:PDF> accessed 3 May 2020.

Other secondary sources

'Rechtspleging Civiel en Bestuur' (Scientific Research and Documentation Center) <https://www.wodc.nl/cijfers-en-prognoses/rechtspleging-civiel-en-bestuur/> accessed 4 May 2020.

Council, 'Recommendation from the Commission to the Council on the modification of the negotiating directives for an Economic Integration Agreement with Canada in order to authorize the Commission to negotiate, on behalf of the Union, on investment' (WTO 270 FDI 19 CDN 5 Services 79 Restreint UE, 2011) <http://data.consilium.europa.eu/doc/document/ST-12838-2011-EXT-2/en/pdf> accessed 21 May 2020.

European Parliament, 'EU investment protection after the ECJ opinion on Singapore: Questions of Competence and Coherence' (Study, PE 603.476, March 2019) <https://www.europarl.europa.eu/RegData/etudes/STUD/2019/603476/EXPO_STU(2019)603476_EN.pdf> accessed 4 May 2020.

European Parliament, TTIP Negotiations on Investment Protection: Investor-State Dispute Settlement (ISDS)' (Legislative Train, June 2020).

European Parliament, 'Legislative Train Schedule – A Balanced and Progressive Trade Policy to Harness Globalisation – EU-Canada Comprehensive Economic and Trade Agreement (CETA)' (20 November 2019) <https://www.europarl.europa.eu/legislative-train/theme-a-balanced-and-progressive-trade-policy-to-harness-globalisation/file-ceta> accessed 19 May 2020.

Eurostat, 'EU Foreign Direct Investment flows in 2018' (17 July 2019) <https://ec.europa.eu/eurostat/web/products-eurostat-news/-/DDN-20190717-1> accessed 21 May 2020.

Government of Canada, 'Assessing the costs and benefits of a closer EU-Canada economic partnership – A Joint Study by the European Commission and Government of Canada' (15 May 2007) <https://www.international.gc.ca/trade-agreements-accords-commerciaux/agr-acc/eu-ue/study-etude.aspx?lang=eng> accessed 4 May 2020.

Government of Canada, 'Canada-EU Summit Declaration – May 6, 2009' <http://www.sice.oas.org/TPD/CAN_EU/Negotiations/Dec2009_Prague_e.pdf> accessed 3 May 2020.

Government of Canada, 'Trade and Investment Agreements' <https:// international.gc.ca/ trade-commerce/trade-agreements-accords-commerciaux/agr-acc/index.aspx?lang=eng> accessed 3 May 2020.

Hindelang S and Sassenrath C, 'The Investment Chapters of the EU's International Trade and Investment Agreements – In a Comparative Perspective' (Study, European Parliament, September 2015).

Kaufmann-Kohler G and Potestà M, 'Can the Mauritius Convention serve as a model for the reform of Investor-State arbitration in connection with the introduction of a permanent investment tribunal or an appeal mechanism? – Analysis and roadmap' (Geneva Centre for International Dispute Settlement, 2016) <https://lk-k.com/wp-content/uploads/2016/05/ KAUFMANN-KOHLER-POTESTA-CIDS-Research-Paper-Reform-of-Investor-State-Arbitration-2016.pdf> accessed 3 May 2020.

Kingsbury B and Schill S, 'Investor-State Arbitration as Governance: Fair and Equitable Treatment, Proportionality and the Emerging Global Administrative Law' (IILJ Working Paper 2009/6, New York University School of Law, 2009).

Lavranos N, 'The New EU Investment Treaties: Convergence towards the NAFTA model as the new Plurilateral Model BIT text?' (Social Science Research Network, 29 March 2013).

NAFTA Free Trade Commission, 'North American Free Trade Agreement – Notes of Interpretation of Certain Chapter 11 Provisions' (31 July 2001) <http://www.sice.oas.org/ tpd/nafta/Commission/CH11understanding_e.asp? accessed 4 May 2020.

Netherlands Model BIT (1997) <https://investmentpolicy.unctad.org/international-investment-agreements/treaty-files/2857/download> accessed 4 May 2020.

OECD, '"Indirect Expropriation" and the "Right to Regulate" in International Investment Law' (OECD Working Papers on International Investment No 2004/04, OECD Publishing) <http://dx.doi.org/10.1787/780155872321> accessed 21 May 2020.

Permanent Court of Arbitration, 'History' <https://pca-cpa.org/en/about/introduction/ history/> accessed 4 May 2020.

Pohl J, 'Temporal Validity of International Investment Agreements: A Large Sample Survey of Treaty Provisions' (OECD Working Papers on International Investment No 2013/04, OECD Publishing, 2013) <https://doi.org/10.1787/5k3tsjsl5fvh-en> accessed 21 May 2020.

SOMO, 'Socializing Losses, Privatizing Gains – How Dutch investment treaties harm the public interest' (Briefing, January 2015) <https://www.somo.nl/wp-content/uploads/2015/ 01/Socialising-losses-privatising-gains.pdf> accessed 21 May 2020.

Tietje C and Crow K, 'The Reform of Investment Protection Rules in CETA, TTIP and other Recent EU-FTAs: Convincing?' (Social Science Research Network, 12 December 2016).

UN, *Enforcing Arbitration Awards under the New York Convention; Experience and Prospects* (United Nations Publications, 1998) <https://www.uncitral.org/pdf/english/texts/ arbitration/NY-conv/NYCDay-e.pdf> accessed 4 May 2020.

UN, 'Report of the International Court of Justice (1 August 2018 – 31 July 2019)' UN Doc Supp No 4 (A/74/4) <https://www.icj-cij.org/files/annual-reports/2018-2019-en.pdf> accessed 4 May 2020

UNCITRAL, 'UNCITRAL Arbitration Rules (with new article 1, paragraph 4, as adopted in 2013)' (United Nations, 2013).

UNCTAD, 'Comprehensive Study of the Interrelationship between Foreign Direct Investment (FDI) and Foreign Portfolio Investment (FPI)' (UNCTAD/GDS/DFSB/5, Staff

Paper by UNCTAD Secretariat, 23 June 1999) <https://unctad.org/en/Docs/pogds
dfsbd5.pdf> accessed 21 May 2020.

UNCTAD, 'Expropriation – UNCTAD Series on Issues in International Investment Agreements II' (United Nations, 2012) <https://unctad.org/en/Docs/unctaddiaeia2011d7_
en.pdf> accessed 21 May 2020.

UNCTAD, 'Fair and Equitable Treatment – UNCTAD Series on Issues in International
Investment Agreements II' (United Nations, 2012) <https://unctad.org/en/Docs/unct
addiaeia2011d5_en.pdf> accessed 21 May 2020.

UNCTAD, 'Review of ISDS Decisions in 2018: Selected IIA Reform Issues' (IIA Issues
Note- International Investment Agreements, Vol 4, July 2019) 1 <https://unctad.org/en/
PublicationsLibrary/diaepcbinf2019d6_en.pdf> accessed 4 May 2020.

CHAPTER 16

Books

Fouret J (ed) *Enforcement of Investment Treaty Arbitration Awards* (Globe Law and Business,
2021).

Gaillard E and Kaiser GE (eds), *The Guide to Challenging and Enforcing Arbitration Awards*
(Law Business Research 2019).

Gómez KF and Rodríguez A (eds), *60 Years of the New York Convention: Key Issues and Future
Challenges* (Kluwer Law 2019).

Keutgen G and Dal G, *Droit belge de l'arbitrage: Tome II Le droit international* (Bruylant 2015).

Ruys T, Angelet N and Ferro L (eds), *The Cambridge Handbook of Immunities and International
Law* (Cambridge University Press 2019).

Van Den Heuvel J (ed), *Liber amicorum* (Kluwer 1999).

Journal articles

'*Civ Bruxelles, 8 June 2017(chambre des saisies)*' (2017) 2 *b-Arbitra*, 301.

'*Civ Bruxelles, 9 décembre 2016 (4e ch*' (2017) 2 *b-Arbitra* 287.

Cullborg JD, 'The role of the Swedish Supreme Court in International Arbitration' (2019) vol
2 *b-Arbitra* 469.

De Boeck M, 'Brussels Court of First Instance Acknowledges EU Law over ICSID: Intra-EU
BIT ICSID awards not so 'Benvenuti' in Belgium' (2016) 1 *b-Arbitra* 35.

de Sadeleer N, 'Le contentieux du droit des investissements dans tous ses états – De la
disparition des tribunaux d'investissement intra-UE à l'avènement d'une Cour multilatérale
d'investissement' (2019) 6 *Revue de droit commercial belge* 742.

Fouchard P '*République Arabe d'Egypte v Société Chromalloy Aéro Services*' (1997) *Revue de
l'arbitrage* 395 (note).

Gaillard E, 'Dialogue des ordres juridiques: ordre juridique arbitral et ordres juridiques
étatiques' (2018) 3 *Revue de l'arbitrage* 510.

Gaillard E, L'exécution des sentences annulées dans leur pays d'origine' (1998) 3 *Journal du
droit International* 49.

Gaillard E, '*Société PT Putrabali Adyamulia v Rena Holding et Société Mnogutia Est Épices*'
(2007) *Revue de l'arbitrage* 507 (note).

Goldman B, '*Société Pabalk Ticaret Ltd Sirketi v Norsolor S.A.*' (1985) *Revue de l'arbitrage* 433.

Grierson J, 'The Court of Justice of the European Union and International Arbitration' (2018) 2 *b-Arbitra* 309.

Hansebout A, *'De actualitiet van de arbitrale uitspraak: een conflict tussen het exequaturvonnis en het vernietingsvonnis'* (2018) vol 1 *b-Arbitra* 93–105.

Jarrosson C, ' *Société Hilmarton v Société Omnium de traitement et de valorisation'* (1994) vol 2 *Revue de l'arbitrage* 327.

Paulsson J, 'May or Must under the New York Convention: An exercise in Syntax and Lingusitics' (1998) 14(2) *Arbitration International* 299.

Reinisch A, 'European Court Practice Concerning State Immunity from Enforcement Measures' (2006) 17(4) *European Journal of International Law* 803.

Struckmann K and others, 'Enforcement of Investor-State Arbitral Awards: More Questions than Answers Annotation on the Judgment of the High Court of England and Wales of 20 January 2017 in *Micula and Others v Romania* [2017] EWHC 31 (Comm)' (2017) 16 *European State Aid Law Quarterly* 316.

van der Haegen O, 'Back to the CJEU's Gazprom judgment: anti-suit injunctions, arbitration and Brussels I' (2016) vol 2 *b-Arbitra* 151.

Commission documents

Micula v Romania (Case State aid SA.38517) Commission Decision of 26 May 2014 ordering Romania to suspend any action which may lead to the execution or implementation of the *Ioan Micula, Viorel Micula and others v Romania* ICSID Case No ARB/05/20 Award of 11 December 2013.

Micula v Romania (Case State aid SA.38517) Commission Decision of 1 October 2014 to initiate the formal investigation procedure; Commission (Letter to Romania) C(2014) 6848 final <https://ec.europa.eu/competition/state_aid/cases/254586/254586_1595781_31_11.pdf> accessed 21 April 2020.

Micula v Romania (Case State aid SA.38517) Commission Decision 2015/1470 [2015] OJ L232/43.

Other secondary sources

European Treaty Series – No 74, 'Explanatory Report to the European Convention on State Immunity' (*Council of Europe*, 16 May1972) <https://www.coe.int/en/web/conventions/full-list/-/conventions/treaty/074> accessed 29 April 2020.

Blogs and websites

'Enforcement against Poland stayed in light of Achmea' (*Global Arbitration Review*, 15 June 2018) <https://globalarbitrationreview.com/article/1170617/enforcement-against-poland-stayed-in-light-of-achmea> accessed 29 April 2020.

Croisant G, 'Micula Case: The UK Supreme Court Rules That The EU Duty Of Sincere Co-operation Does Not Affect The UK's International Obligations Under The ICSID Convention' (*Kluwer Arbitration Blog*, 20 February 2020) <http://arbitrationblog.kluwerarbitration.com/2020/02/20/micula-case-the-uk-supreme-court-rules-that-the-eu-duty-of-sincere-co-operation-does-not-affect-the-uks-international-obligations-under-the-icsid convention/> accessed 27 April 2020.

Dahlquist J, 'Swedish Supreme Court to send Achmea-related question to European Court of Justice' *(Investment Arbitration Reporter*, 14 December 2019) <https://www.iareporter.com/articles/swedish-supreme-court-sends-achmea-related-issue-to-european-court-of-justice/> accessed 29 April 2020.

Jones T, 'Miculas suffer setback in Sweden' (*Global Arbitration Review*, 4 February 2019) <https://globalarbitrationreview.com/article/1179932/miculas-suffer-setback-in-sweden> accessed 28 April 2020.

CHAPTER 17

Books

Beharry CL (ed), *Contemporary and Emerging Issues on the Law of Damages and Valuation in International Investment Arbitration* (Brill Nijhoff 2018).

Cobin JM, *A Primer on Modern Themes in Free Market Economics and Policy* (2nd edn, Universal Publishers 2009).

Fikentscher W and Heinemann A, *Schuldrecht* (10th edn, De Gruyter 2006).

Gisawi F, *Der Grundsatz der Totalreparation*, Gundlagen der Rechtswissenschaft 25 (Mohr Siebeck 2015).

Gordley J, *Foundations of Private Law: Property, Tort, Contract, Unjust Enrichment* (Oxford University Press 2006).

Herrmann Hoppe H, *The Economics and Ethics of Private Property: Studies in Political Economy and Philosophy* (2nd edn, Ludwig van Mises Institute 2006).

Hughes GJ, *The Routledge Guidebook to Aristotle's Nicomachean Ethics* (Taylor & Francis Group 2013).

Krijnen C and Bas Kee (eds), *Philosophy of Economics and Management & Organization Studies: A Critical Introduction* (Kluwer 2009).

Lauterpacht H, *Private Law Sources and Analogies of Law* (Longmans, Green & Co Ltd 1927).

Lauterpacht H, *The Development of International Law by the International Court* (Cambridge University Press 1958).

Marboe I, *Calculation of Compensation and Damages in International Investment Law* (2nd edn, Oxford University Press 2017).

Mommsen F, *Beiträge zum Obligationenrecht: Abth. Zur Lehre von dem Interesse* (E.U. Schwetschke und Sohn 1855).

Reinisch A (ed), *Standards of Investment Protection* (Oxford University Press 2008).

Ribeiro C (ed), *Investment Arbitration and the Energy Charter Treaty* (Juris Publishing 2006).

Sabahi B, *Compensation and Restitution in Investor-State Arbitration* (International Economic Law Series, Oxford University Press 2011).

Trenor JA (ed), *GAR Guide to Damages in International Arbitration* (3rd edn GAR 2019).

Wöss H and others, *Damages in International Arbitration under Complex Long-term Contracts* (Oxford International Arbitration Series, Oxford University Press 2014).

Yannaca-Small K (ed), *Arbitration under International Investment Agreements – A Guide to Key Issues* (2nd edn, Oxford University Press 2018).

Journal articles

Abdala MA and Spiller PT, 'Chorzów's Standard Rejuvenated: Assessing Damages in Investment Treaty Arbitrations' (2008) 25 *Journal of International Arbitration* 1.

Goodman REM and Parkhomenko Y, 'Does the Chorzów Factory Standard Apply in Investment Arbitration? A Contextual Reappraisal' (2017) 32 *ICSID Review* 304.

Kachavani D, 'Compensation for Unlawful Expropriation: Targeting the Illegality' (2017) 32 *ICSID Review* 385.

Lieblich WC, 'Determinations by International Tribunals of the Economic Value of Expropriated Enterprises' (1990) 7 *Journal of International Arbitration* 37.

Nelson TG, 'A Factory in Chorzów: The Silesian Dispute that Continues to Influence International Law and Expropriation Damages Almost a Century Later' (2014) 1 *The Journal of Damages in International Arbitration* 77.

Ripinsky S, 'Damages Assessment in the Spanish Renewable Energy Arbitrations: First Awards and Alternative Compensation Approach Proposal' (2018) *TDM* (provisional), subsequently published in (2020) 2 *TDM*.

San Román A and Wöss H, 'Damages in International Arbitration with Respect to Income Generating Assets or Investments in Commercial and Investment Arbitration' (2015) 2(1) *Journal of Damages in International Arbitration* 37; also published in (2015) 5 *Transnational Dispute Management*.

Smith M and Vikis R, 'Whose Money is it and Should it Matter? An Essay on the Cost of Capital in International Arbitration' (2014) 1(2) *Journal of Damages in International Arbitration* 77.

Wöss H and Bray D, 'Investment Protection and the Mexican Energy Reform' (2018) 12(1) *Dispute Resolution International* 41.

Wöss H, 'Systemic Aspects and the Need for Codification of International Tort Law Standards in Investment Arbitration' (2016) 1 *TDM* (CETA Special Volume).

Ziyaeva D, 'Arbitral Tribunals Tend to Pay Lip Service to the Chorzów Factory Full Reparation Principle, This Regarding the Context and Full Implication of the Dictum' (2015) 2(2) *Journal of Damages in International Arbitration* 121.

Other secondary sources

Franck TM, 'Fairness in the International Legal and Institutional System: General Course on Public International Law' (1993) 240 *Recueil des cours* 26.

Giroux ME and others, 'Hindsight Bias and Law' (2016) 224(3) 190 <https://www.researchgate.net/publication/309539553_Hindsight_Bias_and_Law> accessed 21 July 2019.

Spiller PT, Presentation at the 'DC Bar Advanced Seminar on Damages in International Arbitration' (23 January 2019).

CHAPTER 18

Books

Aquinas T, *Summa Theologiae* (New York: Benziger Brothers 1911–1925) IIa-IIae Q 161.

Brokelind C (ed) *Principles of Law: Function, Status and Impact in EU Tax Law* (IBFD 2014).

Gazzini T (ed) *Interpretation of International Investment Treaties* (Hart Publishing 2016).

Ho J, *State Responsibility for Breaches of Investment Contracts* (CUP 2018).

Kantor M (ed), *Valuation for Arbitration* (Wolters Kluwer 2008).

Lang M et al (eds), *The Impact of Bilateral Investment Treaties on Taxation* (IBFD 2017).

Lang M, 'Has the Case Law of the ECJ on Final Losses Reached the End of the Line?' in Madalina (ed) *ECJ direct tax compass 2014* (IBFD tax travel companions 2014) 530.

Marboe I (ed) *Calculation of Compensation and Damages in International Investment Law* (OUP 2009).

Muchlinski P, Ortino F and Schreuer C (eds), *The Oxford Handbook of Investment Law* (OUP 2008).

OECD, *Model Tax Convention on Income and on Capital* (OECD Publishing 2017).

Rathore S, *International Accounting* (PHI Learning 2009).

Journal articles

Castagna S, 'ICSID Arbitration: BITs, Buts and Taxation: An Introductory Guide' (2016) 7 *Bulletin for Internal Taxation* 375.

Echandi R and Kher P, 'Can International Investor–State Disputes be Prevented? Empirical Evidence from Settlements in ICSID Arbitration' (2014) 29 *ICSID Review* 41.

Martinez-Fraga PJ and Pampin JM, 'Reconceptualising the Statute of Limitations Doctrine in the International Law of Foreign Investment Protection: Reform beyond Historical Legacies' (2018) 50 *NYU Journal of International Law and Politics* 789.

Scherer A and Rayman S, 'Tax Implications of Expropriation' (2008) 56 *Canadian Tax Journal/Revenue Fiscale Canadienne* 870.

Schreuer C, 'Travelling the BIT Route: Of waiting periods, Umbrella Clauses and Forks in the Road' (2004) 5 *Journal of World Investment and Trade* 240.

Simonis P, 'BITs and Taxes' (2014) 42 *Intertax* 234.

Tobis E, 'Avoiding Double Taxation on International Arbitration Awards' (2017) 4 *Journal of Damages in International Arbitration* 16.

Academic/working papers

Alvarez JE, 'Reviewing the Use of "Soft Law" in Investment Arbitration' (NYU School of Law, Public Law Research Paper No 18-46, 2018), available at: <https://ssrn.com/abstract=3258737> accessed 15 May 2020.

Brauch MD, 'Side-by-side Comparison of the Brazil-Mozambique and Brazil-Angola Cooperation and Investment Facilitation Agreements' (International Institute for Sustainable Development, 2015) <http://www.iisd.org/sites/default/files/publications/comparison-cooperation-investment-facilitation-agreements.pdf> accessed 15 May 2020.

Brauch MD, 'Exhaustion of Local Remedies in International Investment Law' (International Institute for Sustainable Development, IISD Best Practices Series, 2017) 2, available at: <https://www.iisd.org/sites/default/files/publications/best-practices-exhaustion-local-remedies-law-investment-en.pdf> accessed 15 May 2020.

Entrate A, 'Circolare N. 11/E. Chiarimenti in tema di Patent Box – Articolo 1, commi da 37 a 45, della legge 23 dicembre 2014, n.190 e successive modificazioni e Decreto del Ministro dello Sviluppo Economico di concerto con il Ministro dell'Economia e delle Finanze del 30 luglio 2015' (7 April 2016), available at: <https://www.agenziaentrate.gov.it/portale/documents/20143/239558/Circolare+11e+7+aprile+2016_AGE.AGEDC001.REGISTRO

+BOZZE.0003638.06-04-2016-B_Circolare+11_sostituita.pdf/521608a1-41d9-c00b-faeb-0419fabd1557> accessed 15 May 2020.

Commission documents

Commission (EU), 'Notice from the Commission: Towards an effective implementation of Commission decisions ordering Member States to recover unlawful and incompatible State aid' [2007] OJ C272/4, para 17, available at: <https://eur-lex.europa.eu/legal-content/EN/TXT/PDF/?uri=CELEX:52007XC1115(01)&from=EN> accessed 15 May 2020.

Commission, 'Guidelines for a Model for A European Taxpayers Code' Ref Ares (2016) 6598744, available at: <https://ec.europa.eu/taxation_customs/business/tax-cooperation-control/guidelines-model-european-taxpayers-code_en> accessed 15 May 2020.

Commission, *'Guidelines for a Model for a European Taxpayers' Code'* (2017) available at: <https://un.org/esa/ffd/wp-content/uploads/2018/05/MDT_2017.pdf> accessed 15 May 2020.

Commission, State aid SA.38375 (2014/C ex 2014/NN) which Luxembourg granted to Fiat (notified under document C (2015) 7152) Commission Decision 2016/2326 [2015] OJ L351/1.

Other secondary sources

Ad Hoc Group of Experts on International Cooperation in Tax Matters, 'Transfer Pricing: History, State of the Art, Perspectives' (2001) UN Doc ST/SG/AC.8/2001/CRP.6 2.

Arnold BJ, 'An introduction to tax treaties', 1 <https://un.org/esa/ffd/wp-content/uploads/2015/10/TT_Introduction_Eng.pdf> accessed 15 May 2020.

Centre for Tax Policy and Administration, 'Forum on Tax Administration – Guidance Note: Guidance on Test Procedures for Tax Audit Assurance' (April 2010) 7, available at: <http://www.oecd.org/tax/administration/45045414.pdf> accessed 15 May 2020.

EU, 'EU Joint Transfer Pricing Forum: Report on the Use of Comparables in the EU' (JTPF/007/2016/FINAL/EN, 2016).

OECD, Multilateral Instrument (MLI) and its Explanatory Statement (adopted on 24 November 2016 and entered into force on 1 July 2018), available at: <https://www.oecd.org/tax/treaties/multilateral-convention-to-implement-tax-treaty-related-measures-to-prevent-beps.htm> accessed 15 May 2020.

OECD, *OECD Transfer Pricing Guidelines for Multinational Enterprises and Tax Administrations* (OECD Publishing 2017).

South African Revenue Service, 'Guide to Capital Gains Tax' (2000) 13, available at: <http://www.treasury.gov.za/documents/national%20budget/2000/cgt/cgt.pdf> accessed 15 May 2020.

UNCITRAL 'UNCITRAL Model Law on Secured Transactions – Guide to Enactment (2017) <https://www.uncitral.org/pdf/english/texts/security/MLST_Guide_to_enactment_E.pdf> accessed 30 May 2020.

UNCITRAL, 'Report of Working Group III (Investor-State Dispute Settlement Reform) on the work of its thirty-sixth session (Vienna, 29 October–2 November 2018)' (A/CN9/964, 6 November 2018), paras 27-38, available at: <https://undocs.org/en/A/CN.9/964> accessed 15 May 2020.

CHAPTER 19

Books

Arsanjani MH et al (eds), *Looking to the Future – Essays on International Law in Honor of W Michael Reisman* (Martinus Nijhoff 2011).

Bianchi A and Peters A (eds), *Transparency in International Law* (CUP 2013).

Binder C et al (eds), *International Investment Law for the 21st Century* (OUP 2009).

Born G, *International Commercial Arbitration – I* (2nd edn, Wolters Kluwer 2014).

Bungenberg M and Reinisch A, *From Bilateral Arbitral Tribunals and Investment Courts to a Multilateral Investment Court: Options Regarding the Institutionalization of Investor-State Dispute Settlement – European Yearbook of International Economic Law* (Springer 2018).

Bungenberg M et al (eds), *European Yearbook of International Economic Law 2017* (Springer 2017).

Bungenberg M et al (eds), *International Investment Law – A Handbook* (Hart Publishing 2015).

Calvo C, *Le Droit International Théroique et Pratique* (VI Publisher 1896).

Crawford J et al (eds), *The Law of International Responsibility* (OUP 2010).

Douglas Z et al (eds), *The Foundations of International Investment Law* (OUP 2014).

Euler D, *Transparency in International Investment Arbitration – A Guide to the UNCITRAL Rules on Transparency in Treaty-Based Investor-State Arbitration* (CUP 2015).

Fahey E (ed), *Institutionalisation beyond the Nation State* (Springer 2018).

Hindelang S and Krajewski M, *Shifting Paradigms in International Investment Law – More Balanced, Less Isolated, Increasingly Diversified* (OUP 2016).

Hofmann R and Tams CJ (eds), *International Investment Law and General International Law – From Clinical Isolation to Systemic Integration?* (Nomos 2011).

Kalicki J and Joubin-Bret A (eds), *Reshaping the Investor-State Dispute Settlement System – Journeys for the 21st Century* (Martinus Nijhoff 2015).

Kulick A (ed), *Reassertion of Control over the Investment Treaty Regime* (CUP 2016).

Müller C and Rigozzi A (eds), *New Developments in International Commercial Arbitration 2013* (Schulthess Juristische Medien 2013).

Nakagawa J (ed), *Transparency in International Trade and Investment Dispute Settlement* (Routledge 2013).

Rovine AW (ed), *The Fordham Papers 2013 – Contemporary Issues in International Arbitration and Mediation* (Martinus Nijhoff 2014).

Salacuse JW, *The Foundations of International Investment Law* (OUP 2010).

Sauvant KP (ed), *Yearbook on International Investment Law & Policy 2010 – 2011* (OUP 2012).

Sauvant KP and Chiswick-Patterson M (eds), *Appeals Mechanism in International Investment Disputes* (OUP 2008).

Schill SW (ed), *International Investment Law and Comparative Public Law* (OUP 2010).

Shan W et al (eds), *Redefining Sovereignty in International Economic Law* (Hart Publishing 2008).

van den Berg (ed), *Yearbook of Commercial Arbitration* (Kluwer Law International 1986).

Vandevelde K, *Bilateral Investment Treaties – History, Policy and Interpretation* (OUP 2010).

von Bogdandy A and Venzke I (eds), *International Judicial Lawmaking – On Public Authority and Democratic Legitimation in Global Governance* (Springer 2012).

Waibel M and Kaushal A (eds), *The Backlash against Investment Arbitration – Perceptions and Reality* (Wolters Kluwer 2010).

Waibel M and Kaushal A (eds), *The Backlash Against Investment Arbitration* (Wolters Kluwer 2010).

Journal articles

'Mexico–United States: Expropriation by Mexico of Agrarian Properties Owned by American Citizens.' *The American Journal of International Law*, vol. 32, no. 4, 1938.

Bernardini P, 'The European Union's Investment Court System – A Critical Analysis' (2017) 35(4) *ASA Bulletin* 812.

Boon K, 'Investment Treaty Arbitration: Making a Place for Small Claims' (2018) 19 *Journal of World Investment & Trade* 667.

Brower CN and Ahmad J, 'From the Two-Headed Nightingale to the Fifteen-Headed Hydra: The Many Follies of the Proposed International Investment Court' (2018) 41 *Fordham International Law Journal* 791.

Calamita NJ, 'The (In) Compatibility of Appellate Mechanisms with Existing Instruments of the Investment Treaty Regime' (2017) 18 *Journal of World Investment & Trade* 585.

Coates P, 'The UNCITRAL Rules on Transparency in Treaty-Based Investor State Arbitration – Continuing the Evolution of Investment Treaty Arbitration' (2014) 17 *International Arbitration Law Review* 113.

Coyne JG, 'The TTIP Investment Court System: An Evolution of Investor-State Dispute Settlement' (2016) 5(2) *European International Arbitration Review* 1.

De Brabandare E, 'The ICSID Rule on Early Dismissal of Unmeritorious Treaty Claims: Preserving the Integrity of ICSID Arbitration' (2012) 9 *Manchester Journal of International Economic Law* 23.

Franck SD, 'The Legitimacy Crisis in Investment Treaty Arbitration: Privatizing Public International Law Through Inconsistent Decisions' (2005) 73 *Fordham Law Review* 1521.

Goldsmith A, 'Trans-Global Petroleum: "Rare Bird" or Significant Step in the Development of Early Merits-Based Claim-Vetting?' (2008) 26 *ASA Bulletin* 667.

Gómez KM, 'Diversity and the Principle of Independence and Impartiality in the Future Multilateral Investment Court' (2018) 17 *The Law and Practice of International Courts and Tribunals* 78.

Heppner S, 'A Critical Appraisal of the Investment Court System Proposed by the European Commission' (2017) 72(2) *Dispute Resolution Journal* 93.

Howard DM, 'Creating Consistency Through a World Investment Court' (2017) 41 *Fordham International Law Journal* 1.

Howse R, 'Designing a Multilateral Investment Court: Issues and Options' (2017) 36 *Yearbook of European Law* 209.

Kaushal A, 'Revisiting History: How the Past Matters for the Present Backlash against the Foreign Investment Regime' (2009) 50 *Harvard International Law Journal* 491.

Knahr C and Reinisch A, 'Transparency in International Investment Arbitration – The Biwater Gauff Compromise' (2007) 6 *Law & Practice of International Courts & Tribunals* 97.

Lavranos N, 'Mixed Exclusivity: The CJEU's Opinion on the EU-Singapore FTA' (2017) 2 *European Investment Law and Arbitration Review* 3.

Ma D, 'A Bit Unfair? An Illustration of the Backlash against Arbitration in Latin America' (2012) *Journal of Dispute Resolution* 571.

Malintoppi L and Limbasan N, 'Living in Glass Houses? The Debate on Transparency in International Investment Arbitration' (2015) 2 *BCDR International Arbitration Review* 31.

Markert L, 'Preliminary Objections pursuant to ICSID Arbitration Rule 41(5) – Soon to Become the Preliminary Objection of Choice?' (2012) 9 *Transnational Dispute Management* 1.

Maxwell I, 'Transparency in Investment Arbitration – Are Amici Curiae the Solution?' (2007) 3 *Asia International Arbitration Journal* 159.

Orellana MA, 'The Right of Access to Information and Investment Arbitration' (2011) 26(2) *ICSID Review* 59.

Potestà M and Sobat M, 'Frivolous claims in international adjudication: a study of ICSID Rule 41(5) and of procedures of other courts and tribunals to dismiss claims summarily' (2012) 3 *Journal of International Dispute Settlement* 137.

Simmons JB, 'The Misdiagnosed Investment Court: The Wrong Remedy for the Right Problem' (2016) 5(2) *European International Arbitration Review* 23.

Simoes FD, 'Hold on to Your Hat! Issue Conflicts in the Investment Court System' (2018) 17 *The Law and Practice of International Courts and Tribunals* 98.

van den Broek N and Morris D, 'The EU's Proposed Investment Court and WTO Dispute Settlement: A Comparison and Lessons Learned' (2017) 2 *European Investment Law and Arbitration Review Online* 35.

Zachariasiewicz M, 'Amicus Curiae in International Investment Arbitration – Can it Enhance the Transparency of Investment Dispute Resolution' (2012) 29 *Journal of International Arbitration* 205.

Commission documents

Commission, 'Investment in TTIP and beyond – the path for reform: Enhancing the right to regulate and moving from current ad hoc arbitration towards an Investment Court' (Concept Paper, May 2015) <https://trade.ec.europa.eu/doclib/docs/2015/may/tradoc_153408.PDF> accessed 4 May 2020.

Commission, New EU-Mexico agreement – The agreement in principle' (21 April 2018), available at <http://trade.ec.europa.eu/doclib/docs/2018/april/tradoc_156791.pdf> accessed 12 September 2016.

Commission, text of the EU-Vietnam trade agreement at the end of the negotiation conducted by the European Commission (made available public solely for information purposes on 18 June 2020) <http://trade.ec.europa.eu/doclib/press/index.cfm?id=1437> accessed 21 November 2020.

Commission, Recommendation for a Council Decision Authorizing the Opening of Negotiations for a Convention Establishing a Multilateral Court for The Settlement of Investment Disputes (Staff Working Document) COM (2017) 493 final.

Commission, Sumary of the negotiating results of the Trade part of the EU-Mexico modernised Global Agreement at the time of the agreement in principle in April 2018 <http://trade.ec.europa.eu/doclib/docs/2018/april/tradoc_156791.pdf> accessed 21 November 2020.

Other secondary sources

Braun T, 'Globalization-Driven Innovation: The Investor as a Partial Subject in Public International Law – An Inquiry into the Nature and Limits of Investor Rights' (Jean Monnet Working Paper 04/13).

Council, 'Council Decision (EU) 2019/1121 of 25 June 2019 on the signing, on behalf of the European Union, of the Free Trade Agreement between the European Union and the Socialist Republic of Vietnam' [2019] OJ L177/1 <https://eur-lex.europa.eu/legal-content/EN/ALL/?uri=OJ:L:2019:177:TOC> accessed 12 September 2016.

Council, 'Negotiating Directives for a Convention establishing a multilateral court for the settlement of investment disputes' (12981/17 ADD 1 DCL 1, 2018).

Draft Text of India's Model BIT (2015).

European Parliament, 'Report containing the European Parliament's recommendations to the European Commission on the negotiations for the Transatlantic Trade and Investment Partnership (TTIP) (2014/2228(INI))' (A8-0175/2015, 1 June 2015) <https://www.europarl.europa.eu/doceo/document/A-8-2015-0175_EN.html> accessed 12 September 2016.

House of Commons Debates, June 25, 1980, vol 112 (3rd Ser), c 444 (statement of Lord Palmerston).

ICSID, 'The ICSID Caseload – Statistics (Issue 2018-2)', 11 <https://icsid.worldbank.org/en/Documents/resources/ICSID%20Web%20Stats%202018-2%20(English).pdf> accessed 3 November 2018.

Kaufmann-Kohler G and Potestà M, 'Can the Mauritius Convention serve as a model for the reform of investor-State arbitration in connection with the introduction of a permanent investment tribunal or an appeal mechanism?' (Geneva Center for International Dispute Settlement, 2016) available at <https://www.cids.ch/images/Documents/CIDS_First_Report_ISDS_2015.pdf> accessed 12 September 2016.

Kaufmann-Kohler G and Potestà M, 'The Composition of a Multilateral Investment Court and of an Appeal Mechanism for Investment Awards – CIDS Supplemental Report' (Geneva Center for International Dispute Settlement) 14, available at <https://www.cids.ch/news/isds-project-cids-supplemental-report> accessed 12 September 2016.

Puig S and Brown C, 'The Power of ICSID Tribunals to Dismiss Proceedings Summarily: An Analysis of Rule 41(5) of the ICSID Arbitration Rules' (Sydney Law School Research Paper No 11/33, 2011).

UN, 'Report of the International Court of Justice – 1 August 2016-31 July 2017' (UN Doc A/72/4, 2017).

UNCITRAL, 'Possible reform of investor-State dispute settlement (ISDS): Consistency and related matters – Note by the Secretariat' (A/CN 9/WG III/WP150, 28 August 2018).

UNCITRAL, 'Possible reform of investor-State dispute settlement (ISDS) – Submission from the European Union' (A/CN 9/WG III/WP145, 12 December 2017) (Submission from the EU).

UNCITRAL, 'Possible reform of investor-State dispute settlement (ISDS) – Ensuring independence and impartiality on the part of arbitrators and decision makers in ISDS- Note by the Secretariat' (A/CN9/WGIII/WP151, 30 August 2018) .

UNCITRAL, 'Possible reform of Investor-State dispute settlement (ISDS) – cost and duration-Note by the Secretariat' (A/CN 9/WG III/WP153, 31 August 2018).

UNCITRAL, 'Possible reform of investor-State dispute settlement (ISDS) – Note by the Secretariat' (A/CN9/WGIII149, 5 September 2018).

UNCITRAL, 'Possible reform of investor-State dispute settlement (ISDS) – Multilateral instrument on ISDS reform-Note by the Secretariat' (A/CN 9/WGIII/WP194, 16 January 2020).

UNCITRAL, 'Report of Working Group II (Arbitration and Conciliation) on the work of its fifty-fourth session (New York, 7–11 February 2011)' (A/CN9/717, 25 February 2011).

UNCITRAL, 'Report of Working Group III (Investor-State Dispute Settlement Reform) on the work of its thirty-fourth session (27 November–1 December 2017) – Part I'(A/CN.9/930/Rev1, 19 December 2017).

UNCITRAL 'Report of Working Group III (Investor-State Dispute Settlement Reform) on the work of its thirty-fifth session (New York, 23–27 April 2018)' (A/CN 9/935, 14 May 2018).

UNCITRAL Rules on Transparency in Treaty Based Investor-State Arbitration, 2013.

UNCITRAL, 'Settlement of commercial disputes – Investor-State Dispute Settlement Framework – Compilation of comments' (A/CN.9/918/Add 3, 31 January 2017), 12 (Comments from Germany).

UNCITRAL, 'Settlement of commercial disputes – Investor-State Dispute Settlement Framework – Compilation of comments' (A/CN 9/918/Add 4, 31 January 2017) 12 (Comments from Thailand).

UNCTAD, 'World Investment Report 2016 – Investor Nationality: Policy Challenges' (United Nations, 2016).

Blogs and websites

Anthea Roberts, 'Would a Multilateral Investment Court be Biased? Shifting to a treaty party framework of analysis' (EJIL: Talk!, 28 April 2017) available at:<https://www.ejiltalk.org/would-a-multilateral-investment-court-be-biased-shifting-to-a-treaty-party-framework-of-analysis/> accessed 12 September 2016.

Mapping BITs <http://mappinginvestmenttreaties.com> accessed 3 November 2018.

CHAPTER 20

Books

Esplugues C, Iglesias J and Palao G (eds), *Civil and Commercial Mediation in Europe: National Mediation Rules and Procedures* (Intersentia 2013).

Hopt KJ and Steffek F (eds), *Mediation, Principles and Regulations in Comparative Perspective* (OUP 2013).

Ingen-Housz A (ed), *ADR in Business, Practice and Issues Across Countries and Cultures* (Wolters Kluwer Law and Business 2011).

Muruga Perumal Ramaswamy MP and Ribeiro J (eds), *Harmonizing Trade Law to Enable Private Sector Regional Development* (UNCITRAL Regional Centre for Asia and the Pacific 2017).

Nadja Alexander A, Walsh S and Svatos M (eds), *EU Mediation Law Handbook, Regulatory Robustness Rating for Mediation Regime* (Wolters Kluwer 2017).

Thaler R and Sunstein C, *Nudge: Improving Decisions about Health, Wealth and Happiness* (Penguin Books 2008).

Titi C and Gomez KF (eds), *Mediation in International Commercial and Investment Disputes* (OUP 2019).

Journal articles

Alexander N and Chong S, 'The New UN Convention on Mediation (aka the 'Singapore Convention') – Why It's Important for Hong Kong' (April 2019) *Hong Kong Lawyer* 26.

Chong S and Steffek F, 'Enforcement of International Settlement Agreements resulting from Mediation under the Singapore Convention: Private international law issues in perspective' (2019) 31 (special issue) *Singapore Academy of Law Journal* 448.

Chua E, 'The Singapore Convention on Mediation – A Brighter Future for Asian Dispute Resolution' (2019) 9 *Asian Journal of International Law* 195 <https://ssrn.com/abstract= 3309433> accessed 27 April 2020.

Johnson E and Goldstein D, 'Do Defaults Save Lives?' (2003) 302 *Science* 1338 <https:// papers.ssrn.com/abstract=1324774> accessed 27 April 2020.

Schnabel T, 'The Singapore Convention on Mediation: A Framework for the Cross-Border Recognition and Enforcement of Mediated Settlements' (2019) 19 *Pepperdine Dispute Resolution Law Journal* 1.

Silvestri E, 'The Singapore Convention on Mediated Settlement Agreements: A new string to the bow of international mediation?' (2019) 2 (3) *Access to Justice in Eastern Europe* 5.

Strong SI, 'Beyond International Commercial Arbitration? The Promise of International Commercial Mediation' (2014) 45 *Washington University Journal of Law and Policy* 11.

Strong SI, 'Realizing Rationality: An Empirical Assessment of International Commercial Mediation' (2016) 73 *Washington and Lee Law Review* 1973 <https://scholarlycommons. law.wlu.edu/wlulr/vol73/iss4/7/> accessed 27 April 2020.

Research papers

Reed L, 'Ultima Thule: Prospects for International Commercial Mediation' (18 January 2019) No. 18/03 NUS Centre for Intl L Research Paper 13 <https://papers.ssrn.com/sol3/ papers.cfm?abstract_id=3339788> accessed 27 April 2020.

Commission documents

Commission, 'Commission Recommendation of 30 March 1998 on the principles applicable to the bodies responsible for out-of-court settlement of consumer disputes' [1998] OJ L115/31.

Commission, 'European Code of Conduct for Mediators – List of Organisations' <https:// kmfcr.cz/download/adr_ec_list_org_en.pdf> accessed 27 April 2020.

Commission, '*Green Paper on alternative dispute resolution in civil and commercial law*' COM/ 2002/ 0196 final.

Commission, 'Proposal for a Directive of the European Parliament and of the Council on certain aspects of mediation in civil and commercial matters' COM (2004) 718 final.

Other secondary sources

ADR Center, 'The cost of Non ADR – Surveying and Showing the Actual Costs of Intra-Community Commercial Litigation' (Survey Data Report, 2010), 42 <https://www. adrcenterfordevelopment.com/wp-content/uploads/2018/06/Survey-Data-Report.pdf> accessed 27 April 2020 (Survey Data Report).

Council Directive 2008/52/EC of the European Parliament and of the Council of 21 May 2008 on certain aspects of mediation in civil and commercial matters [2008] OJ L 136/3 (EU Mediation Directive), art 1(3) (with the exception of Denmark).

Council, 'Recommendation of the Committee of Ministers to Member States on mediation in civil matters (adopted at the 808th meeting of the Ministers' Deputies)' Recommendation Rec (2002) 10.

Dispute Resolution Data (DRD) <www.disputeresolutiondata.com> accessed 27 April 2020.

Einigungsverfahren <www.einigungsverfahren.at> accessed 27 May 2020.

EuroMed Justice, European Code of Conduct for Mediators <https://euromed-justice.eu/en/system/files/20090128130552_adr_ec_code_conduct_en.pdf> accessed 27 April 2020.

European Parliament, 'A ten-year-long "EU Mediation Paradox" when an EU Directive needs to be more … Directive' (PE 608.847, Briefing, November 2018).

European Parliament, 'Quantifying the cost of not using mediation – a data analysis' (PE 453.180, Note, 2011).

European Parliament, 'Rebooting the Mediation Directive: Assessing the Limited Impact of Its Implementation and Proposing Measures to Increase the Number of Mediations in the EU') (PE 493.042, Study, 2014).

European Parliament, 'Resolution of 12 September 2017 on the implementation of Directive 2008/52/EC of the European Parliament and of the Council of 21 May 2008 on certain aspects of mediation in civil and commercial matters (the 'Mediation Directive') (2016/2066(INI))' [2018] OJ C337/01.

European Parliament, 'The Implementation of the Mediation Directive' (PE 571.395, Workshop, 29 November 2016).

Opinion of the European Economic and Social Committee on the Proposal for a Directive of the European Parliament and of the Council on certain aspects of mediation in civil and commercial matters as on the definition of the mediator [2005] OJ C 286/1.

Tampere European Council, 'Presidency conclusions' (15–16 October 1999).

UN, Treaty Collections, details on the status of the Convention on International Settlement Agreements Resulting from Mediation <https://treaties.un.org/pages/ViewDetails.aspx?src=TREATY&mtdsg_no=XXII-4&chapter=22&clang=_en> accessed 27 April 2020.

Umbrella Organization for Out-Of-Court Conflict Resolution in Austria, 'Ethics Guidelines' (2017) <https://www.netzwerk-mediation.at/content/ethikrichtlinien> accessed 27 April 2020.

UNCITRAL, 'Model Law on International Commercial Mediation and International Settlement Agreements Resulting from Mediation, 2018 (amending the UNCITRAL Model Law on International Commercial Conciliation 2002)' A//73/17 <https://uncitral.un.org/sites/uncitral.un.org/files/media-documents/uncitral/en/annex_ii.pdf> accessed 27 April 2020.

UNCITRAL, 'Planned and possible future work – Part III – Proposal by the Government of the United States of America: future work for Working Group II' (A/CN9/822, 2 June 2014) <https://undocs.org/en/A/CN.9/822> accessed 27 April 2020.

UNCITRAL, 'Report of the Working Group II (Arbitration and Conciliation) on the work of its sixty-third session (Vienna, 7–11 September 2015)' (A/CN9/861, 17 September 2015), para 15 <https://undocs.org/en/A/CN.9/861> accessed 27 April 2020.

UNCITRAL, 'Report of Working Group II (Dispute Settlement) on the work of its sixty-seventh session (Vienna, 2–6 October 2017)' (A/CN9/929, 11 October 2017), <https://undocs.org/en/A/CN.9/929> accessed 27 April 2020.

UNCITRAL, 'Report of Working Group II (Dispute Settlement) on the work of its sixty-eighth session (5–9 February 2018)' (A/CN9/934, 19 February 2018), <https://undocs.org/A/CN.9/934> accessed 27 April 2020.

UNCITRAL, 'Report on the work of its forty-eighth session (29 June–16 July 2015)' (A/70/17), paras 135–142 <https://undocs.org/en/A/70/17> accessed 27 April 2020.

UNCITRAL, 'Settlement of Commercial Disputes – International Commercial Conciliation: preparation of an instrument on enforcement of international commercial settlement agreements resulting from conciliation – Note by the Secretariat (12–23 September 2016)' (A/CN9/WGII/WP198, 30 June 2016), para 35 <https://undocs.org/en/A/CN.9/WG.II/WP.198> accessed 27 April 2020.

UNCITRAL, 'Settlement of Commercial Disputes – International Commercial Mediation: Draft UNCITRAL Notes on Mediation – Note by the Secretariat' (A/CN9/987, 18 April 2019) <https://undocs.org/en/A/CN.9/987> accessed 27 April 2020.

UNCITRAL, 'Status: United Nations Convention on International Settlement Agreements Resulting from Mediation' <https://uncitral.un.org/en/texts/mediation/conventions/international_settlement_agreements/status> accessed 27 April 2020.

UNCITRAL, 'UNCITRAL Conciliation Rules' (1980) <https://www.uncitral.org/pdf/english/texts/arbitration/conc-rules/conc-rules-e.pdf> accessed 27 April 2020.

UNCITRAL, 'UNCITRAL Model Law on International Commercial Conciliation with Guide to Enactment and Use' (2002) <https://www.uncitral.org/pdf/english/texts/arbitration/ml-conc/03-90953_Ebook.pdf> accessed 27 April 2020.

UNGA Res 74/182, Report of the UNCITRAL work of its fifty-second session (adopted on 18 December 2019), para 8 <https://undocs.org/en/A/RES/74/182> accessed 27 April 2020.

Blogs and websites

O'Neill J, 'The new Singapore Convention: will it be the New York Convention for Mediation?' (Dispute Resolution Blog, 19 November 2018) <http://disputeresolutionblog.practicallaw.com/the-new-singapore-convention-will-it-be-the-new-york-convention-for-mediation/> accessed 27 April 2020.

Phillips P, 'The European Directive on Commercial Mediation: What it provides and what it doesn't' (Business Conflict Management, 2008) <https://businessconflictmanagement.com/pdf/BCMpress_EUDirective.pdf> accessed 27 April 2020.

Wojtowicz P and Gevaerd F, 'A New Global ADR Star is Born: The Singapore Convention on Mediation' (2019) Wiley Online Library <https://onlinelibrary.wiley.com/doi/abs/10.1002/alt.21810> accessed 27 April 2020.

INDEX

549